A
COMPENDIOUS

Law Dictionary,

Containing both an

EXPLANATION OF THE TERMS

AND THE

LAW ITSELF.

INTENDED FOR THE USE OF

THE COUNTRY GENTLEMAN, THE MERCHANT,

AND

THE PROFESSIONAL MAN.

By THOMAS POTTS, Gent.
FORMERLY OF SKINNERS' HALL.

THE LAWBOOK EXCHANGE, LTD.
Clark, New Jersey

ISBN 978-1-58477-433-4

Lawbook Exchange edition 2004, 2026

The quality of this reprint is equivalent to the quality of the original work.

THE LAWBOOK EXCHANGE, LTD.
33 Terminal Avenue
Clark, New Jersey 07066-1321

Please see our website for a selection of our other publications and fine facsimile reprints of classic works of legal history:
www.lawbookexchange.com

Library of Congress Cataloging-in-Publication Data

Potts, Thomas, 1778-1842.
A compendious law dictionary, containing both an explanation of the terms and the law itself : intended for the use of the country gentleman, the merchant, and the professional man / by Thomas Potts.
p. cm.
Originally published : London : Printed for T. Ostell, 1803.
ISBN 1-58477-433-9 (cloth : acid-free paper)
1. Law—England—Dictionaries. 2. Law—Dictionaries. I. Title.

KD313.P68 2004
349.42'03—dc22 2004040736

Printed in the United States of America on acid-free paper

A

COMPENDIOUS

Law Dictionary,

Containing both an

EXPLANATION OF THE TERMS

AND THE

LAW ITSELF.

INTENDED FOR THE USE OF

THE COUNTRY GENTLEMAN, THE MERCHANT,

AND

THE PROFESSIONAL MAN.

By THOMAS POTTS, Gent.
FORMERLY OF SKINNERS' HALL.

LONDON:

PRINTED FOR T. OSTELL, AVE-MARIA-LANE.

1803.

J. CUNDEE, PRINTER,
Ivy Lane.

TO THE

RIGHT HONOURABLE

LORD ELLENBOROUGH,

BARON ELLENBOROUGH, OF ELLENBOROUGH, IN THE COUNTY OF CUMBERLAND,

Lord Chief Justice of the Court of King's Bench.

MY LORD,

I HAVE presumed to dedicate this trifling Work to your Lordship, as most competent to judge of its public utility. The design of reducing the Law Dictionary into one small volume, will, I trust, merit the approbation of every professional man, and (should it be honoured with your Lordship's patronage) obtain that share of public favour, which would ever constitute the pride and ambition of

My Lord,

Your Lordship's

Most obedient humble Servant,

THE AUTHOR.

Camden Town,
Nov. 1, 1803.

PREFACE.

A DICTIONARY of the Laws of England, undertaken with the view of arranging properly, with regard to matter, and method, and at the same time compressing into a narrow compass, the substance of the many voluminous works written on the Statute, and Common Law, cannot, it is presumed, fail to be acceptable to every one, in any manner engaged in a practical department of the law.

But the author of this work, has not confined it solely to the use of the professional man; as it has been both his aim and wish, to render it equally serviceable to the merchant and trader, who, amidst the variety of business, have little leisure to consult those elaborate works, which comprehend and elucidate commercial legislation, and the almost inexpressibly diversified cases which have been determined constructive of those laws: For their use, therefore, the most eminent writers on the Bankrupt Laws, Insurance, Bills of Exchange, Promissory Notes, &c. have been carefully consulted, and the essential contents briefly given.

As there are however, subjects of the first consequence to the mercantile interest of this kingdom, namely, *the Customs* and *Excise Laws*, which on account of their great length could not be inserted in this Dictionary; the proprietors aware of their great importance, have commenced and will speedily publish, *A complete Abridgment of the Customs, Excise, Import,*

and

and Export Laws, which will form a small additional volume, or may be bound up with this work. The merchant and tradesman will easily perceive the utility of this plan, and as it has been arranged, chiefly with a view to their convenience, it is presumed that the whole will form the most complete *Commercial Assistant* ever published, and merit their unqualified approbation.

The country gentleman will here also find the nature of tenures fully explained under their proper heads, and the County Courts, Courts Baron, Courts Leet, Game, and Tithes, concisely but clearly treated on.

To the professional man, it is not meant to insist, that this production can possibly answer all the purposes of the voluminous library of the lawyer; but as the authorities recited in support of the authenticity of the respective articles, are particularly referred to, it will serve him as a most complete index, whereby he may be enabled immediately to direct his attention to any point under consideration.

As the author has selected this work, from writers of the most acknowledged authority, and has devoted it to the use of the Country Gentleman, the Merchant, and the Professional Man, he trusts it will not be found unworthy of a place, either in the Library, the Counting-house, or Office.

A NEW

LAW DICTIONARY.

ABACTORS, drivers away, and stealers of cattle, or beasts in herds or great numbers.

ABATE, to overthrow, demolish, destroy, or beat down.

ABATEMENT, in its most general signification, relates to writs or plaints, and signifies the quashing the plaintiff's writ or plaint; but is used by our law in three different senses. 1 *Inst.* 134. b. 277.

The first, that of removing a public or private nuisance. If a new gate be erected across the king's high-way (which is a *public* nuisance), any of the king's subjects passing that way may cut it down and destroy it. Or if a house or wall be erected so near to mine that it stop my ancient lights (which is a *private* nuisance), I may enter my neighbours land, and peaceably pull it down. And the reason why the law allows this summary method of doing one's self justice, is, because injuries of this kind require an immediate remedy, and cannot wait for the slow progress of the ordinary forms of justice. 3 *Black.* 5.

The second, the defeating or overthrowing of an *action*, by some defect in the proceedings. The chief pleas in abatement are—To the jurisdiction of the court.—To the person of the plaintiff.—To the person of the defendant — Outlawry — Excommunication Alienage—Attaint—Privilege—Misnomer—Addition—To the writ and action—To the count, or declaration—By the demise of the king. The marriage, or death of the parties; for these and many other causes, the defendant oftentimes prays that the suit of the plaintiff, may for that time cease. And in case of abatement in these respects, all writs and process must begin de novo. In the case of an *indictment*, or a criminal process, the defendant may plead an abatement, that his name is not as in the indictment specified, or that they have given him a wrong addition, as yeoman, instead of gentleman; and, if the jury find it so, the indictment shall abate. But he who *takes advantage of a flaw*, must at the same time shew how it may be amended, so as to give the plaintiff a better writ: which is the intent of all pleas in abatement. 4 *Black.* 355. *Finch* 363. 4 *Durnf. and East* 227.

As pleas in abatement enter not into the *merits of the cause*, but are dilatory, it is enacted, by the statute of 4 and 5 *Ann.* c. 16, that no dilatory plea be received unless upon oath, and probable cause shewn to the court: that no plea in abatement be received after a *respondeas ouster*; that they are to be pleaded before imparlance; that when issue is joined on them, if it be found against him who pleads such dilatory plea, it should be peremptory. 1 *Lutw.* 178. 2 *Lutw.* 1117. 2 *Show. rep.* 42.

The third is, where the rightful possession or freehold of the *heir*, or *devisee*, is defeated or overthrown by the intervention of a stranger. And herein it differs from *intrusion*, which is the entry of a stranger, after a particular estate of freehold is determined before him in *remainder*, or *reversion*. An *abatement*, is always to the prejudice of the *heir* or immediate *devisee*; an intrusion is always to the prejudice of the *remainder-man* or *reversioner*. The remedy in abatement or intrusion, may be by entry, without the parties being compelled to bring their action, for as the entry of the wrong-doer was unlawful, it may be remedied by the mere entry of him who hath right. 3. *Black.* 175.

ABBAT, or Abbot, a spiritual lord or governor, having the rule of a religious house. Of these in England, some were elective, some presentative, some mitred, and others not. Those who were mitred, had episcopal authority within their limits, and exempted from the jurisdiction of the diocesan, but the other abbots were subject to the diocesan, in all spiritual government.

ABBEY-LANDS, before the dissolution of the monasteries, were many of them discharged from the payment of tythes, so long as they remained in the hands of, and were cultivated by the religious societies, and not by their tenants and lessees. These exemptions were continued to the possessors of the said lands by the act of

31 Hen. VIII. c. 13. This act also created a law, that is, *unity of the possession* of the parsonage and land tythable, in the same hand; and though many of the titles of discharge are now lost, yet if the lands of a religious house have been held since the dissolution freed from payment of tythes, it shall be intended they were held so before. *Wood* b. 2, c. 2.

ABBREVIATION, by 4 Geo. II. c. 26. all law proceedings shall be in the English tongue, and written in a common legible hand and character, and in words at length and not abbreviated: but by 6 Geo. II. c. 14. numbers may be expressed by figures, and such abbreviations allowed, as are in common use.

ABUTTALS, the *buttings* and boundings of land, either to the east, west, north, or south, shewing on what other lands, rivers, highways, or other places it does *abut*

The boundaries and abuttals of corporations, church-lands, and parishes, are usually preserved by annual procession.

ABDICATION, in general, is where a magistrate or person in office, renounces and gives up the same before the term of service is expired. This word is frequently confounded with resignation, but differs from it in that *abdication*, is done purely and simply; whereas *resignation*, is in favour of some third person. *Chamb. Dict.* 1 W. and M. *Sess.* 2. c. 2. *sect.* 7.

ABEREMURDER, plain or downright murder; as distinguished from the less heinous crimes of *manslaughter*, and chance *medley*.

ABET, to stir up or incite, encourage or set on: Abettors of murder are such as command, procure, or counsel others to commit a murder; and, in case they are present when the murder is committed, they shall be taken as principals; but, if absent at the time of the fact, they shall be considered as accessaries only. *See Accessary.*

ABEYANCE, is that which is in expectation, remembrance, and intendment of law. By a principal of law, in every land there is a fee simple in somebody, or it is in *abeyance*; that is, though at present it be in no man, yet it is in expectancy, belonging to him that is next to enjoy the land. Thus where no person is seen or known, in whom the *inheritance* can vest, it may be in abeyance, as in a limitation to several persons, and the survivor, and the heirs of such survivor, because it is uncertain who will be the survivor:

 yet

yet the freehold cannot, because there must be a tenant to the præcipe always. 1 *Vezey*. 174.

ABISHERSING, is by old authors termed a freedom or liberty, because whoever hath this word inserted in a charter or grant, hath not only the forfeiture and amerciments of all others within his fee, for transgressions, but also is himself free from the controul of any, within their fee. *Cowel.*

ABJURATION, in the old law, signified a sworn banishment, or an oath taken to forsake the realm for ever.

Anciently, if a person had committed a felony, and fled to a church, or church-yard before he were apprehended, he could not be taken from thence to be tried for his crime; but, on confession thereof before the coroner, he was admitted to his oath to abjure the realm; which privilege he was to have forty days, during which time any persons might give him meat and drink for his sustenance, but not after, on pain of being guilty of felony. But, by 21 *Jac.* c. 28. all privilege of sanctuary, and abjuration thereupon, is utterly abolished.

Abjuration signifies also an oath, whereby every person in office, trust, or employment, abjures the pretender, and recognizes the right of his majesty under the act of settlement, engaging to support him, and promising to disclose all treasons, and traiterous conspiracies against him.

ABOLITION, is the leave given by the king or judges to a criminal to desist, from farther prosecution.

ABORTION, if caused by giving a portion to, or striking a woman big with child, was murder; but now is said to be a great misprision only, and not murder, unless the child be born alive, and die thereof. *Leach's Haw.* 1. 31.

ABRIDGE, in the common law, signifies making a declaration, or count shorter, by taking away or severing some of the substance from it. A man is said to *abridge* his plaint in assize; and a woman her demand in an action of dower, where any land is put into the plaint or demand, which is not in the tenure of the tenant or defendant; for, if the defendant plead nontenure, joint tenancy, &c. in abatement of the writ, the plaintiff may leave out those lands, and pray that the tenant may answer the rest. The reason of this abridgement of the plaint is, because the certainty is not set down in such writs, but they run in general

neral; and, though the demandant hath abridged his plaint in part, yet the writ will be good for the remainder. *Cowel.*

ABROGATE, to abrogate a law, is to lay aside, or repeal it.

ABSQUE HOC, when law proceedings were in Latin, were words of exception made use of in a traverse; as where the defendant pleads that such a thing was done at such a place, *without this,* that it was done at such other place.

ACCAPITUM, a relief due to lords of manors.

ACCEDAS AD CURIAM, a writ that lies for him who has received false judgment, or fears partiality in a court baron, or hundred-court. It is directed to the sheriff, and issued out of chancery; but returnable into B. R. or C. B. and is in the nature a writ *de falso judicio,* which lies for him that had received false judgment, in the county court.

ACCEDAS AD DICECOMITEM, a writ directed to the coroner, commanding him to deliver a writ to the sheriff, who having a *pone* delivered to him suppresses it. *Cowel.* Reg. Orig. 83.

ACCEPTANCE, the taking and accepting of any thing in good part, and, as it were, a tacit agreement to a preceding act, which might have been defeated and avoided, were it not for such acceptance had. If baron and feme, seized of lands in right of feme, join and make a lease of feoffment, reserving rent; and the baron die, after whose death the feme receive, or *accept* the rent; by this the lease or feoffment is confirmed, and it shall bar her. Co. *Litt.* 211.

So if *tenant in dower* lease for years, and die, and the heir accept the rent; but, if a parson make a lease for years not warranted by the statute, acceptance of rent by a new parson, will not make it good. 1 *Saund.* 241.

And if a *tenant for life,* make a lease for years, there no acceptance will make the lease good, because it is void by his death. *Dyer* 239.

But if a tenant in tail make a lease for years, rendering rent, and die, and the *issue* accept the rent, it shall bind him. Should such tenant in tail make a lease for years to commence after his death, rendering rent; in such case, *acceptance* of rent by the *issue,* will not make the lease good to bar him, because the lease did not take effect in the life of his ancestors. *Plowd.* 418.

If a lease be made on condition that the lessee do no *waste,* and, he commit waste, and afterwards the lessor accept the rent, he cannot enter for the condition broken. 1 *Inst.* 211.

Though a lease may be made voidable by the default of the lessee, in not paying his rent according to the covenants therein contained, it can only be rendered void by the act of the lessor, that is by *his entry*: but if the lessor, after such non-payment at the day, and *before re-entry accept* the rent, that which was before voidable, becomes by such acceptance, a good lease; and a landlord *accepting* the last quarter's rent, when there are arrears on a former quarter, precludes himself from demanding the arrears. *Cowp.* 803.

ACCEPTANCE, is that act by which the party upon whom a bill of exchange is drawn, makes himself liable to the amount therein contained. An acceptance may be *absolute* to the bill at all events, or it may be *partial*, as to pay a certain part of it; or, *conditional*, that is to say, upon the performance of a certain condition: in this case, when such condition is performed, the acceptance becomes *absolute*.

An acceptance may also be collateral, as an acceptance *upon protest*. An acceptance may be given either *verbally* or in writing; the latter, however, is the most usual and regular. But, any thing tending to shew that the party means to be bound by his undertaking, such as the signatnre of his initials; the day of the month; keeping the bill a longer time than usual; or any verbal promise, or agreement, will be tantamount to an acceptance. See *Bills of Exchange*.

An *absolute acceptance*, is an engagement to pay the bill according to its tenor; it is usually given by writing upon the bill accepted, with the name or initials of the drawee. The holder of a bill has a right to insist on a written acceptance, which is essentially necessary to give the instrument the full benefit of circulation. In accepting a bill payable after sight, it is customary also to write the day on which the acceptance is made. If the drawee keep the bill a longer time than is usual, or do any other act, which upon a fair construction gives credit to the instrument, and thereby induces the holder not to protest it as dishonoured, this will amount to an absolute acceptance, as will also an agreement to pay it at a future day.

A *conditional acceptance*, is an agreement to pay according to the tenor of the acceptance, as where the party renders himself

liable

liable for payment, on a contingency only. Any act which evinces an intention not to be bound, unless on a certain event, will be sufficient to give the acceptance the operation of a conditional one. Conditional acceptances become absolute as soon as the contingency happens, or the condition is performed.

When a conditional acceptance is made in writing, the party giving it, should also express the condition, otherwise he will not be able to avail himself of such condition, against any other, party. *Doug.* 296.

A *partial acceptance,* is an agreement to pay according to the tenor of the acceptance, and may vary with respect to the sum, time, or place; it may also vary from the tenor, in the manner in which the acceptor undertakes to pay the bill. Either of these acceptances, although the holder may refuse each, will be binding on the acceptor; and the holder of the bill, in either of these cases, if he mean on default of payment to have recourse to the other parties, should give notice to all of them, of such acceptance.

Acceptance upon honour, or supra protest, is a *collateral acceptance,* and may be made where the drawee refuses to accept, and some third person, after protest for non-acceptance, accepts for the honour of the drawer, or any particular indorser; in which latter case, he should immediately send the protest to the indorser. Not only a stranger, but the drawee, may accept a bill for honour of the drawer, or any of the indorsees.

It has been held, that the bill should be left with the drawee twenty-four hours, that he may look into his account, and determine whether he will accept or not; but a bill or note, need not be left on a presentment for payment.

ACCESSARY, one guilty of a felonious offence, not principally, but by participation; as by command, advice, or concealment. *Cowel.*

In the highest capital offence, namely high treason, there are no accessaries before or after; for the consenters, aiders, abettors, and knowing receivers and comforters of traitors, are all principals. *Hale's Hist.* 613.

In cases that are criminal, but not capital, as in *petit-larceny,* and *trespass,* there are no accessaries; for all the accessaries *be-*

fore

fore, are in the same degree as principals; and accessaries after, by receiving the offenders, cannot as such, by law, be under any penalties, unless the act of parliament which induce those penalties, expressly extend to receivers or comforters.

Accessary before the fact, is one, who although absent at the time the felony was committed, doth yet procure, counsel, or abet another to commit a felony. An accessary before, is a greater offender than an accessary after; and therefore, in many cases, clergy is taken away from accessaries *before,* which is not taken away from accessaries *after,* as in petit-treason, murder, and wilful burning. *Hale's pl.* 615.

Accessary after the fact, is where a person knowing the felony to be committed, *receives, relieves, comforts,* or *assists* the felon. Such as furnishing him with a horse to escape his pursuers—money or victuals to support him—a house or other shelter to conceal him—or open force and violence to enable him to break his goal, or to bribe the goaler to let him escape, makes a man accessary to the felony. 4 *Black.* 37.

ACCOMMODATION, signies a friendly agreement or composition between persons at variance.

ACCOMPLICE, one of many equally concerned in a felony; generally applied to those who are admitted to give evidence against their fellow criminals. It is a settled point, that it is no exception against a witness, that he has confessed himself guilty of the same crime, if he have not been indicted for it; for, if no accomplices were to be admitted as witnesses, it would generally be impossible to find evidence, to convict the greatest offenders. *Leach's Haw.* 2. 37.

ACCOMPT, when persons have mutual dealings, signing the accompt is not necessary to make a *stated one*; but the act of keeping it any length of time, without making any objection, binds the person to whom it is sent, and prevents his entering into an open account afterwards. 2 *Atk.* 251.

Among merchants, it is looked upon as an allowance of an account current, if the merchant who receive it do not object to it, in a second or third post. 2 *Vern.* 276.

ACCORD, is an agreement between the party injuring, and the party injured, where one is injured by a trespass, or offence

done

done, or on a contract to satisfy him with some recompence; which, if executed and performed, shall be a good bar in law, if the other party, after the accord performed, bring an action for the same. 3 *Black.* 15.

ACCOUNT, a writ or action which lies against a bailiff, or receiver, who by reason of his office or business, is to render an *account* to another, and refuseth to do it. The proceedings upon this action being difficult, dilatory, and expensive, it is now seldom used, especially if the party have other remedy. 1 *Vern.* 182.

ACCOUNTANT GENERAL, an officer in the court of chancery, appointed by act of parliament, to receive all money lodged in court.

ACCUSATION. By *Magna Charta,* no man shall be imprisoned or condemned on any *accusation,* without trial by his peers, or the law.

AC ETIAM, a clause in a writ, where, to entitle the court to jurisdiction, an additional cause of action is alledged; as where the defendant is required to answer the plaintiff in a plea of trespass, and also (ac etiam) to a bill of debt.

ACKNOWLEDGMENT MONEY, a sum of money, paid by the tenant on the death of the landlord, in *acknowledgment* of the new landlord.

ACQUIETANDIS PLEGIIS. A writ that lies for a surety against a creditor, who refuses to acquit him after the debt is paid. *Cowel.*

ACQUITTAL, in one sense, is to be free from entries and molestations of a superior lord, for services issuing out of land; and, in another, for the deliverance and setting free of a person, from the suspicion of guilt; one acquitted of a felony cannot be tried again for the same offence, as he may plead *auter foits acquit.* *Acquittal in law,* is, when two are indicted, the one as principal, the other as accessary; the principal being discharged, the accessary will, of consequence be *acquitted* by *law.* *Acquittal in fact,* is, when by verdict, a person is found *not guilty* of the offence whereof he is charged. 2 *Inst.* 385.

ACQUITTANCE, a release or discharge in writing for a sum of money; and no one is obliged to pay a sum of money, if the demandant refuse to give an acquittance.

An acquittance given by a servant, for a sum of money received for

for the use of his master, shall be a good discharge for that sum, provided, such servant is in the general practice of receiving his master's rents, debts, &c.

An acquittance in full of *all demands*, will discharge all debts, except such as are on specialty under seal, which can only be destroyed by a general release.

ACT OF PARLIAMENT. By the 33 Geo. III. c. 13. every act of parliament, in which the commencement thereof is not directed to be from a specified time, and which shall pass after the 8th of April, 1793, immediately after the title thereof, shall be endorsed by the clerk of parliament, with the day, month, and year, when the same passed and received the royal assent; which endorsement, shall be taken to be the date of its commencement, where no other commencement shall be therein provided.

ACTION, is defined to be a legal demand of one's right; and implies a recovery of, or restitution to something. The suit till judgment, is properly called an action, but not after; and therefore a release of all actions, is regularly no bar of an execution. *Co. Lit.* 289.

Actions, are divided into *criminal* and *civil; criminal,* are either to have judgment of death, or only to have judgment for damage to the party, fine to the king, imprisonment, &c. *A civil action,* is that which tends only to the recovery of what is due to a person, as action of debt, &c. *Civil actions* are divided into real, personal, and mixed. *Co. Lit.* 284.

Action real, is that which concerns real property only, whereby the plaintiff or demandant, claims title to have any lands or tenements, rents, commons, or other hereditaments, in fee simple, fee-tail, or for term of life. 3 *Black.* 117.

Action personal, is that which one man may have against another, by reason of any contract for money or goods, or for any offence or trespass done by him, or some other, for whose act he is answerable. *Bract.* lib. 3. c. 3.

Mixed actions, are those in which the freehold is recovered, and also damages for the unjust detention of it. *Co. Lit.* 284. For the various kinds of actions, see *Covenant, Debt, Detinue, Slander, Trespass, Trover, &c.*

ACTOR. The proctor, or advocate, in civil law courts.

ACTS OF PARLIAMENT. Statutes, acts, or edicts, made

by

by the king, with the advice and consent of the lords spiritual and temporal, and commons, in parliament assembled. An act of parliament, is the exercise of the highest earthly authority that the kingdom acknowledges. It hath power to bind, not only every subject, but even the king himself, if particularly named therein, and cannot be *altered* or *repealed*, but by the same authority.

Where the common law and a statute differ, the common law gives place to the statute; and an old statute, gives place to a new one. 1 *Black*. 89.

ADDITION, signifies a title given to a man, beside his christian and surname, setting forth his estate, degree, mystery, trade, place of dwelling, and

Additions of estate, are *yeoman, gentleman, esquire*, and the like: additions of degree, are names of dignity, as *knight, baron, earl, marquis, duke*: and additions of mystery are *printer, painter, mason, carpenter, distiller*: additions of towns, as *London, Bristol*, &c. By 1 Hen. V. c. 5. it is provided, that in every original writ of actions, personal, appeals, and indictments, in which the *exigent* shall be awarded, to the names of the defendants of such writs, additions shall be made of their estate, &c.

ADEMPTION, or taking away of a legacy, arises from a supposed alteration, of the testator's intention.

ADJOURNMENT, a putting off until another day, or to another place.

ADJUDICATION, a giving, or pronouncing judgment.

ADMEASUREMENT, is a writ brought for remedy against such persons, as usurp more than their share. It lies in two cases, one is termed *admeasurement of dower*, where the widow of the deceased holds from the heir, or his guardian, more in the name of her dower, than of right belongs to her. The other is *admeasurement of pasture*, which lies between those that have common of pasture appendant to their freeholds, or common of vicinage; in case any one of them surcharge the common with more cattle than they ought. *Regist*. 171 a. F. N. 148.

ADMINISTRATOR, is a person to whose charge is committed, by the ecclesiastical court, the personal property of a person dying intestate, for which he is accountable when thereunto required. See *Executor*.

ADMIRAL, an officer or magistrate of high authority, having the

the government of the royal navy, and in his court, the determination of all causes belonging to the sea, and offences committed thereon. This office is now usually exercised by commissioners, who, by stat. 2 W. & M. c. 2. are declared to have the same authorities, jurisdictions, and power, as the lord high admiral.

ADMIRALTY. The admiralty, and admirals of England, had formerly jurisdiction in all causes of merchants and mariners, both civil and criminal; not only on the main sea, but in all foreign parts, within and without the king's dominions; but by 28 Hen. VII. c. 15. all felonies committed on the sea, shall be tried by commissioners nominated by the lord chancellor.

Civil Jurisdiction of the court. The proceedings are according to the method of the ecclesiastical court, and held at the same place. It is no court of record; and an appeal from its decision lies to the court of delegates. From the sentence of an inferior court of admiralty, an appeal lies to the court of the lord high admiral.

Criminal Jurisdiction. The judge of the admiralty presides in this court, as the deputy of the lord high admiral: and the court may be held in any place. Of the commissioners nominated by the lord chancellor, two common law judges are constantly appointed; and although the judges try the prisoner, yet the judge of the admiralty always presides.

ADMISSION to a benefice, is, when the bishop upon examination, approves of the person presented, as a fit person to serve the cure of the church to which he is appointed.

ADMITTANCE, is the giving possession of a copyhold estate, as livery of seisin is of a freehold. It is of three kinds, upon *a voluntary grant by the lord*---upon *surrender by the former tenant*---*and admittance by descent.* See *Copyhold.*

AD QUOD DAMNUM, a writ issuing out of and returnable into the chancery, directed to the sheriff, to enquire by a jury, what damage it will be to the king, or any other, to grant a liberty, fair, market, highway, or the like.

ADULTERY, is the sin of incontinence between two married persons; and if only one of the persons be married, it is called single adultery, to distinguish it from the other, which is double. It is an additional aggravation to the crime of adultery in a woman, that it not only entails a spurious race on the husband, for whom

he

he is obliged to provide; but also destroys that peace and mutual endearment, which ought always to subsist in the marriage state. This crime was severely punished by the ancient law of the land, but the present proceedings against adulterers, are chiefly in the ecclesiastical courts. The most lucrative method, however, of pursuing the adulterer, seems to be to institute an action against him in one of his Majesty's courts at Westminster, by the husband of the adulteress, for seducing and debauching his wife.

ADVOCATE, the patron of a cause, who assists his client with advice, and pleads for him.

ADVOW, or AVOW, to justify or maintain an act formerly done. As if one take a distress for rent, or other thing, and he that is distrained sues a replevin; he that took the distress, by maintaining the act, is said to *avow*.

ADVOWEE, he that hath the right to present to a benefice.

ADVOWSON, is the right of presentation to a benefice. Advowsons are either *appendant*, or in *gross*. Lords of manors being originally the only founders, and consequently the only patrons of the churches; the right of patronage, or presentation, so long as it continues annexed to the possession of the manor, is called an advowson *appendant;* and it will pass or be conveyed, together with the manor, as incident and *appendant* thereunto, by a grant of the manor only. But where the property of the advowson, hath been once separated from the property of the manor, *by legal conveyance*, it is called an advowson *in gross*, and it never can be appendant any more.

Advowsons are also either *presentative*, *collative*, or *donative*. *Presentative*, where the patron hath a right of presentation to the bishop, or ordinary; *collative*, where the bishop is the patron; and *donative*, when the king, or any subject by his licence, founds a church or chapel, and ordains that it shall be merely in the gift of the patron.

Advowson of religious houses, those who founded any house of religion had thereby the *advowson* or patronage of it.

AFFEERERS, such as are appointed in courts-leet upon oath, to set fines on such as have committed faults.

AFFIDATIO DOMINORUM, an oath taken by the lord in parliament.

AFFIDAVIT, is an oath in writing, sworn before some person

 legally

legally authorized to administer the same: the true place of abode, and addition of the person making such affidavit, is to be inserted therein; it should set forth the matter of fact only, and not the merits of the cause, of which the court is to judge; it must also set forth the matter positively, and all material circumstances attending it, and be absolute, and not couched in words of reference; except in the case of assignees, executors, &c. who may swear to their belief of the matter.

AFFIRM, to ratify or confirm a former law or judgment.

AFFIRMATION, an indulgence allowed by law to the people called Quakers, who, in cases where an oath is required from others, may make a solemn affirmation that what they say is true. But their affirmation is confined to civil cases, and is not allowed in any criminal cause.

AFFORCIAMENTUM CURIÆ, the calling of a court upon a solemn occasion.

AFFOREST, to turn ground into a forest.

AFFRAY, is a public fighting (if it be in private it is no affray, but an assault), and is a public offence to the terror of the king's subjects. All affrays in general, are punishable with fine and imprisonment. 1 *Haw.* 138, and a constable is not only empowered to part an affray *in his presence*, but can justify commitment till the offenders find sureties for the peace. *Cro. Eliz.* 375.

AGE, in the law, is used for those special times, which enable persons, of both sexes, to do certain acts, which before, through want of years and judgment, they are prohibited to do. A man, at twelve years of age, ought to take the oath of allegiance to the king; at fourteen, which is his *age* of discretion, he may consent to marriage, and choose his guardian; and at twenty-one he may alien his lands, goods, and chattels. A woman, at nine years of *age*, is dowable; at twelve she may consent to marriage; at fourteen she is at years of discretion, and may choose a guardian; and at twenty-one may alienate her lands, &c. 1 *Inst.* 78.

AGENT, a person appointed to transact the business of another. It is a principle of law, that whenever a man has a power, as *owner*, to do a thing, he may, as consistent with this right, do it by deputy, either as attorney, *agent*, factor, or servant. It has been asserted, that agents should be appointed by a formal power of attorney; but this is not necessary; for the authority of an agent

agent to draw, indorse, and accept bills in the name of his principal, is usually in words. 7 T. R. 209. 12 *Mod.* 654.

If a person be appointed a *general agent,* the principal is bound by *all* his acts. But an agent, *specially* appointed, cannot bind his principal by an act whereby he *exceeds his authority.* 5 T. R. 757.

AGENT AND PATIENT, is the person who is the doer of a thing, and the party to whom done; thus, if a man be indebted to another, and afterwards make the creditor his executor, and die, the executor, by retaining so much of the goods of the deceased as will satisfy his debt, is both *agent and patient.* But a man shall not be the judge of his own cause. 8 *Rep.* 138.

AGE-PRIER, is where an action is brought against one under age, for lands which he hath by descent, who by petition or motion shews the matter to the court, and prays that the action may stay till his full age, which the court generally agrees to.

AGILD, free from penalties, not subject to the customary fine or imposition.

AGISTMENT, is where other men's cattle are taken into any ground, at a certain rate for their feeding. There is also an *agistment of sea banks,* where lands are charged with a tribute to keep out the sea.

AGNUS DEI, a piece of white wax, stamped with the figure of a lamb, and consecrated by the pope: but not permitted to be brought into this kingdom, on pain of a *præmunire.* 13 *Eliz* c. 2.

AGREEMENT, is a memorandum, article, or minute, importing the consent or concurrence of two or more persons; the one in disposing of, and the other in receiving some property, right, or benefit, and is generally made preparatory to a more formal instrument of conveyance. The requisites of an *agreement* are, parties capable of contracting; and a property, right, or benefit, capable of being contracted for. Every agreement ought to be perfect, full, and complete, so as to shew with precision, what is intended to be stipulated between the parties, and should also make express provision against the possibility of failure in any of the contracting parties.

In many cases, the party injured by breach of an agreement, may have a remedy, either at common law, or in a court of equity. But wherever the matter of the bill is merely in damages, *there* the remedy is at *law,* because the damages cannot be ascertained by the *conscience of the chancellor*, and therefore must be settled by a *jury*. *Abr. Eq.* 16.

Although it is prudent that both parties should actually sign the agreement, it will be binding, notwithstanding the statute of frauds, if it be signed by *one party only*; provided the other party be so circumstanced, that he can have an adequate remedy thereupon. 1 *Doug.* 296.

AID-PRAYER, a term used in pleading, for a petition in court to call in help from another person, that hath an interest in the thing contested.

ALBA FIRMA, a white rent paid in silver, in distinction from that paid in corn, &c.

ALDERMAN, a magistrate subordinate to a mayor of a city or town corporate. This office is for life, so that when one of them dies, or resigns, a ward-mote is called, which returns the person they have chosen to the court of aldermen, who are obliged to admit him to supply the vacancy. All the *aldermen* of *London*, &c. are justices of peace, by charter of 15 Geo. II. and are exempt from serving inferior offices; nor shall they be put upon assizes, or serve on juries, so long as they continue such.

ALEHOUSES. To prevent disorders in alehouses, no licence shall be granted to any person, not licenced the year preceding, unless he produce a certificate, under the hands of the parson, vicar, or curate, and the major part of the churchwardens and overseers, or else of three or four substantial householders and inhabitants of the parish, where such alehouse is to be; setting forth that such person is of good fame, &c. and it shall be mentioned in such licence, that such certificate was produced, otherwise it shall be null and void. 26 Geo. II. c. 31. and by 26 Geo. II. c. 41. Justices, on granting licences, are to take recognizances in 10l. with sureties in the like sum, for the maintenance of good order. Licences to be granted on the 1st of September, or within twenty days after, yearly, and to be for one year only. Penalty for selling ale, &c. without a licence (except at public fairs, during which, on paying the duty for the ale, &c. sold, any one may sell ale, &c. without licence), for the first offence 40s. for second 4l. for the third 6l.; and no person can sell wine by retail, to be drank *in his own house*, who has not also an *ale licence*.

ALE-SILVER, is a rent or tribute paid annually to the lord mayor

mayor of London, by those that sell ale within the liberty of the city.

ALE-TASTER, an officer in every court leet, sworn to look to the assize and goodnesss of *ale* and *beer* within the lordship. In *London* there are *ale conners*, chosen by the livery, to taste ale, beer, &c. in the limits of the city.

ALIAS, is a second writ, after a former one has been sued out without effect.

ALIAS DICTUS, is used in the description of a defendant, where his true name is not certainly known.

ALIENS, are persons not born within the dominions of the crown of England, or within the allegiance of the king; but from this rule of law must be excepted the children of the kings of England, and the children of British ambassadors born abroad. No *alien* can be a revenue officer, or hold any office under the crown. The issue of an *English woman* by an *alien*, born *abroad*, is an *alien*. 4 *Durnf. and East.* 400.

Aliens can have no heirs, because they have not in them any inheritable blood. 2 *Black.* 249.

All persons being *natural born* subjects, may inherit as heirs to their ancestors, though those ancestors were *aliens*.

If an Englishman living beyond the sea, marry a wife there, and have a child by her, and die, this child is born a denizen, and shall be heir to him, notwithstanding the wife was an alien. *Cro. Car.* 601.

If an *alien* be made a *denizen* by letters patent, and *then* purchase lands, his son *born before his denization* shall not inherit those lands; but a son *born afterwards* may, even though his elder brother be living. 2 *Black.* 249.

Every foreign seaman, serving on board an English ship *two years*, in time of war, is, by 13 Geo. II. c. 3. naturalized.

All masters of ships, arriving from foreign parts, are to give an account at every port, of the number and names of every *foreigner* on board, under the penalty of forfeiting ten pounds for each *alien* who has been on board, at the arrival of the ship or vessel. 33 Geo. III. c. 4.

Every *alien* neglecting to pay due obedience to the proclamation of his majesty, &c. directing that any *alien* who may be within this realm, or may hereafter arrive therein, to depart therefrom within a time limited, shall on conviction, for the first offence suffer imprisonment for any time not exceeding one month; and not exceeding twelve months for the second, and at the expiration thereof, depart out of the realm within a time to be limited by the judgment: and if such *alien* be found therein after such time so limited, without lawful cause, being duly convicted thereof, *he* or *she* is to be transported for life. And secretaries of state, or lord lieutenant of Ireland, &c. may grant warrants to conduct such aliens out of the kingdom, as *they apprehend will not pay due obedience* to such proclamation. 42 Geo. III. c. 92.

ALIENATION, transferring the property of any thing from one man to another. All persons who have a right to lands (except tenants for life, &c. which incurs a forfeiture of estate,) may generally alien them to others. Thus to *alien* land in fee, is to sell the fee simple thereof; and to *alien* in mortmain, is to make over lands, &c. to a religious house, or body politic, for which the king's licence is to be obtained. 15 R. II. c. 5. 1 *Inst.* 118.

ALIMONY, is that maintenance, which, after a divorce of husband and wife *a mensa et thoro*, the ecclesiastical judge allows to the woman out of her husband's estate. But in case of an elopement, and living with an adulterer, the law allows her no alimony. 3 *Black.* 94.

ALLAY, or ALLOY, is a mixture of several metals with silver or gold; it is done to augment their weight, and thus defray the charge of coinage, and make it the more fusile. The *allay* in gold coin is silver and copper; and in silver coin, copper alone.

The standard of gold in England is twenty-two carats of fine gold, and two carats of allay, in the pound troy. The standard for silver is eleven ounces two pennyweights, and eighteen pennyweights allay of copper.

ALLEGIANCE, is the lawful duty from the subject to the sovereign; and is either *natural*, *acquired*, or *local*. *Natural*, as every subject born, immediately upon his birth ought to pay a *natural allegiance* to his sovereign. *Acquired*, where a man naturalized, or made a denizen, *acquires allegiance* to the King. *Local*, where a man, who comes under the dominion of the king, ought to pay a *local allegiance*. 7 *Co.* 4, 5, 6.

ALLEGIARE, to defend or justify by due course of law.

ALLEVIARE, to levy or pay an accustomed fine.

ALLO-

ALLOCATIONE FACIENDA. A writ for allowing to an accountant, such sums of money as he hath lawfully expended in his office; directed to the lord treasurer and barons of exchequer, upon complaint made.

ALLOCATO COMMITATU, a new writ of *exigent,* allowed before any other *county court* holden, on the former not being fully served or complied with.

ALLODIAL, entire or absolute property.

ALLUVIAN, is the washing of a sea, or of a river; if land be gained of the sea, by the washing up of sand and earth by imperceptible degrees, so as in time to make a *terra firma,* it shall go to the owner of the land adjoining; but if the *alluvian* be sudden, and considerable, it belongs to the king by his prerogative. 2 *Black.* 262.

ALMANACK, is part of the law of England, of which the courts must take notice in the return of writs, &c. but the almanack to go by, is that annexed to the book of common prayer. The court may judicially take notice of almanacks, for, an almanack, wherein the father had written the day of the nativity of his son, was allowed as evidence to prove the non-age of his son. *Raym.* 84. M. 15. c. 2.

ALMNER, or ALMONER, an officer of the king's house, whose business it is to distribute the king's alms every day; this officer is usually some bishop.

ALNAGE, the measure of an ell, or measuring with an ell.

ALODIUM, signifies a manor.

ALTARAGE, the offerings made upon the *altar,* and the profit that arises to the priest therefrom; this was declared in the exchequer to mean tithes of wool, lambs, colts, calves, pigs, chickens, butter, cheese, fruit, herbs, and other small tithes, with the offerings due; but our parsons have generally contented themselves with the greater profits of glebe, and tenths of corn and hay, and have left the small tithes to the officiating priests. 26 *Crow.* 516.

ALTERATION, when witnesses are examined upon exhibits, &c. they are to remain in the office, and not to be taken back into private hands, by whom they may be *altered.*

AMBASSADOR, is a person appointed by one sovereign

 power

power to another, to superintend his affairs at some foreign court; and supposed to represent the power from which he is sent. The person of an ambassador is inviolable.

AMBIDEXTER, is taken for a juror, or embraceor, who takes money of both parties for giving his verdict; such a one shall forfeit ten times the sum taken. *Crompt. Inst.* 156.

AMENABLE, to be responsible or subject to answer, &c. in a court of justice.

AMENDMENT, is the correction of an error committed in any process, which may be amended after judgment; but if there be any error in giving the judgment, the party is driven to his writ of error; though, where the fault appears to be in the clerk who wrote the record, it may be amended. *Terms of law.*

AMERCEMENT, or AMERCIAMENT, the pecuniary punishment of an offender against the king, or other lord, in his court, that is found to have offended, and to stand at the mercy of the king or lord.

AMICUS CURIÆ. If a judge be doubtful or mistaken, in a matter of law, a bystander may inform the court as *amicus curiæ. Inst.* 178.

AMITTERE LEGEM TERRÆ, to lose and be deprived of the liberty of swearing in any court; such is the punishment of jurors found guilty in a writ of attaint. 5 Eliz. c. 9.

AMNESTY, an act of pardon or oblivion.

AMORTIZATION, an alienation of lands or tenements in mortmain, to any corporation or fraternity, and their successors, &c.

AMPLIATION, a referring of judgment till the cause be further examined.

AMY, is the next friend to be trusted for an infant.

AN, JOUR, ET WASTE, year, day, and waste; a forfeiture of lands to the king by tenants committing felony, and afterwards the lands fall to the lord.

ANCESTOR, one from whom an inheritance is derived.

ANCHORAGE, a duty paid by the ships for the use of the haven where they cast anchor. As all ports and harbours belong to the sovereign, no person can let an anchor fall therein, without paying for the same.

ANCIENTS,

ANCIENTS, gentlemen of the *inns* of *court*. In *Gray's-Inn*, the society consists of *benchers, ancients, barristers*, and *students*, under the bar; here the ancients are of the oldest barristers.

ANCIENT DEMESNE, or DEMAIN, is a certain *tenure*, whereby all manors belonging to the crown in the days of Saint Edward, or William the *Conqueror*, were held, and both their numbers and names were written in the *Domesday-Book* now remaining in the exchequer.

ANGEL, in the computation of money, ten shillings English.

ANGILD, the bare single valuation, or compensation of a criminal.

ANHLOTE, a single tribute, or tax.

ANIENS, void, of no force.

ANNATS, the same meaning with first fruits, because the rate of the first fruits paid for spiritual livings, is after the value of one year's profit.

ANNIENTED, abrogated, frustrated, or brought to nothing.

ANNI NUBILES, when a woman is under the age of twelve years, her age to marry, she is said to be *infra annos nubiles*. 2 *Inst*. 434.

ANNO DOMINI, the computation of time from the incarnation of our Saviour, generally inserted in the dates of all public writings, sometimes with, and sometimes without the king's reign.

ANNOYANCE, any hurt done to a public place, as a highway, bridge, or common river; or to a private, as laying any thing that may breed infection, by encroaching, or the like.

ANNUITY, a yearly rent to be paid for terms of life, or years, or in fee; and is also used for the writ that lies against a man for the recovery of such a rent, if he be not satisfied *yearly* according to the grant.

ANSWER in Chancery. On an indictment for perjury, in an answer in chancery, it is a sufficient proof of *identity*, if the name subscribed be proved to be the hand-writing of the defendant; aud that the same was subscribed by the *master* on being sworn before him.

ANTEJURAMENTUM, the oath sworn by an accuser to prosecute a criminal, and that taken by the accused on the day he was to undergo the ordeal. If the accuser failed to take this oath, the

the criminal was discharged; and if the accused did not take his, he was supposed guilty.

APOTHECARIES, within London and seven miles thereof, being free of the company; and country apothecaries, who have served seven years apprenticeship, shall be exempted from serving offices: their medicines are to be searched and examined by the physicians, chosen by the college of physicians, and if faulty burnt. 32 Hen. VIII. c. 40.

APPARATOR, or APPARITOR, a messenger that serves the process of the spiritual court: his duty is to cite the offenders to appear; to arrest them; and to execute the sentence or decree of the judges.

APPEAL, an accusation of another in a legal form, for a crime by him committed. Formerly there were several kinds of appeals, but those which require any consideration are, death, larceny, and rape, and that of mayhem, which is considered as a trespass; but, on account of the great nicety required in conducting them, these are now entirely disused; and indictment is the only method now taken. 4 *Black.* 313.

Appeal also signifies the removal of a cause to a superior controuling tribunal, where the party bringing the appeal is termed the appellant. An appeal is frequently brought in matters of trade; and, from decision in the plantations, an appeal lies to the king in council.

APPEARANCE, signifies the defendant's filing common or special bail, when he is served with a copy of, or arrested on any process, out of the courts of Westminster. Defendants may *appear in person, by attorney, by guardian, and next friend.*

In person, where the party stands in contempt, for the court will not permit him to appear by attorney: also in capital, and criminal cases; where an act of parliament requires that the party should appear in person; and likewise in appeal or on attachment. 2 *Haw.* P. C. c. 22. s. 1.

By attorney, in all actions real, personal, and mixed, and for any crime whatsoever under the degree of capital, by favour of the court. F. N. B. 26. 1 *Lev.* 146.

By guardian and next friend, when *under age.* *Co. Lit.* 135. b. 2. Inst. 390.

APPELLOR, or APPELLANT, he who has committed some felony,

felony, or other crime, which he confesses and *appeals*; that is, accuses his accomplices.

APPENDANT, any inheritance belonging to another that is superior or more worthy; indifferent to things appendant, and things appurtenant. Thus common of Turbary cannot be *appendant* to land. 4 *Rep.* 37. but *waifs* and *estrays* may be *appendant* to a *leet*, and a *leet* may be appendant to a *manor*. 4 *Rep.* 36. 10 *Rep.* 64.

APPENAGE, or APENAGE, was *formerly* the portion of the younger children of the *kings of France*; where, by a fundamental law, called the law of *appenages*, the younger sons had duchies, counties, or baronies granted to them.

APPORTIONMENT, is a division of rent into parts, according as the land whence the whole issues, is divided among two or more; for on *partition* of lands out of which a rent is issuing, the rent shall be *apportioned*. *Danv. Abr.* 507.

APPOSAL of Sheriffs, the charging them with money received upon their accounts in the exchequer.

APPRAISERS of goods, are sworn to make true *appraisement*; and, if they value the goods *too high*, they shall be obliged to take them at the price *appraised*. Stat. 13 *Ed.* 1.

APPRENTICE, one who is bound by covenant to serve a certain time, upon condition of the master's instructing him in his art or mystery: but he must be retained by the name of an *apprentice expressly*, otherwise he is no apprentice, though he be bound. *Dalt.* c. 58.

An apprenticeship is a personal trust between master and apprentice, and determines by the death of either of them; and where a master dies, an apprentice is not obliged to serve the executors or administrators for the remainder of the term. *Doug.* 1266.

A person cannot be bound *apprentice* but by deed indented; and this must be complied with for all purposes, except for obtaining a settlement. 5 *Eliz.* c. 4. s. 25. But, by 31 Geo. II. c. 11. the apprentice may gain a settlement under such writing, though it be not indented.

Where a premium is given with an apprentice, the indentures must be, if within the bills of mortality, within one month, and elsewhere within two months after the date, taken to the stamp-office

office in the former case; and, in the latter, either to the stamp-office, or the collector of the stamp-duties, and the master or mistress pay a duty of 6d. in the pound upon the premium given, if under 50l. and 1s. for every pound for all above 50l. and, if the full sum given with an apprentice be not inserted, and the duty paid, the indentures are void, and the apprentice not capable of following the trade, and the master liable to a penalty of 50l.

Every indenture for binding a *poor apprentice* must be on a sixpenny stamped piece of paper, or parchment; and an indenture of a *poor or parish apprentice*, assented to by two justices *separately*, is void; and no settlement is gained by serving under it. *Durnf.* and *East* 380. The churchwardens and overseers are not restrained to bind such children to the inhabitants of the parish, but are authorized to apprentice them to *any other persons* wherever resident who are willing to take them. 2 *Durnf.* and *East* 730.

An infant may voluntarily bind himself apprentice by indenture; but no remedy at law lieth against an infant; 5 Eliz. c. 4. If the father covenant, it will of course bind *him*, but the son must be of the party, otherwise it is no apprenticeship. 8 *Mod.* 190.

A man may, by law, chastise and correct his apprentice; but, if the master and his apprentice cannot agree, they may by 2 Geo. II. c. 19. be discharged at their mutual request, either at the quarter sessions, or by one justice with appeal to the sessions; who may, if they think it reasonable, direct restitution of a rateable proportion of the money given with the apprentice. *Salk.* 67. But if an apprentice, with whom less than 10l. has been given, run away from his master, he is compelled to serve out his term of absence, or make satisfaction for the same at any time within seven years after the expiration of the contract. 6 Geo. III. c. 26. And, if an apprentice leave his master's service before his time be expired, his master is entitled to all his earnings, *Ves.* 183. If a person entice away an apprentice he may be indicted, and the master has a remedy for damages by action. 6 *Mod.* 182. Whatever an apprentice gains is for the use of his master. Masters and apprentices in *the city of London* are regulated by the customs of that city. By that custom, every apprentice bound

to

to a freeman must be of 14 years of age, and his agreement must not be for a less term than seven years; and, if he break any of the covenants, an action may be brought against him as if he were of full age. *Green's Privilege of the City*. 27.

An apprentice in London, may be discharged from his master in the following cases: if the master give him unmerciful correction; if he do not provide for him good and wholesome necessaries; if the master turn him away, or refuse to receive him into his service; if he leave off trade, and do not provide another master for the apprentice; if he remove out of the freedom; if he neglect or refuse to instruct the apprentice in his art or trade; if the apprentice shall be under 14 years when bound, or shall be bound for less than seven years; or, if he shall not be enrolled within the first year. *Green's Privilege of the City*.

APPRENTICES, MARINE, *parish* boys *ten years old*, may be bound apprentices to the sea service till *twenty-one*, by the churchwardens and overseers, with the approbation of two justices, or the mayor. 3 *Anne*. c. 6.

Masters of ships from the burthen of 30 to 50 tons, to take *one such apprentice*, and *one more* for the next 50 tons, and *one more* for every 100 tons that such ship shall exceed the burthen of 100 tons. 2 and 3 *Anne* c. 6. s. 7.

No master of a ship is obliged to take an apprentice under 13 years of age, or who is not healthy or strong; and any widow of such master, or his executor, or administrator, who shall have been obliged to take *parish-boys* apprentices, may have the power of assigning them over to another master of a ship: the boy's age to be inserted in the indentures, and the churchwardens and overseers to pay the master 50 shillings for cloathing and bedding for the boy. No such apprentice to be impressed till eighteen years of age, or permitted to enter himself into his Majesty's sea service till that time. 2 and 3 *Anne*, c. 6. s. 2. and 4. and 4 *Anne*, c 19.

Churchwardens shall send the indentures to the collector of the customs, at the port to which the master belongs, who is to register them, and make an indorsement upon the indentures of the registry, and transmit a certificate to the admiralty, containing the apprentice's name and age, and to what ship he belongs, who are to grant protections, from time to time, without fee or reward.

3 Anne, c. 6. s. 5. Collectors refusing or neglecting to register and indorse such indentures, to forfeit five pounds. s. 5.

Voluntary Apprentices, to the sea-service, not to be impressed for three years, reckoning from the dates of their indentures. Indentures to be registered, certificates transmitted, and protections granted for three years.

No apprentices to the sea-service of 18 years of age shall be protected, who shall have been in the sea-service before the date of their indentures.

APPRENTICES to MANUFACTURERS, for the preservation of their health, all rooms and apartments belonging to any mill or factory, shall be washed twice at least in every year, with quick-lime and water, over every part of the walls and cieling thereof; and shall have a sufficient number of windows and openings to insure a proper supply of fresh air. 42 Geo. III. c. 72. Every apprentice shall have one complete suit of cloathing, with suitable linen, stockings, hats, and shoes, delivered to him or her, once at least in every year. s. 3. No apprentice shall be compelled to work more than 12 hours in any day. s. 4. Every such apprentice shall be instructed, for the first four years, at least, of his or her apprenticeship, in the usual hours of work, in reading, writing, and arithmetic, according to their age and abilities; and shall attend for the space of one hour at least every Sunday, and be instructed and examined in the principles of the Christian religion. s. 6. & 8. Apartments of male and female apprentices to be kept distinct, and two only shall sleep in one bed. s. 7. Justices, at their midsummer sessions yearly, shall appoint two visitors of such mills or factories, who shall report the condition thereof to the quarter-sessions.

APPROPRIATION, is the annexing of a benefice to the perpetual use of a religious house, bishopric, college, or *spiritual* person for ever; for which purpose the king's licence was to be obtained in chancery, and also the consent of the ordinary, patron, and incumbent. There are in England 2845 impropriations.

APPROPRIARE COMMUNIAM, to discommon, or inclose any parcel of land that was before laid open.

APPROVE, to approve land, is to make the best benefit of it by increasing the rent.

APPROVEMENT, is where a man hath common in the lord's waste,

waste, and makes an inclosure of part thereof for himself, leaving *sufficient common*, with egress and regress for the commoners.

APPROVER, a person who being indicted of treason or felony, for which he is not in prison, confesses the indictment; and, being sworn to reveal all the treasons and felonies he knows, enters before the coroner his appeal against all his partners in the crime. *Hale*, P. C. 192. All persons may be approvers, except peers of the realm, persons attainted of treason or felony, or outlawed, infants, women, persons non compos, or in holy orders. 3. *Inst.* 129.

Approvers, such as are sent into the counties to increase the farm of hundreds and wapentakes, which were formerly set at a certain rate to the sheriffs.

Approvers to the king, are those that have the letting of the king's demesnes in small manors to his best advantage.

APPURTENANCES, are things both corporeal and incorporeal, appertaining to another thing as principal: as hamlets to a chief manor, common of pasture, piscary, &c. common of estovers to an house; outhouse, yards, orchards, and gardens, are appurtenant to a messuage.

ARAHO, to make an oath in the church, or some other holy place.

ARALIA, arable grounds.

ARATRUM TERRÆ, as much land as can be tilled with one plough.

ARBITRATION, is where the parties submit all matters in dispute, concerning any personal chattels, or personal wrong, to the judgment of one, two, or more arbitrators, who are to decide the controversy; or, if the two do not agree, it is usual to add that another person be called as *umpire*, to whose sole judgment it is then referred. 3 *Black.* 16.

The *submission* to arbitration, is the authority given by the parties in controversy to the arbitrators, to determine and end their grievances; and this being a contract, or agreement, must not be taken strictly, but largely, according to the intent of the parties submitted. *West. Symb.* part 2. s. 1. 2.

An annuity is not determinable by award; neither can *partition* be made by *award.* 1 *Rol. Abr.* Leases for years being chattels real, doubts have arisen if they could be transferred by award.

 It

It seems safest, in every case, that the parties be bound in mutual obligations to perform the award, and if they refuse they forfeit their obligation. Debts on *arrearages of accounts* before auditors, shall not be discharged by award, nor can debts due by *specialty*, except *amongst other things*. 1 *Rol. Abr.* A certain *fixed debt*, cannot be the subject of award. 1 *Bac. Abr. Causes criminal* are not determinable by arbitration, because the perpetrators of crimes should be made known, and punished for the public good. 1 *Bac. Abr.* But, if the party injured proceed by *way of action*, as in assaults and batteries, libels, and the like, the damages may be submitted to arbitration. *Comp. Arbitration. Matrimonial Causes* cannot be submitted to arbitration. 1 *Rol. Abr.* 252. But the damages a person may have sustained by a promise of marriage, or any thing relating to a marriage portion, may. 16 Ed. IV. 2. It is usual to insert, in the *submission*, a clause that no bill in equity shall be filed against the arbitrators: which restriction will be a bar against such bill being brought. 2 *Atkyns*, 395.

ARBITRATOR, is a private extraordinary judge between party and party, chosen by their *mutual consents*, to determine controversies between them. The *award of arbitrators* is definitive, and being chosen by the parties, they are not tied to such formalities of law, as judges in other cases are; and yet they have as great power as other judges, to determine the matter in variance; but their determination must be certain, and it must be according to the express condition of the bond, by which the parties submit themselves to their judgments. 1 *Nels. Abr.* 234. *Dyer* 356.

ARCHBISHOP, the chief bishop in the province. See *Bishop*.

ARCHDEACON, one that hath ecclesiastical dignity and jurisdiction over the clergy and laity next after the bishop throughout the diocese, or in some part of it only. But the power of the archdeacon is different in different dioceses, and therefore, he is to be regulated according to the usage and custom of his own church and diocese.

ARCHERY, a service of keeping a bow for the use of the lord to defend his castle.

ARCHES COURT, the judge whereof is called the *dean of the*

the arches; whose jurisdiction is properly over *the thirteen parishes only*, belonging to the archbishop of Canterbury, in London: but the office of *dean of the arches* having been united with that of the archbishop's *principal official*, he now, in right of his last-mentioned office, receives and determines appeals from the sentences of all inferior ecclesiastical courts within the province.

ARCHIVES, the *rolls*, or any place where ancient records, and charters, and evidences are kept.

AREREIMENT, surprise, affrightment.

ARGENTUM ALBUM, silver coin, in which some rents to the king were paid.

ARGENTUM DEI, money given in earnest upon striking any bargain.

ARMA DARE, to dub, or make a knight.

ARMA LIBERE, a sword and lance, which were usually given to a servant when he was made free.

ARMA MUTARE, a ceremony used to confirm a league of friendship.

ARMIGER, a name of dignity next above the degree of a gentleman, and below a knight; formerly an attendant on the order of knighthood, *bearing their shields*, from thence called scutarius, escuyer, and esquire.

ARMOUR, or ARMS, in the law, are extended to any thing that a man wears for his defence, or takes into his hands, or useth in wrath to cast at, or strike another.

ARMS and AMMUNITION, no merchant-vessel is allowed to carry more than two carriage-guns of 4 pound calibre, nor more than in the proportion of two musquets for every ten men, except ships of marc, or vessels employed in the service of the victualling, ordnance, customs, excise, or post-office, without being regularly licensed for that purpose.. 24 Geo. III. c. 47.

ARRAIGN, or ARRAIN, to *arraign the assise*, is to cause the tenant to be called, to make the plaint, and to set the cause in such order as the tenant may be forced to answer thereto. To *arraign a prisoner*, is to bring him forth to his trial when he is indicted. The prisoner on his arraignment, though under an indictment of the highest crime, must be brought to the bar without irons, and all manner of shackles and bonds: prisoners, however,

 are

are now generally tried in their irons, because taking them off is attended with great pain and trouble.

By the common law, if a principal be acquitted, or pardoned, or die, the accessary shall not be arraigned.

ARRAY, in ancient times it was usual for the king, upon any great emergency, to issue commissions of array, directed to the principal persons in the respective districts, to muster and array all the men capable of bearing arms. *Array* is also applied to a jury, as set in order by the sheriff in his return of the pannel.

ARREARAGES, or ARREARS, denote money unpaid in proper time, as rent behind, the remainder due on account, or a sum of money remaining in the hands of an accomptant.

ARRENTATION, the licensing the owner of lands in the forest, to inclose them with a low hedge and small ditch, according to the assize of the forest, under a yearly rent.

ARREST, *in civil cases,* is a legal restraint of a person charged with some debt to an individual; and, *in criminal cases,* for some crime against the state; and it is executed in pursuance of the command of some court of record, or officer of justice.

Some persons are *privileged from arrests,* as members of parliament, peeresses by birth, marriage, &c. members of convocation actually attending them, ambassadors, domestic servants of ambassadors, king's servants, marshals, or wardens of the fleet, clerks, attornies, or other persons attending the courts of justice, clergymen performing divine service, suitors, witnesses subpœnaed, and other persons necessarily attending any court of record upon business, bankrupts coming to surrender within 42 days after their surrender, witnesses properly summoned before commissioners of bankruptcy, or other commissioners of great seal; sailors and volunteer soldiers, unless the debt be 20l., officers of court, only where they are sued in their rights; but not if as executors or administrators, nor in joint actions.

No writ, process, warrant, &c. (except for treason, felony, or for breach of the peace), shall be served on Sunday; but a person arrested the day before, may be re-taken on the Sunday.

No person can be arrested out of a superior court, unless the cause of action be 10l. and upwards; an arrest must be by corporal seizing, or touching the defendant.

An

An officer cannot justify breaking open an outward door or window to execute process, unless a sranger who is not of the family, *upon a pursuit,* take refuge in the house of another. The chamber of a lodger is not to be considered as *his outer door.* No officer shall carry his prisoner to any tavern without his consent, nor to goal within 24 hours after his arrest, unless he refuse to go to some safe house.

In criminal cases, the causes of suspicion which justify the arrest of a person for felony are, the common fame of the country; the living a vagrant, idle, disorderly life, without any visible means to support it; the being in company with a known offender at the *time of the offence*; the being found in circumstances which induce a strong presumption of guilt; behaviour betraying a consciousness of guilt; and the being pursued by hue and cry. But none of these causes will justify the arresting a man for the *suspicion* of crimes, unless a crime were actually committed.

ARREST OF JUDGMENT, to move *in arrest of judgment,* is to shew cause why judgment should not be stayed, notwithstanding a verdict given; the causes of arrest of judgment, are want of notice of trial; where the plaintiff before trial treats the jury; the record differs from the deed pleaded; for material defect in pleading; where persons are misnamed; more is given and found by the verdict, than laid in, the declaration; or, the declaration doth not lay the thing with certainty, &c.

ARRESTANDIS BONIS NE DISSIPENTUR, a writ which lies for a man whose goods, &c. are taken by another, who during the contest, doth or is like to make them away.

ARRESTANDO IPSUM QUI PECUNIAM RECEPIT, a writ that lieth for apprehending a person, who hath taken the king's prest-money to serve in the wars, and hides himself when he should go.

ARRESTO FACTO SUPER BONIS MERCATORUM ALIENIGENORUM, a writ which lies for a denizen, against the goods of *aliens* found in this kingdom, in recompense of goods taken from him in a foreign country, after denial of restitution.

ARRETTED, is where a man is convened before a judge, and charged with a crime.

ARROWS, by an ancient statute, all heads of *arrows* shall be well

well brazed, and hardened at the point with steel, on pain of imprisonment.

ARSON, is house burning, and burning the *house of another* is felony. *Cr. Law, case* 143. It must be maliciously and voluntarily, and an actual burning; not putting fire only into a house, or any part of it, *without burning*; but if part of the house *be burnt*; or if the fire do burn, and then go out of itself, it is felony. 2 *Inst.* 188. But it is not felony to burn a house (unless done with a fraudulent intent) of which the offender is in possession by virtue of a written agreement, for a lease for three years. *Cr. Law,* 143. If any servant through *carelessness* shall fire any house or outhouse, and be thereof convicted on the oath of one witness, before two justices, he shall forfeit 100l. to the churchwardens of the parish where the fire shall happen, to be by them distributed to the sufferers; and, on non-payment thereof immediately on demand, the said justices shall commit him to some house of correction for 18 months, to be there kept to hard labour.

ARSER IN LE MAINE, burning in the hand, the punishment of criminals that have the benefit of clergy.

ART AND PART, a term used in *Scotland,* when one charged with a crime in committing the same, was both a contriver of, and acted a part in it.

ARTHEL, or ARDDEL, to vouch, one taken with stolen goods in his hands, was to be allowed a lawful *arthel* or voucher, to clear him of the felony. 26 Hen. VIII. c. 6.

ARTICLE, signifies a complaint exhibited in the ecclesiastical court by way of libel.

Articles of the Navy, are rules and orders made by 31 Geo. II. c. 10. for the government of the royal fleet.

Articles of the Peace, are a complaint exhibited in the courts of *Westminster,* in order to compel the defendant to find *sureties of the peace.*

Articles of Religion, are the 39 articles, drawn up by the convocation in 1562, unto which persons admitted into ecclesiastical offices are to subscribe.

Articles of War, a code of laws made by his majesty, from time to time, for the regulation of his land forces, in pursuance of the several annual acts against mutiny and desertion.

ARTIFICERS, a stranger-artificer in London shall not keep more than two stranger servants. 2 Hen. VIII. c. 16.

Persons contracting with *artificers in wool, iron, steel, brass, or other metal*, &c. to go to any foreign country, shall be imprisoned three months; 5 Geo. I. c. 27. and, if any person shall contract with, or encourge any artificers employed in *printing calicoes, cottons, muslins, or linens of any sort*, or in making *any tools or utensils for such manufactory*, to go out of Great Britain to any port beyond the seas, he shall forfeit 500l. and be committed to the common goal of the county for twelve months, and until such forfeiture shall be paid. 22 Geo. III. c. 60. s. 12.

ASPORTATION, a felonious *taking*, and *carrying away* the goods of another; the continuance of the property in the possession of the robber, is not required by the law to compleat the crime.

ASSAULT AND BATTERY, an attempt or offer with force and violence to do a corporal hurt to another; and any injury whatsoever, be it never so small, being actually done to the person of a man, in an angry or revengeful, or rude or insolent manner, are batteries in the eye of the law. 6 *Mod* 149.

A man may justify an assault in defence of his person, or of his wife, or master, or parent, or *child within age*, and even *wounding* may be justified in defence of his *person*, but not of his possessions. 3 *Salk* 46. And if he beat him who committed the assault, he may take advantage thereof, both upon an indictment, and upon an action. 1. *Haw.* 134.

ASSAY, the examination of weights and measures, by the clerks of markets and others.

ASSAYER OF THE KING, an officer of the king's mint, for the trial of silver, gold, &c.

ASSENT. See *Executor, Legacy, Leases*, &c.

ASSESSORS, those that *assess* public taxes, by rating every person according to his estate.

ASSETS, are goods or property in the hands of a person, with which he is enabled to discharge an obligation imposed upon him by another; they may be either *real or personal*. Where a person holds lands in fee simple and dies seized thereof, those lands when they come to the heir, are called *assets*. So far as obligations are left on the part of the deceased to be fulfilled, they are called

called *assets real.* When such assets fall into the management of executors, they are called assets *inter maines.* When the property left, consists of goods, money, or personal property, they are called *assets personal.*

ASSIDERE, or ASSIDARE, to tax equally. Also to sign an annual rent, to be paid out of a particular farm.

ASSIGN, to set over right to another.

ASSIGNMENT, is a transfer or making over to another, of the right one has in any estate; but it is usually applied to an estate for life or years. And it differs in a lease only in this; that by a lease one grants an interest *less* than his own, reserving to himself a reversion; in assignment he parts with the whole property, and the assignee stands to all intents and purposes in the place of the assignor. 2 *Black.* 326.

ASSISE, is taken for the court, place, or time, when and where the writs and processes of assise are handled or taken. Concerning the general assises, all the counties of *England,* are divided into six circuits; and two judges are assigned by the king's commission to every circuit, who hold their assises twice a year in every county (except *Middlesex* where the king's courts of record are held; and his courts for his counties palatine), and have five several commissions.

A *commission of assise* directed to themselves and the clerk of the *assise,* to take the assises, that is to take the verdict of a peculiar species of jury, called an *assise,* summoned for the trial of landed disputes.

A *commission of oyer and terminer,* empowering them to hear and determine treasons, felonies, and other misdemeanors, whether the persons be *in goal or not.*

A *commission of general goal delivery,* to try every prisoner *in the goal* committed for any offence whatsoever, but only such prisoners as *are in goal.*

A *commission or writ of nisi prius,* by which civil causes, brought to issue in the courts above, are tried in the vacation by a jury of twelve men of the county where the action arises, and on return of the verdict of the jury to the *court above,* the judges there give judgment.

A *commission of the peace,* in every county of the circuits; and all justices of the peace of the county are bound to be present at the assises.

ASSISE

ASSISE OF THE FOREST, a statute touching orders to be observed in the king's forest.

ASSISERS, in *Scotland*, the same with jurors.

ASSISUS, rented or farmed out for such an *assise*, or certain assessed rent, in money or provisions.

ASSITHMENT, a wiregild or compensation, by a pecuniary fine.

ASSOCIATION, a writ sent by the king to the justices appointed to take assises, to have others *associated* unto them; as where a justice of assise dies.

ASSOILE, to deliver from excommunication.

ASSUMPSIT, an assumpsit is a voluntary promise made by word, or supposed to be made by word, whereby a person upon some valuable consideration, *assumeth* or undertaketh to perform or pay something to another.

An assumpsit is either *express* or *implied*. Express, is by direct agreement either by word, or by note in writing without seal; as when a person *assumes* or *promises* to pay money upon a bargain or sale, and fails so to do, an action of assumpsit lies against him. 3 *Black.* 157.

Implied contracts, are such as do not arise from the express determination of any court, on the positive directions of any statute; but from natural reason and the just construction of the law; extending to all *presumptive* undertakings and *assumpsits*: which though never, perhaps, actually made, yet constantly arise upon this general *implication* and *intendment* of the courts of judicature; that *every man hath engaged to perform what his duty or justice requires.* Thus where one takes up goods or wares of a tradesman, without expressly agreeing for the price. The law concludes that both parties did intentionally agree, that the real value of the goods should be paid; and an action of assumpsit may be brought accordingly. 3 *Black.* 162.

ASSURANCE OF LANDS, is where lands or tenements, are conveyed by deed; see also *Insurance*.

ASTARIUS HÆRES, where the ancestor by conveyance, hath set his heir apparent and his family in a house in his life-time.

ATTACH, to take or apprehend by commandment of a writ or precept.

ATTACHIAMENTA BONORUM, a distress taken upon goods

goods or chattels, where a man is sued for a personal estate or debt, by the legal *attachiators* or bailiffs, as security to answer an action.

ATTACHMENT, is a process that issues at the discretion of the judges of a court of record, against a person for some contempt; against which all courts of record, but more especially those of *Westminster-hall*, may proceed in a summary way. Thus sheriffs and other officers are liable to an attachment, for an oppressive or illegal practice in the execution of a writ.

ATTACHMENT *foreign*, is an attachment of the goods of foreigners, found in some liberty or city, to satisfy their creditors within such liberty. *Carth. Rep.* 66. And by the custom of some places, as *London*, &c. a man may attach money or goods, in the hands of a stranger; though by the custom of *London* money may be attached *before due as a debt*; but not levied before due. But a *foreign attachment* cannot be had when a suit is depending in any of the courts at *Westminster*; and nothing is attachable but for a certain and due debt. Cro. *Eliz.* 691.

ATTACHMENT OF THE FOREST, is the lowest of the three courts held there. The middle one, is called the *Swainemote*; the highest *the justice in Eyre's seat.*

ATTACHMENT OF PRIVILEGE, is where a man by virtue of his privilege, calls another to that court whereto he himself belongs; and in respect thereof is privileged, there to answer some action.

ATTAINDER, is properly where sentence is pronounced against a person convicted of treason or felony: he is then tainted or stained; whereby his blood is so much corrupted, that by the common law his children or other kindred cannot inherit his estate, nor his wife claim her dower, and the same cannot be restored or saved but by act of parliament.

ATTAINT, is a writ that lies to enquire whether a jury of twelve men gave a false verdict. But this proceeding is now entirely disused; and instead of attaint, motions are usually made for new trials, when a verdict is against evidence. 3 *Black.* 390.

ATTENDANT, one that owes a duty or service to another. Thus there is a *lord, mesne,* and *tenant*; the *tenant* holds of the *mesne* by a penny; the *mesne* holds over by two-pence; the *mesne* releases to the *tenant*, all the right he hath in the land, and the tenant dies; his wife shall be endowed of the land, and she shall be *attendant*, to the *heir* of the third part of the penny, not of the third part of the two-pence, for she shall be endowed of the best possession of her husband.

ATTERMINING, is used for a term granted for payment of a debt.

ATTORNARE REM, to assign or appropriate money or goods, to some particular use and service.

ATTORNATO FACIENDO VEL RECIPIENDO, a writ to command a sheriff or steward of a county, or hundred court, to receive or admit an *attorney*, to appear for the person that owes suit of court.

ATTORNEY, is a person legally authorized, by another to pay or receive monies, sue or transact any other kind of business, in the name of such person as shall appoint him his lawful attorney.

Attorney is either *public*, in the king's courts of record; or *private* upon occasion of any particular business; who is commonly made by virtue of a power of attorney, which must be drawn up in a legal form, adapted to the case.

ATTORNIES AT LAW, are such persons as take upon them the business of other men, by whom they are retained. By the 2 Geo. II. c. 23. s. 5. no person shall be permitted to act as an attorney, or to sue out any process in the name of any other person in any courts of law, unless such person shall have been bound by contract in writing, to serve as a clerk for five years to an attorney duly sworn and admitted in some of the said courts; and such person, during the said term of five years, shall have continued in such service, and unless such person, after the expiration of the said five years, shall be examined, sworn, admitted, and inrolled. And for every piece of vellum, parchment, or paper, upon which shall be written any such contract, whereby any person shall become bound to serve as a clerk aforesaid, in order to his admission as a solicitor or attorney in any of the courts at *Westminster* there shall be charged a stamp-duty of 100l. 34 Geo. III. c. 14. And in order to his admission as a solicitor or attorney in any of the great courts of sessions in *Wales*, or in the counties palatine of *Chester*, *Lancaster*, or *Durham*, or in any court of record in England holding pleas to the amount of forty shillings; and not in any of the said courts of *Westminster*, there shall be charged a stamp duty of fifty pounds. *Id.* Every attorney, solicitor, notary, proctor, agent, or procurator, practising in any of the courts at *Westminster*, ecclesiastical, admiralty, or cinque-port courts, in his majesty's courts in *Scotland*, the great sessions in *Wales*, the courts in the counties Palatine, or any other courts holding pleas to the amount of forty shillings, or more; shall take out a certificate *annually*, upon which there shall be charged if the solicitor, &c. reside *within the bills of mortality* a stamp-duty of five pounds, in any other part of *Great Britain* three pounds, Persons practising after the 1st day of *November* 1797, without obtaining a certificate, shall forfeit fifty pounds, and be incapable of suing for any fees. An attorney shall not be elected into any office against his will, such as constable, overseer of the poor, or churchwarden, or any office within a borough; but his privilege will not exempt him from serving in the militia, or finding a substitute. *Black. Rep.* 1123. See *Arrest and Privilege*.

ATTORNEY OF THE DUCHY COURT OF LANCASTER, is the second officer of that court.

ATTORNEY OF THE WARDS AND LIVERIES, was the third officer of that court.

ATTORNEY-GENERAL, a great officer under the king, made by letters patent; whose office is to exhibit informations and prosecute for the crown in matters criminal; and to file bills in the exchequer, for any thing concerning the king in inheritance or profits; and others may bring bills against the king's attorney.

ATTORNMENT, is the consent of the tenant to the grant of the seigniory or the reversion, putting him into the possession of services due from such tenant.

AVAGE, a rent or payment which every tenant of the manor of *Writtel* in Essex, on the 6th of November pays to the lord for the privilege of pawnage in his woods.

AUCTIONS and AUCTIONEERS, every person exercising the trade of an auctioneer *within the bills of mortality*, shall pay twenty shillings annually for a licence; and without the said bills of mortality five shillings. Auctions and auctioneers are regulated by statutes 29, 30, 32 Geo. III. c. 63, 26, 41.

A bidder

A bidder at an auction, under the usual conditions that the highest bidder shall be the purchaser, may retract his bidding any time *before the hammer is down*.

AUDIENCE COURT, a court belonging to the archbishop of *Canterbury*, having the same authority with the court of arches, but inferior in antiquity and dignity.

AUDIENDO ET TERMINANDO, a commission to certain persons, in case of any insurrection or great riot, for the appeasing and punishment thereof.

AUDITA QUERELA, is, where a defendant against whom judgment is recovered, and who is therefore in danger of execution, or perhaps actually in execution, may be relieved upon good matter of discharge which hath happened since the judgment; as if the plaintiff have given him a release.

AUDITOR, is an officer of the king, or some other great person, who examines yearly the accounts of all under-officers, and makes up a general book, which shews the difference between their receipts and charge; such as the auditors of the exchequer.

AUDITOR OF THE RECEIPTS, an officer of the exchequer, who files the teller's bills, and having made an entry of them, gives the lord-treasurer, &c. a weekly certificate of the money received. 4 *Inst.* 107.

AVENAGE, a certain quantity of oats paid by a tenant to his landlord as a rent.

AVENTURE, a *mischance* or accident causing the death of a man.

AVERAGE, is said to signify service which the tenant owes to his lord by horse or carriage; but is more particularly used for a certain contribution that merchants make proportionably to their losses, who have had their goods cast into the sea in the time of tempest.

AVERAGE OF CORN-FIELDS, the stubble or remainder of straw and grass left in corn-fields, after the harvest is carried away.

AVER-CORN, is a reserved rent in *corn* paid by farmers and tenants to religious houses.

AVERIA, signifies oxen or horses of the plough, and generally any cattle.

AVERIIS CAPTIS IN WITHERNAM, a writ for the taking of cattle to his use, who hath cattle unlawfully distrained by another, and driven out of the county where they were taken, so that they cannot be replevied by the sheriff.

AVERMENT, is an offer of the defendant to justify an exception pleaded in abatement, or bar of the plaintiff's action, and is to ascertain that to the court which is generally or doubtfully alledged, so that the court may not be perplexed *of whom or of what* it ought to be understood. *Heath's Max.* 42.

AVER-PENNY, money paid towards the king's *averages* or carriages.

AVER-SILVER, a custom or rent formerly so called.

AUGMENTATION, the name of a court erected by Hen. VIII. for determining suits and controversies relating to monasteries and abbey lands.

AULA, a court baron.

AULA REGIS, was a court established by *William* the Conqueror in his own hall. It was composed of the king's great officers of state resident in his palace, who usually attended on his person, and followed him in all his progresses and expeditions: which being found inconvenient and burthensome, it was enacted by the great charter, c. 11. that common pleas shall no longer follow the king's court, but shall be holden in some certain place, which certain place was established in Westminster-Hall, where the *aula regis* originally sat when the king resided in that city; and there it has ever since continued. 3 *Black.* 37.

AUMONE, tenure in *aumone* is where lands are given to some church or religious house, on condition, some service or prayers shall be offered at certain times for the repose of the donor's soul.

AUNCEL-WEIGHT, an ancient manner of weighing by hand, but long since prohibited by statute.

AVOIDANCE, is where there is want of a lawful incumbent on a benefice, during which the church is *quasi viduata,* and the possessions belonging to it are in *abeyance.*

AVOWRY, is where one takes distress for rent, or other thing, and the party distrained sues a *replevin,* he who took the distress shall justify his plea for what cause he took it; and if in his own right

right, he must shew the same and *avow* the taking, which is his *avowry*.

AURES, the punishment of cutting off the ears, inflicted by the Saxon laws on those who robbed churches.

AURUM REGINÆ, the queen's gold. This is an ancient perquisite belonging to every queen-consort, during her marriage with the king, and due from every person who has made a voluntary offering or fine to the king, amounting to ten marks or upwards. As where 100 marks in silver be given to the king to have a fair, market, park, chase, or free warren, there the queen is intitled to ten marks in silver, or to one mark in gold.

AUTER DROIT, is where persons sue or are sued in another's rights, as executors, administrators, &c.

AUTERFOITS ACQUIT, is a plea by a criminal, that he was heretofore *acquitted* of the same treason or felony, for no one shall be brought into danger of his life, for the same offence more than once. 3 *Inst.* 213.

AUTHORITY, is a delegated power, by which one person authorizes another to act generally, or especially in his name; and by whose acts, where the authority is strictly pursued, the party delegating such power, will be bound. An authority may be given either verbally or in writing, but the latter is the most usual. Where one person is delegated to act for another, he must not use his own name only, but the name also of the person who gave the authority. 9 *Rep.* 76.

AURITIUM AD FILIUM MILITEM FACIENDUM ET FILIAM MARITANDAM, a writ formerly directed to the sheriff of every county where the king or other lord had any tenements, to levy of them an aid towards the knighting of a son, and the marrying of a daughter.

AURITIUM CURIÆ, a precept or order of court, for the citing of one party, at the suit and request of another, to warrant something.

AURILIUM FACERE ALICUI IN CURIA REGIS, to be another's friend and solicitor in the king's court.

AURILIUM REGIS, the king's aid, or money levied for the king's use, and the public service.

AURILIUM VICE COMITI, a customary aid or duty, anciently

ciently payable to sheriffs out of certain manors, for the better support of their offices.

AWAIT, *way-laying* or laying in *wait*, to execute some mischief. It is enacted that no charter of pardon shall be allowed before any justice, for the death of a man slain by *await*, or malice prepense. 13 Rich. II. c. 1.

AWARD. See *Arbitration.*

B

BAARD an ancient sort of vessel, or transport.

BACCINUM, the service of holding the bason on the day of the king's coronation.

BACHELERIA, the commonalty, or yeomanry.

BACHELOR, an inferior degree taken by students, before they attain to a higher dignity.

BACKVERIND, bearing upon the back, or about a man; as where the thief is apprehended with the stolen goods upon his back.

BACKING, a warrant of the justice of the peace, is, where a warrant granted in one jurisdiction is required to be executed in another; as where a felony has been committed in one county, and the offender resides in another: in which case, on proof of the hand-writing of the justice who granted the warrant, a justice in such other county, indorses, or writes his name at the back of it, thereby giving authority to execute the warrant in such other county.

BADGER, one that buys corn, or victuals, in one place, and carries them to another, to sell and make profit by them. By Stat. 5 and 6 Ed. VI. c. 14. such an one is exempted from the punishment of an ingrosser. But by 5 Eliz. c. 12. and 13 Eliz. c. 25. they are to be annually licensed by justices in the sessions, and must enter into recognizance not to do any thing under colour of their licenses, contrary to the statutes made against forestallers, ingrossers, and regrators.

BAIL, is the freeing, or setting at liberty, of one arrested, or imprisoned,

imprisoned, upon any action, *civil* or *criminal*, on surety taken for his appearance at a day and place certain, or when demanded.

Bail, in *civil cases*, is either *common* or *special*. *Common bail* is a matter of course, being nothing but a *mere form* upon appearance, after personal service of the writ, and notice to appear upon the defendant. If he appear thereto, his attorney puts in imaginary sureties for his future attendance, as John Doe and Richard Roe. But if the plaintiff will make affidavit, that the cause of action amounts to 10l. or upwards, in order to arrest the defendant, and make him put in substantial sureties for his appearance, called *special bail*; it is then required that the true cause of action be expressed in the body of the writ, or process. 3 *Black*. 287.

Special bail, are two or more persons, who, after the arrest, undertake *generally*, or enter into bond to the sheriff in a certain sum, to insure the defendant's appearance at the return of the writ: this obligation is called the *bail bond*.

Bail in criminal cases. Upon offering sufficient surety, bail may be taken either in court, or in some particular cases, by the sheriff, coroner, or other magistrate, but most usually by justices of the peace; in the following cases, *persons* of good fame, charged with *a bare suspicion* of manslaughter, or other inferior homicide. *Persons* charged with petit larceny, or any felony not before specified. *Accessaries* to felony, not being of evil fame, nor under strong presumption of guilt. But *bail cannot be taken* upon an accusation of treason, nor of murder, nor in the case of manslaughter, if the person be clearly the slayer; nor such as being committed for felony have broken prison, nor persons outlawed, nor such as have abjured the realm, nor approvers, nor persons taken with the mainour, or in the fact of felony, nor persons charged with house burning, nor persons taken by writ of *excommunicato capiendo*.

BAILIFF, a keeper, or protector. Hence the Sheriff is considered as bailiff to the crown, and his county, of which he hath the care, and in which he is to execute the king's writ, is called his bailiwick; so also his officers who execute writs, warrants, &c. are called *bailiffs*.

BAILIFFS OF COURTS BARON, summon those courts, and

and execute the process thereof; they present all pound-breaches, cattle strayed, &c.

BAILIWICK, signifies generally that liberty, which is exempted from the sheriff of the county, over which the lord of the liberty appoints a *bailiff*, such as the bailiff of *Westminster*.

BAILMENT, is a delivery of things, whether writings, goods, &c. to another, sometimes to be delivered back to the *bailor*; that is to him who so delivered them; sometimes to the use of the *bailee*; that is, of him to whom they are delivered; and sometimes also to be delivered to a *third person*: this delivery is called a *bailment*. 2 *Black*. 451.

The following rules are laid down as actions in the law of bailments:—

A *Bailee*, who derives no benefit from his undertaking, is responsible only for gross negligence.

A *Bailer*, who alone receives benefit from the bailment, is responsible for slight neglect.

When the *bailment* is beneficial to both parties, the *bailee* must answer for ordinary neglect.

A special agreement of the *bailee* to answer for more or less, is in general, valid.

All *bailers* are answerable for actual fraud, even though the contrary be stipulated.

No *bailee* shall be charged for a loss by inevitable accident, or irresistible force, except by special agreement.

Robbery by Force is considered as irresistible; but a loss by private stealth, is presumptive evidence of ordinary neglect.

Gross Neglect is a violation of good faith.

No action lies to compel performance of a naked contract.

The negligence of a servant acting by his master's orders, expressed or implied, is the negligence of the master.

BAIRMAN, a poor insolvent creditor, left bare and naked.

BALENGER, a barge or water-vessel, and also a man of war.

BALISTARIUS, a cross-bow man.

BALIVO AMOVENDO, a writ to remove a *bailiff* from his office, for want of sufficient land in the bailiwick.

BALLANCE or BALANCE, of trade, a term applied to the money balance to be paid by one nation, trading and carrying on business with another. So far as the articles mutually exported and

and imported pay for each other, there is no balance; but on which ever side the exports fall short in their amount, that nation is said to have the balance against it and vice versa.

BALLAST, gravel or sand thrown into the hold of a ship, to enable her to carry a sufficient quantity of sail, without oversetting. All ships and vessels taking in *ballast* in the river *Thames*, shall pay to the corporation of the *Trinity-house* for all *ballast* demanded, after the rates following. For every ton, consisting of twenty hundred weight carried to any *ship in the coal trade* 1s. For every ton carried to any other *British ship* 1s. 3d. For every ton carried to any *foreign ship* 1s. 7d. The trinity-house shall employ the *ballast-men*, and regulate them; and their lighters are to be marked, so that their tonnage may be clearly ascertained, on pain of forfeiting 10l. 6 Geo. II. c. 29.

BAN, a public notice, summons, or edict; it is most especially used in the publication of intended marriages, which must be done on three several Sundays previous to the marriage, that if any can shew just cause against such marriage they may have an opportunity to make their objections.

BANE, destruction, as he who is the cause of another man's death is said to be *le bane*, that is a malefactor. *Bract. lib. 2. tract* 8. c. 1.

BANERET, is a knight made in the field, with the ceremony of cutting of his standard, and making it a kind of a *banner*; which is deemed so honourable, that they are allowed to display their arms in the king's army as barons do, and may bear arms with supporters.

BANISHMENT, is a forsaking or quitting of the realm; there are two kinds of it, one voluntary called *abjuration*, and the other upon compulsion, for some offence.

By the *habeas corpus act*, 31 Ch. II. c 2. no subject of this realm, who is an inhabitant of England, Wales, or Berwick, shall be sent prisoner into Scotland, Ireland, Jersey, Guernsey, or place beyond the seas, where they cannot have the protection of the *common law*; for by it, every *Englishman* may claim a right to abide in his own country so long as he pleases, and not be banished or driven from it but by sentence of the law. See *Transportation*.

BANK, in the common law, is a seat or bench of judgment.

Bank le roy, the king's-bench; *bank le common pleas*, the bench of common pleas.

BANK OF ENGLAND, is the first bank in point of consequence in Europe; it is managed by a governor and directors, established by act of parliament; with funds for maintenance thereof, appropriated to such persons as were subscribers; and the capital stock, which is enlarged by several statutes, is exempted from taxes. The banking system is founded on the principle of depositing a value, which is forthcoming and answerable for written promises issued, called notes, and which pass from hand to hand as a circulating medium, or as the coin of the country.

BANKRUPT, a trader whom misfortune or extravagance has induced to commit an act of bankruptcy. The benefit of the bankrupt laws is allowed to none but *actual traders*, or such as buy and sell, and gain a livelihood by so doing.

Requisites to constitute a trading, the merchandising, or buying, and selling, must be of that kind, whereby the party gains a credit upon the profits of an uncertain capital stock. Manufacturers, or persons purchasing goods or raw materials to sell again under other forms, or ameliorated by labor, as bakers, brewers, butchers, shoemakers, smiths, tanners, taylors, &c. are also within the statutes.

The following description of persons, are not within the statutes of bankruptcy, viz. proprietors or persons having an interest in land, if buying and selling to whatever extent, for the purposes of disposing merely of the produce and profits of such land; graziers and drovers; owners of coal-mines working and selling the coals; owners or farmers of allum-rocks; farmers who make cheeses for sale, or those who sell cyder made from apples of their own orchard. In all such cases, and others of a similar nature, where the several materials are purchased, and even some kind of manufacture exercised; yet as this is the necessary and customary mode of receiving the benefit arising from the land, such persons are not held to be traders within the statutes; nor are persons buying and selling bank stock or government securities. Buying or selling only, will neither *singly* constitute trading; neither will a single act of buying *and* selling; or drawing or redrawing bills of exchange merely for the purpose of raising money for *private* occasions, and not with a view to gain a profit

upon

upon the exchange. Being a part-owner in a ship, barge, or waggon, does *not constitute* a trader; nor holding a share or interest in a joint stock with others who trade, unless he share in the profit and loss upon the disposition of the capital. The merchandize must also be general, and not in a qualified manner only, as victuallers or innkeepers, schoolmasters, commissioners of the navy who victual the fleet by private contract, the king's butler, steward, or other officers; officers of excise or custom, sutlers of the armies, butlers, stewards of inns of court, clergymen, &c. as acting in such capacities *merely*, are not liable to be made bankrupts; the buying and selling in such cases not being general but in the exercise of particular employments. Neither, upon the same principle, are receivers of the king's taxes, or persons discounting exchequer bills. If the parties above enumerated however, being themselves within the bankrupt laws in any other respect, they will be liable to their operation, although they should evidently not profit by trading, or such trading should be illegal; although the trading should not be wholly carried on in England, buying only in England and selling beyond sea. Any person, native, denizen, or alien, residing in any part of the British dominions, or in foreign countries, though never a resident trader in England, yet if he be a trader, and coming to England commit an act of bankruptcy, he will be subject to the bankrupt laws.

No one can be a bankrupt, on account of any debt, which he is not compellable by law to discharge, as infants or married women. And if a single woman be a trader, and committing any act of bankruptcy, afterwards marry, a commission issued against her after such marriage, cannot be supported. But according to the custom of London, where a married woman is *sole trader*, she is held liable to a commission of bankruptcy like a *feme sole*.

Acts of bankruptcy. Departing the realm. This must be done with intent to defraud or delay creditors; when it appears that there was no such intention, it will not be a departure within the meaning of the statutes. 7 T. R. 509.

Departing from the dwelling-house. Such departure must also be with intent to defraud *and delay* creditors; for the departure with an *intent* to delay, has been held insufficient, without *an actual* delay of some creditors. *Str.* 803.

Beginning

Beginning to keep the house, the being denied to a creditor who calls for money; but an *order* to be denied, is not enough without *an actual denial,* and that also to a creditor who has a debt demandable at the time. 5 T. R. 575.

Voluntary arrest, not only for a fictitious debt, but even for a just one, if done with the intent to delay creditors, is an act of bankruptcy.

Suffering outlawry, with an intent to defraud the creditors, but this will not make a man a bankrupt, if reversed before issuing a commission, or for default of proclamations after it, unless such *outlawry* were originally fraudulent.

Escaping from prison. Being arrested for a just debt of 100l. or upwards, and escaping against the consent of the sheriff.

Fraudulent procurement of goods to be attached or sequestered. A fraudulent execution, though void against creditors, is not within the meaning of the words, *attachment,* or *sequestration,* used in the statute; because they relate only to proceedings used in *London, Bristol,* and other places.

Making any fraudulent conveyance. Any conveyance of property, whether total or partial, made with a view to defeat the claims of creditors, is a fraud, and if it be by deed, is held to be an act of bankruptcy.

A conveyance by a trader of all his effects and stock in trade by deed, to the exclusion of any one or more of his creditors, has been ever held to be an act of bankruptcy.

A mortgage (amongst other things) of all the stock in trade of a tradesman, was held to be an act of bankruptcy, as being an assignment of all the stock in trade, without which he could carry on no business.

A conveyance by a trader, of part of his effects to a particular creditor, carries no evidence whatever of fraud, unless made in contemplation of bankruptcy.

Being arrested for debt, lying in prison two months or more, upon that or any other arrest, or detention in prison for debt, will make the party a bankrupt, from the time of the first arrest: but where the bail is fairly put in, and the party at a future day surrenders in discharge of his bail, the two months are computed from the time of the surrender.

Of proceedings under a commission. The lord chancellor is empowered to issue a commission of bankrupt, and is bound to grant it as matter of right. By 5 Geo. II. c. 30. no commission can issue, unless upon the petition of a single creditor, to whom the bankrupt owes a debt which shall amount to 100l. the debt of two or more, *being partners*, shall amount to 150l. and of three or more to 200l.

If the debt against the bankrupt amount to the sum required, it is not material, though the creditor should have acquired it for less.

If a creditor to the *full amount*, before an act of bankruptcy committed, receive after notice of the bankruptcy a part of his debt, such payment being illegal, cannot be retained, and the original debt remains in force, and will support a commission.

The debt must be a legal and not an equitable one, and if the legal demand be not in its nature assignable, the assignee cannot be the petitioning creditor, as the assignee of a bond.

If the creditor, for a debt at law, have the body of his debtor in execution, he cannot at the same time, sue out a commission upon it; that being, in point of law, a satisfaction for the debt.

Of opening the commission. When the commissioners have received proof of the petitioning creditor's debt, the trading, and act of bankruptcy, they declare and adjudge the party a bankrupt. They are authorized to issue a warrant under their hands and seals, for the seizure of all the bankrupt's effects, books, or writings, and for that purpose to enter the house, or any other place belonging to the bankrupt.

Such debts only can be proved under a commission, as were either debts certainly payable, and which existed at the time of the bankruptcy, or which, although originally contingent, yet, from the contingency happening before the bankruptcy, were become absolute. In every case the amount of the debt must be precisely ascertained.

Time and method of proving. Creditors were formerly precluded from proving after four months, but the court now, except in cases of gross negligence, allows them to come in at any time, whilst any thing remains to be disposed of. The usual proof required, is the oath of the creditor himself, either in person, or by affidavit, if he live remote from the place of meeting, or reside in foreign parts. 5 Geo. II.

Corporations, or *companies,* are generally admitted to prove by a treasurer, clerk, or other officer duly authorized.

Of the assignees. Immediately after declaration of the bankruptcy, the commissioners are to appoint a time and place for the creditors to meet and choose assignees, and are directed to assign the bankrupt's estate and effects to such persons as shall be chosen by the major part in value.

The powers and duties of assignees are principally those of collecting the bankrupt's property, reducing the whole into ready money, and making distribution as early as possible. One assignee is not answerable for the neglect of another. Assignees, if they act improperly, are not only liable at law to the creditors for a breach of trust, but may be removed on account of misbehaviour, &c. by petitioning the lord chancellor. Upon the removal of an assignee, he is directed to join with the remaining one, in assignment to the latter and new assignee.

Provisions for wife, children, &c. By the statute of Eliz. the commissioners may assign any lands, &c. that the bankrupt shall have purchased jointly with his wife, and the assignment shall be effectual, against the bankrupt, his wife, or children; but this shall not extend to conveyances made before the bankruptcy *bona fide,* and not to the use of the bankrupt himself only, or his heirs, and where the party to the conveyance are not privy to the fraudulent purposes to deceive the creditors.

Examination of the bankrupt. By the 5th Geo. II. the commissioners are empowered to examine the bankrupt, and all others, as well by parole, as by interrogations in writing. The said statute requires the bankrupt to discover all his estate and effects, and how, and to whom, and in what manner, on what consideration, and at what time, he has disposed of it; and all books, papers, and writings, relative thereto, of which he was possessed or interested, or whereby he or his family may expect any profit, advantage, &c. and on such examination he shall deliver up to the commissioners all his effects, (except the necessary wearing apparel of himself, his wife, and children,) and all books, papers, and writings relating thereto.

With respect to his privilege from arrest. By the above act, the bankrupt shall be free from all arrest in coming to surrender, and from his actual surrender to the commissioners for and during the forty-two days, or the further time allowed to finish his examination, provided he was not in custody at the time of his surrender.

Books and papers. By 5 Geo. II. c. 30. the bankrupt is entitled, before the expiration of the forty-two days, or enlarged time, to inspect his books and papers, in the presence of the assignees, or some person appointed by them, and make such extracts as he shall deem necessary.

Power of commissioners in case of contumacy. The statutes empower the commissioners to enforce their authority by commitment of the party, in the following cases:..Persons refusing to attend on the commissioners' summons; refusing to be examined, or to be sworn, or to sign and subscribe their examination, or not fully answering to the satisfaction of the commissioners.

Of the certificate. By the 5 Geo. II. a bankrupt surrendering, making a full discovery, and in all things conforming to the directions of the act, may with the consent of his creditors obtain a certificate. If the commissioners certify his conformity, and the same be allowed by the lord chancellor, his person, aud whatever property he may afterwards acquire, will be discharged and exonerated, from all debts owing by him at any time he became a bankrupt. But no bankrupt is entitled to the benefit of the act, unless *four parts in five,* both in number and value of his creditors, who shall be creditors for not less than 20l. respectively, and who shall have duly proved their debts under the commission, or some other person duly authorized by them, shall sign the certificate.

Of the dividends. The assignees are allowed four months from the date of the commission, to make a dividend; and should apply to the commissioners to appoint a meeting for that purpose, or they may be summoned by them, to shew cause why they have not done so.

Allowance to the bankrupt. Every bankrupt surrendering, and in all things conforming to the directions of the act, shall be allowed five per cent. out of the net produce of his estate, provided after such allowance, it be sufficient to pay his creditors ten shillings in the pound, and that the said five per cent. shall not in the whole exceed 200l. Should his estate in like manner pay

 12s.

12s. 6d. in the pound, he shall be allowed seven and an half per cent. so as not to exceed 250l. and if his estate pay 15s. in the pound, he shall be allowed ten per cent. so as not to exceed 300l. But the bankrupt is not entitled to such allowance, till after a second dividend, nor can he be entitled to it till he has received his certificate.

Of the surplus. The commissioners are, on request of a bankrupt, to give a true and particular account of the application and disposal of his estate, and to pay the overplus, if any, to the bankrupt.

Of superseding commissions. Commissions may be superseded, for the want of a sufficient debt of the petitioning creditor, or because he was an infant, or for want of sufficient evidence of the trading or act of bankruptcy, or in cases of fraud, or by agreement or consent of the creditors.

Joint commissions. Partners are liable to a joint commission, or individually, against each; but a joint and separate commission cannot, in point of law, be concurrent. A joint commission must include all partners; if there be three partners, and one of them an infant, there can neither be a commission against the three, nor against the other two.

Felony of bankrupts. If any person, who shall be duly declared a bankrupt, refuse, within forty-two days, after notice left at his place of abode, and in the London Gazette, to surrender himself to the commissioners, and to fully disclose and discover all his estate and effects, real and personal, and all transferrences thereof, and also all books, papers, and writings, relating thereto; and deliver up to the said commissioners, all such estate and effects, books, papers, &c. as are in his power (except his necessary wearing apparel, &c.) or in case he shall conceal, or embezzle, any part of his estate, real or personal, to the value of 20l. or any books of accounts, papers, or writings, relating thereto, with *intent to defraud his creditors*, being lawfully convicted thereof, by judgment or information, shall be adjudged guilty of felony, without benefit of clergy, and his goods divided amongst his creditors. 5 Geo. II. c. 30.

BANKS DESTROYING. If any person shall wilfully or maliciously break, throw down, damage, or destroy any banks, flood-

floodgates, sluices, or any other works, or do any other wilful hurt or mischief thereto, he shall be guilty of felony, and transportation for seven years. 4 G. III. c. 12. s. 5.

BANNIMUS, the form of expulsion of any member from the university of Oxford.

BANNITUS, an outlaw, or banished man.

BAR, a plea, or peremptory exception of a defendant, sufficient to destroy the plaintiff's action.

In *real actions*, a general release, or fine, may be pleaded to bar the plaintiff's title. In *personal actions*, an accord, arbitration, conditions performed, non-age of the defendant, or the statute of limitation may be pleaded in bar.

In *criminal cases*, there are especially four pleas in bar, which go to the merits of the indictment, and give reason why the prisoner ought not to answer it, nor be tried upon it; as a *former acquittal*, a *former conviction*, (though perhaps no judgment were, or will be given,) a *former attainder*, and *a pardon*.

BARCARIUM, a sheep-cote, also a sheep-walk.

BAR-FEE, is a fee of twenty pence, which every prisoner acquitted of felony pays to the gaoler.

BARGAIN and SALE. See *Contract*.

BARON, a degree of nobility next to a viscount, but in point of antiquity the highest. In the house of peers, *dukes, marquisses, earls, viscounts*, and *barons*, are all equals *as members*, whence they are collectively called a house of *peers*, or *equals*; though, in other respects, they claim and enjoy certain honours and distinctions, peculiar to their respective ranks.

The original *barons* by writ, *Camden* refers to king *Hen.* III. and *barons* by letters patent, or creation, commenced 11 Rich II. to these is added a third kind of *barons*, called *Barons by Tenure*. The chief *burgesses* of London were in former times *barons*, before there was a lord-mayor. Hen. III. The earl palatines and marches of England had anciently *their barons* under them; but no *barons*, except those who held immediately of the king, were peers of the realm.

BARON and FEME, are husband and wife by our law, and are adjudged but one person.

BARONET, a dignity, or degree of honour next after barons, having precedency of all knights, except knights baneret. They are created by letters patent, and the dignity usually descends to the issue male.

BARONS OF THE EXCHEQUER. See *Exchequer*.

BARONY, is that honour and territory which gives title to a baron.

BARRASTER, or BARRISTER, a counsellor learned in the law, admitted to plead at the bar, and there to take upon him the protection and defence of clients. *Barrasters* who constantly attend the king's-bench, &c. are to have the privilege of being sued in transitory actions, in the county of Middlesex; but it hath been questioned, whether an action of debt lies for their fees unless it be upon special retainer; for the fees to a counsellor, are not given as a salary or hire, but as a mere gratuity, which a barrister cannot demand, without doing wrong to his reputation *Davis* 23.

BARRATOR, or BARRETER, a person who is a common mover, exciter, or maintainer of suits or quarrels, either in courts or in the country.

A *common barrator*, is said to be a most dangerous oppressor in the law; for he oppresses the innocent by colour of law, which was made to protect them. 8 *Rep*. 37.

If they are common persons, and found guilty on being indicted as public disturbers of the peace, the usual punishment is by fine and imprisonment, and also by binding them to their good behaviour; but if they are of any profession relating to the law, they may be farther punished, by being disabled to practice for the future. 4 *Black*. 134.

BARRATRY, the act of the *barrator*, see *above*. And signifies also, where the master of a ship or the mariners defraud the owners or insurers, whether by running away with the ship, sinking her, deserting her, or embezzling the cargo. See *Marine Insurance*.

BARRIERS, bars or rails, which formerly separated the spectators, from those practising martial exercises. Also places of defence on the frontiers of kingdoms.

BARRISTER. See *Barraster*.

BARTER, an exchange of one species of goods for another, which was the original method of trading before money was in use; but although the invention of money has not altogether put an end to barter, yet it has entirely prevented it from appearing in its real form in the books of merchants; as each article is there stated in its money value, and each sale is supposed to be paid for, in the circulating medium of the country, even in cases where no money whatever is made use of in the transaction.

BARTON, a word used in *Devonshire* for the demesne lands of a manor, sometimes the manor-house itself, and in some places for outhouses and fold-yards.

BAS CHEVALIERS, low and inferior knights by tenure of a bare military fee, as distinguished from *banerets,* the superior knights: hence our simple knights, are called knights bachelors.

BASE COURT, an inferior court not of record, as the court baron.

BASE ESTATE, is that which *base tenants* have in their lands; and *base tenants* are those who perform villainous services to their lords.

BASELS, a coin abolished by Hen. II. *anno* 1158.

BASTARD, one who is born of any woman not married, so that his father is not known by order of the law. A bastard, by our English laws, is one, that is not only *begotten,* but *born* out of lawful matrimony. As all children born before matrimony are bastards, so are all children born so long after the death of the husband, that by the usual course of gestation they could not be begotten by him.

If a man marry a woman grossly big with child by *another,* and within three days afterwards she be delivered, the issue is no bastard. 1 *Danv. Abr.* 729.

If a child be born within a *day after* marriage between parties of full age, if there be no apparent impossibility, that the husband should be the father of it, the child is no bastard, but supposed to be the child of the husband. 1 *Rol. Abr.*

If a bastard die without issue, though the land cannot descend to any heir on the part of the *father,* yet to the heir on the part of the *mother* (being no bastard) it may; because he is of the blood of the mother, but he has no father. 2 *Roll. Abr.*.

If a bastard die intestate, leaving neither widow nor issue; the king is intitled to the personality. 2 *Black.* 505.

The incapacity of a bastard consists principally in this, that he cannot be heir to any one, neither can he have heirs but of his own

own body; for being *nullius filius,* he is therefore of kin to no one, nor has he any ancestor from whom any inheritable blood can be derived. 3 *Salk.* 66.

A bastard may be made legitimate, and capable of inheriting, by the transcendant power of an act of parliament. 1 *Black.* 459.

If any *single woman* be delivered of a bastard-child which shall be chargeable or likely to become chargeable; or shall declare herself to be with child, and that such child is likely to be born a bastard, and to be chargeable; and shall in either of such cases, in an examination to be taken in writing, on oath, before one justice of the peace, of the county, &c. where such parish or place shall lie, charge any person with having gotten her with child; it shall be lawful for such justices, upon application made to him by the overseers of the poor of such parish, or one of them, or by any substantial householder of any extra parochial place; to issue out his warrant for the immediate apprehending such person so charged as aforesaid, and for bringing him before such justice, or before any other justices of the peace of such county, city, or town corporate: And the justice, before whom such person shall be brought, shall commit him to the common goal or house of correction, unless he shall give security to indemnify such parish or place, or shall enter into a recognizance, with sufficient security, upon condition to appear, at the next general quarter-sessions, or general sessions of the peace. 6 Geo. II. c. 31.

Though a bastard-child is a *prima facie settled where born,* yet this rule admits of several exceptions; as where a bastard is born under an order of removal, and before the mother can be sent to her place of settlement; or if a woman be delivered on the road *in transitu,* while the officers are conducting her, by virtue of an order of removal; or if the child be born in the house of correction; or in the house of industry of any hundred or district; or in a lying-in hospital, it shall follow the mother's settlement. 1 Sess. Cr. 33. 94. 2 *Salk.* 474. 13 Geo. III. c. 29. 20 Geo. III. c. 36.

BASTARD EIGNE, is a son born before marriage, whose parents afterwards intermarry, and by the civil law he is *mulier,* or lawful issue; but not by the common law. 2 *Inst.* 99.

BASTON, a staff or club, which also signifies one of the warden's of of the Fleets' servants, or officers who attend the king's courts with red staffs, for taking into custody those who are committed by the court.

BATABLE GROUND, litigious or debatable ground, such as the land which lay between *England* and *Scotland* when they were distinct kingdoms.

BATTEL, a trial by combat, which was anciently allowed of in our laws, where the defendant, in an appeal of murder or felony, might fight with the appellant; and make proof thereby, whether he were culpable or innocent. This mode of trial was used also in one civil case, namely, upon an issue joined in a writ of right. But as the writ of right itself is now disused, this course of trial is only matter of speculation. 3 & 4 *Black.* 377. 346.

BAWDY-HOUSE, a house of ill fame, kept for the resort and commerce of lewd people, of both sexes. The keeping a *bawdy-house*, comes under the cognizance of the temporal law, as a common nuisance, nót only in respect of its endangering the public peace, but by drawing together dissolute and debauched persons, and promoting quarrels, but also in respect to its tendency to corrupt the manners of the people. 3 *Inst.* 205.

Any persons keeping a bawdy-house, gaming-house, or other disorderly house, are punishable, not only with fine and imprisonment, but also with sufficient infamous punishment, as to the court in discretion shall seem proper. 28 Geo. II. c. 19.

BEACON, a signal erected as a sea mark, for the use of mariners, or to give warning of the approach of an enemy. The corporation of the Trinity-house are empowered to set up any beacons, wherever they shall think them necessary; and if any destroy, or take them down, he shall forfeit 100*l.* or be *ipso facto*, outlawed. 1 *Black.* 265.

BEAD, or BEDE, a prayer, or rather prompter in prayer. They are not allowed to be brought into *England*, or any superstitious things to be used here, under penalty of a *præmunire*. Stat. 13 Eliz. c. 2.

BEARERS, oppressors. Justices of assize shall enquire of, hear, and determine maintainors, *bearers*, and conspirators, and of those that commit champerty. 4 Ed. III. c. 11.

BEASTS OF CHACE, the buck, doe, fox, marten, and roe.

BEASTS OF THE FOREST, the hart, hind, boar, and wolf.

BEASTS

BEASTS AND FOWL OF WARREN, the hare, cony, pheasant, and partridge.

BEDEHOUSE, an hospital, or alms-house, for bedesmen, or poor people, who prayed for their founders and benefactors.

BEER AND ALE. By ancient statues, brewers could not raise the assize of *beer and ale*, but according to the price of the corn, whereof the malt was made, under penalty of being fined for the first, second, and third offences, and for the fourth they should suffer the pillory. But by 2 Geo. III. c. 14. strong beer may be reasonably advanced, without subjecting venders to a prosecution. See *Excise*.

BEGGARS. See *Vagrants*.

BEHAVIOUR. See *Good Behaviour*.

BELLS. By a constitution of archbishop *Winchelsea*, the parishioners shall find, at their own expence, bells with ropes.

BELUNDITA, for BIDOWITA, an amerciament for shedding blood.

BENEFICE, is generally taken for all ecclesiastical livings, be they dignities, or other. All church preferments and dignities are benefices; but they must be given for life, not for years, or at will.

BENEVOLENCE, an aid given by the subjects to the king, as a voluntary gratuity, but in reality an extortion and imposition: this has, therefore, been carefully guarded against by several statutes, particularly by the declaration of rights, 1 Wil. st. 2. c. 2. it is insisted, that levying money for, or to the use of the crown, by pretence of prerogative, without grant of parliament, or for longer time, or in other manner than the same is or shall be granted, *is illegal*.

BENEFIT OF CLERGY. By stat. 3 Ed. I. c. 3. it is enacted, that for the scarcity of clergy in the realm of England, to be disposed of in religious houses, or for priests, deacons, and clerks of parishes, there should be a prerogative allowed to the clergy, that if any man that could read as a clerk were to be condemned to death, the bishop of the diocese *might, if he would*, claim him as a clerk; and he was to see him tried in the face of the court if he could read or not, if the prisoner could read, then he was to be delivered over to the bishop, who should dispose of him in some places of the clergy as he should think meet; but if either the

the bishop would not *demand him*, or the prisoner *could not read*, then he was to be put to death.

By the common law a *woman* was not entitled to the benefit of clergy; but by 3 W. c. 9. s 6. a woman convicted, or outlawed, for any felony for which a *man* might have his clergy, shall, upon her prayer to have the benefit of this statute, be subject only to such punishment as a man would in a like case.

But every person (not being within orders) who has been once admitted to his clergy, shall not be admitted to it a second time, 4 Hen. VII. c. 13. and against the defendant's plea of clergy, the prosecutor may file a *counter plea*, alledging some fact, which in law deprives the defendant of the privilege he claims: as he was *before convicted* of an offence, and therefore not entitled to the benefit of the statute. *Leach's Haw.* 2. c. 33. s. 19. n.

In case of high treason against the king, clergy was *never* allowable.

When a person is admitted to his clergy, he forfeits all the goods he possessed at the time of the conviction. 2 H. H. 388. But immediately on his burning in the hand, he ought to be restored to the possession of his lands, 2 H. H. 388. It also restores him to his credit, and consequently enables him to be a good witness. 2 *Haw.* 364.

BEREGAROL, a tribute of barley.

BERGHMASTER, vulgarly BARMASTER and BARMER, a bailiff, or chief officer, among our *Derbyshire miners*, who, among other parts of his office, executes that of coroner.

BERGMOTH, or BERGHMOTE, vulgarly BARMOTE, a court held for deciding pleas and controversies among the *Derbyshire miners*.

BERWICA, an hamlet, or village, appurtenant to some town, or manor.

BERWICK. The town of *Berwick* upon *Tweed*, though originally part of Scotland, is now clearly part of the realm of *England*; being represented by burgesses in the house of commons, and bound by all acts of the British parliament, whether specially named, or otherwise. The *stat.* 20 Geo. II. c. 42. declares, that where *England* only is mentioned in an act of parliament, the same, notwithstanding, hath been, and shall be, deemed to comprehend

prehend the dominion of *Wales* and the town of *Berwick* upon *Tweed*.

BERY, or BURY. The chief house of a manor, or the lord's seat.

BESAILE, a writ that lies where the grandfather was seized in his demesne as of fee, of any lands or tenements in fee simple, the day he died; and after his death a stranger *abates*, or enters the same day upon them, and keeps out his heir.

BESTIALS, all kinds of cattle.

BETACHES, laymen using glebe lands.

BEVERCHES, customary services done at the bidding of the lord, by his inferior tenants.

BID-ALE, or BID-ALL, the invitation friends to drink at some poor man's house, who thereby hopes to receive some assistant benevolence from the guests for his relief.

BIDDING OF THE BEADS, a charge given by the priest to his parishioners to say some particular prayers, on a notice of the festivals in the following week.

BIDENTES, tags, or sheep of the second year; their wool being the first shearing, was sometimes claimed as an *heriot* to the king, on the death of an abbot.

BIGAMUS, one who marries two or more wives successively after each other's death; or a widow.

BIGAMY, is where a person marries a second wife, the first being alive. By the stat. 1 *Jac.* 1. c. 11. it is enacted, that if any person or persons within his majesty's dominions, being married, do marry any person or persons, the former husband or wife being alive, the person or persons so offending, shall suffer death, as in cases of felony. But *it is provided*, that nothing in this statute shall extend to any person or persons, whose husband or wife shall be continually remaining beyond seas by the space of seven years together, or whose husband or wife, shall absent himself or herself from each other, for seven years together; the one of them not knowing the other to be living within that time. *Nor* shall the said statute extend to any person or persons *divorced* by a sentence in the ecclesiastical court; *nor* to any person or persons, for or by reason of any former marriage had or made *within age* of conent.

BILANCUS

BILANCUS DEFERENDIS, a writ directed to a corporation, for the carrying of weights to such a haven, there to weigh the wools that any man is licensed to transport.

BILL, in law proceedings, is a declaration in writing, expressing either the wrong the complainant hath suffered by the party complained of, or some fault committed against some law or statute of the realm; and this bill is sometimes addressed to the lord chancellor, especially for unconscionable wrongs done to the complainant; and sometimes to others having jurisdiction, according as the law directs. It contains the fact complained of, the damages thereby sustained, and petition of process against the defendant for redress; and it is made use of in criminal as well as civil matters. In *criminal cases*, when a grand jury upon presentment, or indictment, finds the same to be true, they indorse on it *billa vera*; and thereupon the offender is said to stand indicted.

Many of the proceedings in the King's Bench are *by bill*, which was the ancient form of proceeding.

BILLS OF EXCEPTIONS TO EVIDENCE. See *Exceptions*.

BILLS OF EXCHANGE. A bill of exchange is an order or request in writing, addressed by one person to another, to pay a certain sum of money on demand, or at a time therein specified, to a third person, or to his order; or it may be made payable to bearer.

If a bill be made payable to bearer, it is assignable by delivery only; but if it be payable to order, it must be transferred by indorsement and delivery.

The person making or drawing the bill, is called the *drawer*; the person to whom it is addressed the *drawee*, who, when he has undertaken to pay the amount, is termed the *acceptor*. The person in whose favour the bill is drawn, is called the *payee*; but if he appoint some other person to receive the money, he is then termed the *indorser*, and the person so appointed the *indorsee*.

No particular form is necessary in a bill of exchange; any order, or promise, which from the time of making it, cannot be complied with, or performed, without *the payment of money*, is a bill or note. *Mod.* 364.

A promissory note, or note of hand, is an engagement in writing, to pay a sum specified at the time therein limited, to a person therein named, or sometimes to his order, or often to the bearer at large: this is also made assignable, and indorsable like a bill of exchange.

Any persons capable of binding themselves by a contract, may be parties to a bill of exchange, or other negotiable instrument, or be in any manner concerned in negotiating either of them. An infant therefore, or a married woman, (except in certain cases, as where by the custom of London she has the privilege of trading as a *feme sole*), as they are incapable of binding themselves by contract, cannot be parties to a negotiable instrument; yet such interest, negotiated by persons incapacitated, will nevertheless *be valid* as to all other *competent* parties. 2 *Atk.* 181.

Bills of exchange are either *foreign* or *inland; foreign* when drawn by a merchant residing abroad upon his correspondent in *England*, or *vice versa;* and inland, when both the drawer and the drawee reside in the kingdom. By 9 & 10. W. III. c. 17. & 3 & 4 Anne, c. 9. all distinctions between foreign and inland bills, as far as respect the custom of merchants, are removed; and the same principles of law are generally applicable to both. See *Stamps.*

Bills or notes must be certain, and not depend on any particular event or contingency. 3 *Wils.* 213.

If a bill or note be made in a foreign country, it must be conformable to the laws of that country, or it will not be valid.

If a bill or note be altered while in the hands of the *payee*, or *any other* holder, in any material instance, as date, sum, &c. without consent of the *drawee*, he will be discharged from his liability, although such bill or note may afterwards come into the hands of an *indorsee* not aware of the alteration; but in this case, if altered *before* acceptance or indorsement, the *acceptor* can take no advantage of the alteration; and the *consent* of any one of the parties to the alteration, will in general preclude him from taking an advantage of it. 4 T. R. 320.

If a bill be made with a proper stamp, and afterwards altered by the consent of the parties, though before negotiation, a new stamp is necessary, as it is a different contract. 5 T. R. 357. If however, there be a stamp of equal or superior value, the proper one may be affixed, on payment of 40s. *before* the instrument is due, and 10l. *after* it is due. But if there is not originally a stamp

stamp amounting to the requisite value, *the omission* can never be legally supplied. *Evans*, p. 6.

The *acceptor* of a bill, is by the custom of merchants as effectually bound by *his acceptance*, as if he had been the original drawer; and having once accepted it, he cannot afterwards revoke it. *Cro. Jac.* 308. See *Acceptance*.

The *indorser* of a bill is as liable as the first drawer; because the *indorsement* is in the nature of a new bill. 1 *Salk*. 125. To indorse a bill, with a fictitious name, is forgery, though such indorsement be useless.

A *presentment*, either for payment or acceptance, must be made at seasonable hours. In case a *bill* be not *regularly paid*, the holder has a right to recover not only the principal, but also in certain cases costs and damages.

Notice is that information, which the holder of a negotiable instrument is bound to give to all the antecedent parties. If the drawee refuse to accept, or having accepted, if he refuse payment, or if he offer an acceptance varying from the bill; in either of the above cases *the bill is dishonoured*; and the holder, in case of neglect to communicate notice within a reasonable time, will not be at liberty to resort to the other parties; who by such negligence, will be discharged from their respective obligations. *Bur.* 2670.

Notice of conditional or partial acceptance should be given to the other parties to the bill, by the *holder* in default of payment; for if under these circumstances a general notice of non-acceptance, be given to any of the parties, omitting to mention in such notice, the nature of the acceptance offered, the acceptor is discharged, by this act of the holder from his acceptance. 1 T. R. 182.

A protest is an act of a notary public, stating that a bill has been presented for acceptance or for payment, and refused; and declaring that the acceptor, indorsers, &c. shall be liable for damages, &c. and to this instrument all foreign courts give entire credit. In the first instance, the notary, marks or *notes* the minute of refusal on the bill itself, and afterwards the instrument is drawn out and attested under his hand and seal. The want of a *protest*, can in no case be supplied by noting, which is a mere preparatory minute, of which the law takes no cognizance as distinguished from a protest.

If there be no notary resident at or near the place, the bill must, when payable, be protested by some substantial resident, in the presence of two or more witnesses, and should in general be made at the place where payment is refused; but when a bill is drawn abroad, directed to the drawee at *Southampton* or *London*, or any other place, requesting him to pay the payee in London, the protest for non-acceptance of such bill, may be made either at Southampton or London.

Notice in case of foreign bills when to be given. Notice should be given on the day of refusal to accept, if any post or ordinary conveyance set out on the day, and if not by the next earliest conveyance. 4 T. R. 174.

An usance is generally understood to mean only a month. *Molloy* 207. 1 *Shaw* 217. Instead of an express limitation by months or days, we continually find the bills drawn or payable at *Amsterdam, Rotterdam, Hamburgh, Altona, Paris,* or any other place in *France, Cadiz, Madrid, Bilboa, Leghorn, Genoa,* or *Venice*, limited by the *usance,* that is the usage between those places and this country.

An usance between this kingdom and *Amsterdam, Rotterdam, Hamburgh, Altona, Paris,* or any place in *France,* is one calendar month from the date of the bill; an *usance* between us and *Cadiz, Madrid,* or *Bilboa,* two; and *an usance* between us and *Leghorn, Genoa,* or *Venice,* three. A *double usance* is double the accustomed time; an *half usance*, half. Upon an *half usance,* if it be necessary to divide a month, the division, notwithstanding the difference of the length of months, shall contain fifteen days. *Blag.* 13.

BILL-BANK, is a note of obligation signed on behalf of the company of the bank of England, by one of the cashiers, for value received; or it is an obligation to pay on demand, either to the bearer or to order.

BILL OF ENTRY, an account of the goods entered at the custom-houses both inwards and outwards. In this bill must be expressed, the merchant exporting or importing, the quantity of merchandizes, and the divers species thereof, and whither or whence transported.

BILL

BILL OF HEALTH. See *Quarantine.*

BILL OF LADING, a memorandum, signed by masters of ships, acknowledging the receipt of the merchant goods, &c. Of this there are usually three parts; one kept by the consignor, one sent to the consignee, and one kept by the captain.

BILLS, NAVY, issued by the navy board, for the payment of the various contractors for stores for the navy, dock-yards, &c.

BILL OF PARCELS, an account given by the seller to the buyer, containing the particulars of the sort and prices of the goods bought.

BILL OF SALE, a solemn contract under seal, whereby, a man passes the right or interest that he hath in goods and chattels. By the statute 13 Eliz. c. 5. all conveyances of lands, goods, and chattels, to avoid the debt or duty of another, shall, as against the party whose debt or duty is so endeavoured to be avoided, *be utterly void*; except grants made *bona fide,* and on *good* (which is constructed a *valuable*) consideration.

BILL OF STORE, a licence granted at the custom-house to merchants, to carry such stores, and provisions as are necessary for their voyage, custom free.

BILL OF SUFFERANCE, a licence granted to a merchant at the custom-house, suffering him to trade from one port to another, without paying custom.

BILLS VICTUALLING, issued by the victualling-board, in payment of contracts made for victualling the navy. They are like navy-bills payable at 90 days, with an interest, of three-pence halfpenny per day on each 100l.

BILLET, bullion of gold or silver in the mass before it is coined.

BILLET-WOOD, must be three feet and four inches longer, and seven inches and an half in compass; any under this size shall be forfeited to the poor. *Stat.* 43 Eliz.

BILLINGSGATE-MARKET, is to be kept every day, and toll is appointed by statute: All persons buying fish in this market, may sell the same in any other market by retail; none but fishmongers shall sell them in shops. If any person shall buy any quantity of fish at Billingsgate to be divided into shares amongst fishmongers or other persons, or any fishmonger shall ingross the market, they incur a penalty of 20l. And fish imported by fo-

 reigners,

reigners (except protestant inhabitants of England), shall be forfeited, and the vessels. And no fish (except stock-fish and live eels) caught by foreigners (except protestant inhabitants of England), shall be imported in any foreign vessel, not being wholly English property, under penalty of forfeiting the vessel and fish. Provided that nothing be construed to prohibit the importation of anchovies, sturgeon, botarjo, or cavear, nor selling of mackarel before and after divine service of a Sunday.

BILLUS, a stick or staff, which in former times, was the only weapon for servants.

BISHOP, signifies an overseer or superintendant; so called from that watchfulness, care, charge, and faithfulness, which by his place and dignity he hath, and oweth to the church.

An archbishop, is the chief of the clergy in his province, who next and immediately under the king hath supreme power, &c. in all causes and things ecclesiastical; and has the inspection of all the bishops of that province. He hath also his own diocese, where he exercises episcopal jurisdiction, as in his province he exercises archiepiscopal. As archbishop, upon receipt of the *king's writ*, he calls the bishops and clergy of his province to meet in convocation: To him all appeals are made from inferior jurisdictions within his province. During the vacancy of any see in his province, he is guardian of the spiritualities thereof. If the archiepiscopal see be vacant, the dean and chapter are the spiritual guardians. The archbishop is entitled to present by lapse, to all the ecclesiastical livings, in the disposal of his diocesan bishops, if not filled within six months. And he has a customary prerogative, when a bishop is consecrated by him, to have the next presentation to such dignity or benefice in the bishop's disposal, as the archbishop shall chuse; which is therefore called his *option*. 1 *Black.* 380. The archbishops may retain and qualify eight chaplains, whereas a bishop can only qualify six.

Bishops are elected by the dean and chapter; in order whereunto, when a bishop dies or is translated, the dean and chapter, certify the king thereof in chancery; upon which the king issues a licence to them to proceed to an election, called a *congé d'elire*; and with it sends a *letter missive*, containing the name of the person whom they *shall* elect; which if they *shall refuse to do*, they incur the penalty of a præmunire.

A bishop

A bishop must be full thirty years of age when consecrated.

A bishop hath his consistory court, to hear ecclesiastical causes; and is to visit the clergy, &c. He consecrates churches, ordains, admits, and institutes priests; confirms, suspends, excommunicates, grants licences for marriage, makes probates of wills, &c. *Co. Lit.* 96. *Rol. Abr.* 230.

BISHOPRIC, the diocese of a bishop.

BISSEXTILE, called leap-year, because the sixth day before the kalends of March is twice reckoned, viz. on the 24th and 25th February: so that the *bissextile year*, hath one day more than other years.

BLACK ACT, is so called, having been occasioned by some devastations committed near *Watham in Hants*, by persons in disguise, or with their faces blacked; to prevent which it is enacted by 31 Geo. II. c. 42. that persons hunting armed and disguised, and killing or stealing deer, or robbing warrens, or stealing fish out of any river, &c. or any person unlawfully hunting in his majesty's forests, or breaking down the head of any fish-pond, or killing, &c. of cattle, or cutting down trees, or setting fire to house, barn, or wood, or shooting at any person, or sending anonymous letters, or letters signed with a fictitious name, demanding money, &c. or rescuing such offenders; are guilty of felony without benefit of clergy.

BLACK BOOK, is a book in the exchequer.

BLACK LEAD, every person who shall unlawfully break into any wad-hole of wad, or black cawke, commonly called black lead, or shall unlawfully take and carry away from thence any wad, black cawke, or black lead, or shall aid or employ others so to do shall be guilty of felony. 25 Geo. II. c. 10.

BLACK MAIL, signifies, in the counties of *Cumberland, Northumberland, Westmoreland*, and the bishopric of *Durham*; a certain rate of money, corn, cattle, or other consideration, paid to some inhabitants near the borders, to be protected from a band of robbers called moss troopers.

Black mail, also signifies the rents formerly paid in provisions of corn and flesh.

BLACK-ROD, or *gentleman usher of the black rod*, is chief gentleman or usher to the king. He hath also the keeping of the chapter-house door, when a *chapter* of the order of the garter is sitting;

sitting; and, in the time of parliament, attends on the *house of peers.*

BLACKWELL-HALL, a repository and market for woollen goods in Basinghall-street, London, established, by 8 and 9 Wm. III. c. 9. which directs that the public market be held there every Thursday, Friday, and Saturday; from 8 to 12 in forenoon, and from 2 to 5 in the afternoon, and no other day or hour.

BLADARIOUS, a corn-monger, mealman, or corn-chandler.

BLANCH FIRMES, anciently the crown rents, were reserved in *libris albis* or *blanch firmes.*

BLANK-BAR, the name of a plea in *bar,* which in action of trespass is put in to compel the plaintiff, to assign the certain place where the trespass was committed.

BLANK FARM, where the rent is paid in silver, not in cattle.

BLANKS, in law proceedings, void spaces left by mistake or sometimes intended to be filled up at a future time. Such blanks are a good cause of demurrer.

BLASPHEMY, all blasphemies against God; all contumelious reproaches of Jesus Christ; all profane scoffing at the holy scriptures, or exposing any part of them to ridicule, are punishable by fine, imprisonment, and such corporal punishment, as to the court shall seem meet, according to the heinousness of the crime. 1 *Haw.* 6.

BLENCH, is the title of a kind of tenure of land, as to hold land in *blench*; is by payment of a sugar-loaf, a beaver-hat, a couple of capons, and such like.

BLOODSHED, the fine imposed for shedding blood, was called, *bloodwit.*

BLOODWIT, or BLOODWITE, a customary fine paid as a composition and atonement, for the shedding or drawing blood, for which the place was answerable, if the party were not discovered.

BLOODY HAND, signifies the apprehension of a trespasser in the forest against venison with his hands or other parts bloody.

BOCKLAND, a possession or inheritance held by instruments in writing; descendible to all sons, and therefore called *gavel kind*; devisable also by will. *Spelman on Feuds.* c. 5.

BOILARY

BOILARY, or BULLIARY OF SALT, a *salt-house*, or *salt-pit*, where salt is boiled.

BOLTING, a term of art formerly used in Gray's Inn, whereby is meant private arguing of cases.

BONA FIDE. That is done *bona fide*, which is done *really*, with a *good faith*, without fraud or deceit.

BONAGHT, or BONAGHTY, an exaction in *Ireland*, imposed at the will of the lord, for relief of the knights called bonaghti, who served in the wars.

BONA NOTABILIA, are such goods as a party dying, has in another diocese, besides that wherein he dies, amounting to 5l. in the whole, which, whoever has, his will must be proved before the archbishop of the province; unless, by composition or custom, other dioceses are ordered to do it, where *bona notabilia* are rated at a greater sum.

Debts owing to the deceased are *bona notabilia*, as well as goods in possession; and they shall be *bona notabilia* in that diocese where the bonds or other specialties are, and not where the debtor inhabits. But bills of exchange, or other debts by simple contract, shall be *bona notabilia*, in that place where the debtor is. 1 *Roll. Abr.* 909.

BONA PATRIA, an assize of countrymen, or good neighbours: when twelve or more are chosen out of the country to pass upon an assize; and they are called *Juratores*, because they swear judicially, in the presence of the party.

BOND, a bond, or obligatian, is a deed whereby the obligor, or person bound, binds himself, his heirs, executors, and administrators, to pay a certain sum of money, or do some other act; and there is generally a condition added, that if he do perform such act, the obligation shall be void, or else remain in full force; as performance of covenants, standing to on award, payment of rent, or repayment of a principal sum of money, with interest, which principal sum is usually half the sum specified in the bond. 2 *Black.* 340.

All persons who are enabled to contract, and whom the law supposes to have sufficient freedom and understanding for that purpose, shall bind themselves in bonds and obligations. 1 *Rol. Abr.* 340.

If the condition of a bond be impossible at the time of making it, it, if it be to do a thing contrary to some rule of law, or to do a thing that is *malum in se*, the obligation itself is void.

The bond of a *feme covert* is void, as is that of *an infant*. If a person be illegally restrained of his liberty, and during such restraint enter into a bond to a person who causes the restraint, the same may be avoided for *duress* of imprisonment. 2 *Inst.* 482.

To avoid controversies, three things are necessary to making a good obligation, signing, sealing, and delivery.

A bond, on which neither principle nor interest has been demanded for *twenty years*, will be presumed in equity to be satisfied.

If several obligors are bound jointly and severally, and the obligee makes one of them his executor, it is a release of the debt, and the executor cannot sue the other obligor. 8 *Cor.* 136.

If one obligor make the executor of an obligee *his* executor, and leave assets, the debt is deemed satisfied; for he has power by way of retainer to satisfy the debt.

A release to one obligor is a release to all, both in law and equity. 1 *Atk.* 294.

BOND, POST OBIT, one and the main condition of which is, that it only becomes payable after the death of some person, whose name is therein specified. The death of any person being uncertain as to time, the risque attached to such bonds, frees them from the shackles of the common law of usury. It has been determined, that bonds bought for half their value did not amount to usury, on account of the risque with which they were attended.

BOOKS. By 8 Anne, c. 19. the author of any book, and his assigns, shall have the sole liberty of printing and reprinting the same for twenty-one years, to commence from the day of the first publication thereof, and no longer; except that if the author be living, at the expiration of the said term, the sole copyright shall return to him for other fourteen years: and if any other person shall print, or import, or shall sell or expose it to sale, he shall forfeit the same, and also one penny for every sheet thereof, found in his possession. But this shall not expose any person to the said forfeitures, unless the title thereof shall be entered in the register book of the company of stationers.

By 41 Geo. III. eleven copies of each book, on the best paper shall, before publication, be delivered to the warehouse-keeper of the

the company of stationers, for the use of the *Royal Library*, the libraries of the two universities in *England*, the four universities in *Scotland*, the library of *Sion College*, the library belonging to the college of advocates in *Edinburgh*, the library of *Trinity College, Dublin*, and the *King's Inns, Dublin*, on pain of forfeiting the value thereof, and also 5l.

By Stat. 34 Geo. III. c. 20. and 41 Geo. III. c. 107. persons importing for sale books first printed within the united kingdom, and reprinted in any other, such books shall be seized and forfeited; and every person so exposing such books to sale, for every such offence shall forfeit the sum of 10l. The penalties not to extend to books not having been printed for twenty years.

By the act of union, 40 Geo. III. c. 67. all prohibitions and bounties on the export of articles (the produce and manufacture of either country) to the other, shall cease; and a countervailing duty of *two-pence* for every pound weight avoirdupoise of books, bound or unbound, and of maps or prints, imported into Great Britain, directly from Ireland, or which shall be imported into Ireland from Great Britain, is substituted.

BOOTING, or BOTING CORN, certain rent-corn so called.

BORDAGIUM, a sort of tenure, subjecting a man to the meanest services; he could not sell his house, without leave of the lord.

BORDARII, or BORDUANNI, boors, husbandmen, or cottagers, who had a *bord*, or cottage, with a small parcel of land allowed to them, on condition they should supply the lord with poulty and eggs, and other small provisions.

BORDEL, a licentious house, the common habitation of prostitutes. See *Bawdy-house* and *Brothel-houses*.

BORD-HALFPENNY, is a small toll paid in fairs and markets, for setting up tables, boards, and stalls, for sale of wares.

BORD-LANDS, the lands which lords keep in their hands for the maintenance of their *board*, or table.

BORDLODE, the quantity of provision which the *bordarii*, or *bordmen*, pay for their *bordlands*; also a service required of the tenant, to carry timber out of the woods of the lord to his house.

BORD-SERVICE, is a tenure of *bord-lands*, by which some lands

lands in the manor of Fulham, and elsewhere, are held of the bishop of *London*; and the tenants now pay sixpence per acre, in lieu of finding provisions for their lord's board, or table.

BOROUGH, or BOROW, is now understood to be a town, either corporate or not, that send burgesses to parliament. 1 *Black.* 114.

BOROUGH ENGLISH, is a custom in divers ancient boroughs, of the youngest son succeeding to the burgage tenement, on the death of his father. 2 *Black.* 83.

BOROUGH GOODS, *devisable.*

BOROUGH HOLDERS, or BORSHOLDERS, are the same officers as those called *borough-heads*, or headboroughs.

BORREL-FOLK, country people.

BORROWING, when money, corn, grain, gold, or any other commodity, merely esteemed according to its price, is borrowed, it is repaid by returning an equal quantity of the same thing, or an equal value in money. And if money be borrowed, it is always understood that interest is payable, and it is by law demandable: but when a horse, a house, or any such property is borrowed, the restoration of the identical property is always understood. Or if a thing be used for any other, or more purposes, than those for which it was *borrowed*, or be lost; the party may have his action on the case for it.

BORSHOLDER. The same with headborough.

BOSCAGE, the food yielded to cattle, &c. by-wood and trees, such as oak and beech mast.

BOSCUS, all manner of wood.

BOTE, a compensation, or amends.

BOTELESS, without emendation.

BOTHAGIUM, customary dues paid to the lord of the manor, for pitching and standing of *booths* in a fair, or market.

BOTTOMRY, the act of borrowing money on a ship's bottom, by engaging the vessel for payment; so that in case she miscarry, the lender loses his money; but if she finish her voyage, and arrive in safety, the borrower is to pay the loan with a premium, or interest, agreed on (which is always adequate to the risk), and if this be denied, or deferred, the lender shall have the ship.

BOVATA TERRÆ, as much as one ox can plough in a year.

BOUCHE OF COURT, an allowance of provision from the king to his knights and servants, that attended him in any military expedition.

BOUND, or BOUNDARY, the utmost limits.

BOW-BEARER, is an under officer of the forest; a kind of sworn keeper.

BOWYERS, one of the ancient companies of the city of London. The *bowyers* of *London* were bound to have each fifty well made bows, under penalty of 10s. for each bow deficient.

BRACINUM, the whole quantity of ale brewed at one time.

BRASIUM, malt; to make malt was a service paid by some tenants to their landlord.

BRASS, must be sold in open fairs, or markets, or in the owners houses, on pain of 10l. Brass, pewter, and bell-metal, &c. shall not be sent out of the kingdom, on pain of forfeiting double the value. 33 Hen. VIII. c. 7.

BREACH OF COVENANT. See *Covenant.*

BREACH OF THE PEACE. See *Peace.*

BREAD, the statutes to regulate the price and assize of bread, and to punish persons who shall adulterate meal, flour, or bread, are 31 Geo. II. c. 29. 13 Geo. III. c. 62. and 37 Geo. III. *but cannot, on account of their great length, be abridged in this work.*

BREAD OF TREET, or TRITE, similar to household bread.

BREAKING PRISON. See *Prison.*

BREDEWHITE, the imposition of a fine, for defaults in the assize of bread.

BREHON, the judges and lawyers in *Ireland* were anciently called *brehons.*

BRENAGUIM, the payment in bran, which the tenant anciently made, to feed the lord's hounds.

BREVE PERQUIRERE, to purchase a writ, or licence of trial, in the king's court. Hence arose the custom of paying 6s. 8d. where the debt is 100l. and so upwards, in suits and trials, for money due upon bond.

BREVE DE REITO, a writ of right for a person ejected, to sue for the possession of an estate detained from him.

BREVIBUS ET ROTULIS LIBERANDIS, a writ to a sheriff, to deliver to the new sheriff chosen in his room, the county, with the appurtenances, *una cum rotulis brevibus;* and other things belonging to that office.

BREWERS. By 24 Geo. III. *st.* 2. c. 41. brewers of strong and small beer, are to take out annual licences from the officers of excise, and are subject to many regulations under the excise laws. The 27 Geo. III. c. 12. settles the duty on beer and ale. By 32 Geo. III. c. 8. s. 1. common brewers must not sell beer in less quantities than 4½ gallons. See *Excise.*

BRIBERY, the receiving, or offering, any undue reward, by or to any person whatsoever, whose ordinary profession or business relates to the administration of public justice, in order to incline him to do a thing against the known rules of honesty and integrity; it also signifies the taking or giving a reward for offices of a public nature.

As to the punishment of bribery, by the common law, *bribery in a judge,* was looked upon as an offence of so heinous a nature, that it was sometimes punished as high treason. 3 *Inst.* 148. and all other kinds of *bribery* are punishable by fine and imprisonment; which may also be inflicted on those who offer a bribe, though not taken. *Black.* 143. 2 *Inst.* 147.

BRIBOR, one that pilfereth other men's goods.

BRICKS and TILES. There shall be paid, by the maker, for every 1000 of bricks made in Great Britain, and so in proportion, an excise duty of 5s. 37 Geo. III. c. 14. For every 1000 of plain tiles 4s. 10d. 37 Geo. III. c. 15. For every 1000 of pan tiles, or ridge tiles, 12s. 10d. 34 Geo. III. c. 15. For every 100 of paving tiles, *not* exceeding ten inches square, 2s. 5d. 34 Geo. III. c. 15. For every 100 of paving tiles, *exceeding* ten inches square, 4s. 10d. 34 Geo. III. c. 15. For every 1000 of tiles, other than such as are before described, by whatsoever name they may be called. 4s. 10d. 34 Geo. III. c. 15.

The foregoing duties are drawn back on exportation; and semieliptical tiles, for the *sole purpose of draining wet or marshy lands,* are exempted from the above duties.

All combinations to inhance the price of bricks or tiles, shall be void; and every brick-maker who shall offend therein shall forfeit 20l. and every clerk, agent, or servant, 10l. half to the poor, and half to the person who shall sue in six calendar months, in one of the courts at Westminster.

BRIDGE,

BRIDGE, public bridges which are of general conveniency, are of common right to be repaired by the inhabitants of that county in which they lie. *Hale's* P. C. 143. Where a person makes a bridge for the common good of the king's subjects, he is not bound to repair it. 2 *Inst.* 700.

No man can be compelled to build or contribute to the charges of building any new bridge, without an act of parliament.

And if none are bounden to repair by tenure or prescription at common law, then the whole county or franchise shall repair it. 2 *Inst.* 701.

Indictments, for not repairing bridges will not lie, but in a case of common bridges on highways, though they will lie for a bridge on a common foot-way. *Mod. Cas.* 256. The defendants to an indictment, for not repairing a bridge, must not only shew, that they are not bound to repair the whole, or any part of the bridge; but also shew, what other person is bound to repair the same. 1 *Haw.* 221.

BRIEF, any writ in writing, issued out of any of the king's courts of record at Westminster, whereby any thing is commanded to be done in order to justice.

Briefs for collecting charity, are to be read in all churches and chapels, within two months after receipt thereof; and the sums thereby collected shall be paid over to the *undertaker* of *briefs*, within six months after the delivery of the briefs under penalty of 20l.

Brief also signifies an abridgment of the client's case made out for the instruction of counsel, on a trial at law, which is to be fully but briefly stated.

BRIGANDINE, a coat of mail.

BRIGANTES, the inhabitants of Yorkshire, Lancashire, Durham, Westmoreland, and Cumberland.

BRIGBOTE, or BRUGBOTE, a fine for not repairing bridges.

BROCAGE, the wages, hire, or trade of a broker.

BROKERS, are those that contrive, make, and conclude bargains and contracts, between merchants and tradesmen, in matters of money and merchandize, for which they have a fee or reward.

Brokers are to be annually licensed in *London*, by the lord mayor and aldermen: If any persons shall act as brokers, without being thus licensed and admitted, they shall forfeit the sum of 500l. and persons employing them 50l. And brokers are to register contracts, &c. under the like penalty: Also they shall not deal for themselves on pain of forfeiting 200l. 6 Anne, c. 16. These are called *Exchange-brokers.*

There are besides persons called *pawn-brokers,* who commonly keep shops and let out money to poor necessitous people upon *pawns,* but these are not of that antiquity or credit as the former. Several late statutes have made divers regulations in their trade, and subjected them to annual licences, and divers penalties on trading without such licences, for which see 29 Geo. III. c. 57.

BROTHEL-HOUSES, are lewd places, the common habitations of prostitutes. They were formerly allowed in certain places, but by a proclamation in the 37th year of the reign of Henry the Eighth they were all suppressed.

BRUSHMENT, BRUSUA, and BRUSULA, browse, or brushwood.

BUCKSTALL, a station to watch the *deer* in hunting; the attending whereof was performed, by the tenants to the lord within the forest.

BUILDINGS. If a house new-built exceed the ancient foundation, and thereby hinder the light or air of another house, action lies against the builder. *Hob.* 131. In *London* a man may place ladders or poles upon the ground, or against houses adjoining, for *building* his own; for which he ought to have a licence from the mayor and aldermen, but he must not break ground. If any person *build* any new house in London, he must erect a party-wall of brick or stone between house and house, and of the thickness of two bricks in length in the ground-story, or he shall forfeit 50l. And pipes are to be fixed on the sides of such houses, for conveying off the water falling thereon, into the channels.

BULL, a brief or mandate of the pope, or bishop of *Rome,* which was formerly of force in this country, but by 28 Hen. VIII. c. 16. made void: And by 13 Eliz. c. 1. and 2. if any person shall obtain from *Rome* any bull or writing, to absolve or reconcile such as forsake their due allegiance, or shall give or receive absolution by colour of such bull, or use or publish such bull, &c. it is *high treason.*

BULL

* BULL AND BOAR, by custom, the parson is obliged in some places to keep a bull and boar, for the use of the parishioners, for the increase of calves and pigs; and every inhabitant prejudiced by his not keeping the same, may have an action on the case against him. 1 *Rol. Abr.* 539.

BULLION, gold or silver in mass or billet.

BUNDLES, a sort of records of the chancery lying in the office of the rolls, in which are contained the files of bills and answers, &c.

BURCIFER REGIS, the king's purse-bearer, or keeper of his privy-purse.

BURGAGE TENURE, is where houses, or lands which were formerly the scite of houses, in an ancient borough, are held of the king or some other lord in common soccage, by a certain established rent. 2 *Black.* 82. See *Borough English.*

BURGHBOTE, a contribution towards the building or repairing of castles or walls of defence, or towards the building of a borough or city.

BURGESSES, those are usually so called, who serve in parliament, for any borough or corporation; although the inhabitants and magistrates were so called formerly.

BURGLARY, the *breaking* and *entering* the mansion-house of another in the *night,* with intent to commit some felony within the same, whether the felonious intent be executed or not. Hale's, *pl.* 79. But there must be a *breaking* and *entry,* to complete this offence. 1 Haw. c. 38, s. 3.

If there be day-light enough, begun or left, to discern a man's face, it is *no burglary.* This however does not extend to moonlight, for then many burglaries would go unpunished. 4 *Black.* 224.

Every entrance into a house by trespass is *not* a *breaking* in this case; for there must be an actual *breaking.* If the door of a mansion should stand open, and the thief enter, this is *not* a *breaking:* or if the window of an house be open, and a thief with a hook or other instrument, should draw out some of the goods of the owner, this is *no burglary,* because there is no actual breaking of the house. But if the thief should break the glass of the window, and with a hook or other instrument draw out some of the goods of the owner, this *is a burglary,* for there is an actual breaking of the house. 3 *Inst.* 64.

The mansion-house, does not only include the dwelling-house, but also the outhouses that are parcel thereof, though not under the same roof, or joining contiguous to it; but if they be far remote from the dwelling-house, and not so near it, as to be reasonably esteemed parcel thereof, then *the breaking is not burglary.* H. H. 553.

To break and enter a *shop,* not parcel of the mansion-house, in which the shop-keeper never lodges, but only works or trades there in the day-time, is *not a burglary,* but only larceny; but if he or his servant, usually or often lodge in the shop at night, it is then a mansion-house, in which a burglary may not be committed. *Id.*

Where the owner leaves his house, and disfurnishes it, without a se ttl resolution of returning, it cannot under *these circumstances* be deemed a *dwelling-house*; but where the owner quits the house in order to return occasionally, though no person be left in it, it may still be considered as his *mansion-house. Fost.* 76.

A chamber in an inn of court, &c. where one usually lodges, is a mansion-house, for every one hath a several property there; but a chamber where any person lodges as an inmate cannot be called *his* mansion; though if a bnrglary be committed in his lodgings, the indictment may lay the offence to be in the mansion-house of him that let them. 3 *Inst.* 65.

If the owner live under the same roof with the inmates, there must be a separate *outer door,* or the whole is the mansion of the owner; but if the owner inhabit no part of the house; or even if he occupy a shop or cellar in it, but do not sleep therein, it is the mansion of each lodger, though there be but *one outer* door. *Leach's Haw.* c. 38, s. 15.

How punishable. By the 18 Eliz. c. 7. s. 1. it is enacted, that if any person shall commit any felonious rape, ravishment, or burglary, and be found guilty by verdict, or shall be outlawed, or shall confess such rape or burglary, every person so found guilty shall suffer death, and forfeit as in cases of felony without benefit of clergy.

But in all cases of burglary, accessaries *after* must have their clergy. 1 *Haw.* 537.

Conviction of a burglar and the reward. The court may allow a prosecutor who hath *bona fide* prosecuted, such sum as they shall think reasonable, not exceeding the expences he was *bona fide* put

 unto;

unto; making also, if he shall appear to be in poor circumstances, a reasonable allowance for his trouble and loss of time. 18 Geo. III. c. 19.

And further, any person who shall apprehend any one guilty of burglary, and prosecute him to conviction, shall have a certificate without fee, to be made out and delivered before the end of the assizes, under the hand of the judge, certifying the conviction, and in what parish the burglary was committed, and that the burglar was taken by the person or persons claiming the reward; and if any dispute should arise between the parties claiming, the judge shall by such certificate, direct the same to be paid and distributed among them as to him shall seem just and reasonable; and on tendering such certificate to the sheriff, and demand made, he shall pay to the person or persons so entitled the sum of 40l. without any deduction. 5 Anne, c. 31. 6 Geo. 23. s. 10. Such certificate shall be inrolled by the clerk of the peace of the county in which it shall be granted, for which he shall have 1s. And the said certificate may be once assigned over; and the original proprietor or assignee of the same, shall by virtue thereof, be discharged from all manner of parish and ward-offices, within the parish and ward where the felony was committed. 10 & 11 Wm. c. 23.

BURIALS, persons dying are to be buried in woollen, or their representatives shall forfeit 5l. and affidavit is to be made thereof before a justice under a like penalty. Minister to keep register, at the parish expence.

BURNING, DESTROYING, or MOLESTING ships, persons convicted thereof, shall be guilty of felony without benefit of clergy. 12 *Anne*, c. 18.

BURNING IN THE HAND. See *Clergy*.

BUTCHER. Butchers within ten miles of *London* may not sell fat cattle *alive or dead* to one another, but they may sell dead calves or sheep. 7 *Anne*, c. 6. No butcher shall be a tanner or currier on pain of 6s. 8d. a day. 1 Jac. c. 22. Every butcher, offering for sale any hide gashed in the flaying thereof, shall forfeit 2s. 6d. for such hide. And any butcher who shall put to sale any hide putrified or rotten shall forfeit 3s. 4d. for each offence. Any butcher who shall kill or sell any victual on the lord's day shall forfeit 6s. 8d.

BUTTERAGE

BUTLERAGE OF WINES, that imposition upon sale wines, brought into the land, which the king's butler, by virtue of his office, may take of every ship: viz. 2s. for every ton of wine imported by strangers. 4 *Inst.* fol. 30.

BUTTER, every cooper making vessels for the packing of butter, shall make them of seasoned wood, and tight; and shall make no others, but tubs, firkins, and half firkins. The tub shall be capable of containing eighty-four pounds of butter, and not less; and shall not of itself weigh less than eleven pounds, nor more than fifteen. The firkin shall be capable of containing fifty-six pounds, and not less; and shall not weigh less than seven pounds, nor more than eleven. The half firkin shall be capable of containing twenty-eight pounds, and not less; and shall weigh not more than four pounds, nor less than six, under the penalty of forfeiting 10s. for every vessel made contrary to the above directions. And every cooper shall brand his christian and surname on the outside of the bottom of each vessel, under the penalty of 10s. Every farmer, and other person, who shall pack up butter for sale, shall pack it in vessels made and marked as aforesaid; and when the same is fully seasoned in water, shall, on bottom, on the inside, and on the top on the outside, brand his christian and surname at length, and shall also brand, both on the top and bouge of the vessel, the weight of the same: and to prevent any of the staves being changed, shall burn both his christian and surname in two separate places across the bouge thereof, under the penalty of forfeiting 5l.

Every farmer, or other person, who shall pack butter for sale, shall pack in every tub eighty-four pounds avoirdupoise net, and not less; in every firkin fifty-six pounds net, and not less; and in every half firkin twenty-eight pounds net, and not less; and shall thereon imprint both his christian and surname, under pain of forfeiting 5l.

And no butter which is old and corrupt, shall be mixed with any butter that is new and sound; nor shall any whey butter be mixed with any butter made of cream, but every cask of butter shall be of one sort or goodness; and no butter shall be salted with any great salt, but with fine small salt; and every person acting contrary to the directions aforesaid shall forfeit 5l.

And every cheesemonger, or other, who shall sell any tub, firkin,

kin, or half firkin of butter, shall deliver therein the full quantity and due quality, or shall be liable to make satisfaction, according to the price thereof.

And no cheesemonger, or other person, shall repack for sale, any butter, in any tub, firkin, or half firkin, on pain of forfeiting double the value thereof.

The prosecution for the offences above, shall be commenced in four months after the sale of the butter.

BUTTONS, the making and sale of these articles are restricted by the statutes 13 & 14 C. II. 4 W. and M. c. 10. 8 Ann. c. 6. 4 & 7 Geo. I. c. 7. & 12. but are seldom enforced.

BUYING and SELLING, a transferring of property from one person to another, in consideration of some price or recompence. On an agreement for goods, the vendee cannot carry them away without payment, unless the vendor agree to trust him. But if any part of the price be laid down, or any portion of the goods delivered by way of earnest, the vendee may recover the goods by action, as well as the vendor may the price of them. By 29 C. II. c. 3. no contract for the sale of goods, to the value of 10l. or upwards, shall be valid, unless the payment or delivery be performed, or unless some note in writing be made and signed by the party, or his agent. But if a vendee, after a bargain is struck, *tender the money*, and the vender refuse it, the property is absolutely vested in the vendee.

BY-LAW, is a private law made by those who are duly authorized so to do by charter, prescription, or custom, for the preservation of order and good government, within some particular place or jurisdiction. *Moor*. 583.

Every corporation, lawfully erected, hath power to make bylaws, or private statutes, for the better government of the corporation; which are binding upon themselves, unless *contrary* to the laws of the land, and then they are void. 11 *Black*. 475.

BYRLAW, or LAWS OF BURLAW, laws made by husbandmen, or townsmen, concerning neighbourhood, to be kept among themselves.

CABBAGES.

C.

CABBAGES. Any person who shall steal, or take away, or maliciously pull up and destroy any turnips, potatoes, *cabbages*, parsnips, pease, or carrots, growing in any lands, &c. shall on conviction before one justice, by confession, or oath of one witness, forfeit, over and above the value of the goods stolen, a sum not exceeding 10s. one half to the owner of the goods, and the other to the poor, and in default of payment thereof, shall be committed to the house of correction, there to be kept to hard labour for one month, unless the penalty be sooner paid.

CABLES AND CORDAGE. By 35 Eliz. c. 8. persons making any cables of any old and overworn stuff, which shall contain above seven inches in compass, shall forfeit four times the value of every such cable so made; and every person tarring any hawsers, or other cordage, made of such old and overworn stuff, of a lesser size, not containing in compass seven inches, or who shall sell such cable, hawser, or other cordage, shall forfeit the treble value thereof.

By 6 Geo. III. c. 45. a bounty of 2s. 4½d. is allowed upon every hundred weight of British cordage exported as merchandize to foreign parts; but nothing in this act to extend the bounties to cordage manufactured from old cables, ropes, or cordage, commonly called twice layed cordage.

By 26 Geo. III. c. 85. no bounty to be paid if made from American hemp, nor for less quantity than three tons weight, continued by 36 Geo. III. c. 108.

CALENDAR, a table containing the divisions or time into days, weeks, months, &c. in one year, in their regular order and succession; the terms, feasts, changes, of the moon, &c. See 24 Geo. II. c. 23. s. 1. the calendar, tables, and rules, mentioned in the act, are prefixed to all the editions of the common prayer book.

CALENDAR OF PRISONERS, a list of the names of the prisoners in the custody of the respective sheriffs of counties, &c.

CALLICO. By 7 Geo. I. c. 7. no person shall wear in apparel

rel any printed or dyed callico, under the penalty of 5l. and drapers selling any such forfeit 20l. by 14 Geo. III. c. 72. shifts wholly made of raw cotton wool within this kingdom, are not to be considered as callicoes, and every person may use the same. These are distinguished by three blue stripes in the selvedge. See *Excise*.

CALLING THE PLAINTIFF, is the form which takes place when the plaintiff is non-suited. It is usual for a plaintiff, when he or his counsel perceives that there is not sufficient evidence to maintain his issue, to be voluntarily non-suited, or withdraw himself, whereupon the cryer is ordered to call the plaintiff, and if neither he, nor any one for him appear, he is nonsuited, the jurors are discharged, the action is at an end, and the defendant recovers his costs; but this is not like a *retraxit*, or a *verdict*, a bar to another action.

CAMBRIC and LAWNS. See *Excise*.

CAMBRIDGE. By *stat.* 34 & 35 Hen. VIII. c. 24. a rent is given to the knights of the shire in the county of *Cambridge*, instead of their wages. All that hold tenements in Cambridge shall repair the pavements, &c. over against their tenements, on pain of forfeiting 6d. for every square yard of pavement, and 12d. for every pole of gravelled lanes.

The vice chancellor and the mayor of Cambridge may act as justices for the county, without the landed qualification.

CAMPUS MARTII, an assembly of the people every year on *May-day*, where they confederated together to defend the kingdom against foreigners and enemies.

CANDLEMAS DAY, the feast of the purification of the blessed Virgin Mary, (Feb. 2).

CANDLES. See *Excise*.

CANFARA, a trial by hot iron, formerly used here. See *Ordeal*.

CANNA, a rod in measure of ground, or distance.

CANON, is a law, or ordinance, of the church. The *canon law* consists partly of certain rules taken out of the scripture, partly of the writings of the ancient fathers of the church, partly of the ordinances of general and provincial councils, and partly of the decrees of the pope in former ages.

Before the 25 Hen. VIII. s. 19. the ecclesiastics might make canons

canons without the king, but are by that statute restrained; but since that statute they may make canons with the assent of the king, so long as they are not contrary to the laws of the land, or derogatory of the king's prerogative.

Ecclesiastical persons are subject to the canons. Those of 1640 have been *questioned*, but no doubt was ever made as to those of 1603 *by the court*. No canons, since 1603, can bind laymen. 6 *Mod.* 190.

CANTRED, or CANTREF, signifies an hundred villages.

CAPACITY, in the law signifies when a man, or body politic, is able to give or take lands, or other things, or to sue actions.

CAPE, is a writ judicial, touching pleas of lands or tenements: it is divided into *cape magnum* and *cape parvum*, both which take hold of things immoveable, and differ from each other in these points, first, because *cape magnum* lieth before appearance, and *cape parvum* afterwards. Secondly, the *cape magnum* summoneth the tenant to answer to the default, and aver to the demandant; *cape parvum* summoneth the tenant to answer to the default only.

CAPE MAGNUM, this writ is awarded, upon the defendant or tenant's not appearing or demanding the view in such real actions, where the original writ does not mention the parcels or particulars demanded.

CAPE PARVUM, this writ lieth in a case where the tenant is summoned in a plea of land, and comes at the summons, and his appearance is afore record; and after he makes default at the day that is given to him; then this writ should issue for the king, &c.

CAPE AD VALENTIAM, is a species of *cape magnum*, and lies *before* appearance, it lies where a person is impleaded of certain lands, and I vouch to warrant another, against whom the summons *ad warrantizandum*, hath been awarded, and the sheriff comes not at the day given; then, if the demandant recover against me, I shall have this writ against the vouchee, and shall recover so much in value of the land of him, if he have so much; and if he have not so much, then I shall have execution of such lands and tenements as descend to him in fee simple; or, if he purchase afterwards, I shall have against him a re-summons, and if he can say nothing, I shall recover the value.

CAPIAS, is a writ of two sorts, one whereof is called *capias ad respondendum*, *before* judgment, where an original is sued out, &c. to take the defendant, and make him answer the plaintiff: and the other a writ of execution, *after* judgment, being of divers kinds.

CAPIAS AD RESPONDENDUM, is a writ commanding the sheriff to take the body of the defendant, if he may be found in his bailiwic, or county, and him safely to keep, so that he may have him in court on the day of the return, to answer to the plaintiff of a plea of debt, or trespass, or the like, as the case may be. And if the sheriff return that he cannot be found, then there issues another writ, called an *alias capias*; and after that another, called *a pluries capias*, and if upon none of these he can be found, then he may be proceeded against unto outlawry. But all this being only to compel an appearance, after the defendant hath appeared, the effect of these writs is taken off, and the defendant shall be put to answer, unless it be in cases where special bail is required, and there the defendant is actually to be taken into custody. 3 *Black.* 212.

CAPIAS AD SATISFACIENDUM, is a writ directed to the sheriff, commanding him to take the body of the defendant, and him safely to keep, so that he may have his body in court at the return of the writ, to make the plaintiff satisfaction for his demand: otherwise he is to remain in custody till he do. When a man is once taken in execution upon this writ, no other process can be sued out against his lands or goods. But if a defendant die whilst charged in execution upon this writ, the plaintiff may, after his death, sue out new executions, against his lands, goods, or chattels. 3 *Black.* 415.

CAPIAS ULTAGATUM, is a writ that lies against a person that is outlawed in any action, whereby the sheriff is commanded to apprehend the body of the party outlawed, and keep him in safe custody, till the day of the return of the writ, and then present him to the court, there to be dealt with for his contempt. But this being only for want of appearance, if he shall afterwards appear, the outlawry is most commonly reversed. 3 *Black.* 284.

CAPIAS IN WITHERNAM, is a writ directed to the sheriff, in case where a distress is carried out of the county, or concealed by the distrainer, so that the sheriff cannot make deliverance of the goods upon a replevin; commanding him to take so many of the distrainer's own goods, by way of reprisal, instead of the other that are so concealed.

CAPITE, *tenure in capite*, is to hold of the king as the *head* of the commonwealth, be it by knight service, or soccage. The ancient *tenure in capite* was of two sorts, the one principal and general, which is of the king; the other *special* and *subaltern*, which was of a particular subject; but *tenure in capite* is now abolished, and by 12 C. II. c. 24. all tenures are turned into free and common soccage; so that the tenures hereafter to be created by the king, are to be in common soccage only, and not by *capite*, knights service, &c.

CAPITILITIUM, *poll money*.

CAPTION, when a commission is executed, and the commissioners names subscribed to a certificate, declaring when and where the commission was executed, that is called the caption.

CAPTION signifies sometimes an arrest.

CAPUT ANNI, new year's day.

CAPUT BARONIÆ, the castle of a nobleman, which is not to be divided among daughters (if there be no son), but must descend to the eldest daughter.

CAPUT JEJUNII, is Ash-Wednesday, in our records.

CARDS and DICE---duty on see *stamps*, selling second-hand cards incurs a penalty of 25l. per pack. 16 Geo. III. c. 34.

CARRICK or CARRACK, a ship of great burthen, used both in trade and war. 2 *Rich.* II. c. 4.

CARRIER, every person carrying goods for hire is deemed a carrier, and as such is liable in law for any loss or damage that may happen to them whilst in his custody. Waggoners, captains of ships, lightermen, &c. are therefore carriers; but a *stage-coachman* is not within the custom as a carrier: neither are *hackney-coachmen* carriers within the custom of the realm, so as to be chargeable for the loss of goods, unless they are expressly paid for that purpose, for their undertaking is only to carry the person.

If a person take hire for carrying goods, although he be not a common carrier, he may nevertheless be charged upon a special assumpsit; for where hire is taken a promise is implied; and where goods are delivered to a carrier, and he is robbed of them, he shall be charged and answer for them on account of the hire, and

and the carrier can be no loser, as he may recover against the hundred.

Goods sent by a carrier cannot be distrained for rent; and any person carrying goods for all persons indifferently, is to be deemed a common carrier as far as relates to this privilege.

A delivery to a servant is a delivery to the master, and if goods are delivered to a carrier's porter and lost, an action will lie against the carrier. 1 *Salk.* 282.

Where a carrier gives notice by printed proposals that he will not be responsible for certain valuable goods if lost, if more than the value of a sum specified, unless entered and paid for as such; and valuable goods of that description are delivered to him, by a person who knows the conditions, but concealing the value, pays no more than the ordinary price of carriage and booking, the carrier is, under such circumstances, neither responsible to the sum specified, nor liable to repay the sum paid for carriage and booking. M. 30 Geo. III. 1. H. B. 298.

A carrier who undertakes for hire to carry goods, is bound to deliver them at all events, unless damaged and destroyed by the act of God, or the king's enemies; and if any accident, however inevitable, happen through the intervention of human means, a *carrier becomes responsible.* 1 T. R. 27.

CARTS, every cart, &c for the carriage of any thing, to and from any place where the streets are paved within the *bills of mortality*, shall contain six inches in the felly; and no person shall drive any cart, &c. within the limits aforesaid, unless the name of the owner and number of such cart, be placed in some conspicuous part thereof, and his name entered with the commissioners of the hackney-coaches, under the penalty of 40s. and any person may seize and detain such cart, till the penalty be paid. 18 Geo. II. c. 33. And if the driver shall ride upon such cart without having a person on foot to guide it, he shall forfeit 10s. and the owner so guilty shall forfeit 20s. On changing property the names of the new owners shall be affixed, and entry shall be made with the commissioners of the hackney-coaches. The entry of all carts *driven* within five miles of Temple Bar, is strictly enjoined by the 24 Geo. III. *st.* 2. *c.* 27.

CARUCAGE, a tribute imposed on every plough, for the public service.

CARUCATE or CARVE OF LAND, is a certain quantity of land, by which the subjects have been sometimes taxed.

CASES or REPORTS IN LAW, published fairly and accurately, seem countenanced by the judges as in the case of Currie and others against Walter.

CASTELLORUM OPERATIO, castle-work, or service and labour done and performed by inferior tenants, for the building and upholding castles and public places of defence: towards which some gave their personal assistance and others paid their contribution.

CASTLE GUARD RENTS, are rents paid to those, who dwell within the precincts of any castle, towards the maintenance of such as watch and ward the castle.

CASU CONSIMILI, a writ of entry granted, where the tenant by courtesy, or for term of life, or for the life of another, aliens in fee, or in tail, or for term of another's life.

CASU PROVISO, is a writ of entry given by the statute of *Gloucester*, c. 7. where a tenant in dower aliens in fee, or for term of life; and it lies for him in reversion against the alienee.

CATALLIS CAPTIS NOMINE DISTRICTIONIS, is a writ that lies within a borough, or within a house, for rent going out of the same, and warrants a man to take the doors, windows, or gates, by way of distress for the rent.

CATALLIS REDDENDIS, a writ which lies where goods are delivered to any man to keep a certain day, and are not upon demand delivered at the day.

CATCH LAND, in Norfolk there are grounds, where it is not known to what parish they certainly belong, so that the minister who first seizes the tythe, by that right of pre-occupation, enjoys it for that one year; whence it is called catch land.

CATCH-POL, though now, a word of contempt, was anciently used without reproach, for serjeants at mace, bailiffs, or sheriff's officers.

CATHEDRAL, after the establishment of Christianity, the emperors and other great men, gave large demesnes and other possessions for the maintenance of the clergy, whereon were built the first places of public worship, which were called *cathedra*, *cathedrals*, *sees* or *seats*, from the bishop and his chief clergy's residence thereon.

CATHE-

CATHEDRATIC, a sum of two shillings, paid to the bishop by the inferior clergy, *in argumentum subjectionis et ob honorem* cathedœ.

CATTLE, by the 3 and 4 *Ed.* VI. c. 19. no person shall buy any ox, steer, runt, or cow, &c. and sell the same again alive, in the same market, or fair, on pain of forfeiting double the value thereof, half to the king, and half to him that shall sue. *This is the only act in force against forestalling, ingrossing, and regrating.*

If any person shall feloniously drive away, or steal, or shall wilfully kill any ox, bull, cow, calf, steer, bullock, heifer, sheep, or lamb, with a felonious intent to steal the whole carcase, or any part thereof, or shall assist in committing any such offence, he shall be guilty of felony without benefit of clergy. 14 and 15 Geo. II. c. 6. and 34.

Any person, who shall unlawfully and maliciously kill, maim, or wound *any cattle*, shall be guilty of felony, without benefit of clergy; and the hundred shall be answerable for the damages, not exceeding 200l. 9 Geo. c. 22. And horses, mares, and colts, are included in the word *cattle*. Every person, who shall apprehend and prosecute to conviction any offender, shall have 10l. reward; to be paid by the sheriff within a month, on his producing a certificate from the judge. The 26 Geo. III. c. 71. to prevent the stealing of horses, &c. for their skin, provides that all persons keeping a slaughter-house for cattle not killed for butcher's meat, shall take out licences, be subject to an inspector, and only slaughter at certain times.

CAVEAT, is a caution, entered in the spiritual court, to stop probates, administrations, licences, dispensations, faculties, institutions, and such like from being granted without the knowledge of the party that enters it. A *caveat* stands in force for three months. 2 *Rol. Rep.* 6.

The entering a *caveat*, being at the instance of the party, is only for the benefit of the ordinary, that he may do no wrong; it is a cautionary act for his better information, to which the temporal courts have no manner of regard; therefore if after a caveat entered, the ordinary should grant administration, or probate of a will, it is not void by our law; it is true it is void by the canon law, but our law takes *no notice* of a *caveat*. *Rol. Rep.* 191.

CAUSA MATRIMONII PRÆLOCUTI, a writ which lies, where a woman gives lands to a man in fee simple to the intent he shall marry her, and being by her thereunto required, he refuses.

CAUSAM NOBIS SIGNIFICES, a writ directed to a mayor of a town or city, &c. that formerly by the king's writ, being commanded to give seisin unto the king's grantee of any lands or tenements, delays so to do, willing him to shew cause, why he so delays the performance of his charge.

CAUSES and EFFECTS. In most cases the law hath respect to the *cause* or beginning of a thing, as the principal part on which all other things are founded; for such as is the *cause* such is the *effect*: where the *cause* ceases, the *effect* or thing will cease, as wedlock or matrimony *ceasing*, the dower *ceases*. 1 *Co. Inst.* 13.

CAUTIONE ADMITTENDA, a writ that lies against the bishop, who holds an excommuniate person in prison for his contempt, notwithstanding he offers sufficient *caution* or security to obey the commandments of the church for the future.

CENEGILD, an expiatory mulct or fine, paid by one who kills another, to the kindred of the deceased.

CENSURE is, in several manors in *Cornwall* and *Devon*, the calling in, of all above the age of sixteen, to swear fealty to the lord, to pay *2d. per poll*, and *1d. per ann.* ever after, as *cert-money*; and the persons thus sworn are called *censors*.

CENTENARII, petty judges under sheriffs of counties, who had rule of a *hundred*.

CEPI CORPUS, a return made by the sheriff, who upon a *capias*, *exigent*, or other process, has taken the body of the party.

CERTAINTY, a convenient *certainty* is required in writs, declarations, pleadings, &c. 11 *Rep.* 25, 121.

CERTIFICANDO DE RECOGNITIONE STAPLUÆ, a writ directed to the mayor of the staple, &c. commanding him to certify the lord chancellor of a statute of the *staple*, taken before him between such and such; where the party himself detains it, and refuse to bring it in.

CERTIFICATE, a writing made in any court, to give notice to another court of any thing done therein, which is usually by way of transcript. And sometimes it is made by an officer of the same court, where matters are referred to him, or a rule of court is obtained for it, containing the tenor and effect of what is done.

CERTIFICATION OF ASSIZE OF NOVEL DISSEISIN, a writ granted for the re-examination or review of a matter passed by *assize* before any justices; as where a man appearing by his bailiff to an *assize* brought by another, hath lost the day, and having something more to plead for himself, as a deed of release, &c. which the bailiff did not or might not plead for him; desires a farther examination of the cause, either before the same justices or others, and obtaineth letters patent to that effect.

CERTIORARI, the writ of *certiorari*, is an original writ, issuing out of the court of chancery or the king's-bench, directed in the king's name, to the judges or officers of inferior courts, commanding them to certify or to return the records of a cause depending before them, to the end, the party may have the more sure and speedy justice, before the king or such justices as he shall assign to determine the cause. 1 *Bac. Abr.*

A *certiorari* lies in all judicial proceedings in which a writ of error does not lie; and it is a consequence of all inferior jurisdictions erected by act of parliament, to have their proceedings returnable in the king's-bench. *Ld. Raym.* 469.

In particular cases, the court will use their discretion to grant a *certiorari*, as if the defendant be of good character, or if the prosecution be malicious, or attended with oppressive circumstances. *Leach's Ham.* 2. c. 27. s. 28. n.

The courts of chancery and king's-bench may award a *certiorari* to remove the proceeding from *any inferior courts*, whether they be of ancient, or newly created jurisdiction, unless the statute or charter which creates them, exempts them from such jurisdiction. 1 *Salk.* 144. *pl.* 3.

CERT-MONEY, head-money. See *Censure.*

CESSAVIT, a writ that lies in many cases, upon this general ground, that he against whom it is brought, has for two years ceased or neglected to perform such service, or to pay such rent as he is tied to by his tenure, and has not upon his lands and tenements sufficient goods or cattle to be distrained.

CESSE, an assessment or tax.

CESSION, is where an ecclesiastical person is created a bishop, or where a parson of a parsonage takes another benefice without

without dispensation, or otherwise not qualified, &c. in both cases, their first benefices are said to be void by *cession:* and to those benefices which the person had who was created a bishop, the king shall present for that time, whosoever is patron of them; and in the other cases the patron may present.

CESSOR, one who neglects so long to perform a duty belonging to him as to be liable to have a writ of *cessavit* brought against him. See *Cessavit.*

CESTUI QUE TRUST, is he to whose use and benefit, another man is enfeoffed of lands or tenements. By 29 Ch. II. c. 3. Lands of *cestui que trust* may be delivered in execution.

CHALDRON, or chalder of coals, by 16 and 17 Ch. II. c. 2. contains thirty-six bushels of coals heaped up, and according to the sealed bushel, kept at *Guildhall, London.*

CHALKING, wounding, and maiming cattle, made felony in *Ireland.*

CHALLENGE, taken either against persons or things: persons, as in assize the jurors, or any one or more of them; or in a case of felony, by a prisoner at the bar.

Challenge of jurors, is of two kinds; either to the *array* by which is meant the whole jury as it stands arrayed in the pannel or little square *pane* of parchment on which the jurors names are written; or to the *polls*; by which are meant the several particular persons or *heads* in the array. 1 *Inst.* 156.

Challenge to the *array* is in respect of the partiality or default of the sheriff, coroner, or other officer that made the return; and it is then two fold: 1st. Principal challenge to the array, which if it be made good, is a sufficient cause of exception, without leaving any thing to the judgment of the triers; as if the sheriff be of kindred to either party; or if any of the jurors be returned at the denomination of either of the parties. 2nd. Challenge to the array *for favor,* which being no principal challenge, must be left to the discretion and conscience of the triers. As where either of the parties suspects that the juror is inclined to favor the opposite party. 1 *Inst.* 158.

Principal challenge to the polls, is where cause is shewn, which if found true, stands sufficient of itself, without leaving any thing to the triers; as if the juror be under the age of twenty-one, it is a good cause of challenge.

Challenge

Challenge to the polls for favor, is when neither party can take any principal challenge; but shews causes of favor, as that the *juror* is a fellow-servant with either party.

In cases of high treason, and misprision of high treason, the prisoner shall have his peremptory challenge to the number of *thirty-five.* 1 *Inst.* 156. But with regard to petit treason, murder, and other felonies, the 22 Hen. VIII. c. 14. continues in force, which takes away the peremptory challenge of more than *twenty.*

CHAMBERLAIN. The office of *lord great chamberlain of England* is hereditary; and where a person dies seized in fee of this office, leaving two sisters, the office belongs to both, and they may execute it by deputy, but such deputy must be approved of by the king, and must not be of a degree inferior to a knight. To the lord chamberlain the keys of *Westminster-hall,* and the court of *requests* are delivered upon all solemn occasions. He disposes of the sword of state to be carried before the king, when he comes to the parliament, and goes on the right-hand of the sword next the king's person. He has the care of providing all things in the house of lords in the time of parliament. To him belong, livery and lodgings in the king's court, &c and the gentleman usher of the black rod, yeoman usher, &c. are under his authority.

The *lord chamberlain of the household,* has also, superintendance of artificers retained in the king's service, messengers, comedians, revels, music, &c.

Chamberlain of London, is commonly the receiver of all rents and revenues belonging to that city, and has great authority in making and determining the rights of freemen, and regulating matters concerning apprentices, orphans, &c.

Chamberlain of Chester, when there is no Prince of *Wales* and *Earl of Chester,* receives and returns all writs, coming thither out of any of the king's courts.

CHAMPARTY, or CHAMPERTY, is the unlawful maintenance of a suit, in consideration of some bargain to have part of the lands or thing in dispute, or part of the gain. By *stat.* 33 Ed. I. *st.* 3. both the champartor, and he who consents thereunto, shall be imprisoned three years, and make fine at the king's pleasure.

CHAM-

CHAMPION OF THE KING, whose office is at the coronation of our kings, to ride into *Westminster-hall* armed *cap a pie*, when the king is at dinner there, and throw down his gauntlet by way of challenge, pronounced by a herald, *that if any man shall deny, or gainsay the king's title to the crown, he is there ready to defend it in single combat*, &c. which being done the king drinks to him, and sends him a gilt cup, with a cover, full of wine, which the champion drinks, and has the cup for his fee. This office is hereditary.

CHANCELLOR and CHANCERY. He that bears the magistracy, is called the *lord high chancellor of England*. By 5 Eliz. c. 18. the *lord chancellor* and keeper had one and the same power, and therefore since that statute there cannot be a *lord chancellor* and *lord keeper* at the same time; and when seals came in use he had always the custody of the king's great seal, so that his office is created by the mere delivery of the king's great seal into his custody; whereby he become without writ or patent, an officer of the greatest weight and power of any now subsisting in the kingdom, and superior in point of precedency to every temporal lord. He is a privy counsellor by his office, and prolocutor of the house of lords by prescription. To him belongs the appointment of all the justices of the peace throughout the kingdom; he is a visitor in right of the king, of all hospitals and colleges of the king's foundation; and patron of all the king's livings, under the value of 20 marks a year in the king's books. He is a general guardian of all infants, idiots, and lunatics; and has the general superintendance of all charitable uses in the kingdom. And all this, over and above the vast and extensive jurisdiction which he exerciseth in his judicial capacity in the court of chancery. All other justices in this kingdom, are tied to the law, but the *chancellor* hath the king's absolute power to moderate the written law, governing his judgment by the law of nature and conscience. 3 *Black*. 46.

In chancery are two courts; one ordinary, being a court of *common law*; the other extraordinary, being a court of *equity*. The ordinary or *common law* court, is a court of record. Its jurisdiction is to hold plea upon a *scire facias*, to repeal and cancel the king's letters patent, when made against law, or upon untrue suggestions; and to hold plea on all personal actions, where any officer

officer of this court is a party; and of executions on statutes, or of recognizances in nature of statutes; and by several acts of parliament, of divers others offences and causes: But this court cannot try a cause by a jury, but the record is to be delivered by the lord chancellor, into the king's-bench to be tried there, and judgment given thereon. And when judgment is given in this common law part of chancery upon demurrer, or the like, a writ of error is returnable into the king's-bench; but this hath not been practised for many years. From this court also proceed all original writs, commissions of charitable uses, bankrupts, sewers, idiots, lunatics, and the like: and for these ends this court is always open. 3 *Black.* 47.

The extraordinary court, is a court of *equity*, and proceeds by the rules of equity and good conscience. This equity consists in abating the rigour of the common law, and giving a remedy in cases where no provision, or not sufficient provision, had been made by the ordinary course of law. The jurisdiction of this court is of vast extent. Almost all causes of weight and moment, first or last, have their determination here. In this court relief is given in the case of infants, married women, and others not capable of acting for themselves. All frauds for which there is no remedy at law, are cognizable here; as also all breaches of trust, and unreasonable or unconscionable engagements. It will compel men to perform their agreements; will remove mortgageors and obligors against penalties and forfeiture, on payment of principal, interest, and costs; will rectify mistakes in conveyances; will grant injunctions to stay waste; and restrain the proceedings of inferior courts, that they exceed not their authority and jurisdiction. 3 *Black.* 48. This court will not retain a suit for any thing under 10l. value, except in cases of charity, nor for lands under 40s. *per annum.*

CHANCELLOR OF THE DUCHY OF LANCASTER. His office is principally, in that court, to judge and determine all controversies, between the king and his tenants, of the duchy lands.

CHANCELLOR OF THE EXCHEQUER, sits in the court, and in the *exchequer-chamber*; and with the rest of the court, orders things to the king's best benefit.

CHANCE-MEDLEY, is the casual killing of a man, not wholly

wholly without the killer's fault, it is also called *manslaughter by misadventure,* for which the offender shall have his pardon of course. 6 Ed. I. c. 9. But here is to be considered, whether the person who commits this manslaughter by *chance-medley,* was doing a lawful thing; for if the act were unlawful it is felony. *Chance-medley,* is properly applied to such killing as happens to self-defence in a sudden rencounter. 4 *Black.* 183.

CHANDLER, tallow-chandlers and wax-chandlers are by 24 Geo. III. *st.* 2. c. 41. to take out annual licences. They shall not use melting-houses, without making a true entry, on pain of 100l. and are to give notice of making candles to the excise-officer for the duties, and of the number, &c. or forfeit 50l. See *Candles, Excise.*

CHAPELS, are of several kinds; *private chapels,* such as belong to noblemen, &c. *free chapels,* so called from their freedom or exemption from all ordinary jurisdiction. The king himself visits his free chapels, and not the ordinary; which office of visitation is executed for the king, by the lord chancellor.

Chapels of ease under the mother-church, built for the ease of the parishioners in large parishes. At the foundation of these chapels, it is generally provided that they shall be no prejudice to the mother-church, either in revenues, or in exemption from subordination and dependance.

CHAPELRY, the precincts and limits of a chapel.

CHAPITERS, in the common law, a summary, or content of such matters, as are to be inquired of, or presented before justices in *eyre,* justices of *assize,* or of *peace,* in their sessions.

CHAPLAIN. The king, queen, prince, princess, &c. may retain as many chaplains as they please: and the king's chaplains, may hold any such number of benefices of the king's gift, as the king shall think fit to bestow upon them. By 21 Hen. VIII. c. 13. an archbishop may retain *eight* chaplains, a duke or bishop *six,* marquis or earl *five*; viscount *four*; baron or knight of the garter, or lord chancellor *three*, duchess, marchioness, countess, baroness (being a widow), the treasurer and controller of the king's house, the king's secretary, dean of the chapel, almoner, and master of the rolls, each of them *two*; the chief justice of the *king's-bench,* and warden of the cinque-ports *one*; all which chaplains may purchase a dispensation, and take two benefices. Every judge

judge of the king's-bench and common-pleas, and the chancellor and chief baron of the exchequer; the attorney and solicitor-general; the groom of the stool; treasurer of the king's chamber and chancellor of the duchy of Lancaster may each retain *one* chaplain, but these chaplains are not entitled to *dispensations*.

CHARACTER, if one person apply to another for the character of a third person, and a good character as to his solvency be given, yet, if in consequence of this opinion, the party asking the question suffer loss through the person's insolvency, no action lies against him who gave the character if it were fairly given. 1 *Esp. Rep.* 442.

But if a man wickedly assert that which he knows to be false, and thereby draws his neighbour into a loss, it is actionable. 3 T. R. 351. But if the party giving credit also knew that the party credited was in bad circumstances an action will not lie. 1. *Esp. Rep.* 290.

CHARGE and DISCHARGE, a *charge* is a thing done that binds him who does it, or that which is his to the performance thereof: and *discharge* is the removal of that *charge*. In all cases where an executory thing is created by deed, *there*, by consent of all the parties, it may by deed, be defeated and *discharged*.

CHARITABLE USES, lands given to alms, and aliened, may be recovered by the donor. 13 Ed. 1. c. 41. Lands, &c. may be given for the maintenance of houses of correction, or of the poor. 35 Eliz. c. 7. Money given to put out apprentices, either by parishes, or public charities to pay no duty. 8 Ann. c. 9.

CHARLOTTE (Queen). By 2 Geo. III. c. 1. his majesty is empowered to grant the queen an annuity of 100,000l. for her life, to take place from his majesty's decease.

CHARTA MAGNA, the great charter of liberties granted first by king *John*, and afterwards, with some alterations confirmed in parliament by king *Henry* the third. It is so called, either for the excellence of the laws therein contained, or because there was another charter, called the *Charter of the Forest*, which was the less of the two; or in regard of the great wars and trouble in obtaining it. The said king Henry the third after it had been several times confirmed by him, and as often broken, at last, in the 37th year of his reign confirmed it in the most solemn manner in *Westminster-hall*. Afterwards King Ed. I. confirming this charter, in the 35th year of his reign, made an explanation of the liberties therein granted to the people; adding some, and in the confirmation, he directed that this charter, should be read twice a year to the people, and sentence of excommunication to be constantly denounced, against all that by word, or deed, or counsel, shall act contrary thereto, or in any degree infringe it.

CHARTER, is a deed whereby the king passeth any grant to any one person or more, or to any body politic.

CHARTER OF FOREST, wherein the laws of the forest, are comprised. *Anno* 9 Hen. III.

CHARTER LAND, is such as a man holds by charter; that is by evidence in writing, otherwise called, freehold. *Stat.* 19 Hen. VII. c. 13.

CHARTER-PARTY, is a contract under hand and seal, executed by the freighter and the master or owner of the ship, containing the terms upon which the ship is hired to freight; the masters and owners usually bind themselves, the ship, tackle, and furniture, that the goods freighted shall be delivered (dangers of the sea excepted) well conditioned at the place of discharge; and they also covenant to provide mariners, tackle, &c. and to equip the ship complete and adequate to the voyage. The freighter stipulates to pay the consideration money for the freight, and penalties are annexed to enforce the reciprocal covenants. A charter-party is the same in the civil law, as an indenture at common law; and is distinguished from a bill of lading, in as much as the former adjusts the term of the freight, and the latter ascertains the contents of the cargo.

CHARTIS REDDENDIS, a writ that lies against him who hath charters of feoffment, delivered him to be kept, and refuses to deliver them.

CHASE, a place of receipt for deer and wild beasts, of a middle nature, between a forest and a park. It is not lawful to make a *chase*, park, or warren, without licence from the king under the broad seal.

CHATTELS or CATALS, all sorts of goods and property, moveable or immoveable, except freehold property.

CHAUNTRY-RENTS, rents paid to the crown by the servants or purchasers of *chauntry-lands*. 22 Ch. II. 16.

CHEAT, a cheat is one who defrauds or endeavours to defraud another

another of his known right, by means of some artful device, contrary to the plain rules of common honesty. By the 30 Geo. II. all persons who knowingly or designedly, by false pretence or pretences, shall obtain from any person money, goods, wares, or merchandizes, with intent to cheat or defraud any person of the same, or shall knowingly tend or deliver any letter or writing, with or without a name subscribed thereto, or signed with a fictitious name, threatening to accuse any person of a crime punishable by law with death, transportation, pillory, or other infamous punishment, with intent to extort from him any money, or other goods, shall be deemed offenders against law and the public peace; and the court before whom any such offender shall be tried, shall, on conviction, order him to be fined and imprisoned, or be put in the pillory, or publicly whipped, or to be transported for seven years.

CHECK ROLL, a *roll* or book, containing the names of such as are attendants, and pay in to the king, or other great persons, as their household servants.

CHECKS or DRAFTS, on bankers, are instruments by means of which, a creditor may assign to a third person, not originally party to the contract, the legal as well as equitable interest in a debt raised by it, so as to vest in such an assignee a right of action against the original debtor. 1 H. B. 602. These instruments are uniformly made payable to bearer, which constitutes a characteristic difference between them and bills of exchange; and the legislature has considered them in a more favourable point of view by exempting them from the stamp duties. They are equally negotiable with bills, although strictly speaking, not due before payment is demanded. When given in payment they are considered as cash; and it is said, may be declared upon as a bill of exchange; and the moment this resemblance begins, they are governed by the same principles of law as bills of exchange.

Checks payable on demand, or where no time of payment is expressed, are payable on presentment, without any indulgence or days of grace; but the presentment should be made within a reasonable time after the receipt, otherwise the party upon whom the check is drawn, will not be responsible, and the person from whom the holder received it will be discharged. Therefore, where circumstances will allow of it, it is advisable for the holder of a check to present it on the same day it is received.

CHESTER, where felony, &c. is committed by any inhabitant of the palatine of *Chester*, in another county, process shall be made to the *exigent* where the offence was done, and if the offenders then fly to the county of *Chester*, the outlawry shall be certified to the officers there. 1 Hen. IV. c. 18.

CHERAGE, tribute, head or poll-money.

CHERISANCE, an unlawful bargain or contract. 37 Hen. VIII. c. 9.

CHILDREN, are in law a man's issue begotten on his wife. In case land be given by will to a man and his *children*, who has such alive, the devisee takes only an estate for life; but if there be no child living, it is held to be an estate tail. 1 *Vent.* 214.

CHILDWIT, a fine paid to the lord of a manor, for every bastard child begotten in the manor.

CHIMIN, in the law signifies way, and is equally applicable to the king's highway, and to a private way.

CHIMMAGE, a toll for way-farage through the forest.

CHIMNEY-MONEY, or hearth-money, was formerly a duty on houses, but long since repealed.

CHIMNEY-SWEEPERS, the overseers, &c. of any parish, may bind any boy of the age of eight years or upwards, who is chargeable to the parish, to any person using the trade of a chimney-sweeper, till he shall attain the age of sixteen years; provided that it be done with the consent of the parent of such boy. And no master shall have more than six apprentices at one time. Every master, shall cause his name and place of abode, to be put upon a brass plate, and to be fixed upon the front of a leathern-cap, which he shall provide for each apprentice, who shall wear the same when out upon his duty; on pain of forfeiting for every such apprentice, above such number, or without having such cap, not exceeding 10l. nor less than 5l.

CHIROGRAPHER OF FINES. The officer in common-pleas, who ingrosses fines in that court, acknowledged into a perpetual record, after they are acknowledged and fully passed by those officers, by whom they were formerly examined, and that write or deliver the indentures of them to the party. This officer also, makes two indentures, one for the buyer and another for the seller, and makes one other indented piece, containing also the effect of the fine, which he delivers over to the *custos brevium*, that is called

called *the foot of the fine*. The chirographer also, or his deputy, proclaims all the fines in the court every term, and then repairing to the *custos brevium*, there indorses the proclamations upon the foot thereof; and always keeps the writ of covenant, and the note of the fine.

CHIVALRY, a tenure of land by knight's service, whereby the tenant is bound to perform some noble or military office unto his lord.

CHOSE, *chose in action*, is a thing incorporeal, and only a right; as an annuity, obligation for debt, a covenant, voucher by warranty, and generally all causes of suit for any debt or duty, tresspass, or wrong, are to be accounted *choses in action*.

CHURCH, the place which Christians consecrate to the worship of God. By the common law and general custom of the realm, it was lawful for earls, barons, and others of the laity, to build churches; but they could not erect a spiritual body politic to continue in succession, and capable of endowment, without the king's licence; and, before the law shall take knowledge of them as such, they must also have the bishop's leave and consent, to be consecrated or dedicated by him. 3 *Inst.* 203.

CHURCHWARDENS, the guardians or keepers of the church, are persons annually chosen in *Easter* week, by the joint consent of the minister and parishioners, or according to the custom of the respective places; to look after the *church* and *church-yard*, and things thereunto belonging. They are entrusted with the care and management of the *goods* and *personal property* of the church, which they are to order for the best advantage of the parishioners; but they have no interest in, or power over the freehold of the church itself, or of any land or other *real* property belonging to it; these are the property of the parson or vicar, who alone is interested in their loss or preservation. The churchwardens therefore, may purchase goods and other articles for the use of the parish; they may likewise with the assent of the parishioners, sell or otherwise dispose of the goods of the church, but without such consent, they are not authorised to alienate any of the property under their care. 4 *Viner Abr.* 526.

All peers of the realm, clergymen, counsellors, attorneys, clerks in court, physicians, surgeons, and apothecaries, are exempt

 from

from serving the office of churchwarden; as is every dissenting teacher, or preacher, in holy orders, or pretended holy orders.

By 2 Geo. III. c. 20. no serjeant, corporal, drummer, or private man, personally serving himself in the militia, during the time of such service shall be liable to serve as churchwarden.

By the 10 & 11 Wm. c. 23. s. 2. persons who have prosecuted a felon to conviction, and the first assignee of the certificate thereof, are exempted.

No person living out of the parish may be chosen churchwarden. *Gibs.* 215.

CINQUE PORTS, five ports or havens that lie on the south-east coast of England, towards France; namely Dover, Hastings, Hythe, Romney, and Sandwich; to which were afterwards added, Winchelsea, Seaford, and Rye. They were distinguished from other ports, on account of their superior importance; in consequence of which they are governed by a *lord warden of the cinque ports*, and have divers privileges granted to them, as a particular jurisdiction, their warden having the authority of admiral among them, and sending out writs in his own name.

Certioraris, to remove indictments taken in the Cinque Ports, must be directed to *the mayor and jurats* before whom they were taken, and not to the *lord warden*, because they hold plea of it as justices of the peace, by virtue of their commission and not by their ancient charter.

CIRCUIT. See *Assize*.

CIRCUITY OF ACTION, is when an *action* is rightfully brought, but in a circuitous way; whereas it might have been as well otherwise answered and determined, and the suit saved.

CIRCUMSTANTIBUS, signifies the supply, or making up of the number of jurors (if any empanelled do not appear; or appearing, be challenged by either party), by adding to them so many other of those that *are present*, or *standing by*, as will serve.

CITATION, is summons to appear, applied particularly to process in the ecclesiastical courts. The party to whom it is directed, shall diligently seek the person to be cited; and when he hath found him, he is to shew him the *citation* under seal, and by virtue thereof, *cite* him to appear at the time and place appointed.

CITY.

CITY, generally signifies such a town corporate, as hath usually a bishop and cathedral church. Formerly there were no *cities* but all great towns were called *burghs*.

CITIZENS, of *London* (see *London*), may prescribe against a statute, because their liberties are reinforced by statute. 1 *Rol. Rep.* 105.

CIVIL LAW, is that *law* which every particular nation, commonwealth, or city, has established peculiarly for itself. The *civil law* is either *written* or unwritten; and the *written law* is public or private; *public*, which immediately regards the state of the commonwealth, as the enacting and execution of laws, consultations about war and peace, establishment of things relating to religion, &c. *private*, that more immediately has respect to the concerns of every particular person. The *unwritten law*, is custom introduced by the tacit consent of the people only, without any particular establishment. The authority of it is great, and it is equal with a written law, if it be wholly uninterrupted, and of a long continuance.

The civil law, is allowed in this kingdom in the two universities, for the training up of students, &c. in matters of foreign treaties between princes; marine affairs, *civil* and criminal; in the ordering of martial causes; the judgment of ensigns and arms, rights of honour, &c.

CLAIM, a challenge of interest in any thing, that is in the possession of another, or at least out of aman'sown; as *claim* by charter, by descent,. &c. By *stat.* 4 Anne *c.* 16. *sect.* 16. no claim or entry shall be of force to avoid any fine levied with proclamation in the common-pleas, or in the court of sessions in the counties palatine, or of grand sessions in *Wales*, or shall be a sufficient entry to claim within the statute of limitation, 21 *Jac.* 1. c. 16. unless upon such entry or claim, an action be commenced within one year after making such entry or claim, and prosecuted with effect. *Plowd.* 359.

CLAMEA ADMITTENDA IN ITINERE PER ATTURNATUM, a writ whereby the king commands the justices in *eyre*, to admit a person's claim by attorney, who is employed in the king's services, and cannot come in his own person.

CLAVES INSULÆ, the keys of the island, in the Isle of *Man*, all

all ambiguous and weighty causes are referred to twelve whom they call *claves insulæ*.

CLAUSUM FREGIT, signifies an action of trespass; and so called, because in the writ, such an one is summoned to answer *quare clausum fregit*, why he made such trespass.

CLERICO ADMITTENDO, a writ to the bishop, for the admission of a *clerk* to a benefice upon a *ne admitteas*, tried and found for the party who procureth the writ.

CLERICO CAPTO PER STATUTAM MERCATORUM, &c. a writ directed to the bishop, for the delivery of a *clerk* out of prison, who is in custody upon a breach of a *statute merchant*.

CLERICO CONVICTO COMMISSO GAOLÆ IN DEFECTU ORDINARII DELIVERANDO, a writ for the delivery of a *clerk* to his ordinary, that was formerly convicted of felony, by reason his ordinary did not challenge him according to the privileges of *clerks*.

CLERICUS SACERDOTIS, a parish-clerk, or inferior assistant to the parochial priest. The *parish-clerks* were formerly to be men of letters, and to teach a school in the parish.

CLERK OF THE ACTS, a respectable officer in the navy-office, who receives and records all orders, contracts, bills, warrants, and other business, transacted by the lords commissioners of the navy. 22 & 23 Geo. II.

CLERK OF THE AFFIDAVITS, in the court of chancery, is an officer who files all affidavits made use of in court.

CLERK OF THE ASSISE, is he that writes all things judicially done by the justices of *assize* in their circuits. Clerk of assize is associated with the judge in the commissions of assize. See *Assize*.

CLERK TO AN ATTORNEY. See *Attorney*.

CLERK OF THE BAILS, an officer formerly belonging to the court of king's-bench.

CLERK OF THE CROWN, a clerk or officer in the king's-bench, whose function is to frame, read, and record all indictments against traitors, felons, and other offenders, there arraigned or indicted upon public crime.

CLERK OF THE CROWN IN CHANCERY, an officer there who by himself or deputy, is continually to attend the lord chancellor

chancellor, or lord keeper, writes and prepares for the great seal of *England*, special matters of state by commission, or the like, either immediately from his majesty, or by order of his council as of well ordinary as extraordinary, *viz.* commissions of lieutenancy, justices itinerant, and of assize of *oyer* and *terminer*, goal delivery, and of the peace, with their writs of association, &c. Also all general pardons upon grants of them, at the king's coronation, or at the parliament, where he sits in the lords house in parliament time, into whose office the writs of parliament, made by the clerks of the petty-bag, with the names of the knights and burgesses elected thereupon are to be returned and filed. He hath also the making of all special pardons, and writs of execution upon bonds of statute-staple forfeited.

CLERK OF THE DECLARATIONS, an officer in the court of king's-bench who files all declarations in causes there depending, after they are ingrossed.

CLERK OF THE ERRORS, in the court of common-pleas, transcribes and certifies into the king's-bench, the tenor of the records of the cause of action; upon which, the *writ of error* (made by the cursitor) is brought, there to be judged and determined. The *clerk of the errors* in the king's-bench, likewise transcribes and certifies the record of such causes in that court into the Exchequer, if the cause of action were by *bill*; if by *original*, the lord chief justice certifies the record in the house of peers in parliament, by taking the transcript from the *clerk of the errors*, and delivering it to the lord keeper.

The *clerk of the errors* in the exchequer, transcribes the records, certified thither out of the king's-bench, and prepares them for judgment in the court of exchequer, to be given by the justices of the common-pleas and barons there.

CLERK OF ESSOINS, an officer belonging to the court of common-pleas, who keeps the essoin rolls. See *Essoin*.

CLERK OF THE ESTREATS, a clerk belonging to the exchequer, who *termly* receives the *estreats* out of the lord treasurer's remembrancer's office, and writes them out to be levied for the king. He also makes schedules of such sums, *estreated* as are to be discharged.

CLERK OF THE HAMPER or HANAPER, an officer in chancery, whose function is to receive all the money due to the king

king for the seals of charters, patents, commissions, and writs, as also fees due to the officers for enrolling and examining the same, &c. His attendance on the lord chancellor or lord keeper is daily required in term time, and at all times of sealing, having with him a leather-bag, wherein are put all charters, &c. after they are sealed; those bags being sealed up with the lord chancellor's private seal, are delivered to the controller of the *hanaper*.

CLERK OF THE JURIES, an officer belonging to the court of common-pleas, who enrolls and exemplifies all fines and recoveries, and returns writs of entry, summons, seisin, &c.

CLERK OF THE JURIES, or JURATA WRITS, an officer belonging to the court of common-pleas, who makes up the writs called *habeas corpora*, and *distringas*, for the appearance of juries, either in court, or at the assizes, after the jury is returned upon the *venire facias*.

CLERK OF THE MARKET, has no concern but with victuals, but formerly their power was much greater. The court of the *clerk of the market*, is incident to every fair and market in the kingdom, to determine all disputes, relative to private or civil property,

CLERK OF THE PEACE, an officer attending upon the justices of the peace in the sessions. He must yearly certify into the king's-bench, the names of all persons outlawed, attainted, or convicted of felony. He must also deliver to the sheriff yearly, a schedule of fines and other forfeitures in sessions, and also a duplicate thereof upon oath into the court of exchequer.

CLOCKS AND WATCHES, no dial-plates and cases shall be exported without the movements; and makers shall engrave their names thereon.

CLOTH, no cloth made beyond sea, shall be brought into the king's dominions on pain of forfeiting the same, and the importers incur further punishment. *Stat.* 12 Ed. III. c. 3. See *Drapery and Woollen Manufactures*.

COACH. *Hackney-coaches*, commissioners are appointed to license and regulate them: the proprietor of each coach to pay 10s. per week. Each coach is to be numbered on both sides, the altering of which incurs a penalty of 5l. The same penalty is incurred by driving or letting to hire a coach without a license.

Mourning-coaches and hearses are within the act. The horses in hackney-coaches, must be fourteen hands high. Coachmen compellable to go in the day ten miles; after dark, but two miles and an half on turnpike-roads; to have check-strings, under the penalty of 5l.

The rate for a mile and a quarter, or less is 1s. from that to two miles 1s. 6d. and for each additional half mile entered upon 6d.

In reckoning by *time*, three quarters of an hour, or less is 1s. between that and an hour 1s. 6d. one hour and twenty minutes 2s. and for each additional twenty minutes entered upon 6d. For a day of twelve hours 14s 6d. and 6d. for each twenty minutes over.

A coachman refusing to go, or exacting more than his fare, forfeits from 10s. to 3l. By misbehaviour or impudence he incurs the same penalty, and subjects his license to be revoked, and himself to be committed to the house of correction. Persons refusing to pay the fare, or defacing the coach, may be compelled by a justice to make satisfaction. The penalties may be recovered before the aldermen of the city, and justices of the peace, as well as before the commissioners. 4, 7, 10, 11, 12, 24, 26, and 32 Geo. III.

Stage-coaches, every person keeping any public stage coach shall pay annually 5s. for a license; and keeping any such public stage without a license, he shall forfeit for every time such carriage is used, 10l. No person licensed, shall by virtue of *one* license, keep more than *one carriage*, on penalty of 10l. Every licensed stage-coach shall pay, *twopence halfpenny* for every mile it travels. Every person licensed shall paint, on the outside pannel of each door, his *christian and surname*, with the name of place from whence he sets out, and to which he is going, on pain of 10l. Should he discontinue such carriage, he shall give seven days previous notice, and have such notice indorsed upon his license, and from thenceforth shall be no longer chargeable.

Drivers of stage-coaches, are not to admit more than *one* outside passenger on the box, and four on the roof of the coach, on the penalty of 5s. for each passenger at every turnpike-gate. See *Taxes*.

COACHMAKER, the wares of coachmakers shall be examined

amined by persons appointed by the sadler's company. 1 *Jac.* c. 22. And every coachmaker shall take out an annual license from the excise-office, and pay a duty of 20s. for every four-wheeled carriage, and 10s. for every two-wheeled carriage built by him for sale.

COACHMAN, opening and partly destroying a parcel left in his coach is guilty of felony.

COALS. Sea-coal brought into the *Thames*, shall be sold by the chaldron containing thirty-six bushels heaped up, according to the bushel sealed for that purpose at *Guildhall.*

Coals within the bills shall be carried in linen sacks, sealed by the proper officer, which shall be at least four feet four inches in length, and twenty-six inches in breadth : and sellers of coals by the chaldron, or less quantity, shall put three bushels of coals into each sack. 3 and 32 Geo. II. c. 26. and 27.

All sellers of coals, are to keep a lawful bushel, which bushel and other measures shall be edged with iron and sealed; and using others, or altering them, incurs a forfeiture of 50l.

Any purchaser dissatisfied with the measure of any coals, may, on delivery to him of the meter's ticket, have the same re-measured, by sending notice thereof to the seller, and to the land coal-meter's office for the district in which the coals were sold; on which a meter (not being the same under whose inspection the coals were originally measured) must within two hours attend to re-measure the coals, and shall re-measure the same sack by sack, in the presence of the seller and purchaser (if they attend), and also in the presence of a meter from the two other districts (whose attendance within London and Westminster is enforced by a penalty of 5l. but not in *Surry*); for this attendance, the purchaser is to pay each coal-meter attending, sixpence per chaldron. If the coals prove deficient in measure, the seller shall forfeit 5l. for every bushel deficient, and also forfeit the coals to the poor. The meter under whose inspection the coals were measured at the wharf, shall also forfeit 5l per bushel deficient, to be recovered (if not in five days) of the principal coal-meter; and coal-porters 2s. 6d. per bushel. The carman is to be paid 2s. 6d for his horses, &c. for each hour, whilst the coals are re-measuring.

Any coal-factor receiving, or coal-owner giving any gratuity, for buying or selling any particular sort of coals, and selling one kind

kind of coals for and as a sort which they really are not, shall forfeit 500l. 3 Geo. II. c. 26.

Owners or masters of ships shall not enhance the price of coals in the river *Thames*, by keeping turn in delivering coals there, under the penalty of 100l. 4 Geo. II. c. 30. Contracts between coal-owners, &c. and merchants of ships for restraining the buying of coals are void, and the parties shall forfeit 100l. 9 Ann. c. 28.

Wilfully and maliciously setting on fire, any mine, pit, or delph of coal, or cannel-coal, is felony without benefit of clergy. 10 Geo. II. c. 32.

Setting fire to, demolishing, or otherwise damaging any engine or any other thing belonging to coal-mines, is felony and transportation for seven years. 9 Geo. III. c. 29.

COCKETT, COCKETTUM, COCKETUM. The custom-house or office, where goods to be transported are first entered, and pay their custom, and are to have a *cokett*, signifying their merchandizes are customed, and may be discharged. See *Custom-House*.

CODICIL, a schedule or supplement to a will. See *Will*.

COFFERER OF THE KING'S HOUSEHOLD, next under the controller, who superintends and pays the other officers of the household their wages.

COGNISOR or CONNUSOR, he that passeth or acknowledgeth a fine of lands or tenements to another. *Cognisee* or *conusee*, is he to whom the fine is acknowledged.

COGNISANCE, sometimes signifies an acknowledgment of fine, and sometimes a power or jurisdiction, as *cognisance of pleas*, is an ability to call a cause or plea out of another court, which no one can do but the king, except he can shew charters for it.

COGNITIONIBUS MITTENDIS, a writ to one of the king's justices of the common-pleas, or other that has power to take a fine, and who having taken it, delays to certify the same, commanding him to certify it.

COGNOVIT ACTIONEM, is an acknowledgment by a defendant, or confession that the plaintiff's cause of action is just, and who to save law expences suffers judgment to be entered against him; in this case the confession generally extends to no more than is contained in the declaration, with costs.

COIF. The serjeants at law, are otherwise called, *serjeants of the coif,* from the lawn coif they wear on their heads, under their caps, when they are created, and always after.

COIN, metallic money, struck with a mark, effigy or inscription, from which its weight, title, and value are known; and though the material of which it is composed, were melted into any other form, still it would preserve the same value, or very nearly so.

Counterfeiting the king's money, or bringing false money into the realm counterfeit to the money of *England,* clipping, washing, rounding, filing, impairing, diminishing, falsifying, scaling, lightening, edging, colouring, gilding, making, mending, or having in one's possession, any puncheon, counter-puncheon, matrix, stamp, dye, pattern, mould, edger, or cutting-engine: all these incur the penalty of high treason. And if any person shall counterfeit any such kind of gold or silver, as are not the proper coin of the realm, but current therein by the king's consent, he shall be guilty of high treason.

If any person shall tender in payment any counterfeit coin, he shall for the first offence, be imprisoned six months; for the second offence two years; and for the third offence shall be guilty of felony without benefit of clergy.

Blanching copper or other base metal, or buying or selling the same; and receiving or paying money at a lower rate than its denomination doth import; and also the offence of counterfeiting copper halfpence and farthings; incur the penalty of felony, but within clergy. Counterfeiting coin not the proper coin of this realm not permitted to be current therein, is misprision of treason. A person buying or selling, or having in his possession, clippings or filings, shall forfeit 500l. and be branded in the cheek with the letter R. And any person having in his possession a coining-press, or casting bars or ingots of silver in imitation of *Spanish* bars or ingots, shall forfeit 500l.

A reward of 40l. is given for convicting a counterfeiter of the gold or silver coin; and 10l. for a counterfeiter of the copper coin. 16 Geo. II. and 13 Geo. III. c. 28. and 77.

COLIBERTUS,

COLIBERTUS, a tenant, who held his freedom of tenure, under condition of particular works and services.

COLLATERAL assurance is that, which is made over and beside the deed itself. See *Security*.

COLLATION OF A BENEFICE, the bestowing of a *benefice* by the bishop, who has it in his own gift or patronage. See *Advowson*.

COLLATIONE FACTA UNI POST MORTEM ALTERIUS, a writ directed to the justices of the common-pleas, commanding them to direct their writ to a bishop, for the admission of a clerk in the place of another presented by the king, who died during the suit between the king and the bishop's clerk.

COLLEGE, a particular corporation, company, or society of men, having certain privileges founded by the king's licence.

Colleges in the universities are generally lay corporations, although the members of the college, may be all ecclesiastical. 2 *Salk*. 672. And in the government thereof, the king's courts cannot interfere, where a visitor is specially appointed. 1 *Black*. 483.

The two universities, in exclusion of the king's courts, enjoy the sole jurisdiction over all civil actions and suits, except where the right of freehold is concerned; and also in criminal offences or misdemeanours under the degree of treason, felony, or maim. 3 *Black*. 83. Their proceedings are in a summary way, according to the practice of the civil law. Wood. b. 4. c. 2. But they have no jurisdiction unless the plaintiff or defendant be a scholar or servant of the university, and resident *in it at the time*. An appeal lies from the chancellor's court to the congregation, thence to the convocation, from thence to the delegates.

COLLEGIATE CHURCH, a church built and endowed for a society, or a body corporate of a dean, or other president, and secular priests, as canons, or prebendaries in the same church.

COLLOQIUM, the affirming of a thing, laid in declarations, as for words in actions of slander, &c.

COLLUSION, a deceitful agreement or compact between two or more, for the one party to bring an action against the other to some evil purpose, as to defraud a third of his right.

COLONIES. See *Plantations*.

COLOUR, in a legal acceptation, a probable plea, but false in in fact, and hath this end to draw the trial of the cause from the jury to the judges.

COLOUR OF OFFICE, generally signifies an act evilly done by the countenance of an office, whereas the office is but as a trick to give plausibility to the falshood. *Plowd. 64. a.*

COMBARONES, the fellow-barons or commonalty of the cinque ports; this title is restrained from the common inhabitants, to distinguish their representatives in parliament.

COMBAT. See *Battel.*

CONBINATIONS, are persons assembled together unlawfully, with an intent to do unlawful acts, and these offences are punishable before such acts are carried into effect, in order to prevent the consequence of *combinations,* and conspiracies. 9 *Rep.* 57.

COMBUSTIA PECUNIÆ, the ancient method of trying mixed and corrupt money, *Temp.* H. II. by melting it down, upon payment into the exchequer.

COMITATU COMMISSO, a writ or commission, whereby the sheriff is authorised to take upon him the command of the county.

COMITATU ET CASTRO COMMISSO, a writ whereby the charge of a county together with the keeping of a castle, is committed to the sheriff.

COMMANDMENT, of the justices, is either *absolute* or *ordinary.*

Absolute, as when upon their own authority, in their wisdom and discretion, they commit a man to prison for a punishment. *Ordinary* is when they commit him rather for safe custody than as a punishment: and a man committed upon an *ordinary commandment* is bailable. *Staund. pl. cor.* 73. *commandment* is also used for the offence of one encouraging another to transgress or do any thing contrary to law, as theft, murder, and such like. See *Accessary.*

COMMANDRY, was any manor or chief messuage with lands and tenements appertaining thereto, belonging to the priory of *St. John of Jerusalem* in *England.*

COMMEATURA, a commandry, for the accommodation of the knights templars.

COMMENDAM, a benefice or church-living, being either void,

void, or to prevent it's becoming void, is *commended* to the charge of some sufficient clerk, to be supplied, till it may be conveniently provided with a pastor. When a parson is made bishop, there is a cession of his benefice by the promotion; but if the king give him power to retain his benefice, he shall continue parson, and is said to hold it in *commendam*; but it must be always before consecration; for afterwards it comes too late, because the benefice is then absolutely void.

COMMENTARY, one that has a church-living in *commendam.*

COMMENDATORY LETTERS, are such as are written by one bishop to another in behalf of any of his clergy, or other of his diocese, travelling thither, or that the clerk may be promoted, &c.

COMMENDATUS, one who lives under the protection of a great man.

COMMINALTY, are such of the commons, as, raised beyond the common peasants, come to have the managing of offices, and by that means are a degree under burgesses.

COMMISSARY, a title of ecclesiastical jurisdiction, appertaining to one who exercises spiritual jurisdiction in places so remote from the chief city, that the chancellor cannot call the subjects to the bishops principal consistory, without subjecting them to great inconvenience.

COMMISSION, is taken for the warrant or letters patent, that all men exercising jurisdiction either ordinary or extraordinary, have for their power to hear or determine any cause or action; thus the judges and most of the great officers judicial and ministerial of this realm, are made by commission.

COMMISSIONERS OF THE ADMIRALTY. See *Admiral.*

Commissioners of the Excise. See *Excise.*

Commissioners of the Great Seal, persons appointed to execute the office of lord chancellor. See 1 W. & M. *sess.* 1. c. 21.

COMMITMENT, is the sending a person to prison by warrant or order, either for a crime or for contumacy. If for *a crime* the warrant must be until *discharged according to law*; but for contumacy, until *he comply,* and perform the thing required. *Carth.* 153. The *commitment* should be in writing, otherwise by the

the *habeas corpus act*, the prisoner may be admitted to bail whatever his offence may have been. 1 *Burn*. 379.

Who may commit. Wheresoever a constable or person may justify the arresting another for a felony, or treason, he may justify the sending him or bringing him to the common goal. 2 *Haw*. 116. But it is most adviseable, for any private person who arrests another for felony, to cause him to be brought as soon as possible before some justice of peace, that he may be committed or bailed by him. *Dall*. c. 118.

The privy-council, or any one or two of them, or a secretary of state, may lawfully commit persons for treason, and for other offences against the state. 2 *Haw*. 117.

To what place. All felons shall be committed to the common goal and not elsewhere. 5 Hen. IV. c. 10. But vagrants and other criminals, offenders, and persons charged with small offences, may, for such offences, or for want of sureties, be committed either to the common goal or house of correction, as the justices in their judgment shall think proper. 6 G. c. 19.

Who may be committed. All persons who are apprehended for offences *not bailable*, and those who neglect to *offer bail* for offences which are bailable, must be committed; and wheresoever a justice of peace is empowered to bind a person over, or to cause him to do a certain thing, he may commit him, if in his presence he shall refuse to be so bound, or do such a thing. 2 *Haw*. 116.

Observations respecting commitment. A commitment must be in writing, either in the name of the king, and only tested by the person who makes it; or it may be made by such person in his own name, expressing his office or authority, and must be directed to the *goaler or keeper of the prison*. 2 *Haw*. 119. The commitment should contain the name and surname of the party committed, if known; if not known, it may be sufficient to describe the person by his age, &c. and to add, that he refuses to tell his name. 1 H. H. 557. It ought to contain the cause as for treason or felony, or suspicion thereof; and also the special nature of the felony, briefly, *as for felony for the death of such an one*, or for burglary, *in breaking the house of such an one*. 2. H. H. 122. A commitment must also have an apt conclusion; as if it be for felony, till he be thence delivered by due course of of law. 2 H. H. 123. All commitments grounded on acts of parliament ought to be conformable to the method prescribed by them. 2 *Haw. Not.* 33. And where a statute appoints imprisonment, but does not limit the time, in such case the prisoner must remain at the discretion of the court. *Dalt. c.* 170.

The duty of a goaler respecting commitments. If the goaler shall refuse to receive a felon, or take any thing for receiving him, he shall be punished for the same by the justices of goal delivery. 4 Ed. III. c. 9. But no person can justify the detaining a prisoner in custody, out of the common goal, unless there be some particular reason for so doing; as if the party should be so dangerously ill, that it would apparently hazard his life to send him to goal, or that there be evident danger of a rescue from rebels or the like. 1 *Haw.* 118. By the 3 Hen. VII. *c.* 3. the sheriff or goaler, shall certify the commitment to the next goal delivery.

By the *habeas corpus act,* the charge of conveying an offender, is limited not to exceed 12d. a mile.

Commitment discharged. A person legally committed for a crime, certainly appearing to have been done by some person or other, cannot be lawfully discharged but by the king, till he be acquitted upon his trial, or have an *ignoramus* found by the grand jury, or none shall prosecute him, on a proclamation for that purpose by the justices of goal delivery. 2 *Haw.* 121.

COMMON, is a right of privilege which one or more persons claim to take or use, in some part or portion of that, which another man's lands, waters, woods, &c. naturally produce; without having an absolute property in such lands, woods, waters, &c. 2 *Inst.* 65.

Of the several kinds of commons. The general division, of common, is into *common of pasture,* which is a right or liberty that one or more have to feed or fodder their beasts or cattle in another man's land. *Common of turbary,* or a liberty of cutting turves in another man's land or soil. *Common of piscary,* or a right and liberty of taking fish in another's fish-pond, pool, or river. *Common of estovers,* which is a right of taking trees or loppings, shrubs, and underwood, in another's woods, coppices, &c. and *lastly,* a liberty which the tenants have in some manors, of of digging and taking sand, gravel, stone, &c. in the lord's soil. 1 *Bac. Abr.* 385.

But the word *common* is usually understood of common of pasture, of which there are four kinds; *common appendant*; *common appurtenant*; *common in gross*; and *common by reason of vicinage*.

Common appendant, is a right belonging to the owners or occupiers of arable land, to put commonable beasts upon the lord's waste, and upon the lands of other persons within the same manor. Commonable beasts, are either beasts of the plough, or such as manure the land. 1 *Inst.* 122.

Common appurtenant, can only be claimed by prescription, and is a right of commonage for beasts, not only commonable, as horses, oxen, cows, and sheep, but likewise for beasts not commonable, as swine, goats, and geese. *Co. Lit.* 122.

Common in gross, is a right of commonage which must be claimed by deed or prescription, and has no relation to any land belonging to the commoner; it may be for a certain number of cattle, or without number. He that hath *common in gross* for a certain number of cattle, may put in the cattle of a stranger, and use the common with them. 2 *Inst.* 427. 2 *Rol. Abr.* 402.

Common by reason of vicinage, is a liberty that the tenants of one lord, in one town, have to common with the tenants of another lord in another town. Those who challenge this kind of common (which is usually called intercommoning) may not put their cattle in the common of the other town; for then they are distrainable; but turning them into their own fields, if they stray into the neighbour common, they must be suffered. *Cowel.*

How far the commoner is interested in the soil, a commoner hath only a special and limited interest in the soil, but yet he shall have such remedies as are commensurate to his right, and therefore may distrain beasts *damage-feasant*, bring an action on the case, &c. but not being absolute owner of the soil, he cannot bring a general action of trespass, for a trespass done upon the common. Nor can he do any thing to the soil which tends to the melioration or improvement thereof, as cutting down of bushes, fern, &c. *Commoner* may abate hedges made on his common; and may *drive the beasts* of a commoner mixed with the beasts of

a *stranger*

a *stranger* to a convenient place to sever them, and may drive the beasts of the stranger out of the common, without any custom. *Godb.* 123. 2 Mod. 65. 3 *Lev.* 40. It is a general rule, that a commoner cannot distrain or chase out the cattle of the lord, or *terre tenant,* damage-feasant; and if the lord surcharge the common, his proper remedy is an action on the case. *Godb.* 182.

COMMON INTENDMENT, is common meaning or understanding according to the subject matter, and not strained to an extraordinary or foreign sense.

COMMON LAW. The common law of England, is the common rule for administering justice within this kingdom, and asserts the king's royal prerogatives, and likewise the rights and liberties of the subject: it is generally that law by which the determination in the king's ordinary courts are guided. It is distinguished from the *statute* laws or acts of parliament, as having been the law of the land, before any acts of parliament which are now extant were made. *Hale's Hist.* 24. 44. 45.

COMMON PLEAS, pleas or suits are regularly divided into two sorts; *pleas of the crown,* which comprehend all crimes and misdemeanours wherein the king (on behalf of the public) is plaintiff; and *common-pleas,* which include all civil actions depending between subject and subject. The former of these were the proper object of the court of king's-bench, the latter of the court of *common-pleas,* and in this court only can *real* actions, that is actions which concern the right of freehold or the *reality,* be originally brought; and in this court also, all other or *personal* pleas between man and man are determined, but in some of these the court of king's-bench hath a concurrent authority. But a writ of error, in the nature of an appeal, lies from the court of common-pleas to the court of king's-bench. 3 *Black.* 37. This court can hear and determine causes removed out of inferior courts by *pone, recordare,* or other like writs. They can also grant prohibitions, to keep other courts as well ecclesiastical as temporal, within due bounds.

In this court are four judges, created by letters patent; the seal of the court is committed to the custody of the chief justice.

COMMON PRAYER. It is the particular duty of a clergyman

man every *Sunday*, &c. to use the public form of prayer, prescribed by the book of common prayer. And the 13 & 14 Ch. II. enacts that every incumbent residing upon a living and keeping a curate, shall at least once a month, publicly read the *common prayer*, and if there be occasion, administer the sacraments, and other rights of the church, on pain of 5l. to the poor, on confession or conviction thereof before two justices.

COMMON RECOVERY. See *Fine*.

COMMONWEAL, the public good. The law tolerates many things to be done for *common good*, which otherwise might not be done: and hence it is that monopolies are void in law, and that bonds and covenants to restrain free trade, tillage, or the like, are adjudged void. 11 *Co. Rep.* 50.

COMMORANCY, a dwelling in any place, as an inhabitant of a house in a vill. *Commorancy* for a certain time may make a settlement in a parish. 4 *Black.* 273.

COMMOTE, in Wales, is half a *cantred* or hundred, containing fifty villages. See *Cantred*.

COMMUNITAS REGNI. See *Comminalty*.

COMPOSITION, an agreement or contract between a parson, patron, and ordinary, &c. for money or other things in lieu of tithes. The *compositions* for tithes, made by the consent of the parson, patron, and ordinary, by virtue of 13 Eliz. c. 10. shall not bind the successor unless made for twenty-one years or three lives, as in case of leases of ecclesiastical corporations, &c.

COMPRINT, usually means, a surreptitious *printing* of another's copy. See *Books*.

COMPROMISE, a mutual promise of two or more parties at difference, to refer the ending of their controversies, to the arbitrament and equity of one or more arbitrators. See *Arbitration*.

COMPOSITION, an agreement between a debtor and creditor, to accept a certain sum in discharge of all demands. It has been questioned, whether even agreement by creditors to take a composition in discharge of their debts, be not binding; though no fund be appropriated for the payment of the composition. 6 T. R. 263.

COMPURGATOR, one who by oath justifies another's innocence. See *Oath*.

COMPUTATION is used in the common law, for the true account

count and construction of time, so that neither the one party nor the other shall do wrong, nor the determination of time referred at large, be taken one way or other; but computed according to the best judgment of the law.

CONCEALERS, such as find out *concealed* lands, which are kept from the king by common persons, having nothing to shew for their title or estate therein. 39 Eliz. c. 22. & 21 Jac. c. 2.

CONCORD, the agreement between parties, that intend the levying of a fine of lands one to the other, how and in what manner the land shall pass.

CONCUBINAGE, is used as an exception against one suing for dower, alledging thereby, that she was not a wife, lawfully married to the party, in whose lands she seeks to be endowed, but his *concubine*.

CONDITION, a restraint annexed to a thing, so that by the non-performance the party to it shall sustain loss, and by the performance receive advantage; or it is a restriction of men's acts, qualifying or suspending the same, and making them uncertain whether they shall take effect or not. Also it is defined to be, what is referred to a contingency, which may or may not take place.

CONE AND KEY, accounts and key. A woman at the age of 14 or 15, might take the charge of her house and receive *cone and key*, so that a woman was held to be of competent years, when she was able to keep the *accounts* and *key* of her house.

CONFEDERACY, is when two or more confederate, to do any damage or injury to another, or to commit any unlawful act. And though a writ of confederacy do not lie if the party be not indicted and in a lawful manner acquitted, yet false confederacy between divers persons shall be punished, though nothing be put in execution.

CONFESSION OF OFFENCE, is when a prisoner is appealed or indicted of treason or felony, and brought to the bar to be arraigned, and his indictment being read to him, the court demands what he can say thereto: then either he confesses the offence, and the indictment to be true, or pleads not guilty.

Confession, is two fold, either *express* or *implied*. An *express* confession is, where a person directly confesses the crime with which he is charged, which is the highest conviction that can be.

2 Haw.

2 *Haw.* 333. But it is usual for the court, especially if it be out of clergy, to advise the party to plead, and put himself upon his trial, and not immediately to record his confession, but to admit him to plead. 2 H. H. 225. An *implied* confession is, where a defendant in a case not capital, does not directly own himself guilty, but in a manner admits it, by yielding to the king's mercy, and desiring to submit to a small fine; which submission the court may accept if they think fit, without putting him to a direct confession. 2 Haw. 233.

Confession in a civil action. Sometimes there is a confession in a civil action, but not usually of the whole complaint, for then the defendant would probably end the matter sooner, or not plead at all, but suffer judgment to go by default; but sometimes, after tender and refusal of debt, if the creditor harass his debtor with an action, it then becomes necessary for the defendant to confess the debt and plead the tender; for a tender by the debtor, and refusal by the creditor, will in all cases discharge the costs. 4 *Black.* 303. So in order to strengthen the creditor's security, it is usual for the debtor, to execute a warrant of attorney to confess judgment in an action to be brought by such creditor; which judgment when confessed, is compleat and binding. 3 *Black.* 397.

CONFIRMATION, is a conveyance of an estate or right *in esse*, whereby a voidable estate is made sure and unavoidable, or whereby a particular estate is increased. Thus a bishop grants his chancellorship by patent, for the term of the patentee's life; this is no void grant, but voidable by the bishop's death, except it be strengthened by the *confirmation* of the dean and chapter. 2 *Black.* 325.

CONFISCATE, if a man be indicted that he feloniously stole the goods of another man, when in truth they are the proper goods of him indicted, and which being brought into court against him, he *disclaims* them, by this *disclaimer* he shall lose the goods, although afterwards he be acquitted of the felony, and the king shall have them as *confiscated.* *Staundf. pl. cor. l.* c. 24.

CONGE' D'ESLIRE. The king's permission royal to a dean and chapter, in time of vacation, to choose or elect a bishop. See *Bishop.*

CONJURATION. The using of witchcraft, *conjuration*, &c. was

was made felony by the 1 *Jac. c.* 12. but that superstitious statute having produced many pernicious effects, it was wisely repealed by the 9 Geo. II. c. 5. wherein it is enacted, that no prosecution, suit, or proceeding shall be commenced, or carried on, against any person for witchcraft, sorcery, inchantment, or conjuration, or for charging another with any such offence, in any court whatsoever.

But, by the same statute, if any person shall *pretend* to exercise or use any kind of witchcraft, sorcery, inchantment, or conjuration; or undertake to tell fortunes; or pretend from his skill or knowledge in any occult or crafty science, to discover where, or in what manner, any goods or chattels supposed to have been stolen or lost, may be found; every person so offending, being convicted on indictment or information, shall suffer imprisonment for a year without bail or mainprize, and once in each quarter of the year, in some market town of the proper county, upon the market-day there, stand openly on the pillory for one hour; and shall also, (if the court by which such judgment shall be given shall think fit) be obliged to give sureties for his good behaviour, in such sum and for such time, as the court shall judge proper, according to the circumstances of the offence; and in such case shall be further imprisoned, till such sureties shall be given. 4 *Black.* 60.

CONSANGUINITY, or kindred, is the connexion or relation of persons descended from the same stock or common ancestor; and is either *lineal* or *collateral. Lineal* consanguinity, is that which subsists between persons, of whom one is descended in a direct line from the other, as grandfather, father, and son. *Collateral* consanguinity, is that which subsists between persons descended from the same common ancestor, but not from one another; as brothers, uncles, and nephews. 2 *Black.* 204.

CONSENT, in all cases where any *thing executory* is created by *deed,* it may by consent of all persons that were parties to the creation of it, by *their* deed be *defeated and annulled.* 1 Rep. 113.

CONSEQUENTIAL LOSSES OR DAMAGES. It is a fundamental principle of law and reason, that he who does the first wrong, shall answer for all the consequential damages. 12 *Mod.* 639. But this admits of limitation. Though a man do a lawful thing, yet, if any damage thereby befal another, he shall answer *if he could have avoided it.*

CONSERVATOR OF THE PEACE, before justices of the peace were appointed (*Temp.* Ed. III.) there were persons that by the common law, had interest in keeping the peace, some of these were therefore named *custodes pacis,* wardens or *conservators* of the peace.

CONSIDERATIO CURIÆ, is the judgment of the court.

CONSIDERATION, is the material cause of a contract, without which it would not be effectual or binding. Consideration in *contracts,* is something given in exchange, something that is mutual and reciprocal; as money given for goods sold, work performed for wages. And a consideration of some sort or other is so absolutely necessary to the forming a contract, that a *nudum pactum,* or agreement to do or pay any thing on one side, without any compensation on the other, is totally void in law; and a man cannot be compelled to perform it. 2 *Black.* 445. A consideration is necessary to create a debt, otherwise it is a *nudum pactum.* *Jenk.* 290. *in pl.* 27.

CONSIGNMENT, the sending, delivering over goods, money, or other property, to another person. It may be either consigned unconditionally, or for some particular purpose. Consigned goods are supposed in general, to be the property of him, *by* whom they are consigned, but to be at the disposal of him, *to* whom they are consigned.

CONSILIUM, is now used to signify a speedy day appointed to argue a demurrer; which the court grants after the demurrer joined, on reading the records of the cause.

CONSISTORY, a tribunal; every archbishop and bishop of every diocese hath a *consistory court,* held before his chancellor or commissary in his cathedral church, or other convenient place of his diocese, for ecclesiastical causes. From the bishop's court the appeal is to the archbishop; from the archbishop's court to the delegates.

CONSOLIDATION, is used for uniting two benefices into one.

CONSPIRACY, is the act of those that confederate or bind themselves by oath, covenant, or other alliance, that every of them

them shall aid and bear the other falsely and maliciously, to indict, or cause to be indicted, or falsely to move or maintain pleas. From which it seems clearly to follow, that not only those who actually cause an innocent man to be indicted, and also to be tried upon the indictment, (whereupon he is lawfully acquitted) are properly conspirators; but that those also are guilty of this offence who basely conspire to indict a man falsely and maliciously, whether they do any act in prosecution of such confederacy or not. 1 *Haw.* 189. For this offence the conspirators (for there must be at least two to form a conspiracy) may be indicted at the suit of the king, and may be sentenced to fine, imprisonment, and pillory. 4 *Black.* 136.

CONSTABLE, by the laws of *Alfred*, the freemen were to distribute themselves into *decennaries*, and *hundreds*; and every ten freeholders chose an annual officer, whom they called *constable*, borsholder, tithingman, or headborough, as the head of the *decennary* or *ten*. These in every hundred where there was a feudal lord, were sworn in and admitted by the lord or his steward, in his leet; but where there was no feudal lord, the sheriff, in his *torn* had the swearing of them in. So if there were no feudal lord of the hundred, an annual officer was chosen, who was to preside over the whole hundred and was called the *high constable*.

Who may or may not be chosen constables. The ancient officers of any of the colleges in the two universities are exempted from this office. *Doug.* 531. Any person of the age of 63 years or upwards, is not compellable to serve the office of constable within the city of *Westminster*. No person born out of the kingdom of England or the dominions thereof (except he be born of English parents, see *Aliens*), is eligible to serve this office, even though he be naturalized. 5 *Bur.* 2790. Counsellors, attornies, and all other officers whose attendance is required in the courts of *Westminster-hall*, aldermen of London, the president and fellows of the fellowship of physic in *London*, surgeons and apothecaries in *London*, and within seven miles thereof being free of the company of apothecaries, and teachers, or preachers in holy orders, in a congregation legally tolerated, shall be exempted from the office of a constable. The prosecutor of a felon to conviction, or the person to whom he shall assign the certificate thereof, shall be discharged from the office of constable.

But generally speaking, every housekeeper, inhabitant of the parish, and of full age, is liable to fill the office of constable: he ought however to be of the abler sort of parishioners, as being more likely to perform his duty with probity and discretion. 8 Co. 42.

Mode of choosing constables. It seems regularly, that the petty constable ought to be chosen in the leet and the high constable in the torn which is the general leet of the whole hundred; and if there be no leet, then, that the petty constable ought to be chosen also in the torn. 1 *Burn.* 400.

The high constables of hundreds are generally chosen either at the sessions, or by the greater number of the justices of the division; and they may be sworn at sessions, or by warrant from the sessions, which course has often been allowed and commended, by the justices of assize. *Dalt.* c. 28. The office of *petty constable,* being very necessary for the preservation of the peace, the justices of the peace have ever since the institution of their office, taken upon them as conservators of the peace, not only to swear the petty constables who have been chosen at a torn or leet, but also to nominate and swear those, who have not been chosen at any such court, on neglect of the sheriffs or lords to hold their courts, or to take care that such officers are appointed in them. And this power of the justices, having been confirmed by the uninterrupted usage of many ages, shall not now be disputed. 2 *Haw.* 65.

The office, duty, power, &c. of constables. The original and proper authority of a high constable, as such, seems to be the very same within his hundred, as that of the petty constable within his *vill.* The other branches of his office, such as the surveying of bridges, levying county rates, the issuing precepts concerning the appointment of the overseers of the poor, surveyors of highways, assessors and collectors of the land-tax and window duties, &c. are in him, not of necessity, but as matter of convenience. 4 *Inst.* 265. Every high and petty constable, is by common law a conservator of the peace. 2 *Haw.* 33. The general duty of constables is to preserve the king's peace in their several districts, for which purpose they are armed, as well by the common law as by the legislature, with the very large and serious powers of arresting and imprisoning their fellow-subjects, forcibly entering their dwellings, and other extensive authorities,

which

which it is highly their duty to exercise with becoming moderation, and humanity. The high constable, is as much the officer of the justices of the peace, as the constable of the *vill*. *Fort.* 128.

The constable is the proper officer to the justices of peace and bound to execute his warrants. Hence it has been resolved, that where the statute authorities a justice of the peace to convict a man, of a crime, and to levy the penalty by warrant of distress, without saying to whom such warrant shall be directed, or by whom it shall be executed, the constable is the proper officer to serve such warrant, and indictable for disobeying it. 2 *Haw.* 262.

But as the office of constable is by no means judicial, but wholly ministerial, he may execute such warrants, &c. directed to him, by deputy, if on account of indisposition, absence or other special cause, he cannot conveniently do it in person. 2 *Bur.* 1259.

The high constables shall, at the general or quarter-sessions, if required, account for the general county rate by them received, on pain of being committed to goal till they shall account, and shall pay over the money in their hands, according to the order of the said court, on like pain of imprisonment. And all their accounts and vouchers shall, after having been passed at such sessions, be deposited with the clerk of the peace, to be kept among the records; and be inspected by any justice without fee. 12 Geo. II. c. 29. s. 8.

Constables should be very careful to keep in their custody, whatever things they take upon felons; the same caution is to be observed, in respect of such stolen goods as they take in the execution of such warrants. The law strictly requires this, that they may be produced in evidence upon the trial of the prisoner: for the identity of such things is to be proved upon the constable's oath, as well as the time when taken, and place where: if therefore he suffer such goods to go even out of his sight, he weakens his evidence, if he do not destroy it; and should the goods be by accident, or otherwise lost, he is not only answerable to the court for acting wrong, which may defeat the prosecution, but also to the presecutor for the value of the goods; nor will it be a sufficient plea to the court that he left them in the hands of justice, even by his command; for as they were taken by him, the law requires them at his hands. And as the goods, taken on persons charged with felony, or by search-warrants, are, as the law terms it, *in abeyance* ; after the jury have returned their verdict, if the prisoner be convicted, the constable is to deliver such goods to the prosecutor; on the contrary, if the prisoner be acquitted, the goods revert to him, the cause of seizure being discharged. But if any difficulty should arise the safest way is to pray the direction of the court. The duty of the constable indeed, absolutely obliges him to produce such goods at the trial; but after this is over, he should be careful how he brings them out of court, lest he should suffer by actions at law, from both parties.

An officer who has *negligently* suffered a prisoner to escape, may take him wherever he finds him, without mentioning any fresh pursuit.

A person found guilty, upon an indictment or presentment of a negligent escape of a criminal, actually in his custody, is punishable by fine and imprisonment, according to the quality of the offence. 2 *Haw.* 134.

But a voluntary escape is no felony, if the act done were not felony at the time of the escape made, as in case of a mortal wound given, and the party not dying till after the escape; so that the offence was but a trespass at the time of the escape: but the officer may be fined to the value of his goods. *Dalt.* c. 129.

An action brought against a constable, headborough, or tithingman, for any matter done by virtue of their office, shall be laid *in the county where the fact was committed*, and not elsewhere. 21 *Jac.* c. 12. s. 5.

The constable executing a justice's warrant, for levying a penalty, or other sum of money directed by an act of parliament, by distress, may deduct his own reasonable charges of taking, keeping, and selling the goods distrained; returning the overplus on demand. 27 Geo. II.

The sheriff or steward of the leet, having power to place a constable in his office, has consequently a power of removing him. 2 *Haw.* 63. And it has been the practice of the justices of the peace, for good cause, to displace such constables as have been chosen, and sworn by them. 2 *Haw.* 65.

If a constable shall continue more than a year in his office, the sessions may discharge him, and put another in his place, till the lord shall hold a leet, and should the court, or judge, refuse to discharge a constable, the king's-bench may compel them by mandamus. *2 Haw.* 65.

In the manner that constables are chosen, they may be removed, and by the like authority; therefore, if there should be cause to remove an high constable, it has not been thought fit that any one or two justices should do it upon their discretion; but that it should be done by the greater part of the justices of that division, or at the sessions. *Dalt c.* 28.

Of London constables. The constables must be freemen of the city, and nominated by the inhabitants of the ward on St. Thomas's day, confirmed or disallowed at the next wardmote, and afterwards sworn into office at the next court of aldermen on the *Monday* ensuing twelfth-day.

They swear to keep the king's peace to the utmost of their power, to arrest affrayers, rioters, and such as make contests to the breach of the peace, and carry them to the house of correction, or compter of one of the sheriffs; and in case of resistance, to make outcry to them, and pursue them from street to street, and from ward to ward till they are arrested: to search for common nuisances in their respective wards, being required by scavengers, &c. and upon request, to assist the beadle and raker in collecting their salaries and quarterage, to present to the lord mayor and ministers of the city, defaults relating to the ordinances of the city. They are to certify to the mayor's court, once a month, the names and surnames of all freemen deceased, and also of the children of such freemen, being orphans. They are to certify the name, surname, place of dwelling, profession and trade of every person who shall just come into the ward, and keep a roll thereof; for which purpose they are to enquire once a month, into what persons are come into the said ward; and if such persons are found to be ejected from any other ward for any misdemeanor, and refuse sureties for their good behaviour, they are to give them and their landlords warning to depart; and on refusal, they may be imprisoned, and the landlords fined a year's rent. *Rep.* 129. 138.

Constables are to keep watch and ward from the 10th of *September* to the 10th of *March*, from nine in the evening till seven the next morning; and from the 10th of *March* to the 10th of *September*

September, from ten in the evening, till five next morning. They shall use their best endeavours for preventing fires, robberies, and disorders, and arrest malefactors; and go twice or oftener about their wards in every night; and the watchmen are to apprehend all suspected persons, &c. and deliver them to the constable of the night, who shall carry them before a justice of the peace: Constables misbehaving themselves, to forfeit 20s. and the lord mayor, or two justices for the city, may hear and determine offences, and levy penalties by distress and sale of goods, &c. They must place the king's arms, and the arms of the city, over their doors; and if they reside in alleys, at the ends of such alleys towards the streets, to signify that a constable lives there.

CONSTAT, is the name of a certificate, which the clerk of the pipe and the auditors of the exchequer, make at the request of any person who intends to plead or move in that court, for the discharge of any thing.

CONSUETUDINIBUS ET SERVICIIS, a writ of right close, which lies against the tenant that deforces his lord of the rent or service due to him.

CONSULTATION, a writ, whereby a cause being formerly removed by prohibition from the ecclesiastical court, to the king's court at Westminster is returned thither again.

CONTEMPT, is a disobedience to the rules and order of the court, which hath power to punish such offence; and a person may be fined or imprisoned for a *contempt* done in a court. *Cro. Eliz.* 689.

CONTENEMENT, signifies that which is necessary for the support and maintenance of men, according to their several qualities, conditions, or state of life.

CONTINGENT LEGACY, is a legacy which may, or may not happen. If a legacy be left to one *when* he shall attain, or *if* he shall attain the age of twenty-one years this is a contingent legacy, and if the legatee die before that time, the legacy shall not vest. But a legacy to one *to be paid* when he attains the age of twenty-one years, is a vested legacy; an interest which commences in *præsenti*, although it be *solvendum in futuro*: and if the legatee die before that age, his representatives shall receive it out of the testator's personal estate, at the same time,

time, that it would have become payable in case the legatee had lived.

CONTINGENT REMAINDER, is where no present interest passes, but the estate is limitted to take effect, either to a dubious and uncertain *person*, or upon a dubious and uncertain *event*, so that the particular estate, may chance to be determined, and the remainder never take effect.

CONTINGENT USE, a *use* limited in a conveyance of land, which may or may not happen to vest, according to the contingency expressed in the limitation of such *use*.

CONTINUAL CLAIM, a claim made from time to time within every year and day to land or other thing, to save the right of entry to an heir.

CONTINUANCE, of a writ or action, is from one term to another, in case where the sheriff hath not returned or executed a former writ, issued in the same action.

CONTINUANDO, is a word used in a special declaration of trespass, when the plaintiff would recover damages for several trespasses in the same action.

CONTRABAND GOODS, are goods which are prohibited by act of parliament, or the king's proclamation, to be imported or exported. See *Smuggling*.

CONTRACT, a covenant or agreement between two or more persons, with a lawful consideration or cause. *Contracts* are two-fold; either *express* or *implied*. *Express contracts*, are, where the terms of the agreement are openly uttered, as to pay a stated price for certain goods. *Implied*, are such as reason and justice dictate, and which therefore, the law presumes that every man undertakes to perform: thus if a man take up wares from a tradesman, without any agreement of price, the law concludes, that he contracted to pay their real value. 2 *Black.* 443.

CONTRA FORMAM COLLATIONIS, a writ, that lies where a man had given lands to the warden and master of an hospital, to support certain poor men; if they alienated the land, then the donor or his heirs should bring this writ, to recover them.

CONTRA FORMAM STATUTI, the usual conclusion of every indictment for an offence created by statute.

CONTRAMANDATIO PLACITI, countermanding what was formerly ordered, and giving the defendant further time to answer.

CONTRA-

CONTRAMANDATUM, a lawful excuse, which the defendant in a suit by attorney alleges for himself, to shew that the plaintiff hath no cause of complaint.

CONTRIBUTION, is where every one pays his share, or contributes his part to any thing. One parcener shall have *contribution* against another; one heir have *contribution* against another heir in equal degree; and one purchaser have *contribution* against another.

CONTRIBUTIONE FACIENDA, is a writ that lies where there are tenants in common who are bound to do one thing, and yet one is put to the burden.

CONTROLLER, an overseer, or officer, relating to public accounts; such as the controller of the king's navy, controller of the customs, &c.

CONTROVER, he that devises or invents false or feigned news. 2 *Inst.* 227.

CONVENABLE, agreeable, suitable, convenient. 27 Edw. III. c. 21, and 2. H. VI. c. 2.

CONVENTICLE, a term applied to the illegal meetings of the nonconformists; by the 22 Car. II. c. 1, any one being present at a *conventicle*, was liable to the penalty of 5s. for the first offence, and 10s. for the second; and persons preaching incurred a penalty of 20l. Also suffering a meeting to be held in a house was liable to a like penalty of 20l. and justices of the peace, had power to enter such houses and seize the persons assembled, or neglecting so to do incurred the penalty of 100l. But by 1 W. and M. c. 18, all protestant dissenters are exempted from penalties, though if they meet in a house, with the doors locked, barred, or bolted, they shall receive no benefit from the act.

CONVENTIONE, is a writ that lies for any covenant in writing, not performed.

CONVENTION PARLIAMENT, on the abdication of king James II. in 1689. The assembly of the states of the kingdom; to take care of their rights and liberties, and who settled king *William* and queen *Mary* on the throne, was called the *Convention*.

CONVERSOS, the Jews in England, because they were converted to the christian religion, were formerly called *conversos*.

CONVEYANCE, a deed which passes land from one to another.

ther. The most common *conveyances* now in use are, *deeds of gift, bargain and sale, lease and release, fines and recoveries, settlements to uses,* &c. A *conveyance,* cannot be fraudulent in part, and good as to the rest; for if it be fraudulent and void in part, it is void in all, and it cannot be divided. Fraudulent conveyances to deceive creditors, defraud purchasers, &c. are void, by stat. 50 *Ed. III.* c. 6. 13 *Eliz.* c. 5—27. *Eliz.* c. 4.

CONVICTION is either where a man is outlawed, or appeareth and confesseth, or else is found guilty by the inquest. *Cromp. Inst.* 9.

Summary proceedings are directed by several acts of parliament, for the conviction of offenders, and the inflicting certain penalties imposed by those acts. In those there is no intervention of a Jury, but the party accused, is acquitted or condemned by the suffrage of such person only as the statute has appointed for his judge.

The law implies that there must be a *conviction* before judgment, though not so mentioned in a statute; and where any statute, makes a second offence felony, or subject to an heavier penalty than the first, it is always implied, that such second offence ought to be committed after a conviction for the first. 1 *How.* 13—107. Judgment amounts to a conviction, though it does not follow that every one who is convict, is adjudged. 1 *Horn.* 14.

A *conviction* ought to be in the present tense, and not in the time past. *Ld. Raym.* 1376. Str. 608. A *conviction,* ought to be on an information or claim precedent *Ld. Raym.* 510.

When an act of parliament, orders the *conviction* of offenders before justices of the peace &c. it must be intended *after summons* to bring them in, that they may have an opportunity of making their defence; and if it be otherwise, the conviction shall be quashed.

CONVICT RECUSANT, one who has been legally presented, indicted, and *convict,* for refusing to come to church to hear the *common prayer,* according to the several statutes of 1 Eliz. 2. 23 *Eliz.* 1, and 3 *Jac.* 1.

CONVIVIUM, is when the tenant, by reason of his tenure, is bound to provide meat and drink for his lord, once or oftener in the year.

CONVOCATION,

CONVOCATION, is the assembly of all the clergy to consult of ecclesiastical matters, in time of parliament. There are two houses of *convocation,* the one called the higher *convocation house,* where all the archbishops and bishops sit severally by themselves; the other the *lower convocation house,* where all the rest of the clergy sit; that is, all the deans and archdeacons, one proctor for every chapter, and two proctors for all the clergy of each diocese; in all one hundred and sixty-six persons.

The archbishop of *Canterbury* is the president of the convocation, and prorogues and dissolves it by mandate from the king. The *convocation* is not only to be assembled by the king's writ but the canons made by them are to have the royal assent. They are to have the examining and censuring of heretical and schismatical books, and persons, &c. but appeal lies to the king in chancery, or to his delegates, 4 *Inst.* 322. 2 *Rol. Abr.* 225. The clergy called to the *convocation,* and their servants, &c. have the same privileges as members of parliament. Stat. 8, H. VI. c. 1.

CONNUSANCE OF PLEAS, is when one living within a jurisdiction, may implead another within it, or for a cause arising there.

COOPERS. By 23. H. VIII. c. 4, coopers shall make their vessels of seasonable woods, and make them with their own marks, on forfeiture of 3s. 4d. and the contents of vessels are appointed to be observed, under like penalty.

COPARCENARY, an estate held in *coparcenary,* is, where lands of inheritance descend from the ancestor to two or more persons. It arises either by common law, or particular custom. By common law, as where a person seized in fee-simple or fee-tail dies, and his next heirs are two or more females, his daughters, sisters, aunts, cousins, or their representatives; in this case they shall all inherit. And these co-heirs are then called *coparceners*; or for brevity sake *parceners. Parceners* by particular custom, are, where lands descend, as in gavel-kind, to all the males in equal degree, as sons, brothers, uncles, or other kindred; and in either of these cases, all the parceners put together make but one heir, and have but one estate among them. 2 *Black* 187.

COPARCENERS, in the common law, are such as have equal portions in the inheritance of their ancestor—see *coparcenary.*

COPARTNERSHIP is when two or more persons unite together,

ther, *and agree to participate in profit and loss,* according to their respective shares in a capital or joint stock ; but this is absolutely necessary to constitute a *copartnership.* 1 H. B. 43, 48.

COPY, in a legal sense, is the transcript of an original writing; as the *copy* of a *patent,* of a *charter, deed,* &c. but a clause out of either, cannot be given in evidence to prove the original, as it must be absolutely a *true office copy of the whole.*

COPYHOLD, a tenure for which the tenant hath nothing to shew but the *copy* of the rolls made by the steward, as he inrolls and makes remembrances of all other things done in the lord's court; thus a tenant by *copy of court roll,* is he who is admitted a tenant of any lands or tenements within a manor, that, time out of mind, by use and custom of the manor, have been demisable, and demised to such as will take the same in fee, or fee tail, for life, years, or at will, according to the custom of the manor, by copy of court-roll of the said manor.

The customs of manors, differ as much as the humour and temper of the respective ancient lords, so a *copyholder,* by custom may be tenant in fee-simple, in fee-tail, for life, by the courtesy, in dower, for years, at sufferance, or on condition; subject however, to be deprived of these estates upon the concurrence of those circumstances, which the will of the lords promulged by immemorial custom, hath declared to be a forfeiture or absolute determination of those interests; as in some manors the want of issue, in others the want of issue male, in others, the cutting down timber, in others the nonpayment of rent or fine. Yet none of these interests amount to freehold; for the freehold of the whole manor abides always with the lord only, who hath granted out the use of occupation, but not the corporeal seizin, or true possession of certain parts or parcels thereof, to these his customary tenants at will. 2 *Black* 148.

Where, by special custom, a descent of copyholds may be contrary to the common law, such custom shall be interpreted strictly: but otherwise, the lands must descend according to the rules of the common law. *Durnf. and East,* 466.

Copyholds are not transferable by matter of record, even in the king's courts; but only in the court baron of the lord, by surrender and admittance. 2 Black, 366.

If one would *exchange* a copyhold with another, both must surrender to each others use, and the lord admit accordingly. *Co. Copyhold s.* 36, 39.

If a man will *devise* his copyhold estate, he cannot do it by his will, but he must surrender to the use of his will, and in it declare his intent. *Id.* But when the legal estate is in *trustees*, a man cannot in that case, surrender the copyhold lands to the use of his will; but they will pass by his will only. 2 *Atk.* 38. 1 *Vez.* 489.

So a *mortgager* may dispose of the equity of redemption by will, without surrender; for he hath at that time no estate in the land whereof to make a surrender.

A devise of a copyhold to the *heir* is void; for where two titles meet the worthier is to be preferred. *Str.* 489.

A copyhold may be *intailed* by special custom, and the intail cut off by recovery or surrender in the lord's court. But a recovery in the lord's court, without custom to warrant it, will not be a bar to the intail; but a surrender in that case will bar it. 2 *Vez.* 603. But where there are two customs to bar estates tail, one by recovery, and the other by surrender, either of them may be pursued. *Str.* 1197.

Recovery in the lord's court, differs in nothing that is material, from recoveries of freehold land in the king's court; but the method of surrender is easier and cheaper. 2 *Black,* 365.

A copyhold is not barred by fine, and five years nonclaim. *Noy.*

Surrender, is yielding up the estate by the tenant into the hands of the lord, for such purposes, as in the surrender are expressed.

A steward of a manor, may take a surrender out of the manor, but cannot admit out of the manor. 4 *Co.* 26. A femme covert, is to be secretly examined by the steward, in her surrendering her estate. 1 *Inst.* 59.

Until admittance of the *surrendree,* the *surrenderor* continues tenant, and shall receive the profits, and discharge all services due to the lord; but he cannot revoke his surrender, except in the case of a surrender to the use of his will, which is always revocable. And if the lord will not admit the surrendree, he may be compelled to it by a bill in chancery or mandamus. 2 *Black,* 368

And

And this method of conveyance, by surrender and admittance, is so essential to the nature of a copyhold estate, that it cannot possibly be transferred by any other assurance. No feoffment, fine, or recovery, in the king's courts, has any operation upon it. *Ibid.* Upon admittance, the tenant pays a fine to the lord, according to the custom of the manor, and takes the oath of fealty. *Id.* If a copyholder, do not pay the services due to the lord, or refuse to attend at the lord's court, or to be of homage, or to pay his fine for admittance, or to do suit at the lord's mill, or the like, it is in law a forfeiture. *Rol. Abr.* 509.

If there be a tenant for life, remainder in fee, and tenant for life commit a forfeiture, by which his estate for life be forfeited; the lord enters for the forfeiture; yet this shall not bind him in the remainder, but only the tenant for life *Ibid.*

If a copyholder commit a felony or treason, he forfeits his copyhold to the lord, without any particular custom; only the king shall first have thereof the year, day, and waste. *Gibb. Ter.* 226.

If a copyhold escheat, the lord may grant it out again with what improved fine he will. *Hil.* 6.

COPY-RIGHT, the exclusive right of printing and publishing copies of any literary performance, for a limited time. See *Books* and *Literary Property.*

CORAAGE, is an imposition extraordinary, growing upon some unusual occasion, and generally, certain measures of corn. *Bract.*

CORAM NON JUDICE, when a cause is brought into a court, whereof the judges have not any jurisdiction, it is said to be *coram non judice.*

CORD OF WOOD, ought to be eight feet long, four feet broad, and four feet high, by statute.

CORDAGE, for penalties and punishments incurred, by fraudulently manufacturing *cordage. See* 25 *G. III. c.* 56. *See Cables.*

CORN. It is against the common law of England to buy or sell corn in the sheaf, before it is threshed and measured; the reason whereof seems to be, because by such sale, the market is in effect forestalled. 3 *Inst.* 197.

Every person who shall sell or buy corn without measuring, or otherwise than the Winchester measure, scaled and stricken by the brim, shall on conviction before one justice on the oath of one witness, forfeit 40s. besides the whole of the corn so sold or bought, or the value thereof, half to the poor, and half to the informer.

On complaint to a justice, that corn has been bought, sold, or delivered, contrary to the act, the proof shall lie upon the defendant, to make it appear by oath of one witness, that he sold or bought the same lawfully: and if he shall fail therein, he shall forfeit, as before mentioned, to be levied by distress and sale. 22 and 23. C. II. c. 8 and 12, and K. v. Arnold. T. 33, G. III.

And if any mayor, or other head officer, shall knowingly permit the same, he shall upon conviction at the county sessions, forfeit 50l. half to the prosecutor and half to the poor, by distress and sale. For want of distress, to be imprisoned by warrant of the justices, till payment be made. 22 C. II. c. 8. s. 3.

The last acts now in force to regulate the returns of the prices of grain, are statutes 31 G. III. c. 30: 33 G. III. c. 65. By the former the statutes 1. Jac. II. c. 19: 1 W. and M. c. 12: 5 G. II. c. 12: 10 G. III. c. 39: 13 G. III. c. 43: 21 G. III. c. 50 and 29. G. III. c. 58, are all repealed; as also every provision in any other act for regulating the importation of wheat, &c. except such as relate to the making of *malt* for exportation, and the exportation thereof. So much of the 15 Car. II. as prohibits the buying of corn to sell again, and the laying it up in granaries is also repealed.

By the statutes of 31 G. III. c. 30, and 33 G. III. c. 65, bounties are granted on exportation at certain prices, and the exportation prohibited when at higher prices: the quantity of corn to be exported to foreign countries is settled; the maritime counties of England are divided into districts. The exportation of corn to be regulated in *London*, *Kent*, *Essex*, and *Sussex*, by the prices at the corn exchange; the proprietors of which are to appoint an inspector of corn returns, to whom weekly returns are to be made by the factors: and he is to make weekly accounts, and transmit the average price to the receiver of the returns, to be transmitted to the officers of the customs, and inserted in the *London Gazette*. The exportation in other districts and in Scotland, to be regulated by the prices at different appointed places, for which mayors, justices, &c. are to elect inspectors. Declarations are to be truly

made

made by factors of the corn sold by them. Orders of council may be made to regulate importation, or exportation, from time to time: such orders to be laid before parliament respecting the exportation of wheat, and trans-shipping of corn brought coastwise. See 32 G. III. c. 50, and 33 G. III. c. 3.

CORNAGE, a kind of *grand serjeanty*, the service of which tenure was to blow a horn, when any invasion of the northern enemy was perceived. By this many persons held their land northward about the wall, commonly called the Picts wall. *Littl.* 65.

CORNWALL, a royal duchy belonging to the prince of Wales, abounding with mines, and having stanary courts, &c. It yields a great revenue to the prince. Several statutes have been issued respecting leases and grants in this duchy, and particularly the stat. of 39 G. II. c. 10.

CORODY, a sum of money, or allowance of meat, drink, or cloathing, due to the king from an abbey or other house of religion, whereof he is the founder, towards the reasonable sustenance of such a one of his servants, being put to his pension, as he thinks good to bestow it on. *Corodies*, belonged sometimes to bishops and noblemen from monasteries. But these *corodies* are now totally fallen into disuse. 1 *Black*, 283.

CORONARE FILIOS, the old *villains*, or those who held in villenage, were forbid *conare filios*, to make their sons priests, that is, to let them be ordained; because ordination changed their condition, and gave them liberty to the prejudice of the lord, who could before claim them as his natives, or born servants.

CORONATORE ELIGENDO, a writ, which, after the death or discharge of any *coroner*, is directed to the sheriff out of the chancery, for the choice of a new *coroner*, and to certify into the chancery, both the election, and name of the party elected, and to give him his oath.

CORONER, a very ancient officer at the common law, he is called *coroner*, because he deals principally with the pleas of the crown; and coroners were of old time the conservators of the peace. This officer, ought to be a sufficient person, that is, the most wise and discreet knight, that best would and might attend upon such an office. *St. Westm.* c. 10. By the 14 Ed. III. *st.* 1, c. 8. No coroner shall be chosen, unless he shall have land in fee sufficient, in the same county wherein he may answer to all manner of people. The lord chief justice of the king's bench is the sovereign coroner of the whole realm.

How elected. In ancient times, none under the degree of knight were chosen. 2 *Inst.* 32. 176. But as the chief intent was to prevent the choosing of persons of mean ability, it seems the design of it is sufficiently answered, by choosing men of substance and credit; and as the constant usage for several ages past has been accordingly, it seems to be no objection at this day, that the person chosen is not a knight. 2 *Haw.* 42. 43.

By the 28 Ed. III. c. 6. it is enacted, that all coroners of the counties, shall be chosen in full counties, by the commoners of the said counties, of the most meet and lawful people that shall be found in the same, to execute the said office. But though they are chosen by the county, it must be pursuant to the king's writ, issuing out of and returnable into chancery; and none but freeholders have a voice at such election, for they only are suitors to the county court. 2 *Inst.* 99. 2. *Haw.* 43. 44. When chosen they shall be sworn by the sheriff, for the due execution of their office. 2 *Hale.* H. 55.

His duty in taking inquisitions. When any person comes to an untimely death, the township shall give notice thereof to the coroner: otherwise if the body be interred before he come, the township shall be amerced. *Hale's Pl.* 170. And if the township shall suffer the body to lie till putrefaction, without sending for him, they shall be amerced. 2 *Haw.* 48.

When the coroner has received notice, he shall issue a precept to the constables of the four, five, or six next townships, to return a competent number of good and lawful men of their townships, to appear before him in such a place, to make an inquisition touching that matter. 4 Ed. I. *st.* 2. Or he may send a precept, to the constable of the hundred. *Wood b.* 4. c. 1. And there must be twelve jurors at the least. 2 *Inst.* 148. If the constables make no return, or if the jurors returned, shall not appear, their defaults are to be returned to the coroner, and they shall be amerced before the judges of the assize. 2 H. H. 55.

The jury after being sworn, is to be charged by the coroner to inquire, upon the view of the body, how the party came by his death. 2 H. H. 60.

Every

Every coroner upon an inquisition before him found, whereby any person shall be indicted for murder or manslaughter, or as an accessary before the offence committed, shall put in writing the effect of the evidence given to the jury before him, being material; and shall bind over the witnesses to the next general goal delivery to give evidence; and shall certify the evidence, the recognizance, and the inquisition or indictment before him taken and found, at or before the trial, on pain of being fined by the court. 1 & 2 P. & M. c 13. s. 5.

But the coroner cannot enquire of accessaries *after* the fact. He ought to enquire into the death of all persons dying in prison, that it may be known, whether they died by violence or any unreasonable hardships.

His general power and duty. Besides his judicial place, the coroner has an authority ministerial, as a sheriff; namely, when there is a just exception taken to the sheriff, judicial process shall be awarded to the coroner for the execution of the king's writ: and in some special cases, the king's original writ, shall be immediately directed to him. 4 *Inst.* 271. He is bound to be present in the county court, to pronounce judgment of outlawry upon the exigent, after *quinto exactus*, at the fifth court, if the defendant do not appear. *Wood.* b. 4. c. 1.

It is his duty to enquire of treasure that is found, who were the finders, and likewise who is suspected thereof. He may also receive the appeal of an approver, for an offence in the same, or in a different county, and if the appellel be in the same county, he may award process against him to the sheriff till it come to the exigent; but if the appellee, be in a foreign connty, the coroner cannot award process against him, but must leave it to the justices of a goal delivery, before whom the appeal is afterwards recorded 2 *Haw.* 52.

Punishment for misdemeanour. Justices of assize and peace, have power to enquire of and punish the defaults and extortions of coroners. 1 Hen. VIII. c. 7. and 25 Geo. II. c. 29. *s.* 6.

His fees. The coroner shall have for his fee, upon every inquisition taken upon the view of the body slain, 13s. 4d. of the goods and chattels of him that is the slayer and murderer, if he have any goods; and if he have no goods, of such amerciament, as should fortune any township to be amerced for the escape of the murderer. 3 Hen. VII. But as the said fee of 13s. 4d. is not an adequate

adequate reward for the general execution of the said office, therefore for every inquisition, not taken upon view of a body dying in goal, the coroner shall have 20s. and also 9d. for every mile he shall be compelled to travel from his usual place of abode to take such inquisition; to be paid by order of the justices in sessions, out of the county rates. 25 Geo. II. c. 29. s. 1.

CORPORATION, a body politic or incorporated, consisting of a number of persons empowered by the law of the land to act under one name, and as one person. Corporations are established by act of parliament, and their functions or powers are limited by the act of their creation or charter. See *Charter*.

The magistrates of a town or city act in a corporate capacity, for the advantage and administration of affairs within their liberties.

CORPOREAL INHERITANCE. See *Inheritance*.

CORPSE, if any person steal the shroud or other apparel from a dead body, it will be a felony. 3 *Inst.* 110. 12 *Rep.* 113. But stealing the corpse itself, *only*, is not felony, but it is punishable as a misdemeanour, by indictment at common law. 2 *Black.* 236.

CORPUS CUM CAUSA, a writ issuing out of chancery, to remove both the body and the record, touching the cause of any man lying in execution upon a judgment for debt in the king's-bench, &c. there to lie, until he have satisfied the judgment.

CORRECTOR OF THE STAPLE, a clerk belonging to the *staple*, who writes and records the bargains of merchants there made.

CORRUPTION OF BLOOD, an infection growing to the state of a man attainted of felony or treason. Restitution of blood, in its true nature and extent, can only be by act of parliament. 4 *Black.* 388. See *Attainder*.

CORSNED BREAD, was a kind of superstitious trial, used by our Saxon ancestors, by a piece of barley bread, first execrated by the priest, and then offered to the suspected guilty person, to be swallowed by way of purgation: for they believed a person, if guilty, could not possibly swallow a morsel so accursed; or if he did, it would choak him.

CORSEPRESENT, at any man's death, the *body* of the best, or second-best beast, was according to the custom, offered, or presented

presented to the priest, and carried with the corpse, as a *corse-present.*

COSENING, an offence whereby any thing is done deceitfully, whether belonging to contracts or not, which cannot be properly termed by any special name.

COSHERING, a seniorial prerogative, whereby the lord and his followers, lay and feasted themselves at his tenant's house.

COSINAGE, a writ that lies where the *tresayle* or great-grandfather is seized in his demesne, as of fee at the day of his death, of certain lands or tenements, and dies, and then a stranger enters, and abates; for then shall his heir have this writ of *cosinage.*

COSTS. By the statute of *Gloucester,* 6 Ed. I. c. 1. it is provided that the demandant may recover against the tenant, the costs of his writ, together with his damage; and that this act shall hold place in all cases, when the party is to recover damages. 1 *New. Abr.* 511.

Costs of the writ, extends to all legal costs of suit, but not expences of travel, loss of time, &c. 2 *Inst.* 288.

When double damages are given by act of parliament, the costs shall be doubled also; for damages include costs. *Str.* 1048.

Persons suing in *forma pauperis,* shall not pay costs. 3 *Black.* 400.

If it be an action, wherein there can be no such certifying, as debt, assumpsit, trover, trespass for taking goods, trespass for spoiling goods, trespass for beating a servant, whereby he lost his service, it is out of the statute, and the plaintiff may have full costs. Salk. 208.

Where costs are allowed, it is not necessary for the jury to give them, but they may leave it to the court to do it, who are the best able to judge of what costs are fitting to be given. It is the course of the court of king's-bench, to refer the taxation of costs to the proper officer of the court, and not to make any special rules for such matters, except it be in extraordinary cases. 1 *Litl. Abr.* 338.

The matter of costs in *equity,* is not held to a point of right, but merely discretionary, according to the circumstances of the case,

case, as they appear more or less favourable to the party vanquished. 3 *Black*. 451.

If costs be refused to be paid, an attachment lies. 1 *Nels. Abr*. 550.

The king and any person suing to his use, shall neither pay nor receive costs. Stat. 24 H. VIII. c. 8.

The 18 Geo. III. c. 19. authorizes any justice, who shall have heard and determined the matter of a complaint made before him, to award such costs to be paid by either party, and in such manner, as to him shall seem meet, to the party injured: and if the person so ordered by the justice, shall not forthwith pay, or give satisfaction to the justice, the same shall be levied by distress: and if goods and chattels of such person cannot be found, the justice shall commit him to the house of correction for the place where such person shall reside: to be kept to hard labour for any time not exceeding one month, nor less than ten days, or till such sum, with the expences attending the commitment be first paid.

Provided, that upon the conviction of any person upon a penal statute, where the penalty shall be at or exceed the sum of 5*l*. the said costs shall be deducted by the justice, at his discretion out of the penalty, so that such deduction shall not exceed one-fifth part of the penalty; and the remainder of the penalty, shall be divided among the persons who would have been entitled to the whole thereof, if this act had not been made.

Costs double or treble are allowed to defendants sued for acting under almost every statute relating to officers of justice, customs, or other duties, highways, paving, &c.

For more matter concerning Costs see Bac. Abr. & 6 Vin. Abr. tit. COSTS.

COTERELLI, a sort of wandering thieves and plunderers, who seem at first to have been cottagers and country-fellows.

COTLRELLUS, a mean, servile tenant, who seemed to have lived in mere villenage, and had his person and issue, and goods, disposed at the pleasure of the lord.

COTTAGE. By 31 *Eliz*. c. 7. it was enacted that no person should build or erect any manner of cottage, without laying at least four acres of land to the same, but that act was repealed by

15 Geo.

15 Geo. III. c. 32. on its having been suggested, that it had laid the industrious poor under great difficulties to procure habitations; that it tended much to lessen population, and in many other respects, was inconvenient to the labouring part of the people.

COVENABLE, fit, convenient, or suitable.

COVENANT, the agreement or consent of two or more by deed in writing, sealed and delivered; whereby either, or one of the parties, promises to the other, that something is done already, or shall be done afterwards: he that makes the covenant, is called the *covenantor*, and he to whom it is made the *covenantee*. *Shep. Touch*. 160.

A *covenant* is generally either *in fact*, or *in law*. In *fact*, is that which is expressly agreed between the parties, and inserted in the deed. In *law*, is that covenant which the law intends and implies, though it be not expressed in words, as if a lessor demise and grant to his lessee, an house or lands for a certain term, the law will intend a covenant on the lessor's part, and the lessee shall, during the term, quietly enjoy the same against all incumbrances. 1 *Inst*. 384.

COVENANT TO STAND SEISED TO USES, is when a man that hath a wife, children, brother, sister, or kindred, doth by covenant in writing under hand and seal agree, that for their, or any of their provision or preferment, he or his heirs, will stand seised of land to their use, either in fee-simple, fee-tail, or for life.

COVERTURE, in law is applied to the condition of a married woman, who by the laws of this realm is *sub potestate viri*, and therefore disabled to make bargain with any, to the prejudice of herself or her husband, without his assent and privity, or at least without his allowance and confirmation.

COVIN, is a deceitful assent or agreement between two or more, to the prejudice of another. As if a tenant for term of life, or tenant in tail, will secretly conspire with another, that the other will recover against the tenant for life, the lands which he holds, &c. in prejudice of him in the reversion.

COUNCIL. Rioters shall answer before the council, on certificate of the justices. 13 Hen. IV. c. 7. *sect*. 21. Conspiracies against privy counsellors, see 3 Hen. VII. c. 14.

COUNCIL

COUNCIL, in the city of *London*, there are *common council-men* chosen in every ward, at a court of wardmote held by the aldermen of the respective wards, on St. Thomas's day yearly; they are to be chosen out of the most sufficient men; and sworn to give true *counsel* for the common profit of the city. In the court of *common council*, are made laws for the advancement of trade, and committees yearly appointed, &c. but acts made by them, are to have the assent of the lord mayor and aldermen by stat. 21 Geo. I.

COUNSEL, for *prisoners*. The judges never scruple to allow a prisoner counsel, to instruct him what questions to ask, or even to ask questions for him with respect to matters of fact, for as to matters of law, arising on the trial, they are *entitled* to the assistance of a counsel. 4 *Black*. 335.

COUNSELLOR, one retained by a client, to plead his cause in a court of judicature. A counsellor in law retained, has a privilege to enforce any thing, which he is informed of by his client, and to give it in evidence, it being pertinent to the matter in question, and not to examine whether it be true or false; but it is at the peril of him who informs him; for a counsellor is at his peril to give in evidence, that which his client informs him, being pertinent to the matter in question, otherwise action upon the case lies against him by his client. *Cro. Jac.* 90.

The *fees to counsellors are not in the nature of wages or pay*, or that which we call *salary or hire*, which are duties certain, and grow due by contract for labour or service; but *what is given them, is honorium*, not *merces*; being a gift, which gives honour as well to the taker as the giver; nor is it certain or contracted; for no price or rate can be set upon counsel which is invaluable and inestimable, so as it is more or less according to the circumstances, namely, the ability of the client, the worthiness of the counsellor, the weightiness of the cause, and the custom of the country. It is a gift of such a nature, that the able client may not neglect to give it, without ingratitude, for it is but a gratuity or token of thankfulness: yet the worthy counsellor may not demand it without doing wrong to his reputation. *Præf. to Dav. Rep.* 22. 23.

COUNT, signifies as much as the original declaration in a process,

cess, though more used in *real* than *personal* actions, as a declaration is more applied to personal, than real.

COUNTEE, was the most eminent dignity of a subject before the conquest: and those who in ancient time were created *countees*, were men of great estate and dignity. The *countee*, was *prefectus* or *prepositus comitatus*, and had the charge and custody of the county, whose authority the sheriff now hath. 9 *Rep.* 46 n.

COUNTENANCE, was anciently used for credit or estimation. 1 Ed. III. *st.* 2. c. 4.

COUNTER, lately used for the name of two city prisons---the Poultry and Giltspur-street counters.

COUNTERFEITS, persons obtaining any money, goods, &c by *counterfeit* letters or false tokens, being convicted before justices of assize, or justices of peace, are to suffer such punishments as shall be thought fit, short of death; as imprisonment, pillory, &c. Stat. 33 Hen. VIII. c. 1. The obtaining money from one man, to another's use, upon a false pretence of having a message and verbal order to that purpose, is not punishable by criminal prosecution; it depending on a bare naked lie, against which common prudence and caution may be a security. 6 *Mod.* 105. 1 *Haw.* 188.

COUNTERMAND, is where a thing formerly executed, is afterwards by some act or ceremony made void, by the party that had first done it.

COUNTERPART, when the several parts of an indenture, are interchangeably executed by the several parties, that part or copy which is executed by the grantor, is usually called the original, and the rest are *counterparts.*

But a better practice is lately adopted for all the parties to execute every part; which renders them all originals. 2 *Black.* 296. If an original deed is in being, or may be had, the *counterpart* cannot be produced as evidence; otherwise, where the original cannot by any means be procured. *Wood.* b. 4. c. 4.

COUNTERPLEA, is in law a replication to *aid prier*, as is also a *counterplea* to the plea of *clergy.*

COUNTER-ROLLS, the rolls which sheriffs of counties, have with coroners of their proceedings, as well of appeals as of inquest, &c. 3 Ed. I. c. 10.

COUNTIES PALATINE, are those of *Chester, Durham,* and *Lancaster*. Of these three, the county of *Durham* is now the only one, remaining in the hands of a subject; for the earldom of *Chester* was united to the crown by king Henry III. and hath even since given title to the king's eldest son. And the county Palatine or duchy of *Lancaster*, in the reign of king *Edward* IV. was by act of parliament, vested in the king, and his heirs kings of *England*, for ever. 1 *Black*, 118.

There is a court of chancery, in the counties Palatine of *Lancaster* and *Durham*, over which there are chancellors; that of *Lancaster* called the chancellor of the duchy. And there is a court of exchequer at *Chester*, of a mixed nature for law and equity, of which the chamberlain of Chester is judge. There is also a chief justice of Chester; and other justices in the other counties palatine, to determine civil actions and pleas of the crown. In all of these the king's ordinary writs are of no force. And the judges of assise, who sit within these franchises, sit by virtue of a special commission from the owners thereof, and under the seal thereof, and not by the usual commission under the great seal of England. 3 *Black*. 79.

COUNTY signifies the same as shire, and contains a circuit or portion of the realm, into which the whole land is divided, for the better government of it, and the more easy administration of justice; so that there is no part of this nation which is not within some county; and every county is governed by a yearly officer, whom we call a sheriff. See *Sheriff*. *Fortescue*, c. 24.

COUNTY COURT, this was anciently a court of great dignity and splendor; the bishop and the earl, with the principal gentlemen of the shire, sitting therein to administer justice, both in lay and ecclesiastical causes. But its dignity was much impaired, when the bishop was prohibited, and the earl neglected to attend it. And in modern times, as the proceedings are removable from hence into the king's superior courts, by writ of *pone*, or *recordare*, this hath occasioned the business of the county court, in a great measure to decline,

By the 2 and 3 Edw. VI. c. 25, no county court shall be longer deferred than one month from court to court; so that the county court, shall be kept every month, and not otherwise. And only twenty-eight days shall be reckoned to the month. 2 *Inst*. 71.

And

And it may be kept at any place within the county, unless restrained by statute. *Wood* c. 4. c. 1.

The suitors, that is, the freeholders, are the judges of this court; except that in re-disseisin, by the statute of *Merton*, the sheriff is judge.

The jury in this court ought to be freeholders, but the quantum of their estate is not material.

This court shall hold pleas between party and party, where the debt, or damage is under 40s. 4 *Inst.* 266.

But in replevin the sum may exceed 40s. *Id.*

It has not cognizance of trespass *vi et armis*, because a fine is thereby due to the king, which it cannot impose. *Id.*

But by virtue of a writ of *justicies* the court may hold plea of trespass *vi et armis*, and of any sum, or of all actions personal above 40s. *Id.*

Causes may be removed from this court by a writ of *recordare*, issuing out of the chancery, directed to the sheriff, commanding him to send the plaint that is before him in his county court (without writ of *justicies*) into the court of king's bench or common pleas, to the end that the cause may be there determined: whereupon, the sheriff is to summon the other party to be in that court (into which the plaint is to be sent) at a day certain; and he is to make certificate of all this under his own seal, and the seal of four suitors of the same court. *Read. County. C.*

Causes, may also be removed by *pone*, which differs in nothing from a *recordare*, except that it removes such suits as are before the sheriff by *writ of justicies*, and a *recordare* is to remove the suit that is by *plaint* only, without a writ. *Id.* And though the plea be discontinued in the county, yet the plaintiff or defendant may remove the plaint into the common pleas or king's bench, and it shall be good, and he shall declare upon the same. *Id.*

COUNTY RATE, by the 12 G. II. c. 29, the justices at their general or quarter sessions, or the greater part of them (and by 13 G. II. c. 18, justices of liberties and franchises not subject to the county commissioners) shall have power to make one general county rate, to answer all former distinct rates, which shall be assessed on every parish, &c. and collected and paid by the high constables of hundreds to treasurers appointed by the justices; which money shall be deemed the public stock, &c. But appeal lies by the churchwardens and overseers, against the rate of any particular parish. 22 G. III. c. 17.

For the repairing of bridges, and highways thereto adjoining, and salaries for the surveyors of bridges. *For* building and repairing county goals. *For* repairing shire halls. *For* the salary of the master of the house of correction, and relieving the weak and sick in his custody. *For* the relief of the prisoners in the king's bench and marshalsea prisons; and of poor hospitals in the county, and of those who shall sustain losses by fire, water, the sea, or other casualties, and other charitable purposes for the relief of the poor, as the justices in sessions shall think fit. *For* the relief of the prisoners in the county goal. *For* the preservation of the health of the prisoners. *For* the salary of the chaplain of the county goal. *For* setting prisoners to work. *For* the treasurer's salary. *For* salary of persons making returns for the prices of corn. *For* charges attending the removal of any of the said general county rates by *certiorari*. *For* money for purchasing lands at the ends of county bridges. *For* charges of rebuilding or repairing houses of correction, and for fitting up and furnishing the same, and employing the persons sent thither. *For* charges of apprehending, conveying, and maintaining rogues and vagabonds. *For* charges of soldiers carriages, over and above the officers pay for the same, by the several yearly acts against mutiny and desertion, and by the militia act. For the coroner's fee of 9d. a mile for travelling to take an inquisition, and 20s. for taking it. *For* charges of carrying persons to the goal, or house of correction. *For* the goaler's fees for persons acquitted of felony, or discharged by proclamation. *For* charges of prosecuting and convicting felons. *For* charges of prosecuting and convicting persons plundering shipwrecked goods. *For* charges of maintaining the militia-men's families, by the several militia acts. *For* charges of bringing insolvent debtors to the assises, in order to their discharge, if themselves are not able to pay. *For* the charges of transporting felons, or conveying them to the places of labour and confinement. *For* charges of carrying parish apprentices, bound to the sea service, to the port to which the master belongeth.

By the 12 G. II. c. 29, the churchwardens and overseers shall, in thirty days after demand made, out of the money collected for relief of the poor, pay the sums so assessed on each parish or place,

place. And if they shall neglect or refuse so to pay, the high constable shall levy the same by distress and sale of their goods, by warrant of two or more justices residing in or near such parish or place. Where there is no poor-rate, the justices, in their general or quarter sessions, shall by their order direct the sum assessed on such parish, township, or place, to be rated and levied by the petty constable, or other peace officer, as money for the relief of the poor is by law to be rated or levied. The high constables, at or before the next sessions respectively after they have received the money, shall pay the same to the treasurer; and the money so paid, shall be deemed the public stock. And the said high constables shall deliver in a true account on oath (if required) of the money by them received, before the said justices at their general or quarter sessions. The treasurer shall pay so much of the money in his hands, to such persons as the justices in sessions shall from time to time appoint, for any uses and purposes, to which the public stock of any county, city, division, or liberty, is or shall be applicable. And shall deliver in a true account on oath (if required), of his receipts and disbursements, to the justices at every general or quarter sessions, and also the proper vouchers for the same, to be kept amongst the records of the sessions. And the discharge of the said justices, by their order at their general or quarter sessions, shall be a sufficient discharge to the treasurer. And *no new rate* shall be made, until it appear by the treasurer's accounts or otherwise, that three fourths of the money collected, have been expended for the purposes aforesaid. If the churchwardens and overseers of any parish or place, shall think such parish or place is overrated, they may appeal to the next general or quarter sessions.

COURT, a court is defined to be a place, appropriated to the judicial administration of justice. The law has appointed a considerable number of courts, some with a more limited, others with a more extensive jurisdiction; some of these are appropriated to enquire only, others to hear and determine; some to determine in the first instance, others upon appeal and by way of review.

The most general division of our courts, is, into such as are of record, or not; those of record, are again divided into such as are *supreme, superior,* or *inferior.*

The supreme court of this kingdom, is the high court of parliament, consisting of the king, lords, and commons, who are vested with a kind of omnipotency in making new laws, repealing and reviving old ones; and on the right balance of these, depends the very being of our constitution.

Superior courts of record are again, those that are more or less principal: the *more principal* ones are the lords house in parliament, the chancery, king's bench, common pleas, and exchequer: the *less principal* ones are such as are held by commission of *goal delivery, oyer* and *terminer, assise, nisi prius,* &c. by custom or charter, as the courts of the palatine of *Lancaster, Chester, Durham*; or by virtue of acts of parliament, and the king's commission, as the court of *sewers, justices of the peace,* &c.

The inferior courts of record, as ordinarily so called, are corporation courts, courts leet, and sheriffs torn, &c.

Courts not of record, are the courts baron, county courts, hundred courts, &c.

Also the admiralty, and ecclesiastical courts, which are not courts of record, but derive their authority from the crown, and are subject to the controul of the king's temporal courts, where they exceed their jurisdiction. All these are bounded and circumscribed by certain laws and stated rules, to which in all their proceedings and judicial determinations, they must square themselves. *Hale's. An.* 35.

And here it may be proper to observe, that where a statute prohibits a thing, and appoints that the offence shall be heard and determined in any of the king's courts of record, it can be proceeded against, only, in one of the courts of *Westminster Hall, Dyer,* 236.

Every court of record is the king's court, though the profits may be another's; if the judges of such courts err, a writ of error lies; the truth of its records, shall be tried by the records themselves, and there shall be no averment against the truth of the matter recorded. *Co. Lit.* 17. All such courts are created by act of parliament, letters patent, or prescription, and every court by having power given it to fine and imprison, is thereby made a court of record; the proceedings of which, can only be removed by writ of error or *certiorari*. *Co. Lit.* 260.

A court, that is not a court of record, cannot impose any fine on an offender, nor award a *capias* against him, nor hold plea of debt

debt or trespass, if the debt or damages amount to 40s. nor of trespass done *vi et armis*, though the damages are laid to be under 40s.

COURT BARON, is a court which every lord of the manor (anciently called the barons) hath within his own precincts. This court is an inseparable ingredient of every manor; and if the number of the suitors should so fail, as not to leave sufficient to make a jury or homage, that is, two tenants at the least, the manor itself is lost. 2 *Black*. 90.

The court baron is of two natures; the one is a customary court, appertaining entirely to the copyholders or other customary tenants; and of this the lord, or his steward is the judge; the other is a court of common law, and is before the freeholders who owe suit and service to the manor, the steward being rather register than judge.

The copy-holders or customary court, is for grants and admittances upon surrenders and descents, no presentment of the homage or jury. The homage may enquire of the death of tenants after the last court, and who is the next heir; of fraudulent alienation of lands, to defeat the lord of his profits; of rent or service withdrawn; of escheats and forfeitures; of cutting down trees without license or consent; of suit not performed at the lord's mill; of waste by tenant for life; of surcharge of common; of trespass in corn, grass, meadow, woods, hedges; of pound breach; of removing mere stones and land marks; of by-laws not observed and the like. The method of punishment is by amercement.

COURT OF CHANCERY. See *Chancellor* and *Chancery*.

COURT OF CHIVALRY, otherwise called the *marshal court*; the judges of which were the lord *constable* of *England*, and the earl *marshal* of *England*: but since the extinguishment of the hereditary office of constable, in the reign of *Henry* VIII. this court has been holden before the earl marshal only, and if it exceed its jurisdiction, it may be prohibited by the common law courts. 2 *Haw*. 602. It seems at this day to have a jurisdiction, as to disputes concerning precedency and points of honor, and satisfaction therein; and may proceed against persons, for falsely assuming the name and arms of honourable persons. 2 *Haw*. 11. This court is to be governed by its own usages, as far as they go, and

and in other cases by the civil law; but since it is no court of common law, no condemnation in it causes any forfeiture of lands, or corruption of blood; neither can an error in it be remedied by a writ of error, but only by appeal to the king; yet the judges of the common law take notice of its jurisdiction, and give credit to a certificate of its judges.

COURT CHRISTIAN, so called, because as in *secular* courts the king's laws sway and decide causes, so in ecclesiastical courts, the laws of Christ should rule and direct; for which cause, the judges in these courts are divines, as archbishops, bishops, archdeacons, &c.

COURT OF COMMON PLEAS. See *common pleas.*

COURT OF DELEGATES, is the highest court for civil affairs, that concern the church. See *Delegates.*

COURTS ECCLESIASTICAL, are those courts which are held by the king's authority, as supreme governor of the church, for matters which chiefly concern religion. As to suits in *spiritual,* or *ecclesiastical* courts, they are for the reformation of manners; as for punishing of heresy, defamation, laying violent hands on a clerk, and the like; and some of their suits are to recover something demanded, as tithes, a legacy, contract of marriage, &c. and in cases of this nature, the court may give costs, but not damages: the proceedings in the ecclesiastical courts, are according to the civil and canon law; they are not courts of record.

COURT OF EXCHEQUER. See *Exchequer.*

COURT OF HUSTINGS, the highest court of record holden at Guildhall, for the city of *London,* before the lord mayor and aldermen, the sheriffs and recorder. 4 *Inst.* 247. This court determines all pleas, real and mixed; and here all lands, tenements, and hereditaments, rents and services, within the city of London and suburbs of the same, are pleadable in two *hustings*; one called *hustings of the plea of lands,* and the other, *hustings of the common pleas.* In the hustings of *plea of lands,* are brought *writs of right patent,* directed to the sheriffs of London. In the hustings of *common pleas,* are pleaded *writs ex gravi querela,* writs of *gravelet,* of *dower, waste,* &c. If an erroneous judgment be given in the hustings, the party grieved may sue a commission out of chancery, directed to certain persons, to examine the record, and thereupon do right.

COURT

COURT OF KING'S BENCH. See *King's Bench.*

COURT OF THE LEGATE, was a court obtained by Cardinal *Wolsey*, of pope *Leo* the tenth, 9 H. VIII. wherein he had power to prove wills, and dispense with offences against the spiritual laws, &c. This court, was however of short continuance.

COURT OF MARSHALSEA. See *Marshalsea.*

COURT MARSHAL, is a court for punishing the offences of officers and soldiers in time of war. See 22, 29, and 32 G. II. c. 3, 6, 25, and 34.

COURT OF NISI PRIUS. See *nisi prius.*

COURT OF PECULIARS, a *spiritual court*, held in such parishes as are exempt from the jurisdiction of the bishops, and are peculiarly belonging to the archbishop of *Canterbury*, in whose province, there are fifty-seven such peculiars.

COURT OF PIEPOWDER, a court held in fairs, to do justice to buyers and sellers, and for redress of disorders committed in them, so called because they are most usual in summer, when the suitors to the court have dusty feet; and from the expedition in hearing causes proper thereunto, before the dust goes off the feet of the plaintiff and defendant. The court of *piepowder*, may hold plea of a sum above 40s. The steward before whom the court is held, is the judge, and the trial is by merchants and traders in the fair; and the judgment against the defendant shall be, *quod amercietur*. If the steward proceed contrary to the stat. 17 E. IV. he shall forfeit 5l.

COURT OF REQUESTS, was a court of equity, of the same nature with the court of chancery but inferior to it. This court having assumed great power to itself, so that it became burthensome, *Mich. anno* 40 and 41 *Eliz.* in the court of common pleas, it was upon solemn argument adjudged, that the court of requests was no court of judicature, &c. and by the stat. 16 and 17, C. I. c. 10, it was taken away. 4 *Inst.* 97.

Court of Requests, by 41 G. III. c. 14, for extending the powers of the court of requests within the city of *London*, all debts amounting to 5l. due from any person resident within the jurisdiction of the city, are to be exclusively sued for and recovered. Two aldermen, and not less than twenty inhabitants householders of the several wards and districts, are appointed commissioners, and sit in rotation. The process is by summons,

and

and the commissioners have power to award payment by such instalments, as are consistent with the circumstances and ability of the debtor. In this court, an attorney's privilege is of no avail.

COURT OF SESSION IN SCOTLAND. See *Scotland*.

COURT OF THE LORD STEWARD OF THE KING'S HOUSE. The lord steward, or in his absence, the treasurer and comptroller of the king's house, and steward of the marshalsea, may inquire of, hear and determine, in this court, all treasons, murders, manslaughters, bloodsheds, and other malicious strikings, whereby blood shall be shed, in any of the palaces, and houses of the king, or in any other house wherein his royal person shall abide.

COURT OF STAR-CHAMBER, a court erected by 3 H. VII. c. 8, for punishing persons unlawfully assembling, and for other misdemeanors. But the act was repealed, and the court dissolved, by stat. 17, C. I. c. 10.

COURTS OF UNIVERSITIES, these courts are called the *chancellor's courts*, and are kept by the vice chancellors of Oxford and Cambridge. Their jurisdiction extends to all causes ecclesiastical and civil (except for maihem, felony, and relating to freehold) where a scholar, servant, or minister of the universities, is one of the parties to the suit. They proceed in a summary way, according to the practice of the civil law; and the judges in their sentences follow the justice and equity of the civil law, or the laws, statutes and customs of the universities, or the laws of the land at their discretion. If any erroneous judgment be given in these courts, appeal lies to the *congregation*; thence to the *convocation*; and thence to the king in chancery by his delegates.

COURTS OF WALES, by 34 and 35 H.VIII. c. 26, it is enacted, that there shall be a *court of great sessions*, kept twice in every year in every of the twelve counties of Wales; and the justices of those courts, may hold pleas of the crown in as large a manner as the king's bench, &c. and also pleas of assise, and all other pleas and actions real and personal, in as large a manner as the common pleas, &c.

Writs of error shall lie from judgments in this great sessions, it being a court of record, to the court of king's bench at *Westminster*. But the ordinary original writs of process from the king's courts at *Westminster* do not run into the principality of *Wales*, though pro-

cess

cess or execution does, as do also prerogative writs, as writs of *certiorari, quo minus, mandamus,* and the like.

COURT OF WARDS AND LIVERIES, abolished by 12 C. II. c. 24. See *Tenure.*

COURTESY, or CURTESY OF ENGLAND, is where a man takes a wife seized of fee simple, fee-tail general, or as heir in tail-special, and hath issue by her, male or female *born alive*; if the wife die, the husband shall hold the land during his life by the law of *England,* and he is tenant by the courtesy of England.

COURT LANDS, demesnes, or land kept in demesnes, or in the lord's own hands, to serve his family.

COWS. See *Cattle.*

CRANAGE, is a liberty to use a *crane,* for the drawing up of wares from vessels at any creek, of the sea or wharf, to the land, and make profit of it. It signifies also the money taken, and paid for the same. *Stat.* 22, C. II. c. 11.

CRASTINO SANCTI VINCENTII, the morrow after the feast of St. Vincent the martyr, (Jan. 22.) and is the date of the statute made at *Merton.* Anno 20. H. III.

CRAVENT OR CRAVEN. In a trial by battle upon a writ of right, if the appellant join in battle and cry *craven,* he shall lose *liberam legem,* that is become infamous, but if the appellee cry *craven,* he shall have judgment to be hanged. The word *craven* is still used for a coward.

CREAST or CREST, a word adopted by *heralds,* and applied to the device set over a coat of arms.

CREDITORS, shall recover their debts of executors, or administrators, who in their own wrong, waste, or convert to their use the estate of the deceased 30 C. II. c. 7. Wills and devises of lands, &c. as to creditors on bonds, or other specialties, are declared void: and the *creditors,* may have actions of debt against the heir at law and devisees; 3 & 4 W. & M. c. 14, and in favour of *creditors,* whenever it appears to be the testator's intent, in a will, that his land should be liable for paying his debts, in such case equity will make them subject, though there are no express words, but there must be more than a bare declaration, or it shall be intended out of the personal estate. 2 *Vern. Rep.* 708, where one devises that all his debts, &c. shall be first paid, if his personal estate

estate, is not sufficient to pay the *creditors*, it shall amount to a charge on his real estate for that purpose. *Preced. Chanc.* 430.

CRIMINAL CONVERSATION. See *Adultery*. An action for criminal conversation, is the only *civil case*, where an actual marriage need be proved; for in every other case, general reputation, the acknowledgment of the parties themselves, and reception by their family and friends as man and wife, is *prima facie*, good and admissible evidence of a marriage, though no register whatever be produced. *Espinasses cases* at N. P. 214. 354.

CROCUIM, CROCIA, the crosier or pastoral staff, which bishops and abbots had the privilege to carry, as the common ensign of their religious office.

CROFT, a little close, inclosed near a dwelling-house, for any particular use.

CROISES, signify *pilgrims*, and also the knights of St. *John of Jerusalem*, because they wear the sign of the cross.

CROSSES, beads, &c. used by the Roman Catholics, are prohibited to be brought into this kingdom, on pain of *præmunire*, &c.

CROWN-OFFICE. The court of king's-bench, is divided into the *plea side*, and the *crown side*. In the *plea* side it takes cognizance of civil causes, in the *crown* side, it takes cognizance of criminal causes, and is thereupon called the *crown-office*. In the crown-office are exhibited informations in the name of the king, of which there are two kinds; 1. Those which are truly and properly the king's own suits, and filed *ex-officio* by his own immediate officer, the attorney-general. 2. Those in which, though the king is the nominal prosecutor, yet it is at the relation of some private person or common informer: and these are filed by the king's coroner and attorney, usually called the master of the crown-office.

CUI ANTE DIVORTIUM, is a writ, that a woman divorced from her husband, hath to recover lands or tenements from him, to whom her husband had alienated during the marriage, because she could not gainsay it.

CUI IN VITA, is a writ of entry, which a widow hath against him, to whom her husband alienated her lands or tenements in his life time; which must contain in it, that during his life (cui in vita) she could not withstand it.

CULPRIT

CULPRIT, is not (as is vulgarly imagined) an opprobrious name given to the prisoner before he is found guilty, but it is the reply of the clerk of arraigns to the prisoner, after he had pleaded not guilty: which plea was anciently entered upon the minutes in an abbreviated form, *non cul'*; upon which the clerk of the arraigns, on behalf of the crown, replies that the prisoner is guilty, and that he is ready to prove him so; which is done by a like kind of abbreviation, *cul'prit*, signifying that the king is ready to prove him guilty (from *cul* that is *culpabilis*, guilty; and *prit*, *præsto sum*, I am ready to verify it). 4 *Black.* 339.

CULVERTAGE, was a *Norman* feudal term, for lands of the vassal escheated to the lord; and signified, confiscation, or forfeiture of lands and goods.

CURATE, is he who represents the incumbent of a church, parson, or vicar, and officiates divine service in his stead: and in case of pluralities of livings, or where a clergyman is old and infirm, it is requisite there should be a *curate* to perform the cure of the church. He is to be licensed and admitted by the bishop of the diocese, or by an ordinary, having episcopal jurisdiction: and when a curate hath the approbation of the bishop, he usually appoints the salary too; and in such case, if he be not paid, the curate hath a proper remedy in the ecclesiastical court, by a sequestration of the profits of the benefice; but if he have no licence from the bishop, he is put to his remedy at common law, where he must prove the agreement.

CURFEU, was an institution of *William* the *Conqueror*, who required, by ringing a bell at eight o'clock every evening, that all companies should immediately disperse and fire and candle be extinguished.

CURIA, it was usual for the king of *England* to assemble the bishops, peers, and other great men of the kingdom to some particular place, at the chief festivals in the year, and this was called *curia*; because they consulted about the weighty affairs of the nation.

CURIA ADVISARE VULT, a deliberation which the court sometimes takes, before they give judgment in a cause. And when judgment is stayed, upon motion to arrest it; then it is entered by the judges, *curia advisare vult*.

CURIA CLAUDENDA, a writ that lies against him who should fence and close up his ground, if he refuse or defer to do it.

CURIA DOMINI, the lord's court, where all the tenants, if required, were bound to attend every three weeks.

CURIA MILITUM, a court so called, anciently held a *Carisbroke-castle*, in the Isle of Wight.

CURRIERS. No currier shall use the trade of a butcher, tanner, &c. or shall curry skins insufficiently tanned, or gash any hide of leather, on pain of forfeiting for every hide or skin, 6s. 8d. If any currier, do not curry leather sent to him, within sixteen days between Michaelmas and Lady-day, and in eight days at other times, he shall on conviction thereof forfeit 5l. Geo. II. c. 25. Every currier or dresser of hides in oil, shall annually take out a licence from the commissioners or officers of excise.

CURSITOR, an officer or clerk belonging to the chancery, who makes out original writs; of these there are twenty-four in number, and to each allotted several counties.

CURTEYNE. The name of King *Edward* the Confessor's sword, which is the first sword carried before the kings of England at the coronation.

CURTILAGE, a yard, backside, or piece of ground, lying near a dwelling-house.

CURTILES TERRÆ, court lands. See *Court Lands.*

CUSTODE ADMITTENDO ET CUSTODE AMOVENDO, are writs for the admitting or removing of guardians.

CUSTODES LIBERTATIS ANGLIÆ, AUTHORITATE PARLIAMENTI, was the stile wherein writs and other judicial proceedings ran during the times of trouble from the murder of King *Charles* the First, till the usurpation by *Cromwell*, declared traiterous by 12 C. II c. 3.

CUSTOM, is a law or right, not written, which being established by long use, and the consent of our ancestors, hath been, and is daily practised. If it is to be proved by record, the continuance of an hundred years will serve. *Custom* is either *general* or *particular*. *General*, when allowed through all England. *Particular* is that, which belongs to this or that county, as *gavelkind* to *Kent*

General

General customs which are used throughout *England*, and are the common law, are to be determined by the judges: but *particular customs*, such as are used in some certain towns, boroughs, cities, &c. shall be determined by a jury. 1 *Inst.* 110. But the judges of the courts of king's-bench, and common-pleas, can overrule a custom, though it be one of the customs of *London*, if it be against natural reason. 1 *Mod.* 212.

CUSTOM OF LONDON. The ancient city of London, being the metropolis and chief town for trade and commerce within the kingdom, it was necessary, that it should have certain customs and privileges for its better government, which though derogatory from the general law of the realm, yet, being for the benefit of the citizens, and for the advantage of those who trade to, and from the city, have not only been allowed good, by the judgments in the superior courts, but have also been confirmed by several acts of parliament.

The customs of London differ from all others in point of trial, for if any of the customs be pleaded, and denied, and issue be taken thereupon, the existence of such customs shall be tried by a writ directed to the mayor and aldermen, to certify whether there is such a custom or not, and they shall make their certificate by the mouth of the recorder.

These customs of London, relate to divers particulars with regard to trade, apprentices, widows, orphans, and a variety of other matters; the custom relative to the distribution of a freeman's estate, extends only to cases of intestacy, or express agreements made in consideration of marriage. *For an account of the customs of London, see* Laws and Customs, &c. of London.

CUSTOMS OF MERCHANTS. See *Bills of Exchange, Bankrupts, Insurance, &c.*

CUSTOMS, are used for the tribute or toll that merchants pay to the king, for carrying out and bringing in merchandize.

Tonnage is a duty on wine imported, at so much a *tun*. *Poundage* a duty *ad valorem*, on all other merchandize at so much a pound. 1 *Black.* 314.

CUSTOMARY TENANTS, such tenants as hold by the *custom* of the manor, as special evidence.

CUSTOM HOUSE, a house in several cities and port-towns,

as *London*, &c. where the king's customs are received, and all business relative thereunto transacted.

CUSTOS BREVIUM, a principal clerk belonging to the court of common-pleas, whose office is, to receive and keep all the writs returnable in that court, and put them on files, every return by itself; and at the end of every term, to receive of the *prothonotaries*, all the records of *nisi prius*, called the *postea*. The *custos brevium*, also makes entry of the writs of covenant, and the concord upon every fine, and makes forth exemplifications and copies of all writs and records in his office, and of all fines levied. The fines after they are ingrossed, are to be divided between the *custos brevium* and *chirographer*; whereof the *chirographer* keeps always the writ of covenant, and the note; the *custos brevium* keeps the concord and foot of the fine. This office is in the king's gift. There is also a *custos brevium et rotulorum* in the king's-bench, who files such writs as are there used to be filed, and all warrants of attorney, and transcribes, or makes out the records of *nisi prius*, &c.

CUSTOS PLACITORUM CORONÆ, this is the same as the *custos rotulorum.*

CUSTOS ROTULORUM. This officer has the custody of the rolls, or records of the session of the peace. He is always a justice of the peace, and *quorum* in the county where he has his office.

CUSTOS OF THE SPIRITUALITIES. He who exercises spiritual or ecclesiastical jurisdiction of any diocese, during the vacancy of the see.

CUSTOS TEMPORALIUM, the person to whose custody a vacant see was committed by the king, as supreme lord; who as steward gave an account of the goods and profits to the *escheator*, and he into the exchequer.

CUTTER OF THE TALLIES, an officer in the exchequer, who provides wood for the tallies, and cuts the sum paid upon them, and takes them into the court to be written upon.

D.

DAIRIES, by 36 Geo. III. dairies or places kept solely for drying, keeping, and making cheese and butter, are exempted from the duties on windows.

DAMAGE-FEASANT or FAISANT, is where the beasts of another come upon a man's land, and do there feed, tread, or spoil, his corn or grass there growing; in which case, the owner of the ground, may distrain and impound them, till satisfaction be made. *Wood. b.* 4. *c.* 4.

DAMAGE, generally signifies any hurt, or hindrance that a man receives in his estate; but in the *plural* in common law, are the recompence that is given to a man, by a jury, as a satisfaction for some injury sustained; as for a battery, imprisonment, slander, or trespass. 2 *Black.* 438.

In actions upon the case, the jury may find less damages than the plaintiff lays in his declaration, though they cannot find more; but costs may be increased beyond the sum mentioned in the declaration for damages; for costs are given in respect of the plaintiff's suit to recover his damages, which may be sometimes greater than the damage. 10 *Co.* 115.

A jury may, and now frequently do, give interest on book-debts, in the name of damages.

For a more general account of damages, see 7 *Vin. Abr.* and 2 *Bac. Abr.* title, Damage.

DAMAGE CLEER, was formerly a fee or gratuity (generally a *tenth* part of the damages recovered) paid to the prothonotaries or clerks of the king's-bench, common-pleas, and exchequer. But this is abolished by 17. C. II. c. 6. *s.* 2. And if any officer shall take any money in the name of *damage cleer*, or in lieu thereof; or shall delay to sign any judgment until *damage cleer* be paid, he shall forfeit treble the sum so taken, or demanded, to the party grieved.

DANE-GELT or DANE-GELD, a tribute imposed upon our ancestors of 1s. for every hide of land, through the realm, for clearing the seas of *Danish* pirates, which heretofore greatly an-

 noyed

noyed our coasts. This *Dane-gelt*, was released by St. *Edward* the Confessor, but levied again by William the First and Second, released by *Henry* the First, and finally by king *Stephen*.

DANGER, a payment in money, made by the forest tenants to the lord, that they might have leave, to plough and sow in time of *pannage*, or mast-feeding.

DATE OF A DEED, is a description of the time, viz. the day, month, year of our lord, year of the reign, &c. in which the deed was made, either expressly, or by reference to some day or year mentioned in the deed before. 2 *Black.* 304.

A deed may be *dated* at one time, and sealed and delivered at another; but every deed shall be intended to be delivered, on the very same day it bears date, unless the contrary be proved. 2 *Inst.* 670. Though there can be no delivery of a deed, before the day of the date, yet after there may. *Yelv.* 138.

DAY, is either natural or artificial, the *natural* day consists of twenty-four hours, and contains the day solar and the night. The *artificial* or solar day begins at sun-rise and ends at sun-set.

In order to avoid disputes, the law generally rejects all fractions of a day: therefore if I am bound to pay monies on a certain day, I discharge the obligation if I pay it before 12 o'clock at night; after which the following day commences. 2 *Black.* 141.

Days in bank, are days of appearance in the court of common-pleas.

To be dismissed *without day*, is to be finally dismissed the court.

Days of grace. See *Bills of Exchange*

DAY-LIGHT, before *sun-rising*, and after *sun-setting*, and as long as the day continues, whereby a man's countenance may be discerned; is accounted part of the common law, as to *robberies*, committed in the day-time, when the *hundred* is liable.

DAY WRIT. The king may grant a *writ of warrantia diei* to any person, which shall save his default for one day, be it in plea of land, or other action, and be the cause true or not; and this by his prerogative.

DAYMERE OF LAND, as much arable land, as can be ploughed in one day's work.

DEADLY FEUD, a profession of an irreconcileable enmity till

till revenge be obtained, even by the the death of that enemy, and allowed by our ancient *Saxon* laws till pecuniary satisfaction were made to the kindred.

DEAF, DUMB, AND BLIND, a man born deaf, dumb, and blind, is considered by the law as an idiot; he being supposed incapable of understanding, as not having those senses which furnish the mind with ideas. *Black.* 308.

DEAFORESTED, discharged from being *forest,* or exempted from the *forest laws.*

DEAN, an ecclesiastical magistrate, or dignitary, he is next under the bishop, and chief of the chapter, ordinarily in a cathedral church.

There are four sorts of deans and deaneries. The *first* is a dean who hath *a chapter* consisting of prebendaries or canons, subordinate to the bishop, as a council assistant to him in matters spiritual, relating to religion, and in matters temporal, relating to the temporalities of his bishopric: The *second* is a dean who hath *no chapter,* and yet he is *presentative* and hath *cure of souls,* he hath a peculiar, and a court wherein he holds ecclesiastical jurisdiction; but he is not subject to the visitation of the bishop or ordinary; such is the dean of *Battle in Sussex*: The *third* dean is also ecclesiastical, but the deanery is not *presentative,* but donative, nor hath *any cure of souls,* but he is only by covenant or condition; and he hath also a court and peculiar, in which he holds plea and jurisdiction, of all such matters and things as are ecclesiastical, and which arise within his peculiar, which oftentimes extends over many parishes; such a dean constituted by commission from the metropolitan of the province, is the dean of the *Arches,* and the dean of *Bocking* in Essex. The *fourth* sort of of dean, is he, who is usually called the rural dean; having no absolute judicial power in himself, but is to order the ecclesiastical affairs within his deanery and precinct, by the direction of the bishop or of the archdeacon; and is a substitute of the bishop in many cases.

DEATH OF PERSONS, there is a *natural* death of a man, and a *civil* death; *natural* where nature itself expires and extinguishes; and *civil,* where a man is not actually dead but is adjudged so by law. If any person, for whose life any estate hath been

been granted, remain beyond sea, or is otherwise absent seven years, and no proof made of his being alive; such person shall be accounted naturally dead; though if the party be afterwards proved living at the time of eviction of any person, then the tenant, &c. may re-enter and recover the profits. *Stat.* 19. C. II. c. 6.

And persons in reversion or remainder, after the death of another, upon affidavit that they have cause to believe such other dead, may move the lord chancellor to order the person to be produced; and if he be not produced, he shall be taken as dead; and those claiming may enter, &c. 6 *Anne*, c. 18.

DEATH'S PART, or *deadman's part*, is that portion of his personal estate, which remained after his wife and children had received thereout their respective reasonable parts; which was, if he had both a wife and a child, or children, one third part; if a wife and no child, or a child or children, and no wife, one half; if neither wife nor child, he had the whole to dispose of by his last will and testament; and if he made no will, the same was to go to his administrators. And within the city of *London*, and throughout the province of *York*, at this day in case of intestacy, the wife and children are entitled to their said reasonable part, and the residue only is disputable by the *Statute of Distribution*.

DEAWARRENNATS, diswarrened, as when a warren were broke up.

DE BENE ESSE, in law signification, is to accept or allow a thing as well done for the present, thus judges frequently take bail, and declarations are frequently delivered *de bene esse*, or conditionally, until special or common bail be filed.

DEBENTURE, is a certificate delivered at the custom-house, when the exporter of any goods or merchandize has complied with the regulations prescribed by certain acts of parliament, in consequence of which, he is entitled to a bounty or drawback on the exportation.

Stealing debentures was made felony by 2 Geo. II. c. 25. s. 3.

DEBET ET DETINET, are *Latin* words used in the bringing of writs and actions. And an action shall always be in the *debet et detinet*, when he who makes a bargain or contract, or lends money

money to another, or he to whom a bond is made, brings the action against him who is bounden, or party to the contract or bargain, or unto the lending of money, &c.

DEBET ET SOLET, if a man sue to recover any right by writ, whereof his ancestor was disseised by the tenant or his ancestor, then he uses only the word *debet* in his writ; because *solet* is improper, as his ancestor was disseised, and the custom discontinued; but if he sue for any thing that is now first of all denied, then he uses both these words *debet et solet*; because his ancestor before him, and he himself usually enjoyed the thing sued for.

DEBT, a sum due from one person to another, in consequence of work done, goods delivered, or money or other value, for which reimbursement has not been made.

The non-payment in these cases, is an injury, for which the proper remedy is by *action of debt*, to compel the performance of the contract, and recover the special sum due. 4 *Co.* 90.

Actions of debt are now seldom brought but upon special contracts under seal; wherein the sum due, is clearly and precisely expressed: for in case of such an action upon simple contract, the plaintiff labours under two difficulties; first, the defendant has here the same advantage as in an action of detinue, that of waging his law, namely, purging himself of the debt by oath, if he think proper; secondly, in an action of debt, the plaintiff must recover the whole debt he claims, or nothing at all. For the debt is one single cause of action, fixed, and determined; but in an action upon the case, or what is called an *indebitatus assumpsit*, which is not brought to compel a specific performance of the contract, but to recover damages for its non-performance; these damages are in their nature indeterminate, and will therefore adapt and proportion themselves to the truth of the case, which shall be proved; without being confined to the precise demand stated in the declaration. 3 *Black.* 154.

DEBTOR. The gaoler shall not put, keep, or lodge prisoners for debt, and felons, together in one room or chamber, on pain of forfeiting bis office, and treble damages to the party grieved. 22 & 23 C. II. c. 20.

But every goaler ought to keep such prisoner in safe and close custody;

custody; safe, that he cannot escape; and close, without conference with others, or intelligence of things abroad. *Dalt.* c. 170.

DECENNARY, was originally a district of ten men with their families, the inhabitants whereof living together, were sureties or pledges for each others good behaviour. See *Constable.*

DECEPTIONE, a writ that lies properly against him who deceitfully does any thing in the name of another, for one that receives damage or hurt thereby.

DECIES TANTUM, a writ that lies against a juror, who hath taken money for giving his verdict, called so of the effect, because it is to recover ten times as much as he took. *Stat.* 98. Edw. III. c. 12 and 13. *Decies tantum* lies against sheriffs taking a reward for arraying a pannel. 11 H. VI. c. 14. See *Vin. Abr.* 378, & 382.

DECINERS, DECENNIERS, or DOSINERS, such as were anciently, appointed to have the oversight and check of ten *friburghs* for the maintenance of the king's peace.

DECLARATION, is a shewing in writing the grief and complaint of the demandant, or plaintiff, against the defendant or tenant wherein he is supposed to have done some wrong. And this ought to be plain and certain, both because it impeaches the defendant, and also compels him to answer thereto. Such a *declaration* in an action real, is termed a *count,* and it is essential, that the *count* or *declaration* ought to contain, *demonstration, declaration,* and *conclusion*; and in the *conclusion* the plaintiff ought to aver, and offer to prove his suit, and shew the damages he has sustained by the wrong done him. *Declaration,* must be *certain,* containing; 1. such sufficient *certainty whereby the court may give a peremptory and final judgment* upon the matter in controversy. 2. *The defendant may make a direct answer* to the matter contained therein. 3. *That the jury,* after issue joined, *may give a compleat verdict* thereupon. 4. *No blank* or space, *to be left therein. Brown's Annal.* 3.

By the general rules of law, a plaintiff must declare against a defendant, within twelve months after the return of the writ: but by the rules of court, if he do not deliver his declaration within two terms, the defendant may sign judgment of *non pros,* though unless he take such advantage of the plaintiff's neglect, the plaintiff

tiff may still deliver a declaration within the year. 2 *Durnf.* and *East.* 112 and 3 *Durnf.* and *East.* 123.

DECREE is a sentence pronounced by the lord chancellor in the court of chancery, and it is equally binding upon the parties, as a judgment in a court of law.

By the laws of *England*, a *decree* (notwithstanding any contempts thereof) shall *not bind the goods* or moveables, but only charge the person. *Chan. Rep.* 193.

If a *decree* be obtained and inrolled, so that the cause cannot be reheard, then there is no remedy but by *bill of review*, which must be on error appearing on the face of the decree, or on matters subsequent thereto, as a release or a receipt discovered since. 3 *M'm's. Rep.* 371.

DECRETALS, a volume of the canon laws, containing the decrees of sundry popes. See *Canon Law.*

DEDBANNA, an actual homicide or manslaughter.

DEDI, a warrant in law, to the feoffee and his heirs; as if it be said in a feoffment, *A. B. hath given and granted, &c.*

DEED, is a written contract sealed and delivered. It must be written before the sealing and delivery, otherwise it is no deed; and after it is once formally executed by the parties, nothing can be added or interlined; and therefore, if a deed be sealed and delivered with a blank left for the sum, which the obligee fills up after sealing and delivery, this will make the deed void.

A deed must be made by parties capable of contracting, and upon a good consideration; and the subject matter must be legally and formally set out.

The formal parts of a deed are:

The *premises*, containing the number, names, additions, and titles of the parties.

The *habendum*, which determines the estate and interest intended to be granted by the deed.

The *reddendum*, or reservation, whereby the grantor reserves to himself something out of the thing granted.

A *condition*, which is a clause of contingency, on the happening of which, the estate granted, may be defeated.

The *warranty*, whereby the grantor for himself, and heirs, warrants or secures to the grantee, the estate so granted.

The *covenants*, which are clauses of agreement contained in the

 deed,

deed, whereby the contracting parties stipulate for the truth of certain facts, or bind themselves to the performance of some specific acts.

The *conclusion*, which mentions the execution and date of the deed, or the time of its being given or executed, either expressly or with reference to some day and year before mentioned.

A deed may be either an indenture, or a deed-poll. The former derives its name, from being indented or cut in an uneven manner, so as to tally with the counterparts, of which there ought to be as many as there are parties; the latter, or deed-poll, of which there is one part only, is so called from its being polled or shaven quite even.

A deed is the most solemn act of law which a man can perform with respect to the disposition of his property, and therefore no person shall be permitted to aver or prove any thing against his own deed.

All the parts of a deed indented, constitute in law but one entire deed; but every part has the same operative force as all the parts taken together, and they are deemed the mutual or reciprocal acts of either of the parties, who may be bound by either part of the same, and the words of the indenture may be considered as the words of either party.

If the name of baptism or surname of a party to a deed be mistaken, as John for Thomas, &c. this has been held to be dangerous. 2 *Bulst.* 70.

But any mistake as spelling &c. not deviating from the substance of the deed, will not render it void.

If a man get another name in common esteem than his right name, any deed made to him under such name, will be valid.

Every deed must be founded upon good and sufficient consideration; not upon an usurious contract, nor upon fraud or collusion, either to deceive *bona fide* purchasers, or just and lawful creditors; any of which considerations will vacate the deed, and subject the parties to forfeiture, and in some cases to imprisonment.

A deed also without any consideration is void, and is construed to enure only to the benefit of the party making it.

Considerations may be *express* or *implied*. An *express* consideration, is where a man contracts to do a certain act for a certain

sum

sum of money, or other equivalent act; and an *implied* consideration, is, when it may be enforced by law; thus if a person do any work, or receive any goods from another, the law implies a consideration, which it will enforce, although there was no specific agreement for remuneration.

A deed must be written upon the proper stamps prescribed by the legislature, otherwise it cannot be given in evidence. See *Stamps*.

The written matter of a deed, must be set forth in a legal and orderly manner, so as that there are words sufficient to explain the meaning of the parties, and at the same time to bind them to the execution of their contract; and of this sufficiency the courts of law are to determine. Although it is not indeed absolutely necessary in law, to have all the formal words which are usually drawn out in deeds, provided there be sufficient words legally and clearly to explain the meaning of the parties, yet as these formal or orderly parts, are calculated to convey the meaning of the parties in the most clear, distinct, and effectual manner, and have been well considered and sanctioned by the wisdom of successive ages, it is prudent not to depart from these without good reason, and the most urgent necessity.

The force and effect which the law of *England* gives to a deed under seal, cannot exist, unless such deed be executed by the party himself, or by another for him, in his presence, or with his direction, or in his absence, by an agent authorized so to do, by another deed also under seal, and in every such case, the deed must be made and executed in the name of the principal.

A deed takes effect only from the day of delivery, and therefore if it have no date, or a date impossible, the delivery will in all cases ascertain the date of it; and if another party seal the deed, yet if the party deliver it himself, he thereby adopts the sealing and signing, and by such delivery makes them both his own.

The delivery of a deed may be alledged at any time after the date, but, unless it be sealed, and regularly delivered, it is no deed.

Another requisite of a deed is, that it be properly witnessed or attested; the attestation, is however, necessary, rather for preserving the evidence, than as intrinsically essential to the validity of the instrument.

There are four principles adopted by the courts of law for the exposition of deeds; viz.

That they be beneficial to the grantee or person in whose favor they are intended to operate.

That where the words may be employed to some interest, they shall not be void.

That the words be construed according to the meaning of the parties, and not otherwise; and the intent of the parties shall be carried into effect, provided such intent can possibly stand at law.

That they are to be consonant to the rules of law, and deeds shall be expounded reasonably without injury to the grantor, and to the greatest advantage of the grantee. Deeds are further expounded upon the whole; and, if the second part coutradict the first, such second part shall be void; but if the latter expound or explain the former, which it may, both parts may stand.

In construction of law, the first deed and the last, will stand in force; and where a deed is by indenture between parties, none can have an action upon such deed, but the person who is a party to it. In a deed-poll however, one person may covenant with another who is not a party, to do certain acts; for the nonperformance of which he may bring his action.

Where a man justifies title under any deed, he ought to produce that deed; if it be alledged in pleading, it must be produced to the court, that it may determine whether the deed contain sufficient words to make a valid contract.

DEED-POLL, is a deed *polled*, or *shaven*, quite even, in contradistinction from an *indenture*, which is cut unevenly, and answerable to another writing that comprehends the same words. A *deed-poll* is properly single, and but of one part, and is intended for the use of the feoffee, grantee, or lessee; an indenture always consists of two or more parts and parties. Every deed that is pleaded, shall be intended to be a *deed-poll*, unless it be alledged to be indented. See *Deed, and Stamp.*

DEEMSTERS, or DEMSTERS, *all controversies* in the Isle of Man, *are decided without process*, writings, or *any charges*, by certain

certain judges called *Deemsters* whom they choose from among themselves.

DEER. See *Forest.*

DE EFFENDO QUIETUM DE TELONIO. A writ which lies for those who are by privilege freed from the payment of toll.

DE EXPENSIS MILITUM, a writ commanding the sheriff to levy so much a day for the expences of a knight of the shire, and a like writ to levy two shillings a day for every citizen and burgess, called *de expensis civium et burgensium.* 4 *Inst.* 46.

DEFACTO. A thing really and actually done.

DEFAMATION, the offence of speaking slanderous words of another; and where any person circulates any report injurious to the credit or character of another, the party injured, may bring an action to recover damages proportioned to the injury he has sustained; but it is incumbent upon the party, to prove that he has sustained an injury, to entitle him to damages. In some cases however, as for words spoken which by law, are in themselves actionable, as calling a tradesman a bankrupt, cheat, or swindler, &c. there is no occasion to prove any particular damage, but the plaintiff must be particularly attentive to state words precisely as they were spoken, otherwise he will be nonsuited.

DEFAULT, is commonly taken for *non-appearance* in court at a day assigned, if a plaintiff make *default* in appearance in a trial at law, he will be non-suited; and where a defendant makes a *default,* judgment shall be had against him by *default.*

DEFAULT IN CRIMINAL CASES. If an offender, being indicted, appear at the *capias,* and plead to issue, and is let to bail to attend his trial, and then make *default*; here the inquest, in case of felony, shall never be taken by default, but a *capias ad audiendum juratum* shall issue, and if the party be not taken, an *exigent*; and if he appeared on that writ, and then make *default,* an *exigi facias de novo* may be granted: but where, upon the *capias* on *exigent,* the sheriff returns *cepi corpus,* and at the day hath not his body, the sheriff shall be punished, but no new *exigent* awarded because in custody of record. 2 H. H. 202.

DEFAULT OF JURORS. If jurors make default in their appearance for trying of causes, they shall forfeit their *issues,* unless they have any reasonable excuse proved by witnesses, in which case the justices may discharge the issues for default. *Stat.* 35 H. VIII. c. 6.

DEFEASANCE, a condition relating to a deed, as to a recognizance or statute, which being performed by the recognizor, the deed is defeated, and made void, as if it had never been done. The difference between a *proviso*, or a condition in a deed, and a *defeasance*, is, that the condition is annexed to, or inserted in the deed or grant; and a *defeasance* is a deed by itself, concluded and agreed on between the parties, and having relation to another deed.

DEFENCE, in its legal signification, is merely an *opposing* or *denial* of the truth or validity of the declaration; or a general assertion that the plaintiff hath no ground of action; which assertion is afterwards extended and maintained in his plea.

DEFENDANT, is the party that is sued in an action personal; as tenant is he that is sued in an action real.

DEFENDEMUS, is a word used in a feoffment or donation, and hath this force, that it binds the donor and his heirs to defend the donee, if any man go about to lay any servitude upon the thing given, other than is contained in the donation.

DEFENDER OF THE FAITH, a peculiar title given to the king of England by pope *Leo* the tenth to king Henry the eighth, for writing against *Martin Luther* in behalf of the church of Rome, then accounted *domicilium fidei catholicæ*.

DEFENDERE SE PER CORPUS SUUM, to offer duel or combat, as a legal trial on appeal. See *Battel*.

DEFENSA, a park or place fenced in for deer, and defended as a property, and peculiar for that use and service.

DEFENSIVA, the lords or earls of the marches, the wardens and defenders of the country.

DEFORCEMENT, a withholding lands or tenements by force from the right owner.

DEFORCEANT or DEFORCEOR, one who overcomes and casts out by force, and differs from a disseisor, because, a man may disseise another without force, but a man may *deforce* another that never was in possession; as, if many have a right to lands as common heirs, and one entering keep out the rest, the law saith, that he *deforceth* them, though he do not *disseise* them.

DEGRADATION, an ecclesiastical censure, whereby a clergyman

gyman is deprived of his holy orders which formerly he had, as of priest, or deacon. *Cod. Rep.* 309.

DEI JUDICIUM, the *ordeal*, was so called, because it was thought an appeal to God for the justice of a cause. See *Ordeal.*

DELEGATES, court of, is so called, because by stat. 26 H. VIII. c. 19, the judges thereof, are *delegated* by the king's commission under the great seal, to hear and determine appeals in the three following cases: 1. where a sentence is given in any ecclesiastical cause by the archbishop or his official. 2. When any sentence is given in any ecclesiastical cause in the places exempt. 3. When a sentence is given in the admiral's court, in suits civil and marine, by order of the civil law. This commission is usually filled with lords spiritual and tempóral, judges of the courts at *Westminster*, and doctors of the civil law. 4 *Inst.* 339.

DELIVERANCE, a criminal brought to trial, to which pleading not guilty, he puts himself on God and his country; the clerk of the crown wishes him a good *deliverance.*

DELIVERY OF DEEDS. See *Deed.*

DELIVERY OF GOODS. See *Sale of Goods.*

DEMAIN or DEMESNE, signify the king's lands appertaining to him in property. No common person hath any *demains* simply understood, for we have no land (that of the crown only excepted) which is not holden of a superior, for all depends either mediately, or immediately of the crown: thus, when a man in pleading would signify his land to be his own, he says that he is or was seized thereof in his *demain* as of fee; whereby he means, that although his land be to him and his heirs for ever, yet it is not true *demain*, but depending upon a superior lord, and holding by service, or rent in lieu of service, or by both service and rent.

DEMAND, calling upon a man for any sum or sums of money, or any other thing due. By the several statutes of limitation, debts, claims, &c. are to be demanded and made in time, or they will be lost by law.

There are two manner of demands, the one in *deed*, the other in *law*; *in deed*, as in every *precepe* there is an express *demand*; *in law*, as in every entry in land, distress for rent, taking or seizing of goods, and such like acts, which may be done without any words, are *demands in law.*

Where there is a duty which the law makes payable on demand,

 no

no demand need be made; but if there be no duty till demand, in such case there must be a demand to make the duty. 1 *Lit.* 432. Upon a penalty the party need not make a demand; as if a man be found to pay 20l. on such a day, and in default thereof to pay 40l. the 40l. must be paid without demand.

If a person release to another all *demands*, this is the best release, the releasee can have, as he is thereby excluded from all actions, duties, and seizures.

DEMANDANT, the plaintiff in a real action, so called because he *demandeth* lands, &c.

DEMISE, is applied to an estate in fee simple, fee tail, or for term of life, and so it is commonly taken in many writs. 2 *Inst.* 483.

The king's death is in law termed *the devise of the king to his successor*.

DEMURRAGE, is an allowance made to the master of a ship by the merchants, for being detained in port longer than the time appointed and agreed for his departure. The rate of this allowance, is generally settled in the charter party.

It is now firmly established that the claim of demurrage ceases, as soon as the ship is cleared out, and ready for sailing. *Jameson v. Lawrie.* House of lords, Nov. 10, 1796.

DEMURRER, is a kind of pause or stop, put to the proceedings of an action upon a point of difficulty, which must be determined by the court, before any farther proceedings can be had therein.

He that demurs in law, confesses the facts to be true, as stated by the opposite party; but denies that by the law arising upon those facts, any injury is done to the plaintiff, or that the defendant has made out a lawful excuse. As if the matter of the plaintiff's declaration be insufficient in law, then the defendant demurs to the declaration; if, on the other hand, the defendant's excuse or plea be invalid, the plaintiff demurs in law to the plea; and so in every other part of the proceedings, where either side perceives any material objection in point of law, upon which he may rest his case. 3 *Black*, 314.

General demurrer being entered, it cannot be afterwards waved, without leave of the court; but a *special* demurrer generally

rally may, unless the plaintiff have lost a term, or the assizes, by the defendant's demurring. *Impey.* i. K. B.

And upon either a *general* or *special demurrer*, the opposite party avers it to be sufficient, which is called a *rejoinder in demurrer*, and then the parties are at issue in point of law: which issue in law, or demurrer, is argued by counsel on both sides; and if the points be difficult, then it is argued openly by the judges of the court, and if they, or the majority of them concur in opinion, accordingly judgment is given: but in case of great difficulty, they may adjourn into the exchequer chamber, where it shall be argued by all the judges. 1 *Inst.* 71.

DEMURRER TO EVIDENCE, is where a question of law arises thereon, and because juries, by direction of the court, usually find a doubtful matter specially, *demurrers upon evidence* are now seldom used. 5 *Rep.* 104.

DEMURRER TO INDICTMENTS, if a criminal join issue upon a point of law in an indictment or appeal, allowing the fact to be true as laid therein, this is a demurrer in law: by which he insists that the fact as stated, is no felony or treason, or whatever the crime is alledged to be. But *demurrer to indictments* are seldom used, since the same advantages may be taken upon a plea of not guilty; or afterwards in arrest of judgment, where the verdict has established the fact. 4 *Black.* 333.

DEMY SANGUE, of the half blood, as when a man marries a woman, and hath issue by her a son or a daughter, and the wife dying, he takes another woman, and hath by her also a son or daughter; now these two sons or daughters, are but of *the half blood,* because they are not brothers or sisters by the mother's side, as having different mothers, and therefore cannot be heirs to one another; for he that shall claim as heir to one by descent, must be of the whole blood to him from whom he claims. *Cowel.*

DEN AND STROND, liberty for ships or vessels to run aground, or come ashore. This privilege was granted to the barons of the cinque ports by king Edw. I.

DENARIUS, an English penny. Stat. Edw. I. &c. *de compositione mensurarum.*

DENARIUS DEI, God's penny, or earnest money given and received to enforce contracts.

DENELAGE

DENELAGE or DANELAGE, the law that the Danes made in *England*.

DENIZEN, a Denizen is an alien born, who has obtained letters patent whereby he is constituted an *English* subject. A Denizen is in a middle state, between an alien and a natural born or naturalized subject, partaking of the nature of both. He may take lands by purchase, or derive a title by descent through his parents or any ancestor, though they be aliens. By Stat 25 G. II. c. 39, no natural born subject shall derive a title through an alien parent or ancestor, unless he be born at the time of the death of the ancestor, who dies seized of the estate which he claims by descent; with this exception, that if a descent shall be cast upon a daughter of an alien, it shall be divested in favor of an after-born son, and in case of an after born daughter or daughter only, all the sisters shall be coparceners. The children born previous to the dezination of their parent cannot inherit by descent, whilst those of a foreigner naturalized, are in every respect, entitled to the same privileges as British subjects. See *Alien.*

DEODAND, is where any moveable thing inanimate, or beast animate, moves or causes the death of any reasonable creature, by mischance, without the will or fault of himself, or of any person. 3 *Inst.* 57.

Formerly wherever the thing which was the occasion of a man's death was in motion at the time, not only that part thereof which immediately wounded him, but all things which moved together with it, and helped to make the wound more dangerous, were forfeited also. 1 *Haw.* 66. But juries have lately determined very differently. As these forfeitures seem to have been originally founded in the superstition of an age of ignorance, they are now discountenanced in *Westminster hall. Fost.* 266.

DE EONERANDA PRO RATA PORTIONIS, is a writ that lies where one is distrained for a rent, that ought to be paid by others *proportionably* with him.

DEPARTURE from a plea or matter, is where a man pleads a plea in bar of an action, which being replied to, doth in his rejoinder shew another matter contrary to his first plea, that is called a *departure from his bar.* It may also be applied to a plaintiff, who in his replication shews new matter from his declaration. *Plowd. Com.* 7, 8. Co. 2. par. *Fo.* 147.

DEPOSITION.

DEPOSITION. Proof in the high court of chancery is by the *depositions* of witnesses; and the copies of such, regularly taken and published, are read as evidence at the hearing. For the purpose of examining witnesses in or near *London*, there is an examiner's office appointed: but for such as live in the country, a commission to examine witnesses is usually granted to four commissioners, two named on each side, or any three or two of them to take the depositions there. And if the witnesses reside beyond sea, a commission may be had to examine them there, upon their own oaths; and, if foreigners, upon the oaths of two skilful interpreters. The commissioners are sworn to take the examinations truly and without partiality, and not to divulge them till published in the court of chancery; and their clerks are also sworn to secrecy. The witnesses are compellable by process of *subpœna*, as in the courts of common law, to appear and submit to examination. And when their depositions are taken, they are transmitted to the court with the same care, that the answer of a defendant is sent. 3 *Black*, 445.

DEPRIVATION, is an ecclesiastical censure, whereby a clergyman is deprived of his parsonage, vicarage, or other spiritual promotion of dignity. *Degg's Parson's Counsellor*. C. 9.

Causes of deprivation: if a clerk obtain preferment in the church by simonical contract, if he be an excommunicate, a drunkard, fornicator, adulterer, infidel, or heretic; or guilty of murder, manslaughter, perjury, forgery, &c. if a clerk be illiterate, and not able to perform the duty of his church; if he be a scandalous person in life and conversation; or bastardy is objected against him; if he be under age, *viz.* the age of *twenty-three* years; be disobedient and incorrigible to his ordinary; or a nonconformist to the canons; if he refuse to use the common prayer; or preach in derogation of it; do not administer the sacrament, or read the articles of religion, &c. if any parson, vicar, &c. have one benefice with cure of souls, and take plurality, without a faculty or dispensation: or if he commit waste in the houses and lands of the church, called dilapidations; all these have been held good causes for *deprivations* of priests. *Deg. Par. Coun.* 98, 99.

DEPUTY, one who performs an office or duty in another's right: where an office is granted to a man and his heirs, he may make an assignee of that office, and consequently a deputy. 9 *Rep.* 47.

There

There is great difference between a *deputy*, and *assignee* of an office; for an *assignee* hath an interest in the office itself, and does all things in his own name; for which his grantor shall not answer unless in special cases; but a *deputy* hath not any interest in the office, but is only the shadow of an officer, in whose name he does all things. 9 *Rep*. 49.

A superior officer must answer for his deputy in civil actions, if he be not sufficient: but in criminal cases it is otherwise, where deputies are to answer for themselves. 2 *Inst*. 191.

DE QUIBUS SUR DISSESIN, a writ of entry.

DESCENT, or hereditary succession, is the title of which a man on the death of his ancestor, acquires his estate by right of representation, as his heir at law: and an estate so descending to the heir, is in law called the inheritance. 2 *Black*, 201.

Descent is of three kinds; by *common law*, by *custom*, or by *statute*. By *common law*, as where one hath land of inheritance in fee-simple, and dieth without disposing thereof in his life time, and the land goes to the eldest son and heir of course, being cast upon him by the law.

Descent of fee-simple by *custom*, is sometimes to all the sons, or to all the brothers (where one brother dieth without issue), as in gavel-kind; sometimes to the youngest son, as in borough English; and sometimes to the eldest daughter, or the youngest, according to the customs of particular places. Descent by *statute* is of fee-tail, as directed by the statute of *Westminster*, 2. *de donis*.

Descent at common law is either *lineal*, or *collateral*: *lineal* consanguinity, is that which subsists between persons, of whom one is descended in direct line from the other, as between a man and his father, grandfather, and great-grandfather, and so upwards, in a direct *ascending* line; or between a man and his son, grandson, great-grandson, and so downwards in the direct *descending* line. Every generation, in this *lineal* direct consanguinity, constitutes a different degree, reckoned either upwards or downwards; the father is related in the first degree, and so likewise is the son, grandsire and grandson in the second; great-grandsire, and great-grandson in the third. This is the only natural way of reckoning the degrees in the direct line, and therefore universally obtains, as well in the *civil* and *canon*, as in the *common law*.

Collateral kindred answers to the same description: collateral relations

relations agreeing with the lenial in this, that they descend from the same stock or ancestor; but different in this, that they do not descend one from the other. Collateral kinsmen are therefore such as lineally spring from one and the same ancestor, who is the *stirps* or root, *stipes*, trunk or common stock, from whence these relations are branched out. As if a man have two sons, who have each a different issue; both these issues are lineally descended from him as their common ancestor; and they are *collateral* kinsmen to each other, because they are all descended from this common ancestor, and all have a portion of his blood in their veins, which denominates them *consanguineors*.

Inheritances shall lineally *descend* to the issue of the person last actually seized, *in infinitum*, but shall never lineally *ascend*. 3 *Black*, 208.

The male issue shall be admitted before the female; and where there are two or more males in equal degree, the eldest only shall inherit (except where there are particular local customs to the contrary): but the females shall inherit all together, except in case of succession to the crown, which is indivisible; and of succession to dignities and titles of honour: yet where a man holds an earldom to him and the heirs of his body, and dies, his eldest daughter shall not succeed of course to the title of countess, but the dignity is in suspence or abeyance, till the king shall declare which of the daughters shall have that title. 2 *Black*, 216.

DESCENT OF CROWN LANDS, all the lands whereof the king if seized *in jure coronæ*, shall attend upon and follow the crown; so that to whomsoever the crown descends, those lands and possessions descend also. *Plowd.* 247.

DESCENT OF DIGNITIES, the dignity of peerage is personal, annexed to the blood, and so inseparable, that it cannot be transferred to any person, or surrendered even to the crown; it can move neither backward nor forward, but only downward to posterity; and nothing but corruption of blood, as if the ancestor be attainted of treason or felony, can hinder the descent to the right heir. *Lex. Const.* 85.

DESCRIPTION. In deeds and grants there must be a *certain description* of the *lands* granted, the *places* where they lie, and the *persons* to whom granted, &c. to make them good. But wills are more favoured than grants as to those *descriptions*; and a wrong

descripption

description of the person, will not make a devise void, if there be otherwise a sufficient certainty, what person was intended by the testator. 1 *Nels. Abr.* 647.

Where a *first* description of land, &c. is false, though the *second* be true, a deed will be void: *contra,* if the *first* be true, and the second false. 3 *Rep.* 2, 3. 8 and 10.

DE SON TORT DEMESNE, words of form used in an action of trespass, by way of reply to the defendant's plea.

DETINUE is a writ which lies where any man comes to goods or chattels either by delivery, or by finding, and refuseth to redeliver them; and it lies only for the *detaining,* when the detaining was lawful. 1 *Inst.* 286.

In this writ the plaintiff shall recover the thing detained; and therefore it must be so certain, as that it may be specifically known. Therefore it cannot be brought for money, corn, or the like, for that cannot be known from other money or corn, unless it be in a bag or sack, for then it may be distinguishably marked. *Ibid.*

But detinue may be brought for a piece of gold of the price of 21s. though not for 21s. in money; for here is a demand of a particular piece. *Buller.* N. P. 50.

In order therefore to ground an action of detinue, which is only for the detaining, these points are necessary: 1. That the defendant came lawfully by the goods, as either by delivery to him, or finding them. 2. That the plaintiff have a property. 3. That the goods themselves be of value. And 4. that they be ascertained in point of identity. Upon this, the jury, if they find for the plaintiff, assess the respective values of the several parcels detained, and also damages for the detension, and the judgment is conditional, that the plaintiff recover the said goods, or (if they cannot be had) their respective values, and also the damages for detaining them. *Id.*

DETINUE OF CHARTERS, an action of detinue lies for charters which make the title of lands; and the heir may have *detinue of charters,* although he have not the land. But if they concern the freehold, the action must be in the common-pleas, and no other court.

DETINUE OF GOODS IN FRANK MARRIAGE, is when a divorce has taken place betwixt a man and his wife, after

which,

which, the wife shall have this writ of *detinue*, for the *goods* given with her in marriage.

DEVASTAVIT or DEVASTAVERUNT BONA TESTATORIS, is a writ that lies against executors, for paying debts of simple contract, before debts on bonds, and specialities, or the like; for in this place the executors are liable to action, as if they had wasted the goods of the testator riotously, or converted them to their own use; and are compellable to pay such debts by speciality out of their own goods, to the value of what they paid so illegally. *Cowel.*

By the 30 C. II. c. 7. if an executor *de son tort* waste the goods, and die, his executors, shall be liable in the same manner as their testator would have been, if he had been living. And it has been since adjudged, that a rightful executor, who wastes the goods of the testator, is in effect an executor *de son tort*, for abusing his trust. 3 *Mod.* 113. and his executor or administrator is made liable to a devastavit by 4 & 5 W. & M. c. 24.

DEVENERUNT, a writ directed to the escheator, when any tenant of the king holding in *capite*, died; and when his son and heir, within age, and in the king's custody, died; then this writ issued, commanding the escheator, that he, by the oath of good and lawful men, inquire what lands and tenements, by the death of the tenant, *came to the king*. *Dyer*. 360. *pl.* 4.

DEVISE, is a disposition of lands, &c. by a last will and testament, to take effect after the death of the deviser. *Co. Lit.* 111. *a.*

DIAMOND, diamonds and precious stones, may be imported duty free, saving the duty granted to the East-India company, on diamonds imported from any place within the limits of their charter. 6 Geo. II. *c.* 7. *s.* 1. 2.

DICTUM DE KENELWORTH, an edict or award between king Henry III. and the barons, and others, who had been in arms against him, containing a composition for five years rent, for the lands and estates of those, who had forfeited them in that rebellion; so called, because it was made at *Kenelworth Castle in Warwickshire.*

DIEM CLAUSIT EXTREMUM, a writ issuing out of Chancery to the escheator of the county, upon the death of any of the king's tenants *in capite*, to inquire by a jury of what lands he died seised, and of what value, and who was next heir to him.

DIES, there are many fee-farm rents, as they are called, reserved to the king in so many *days* and nights provision.

DIES MARCHIÆ, the day of congress between the *English* and *Scotch*, appointed to be holden annually on the *marches*, or borders, to adjust all differences.

DIEU ET MON DROIT, *God and my right*, the motto of the royal arms; intimating, that the king of England holds his empire of none but God. It was assumed by *Richard the First*.

DIEU SON ACT, are words often used in our law; and it is a maxim, that the act of God shall prejudice no man: and therefore if a house be beaten down by tempest or other act of God, the lessee for life, or years, shall not only be quiet in action of waste brought against him, but hath by law a special interest, to take timber to build the house again, if he will, for the habitation. *Co. lib.* 4. 63. When the condition of a bond or obligation, consists of two parts disjunctive, and both are possible at the time of the obligation made, and afterwards one of them becomes impossible by the *act of God*, the obligor is not bound to perform the other part, for the condition shall be taken beneficially for him. *Co. lib.* 5. 22.

DIGNITY, signifies honour and authority, &c. and may be divided into superior and inferior: as the titles of duke, earl, viscount, baron, &c. are the highest names of *dignity*; and those of baronet, knight, esquire, &c. are the lowest order. Nobility only, can give so high a name of *dignity*, as to supply the want of a surname in legal proceedings: and as the omission of a name of *dignity*, may be pleaded in abatement of a writ, &c. so it may be where a peer, who has more than one name of *dignity*, is not named by the most noble. 2 *Haw.* P. C. 185. 239. No temporal *dignity* of any foreign nation, can give a man a higher title than that of esquire. 2 *Inst.* 667. See *Addition*.

DIGNITY ECCLESIASTICAL, ecclesiastical dignities, are those of archbishop, bishop, dean, archdeacon, and prebendary, and the possessor of these dignities are called *dignitaries*. Of *dignities* and prebends, *Camden* reckons 544 in *England*.

DIKES, broken down secretly, to be repaired by the towns adjoining. *St. West.* 2. 13 Ed. I. c. 46. 6 Geo. I. c. 16.

DILAPI-

DILAPIDATION, is where an incumbent of a church-living, suffers the parsonage-house or out-houses to fall down, or be in decay for want of necessary reparations; or it is the pulling down or destroying any of the houses or buildings belonging to a spiritual living, or destroying of the woods, trees, &c. appertaining to the same; for it is said to extend to committing or suffering any wilful waste, in or upon the inheritance of the church. *Deg. Pars. couns.* 89.

By 13 Eliz. c. 10. if any ecclesiastical persons, who are bound to repair the buildings, whereof they are seised in right of their place or function, suffer them to fall into decay for want of repair, and make fraudulent gifts of their personal estate, with intent to hinder their successors from recovering dilapidations against their executors or administrators, in such case the successors shall have like remedy in the ecclesiastical court, against the grantee of such personal estate, as he might have against the executor or administrator of the predecessor.

By 14 Eliz. c. 11. all monies recovered by dilapidations, shall within two years be employed upon the buildings for which they were paid, on pain of forfeiting double so much as shall not be so employed, to the *queen*.

DILATORY PLEAS, are such as are put in merely for delay, and are of three kinds. 1. To the jurisdiction of the court, alledging, that it ought not to hold plea of the matter in hand, as belonging to some other court. 2. To the disability of the plaintiff, by reason whereof he is unable to commence or continue the suit, as that he is ontlawed, attainted, an infant, or the like. 3. In *abatement*, as for some defect in the writ, as a misnomer of the defendant, or other want of form in any material respect. These pleas were formerly used as merely dilatory, without any foundation of truth, and calculated only for delay; but now by *Stat.* 4 & 5 *Anne*, c. 16. no dilatory plea shall be admitted, without affidavit made of the truth thereof, or some probable matter shewn to the court to induce them to believe it true. 3 *Black.* 301. See *Abatement.*

DIMINUTION, is where the plaintiff or defendant in a writ of error, alledges on an appeal to a superior court, that part of the record is omitted, and remains in the inferior court not certified; whereon he prays that it may be certified by *certiorari*. *Co. Ent.* 222. 242.

DIMISSORY LETTERS, are such as are used where a candidate for holy orders, hath a title in one diocese, and is to be ordained in another; the proper diocesan sends *his letters dimissory*, directed to some other ordaining bishop, giving leave that the bearer may be ordained, and have such a cure within his district.

DIOCESE, the circuit of every bishop's jurisdiction. For this realm hath two sorts of divisions; one into shires or counties, in respect of the temporal state; and another into provinces, in regard to the ecclesiastical state; which provinces are divided into dioceses. The provinces are *two; Canterbury*, and *York*, whereof *Canterbury* includes twenty-one dioceses, or sees of suffragan bishops; and *York* three, besides the bishopric of the Isle of *Man*, which was annexed to the province of *York* by king Henry the Eighth. 1 *Inst.* 94.

DISABILITY, an incapacity in a man to inherit or take a benefit which otherwise he might have done, which may happen four ways; by the act of the ancestor, by the act of the party, by the act of law, and by the act of God. 1. *Disability* by the act of the ancestor; as if a man be attainted of treason or felony; by this attainder his blood is corrupt, and himself and his children *disabled* to inherit. 2. *Disability* by the act of the party himself; as if one make a feoffment to another who then is sole, upon condition, that he shall enfeoff a third before marriage, and before the feoffment made, the feoffee takes a wife; he hath by that *disabled* himself to perform the condition according to the trust reposed in him, and therefore, the feoffer may enter, and oust him. *Lit.* 357. 3. *Disability* by act of law, is when a man by the sole act of the law is disabled, as an alien born, &c. 4. *Disability* by the act of God, is where a person is of *non-sane* memory, and in cases of idiocy, &c. But it is a maxim in our law, that a *man of full age, shall never be received to disable his own person. Co. lib.* 4. 123. 124. See also *Aliens, Dissenters, Idiocy*, and *Infamy*.

DISAGREEMENT, will make a nullity of a thing that had effect before: and disagreement may be to certain acts to make them void, &c. *Co. Lit.* 380.

DISCHARGE

DISCHARGE, is where a man confined by some legal process, performs that which the law requires, and is released from the matter for which he is confined. If an obligee, discharge one obligor where several are jointly bound, it discharges the others. See *Arrest, Bond, Payment.*

DISCLAIMER, is a plea containing an express denial, renouncing or *disclaiming*; as if the tenant sue a replevin upon a distress taken by the lord, and the lord avow, saying that he holds of him as his lord, and that he distrained for rent not paid, or service not performed; then the tenant denying to hold of such lord, is said to *disclaim*; and the lord proving the tenant to hold of him the tenant loseth his land. *Co. on Lit.* 102.

DISCONTINUANCE OF POSSESSION, a man may not enter upon his own lands or tenements alienated (such alienation being a *discontinuance of possession*), whatsoever his right be to them, of his own self or by his own authority, but must bring his writ, and seek to recover *possession* by law. *Co. Rep. lib.* 3. 85.

DISCONTINUANCE OF PROCESS, is where the plaintiff leaves a chasm in the proceedings of his cause, whereby the opportunity of prosecution is lost for that time, in which case he must begin again, and usually pays costs to the defendant; or the plaintiff is dismissed the court, &c. Every suit whether civil or criminal, and every process therein, ought to be properly continued from day to day, &c. from its commencement to its conclusion: and the suffering any default or gap herein, is called a *discontinuance.* 2 *Haw.* 298.

DISCONTINUANCE OF PLEA, if where divers things should be pleaded to, and some are omitted; this is a *discontinuance.* 1 *Nels. Abr.* 660. 661.

DISCOVERT, a woman unmarried, or a widow; one not within the bonds of matrimony.

DISCOVERY, the act of revealing or disclosing any matter by defendant, in his answer to a bill filed against him in a court of equity.

A bill for a discovery, must shew an interest in the plaintiff in the subject, to which the required discovery relates: and such an interest as intitles him to call on the defendant for the discovery. *Finch. Rep.* 36. 44. 1 *Vern.* 399.

It is a general rule, that no one is bound to answer so as to

 subject

subject himself to punishment, in whatever manner that punishment may arise. 2 *Vez.* 245. 451. 1 *Atk.* 450. 2 *Atk.* 393.

DISCRETION, is to discern between right and wrong; and therefore whoever hath power to act at *discretion*, is bound by the rule of reason and law. 2 *Inst.* 56. 298. And the court of *king's-bench*, hath a power to redress things that are otherwise done, notwithstanding they are left to the discretion of those that do them. 1 *Lill. Abr.* 477.

DISFRANCHISE, to take away from any one his privilege or freedom. 14 C. II. c. 31.

DISFRANCHISEMENT, is the taking away a man's freedom or privilege. Corporations generally have power by their charter or prescription, to disfranchise a member for doing any thing against the duty of his office as citizen or burgess, and to the prejudice of the public weal of the city or borough, and against his oath, which he took when he was sworn a freeman thereof. But the matter which shall be the cause of his disfranchisement, ought to be *an act* or *deed*, and not an endeavour or enterprize whereof he may repent, before the execution thereof, and of which no prejudice doth ensue. 11 *Co.* 98.

DISGUISED PERSONS, not to hunt in park or warren, under severe penalties; prosecutions against them must be within three years, and the trial may be in any county. 9 Geo. I. c. 22. See *Black Act*.

DISHERITOR, one who disinherits, or puts another out of his inheritance

DISMES, tithes or the tenth part of the fruits of the earth, and of beasts, or labour, due to the clergy.

DISPAUPER, when any person, on account of poverty, attested by his own oath, of not being worth 5l. his debts being paid, is admitted to sue in *forma pauperis*, if afterwards, before the suit be ended, he have any lands, or personal estate fallen to him, or that the court, where the suit depends, thinks fit for that or any other reason, to take away that privilege from him, then he is said to be dispaupered, and can no longer sue in *forma pauperis*.

DISPENSATION, the archbishop of *Canterbury* has now power of *dispensing* in any case, wherein *dispensations* were formerly granted by the see of Rome; and may grant *dispensations* to to the king, as well as to his subjects; but such dispensations shall not be granted out of the realm, &c. and by 28 H. VIII. c. 16. *dispensations* to be confirmed under the great seal. *Wood's Inst.* 26.

DISPENSATIONS OF THE KING. The dispensation of the king, &c. makes a thing prohibited, lawful to be done by him who hath it: but *malum in se* will not admit of a dispensation. *March. Rep.* 213.

DISPENSING POWER OF THE CROWN, if any statute tend to restrain some prerogative incident to the person of the king, as the right of pardoning, or of commanding the service of the subject for the public weal, &c. which are inseparable from the king; by a clause of *non obstante,* he may dsipense with it. 2 *Haw.* 390. But the pretended power of suspending laws, or the execution of laws, by regal authority, without consent of parliament, is illegal. 1 W. and M. Sess. 2. c. 2.

DISSEISIN, is a wrongful putting out of him that is seized of the freehold, which may be effected either in *corporeal* inheritances, or *incorporeal.* Disseisin of things *corporeal*: as of houses and lands must be by entry and actual dispossession of the freehold. Disseisin of *incorporeal* hereditaments, cannot be an actual dispossession, for the subject itself, is neither capable of actual bodily possession, or dispossession, but is only at the election and choice of the party injured, if, for the sake of more easily trying the right, he is pleased to suppose himself disseised. And so also even in *corporeal* hereditaments, a man may frequently suppose himself to be disseised, when he is not so in fact, for the sake of entitling himself to the more easy and commodious remedy of an assise of *novel disseisin,* instead of being driven to the more tedious process of a writ of entry. 3 *Black,* 169.

DISTILLERS, by stat. 2 G. III. c. 5, s. 12, persons who sell liquors chargeable with duty, and distil spirits, are deemed common distillers, and are liable to surveys, penalties, &c. See *Excise.*

DISSENTERS, before the revolution, many statutes were in force against dissenters, but by 1 W. stat. 1. c. 18, commonly called the *toleration act,* it is enacted, that none of the acts made against persons dissenting from the church of *England,* (except the test acts 25 C. II. c. 2. and 30 C. II. st. 2. c. 1.) shall extend to

any

any person dissenting from the church of *England,* who shall at the general sessions of the peace, to be held for the county or place where such person shall live, take the oaths of allegiance and supremacy, and subscribe the declaration against popery, of which the court shall keep a register; and no officer shall take more than 6d. for registering the same, and 6d. for a certificate thereof signed by such officer.

Provided that the place of meeting be certified to the bishop of the diocese, or to the archdeacon of the archdeaconry, or to the justices of the peace at the general or quarter sessions; and the register or clerk of the peace, shall register on record the same, and give certificate thereof to any one who shall demand the same; for which no greater fee than 6d. shall be taken: and provided that during the time of meeting, the doors shall not be locked, barred, or bolted. See *Conventicle.*

Dissenters chosen to any *parochial* or *ward offices,* and scrupling to take the oaths, may execute the office by deputy, who shall comply with the law in this behalf. 1 W. c. 18. But it seems they are not subject to fine, on refusing to serve corporation offices; for they may object to the validity of their election, on the ground of their own nonconformity. 3 *Bro.* P. C. 465.

DISTRESS, in law, is the taking of a personal chattel, out of the possession of the wrong doer, into the custody of the person who is injured, to procure a satisfaction for the wrong committed. It is of two kinds; cattle for trespassing and doing damage, or for nonpayment of rent or other duties. But the most usual injury for which a distress may be taken, is that of nonpayment of rent.

A *distress,* may now be taken for any kind of rent in arrear, the detaining of which, beyond the day of payment, is an injury to him that is intitled to receive it. 4 G. II. c. 28. This is the most common and best remedy, for the recovery of rent in arrear; and the effect of it is, to compel the party to *replevy* the *distress,* and contest the taking in an action against the distrainer; or which is more usual, to compound or pay the debt or duty for which he was distrained. 3 *Black.* 6.

Distress infinite, is a process commanding the sheriff to distrain a person from time to time, and continually afterwards, by taking his goods by way of pledge, to enforce the performance of something due,

due, from the party distrained upon. Generally, it is provided that distress shall be reasonable and moderate; but in case of distress for suit of court, or for defect of appearance, in several cases, where this is the only method of enforcing compliance, no distress can be immoderate; because be it of what value it will, it cannot be sold, but shall be immediately restored, on satisfaction made. 3 *Black.* 231.

Who may distrain for rent. By the common law, and the various statutes in favor of this species of remedy for recovery of rent; all persons having the reversion or remainder of lands, &c. after the determination of the particular estate, or existing term therein, may of common right distrain for rent in arrear, without any clause for that purpose contained in the lease. *Co. Lit.* 142.

What may or may not be distrained. Every thing upon the premises, is liable to the landlord's distress for rent, whether they are the effects of a tenant or a stranger, because of the lien the landlord has on them, in respect of the place where the goods are found, and not in respect of the person to whom they belong. *Co. Lit.* 47. 3 *Bur.* 1502. 3 *Durnf.* and *East.* 601.

Things not distrainable, are tools of a man's trade, corn sent to a mill, a horse sent to a smith's shop, or in a common inn, cloth at a taylor's, goods in the hands of a carrier. 1 *Salk.* 249. 1 *Esp. Rep.* 206. 4 T. R. 569. Dogs, rabbits, beasts of the plough, milk, fruit, and things fixed to the freehold. 3 *Black,* 8 and 9. 4 T. R. 569. But beasts of the plough, and working tools, if not actually in use at the time, may be distrained, if there be not sufficient without them. 4 T. R. 569. So may wearing apparel not actually in use. 1 *Esp. Rep.* 206. Money in a bag sealed, may be distrained.

Horses and carriages sent to stand at livery, are distrainable by the landlord. 3 *Bur.* 1498.

Of the time, &c. and manner of taking the distress. Distress for rent must be in the day-time, for if made at night it will be bad. *Co. Lit.* 142.

Strictly, the rent is *demandable,* and *payable,* before the time of sun-set, of the day whereon it is reserved. Yet the rent is not due, till the last minute of the natural day. 2 *Black.* 42.

Distress cannot be made therefore, till the day after that, on which

which the rent is reserved in the lease; for though payable, it is not strictly due till midnight of the day upon which it is reserved.

Distress, cannot be made after the rent has been tendered: if the landord come to distrain, the tenant may, before the distress made, tender the arrears; and if the *distress* be afterwards taken it is illegal; and so if *after* the *distress*, and *before* it is impounded, the tenant tender payment, the landlord ought to deliver up the distress; and if he do not the detainer is unlawful. 2 *Inst.* 107.

Parole authority to distrain is sufficient, or any authority that can be proved.

By 2 G. II. c. 19. landlords may by the assistance of a peace officer of the parish, break open in the day-time, any place where goods are fraudulently removed and locked up *to prevent a distress*, oath being first made in case it be a dwelling-house, of a reasonable ground to suspect that such goods are concealed therein.

By stat. 8 Anne, c. 14. rent accruing due under a lease, must be distrained for, within six months after its determination.

If a tenant fraudulently remove goods off the premises, the landlord may seize them within thirty days. But such seizure can only be made, where the rent was actually due before the removal.

If a landlord seize only a part of the goods, &c. of his tenant for rent, in the name of them all, it will be a good seizure of the whole. 6 *Mod.* 215.

Distresses ought not to be *excessive*, but in proportion to the duty distrained for. 2 *Inst.* 106.

The remedy for *excessive distresses*, is, by a special action on the *stat.* of *Malbridge*, for an action of trespass is not maintainable upon this account, it being no injury at common law. 1 *Vent.* 104. *Fitzgib.* 85. 4 *Bur.* 590.

Where any distress shall be made for rent justly due, and any irregularity or unlawful act shall be afterwards committed by the party distraining, or his agents; the distress itself shall not on that account be deemed unlawful, nor the party a trespasser from the first, but the person aggrieved shall recover full satisfaction for the *special* damage sustained by such irregularity, and no more, with full costs of suit. 11 G. II. c. 19.

Haw

How a distress is to be disposed of. Persons distraining for rent, may impound the distress on any convenient part of the land, chargeable with the distress, otherwise the goods must be removed to a pound *covert*, and notice given where they are, unless the tenant consent to a person remaining in possession on the premises. *Wood's Inst.* 191.

All living chattels distrained, are regularly to be put in the pound *covert*, because the owner at his peril, is to sustain them, and therefore they ought to be put in such an open place, as that he may have resort to them for that purpose. *Co. Lit.* 47, b.

Household goods, and such other things as would be damaged by the weather, must be impounded in the pound *covert*, otherwise if they be damaged, the distrainer will be answerable for the loss. 1 *Inst.* 47.

If the *distress* for rent, die, or be damaged in the pound, without any default of the distrainer, he may make a fresh distress. 1 *Salk.* 248.

By 2 W. and M. it is provided, that where any goods or chattels, shall be distrained for rent due on any demise, lease, or contract whatsoever, and the owner shall not, within five days next after such distress taken and notice thereof, and of the cause of the the taking left at the dwelling house, or other most notorious place on the premises charged with the rent, *replevy* the same, that then at the expiration of the said five days, the distrainer may with the assistance of the sheriff, undersheriff, or constable; cause the goods and chattels so distrained to be *appraised* by two sworn appraisers, and sold for the best price that can be got for the same, towards satisfaction of the rent for which the said goods and chattels have been distrained, and the costs and charges of such distress, appraisement, and sale, leaving the overplus, if any, in the hands of the said sheriff, or constable, for the use of the owner.

By stat. 2 W. c. 5, on any pound-breach or rescous, of goods distrained for rent, the person grieved thereby, shall in a special action on the case, recover *treble damages and costs* against the offender, or against the owner of the goods, if they are afterwards found to have come to his use or possession.

DISTRESS FOR PENALTIES, by 27 G. II. c. 20. *s.* 1. In all cases where any justice of the peace shall be required or empowered

powered by any act of parliament, to issue a warrant of distress for the levying any penalty inflicted, or any sum of money directed to be paid by such act; it shall be lawful for the justice granting such warrant, therein to order and direct the goods and chattels so to be distrained, to be sold and disposed of within a certain time to be limited in such warrant, so as such time be not less than four days, nor more than eight days, unless the penalty, or sum of money for which the distress shall be made, together with the reasonable charges of taking and keeping such distress, be sooner paid.

DISTRESS OF THE KING, by the common law, no subject can distrain out of his fee or seigniory, unless cattle are driven to a place out of the fee, to hinder the lord's distress, &c. But the king may distrain for rent service, or fee farm, in all the lands of the tenant, wheresoever they be; not only on lands held of himself, but others, where his tenant is in actual possession, and the land manured with his own beasts. 2 *Inst.* 132.

DISTRIBUTION OF INTESTATE'S EFFECTS, after payment of the debts of the deceased, is to be made according to the *stat.* 22 and 23 C. II. c. 10, in manner following: one third shall go to the widow of the intestate, and the residue in equal proportions to his children; or if dead to their representatives; that is, their lineal descendants: if there be no children, or legal representatives, then a moiety shall go to the widow, and a moiety to the next kindred in equal degree, or their representatives: if no widow, the whole shall go to the children: if neither widow nor child, the whole shall be distributed amongst the next kindred in equal degree and their representatives: but no representatives are admitted among collaterals, farther than the children of the intestate's brothers and sisters. The father succeeds to the whole personal effects of his children, if they die intestate, and without issue; but if the father be dead, and the mother survive, she shall only come in for a share equally with each of the remaining children.

DISTRICT, a territory or place of jurisdiction. See *Circuit.*

DISTRINGAS, is a writ directed to the sheriff, commanding him to *distrain* one by his goods and chattels, to enforce his compliance with what is required of him.

Distringas is also issued against peers and persons entitled to

 privilege

privilege of parliament, by which the effects levied, may be sold to pay the plaintiff's costs. 10 G. III. c. 50.

DISTRINGAS JURATORES, a writ directed to the sheriff, to distrain upon a *jury* to appear; and return issues on their lands &c. for nonappearance.

DIVIDEND IN THE EXCHEQUER, one part of an indenture. 10 Ed. I. c. 11.

DIVIDEND OF BANKRUPTS. See *Bankrupts.*

DIVIDEND IN STOCKS, a *dividable* proportionate share of the *interest of stocks*, erected on the public funds.

DIVORCE, a separation of two *de facto* married together; of which there are two kinds; one *a vinculo matrimonii*, from the very *bond of marriage*: the other *a mensa et thora* from *bed and board.*

Causes for separation *a vinculo*, are consanguinity or affinity within the degrees prohibited, also *impuberty* or *frigidity*; where the marriage was merely void *ab initio*, and the sentence of divorce only declaratory of its being so.

This *divorce* enables the parties to marry again: but in the other case a power for so doing must be obtained by act of parliament.

The woman divorced *a vinculo matrimonii*, receives all again she brought with her.

Divorce *a mensa et thora*, is where the use of matrimony, as the use of cohabitation of the married persons, on their mutual conversation, is prohibited for a time, or without limitation of time. And this is in cases of adultery, cruelty, or the like; in which case the marriage having been originally good, is not dissolved or affected as to the *vinculum* or bond.

The woman under separation by this *divorce*, may sue by her next friend; and she may sue her husband in her own name for alimony. *Wood's Inst.* 62.

But the children which she hath after the divorce, shall be deemed bastards; for a due obedience to the sentence will be intended, unless the contrary be shewn. *Walk.* 123.

DOCKET or DOGGET, a brief in writing, on a small piece of paper or parchment, containing the effect of a larger writing, and annexed to other papers for particular purposes. In law a docket is necessary in all judgments, and no debts will be entitled to a preference in debts, due from a party deceased, as judgment debts, unless such judgments be regularly docketed.

DOCTORS and bachelors of divinity and law, may have a dispensation for nonresidence. 21 H. VIII. c. 13. Doctors of civil law, may exercise ecclesiastical jurisdiction, although laymen. 37 H. VIII. c. 17.

DOCTORS COMMONS, is the college of civilians in London.

DOGS. The owner of a dog is bound to muzzle him, if mischievous, but not otherwise; and if a man keep a dog that is known to bite cattle, &c. if, after notice given to him of it, his dog shall do any hurt, the master shall answer for it.

The duty on dogs. The act of 36 G. III. contains the following provisions:

1. That the duty shall not extend to dogs not six months old, the proof of which is to lie on the owner, on an appeal to the commissioners.

2. If any person shall be desirous of compounding for the number of hounds by him kept, and shall give notice thereof to the collector, and shall pay within thirty days after *April* 5, yearly, the sum of 30l. such person shall not be liable to be assessed in respect of any hounds by him kept in the preceding year; and if they are kept in two or more parishes, he shall give notice in which parish, such composition is intended to be made.

By 42 G. III. c. 17, any person keeping two or more dogs, shall pay annually for every greyhound, pointer, setting dog, spaniel, lurcher, or terrier, and for every dog of whatsoever description, or denomination the same may be, the sum of 10s.

And for any dog (not being a greyhound, hound, setting dog, spaniel, lurcher, or terrier), kept by or for the use of any person inhabiting a dwelling house assessed to any of the duties, on houses, windows, or lights, where one such dog and no more shall be kept by or for the use of such person, the annual sum of 6s.

DOMESDAY, is a very ancient record, made in *William the Conqueror's* time, and now remaining in the exchequer fair and legible, consisting of two volumes, containing a survey of all the lands in England. It was begun by five justices, assigned for that purpose in each county, in the year 1081, and finished in 1086.

It is generally known, that the question whether lands are ancient demesne or not, is to be decided by the *Domesday book* of

William

William the Conqueror; from whence there is no appeal. And it is a book of that authority, that even the conqueror himself submitted in some cases, wherein he was concerned, to be determined by it.

DOMICELLUS, signifies a young soldier not yet knighted, and was anciently given as an appellation or addition to the king's *natural* sons in *France*, and sometimes to the eldest sons of noblemen there.

DOMINA, a title given to those honourable women, who in the right of inheritance held a barony.

DOMINUS, a title given to a knight, or a man of quality, the lord of a manor, or to a clergyman.

DOMO REPARANDA, a writ for one against his neighbour, by the fall of whose house he apprehends injury to his own.

DONATIO CAUSA MORTIS, a gift in prospect of death; where a person moved with the consideration of his mortality, gives, and delivers, something to another to keep in case of his decease, but if he live he is to have it again. *Law of Test.* 179.

DONATIVE, is a spiritual preferment, be it church, chapel, or vicarage, which is in the free gift or collation of a patron, without making any presentation to the bishop; and without admission, institution, or induction, by any mandate from the bishop or other; but the *donee* may by the patron, or by any other authorized by the patron, be put into possession. *Deg. Pars. Couns.* 1. c. 13. See *Advowson.*

DONOR AND DONEE, *Donor* is one who gives lands or tenements to another; and he to whom the same is given is the *donee.*

DOTE ASSIGNANDA, is a writ that lay for a widow, where it was found by office, that the king's tenant was seized of tenements in fee or fee-tail at the day of his death; and that he held of the king in chief, &c. In which case the widow came into the chancery, and there made oath, that she would not marry without the king's leave; and hereupon, she had this writ to the escheator. 15 Ed. III. c. 4.

DOTE UNDE NIHIL HABET, a writ of dower that lies for the widow against the tenant, who bought land of her husband in his life time, whereof he was seized solely in fee-simple or fee-tail, in such sort, as the issue of them both might have inherited it. F. N. B. 147.

DOUBLE PLEA, is that, wherein the defendant alledgeth for himself two several matters in *bar* of the plaintiff's action, whereof either is sufficient to effect his desire, which shall not be admitted for a plea.

DOUBLE QUARREL, is a complaint made by any clerk, or other to the archbishop of the province against an inferior ordinary, for delaying justice in any cause ecclesiastical; as to give sentence, to institute a clerk presented, or the like: the effect whereof is, that the archbishop taking notice of such delay, directs his letters under his authentic seal, to all and singular clerks of his province, thereby commanding and anthorizing them, and every of them to admonish the said ordinary, within a certain time; nine days, to do the justice required, or otherwise to cite them to appear before him the said archbishop, or his official, at a day in the said letters prefixed, and there to alledge the cause of his delay. And lastly, to intimate to the said ordinary, that, if he neither perform the thing enjoined, nor appear at the day assigned, he himself will without delay proceed to perform the justice required; and this seems to be termed a *double quarrel*, because it is most commonly made both against the judge and him at whose petition justice is delayed. *Clark's Prax. Tit.* 84. 5.

DOUBLES, nearly the same as letters patent. Stat. 14 H. VI. c. 6.

DOWAGER, a widow endowed, or that hath a jointure; also a title or addition, applied to the widows of princes, dukes, earls, and persons of honour only.

DOWAGER QUEEN, is the widow of the king, and as such enjoys most of the privileges belonging to her as queen consort. But it is not high treason to conspire her death, or violate her chastity; because the succession to the crown is not thereby endangered. But no man can marry her without special licence from the king, on pain of forfeiting his lands and goods. 1 *Black*. 223.

DOWER, the portion which a widow hath of the lands of her husband, after his decease, for the sustenance of herself, and the education of her children.

To

To the consummation of dower, three things are necessary, viz. *marriage, seisin*, and the *husband's death*.

There were formerly five kinds of dower in this kingdom, viz. 1. *Dower by the common law*. 2. *Dower by custom*. 3. *Dower ad ostium ecclesiæ*. 4. *Dower ex assensu patris*, and 5. *Dower de la plus belle*. But of all these kinds of dower, only the two first are now in use.

Dower by the common law, is a third part of such lands or tenements whereof the husband was sole seized in fee-simple, or fee-tail, during the marriage, which the wife is to enjoy during her life; for which there lies a writ of dower. See *Distribution of Intestate's Effects*.

Dower by Custom. This kind of dower varies according to the custom and usage of the place, and is to be governed accordingly; and where such custom prevails, the wife cannot wave the provision thereby made for her, and claim her thirds at common law, because all customs are equally ancient with the common law, itself. *Co. Lit.* 39 *b*.

Dower ad ostium ecclesiæ, is where a man of full age, seized of lands in fee, after marriage, endows his wife at the church door of a moiety, a third, or other part of his lands, declaring them in certainty; in which case, after her husband's death, she may enter into such lands without any other assignment, because the solemn assignment at the church door, is equivalent to the assignment *in pais* by metes and bounds; but this assignment cannot be made before marriage, because *before*, she is not entitled to dower. *Lit. Sect.* 39.

Dower ex assunsu patris, is where the father is seised of lands in fee; and his son and heir apparent *after* marriage endows his wife by his father's assent, *ad ostium ecclesiæ*, of a certain quantity of them; in which case after the death of the son, his wife may enter into such parcel without any other assignment, though the father be living; but this assent of the father's must be by deed, because his estate is to be charged *in futuro*, and this may likewise be of more than a third part. *Co. Lit.* 35, 36.

The dowers *ad ostium ecclesiæ*, or *ex assensu patris*, if the wife enter and assent to them, are a good bar of her in common law; but she may if she will, wave them, and claim her dower at com-

S 3 mon

mon law, because being made after marriage, she is not bound by them. *Br.* 97.

Dower de la plus belle, is, where there is a guardian in chivalry, and the wife occupies lands of the heir as guardian in soccage; if the wife bring a writ of dower against such guardian in chivalry, he may shew this matter, and pray that the wife may be endowed *de la plus belle* of the tenements in soccage; and it will be adjudged accordingly; and the reason of this endowment, was to prevent the dismembering of the lands holden in chivalry, which are *pro bono publico,* and for the defence of the realm. *Lit. Sect.* 48.

After judgment given, the wife may take her neighbours, and in their presence endow herself of the *plus belle,* or *fairest* part of the tenements, which she hath in soccage, for her life. *Lit. Sect.* 48.

DOWRY, in ancient time applied to that which the wife brings her husband in marriage; otherwise called *maritagium,* or marriage goods: but these are termed more properly, goods given in marriage, and the marriage portion. 1 *Inst.* 31.

DOZEIN, one of the articles for stewards in their leets to enquire of, is, if all the *dozeins* (or deciners) be in the assize of our lord the king, and which not, and who receive them. See *Deciners.*

DRAWLATCHES, thieves and robbers, they are mentioned in stat. 5, Ed. III. c. 14.

DREIT DREIT or DROIT DROIT, signifies a double right, that is, *jus possessionis et jus domini.* *Bract. Lib.* 4. c. 27.

DRIFT OF THE FOREST, a view or examination of what cattle are in the forest, that it may be known whether it be overcharged, or not, and whose the beasts are; and whether they are commonable beasts, &c. 4 *Inst.* 309.

DROFLAND or DRYFLAND, an ancient quit rent, or yearly payment made by some tenants to the king, or their landlords, for driving their cattle through the manor to fair, or markets. *Cowel.*

DROIT, right, it is the highest of all real writs whatsoever, and has the greatest respect, and the most assured and final judgment; and therefore is called a writ of right, and in the old books

droit.

droit. 1 *Inst.* 158. There are divers of these writs used in our law, as *droit* de advowson, *droit* de gard, *droit* patent, *droit* rationabili, *droit* sur disclaimer, &c.

DRUNKENNESS, excuseth no crime; but he who is guilty of any crime whatever, through his voluntary drunkenness, shall be punished for it as much as if he had been sober; for the law, seeing how easy it is to counterfeit this excuse, and how weak an excuse it is (though real), will not suffer any man thus to privilege one crime by another. 4 *Black.* 26.

By several statutes *temp. Jac.* every person convicted of drunkenness shall forfeit 5s. or be committed to the stocks for six hours, and offending a second time, shall be bound in a recognizance of 10l. for future good behaviour. And an alehouse-keeper, convicted of drunkenness, shall besides the other penalties, be disabled to keep any such alehouse for three years.

DUCES TECUM, is a writ out of chancery, commanding a person to appear at a certain day in court, and *bring with him* some writings, evidences, or other things, to be inspected and examined in court.

DUELLING, or single combat, between any of the king's subjects, of their own heads, and for private malice or displeasure, is prohibited by the laws of this realm; for in a settled state governed by law, no man, for any injury whatever ought to use private revenge. 3 *Inst.* 157.

And where one party kills the other, it comes within the notion of murder, as being committed by malice afore thought; where the parties meet with an intent to murder, thinking it their duty as gentlemen, and claiming it as their right, to wanton with their own lives, and the lives of others, without any warrant for it either human, or divine; and therefore the law hath justly fixed on them the crime and punishment of murder. 4 *Black.* 199.

And the law so far abhors all duelling in cold blood, that not only the principal, who actually kills the other, but also his seconds, are guilty of murder whether they fought or not; and it is holden that the seconds of the party slain, are likewise guilty as accessaries. 12 *Haw.* 8.

DUKE, in *England,* duke is the next secular dignity to the Prince of Wales.

DUM FUIT INFRA ÆTATEM, a writ that lies for him, that before he came to his full age, made a feoffment of his land in fee, or for term of life, or in tail, to recover them again from him, to whom he conveyed them.

DUM NON FUIT COMPOS MENTIS, a writ that lies against the alienee, or lessee, for him that not being of sound memory, aliened any lands or tenements in fee-simple, fee-tail, or for term of life, or for years.

DURESS, is where a man is kept in prison, or restrained of his liberty, contrary to the order of law, or threatened to be killed, maimed, or beaten; and if such person so in prison, or in fear of such threats, make any specialty or obligation by reason thereof, such deed is void in law; and in any action brought upon such specialty, the party may plead, that it was made by *duress*, and so he may avoid the action. *Cowel.*

Every legal contract must be the act of the understanding, which they are incapable of using, who are under restraint and terrors; and therefore the law requires the free assent of the parties as essential to every contract, and that they be not under any force or violence 2 *Bac. Abr.* 155.

DURHAM. See *Counties Palatine.*

DUTCHY COURT, a court wherein all matters appertaining to the dutchy or county palatine of *Lancaster*, are decided by the decree of the chancellor of that court. See *Counties Palatine.*

DUTIES, sums payable on importing, exporting, or manufacturing an article as a tax. The word is most generally applied to taxes on exports and imports.

There are also various *assessed duties* on private property, both real and funded, on carriages, horses, houses, windows, &c. &c. which on account of the political changes daily occurring, cannot with propriety be entered into, in this book.

DYERS, by Stat. 3 & 4 Ed. VI. c. 2. no dyer may dye any cloth with orchel, or with brazil, to make a false colour in cloth, wool, &c. on penalty of 20s. By Stat. 23 Eliz. c. 9. dyers are to fix a seal of lead to cloths, with the letter M, to shew that they are well mathered, &c. or forfeit 3s. 4d. per yard. By Stat. 23 Geo. III. c. 15. several penalties are inflicted on dyers who dye any cloths deceitfully, and not woaded throughout with indigo and mather. Dying blue with logwo od to forfeit 20l. Dyers in *London*, are subject to the inspection of the dyers company, who may appoint searchers; and out of their limits, justices of the peace in sessions are to appoint them. Opposing the searchers incurs a penalty of 10l.

E.

EALDERMAN, a man chosen to a place of superiority, on account of his age and experience: hence the word alderman in corporations. See *Alderman*.

EARLE, a great title, and is the most ancient of any of the peerage; and, anciently, there was no earl, but who had a shire or county for his earldom. But of later times the number of earls greatly encreasing, they have sometimes for their title some particular part of a county, town, village, or place of residence. Their place is next to a marquis, and before a viscount. See *Selden's Titles of Honour*. 676.

EARNEST, is the money advanced to bind the parties to the performance of a verbal agreement. The person who gives it, is in strictness obliged to abide by his bargain; and in case he declines, is not discharged upon forfeiting his earnest, but may be sued for the whole money stipulated, and damages; and by the statute of frauds 29 C. II. c. 3. no contract for sale of goods to the value of 10l. or more, to be valid, unless such earnest is given.

EASEMENT, a service or convenience, which one neighbour has of another by charter, or prescription, without profit; as a way through his ground, a sink, or the like.

EAST-INDIA COMPANY, a corporation, or united company of merchants of England trading to the East-Indies; which name is given them in Stat. 6 Anne, c. 17. s. 13. more explicitly, according to their charter and adjustment of their rights, by stat. 9 & 10 W. III. c. 44. s. 61. trading into and from the East-Indies, in the countries and ports of Asia and Africa, and into and from the islands, ports, havens, cities, creeks, towns, and places of Asia, Africa, and America, or any of them, beyond the Cape of Good

Good Hope, to the straights of Magellan, where any trade or traffic of merchandize is or may be used and had, to and from every of them.

The temporary rights of the company consist of 1st. the sole and exclusive trade with *India*, and other parts within the limits already described; so that no other of the king's subjects can go thither, or trade there, but by permission of the company; or pursuant to the directions of stat. 33 Geo. III. c. 52. 2dly. They have the administration of the government and revenues of the territories in *India*, acquired by their conquests during their term in the exclusive trade; subject nevertheless to the various checks and restrictions contained in the several statutes, which vest that administration in them.

The rights in perpetuity, are to be a body corporate and politic, with perpetual succession; to purchase, acquire, and dispose at will of lands and tenements in Great Britain, so that the value therein do not exceed 10,000l. per annum; to make settlements to any extent, within the limits of their exclusive trade; build forts and fortifications; appoint governors; erect courts of judicature; coin money; raise, train, and muster forces at sea and land; repel wrongs and injuries; make reprisals on the invaders or disturbers of their peace; and continue to trade within the said limits, *with a joint stock for ever*, although their exclusive right of trading shall be determined by parliament.

The only privileges they can be constitutionally deprived of, are those of trading to the *exclusion of others*, and of governing the countries, and collecting and appropriating the revenues of *India*. *For further particulars concerning the East-India Company*, see Stat. 9 & 10 W. c. 44. s. 69. 6 Anne, c. 3. 7 Geo. I. c. 5. 25 Geo. II. c. 26. 7 Geo. III. c. 47. 12 Geo. III. c. 54. 13 Geo. III. c. 63. 17 Geo. III. c. 8. 21 Geo. III. c. 70. 24 Geo. III. c. 25. and 33 Geo. III. c. 52.

EASTLAND TRADE, all the king's subjects may use the *Eastland trade*, or be admitted a free member of the company, for which purpose it is only necessary to pay 40s.

ECCLESIA, is generally used for the place where the Almighty is worshipped; a church.

ECCLESIASTICAL COURTS. See *Courts Ecclesiastical.*

ECCLE-

ECCLESIASTICAL JURISDICTION, the doctors of the civil law, although laymen may exercise ecclesiastical jurisdiction. 37 H. VIII. c. 17.

EGYPTIANS (Gipsies), are a kind of commonwealth among themselves of wandering impostures and jugglers, who made their first appearance in *Germany*, about the beginning of the sixteenth century, and have since spread themselves over all *Europe* and *Asia*. By the laws of *England*, gipsies were formerly subject to imprisonment and forfeiture of goods, but they are now considered chiefly as *rogues* and *vagabonds*, and are described as such in the vagrant act. 4 *Black*. 166.

EJECTIONE CUSTODIÆ, a writ which lies against him, who casts out the guardian from any land during the minority of the heir.

EJECTMENT, an ejectment is a mixed action, by which a lessee for years, when ousted, may recover his term and damages; it is *real* in respect of the lands, but *personal* in respect of the damages. Since the disuse of real action, this mixed proceeding is become the common method of trying the *title* to lands or tenements. *Runnington on Ejectments*.

The modern method of proceeding in ejectment, entirely depends on a string of legal fictions; no actual *lease* is made; no actual *entry* by the plaintiff; no actual *ouster* by the defendant; but all are merely ideal for the sole purpose of trying the *title*. To this end, a lease for a term of years is stated in the proceedings, to have been made by him who claims title to the *plaintiff*, who is generally an ideal fictitious person, who has no existence; though it ought to be a real person to answer for the defendant's costs. In this proceeding, which is the *declaration*; (for there is no other process in this action) it is also stated, that the *lessee*, in consequence of the demise to him made, entered into the premises; and that the defendant who is also now another ideal fictitious person, and who is called the *casual ejector*, afterwards entered thereon and ousted the plaintiff; for which ouster the plaintiff brings this action. Under this declaration is written *a notice*, supposed to be written by this casual ejector, directed to the *tenant in possession* of the premises; in which notice the casual ejector informs the tenant, of the action brought by *the lessee*, and assures him, that as he the casual ejector, has no title at all to the premises

premises, he shall make no defence, and therefore, he advises the *tenant* to appear in court, at a certain time and defend his own title, otherwise *he* the casual-ejector, will suffer judgment to be had against *him*, by which the *actual tenant* will inevitably be turned out of possession. 2 *Cromp. Prac.* 152.

The ancient way of proceeding, was by actually sealing a lease on the premises, by the party in interest who was to try the titles; and this method is still in use in the following cases:

First, where the house or thing for which ejectment is brought is empty.

Secondly, when a corporation is lessor of the plaintiff, they must give a letter of attorney to some person to enter and seal a lease on the land; for a corporation cannot make an attorney or a bailiff except by deed, nor can they appear but by making a proper person their attorney by deed; therefore they cannot enter and demise upon the land as natural persons can. *L. Raym.* 135.

Thirdly, when the several interests of the lessor of the plaintiff are not known, for in that case, it is proper to seal a lease on the premises; lest they should fail in setting out in their declaration, the several interest which each man passes.

Fourthly, where the proceedings are in an inferior court, they must proceed by actually sealing a lease, because they cannot make rules confess lease, entry, and ouster, inasmuch as inferior courts have not authority to imprison for disobedience to their rules.

It is a general rule, that no person can in any case, bring an *ejectment*, unless he have in himself at the time, a right of *entry*; for although by the modern practice, the defendant is obliged by rule of court, to confess lease, entry, and ouster; yet that rule was only designed to expedite the trial of the plaintiff's right, and not to give him a right which he had not before; and therefore, when it happens that the person claiming title to the lands, has *no right of entry*, he cannot maintain his action. 3 *Black.* 206.

The damages recovered in these actions, though formerly their only intent, are now usually (since the title has been considered as the principal question) very small and inadequate, amounting commonly to one shilling, or some other trivial sum. In order therefore to complete the remedy, when the possession has been long detained from him that has right, an action of trespass also lies,

lies, after a recovery in ejectment to recover the mesne profits which the tenant in possession nad wrongfully received; which action may be brought in the name of either the nominal plaintiff in the ejectment, or his lessor, against the tenant in possession, whether he be made party to the ejectment, or suffer judgment to go by default.

EIGNE, the eldest, or first born.

EIRE or EYRE, signifies the court of justice *itinerant*. *Eyer* is also taken to signify the *justice seat*. See *Justices in Eyre*.

ELECTION, is where a person has by law two remedies, and is compelled to declare which he will abide by: Thus a creditor, in cases of bankruptcy, may either prove his debt under the commission, or proceed at law; but in this case he is compelled to to make his *election*. Where also a person having obtained a judgment, and is entitled to execution, he may either take his remedy against the goods or the person, and he may choose either; but if he proved against the person in the first instance, he cannot afterwards have recourse to the goods; but if he take the goods, and these should be found inadequate to his demand, he may afterwards take the body.

ELECTION OF BISHOPS. See *Bishops*.

ELECTION OF A CLERK OF STATUTES MERCHANT, a writ that lies for the choice of a clerk assigned to take and make bonds, called *statutes merchant*, and is granted out of the chancery upon suggestion made, that the clerk formerly assigned is gone to dwell in another place, or is hindered from following that business, or hath not land sufficient to answer his transgression if he should deal amiss. F. N. B. 164.

ELECTION OF ECCLESIASTICAL PERSONS. If any person that hath a voice in elections, take any reward for an election in any church, college, school, &c. such election shall be void: and if any such societies resign their places to others for reward, they incur a forfeiture of double the sum: and the party giving, and the party taking it, are thereby rendered incapable of such place. 31 Eliz. c. 6. See *Bishops*.

ELECTION OF MEMBERS OF PARLIAMENT. *Qualification of the candidates*. No member shall sit or vote in either house of parliament, unless he be *twenty-one* years of age. 4 *Inst*. 47

They must not be aliens born: they must not be any of the twelve judges; because they sit in the lord's house. But persons who have judicial places in the other courts, ecclesiastical or civil, are eligible. 4 *Inst*. 47. Nor of the clergy; the reason assigned for which, is, that they might sit in the convocation. Nor persons attainted of treason or felony, for they are unfit to sit any where. *Id*.

By the 30 C. II. *st*. 2. c. 1. and 1 Geo. I. c. 13. in order to prevent *papists* from sitting in either house of parliament, no person shall sit or vote in either, till he hath in the presence of the house, taken the oaths of allegiance, supremacy, and abjuration, &c.

Sheriffs of counties, and mayors and bailiffs of boroughs, are not eligible in their respective jurisdictions, as being returning officers; but a sheriff of one county may be chosen knight of another. 1 *Black*. 175.

By several statutes, no persons concerned in the management of any duties or taxes created since 1692, except the commissioners of the treasury; nor any of the officers following, viz. commissioners of prizes, transports, sick and wounded, wine licences navy and victualling; secretaries or receivers of prizes; comptrollers of the army accounts; agents for regiments; governors of plantations; officers of *Minorca* or *Gibraltar*; officers of the excise and customs; clerks or deputies in the several offices of the treasury, exchequer, navy, victualling, admiralty, pay of the army or navy, secretaries of state, salt, stamps, appeals, wine licences, hackney-coaches, hawkers and pedlars; nor any persons that hold any new office under the crown, created since 1705, are capable of being elected. 1 *Black*. 175.

But this shall not extend to, or exclude the treasurer or comptroller of the navy, secretaries of the treasury, secretary to the chancellor of the exchequer, secretaries of the admiralty, under secretary of state, deputy paymaster of the army, or any person holding any office for life, or so long as he shall behave himself well in his office. 15 Geo. II. c. 22.

By the 6 Anne, c. 7. s. 26. if any member shall accept an office of profit under the crown, except an officer of the army or navy accepting a new commission, his election shall be void: but he shall be capable of being re-elected.

No

No person having a pension from the crown during pleasure, shall be capable of being elected. 6 Anne, c. 7. s. 25.

By the 22 Geo. III. c. 45. no contractor with the officers of government, or with any other person for the service of the public, shall be capable of being elected, or of sitting in the house, as long as he holds any such contract, or derives any benefit from it. But this does not extend to contracts with corporations, or with companies, which then consisted of ten partners; or to any person to whom the interest of such a contract shall accrue by marriage or operation of law, for the first twelve months. And if any person disqualified by such a contract shall sit in the house, he shall forfeit 500l. for every day; and if any person who engages in a contract with government, admit any member of parliament to a share of it, he shall forfeit 500l. to the prosecutor.

No person shall be capable to sit or vote in the house of commons, for a county, unless he have an estate freehold or copyhold, for his life, or some greater estate, of the clear yearly value of 600l. nor for a city or borough, unless he have a like estate of 300l. and any other candidate, or two electors, may require him to make oath thereof at the time of election, or before the day of the meeting of parliament; and before he shall vote in the house of commons, he shall deliver in an account of his qualification, and the value thereof under his hand, and make oath of the truth of the same. But this shall not extend to the eldest son or heir apparent of a peer, or of any person qualified to serve as knight of a shire, nor to the members of either of the two universities. 9 Anne, c. 5. 33 Geo. II. c. 20.

Qualifications of Electors. No person shall be admitted to vote, under the age of twenty-one years. This extends to all sorts of members, as well for boroughs as counties. 7 & 8 W. c. 25.

Every elector of a knight of a shire, shall have freehold to the value of 40s. a year within the county; which is to be clear of all charges and deductions, except parliamentary and parochial taxes. 1 *Black.* 172.

No person shall vote in right of any freehold, granted to have fraudulently, to qualify him to vote, and every person who shall prepare or execute such conveyance, or shall give his vote under it, shall forfeit 40l. 10 Anne, c. 23.

No person shall vote for a knight of the shire, without having been in the actual possession of the estate for which he votes, or in the receipt of the rents or profits thereof to his own use, above twelve calendar months; unless it come to him by descent, marriage, marriage-settlement, devise, or promotion to a benefice or office. 18 Geo. II. c. 1.

No person convicted of perjury, shall be capable of voting at an election.

No person shall vote in respect of an annuity or rent-charge, unless registered with the clerk of the peace twelve calendar months before. Such annuity or rent-charge issuing out of a freehold estate.

No person shall vote for a knight of a shire, in respect of any messuages, lands, or tenements, which have not been charged to the land-tax, six calendar months before. 20 Geo. III. c. 17.

No person shall vote, for any estate holden by copy of court roll. 31 Geo. II. c. 14.

In mortgaged, or trust-estates, the mortgagor, *cestuy que trust*, shall vote, and not the trustee or mortgagee unless they be in actual possession.

All conveyances to multiply voices, or to split votes, shall be void; and no more than one voice shall be admitted for one and the same house or tenement.

The right of election in *boroughs* is various, depending entirely on the several charters, customs, and constitutions of the respective places; but by 2 Geo. II. c. 24! this right of voting, for the future shall be allowed according to the last determination of the house of commons concerning it.

And no person, claiming to vote in right of his being a *freeman* of a corporation (other than such as claim by *birth, marriage*, or *servitude*), shall be allowed, unless he have been admitted to his freedom, twelve calendar months before. 3 Geo. III. c. 15.

Of election, as it is essential to the very being of parliaments that election should be absolutely free, all undue influence whatever upon the electors, is illegal, and strongly prohibited. As soon, therefore, as the time and place of election within counties or boroughs, are fixed, all soldiers quartered in the place are to remove, at least one day before the election, to the distance of two miles or more, and not to return till one day after the poll

be

be ended; except in the liberty of *Westminster*, or other residence of the royal family, in respect of his majesty's guards, and in fortified places. 8 Geo. II. c. 30.

By the 7 & 8 W. c. 4. to prevent bribery and corruption, no candidate, after teste of the writ of summons, or after a place becomes vacant in parliament time, shall, by himself, or by any other ways or means on his behalf, or at his charge, before his election, directly, or indirectly, give, or promise to give, to any elector any money, meat, drink, provision, present, reward, or entertainment, to or for any such elector in particular; or to any county, city, town, borough, port, or place in general, in order to his being elected, on pain of being incapacitated.

To guard still more against gross and flagrant acts of bribery, it is enacted by 2 Geo. II. c. 24. explained and enlarged by 9 Geo. II. c. 38. and 16 Geo. III. c. 11. that if any money, gift, office, employment, or reward, *be given*, or *promised to be given*, to any voter, at any time in order to influence him, to give or withhold his vote, as well he that takes, as he that offers such a bribe, forfeits 500l. and is for ever disabled from voting and holding any office in any corporation; unless before conviction, he will discover some other offender of the same kind, and then he is indemnified for his own offence.

If the election shall not be determined upon view, with the consent of the freeholders there present, but a poll shall be demanded, the same shall commence on the day on which such demand is made, or on the next day at farthest (if it be not *Sunday*, and then on the day after), and shall be proceeded in from day to day (*Sundays* excepted) until it be finished, and shall not continue more than fifteen days (*Sundays* excepted); and the poll shall be kept open seven hours at least each day, between eight in the morning and eight in the evening. 25 Geo. III. c. 84. The sheriff shall allow a *cheque-book* for every poll-book for each candidate, to be kept by their inspectors at the place of taking the poll. 19 Geo. II. c. 28.

By the 34 Geo. III. c. 73. in order to expedite the business at elections, the returning officers are enabled, on request of the candidates, to appoint persons to administer to voters, the oaths of allegiance, supremacy, the declaration of fidelity, the oath of

 abjuration,

abjuration, and the declaration or affirmation of the effect thereof, *previously to their coming to vote*; and to grant the voters certificates of their having taken the said oath; without which certificate, they shall not be permitted to vote, if they are required to take the oaths.

And every *freeholder*, before he shall be admitted to poll for a knight of the shire, shall, if required by a candidate, or any elector, make oath of his qualification to vote; in which case the sheriff and clerks shall enter the place of his freehold, and the place of his abode, as he shall disclose the same at the time of giving his vote; and shall enter *jurat* against the name of every such voter who shall have taken the oath. 10 Anne, c. 23. s. 5.

Of the return. After the election, the names of the persons chosen shall be written in an indenture, under the seals of the electors, and tacked to the writ.

The election being closed, the returning officer in boroughs, returns his precept to the sheriff, with the persons elected by the majority. And the sheriff returns the whole, together with the writ for the county, and the names of the knights elected thereupon, to the clerk of the crown in chancery, before the day of meeting if it be a new parliament; or within fourteen days after the election, if it be an occasional vacancy; and this under the penalty of 500l. If the sheriff do not return such knights only as are duly elected, he forfeits by stat. H. VI. 100l. and the returning officer of a borough, for a like false return 40l. and by the late statutes they are liable to an action at the suit of the party duly elected, and to pay double damages, and the like remedy shall be against an officer making a double return. 1 *Black.* 180.

If two or more sets of electors make each a return of a different member (which is called a *double election*), that return only, which the returning officer to whom the sheriff's precept was directed, has signed and sealed, is good; and the members by him returned shall sit, until displaced on petition. *Sim.* 184.

On petition to the house of commons, complaining of an undue election, forty-nine members shall be chosen by ballot, out of whom each party shall alternately strike out one, till they are reduced to thirteen, who, together with two more, of whom each party

party shall nominate one, shall be a select committee for determining such controverted election, 10 and 11 G. III. c. 16 and 42. See *Parliament.*

ELEEMOSINARIUS, the almoner, who received the eleemosinary rents and gifts, and duly distributed them to pious and charitable uses.

ELEGIT, is a writ of execution, either upon a judgment for debt on damages, or upon a forfeiture of the recognizance taken in the king's court. 1 *Inst.* 289.

By the common law, a man could only have satisfaction of goods, chattels, and the present profits of lands, by the writs of *fieri facias* or *leveri facias*; but not the possession of the lands themselves: so that if the defendant aliened his lands, the plaintiff was ousted of his remedy.

The statute 13 Ed. I. c. 18, therefore granted this writ, which is called an *elegit*, because it is in the *election* of the plaintiff, whether he will sue out this writ or one of the former. 3 *Black.* 418.

ELOPEMENT, is, when a married woman of her own accord departs from her husband, and dwells with an adulterer; for which without voluntary reconciliation to the husband, she shall lose her dower by the statute of *Westminster* 2, c. 34.

If a wife willingly leave her husband, and go away and continue with her avouterer, she shall be barred for ever of action to demand her dower that she ought to have of her husband's lands, if she be convicted thereof; except that her husband willingly and without coercion of the church, reconcile her, and suffer her to dwell with him, in which case, she shall be restored to her action. 13 Ed. I. st. 1. c. 34. See *Adultery.*

EMBEZZLEMENT, by stat. 39 G. III. c. 85, for protecting masters against embezzlements by their clerks and servants; servants or clerks, or persons employed for the purpose or in the capacity of servants or clerks, who shall, by virtue of such employment, receive or take into their possession, any money, goods, bond, bill, note, banker's draft, or other valuable security or effects, for or in the name, or on the account of their master or employer, or who shall fraudulently embezzle, secret, or make away with the same, or any part thereof; every such offender, shall be deemed to have feloniously stolen the same from his master or employer, for whose use, or on whose account the same was delivered

livered to, or taken into the possession of such servant, clerk, or other person so employed, although such money, goods, bond, bill, note, banker's draft, or other valuable security, was or were no otherwise received into the possession of his or their servants, clerk, or other person so employed; and every such offender, his adviser, procurer, aider, or abetter, being thereof lawfully convicted or attainted, shall be liable to be transported to such part, beyond the seas, as his majesty, by and with the advice of his privy council, shall appoint; for any term not exceeding fourteen years, in the discretion of the court before whom such offender shall be convicted or adjudged.

EMBLEMENTS, signify the profits of land sown; but the word is sometimes used more largely, for any profits that arise and grow naturally from the ground, as grass, fruit, hemp, flax, &c. *Cowel.*

EMBRACERY, is an attempt to corrupt or influence a jury, or any way incline them to be more favorable to the one side than the other, by money, promises, letters, threats, or persuasions; whether the juror on whom such attempt is made, give verdict or not, or whether the verdict given be true or false. 1 *Haw.* 259.

The punishment of an *embracer* or *embraceor* is by fine and imprisonment; and for the juror so embraced, if it be by taking money, the punishment is (by divers statutes) perpetual infamy, imprisonment for a year, and forfeiture of tenfold the value. 4 *Black.* 140.

EMBROIDERY, no foreign embroidery, or gold or silver brocade, is permitted, to be imported into this kingdom on pain of being seized and burned, and a penalty of 100l. for each piece. No person is allowed to sell any foreign embroidery, gold or silver thread, lace, fringe, brocade, or make up the same into any garment, upon pain of having it burned, and penalty of 100l.

EMPARLANCE. See *Imparlance.*

ENCROACHMENT, an unlawful gaining upon the rights or possessions of another.

ENDEAVOUR, where one who has the use of his reason, *endeavours* to commit felony, &c. he shall be punished by our laws, but not to that degree as if he had actually committed it. 3 *Inst.* 68, 69.

ENDORSEMENT. See *Indorsement, Bills of Exchange,* and *Acceptance*

ENDOWMENT, is the widow's portion; being a third part of all the freehold lands and tenements, of which her husband was seized at any time during the coverture. Of lands not freehold, her portion varies according to the custom in different places.

ENEMY, is properly an alien or foreigner, who in a public capacity, and in an hostile manner, invades any kingdom or country. If a prisoner be rescued by enemies, the goaler is not guilty of an escape; as he would have been if subjects had made the rescue, when he might have a legal remedy against them. 2 *Haw.* 130.

ENFRANCHISEMENT, the incorporating a person into any society or body politic; thus is *the enfranchisement* of one made a citizen of *London*, or other city, or burgess of any town corporate, because he is made partaker of the liberties which appertain to the corporation, wherein he is *enfranchised.*

ENTAIL, signifies *fee-tail,* or *fee-intailed.* See *Estate.*

ENTIERTY, denotes the whole, in contradistinction to moiety which denotes the half.

ENTIRE TENANCY signifies a sole possession in one man.

ENTRY, writ of, is a writ directed to the sheriff, requiring him to command the tenant of the land, that he render to the demandant the premises in question, or appear in court on such a day, and shew why he hath not done it. Of this writ there are four kinds. 1. A writ of entry *sur dissesin,* that lies for the disseisee against the disseisor, upon a disseisin done by himself; and this is called a writ of entry in the nature of an assize. 2. A writ of entry *sur disseisin in the per,* for the heir by descent, who is said to be in the *per,* as he comes in *by* his ancestor. 3. A writ of entry *sur disseisin in the per and cui,* where the feoffee of a disseisor maketh a feoffment over to another; and then the form of a writ is, that the tenant had no title to enter, but *by* a prior alience, *to whom* the intruder demised it. 4. A writ of entry *sur disseisin in the post,* which lies when *after* a disseisin, the land is removed from hand to hand, in case of a more remote seisin, whereunto the other three degrees do not extend. 1 *Inst* 238.

But all these writs are now diseised, as the title of lands is now usually tried upon actions of ejectment or trespass.

ENTRY AD COMMUNEM LEGEM. The writ of entry *ad communem legem* lies, where tenant in dower, or tenant by the courtesy, or for life, aliens in fee, or for the life of another, or in tail, the lands which they hold, &c. after their death, he in the reversion who has it in fee, or for life, shall have this writ against whomsoever is in possession of the land.

ENTRY AD TERMINUM QUI PRÆTERIIT, a writ of entry *ad terminum qui præteriit,* lies where a man leases lands or tenements for term of life, or years, and afterwards the term expires, and he to whom the lease was made, or a stranger, enters upon the land, and occupies the same, and deforces the lessor; the lessor or his heirs shall have the writ. And this writ lies in the *per, cui,* and *post*; for if the lessee hold over his term, and afterwards make a feoffment; the lessor or heirs, may have this writ against the feoffee in the *per*; and if the feoffee make a feoffment over, he may have it against the second feoffee in the *per* and *cui,* and against the third feoffee in the *post.*

ENTRY IN CASU CONSIMILI, a writ of entry *in casu consimili* lies where tenant by the courtesy, or for life, or for another's life, aliens in fee, or in tail, or for life; now he in the reversion, who has an estate there for life, or in fee simple, or in tail, shall have that writ during the life of the tenant for life, who aliened.

ENTRY IN CASU PROVISO. The writ of entry *in casu proviso,* lies where tenant in dower aliens in fee, for life, or in tail, the land which he holds in dower; he who hath the reversion in fee, or in tail, or for life, shall maintain that writ against the alience, and against him who is the tenant of the freehold of land during the life of the tenant in dower, &c. and the writ, may be made in the *per, cui,* and *post.*

ENTRY CAUSA MATRIMOMII PRÆLOCUTI, lies where lands or tenements are given to a man, on condition, that he shall take the donor to his wife within a certain time, and he does not espouse her within the limited time, or espouses another, or otherwise disables himself, that he cannot take her according to the said condition; then the donor and her heirs shall have the said writ against him, or against whoever else is in the said land.

ENURE, to take place or effect, as a release made to a tenant for a term of life, shall *enure* to him in the reversion.

EQUALITY. The law delights in equality, so that when a charge

charge is laid upon one, and many ought to bear it he shall have relief against the rest. 2 *Rep.* 25.

EQUITY, is a construction made by the judges, that cases out of the letter of a statute, yet being within the same mischief or cause of making the same, shall be within the same remedy that the statute provideth. And the reason hereof is, that the law maker could not possibly set down all cases in express terms: thus though it may be unlawful to kill a man, yet it is not unlawful for one to kill another assaulting him, in order to preserve his own life. 4 *Inst.* 24.

EQUITY OF REDEMPTION ON MORTGAGES, if where money is due on a mortgage, the mortgagee is desirous to bar the *equity of redemption*, he may oblige the mortgagor either to pay the money, or be foreclosed of his equity, which is done by proceedings in the court of chancery.

ERROR, signifies an *error* in pleading, or in the process; and the writ which is brought for remedy thereof, is called a *writ of error*.

A *writ of error*, is a commission to judges of a *superior court*, by which they are authorized to examine the *record*, upon which a judgment was given in an *inferior court*, and on such examination, to affirm or reserve the same according to law. *Jenk. Rep.* 25. *For particulars as to the practice of writs of error,* see *Impey's* K.B. & C. P.

ESCAPE, an escape is, where one who is arrested gains his liberty, before he is delivered by course of law.

Escapes are either in *civil* or *criminal* cases; and in both respects, escapes may be distinguished into *voluntary* and *negligent*; *voluntary*, where it is with the consent of the keeper; *negligent* where it is for want of due care in him.

In civil cases: after the prisoner hath been suffered *voluntarily* to escape, the sheriff can never after retake him, but must answer for the debt; but the plaintiff may retake him at any time. In the case of a *negligent escape*, the sheriff upon fresh pursuit, may retake the prisoner; and the sheriff shall be excused, if he hath him again before any action brought against himself for the escape.

When a defendant is once in custody in execution, upon a *capias ad satisfaciendum*, he is to be kept in close and safe custody; and

and if he be afterwards seen at large, it is an escape; and the plaintiff may have an action thereupon for his whole debt: for though upon arrests, and what is called *mesne process*, being such as intervenes between the commencement and end of a suit, the sheriff, till the statute 8 and 9 W. c. 27, might have indulged the defendant as he pleased, so as he produced him in court to answer the plaintiff at the return of the writ; yet, upon a taking in execution, he could never give any indulgence; for in that case, confinement is the whole of the debtor's punishment, and of the satisfaction made to the creditor.

A rescue of a prisoner in execution, either in going to goal, or in goal, or a breach of prison, will not excuse the sheriff from being guilty of and answering for the escape; for he ought to have sufficient force to keep him, seeing he may command the power of the county. 3 *Black* 415 and 6.

In criminal cases: an escape of a person arrested, by eluding the vigilance of his keeper before he is put in hold, is an offence against public justice, and the party himself is punishable by fine and imprisonment: but the officer permitting such escape, either by negligence or connivance, is much more culpable than the prisoner, who has the natural desire of liberty to plead in his behalf. Officers therefore, who after arrest *negligently* permit a felon to escape, are also punishable by fine; but *voluntary escapes*, amount to the same kind of offence, and are punishable in the same degree, as the offence of which the prisoner is guilty, and for which he is in custody, whether treason, felony, or trespass; and this whether he was actually committed to goal, or only under a bare arrest. But the officer cannot be thus punished, till the original delinquent is actually found guilty or convicted by verdict, confession, or outlawry; otherwise, it might happen that the officer should be punished for treason or felony, and the party escaping turn out to be an innocent man. But before the conviction of the principal party, the officer thus neglecting his duty, may be fined and imprisoned for a misdemeanor. 4 *Black.* 129.

If any person shall convey or cause to be conveyed into any goal, any *disguise*, *instrument*, or *arms*, proper to facilitate the escape of prisoners, attainted or convicted of treason or felony, *although no escape or attempt to escape be made*; such person so offending,

offending, and convicted, shall be deemed guilty of felony and be transported for seven years. 16 G. II. c. 31.

ESCHEAT, in our law, denotes an obstruction of the course of descent, and a consequent determination of the tenure, by some unforeseen contingency; in which case, the land naturally results back, by a kind of reversion, to the original grantor, or lord of the fee. 2 *Black*, 244.

Escheat happens either for *want of heirs* of the person last seized, or by his *attainder* for a crime by him committed; in which latter case, the blood is tainted, stained, or corrupted, and the inheritable quality of it is thereby extinguished.

For want of heirs, is where the tenant dies without any relations on the part of any of his ancestors, or where he dies without any relations of those ancestors, paternal or maternal, from whom his estate descended; or where he dies without any relations of the whole blood. Bastards are also incapable of inheritance; and therefore if there be no other claimant than such illegitimate children, the land shall escheat to the lord; and, as bastards cannot be heirs to themselves, so neither can they have any heirs, but those of their own bodies, and therefore if a bastard purchase lands, and die seized thereof without issue and intestate, the land shall *escheat* to the lord of the fee. Aliens also, that is persons born out of the king's allegiance, are incapable of taking by descent; and unless naturalized, are also incapable of taking by purchase; and therefore, if there be no natural born subjects to claim, such lands shall in like manner escheat.

By attainder for treason or other felony, the blood of the person attainded is corrupted and stained, and the original donation of the feud is thereby determined, it being always granted to the vassal on the implied condition of his well demeaning himself. In consequence of which corruption and extinction of hereditary blood, the land of all felons would immediately revert in the lord, but that the superior law of forfeiture intervenes, and intercepts it in his passage; in case of treason, for ever; in case of other felony, for only a year and a day; after which time it goes to the lord, in a regular course of escheat. 2 *Black*, c. 15.

ESCHEATOR, was an ancient officer, so called because his office was properly to look to *escheats*, *wardships*, and other casualties belonging to the crown. This office having its chief dependance on the courts of wards is now out of date. *Co. Lit.* 13 b. 4 *Inst.* 225.

ESCUAGE, signifies a kind of knight's service, called *service of the shield,* whereby the tenant is bound to follow his lord into the *Scotch* or *Welsh* wars, at his own expense. He who held a whole knight's fee, was bound to serve with horse and arms forty days at his own charge, and he who held half a knight's fee, was to serve twenty days.

ESQUIRE, is a name of dignity, next above the common title of *gentleman,* and below a *knight*; heretofore it signified one that was attendant, and had his employment as a servant, waiting on such as had the order of knighthood, bearing their shields, and helping him to horse and such like.

All *Irish* and foreign peers, are only *esquires* in our law, and must be so named in all legal proceedings. 1 *Black.* 406.

ESQUIRES OF THE KING, are such who have the title by creation: these when they are created, have a collar of SS. put about their necks, and a pair of silver spurs is bestowed on them; and they were wont to bear before the prince in war, a shield or lance. There are four *esquires* of the king's body to attend on his majesty's person.

ESSENDI QUIETUM DE TELONIO, a writ that lies for citizens and burgesses of any city or town, that have a charter or prescription to exempt them from toll through the whole realm, if it happened to be any where exacted of them.

ESSOIN, signifies the allegation of an excuse for him that is summoned, or sought for; to appear and answer to an action real, or to perform suit to a court baron, upon just cause of absence. The causes that serve to *essoin* any man summoned are the following:

ESSOIN DE MALO LECTI, is when the defendant is sick in bed.

ESSOIN DE MALO VENIENDI, is when the defendant is infirm in body, and not able to come.

ESSOIN DE MALO VILLÆ, is when the defendant appears in court the first day, but departed without pleading, and being afterwards surprised by sickness, or other infirmity, cannot attend the court, but sends two *essoiners,* who openly protest in court that he is detained by sickness in such a village, that he cannot

come

come, *pro lucrari et pro perdere*; and this must be admitted for full proof, without any farther surety, for it is incumbent on the plaintiff to prove whether the *essoin* be true or not.

ESSOIN PER SERVITIUM REGIS, is when the defendant is in the king's service.

ESSOIN DE ULTRA MARE, when the defendant is beyond sea.

ESSONIO DE MALO LECTI, a writ directed to the sheriff, for the sending of four lawful knights to view one that had *essoined* himself, *de malo lecti*.

ESTABLISHMENT OF DOWER. The assurance of dower made to the wife by the husband, or his friends, before or at marriage; and *assignment* of dower, is the setting it out by the heir afterwards, according to the establishment.

ESTATE, signifies such inheritance, freehold, term for years, tenancy by statute merchant, staple, elegit, or the like, as any man hath in lands and tenements. Estates are *real*, of lands, tenements, &c. or *personal* of goods, or chattels; otherwise distinguished into freeholds that descend to the heir, and chattels which go to the executors. *Co. Lit.* 315.

Of estate in fee-simple; an estate in fee-simple, is an estate lands, tenements, lordships, advowsons, commons, estovers, and all hereditaments, to a man and his heirs for ever: also, where a corporation sole or aggregate arecapable of holding in succession, and lands are given to them and their successors, thy are said to have a fee-simple. 2 *Bac. Abr.* 249.

Of estate in tail; an estate is said to be *intailed*, when it is ascertained what issue shall inherit it.

What things may be intailed by the statute of intails. The statute makes use of the word *tenementum*, and therefore the estate to be intailed, may be as well incorporeal as corporeal inheritances, because the word *tenementum*, comprehends the one as well as the other, and consequently, not only lands may be intailed, but all rents, commons, estovers, or other profits arising from lands. *Co. Lit.* 19, *b.* 20, *a.*

What words create an estate tail. When the notion of succession prevailed, it was necessary in feudal donations to use the word *heirs*, to distinguish such descendible feud from that, which was granted only for life; but as to the word *body*, it was necessary to make use of that in the donation, but it might be expres-

 sed

sed by any equivalent words, and therefore a gift to a man, and *hæredibus de se*, or *de carne quo sibi contigerit habere*, or *procreavit*, is a good estate tail; for these sufficiently circumscribe the word *heirs*, to the descendants of the feudatory: and the reason of the difference is, for that inheritances being only derived from the law, and the law requires the word *heirs*, that comprehends the whole notion of such legal representation; but the limiting the inheritance to the descendants of this or the other body, is only the particular intention of the person that forms the gift, and therefore the law leaves every man, to express himself in such manner as may manifest that intention. 2 *Bac. Abr.* 259.

Of tenant in tail changing his estate. The statute *de donis*, affecting a perpetuity, restrained the donee in tail, either from alienating or charging his estate tail; and by that act the tenant in tail, was likewise to leave the land to his heirs, as he received it from the donor; and upon that statute, the heir in tail might have avoided any alienation or incumbrance of his ancestor; and as the law stood upon that act, so might he in reversion, when the heirs of the donee failed, which were inheritable to the gift. The crown long struggled to break through the perpetuity which was established by this law; and in the reign of Ed. IV. we find the pretended recompence given against the vouchee in the common recovery, to be allowed an equivalent for the estate tail; and because this recompence was to go in succession as the land in tail should have done, therefore they allowed the recovery to bar the reversion as well as the issue in tail, because he in the reversion was to have the recompense in failure of issue of the donee. 2 *Bac. Abr.* 265.

ESTOPPEL, an impediment or bar of action, arising from the act of him that either hath, or might have had his action. For example; a tenant makes a feoffment by collusion to one, the lord accepts the services of the feoffee; by this he debars himself of the worship of the tenant's heir. There are three kinds of *estoppels*, viz.

By matter of record, as by letters patent, fine, recovery, pleading, taking of continuance, confession, imparlance, warrant of attorney, admittance.

By matter in writing, as by deed indented, by making of an acquittance

quittance by deed indented or deed poll, by defeasance by deed indented, or deed poll.

By matter in pais, as by livery, by entry, by acceptance of rent, by partition, and by acceptance of an estate. *Co. Lit.* 352.

Every *estoppel*, because it concludes a man to alledge the truth, must be *certain to every intent*, and not to be taken by argument or inference. *Id.*

ESTOVERS, is a liberty of taking necessary wood for the use or furniture of an house or farm. And this any tenant may take from off the land let or demised to him, without waiting for any leave, assignment, or appointment of the lessor, unless he be restrained by special covenant to the contrary. 2 *Black.* 35.

ESTRAYS AND WAIFS. *Estrays* are where any horses, sheep, hogs, beasts, or swans, or any beast that is not wild, come into a lordship, and are not owned by any man. *Kitch.* 23.

The reason of estray is, because when no person can make title to the thing, the law gives it to the king, if the owner do not claim it within a year and a day.

Waifs are goods which are stolen, and waved, or left by the felon, on his being pursued, for fear of being apprehended; and forfeited to the king or lord of the manor; and though *waifs*, are generally spoken of things stolen; yet if a man be pursued with hue and cry as a felon, and he flies and leaves *his own goods*, these will be forfeited as goods stolen: but they are properly the fugitive's goods, and not forfeited, till it be found before the coroner, or otherwise of record, that he fled for the felony. 2 *Haw.* 450.

Waifs and *strays*, were *anciently* the property of the finders, by the law of nature; and afterwards the property of the king by the law of nations. *Dalt. Sher.* 79.

Waifs and *strays*, not claimed within the year and day, are the lord's. For where the lord has a beast a year and a day, and it has been cried in the church and markets, the property is changed. *Kitch.* 80.

But it must be a year and a day from the time of proclamation, and not from the time of seizure; for it does not become an *estray* till after the first proclamation. 11 *Mod.* 89.

ESTREAT, is a true copy or note of some original writing on

record, and especially of fines and amercements imposed in the rolls of a court, and *extracted* or drawn out from thence, and certified into the court of exchequer; whereupon, process is awarded to the sheriff to levy the same.

ESTREPEMENT or ESTREPAMENT, the spoil made by a tenant for life, upon any lands or woods to the prejudice of the reversioner.

Estrepement, also signifies a writ, which lies in two cases; the one is, when the person having an action depending (as a *formedon*, or *dum fuit infra ætatem*, or *writ of right*, or any other) wherein the demandant is not to recover damages, sues to inhibit the tenant from making waste during the suit. The other is for the demandant, that is adjudged to recover seisin of the land in question, and before execution sued by the writ *habere facias seisinam*, for fear of waste to be made before he can get possession, he then sues out this writ.

EVES-DROPPERS, are such as stand under walls or windows, by night or day, to hear news, and to carry them to others, to cause strife and contention among neighbours. These are evil members in the commonwealth, and therefore by stat. *Westminster* 1. c. 33, are to be punished: and this misdemeanor is presentable and punishable in the court leet.

EVIDENCE, is the testimony adduced before a court or magistrate of competent jurisdiction, by which such court or magistrate are enabled to ascertain any fact which may be litigated between the parties.

This may be of two kinds, viz. *written* or *verbal*, the former by deeds, bonds, or other written documents, the latter by witnesses examined *viva voce*.

Evidence may be further divided into *absolute* and *presumptive*; the former is direct, in positive or absolute affirmance or denial of any particular fact; the latter collateral, and from the conduct of the parties, affords an inference that such a particular fact, did or did not occur.

The party making an affirmative allegation which is denied by his adversary, is in general required to prove it, unless indeed a man be charged with not doing an act, which by law he is required to do; for here a different rule must necessarily prevail, and the rule is, that the evidence must be applied to the particu-

lar

lar fact in dispute; and therefore no evidence not relating to the issue, or in some manner connected with it, can be received; nor can the character of either party, unless put in issue by the very proceeding itself, be called in question; for the cause is to be decided on its own circumstances, and not to be prejudiced by any matter foreign to it.

It is an established principle, that the best evidence the nature of the case will admit shall be produced, for if it appear, that better evidence might have been brought forward, the very circumstance of its being withheld, furnishes a suspicion that it would have prejudiced the party in whose power it is, had he produced it. Thus if a written contract be in the custody of the party, no verbal testimony can be received of its contents.

The law never gives credit to the bare assertion of any one, however high his rank or pure his morals; but requires (except in particular cases with respect to quakers) the sanction of an oath, the personal attendance of the party in court that he may be examined and cross-examined by the different parties; and therefore in cases depending on parole or verbal evidence, the testimony of persons who are themselves conversant with the facts they relate, must be produced, the law paying no regard, except under very special circumstances, to the hearsay evidence. Thus in some cases, the memorandum in writing made at the time, by a person since deceased, in the ordinary way of his business, and which is corroborated by other circumstances, will be admitted as evidence of the fact.

What a party himself has been heard to say, does not fall within the objection. As to hearsay evidence, any thing therefore which the party admits, or which another asserts in his presence, and he does not contradict, is received as evidence against him; but what is said by his wife, or any other member of his family in his absence, will be rejected.

But a distinction must be made between admission, and an offer of compromise, after a dispute has arisen. An offer to pay a sum of money in order to get rid of an action, is not received in evidence of a debt, because such offers are made to stop litigation, without regard to the question whether any thing, or what is due.

Admission of particular articles before arbitration are also good evidence,

evidence, for they are not made with a view to compromise, but the parties are contesting their rights as much as they could do on a trial.

In cases where positive and direct evidence is not to be looked for, the proof of circumstance and fact consistent with the claim of one party, and inconsistent with that of the other, is deemed sufficient to enable the jury, under the direction of the court of justice, to presume the particular fact, which is the subject of controversy; for the mind comparing the circumstances of the particular case, judges therefrom as to the probability of the story, and for want of better evidence, draws a conclusion from that before it.

Written evidence has been divided into two classes; the one that which is public, the other private; and this first, has been subdivided into matters of record, and others of an inferior nature.

The memorials of the legislature, such as acts of parliament, and other proceedings of the two houses, where acting in a legislative character; and judgment of the king's superior courts of justice, are denominated records, and are so respected by the law, that no evidence whatsoever can be received in contradiction of them; but these are not permitted to be removed from place to place, to serve a private purpose, and are therefore proved by copies of them, which in the absence of the original, is the next best evidence.

Of persons incompetent to give evidence. All persons who are examined as witnesses, must be fully possessed of their understanding; that is such an understanding as enables them to retain in memory, the events of which they have been witnesses, and give them a knowledge of right and wrong.

A conviction of treason or felony, and every species thereof, such as perjury, conspiracy, barratry, &c. prevents a man when convicted of them, from being examined in a court of justice. When a man is convicted of any of the offences before mentioned, and judgment entered up, he is for ever after incompetent to give evidence, unless the stigma be removed, which in case of a conviction of perjury, on the stat. of 5 Eliz. c. 9. can never be by any means short of a reversal of the judgment, for the statute has in this case, made his incompetency part of his punishment, but if a man be convicted of perjury, or any other offence at the common law, and the king pardons him in particular, or grants a general pardon to all such convicts, this restores him to his credit, and the judgment no longer forms an objection to his testimony; but an actual pardon must be shewn under the great seal, the warrant for it under the king's sign manual not being sufficient. To found this objection to the testimony of a witness, the party who intends to make it, should be prepared with a copy of the judgment regularly entered upon the verdict of conviction, for until such judgment be entered, the witness is not deprived of his legal privileges.

Persons may also be incompetent witnesses, by reason of their interest in the cause. The rule which has the most extensive operation in the exclusion of witnesses, and which has been found most difficult in its application, is that which prevents persons interested in the event of a suit, unless in a few excepted cases of evident necessity, from being witness in it. Of late years the courts have endeavoured, as far as possible consistent with authorities, to let the objection go to the credit rather than the competency of a witness; and the general rule now established is, that no objection can be made to a witness on this ground, unless he be distinctly interested, that is, unless he may be immediately benefitted or injured by the event of the suit, or unless the verdict to be obtained by his evidence, or given against it, will be evidence for or against him in another action, in which he may afterwards be a party; any smaller degree of interest, as the possibility that he may be liable to an action in a certain event, or that, standing in a similar situation with the party by whom he is called, the decision in that cause, may by possibility influence the minds of a jury in his own, or the like, though it furnish a strong argument against his credibility, does not destroy his competency.

On the question, how far persons who have been defrauded of securities, or injured by a perjury or other crime, can be witnessess in prosecuting for those offences, the event of which might possibly exonerate them from the obligation they are charged to have entered into, or restore to them money which they have been obliged to pay; the general principle now established is this, the question in a criminal prosecution or personal act being

the

the same with that in a civil cause, in which the witnesses are interested, goes generally to the credit, unless the judgment in the prosecution where they are witnesses, can be given in evidence in this cause wherein they are interested. But though this is the general rule, an exception to it seems to be established in the case of forgery; for many cases have been decided, that a person whose hand-writing has been forged to an instrument, whereby if good he would be charged with a sum of money, or one who has paid money in consequence of such forgery, cannot be a witness on the indictment. In cases where the party injured cannot by possibility derive any benefit from the verdict in the prosecution, as in indictments for assault, and the like personal injury, his competence has never been doubted. It is a general rule that a party cannot be examined as a witness, for he is in the highest degree interested in the event of it; but where a man is not in point of fact interested, but only a nominal party, as where members of a charitable institution are defendants in their corporal character, there is no objection to an individual member being examined as a witness for the corporation, for in this case he is giving evidence for the public body only, and not for himself as an individual. *Peake's* N P. *Cas.* 153. *Bul.* N. P. 293.

But instances sometimes occur, in which persons substantially interested, and even parties in a cause, are permitted to be examined from the necessity of the case, and absolute impossibility of procuring other evidence.

In an action on the statute of *Winton*, the party robbed is a witness: and on the same principle of necessity it has been holden, that persons who become interested in the common course of business, and who alone can have knowledge of the fact, may be called as witnesses to prove it, as in the case of a servant who has been paid money, or a porter who in the way of his business, delivers out or receives parcels, though the evidence whereby he charges another with the money or goods, exonerates himself from his liability to account to his master for them; for if this interest were to exclude testimony, there would never be evidence of any such facts. *Bul.* N. P. 289.

As no one can be witness for himself, it follows of course husband and wife, whose interest the law has united, are incompetent to give evidence on behalf of each other, or of any person

whose

whose interest is the same, and the law, considering the policy of marriage, also prevents them giving evidence against each other, for it would be hard that a wife, who could not be a witness for her husband, should be a witness against him; such a rule would occasion implacable divisions and quarrels between them. In like manner, as the law respects the private peace of men, it considers the confidential communications made for the purpose of defence in a court of justice. By permitting a party to intrust the cause in the hands of a third person, it establishes a confidence and trust between the client and person so employed.

Barristers and attornies, to whom facts are related professionally during a cause, or in contemplation of it, are neither obliged nor permitted to disclose the facts so divulged during the pendency of that cause, or at any future time; and if a foreigner, in communication with his attorney, have recourse to an interpreter, he is equally bound to secrecy.

Where a man has by putting his name to an instrument, given a sanction to it, he has been held by some judges to be precluded, or stopped from giving any evidence in a court of justice which may invalidate it; as in the case of a party to a bill of exchange or promisory note, who has been said not to be an admissible witness to destroy it, on the grounds that it would enable two persons to combine together; and by holding out a false credit to the world, deceive and impose on mankind. On this principle it was held, that an indorser could not be a witness to prove notes usurious, in an action or a bond founded on such notes, though the notes themselves had been delivered up, on the execution of the bond. At one time this seems to have been understood as a general principle applicable to all instruments; but in a case where an underwriter of a policy of insurance, was called to prove the instrument void as against another underwriter, and objected to on this ground; the court declared, that it extended only to *negotiable instruments*, and he was admitted to give evidence destructive of the policy.

When a witness is not liable to any legal objection, he is first examined by the counsel for the party on whose behalf he comes to give evidence, as to his knowledge of the fact he is to prove. This examination in cases of any intricacy, is a duty of no small

importance

importance in the counsel; for as on the one hand, the law will not allow him to put what are called leading questions, viz. to form them in such a way as would instruct the witnesses in the answers he is to give; so on the other, he should be careful that he make himself sufficiently understood by the witness, who may otherwise omit some material circumstance of the case.

The party examined must depose those facts only of which he has an immediate knowledge and recollection; he may refresh his memory with a copy taken by himself from a day-book; and if he can then speak positively as to his recollection, it is sufficient; but if he have no recollection further than finding the entry in his book, the book itself must be produced. Where the defendant had signed acknowledgments of having received money, in a day-book of the plaintiff, and the plaintiff's clerk afterwards read over the items to him, and he acknowledged them all right, it was held, that the witness might refresh his memory by referring to the books, although there were no stop to the items on which the receipt was written, for this was only proving a verbal acknowledgment, and not a written receipt.

Lord Ellenborough, upon the authority of Lord Chief Justice Tully, has recently laid down a very important doctrine, viz. that no witness shall be bound to answer any question which tends to degrade himself, or to shew him to be infamous.

EXACTION, a wrong done by an officer, or one pretending to have authority, by taking a reward or fee, for that which the law allows not.

EXAMINATION, justices before whom any person shall be brought for manslaughter or felony, or for suspicion thereof, before they commit such prisoner, shall take his examination, and information of those who bring him, of the fact and circumstances; and as much thereof as shall be material to prove the felony, shall be put in writing within two days after the examination, and the same shall certify in such manner as they should do, if such prisoner had been bailed, upon such pain, as in the act 1 & 2 P. & M. c. 13. is limited.

EXAMINERS IN CHANCERY, are two officers who examine upon oath witnesses produced on either side in *London*, or near it, upon such interrogatories as the parties to any suit exhibit

hibit for that purpose. In the country witnesses are examined by commissioners, usually attornies not concerned in the cause, on the parties joining in commission, &c.

EXCEPTION, is a stop or stay to any action. In law proceedings, it is a denial of a matter alledged in bar to an action; and in chancery, it is what is alledged against the sufficiency of an answer.

EXCEPTION TO EVIDENCE, at common law a writ of error, lay for an error in law, apparent on the record, or for an error in fact, where either party died before judgment; yet it lay not for an error in law not appearing on the record. 2 *Inst.* 426.

By the stat. of *Westminster*, 2. when one impleaded before any of the justices, alledges an exception, praying they will allow it, and if they will not, if he that alledges the exception writes the same, and requires the justices will put thereto their seals, the justices shall so do, and if upon complaint made of the justice, the king cause the record to come before him, and the exception be not found in the roll, and the plaintiff shew the written exception, with the seal of the justices thereto put, the justice shall be commanded to appear at a certain day, either to confess or deny his seal, and if he cannot deny his seal, they shall proceed to judgment according to the exception, as it ought to be allowed or disallowed.

The statute extends to the plaintiff as well as the defendant, also to him who comes in *loco tenentis*, as one that prays to be received, or the vouchee; and in all actions, whether real, personal, or mixt. 2 *Inst.* 427.

EXCEPTION IN DEEDS AND WRITINGS, the exception is a clause whereby the donor, feoffor, grantor, or other person contracting, excepts, or takes a particular thing out of a general thing granted or conveyed. The thing excepted is exempted, and does no pass by the grant, neither is it parcel of the thing granted; as if a manor be granted, excepting one acre thereof, hereby in judgment of law, that acre is severed from the manor. 1 *Wood's Convey*. 241.

Exception, must be of such a thing as he who makes it may have, and does belong to him.

It must not be the whole thing granted, but part thereof only.

The thing that is excepted, must be part of the thing granted before, and not of some other thing.

The thing excepted, must be of such a thing as may be severed from the thing granted, and not inseparable incidents.

It must be of a particular thing out of a general, or of an entire thing, and not of a particular out of a particular, or the whole thing itself granted.

An exception, must be conformable to the grant, and not repugnant thereto; and

The thing excepted must be certainly described and set down.

EXCHANGE, an exchange is a mutual grant of equal interests, the one in consideration of the other. *2 Black.* 323.

An exchange may be made of things that lie either in grant or in livery. But no livery of seisin, even in exchanges of freehold, is necessary to perfect the conveyance: for each party stands in the place of the other, and occupies his right, and each of them hath already had corporal possession of his own land. But entry must be made on both sides; for if either party die before the entry, exchange is void, for want of sufficient notoriety. *Id.*

In exchange, the estates of both parties should be equal; that is if the one hath a fee simple in the one land, the other should have like estate in the other land; and if the one have fee-tail in the one land, the other ought to have the like estate in the other land: and so of other estates. But it is not material in the exchange, that the lands be of equal value, but only that they be equal in kind and manner of the estate given and taken. 1 *Inst.* 51.

Exchange among merchants, is a commerce of money, or a bartering or exchanging the money of one city or country for that of another: money, in this sense, is either real or imaginary; *real,* any real specie current in any country at a certain price, at which it passes by the authority of the state, and of its own intrinsic value; by *imaginary* money, is understood all the denominations made use of to express any sum of money, which is not the just value of any real specie.

Whatever may be the denomination or value of the coin circulating in any country, there is always a rate of exchange, founded upon its intrinsic value, which is called par, between every two countries; but in proportion as the demand may be greater or smaller between one country and another, bills or money become plenty or scarce. When in the market or upon 'Change, which is the money-market, the bills drawn are in greater quantities than the remittances, then they sink in value, and the rate of exchange is said to be against the place. When on the contrary there are more bills wanted than can easily be obtained, the rate of exchange is said to be favourable, and is above par.

Re-exchange, is when the holder of a bill, finds it not paid by the acceptor, then it becomes necessary to take those steps which the circumstances of the case, the law of the land, and the usage of merchants authorize.

The holder of a bill, upon payment being refused, may lawfully take up from a banker, in the place where it is payable, the amount of the bill, and give in return a bill payable upon sight, upon the party from whom the first bill was received, or upon any other person. If he be obliged in consequence of the course of exchange, and the balance being in favour of cash, to pay a price for the money which he receives, that price is the *re-exchange*, which must be compensated by the preceding parties to the bill.

EXCHANGE OF CHURCH LIVINGS, is where two persons having procured licence from the ordinary to treat of and exchange, do by one instrument in writing, agree to exchange their benefices, being both spiritual, and in order thereunto resign them into the hands of the ordinary: such *exchange* being executed, the resignations are good. *Wats.* c. 4.

These exchanges are now seldom used.

EXCHEQUER. This which is a court of law and equity, is a very ancient court of record, established by *William the Conqueror*, as a part of the *aula regis*, though regulated and reduced to its present state by Ed. I. and intended principally to order the revenues of the crown, and to recover the king's debts and duties.

The court consists of two divisions, viz. the receipt of the exchequer, which manages the royal revenue; and the judicial, which is again subdivided into a court of equity, and a court of common law.

The court of equity is held in the exchequer, before the lord treasurer, the chancellor of the exchequer, the chief baron, and three *puisné* barons. The primary and original business of this court was to call the king's debtors to account, by bill filed by the attorney general, and to recover any lands, tenements, or hereditaments, goods, chattels, or other profits or benefits, belonging to the crown.

This court, which was established merely for the benefit of the king's accountant, is thrown open; and now, by suggestion of privilege, any person may be admitted to sue here, as well as the king's accountant.

An appeal from the equity side of this court, lies immediately to the house of peers; but from the common law side, pursuant to 31 Ed. III. c. 12. a writ of error must first be brought into the court of exchequer chamber, from whence, in the dernier resort, there lies an appeal to the House of Lords.

EXCHEQUER CHAMBER, this court has no original jurisdiction, but is merely a court of appeal, to correct the errors of other jurisdictions; and consists of the lord chancellor, the lord treasurer, with the justices of the king's-bench and common-pleas. In imitation of this, a second court of exchequer-chamber was erected by 27 Eliz. c. 8. consisting of the justices of the common-pleas, and the barons of the exchequer; before whom writs of error may be brought, to reverse judgments in certain suits commenced originally in the court of king's-bench. Into the exchequer-chamber, are sometimes adjourned from the other courts, such causes, as the judges upon argument find to be of great weight and difficulty, before any judgment is given upon them in the court.

EXCISE, is an inland imposition, sometimes paid upon the consumption of the commodity, or frequently upon the retail sale, which is the last stage previous to the consumption.

For more easily levying the revenue of the excise, the kingdom of *England* and *Wales*, is divided into about fifty *collections*, some of which are called by the names of particular counties, others by the names of great towns; where one county is divided into several collections, or where a collection comprehends the contiguous parts of several counties, every such collection is subdivided into several *districts*, within which there is a *supervisor*; and each district is again subdivided into *outrides* and *foot-walks*, within each of which there is a *gauger* or surveying officer.

The commissioners or sub-commissioners in their respective circuits

cuits and divisions, shall constitute, under their hands and seals, so many gaugers as they shall find needful.

Arrears of duties. By several acts of parliament, all articles in the possession of persons subject to the excise laws, together with all the materials and utensils of whatsoever description, are made liable for the arrears of duties, whether these be single or double duties; and if a trader, being in arrears for the single duties, become a bankrupt, and is convicted after the assignment of his effects, the double duties are a lien upon the exciseable commodities, utensils, and materials in the hands of his assignees, and the commissioners or magistrates, may authorize the penalty to be levied upon all such commodities, and all the materials, preparations, utensils, and vessels for making thereof, in the custody of the bankrupt, or any person or persons in trust for him. 2 *Doug.* 411.

Bonds, for the exportation of exciseable commodities, are to be taken by officers of excise, and they are to be given generally upon all exciseable articles, at the place where exported.

Forgery, of any stamps, licences, certificates, permits, or any other excise documents, is by various statutes made a capital felony.

Licences, in all cases where licences are required, the licence will only sanction the business carried on in that particular place, for which such licence was granted; but when the business is carried on by partners, one licence will be sufficient to cover the firm.

Officers of excise. The officers of excise are to be appointed, and may be dismissed, replaced, or altered, by the commissioners under their hands and seals; their salaries are allowed and established by the treasury; and by 1 W. & M. c. 24. s. 15. if it be proved by two witnesses, that any officer has demanded or taken any money, or other reward whatever, except of the king, such offender shall forfeit his office.

By several statutes, no process can be sued out against any officers of excise, for any act done in the execution of his office, until one month after notice given, specifying the cause of action, and the name and abode of the person who is to begin, and the attorney who is to conduct the action; and within one month after such notice, the officer may tender amends, and plead such tender in bar; and having tendered insufficient or no amends, he may with leave of the court, *before issue joined,* pay money into court.

Officers of excise, are empowered to search at all times of the day, entered warehouses, or places for tea, coffee, &c. But private houses can only be searched upon oath of the suspicion before a commissioner or justice of peace, who can by their warrant authorize a search.

Permits, persons dealing in exciseable commodities are entitled to permits for removing the same to different places in certain quantities, and under certain regulations. These permits are written upon a peculiar species of paper, and manufactured expressly for the purpose; and by 23 Geo. III. c. 70. s. 11. no permit paper is to be delivered out before it shall be filled up agreeable to the request note of a trader; and officers knowingly granting any false permit, making false entries in the counter part thereof, or receiving any commodities into stock with a false or forged permit, are to be transported for seven years.

Samples. Officers of excise, are by various acts empowered to take samples of exciseable commodities, paying the prices therein regulated for the same.

Seizures When an officer makes a seizure of any spirits or other articles, he must lay his hand on the casks, vessels, &c. so seized, and declare that he seizes such spirits, &c. and the casks or vessels containing the same, for the use of his majesty and of himself; but if the officer happen to be alone when he makes such seizure, he must afterwards in the presence of witnesses, again lay his hand on such cask, vessel, &c. and repeat the former declaration of seizure.

All informations on seizures, must be laid in the names of the officers making the same.

By 41 Geo. III. c. 96. commissioners of excise are empowered to make restitution of exciseable goods.

Scales and weights. By various acts of parliament, traders subject to the excise laws, are to keep just and sufficient scales and weights, under penalty of 100l. for every such offence, and the scales and weights may be seized by the officer.

Traders, manufacturers, and dealers liable to the excise duties, are to assist the officers in weighing stock; and forcibly obstruct-

ing,

ing, or using any act or contrivance to prevent or impede the officer from taking a true account, incurs a penalty of 100l. *For particulars respecting the excise laws, see The Complete Abridgment of* the Excise Laws.

EXCOMMUNICATION, is the highest ecclesiastical censure, which can be pronounced by a spiritual judge against a christian; for thereby he is excluded from the body of the church, and disabled to bring any action, or sue any person in the common law courts. *Co. Lit.* 133.

The sentence of *excommunication*, was instituted originally for preserving the purity of the church; and it seems agreed, that wherever the spiritual court hath jurisdiction in any cause, and the party refuses to appear to their citation, or after sentence, being admonished to obey their decree, that he may be excommunicated. 1 *Rol. Abr.* 883.

A person excommunicated, is thereby disabled to be a witness in any cause; he cannot be attorney or procurator for another; he is to be turned out of the church by the churchwardens, and not to be allowed christian burial. *Gibs. Cod.* 435.

The sentence of *excommunication*, can only be pronounced by the bishop, or other person in holy orders, being a master of arts at least; also the priest's name pronouncing such sentence, is to be expressed in the instrument issuing under seal out of the court. *Gibs. Cod.* 1095.

EXCOMMUNICATO CAPIENDO, a writ directed to the sheriff, for apprehending him who stands obstinately *excommunicated*, forty days; for such an one not seeking absolution, hath, or may have, his contempt certified into the chancery; whence issueth this writ, for imprisoning him without bail or main-prize until he conform. 5 Eliz. c. 23.

EXCOMMUNICATO DELIBERANDO, a writ to the sheriff, for the delivery of an *excommunicate* person out of prison, upon certificate of the ordinary, of his conformity to the jurisdiction ecclesiastical. F. N. B. 63.

EXCOMMUNICATO RECIPIENDO, a writ whereby persons *excommunicate*, being for their obstinacy committed to prison, and unlawfully delivered thence, before they have given caution to obey the authority of the church, are commanded to be sought for and imprisoned again.

EXECUTION is a judicial writ, grounded on the judgment of the

the court from whence it issues: and is supposed to be granted by the court at the request of the party, at whose suit it is issued, to give him satisfaction on the judgment which he hath obtained: and therefore an execution cannot be sued out in one court; upon a judgment obtained in another. *Impey*, K. B.

Executions in actions where money is recovered, as a debt or damages, are of five sorts: 1. against the *body* of the defendant; 2. or against his *goods* or *chattels*; 3. against his *goods* and the *profits* of his lands; 4. against the *goods* and the *possession* of his land; 5. against all three, his *body*, *lands*, and *goods*. 3 *Black*. 414. See *Capias ad satisfaciendum*, *fieri facias*, *levari facias*, and *elegit*.

EXECUTION OF CRIMINALS, must be according to the judgment; and the king cannot alter a judgment from hanging to beheading, because no execution can be warranted, unless it be pursuant to the judgment. 3 *Inst*. 52.

Execution of criminals is the completion of human punishment; and this in all cases, as well capital as otherwise, must be performed by the legal officer, the sheriff, or his deputy. 4 *Black*. 405.

EXECUTIONE FACIENDA IN WITHERNAMIUM, a writ that lies for taking his cattle, who formerly had conveyed out of the county the cattle of another: so that the bailiff, having authority from the sheriff to replevy the cattle so conveyed away, could not execute his charge.

EXECUTIONE JUDICII, a writ which lies where judgment is given in any court of record, and the sheriff or bailiff neglecting to do execution of the judgment, the party shall then have this writ directed to the said sheriff or bailiff; and if they shall not do execution, he shall have an *alias*, and *pluries*. And if upon this writ execution is not done, or some reasonable cause returned why it is delayed, the judges of the court may amerce them.

EXECUTOR, is a person appointed by the testator, to carry into execution his will and testament after his decease. The regular mode of appointing an executor, is by naming him expressly in the will; but any words indicating an intention of the testator to appoint an executor, will be deemed a sufficient appointment.

Any person capable of making a will, is also capable of being an executor; but in some cases, persons who are incapable of making a will, may nevertheless act as executors, as infants, or married

married women; to obviate however, inconveniences which have occurred respecting the former, it is enacted by stat. 38 G. III. c. 89, that where an infant is sole executor, administration, with the will annexed, shall be granted to the guardian of such infant, or such other person, as the spiritual court shall think fit, until such infant shall have attained the age of twenty-one; when, and not before, probate of the will shall be granted him.

An executor derives his authority from the will and not from the probate, and is therefore authorized to do many acts in execution of the will, even before it is proved, such as releasing, paying, or receiving of debts, assenting to licences, &c. but he cannot proceed until he have obtained probate.

If an executor die before probate, administration must be taken out with the will annexed; but if an executor die, his executor, will be executor to the first testator, and no fresh probate will be needed. It will be sufficient if one only of the executors prove the will; but if all refuse to prove, they cannot afterwards administer, or in any respect act as executors.

If an executor become a bankrupt, the court of chancery will appoint a receiver of the testator's effects, as it will also upon the application of a creditor, if he appear to be wasting the assets.

If an executor once administer, he cannot afterwards renounce; and the ordinary may in such case, issue process to compel him to prove the will. 1 *Mod.* 213.

If an executor refuse to take upon him the execution of the will, he shall lose the legacy therein contained.

If a creditor constitute his debtor his executor, this is at law a discharge of the debt, whether the executor act or not, provided however, there be assets sufficient to discharge the debts of the testator.

The first duty of an executor or administrator is to bury the deceased in a suitable manner; and if the executor exceed what is necessary in this respect, it will be a waste of the substance of the testator.

The next thing to be done by the executor, is to prove the will, which may be done either in the common form, by taking the oath to make due distribution, &c. or in a more solemn mode, by witnesses to its execution.

By stat. 37 G. III. c. 9, s. 10, every person who shall administer

nister the personal estate of any person dying without proving the will of the deceased, or taking out letters of administation within six calendar months after such person's decease, shall forfeit 50l.

Upon proving the will, the original is to be deposited in the registry of the ordinary, by whom a copy is made upon parchment under his seal, and delivered to the executor or administrator, together with a certificate of its having been proved before him, and this is termed the probate.

If all the goods of the deceased lie within the same jurisdiction, the probate is to be made before the ordinary or bishop of the diocese, where the deceased resided; but if he had goods and chattels to the value of 5l. in two distinct dioceses or jurisdictions, the will may be proved before the metropolitan or archbishop of the province in which the deceased died.

An executor, by virtue of the will of the testator, has an interest in all the goods and chattels, whether real or personal, in possession or in action of the deceased; and all goods and effects coming to his hands will be the assets to make him chargeable to creditors and legatees.

An executor or administrator, stands personally responsible for the due discharge of his duty; if, therefore the property of the deceased be lost, or through his wilful negligence become otherwise irrecoverable, he will be liable to make it good; and also where he retains money in his hands longer than is necessary, he will be chargeable not only with interest but costs, if any have been incurred.

But one executor shall not be answerable for money received, or detriment occasioned by the other, unless it have been by some act done between them jointly.

An executor or administrator, has the same remedy for recovering debts and duties, as the deceased would have had if living.

Neither an executor or administrator can maintain any action, for a personal injury done to the deceased, when such injury is of such a nature for which damages may be received: in actions however, which have their origin in breach of promise, although the suit may abate by the death of the party, yet it may be revived either by his executors or administrators, who may also sue for rent in arrear, and due to the deceased in his life time.

By

By the custom of merchants, an executor or administrator may indorse over a bill of exchange, or promissory note.

An executor or administrator may also, on the death of a lessee for years, assign over the lease, and shall not be answerable for rent after such assignment, nor shall he be liable for rent due after the lessee's death, from premises which in his life time he had assigned to another.

An executor or administrator, is bound only by such covenants in a lease, as are said to run with the land.

The executor or administrator, previous to the distribution of the property of the deceased, must take an inventory of all his goods and chattels, which must, if required, be delivered to the ordinary upon oath.

He must then collect, with all possible convenience, all the goods and effects contained in such an inventory; and whatever is so recovered that is of a saleable nature, and can be converted into money, is termed assets, and makes him responsible to such amount to the creditors, legatees, and kindred of the deceased.

The executor or administrator, having collected in the property, is to proceed to discharge the debts of the deceased, which he must do according to the following priorities, otherwise he will be personally responsible.

1. Funeral expences, charges of proving the will, and other expenditures incurred by the execution of his trust.

2. Debts due to the king on record, or by speciality.

3. Debts due by particular statutes, as by 30 C. II. c. 23. Forfeitures for not burying in woollen, money due for poor-rates, and money due to the po t-office.

4. Debts of record, as judgments, statutes, recognizances, and those recognized by a decree of a court of equity: and debts due on mortgage. 3 *Peere Wms*, 401.

5. Debts on special contract, as bonds or other instruments under seal, and also rent in arrear.

6. Debts on simple contract, viz. such as debts arising by mere verbal promise, or by writing not under seal, as notes of hand, servants' wages, &c.

The executor is bound at his peril to take notice of debts on record, but not of other special contracts, unless he receives notice.

If

If no suit be actually commenced against an executor or administrator, he may pay one creditor in equal degree the whole debt, though there should be insufficient remaining to pay the rest, and even after the commencement of a suit, he may by confessing judgment to other creditors of the same degree, give them a preference.

Executors and administrators are also allowed, amongst debts of equal degree, to pay themselves first, but they are not allowed to retain their own debt, to the prejudice of others in a higher degree; neither shall they be permitted to retain their own debts, in preference to that of their co-executor or co-administrator of equal degree, but both shall be charged in equal proportion.

A mortgage made by the testator must be discharged by the representative out of the personal estate, if there be sufficient to pay the rest of the creditors and legatees. Where such mortgage, however, was not incurred by the deceased, it is not payable out of the personal estate. See *Legacies* and *Assets*.

EXECUTORY ESTATE, estates *executed*, are when they pass presently to the person to whom conveyed, without any after-act. 2 *Inst.* 513, and leases for years, rents, annuities, conditions, &c. are called inheritances *executory*. *Id.* 293.

EXECUTORY DEVISE, is defined a future interest, which cannot vest at the death of a testator, but depends upon some contingency which must happen before it can vest. *Abr. Eq.* 186.

An executory devise differs from a remainder, in three very material points: 1. that it needs not any particular estate to support it. 2. That by it a fee-simple, or other less estate, may be limited after a fee-simple. 3. That hereby a remainder may be limited of a chattel interest, after a particular estate for life created in the same. 2 *Black*, 172.

Executory devises of terms for years. If a farmer devise his term to *A.* for life, the remainder to another, though *A.* have the whole estate (for that is in him during his life) and so no remainder can be limited over, at common law, yet is good by way of *executory devise.* 1 *Rol. Abr.* 610.

EXEMPLIFICATION OF LETTERS PATENT, a copy or duplicate of *letters patent* made from the inrollment thereof, and sealed with the great seal of *England*, which *exemplifications*, are

as

as effectual to be shewn or pleaded, as the originals themselves. See *Evidence.*

EXEMPTION, a privilege to be free from service or appearance. See *Privilege.*

EX GRAVI QUERELA, a writ that lies for him, to whom any lands or tenements in fee, within a city, town, or borough, are devised by will, and the heir of the devisor enters into them, and detains them from him. *Reg. Orig.* 244.

EXHIBIT, when a deed, acquittance, or other writing, is in a *chancery suit, exhibited* to be proved by witnesses, and the examiner writes on the back, that it was shewn to such an one at the time of his examination; this is there called an *exhibit.*

EXIGENT, a writ that lies where the defendant in an action personal cannot be found, nor any thing within that county, whereby he may be attached or distrained; and is directed to the sheriff, to proclaim and call him, five county court days one after another, charging him to appear on pain of outlawry; and if he come not at the last day's proclamation, he is said to be *quinquies exactus* (five times exacted) and then is outlawed.

This writ, lies also in an indictment of felony, where the party indicted cannot be found.

EXIGENTER, is an officer of the court of common pleas, of whom there are four in number: they make *exigents* and proclamations in all actions where process of outlawry lies.

EXILE, is either *voluntary* as where a man leaves his country upon disgust, or by *restraint,* as when forbidden by government. See *Banishment.*

EXILIUM, is spoken of in our old law books, in reference to tenants or villains being injuriously driven out, or exiled from their tenements.

EX MERO MOTU, words formally used in the king's charter, to signify that he grants them of his *own will* and *mere motion,* without petition or suggestion made by any other; and the effect of these words, are to bar all exceptions, that might be taken to the charters, &c. by alledging that the king in granting them, was abused by any false suggestion.

EX OFFICIO, is so called from the power which an officer hath, by virtue of his office, to do certain acts without being particularly applied to; as, a justice of the peace may not only grant surety of the peace at the complaint or request of any person, but he may in several instances, demand and take it *ex officio*.

EXONERATIONE SECTÆ, is a writ that lay for the king's ward, to be disburthened of all suit, &c to the county, hundred, leet, or court baron, during the time of his wardship.

EXPARTE, of one part, as in the court of *chancery*, a commission *ex-parte*, is that which is taken out and executed by *one party only*; the other party neglecting or refusing to join.

EXPARTE TALIS, a writ that lies for a bailiff, or receiver, who having auditors assigned to take his account, cannot obtain of them reasonable allowance, but is cast into prison by them. F. N. B. 129.

EXPECTANT, is used in common law with the word *fee*, and then is opposite to fee-simple. For example, lands are given to a man and his wife in *frank-marriage to have* and *to hold* to them and their heirs; in this case, they have fee-simple; but if it be given to them, and the heirs of their body, &c. they have tail, and fee *expectant*. *Kitchin*, 153.

EXPECTANCY, signifies having relation or dependance upon something future. See *Expectant*.

EXPEDITATE, in the forest laws, signifies to cut out the ball of dogs fore feet, for the preservation of the king's game. And every one who keeps a great dog not *expeditated*, forfeits three shillings and four-pence to the king. 4 *Inst.* 308.

EXPENDITORS, the stewards or sworn-officers, who supervise the repair of the banks and water-courses in *Romney Marsh*.

EXPENSIS MILITUM LEVANDIS, an ancient writ directed to the sheriff for levying the allowance for knights of the parliament.

EXPENSIS MILITUM NON LEVANDIS, a writ to prohibit the sheriff from levying any allowance for knights of the shire, upon those that hold in ancient demesne.

EXPORTATION, the shipping or carrying out the native commodities of *England*, to other countries.

The law, relative to exports, consists principally of prohibitory or restorative regulations with respect to bullion, corn, wool, tools, raw materials for manufacturing, machinery, &c. the exportation of which might diminish the necessary supply of provi-

sions

sions at *home,* or enable foreigners to depreciate the wealth of the country, by impairing its manufactures.

EXPOSITION OF DEEDS, in the construction of deeds, it must be considered, how a deed in the gross shall be taken and enure; and how it shall be taken and expounded in the several parts and pieces of it. If several join in a deed, and some are able to make such a deed, and some are not, this shall be said to be the deed of those alone who are able. And so *e converso,* if a deed be made to one that is incapable, and to others that are capable, in this case, it shall enure only to him that is capable. *Co. Lit.* 302.

EXPOSITION OF WORDS AND SENTENCES. Words and sentences, that may be employed to some intent, shall never be void: and words tending to enlargement, shall not be construed restraint of a former clause. L. *Raym*, 269.

EX POST FACTO, a term in law signifying something done after another thing done, that was committed before.

EXTEND, signifies in a legal sense, to value the lands or tenements of one bound by statute, &c. (that hath forfeited his bond) at such an indifferent rate, as by the yearly rent the creditor in time be paid his debt.

EXTENT, sometimes means a writ or commission to the sheriff, for the valuing of lands or tenements; sometimes the act of the sheriff upon this writ.

EXTINGUISHMENT, wherever a right, title, or interest is destroyed, or taken away by the act of God, operation of law, or act of the party; this is called an *extinguishment.*

Of the extinguishment of rents, if a lessor purchase the tenancy from his lessee, he cannot have both the rent and the land, nor can the tenant be under any obligation to pay the rent, when the land which was the consideration thereof, is returned by the lessor into his own hands; and this resumption or purchase of the tenancy, makes what is properly called *an extinguishment of the rent.*

Of the extinguishment of copy-holds. As to the extinguishment of copyholds, it is laid down as a general rule, that any act of the copyholder, which denotes his intention to hold no longer of his lord, amounting to a determination of his will, is an extinguishment of his copyhold. *Hutt.* 81.

Of the extinguishment of common, if a commoner release his common in one acre, it is *an extinguishment of the whole common. Show.* 350.

Of the extinguishment of debts. A creditor's accepting an higher security than he had before, is an extinguishment of the first debt; as if a creditor by simple contract accept an obligation, this extinguishes the simple contract debt. 1 *Rol. Abr.* 470 and 471.

EXTINGUISHMENT OF SERVICES. The lord purchases or accepts parcel of the tenancy, out of which an entire service is to be paid or done: by this the whole service will be extinct: but if the service be *pro bono publico,* then no part of it shall be *extinguished*; and homage and fealty are not subject to *extinguishment,* by the lord's purchasing part of the land. 6 *Rep.* 105.

EXTINGUISHMENT OF WAYS, if a man have an highway as appendant, and after purchase the land wherein this way is, the way is extinct. Though a way of necessity, to market, or to church, or to arable land, &c. is not extinguished by purchase of grounds, or unity of possession. 1 *Inst.* 155.

EXTORTION, signifies any oppression by colour or pretence of right, and in this respect it is said to be more heinous than robbery itself, as also that it is usually attended with the aggravating sin of perjury. *Co. Lit.* 368.

At common law, extortion is severely punishable at the king's suit, by fine and imprisonment, and by a removal from the office in the execution whereof it was committed. 31 Eliz. c. 5. And this statute adds a greater penalty than the common law gave; for hereby the plaintiff shall recover his double damages. 2 *Inst.* 210. See *Colour of Office.*

EXTRA-JUDICIAL, is when judgment is given in a cause or case not depending in that court, where such judgment is given, or wherein the judge has no jurisdiction.

EXTRA-PAROCHIAL, out of any parish; privileged or exempted from the duties of a parish.

If a place be extra-parochial, and have not the face of a parish, the justices have no authority to send any poor person thither; possibly a place extra-parochial may be taxed in aid of a parish, but a parish shall not in aid of that. 2 *Salk.* 486.

If a place be a reputed parish, and have churchwardens and overseers

overseers of the poor, it is within 43 Eliz. though in truth it be no parish; but if it be merely extra-parochial; as the justices cannot send to such place so they cannot send from it; as it is exempt from receiving, it shall not have the benefit of removing, for they have not proper persons to complain; persons in extra-parochial places must subsist on private charity, as all persons did at common law before 43 Eliz. which enacts that every parish shall keep their own poor; and that act does not extend to extra-parochial places. 2 *Salk*, 487.

EYRE. See *Justices in Eyre*. See also *Eyre*.

F.

FACTOR. A factor is a merchants' agent or correspondent residing beyond the seas, or in any remote parts of the country, and in some cases, constitutes by letter of attorney to sell goods and merchandize, and otherwise act for his principal, either with a stipulated salary or allowance for his care, or commission. He must pursue his orders strictly, and may be concerned for several merchants. In commissions granted to factors, &c. it is customary to give them an authority in express words to dispose of the merchandize, and deal therein as if it were their own, by which the factor's actions will be excused, though they occasion loss to their principals. Goods remitted to a factor, ought to be carefully preserved; and he is accountable for all lawful goods which shall be consigned and come to his hands; yet if the factor buy goods for his principal, and they receive damage in his possession, through no negligence of his, the principal shall bear the loss; and if a factor be robbed, he shall be discharged in account brought against him by his principal. If a factor act contrary to his orders in selling goods, he is liable for the loss accrued therein, and shall answer to his principal out of his own estate. No factor acting on another man's account, can justify seceding from the orders of his principal, though there may be a probability of advantage by it If a principal give orders to his factor, that he shall make an insurance on his ship and goods as soon as laden, and having money in his hands, he neglects to make such insurance; if if the ship be lost, &c. the factor shall answer for it; so, if a factor make any composition with the insurers, after he hath insured the goods, without order or commission from his principal, he is answerable for the loss.

FACTORAGE, the wages or allowance paid and made to a factor by the merchant. The gain of factorage is certain, however the success proves to the merchant; but the commissions and allowances vary, according to the customs and distance of the country, in the several places where factors are resident, and are often from about two to seven or eight per cent. *Lex. Mercat.* 155.

FACULTY, is used for a privilege, or special power granted to a man by favor, such as to hold two or more ecclesiastical livings and the like. And for granting these, there is an especial court under the archbishop of *Canterbury*, called *the Court of the Faculties*, and the chief officer thereof, *the Master of the Faculties*, whose power to grant such dispensations was given by 25 H. VIII. c. 21.

FAILURE OF RECORD, is where an action is brought against a man, who alledges in his plea matter of record, in bar of the action, and avers to prove it by the record; but the plaintiff saith, *nul tiel record*, viz. denies there is any such record: upon which the defendant hath day given him by the court to bring it in; and if he fail to do it, then he is said *to fail of his record*, and the plaintiff shall have judgment to recover.

FAINT ACTION, a feigned action, or such action, as, although the words of the writ be true, yet for certain causes a man has no title to recover thereby.

FAIRS AND MARKETS, were instituted for the better regulation of trade and commerce, and that merchants and traders may be furnished with such commodities as they want, at a particular mart, without that trouble and loss of time, which must necessarily attend travelling about from place to place; and therefore as this is a matter of universal concern to the commonwealth, so it hath always been held, that no person can claim a fair or market, unless it be by grant from the king, or by prescription which supposes such grant. 2 *Inst.* 220.

Owners and governors of fairs are to take care that every thing be sold according to just weight and measure, and for that and other purposes may appoint a clerk of the fair or market, who i is to mark and allow such weights, and for his duty herein can only take his reasonable and just fees. 4 *Inst.* 274. See *Clerk of the Market*, and *Court of pie poudre*.

Toll is a matter of private benefit to the owner of the fair or market, and not incident to it; therefore if the king grant a fair or market, and grant no toll, the patentee can have none, and such fair or market is counted a free fair or market. 2 *Inst.* 220.

No toll shall be paid for any thing brought to fair or market, before the same is sold, unless it be by custom time out of mind, and upon such sale, the toll is to be paid by the buyer. 2 *Inst.* 221.

Goods in a fair or market cannot be distrained for rent, for they are brought thither for the good of the public: but if they are driving to market, and by the way are put into a pasture, it is otherwise. *Wood.* b. 2, c. 2.

Generally, all sales and contracts of all things vendible in fairs or open markets, shall be good not only between the parties, but also binding on all those that have any right or property therein. 2 *Black.* 449.

FAIT, a deed or writing sealed and delivered to prove and testify the agreement of the parties, whose deed it is; and consists of three principal points, *writing*, *sealing*, and *delivery*. By *writing*, are shewn the parties names to the deed, their dwelling places, degrees, things granted, upon what consideration, the estate limited, the time when granted, and whether simply, or upon condition.

Sealing, is a farther testimony of their consents, and *delivery*, though last, is not the least important; for after a deed is written and sealed, if it be not *delivered*, it is to no purpose: and in all deeds, care must be taken that the delivery be well proved. See *Deeds*.

FALKLAND. See *Freehold*.

FALSE ACTION, if an action be brought against any one whereby he is cast into prison, and dies pending the suit, the law gives no remedy; because the truth or falsehood of the matter, cannot appear before it is tried. And if the plaintiff be barred or nonsuited at common law, regularly, all the punishment is amercement. *Jenk. Cent.* 161.

But if a bailable action be commenced against another, and he is is held to bail thereon, either without a reasonable cause, or for something considerably more than what is *bona fide* due, an action upon the case will lie for the vexation and injury.

FALSE CHARACTER. See *Character.*

FALSE IMPRISONMENT. To constitute the injury of false imprisonment, two points are necessary: the detention of the person, and the unlawfulness of such detention. Every confinement of the person is imprisonment, whether it be in a common prison, or in a private house, or in the stocks, or even by forcibly detaining one in the streets. 2 *Inst.* 589.

By *magna charta,* no freeman shall be taken and imprisoned, but by the lawful judgment of his equals, or by the law of the land: and by the petition of right, 3 C. I. no freeman shall be imprisoned or detained without cause shewn, to which he may make answer according to law. And by the 16 C. I. c. 10, if any person be restrained of his liberty, he may, upon application by his counsel, have a writ of *habeas corpus,* to bring him before the court of king's bench or common pleas, who shall determine whether the cause of his commitment be just, and thereupon do as to justice doth appertain.

For *false imprisonment,* the law hath not only decreed a punishment by fine and imprisonment, as a heinous public crime, but hath also given a private reparation to the party by action at law, wherein he shall recover damages for the loss of his time and liberty. 3 *Black,* 127.

FALSE JUDGMENT. A writ of *false judgment* lies, where false judgment is given in the county court, or other court which is not a court of record, in a plea real or personal, and returnable into the court of common pleas.

FALSE LATIN. Before the statute directing law proceedings to be in *English,* if a *Latin* word were significant, though not good *Latin,* yet an indictment, declaration, or fine, should not be made void by it.

FALSE NEWS, slanderous to the king, or to make discord between the king and nobility, &c. to be punishable by imprisonment. 3 Edw. I. c. 34.

FALSE OATH. If a person take a false oath, he is punishable for it by action on the case if it be not perjury for which he may be indicted; for there is a difference between a false oath

2 and

and perjury; for one is *judicial*, the other is *extra-judicial*. And the law inflicts greater punishment for a false oath made in a court of justice than elsewhere, because of the preservation of justice. *Str.* 337.

FALSE PLEA. See *Pleading*.

FALSIFYING A RECORD. It is held, that he who purchases land of a person, who afterwards is outlawed of felony, or condemned upon his own confession, may *falsify the record*, not only as to the time wherein the felony is supposed to have been committed, but also as to the point of the offence. But it is agreed, that where a man is found guilty by verdict, a purchaser cannot falsify as to the point of the offence, though he may falsify for the time, where the party is found guilty generally of the offence in the appeal or indictment, because the time is not material upon evidence. 2 *Haw.* 459.

FALSIFYING A RECOVERY. Issue in tail may falsify a recovery, suffered by tenants for life, &c. And it has been held that a person may falsify a recovery had by the issue in tail, where an estate tail is before bound by a fine. 2 *Nels. Abr.* 831.

FALSIFYING A VERDICT, where there is a verdict against tenant in tail, in real action, the issue can never falsify such verdict in the point directly tried; but only in a special manner, as by saying that some evidence was omitted, &c. 2 *L. Raym.* 1050.

FARLEY or FARLEU, in some manors in the west of England, they distinguish *farley* or *farleu* as the best of the goods, as *Heriot* is the best beast, payable at the tenant's death.

FARM. By stat. 21 H. VIII. c. 13, no parson, or spiritual person may take, farms or leases of lands, on pain of forfeiting 10l. per month.

FATHER AND SON. The father shall not have action for taking any of his children, except his heir; and that is, because the marriage of his heir belongs to the father; but not of any other of his sons or daughters. And the father has no property or interest in the other children, which the law accounts may be taken from him. *Cro. Eliz.* 770.

The father is obliged by the common law to provide for his children. *Lord Raym.* 41.

Justices cannot order a maintenance for a child to be paid by the father, without adjudging that the child is poor, or likely to become chargeable. *Id.* 669.

FEALTY, signifies an oath taken at the admittance of every tenant, to be true to the lord, of whom he holds his land: and he that holds land by this oath only, holds in a manner the more perfectly free, than any in England under the king may hold.

The oath is now neglected in many places, but it is yet undoubtedly in force. 1 & 2 *Black.* 366. & 86.

FEASTS, the four feasts which our law especially takes notice of, are the feasts of the annunciation of the blessed Virgin Mary; of the nativity of St. John the Baptist, of St. Michael the Archangel, and of St. Thomas the Apostle, or in lieu thereof Christmas Day; on which quarterly days, rent on leases is usually reserved to be paid.

FEE, all our land here in England (the crown-lands being in the king's own hands, in right of his crown, excepted) is in the nature of *feudum* or *fee*; for though many have land by descent from their ancestors, and others have clearly purchased land with their money, yet is the land of such a nature, that it cannot come to any, either by descent or purchase, but with the burthen that was laid upon him who had *novel fee*, or first of all received it as a benefit from his lord to him, and to all such to whom it might descend, or any way be conveyed from him; so that in truth, no man hath *directum dominum*, the very property or demesne in any land, but only the prince in right of his crown. *Cam. Brit.* 93.

FEE SIMPLE, is an estate of inheritance whereby a person is seised of lands, tenements, or hereditaments, *to hold him and his heirs for ever*, generally, absolutely, and entirely; without mentioning *what heirs*, but referring that to his own pleasure, or to the disposition of the law. It is the most perfect tenure of any, when unincumbered; but although the greatest interests which by our law, a subject can possess; yet it may be forfeited for *treason* or *felony*. To constitute an estate in *fee*, or of inheritance, the word *heir* is necessary in the grant or donation. *Co. Lit.* 1. *Plowd.* 498. 2 *Black.* 48.

Fee qualified, is such a freehold estate, as has a qualification subjoined

subjoined to it, and which therefore must determine whenever the qualification is at an end. *Co. Lit.* 27.

Fee, conditional. This estate was at the common law, a fee restrained to some particular heirs exclusive of others; as to the heirs of a *man's body*, or to the heirs male of his body, in which cases it was held, that as soon as the grantee had issue born, the estate was thereby converted into fee simple, at least so far as to enable him to sell it, to forfeit it by treason, or to charge it with incumbrances. But the statute *de donis* having enacted, that such estates so given, *to a man, and the heirs of his body*, should at all events go to the issue, if there were any, or if none, should revert to the donor; this was by the judges denominated an estate in tail. *Plowd.* 251. See *Estate.*

FEE FARM, is, when the lord, upon the creation of the tenancy, reserves to himself and his heirs, either the rent for which it was before let to farm, or at least a fourth part of that farm rent.

FEE FARM RENT, so called, because a *farm rent* is reserved upon a grant in *fee.*

FEES, are certain perquisites, allowed to officers in the administration of justice, as a recompence for their labour and trouble; and these are either ascertained by acts of parliament, or established by ancient usage, which gives them an equal sanction with an act of parliament. See *Vin. Abr. Tit. Fees.*

FEIGNED ACTION. See *Faint Action*

FEIGNED ISSUE, is that whereby an action is feigned to be brought by consent of the parties, to determine some disputed right; without the formality of pleading, and thereby to save much time and expence in the decision of a cause. 3 *Black.* 452.

FELO DE SE, *a felon of himself*, is a person who being of sound mind, and of the age of discretion, voluntarily kills himself; for if a person be insane at the time, it is no crime. But this ought not to be extended so far as the coroners juries sometimes carry it, who suppose that the very act of self-murder is an evidence of insanity; as if every man who acts contrary to reason had no reason at all; for the same argument would prove every other criminal *non compos*, as well as the self-murderer. 3 *Inst.* 54.

All inquisitions of the offence, being in the nature of indictments

ments, ought particularly and certainly to set forth the circumstances of the fact; as the particular manner of the wound, and that it was mortal, &c. and in conclusion add, that the party in such manner murdered himself. 1 *Salk.* 377.

A *felo de se*, forfeits all chattels real and personal, which he hath in his own right, and also all such chattels real whereof he is possessed, either jointly with his wife, or in her right; and also all bonds, and other personal things in action, belonging solely to himself; and also all personal things in action, and entire chattels in possession, to which he was entitled jointly with another, or any account, except that of merchandize; but it is said that he shall forfeit a moiety only of such joint chattels as may be severed, and nothing at all of what he was possessed of as executor or administrator. *Stamdf.* P. C. 188. 189. *Plow.* 243. 262. 3 *Inst.* 55.

FELONS GOODS, are not forfeited, till it is found by indictment that he fled for the felony, and therefore they cannot be claimed by prescription. See *Estrays and Waifs.*

FELONY, in the general acceptation of law, comprises every species of crime which occasioned at common law the forfeiture of lands or goods. This most frequently happens in those for which a capital punishment either was or is liable to be inflicted: for those felonies which are called clergyble, or to which the benefit of clergy extends, were anciently punished with death in lay or unlearned offenders; though now by the statute law, that punishment is for the first offence universally remitted.

Felony is always accompanied with an evil intention, and therefore shall not be imputed to a mere mistake or misanimadversion; as where persons break open a door to execute a warrant, which will not justify such a proceeding. But the bare intention to commit a felony, is so very criminal, that at the common law it was punishable as felony, where it missed its effect through some accident, which no way lessened the guilt of the offender: but it seems agreed at this day, that felony shall not be imputed to a bare intention to commit it, yet it is certain that the party may be very severely fined for such an intention. 1 *Haw.* 65.

The punishment of a person for felony, by our ancient books is 1st, to lose his life; 2ndly, to lose his blood, as to his ancestry, and so to have neither heir nor posterity; 3dly, to lose his goods;

4thly

4thly, to lose his lands, and the king shall have *year, day* and *waste*, to the intent that his wife and children be cast out of the house, his house pulled down, and all that he had for his comfort and delight destroyed. 4 *Rep.* 124. A felony by statute incidentally implies, that the offender shall be subject to the like attainder and forfeiture, &c. as is incident to a felon at common law. 3 *Inst.* 47. See *Burglary, Forgery, Homicide, Petit Treason, Rape, Robbery,* &c.

FELONY UNDER COLOUR OF LAW, such is coming into an house by colour of writ of execution, and carrying away the goods.

A special trust prevents the felony, until such special trust is determined. 8 *Mod.* 76.

FEME COVERT, a married woman, so called from being under the *cover*, protection, and influence, of her husband. See *Husband and Wife.*

FEME SOLE, a single or unmarried woman; a *feme sole* is liable to perform parish offices, the act only requiring the person to be a substantial householder, without reference to sex.

FEME SOLE TRADER, a married woman, who, by the custom of London, trades on her own account, independent of her husband. See *Bankruptcy.*

FENCE, where a hedge and ditch join together, in whose ground or side the ditch is, to the owner of that land belongs the keeping of the same hedge or fence, and the ditch belonging to it on the other side in repair and scoured. *P. Off.* 188.

An action on the case or trespass, lies for not repairing fences, whereby cattle come into the ground of another, and do damage. Also it is presentable in the court baron. 1 *Salk.* 335.

FENCE MONTH, a month wherein it is unlawful to hunt in the forest, because the female deer fawn in that time. It being always according to the charter of the forest, fifteen days before, and ending fifteen days after midsummer.

FENS, any person convicted of maliciously cutting or destroying any bank, mill, engine, floodgate, or sluice for draining *fens*, shall be guilty of felony without benefit of clergy. 27 Geo. II. c. 19.

FEOD or FEUD, a right which the vassal hath in land, or some immoveable thing of his lord's, to use the same, and take the profits thereof hereditarily; rendering to his lord such feodal duties and services as belong to military tenure; the mere propriety of the soil always remaining unto the lord. See *Fee.*

FEODATORY, the tenant who held his estate by *feodal* service.

FEOFFMENT, may be defined to be the gift of any *corporeal* hereditament to another. He that so gives or enfeoffs, is called the *feoffor*; and the person enfeoffed is denominated the *feoffee.* *2 Black.* 20.

But by the mere words of the deed, the feoffment is by no means perfected. There remains a very material ceremony to be performed, called *livery of seisin*; without which, the feoffee hath but a mere estate at will. *Id.*

The end and design of this institution was, by this sort of ceremony or solemnity, to give notice of the translation of the feud from one hand to another; because if the possession might be changed by the private agreement of the parties, such secret contracts would make it difficult and uncertain to discover in whom the estate was lodged, and consequently the lord would be at a loss of whom to demand his services; and strangers equally perplexed, to discover against whom to commence their actions for the prosecution and recovery of their right; to prevent therefore this uncertainty, the ceremony of livery and seisin was instituted. *2 Bac. Abr.* 482.

Of the several sorts of livery. The *livery in deed,* is the actual tradition of the land, and is made either by the delivery of a branch of a tree or a turf of the land, or some other thing, in the name of all the lands and tenements contained in the deed; and it may be made by words only, without the delivery of any thing; as if the feoffor upon the land, or at the door of the house, says to the feoffee, *I am content that you should enjoy this land according to the deed,* this is a good livery to pass the freehold. *Co. Lit.* 48. *a.*

The livery within view, or the livery in law, is when the feoffor is not actually on the land, or in the house, but being in sight of it, says to the feoffee, *I give you yonder house,* or *land, go and enter into the same and take possession of it accordingly;* this livery in law cannot be given or received by an attorney, but only by the parties themselves. *Pollex.* 47.

But

But this sort of livery is not perfect to carry the freehold, till an actual entry made by the feoffee, because the possession is not actually delivered to him, but only a licence or power given him by the feoffor to take possession of it; and therefore if either the feoffor or feoffee die before livery, and entry made by the feoffee, the livery within the view becomes ineffectual and void; for if the feoffor die before entry, the feoffee cannot afterwards enter, because then the land immediately descends upon his heir, and consequently no person can take possession of his land without an authority delegated from him who is the proprietor; nor can the heir of the feoffee enter, because he is not the person to whom the feoffor intended to convey his land, nor had he an authority from the feoffor to take the possession; besides if the heir of the feoffee were admitted to take possession after his father's death, he would come in as a purchaser, whereas he was mentioned in the feoffment, to take as the representative of his ancestor, which he cannot do, since the estate was never vested in his ancestor. *Co. Lit.* 48 *b.*

A feoffment, cannot be made of a thing of which livery cannot be given, as of *incorporeal* inheritances, such as *rent, advowson, common*, &c. 2 *Rol.* 1. *l.* 20. Though it be an advowson, &c. in gross. 21 *Id.*

A man may either give or receive *livery in deed*, by letter of attorney; for since a contract is no more than the consent of a man's mind to a thing, where that consent or concurrence appears, it were most unreasonable to oblige each person to be present at the execution of the contract, since it may as well be performed by any other person delegated for that purpose, by the parties to the contract. *Co. Lit.* 52.

There are few or no persons excluded from exercising this power of delivering seisin, for monks, infants, femes covert, persons attainted, outlawed, excommunicated, villains, aliens, &c. may be attornies; for this being only a naked authority, the execution of it can be attended with no manner of prejudice to the persons under these incapacities or disabilities, or to any other person, who by law may claim any interest of such disabled persons after their death. *Co. Lit.* 52. *a.* See *Fine.*

FEOFFOR AND FEOFFEE, *feoffor*, he who infeoffs, or makes

 a feoffment

a feoffment to another of lands or tenements in fee simple. And *feoffee* is the person infeoffed, or to whom the feoffment is made. See *Feoffment*.

FERÆ NATURÆ, animals, *feræ naturæ*, of a wild nature, are those in which a man hath not an absolute, but only a qualified and limitted property, which sometimes subsists, and at other times doth not subsist. And this qualified property is obtained either by the art and industry of man, or the impotence of the animals themselves, or by special privilege.

A qualified property may subsist in animals, *feræ naturæ*, by the art and industry of man, either by his reclaiming and making them tame, or by so confining them that they cannot escape and use their natural liberty; such as deer in a park, hares or conies in an enclosed warren, doves in a dove-house, pheasants or partridges in a mew, hawks that are fed and commanded by the owner, and fish in a private pond, or in trunks. These are no longer the property of a man, than while they continue in his keeping, or actual possession; but if at any time they regain their natural liberty, his property instantly ceases; unless they have *animum revertendi*, which is only to be known by their usual custom of returning.

A man may have a qualified property in animals, *feræ naturæ*, by special privilege; that is, he may have the privilege, of hunting, taking and killing them, in exclusion of other persons. Under which head may be considered, all those animals which come under the denomination of game. Here a man may have a transient property in these animals, so long as they continue within his liberty, and may restrain any strangers from taking them therein: but the instant they depart into another liberty, this qualified property ceases. 2 *Black.* 391.

Larceny cannot be committed of things *feræ naturæ*, while at their natural liberty; but if they are made fit for food, and reduced to tameness, and known by the taker to be so, it may be larceny to take them. 1 *Haw.* 94. See *Game*.

FERRY, is a liberty by prescription, or the king's grant, to have a boat for passage upon a river, for carriage of horses and men, for reasonable toll. *Savil.* 11 & 14.

Owner of a ferry cannot suppress that ferry, and put up a bridge in its place without a licence. *Show.* 243. 257.

Ad

And if a ferry be granted at this day, he who accepts such grant, is bound to keep a boat for the public good. *Id.*

FEUDAL BARONIES, *feudal baronies* were, when the king in the creation of baronies, gave rent and land to hold of him for the defence of the realm. There is no feudal barony remaining at this time, except *Arundel.* 1 *Salk.* 353.

FEUD BOTE, a recompense for engaging in a feud or faction, and the contingent damages; it having been the custom of ancient times, for all the kindred to engage in the kinsman's quarrel.

FEUDS, estates in lands were originally at will, and then they were called *munera* ; afterwards they were for life, and then they were called *beneficia* ; and for that reason the livings of clergymen are so called at this day ; afterwards they were made hereditary, when they were called *feoda,* and in our law fee simple. See *Fee Simple.* 3 *Salk.* 165.

FIAT, a short order or warrant of some judge, for making out and allowing certain processes.

FIAT JUSTICIA, on a petition to the king, for his warrant to bring a writ of error in parliament, he writes on the top of the petition, *fiat justicia,* and then the writ of error is made out, &c. *Staundf. Prærog. Reg.* 22.

FICTION OF LAW, is allowed of in several cases: but it must be framed according to the rules of law ; and there ought to be equity and possibility in every legal fiction.

Fictions, were invented to avoid inconvenience; and it is a maxim invariably observed, that no fiction shall extend to work an injury; its proper operation being to prevent a mischief, or remedy an inconvenience, that might result from the general rule of law. 3 *Black.* 434.

All fictions of law, are to certain respects and purposes, and extend only to certain persons ; as, the law supposes the vouchee to be tenant of the land, where *in rei veritate* he is not ; but this is as to the demandant himself, and to enable him to do things as to the demandant, and which the demandant may do to him ; and therefore a fine levied by vouchee to the demandant, or fine or release from the defendant to the vouchee, is good ; but fine levied by the vouchee to a stranger, or lease made to him by a stranger is void. 3 *Rep.* 29.

FIERI FACIAS, a writ judicial, that lies at all times within the year and day, for him who hath recovered in an action of debt or damages, to the sheriff, to command him to levy the debt or damages, of his goods against whom the recovery was had.

Upon a *fieri facias*, the sheriff cannot deliver the defendant's goods to the plaintiff in satisfaction of his debt; nor ought he to deliver them to the defendant against whom execution is; but the goods are to be sold, and in strictness, the money is to be brought into court. *Cro. Eliz.* 504.

If the defendant die after the execution awarded, and before it be served, yet it may be served upon his goods in the hands of his executor or administrator; for if the execution be awarded, the goods are bound, and the sheriff need not take notice of his death. 1 *Mod.* 188.

And upon a *fieri facias*, the sheriff may take any thing but wearing cloaths. *Cumb.* 356.

FIGURES, figures are not allowed to express numbers in indictments, but numbers must be expressed in words. *Cro. Car.* 109.

Roman figures are good in pleading, but otherwise of *English* figures. 2 *Lev.* 102.

FILACER or FILIZER, an officer of the court of common-pleas, so called because he files those writs, whereon he makes out process. There are fourteen of them in their several divisions and counties; and they make out all writs and processes upon original writs, issuing out of chancery, as well in real, as in personal and mixed actions; and in actions merely personal, where the defendants are returned summoned, they make out *pones* and attachments, which being returned and executed, if the defendant appear not, they make forth a *distringas*, and so *ad infinitum*, or until he doth appear; if he be returned *nihil*, then process of *capias* infinite, &c. They enter all appearances and special bails, upon any process made by them. They make the first *scire facias* upon special bails, writs of *habeas corpus, distringas, nuper vicecomitem vel ballivum*, and *duces tecum*, and all *super sedeas* upon special bail or otherwise; writs of *habeas corpus cum causa*, upon the sheriff's return, that the defendant is detained with other actions; writs of adjournment of a term, in case of pestilence, war, or public disturbance.

FILE,

FILE, a *file* is a record of the court, and the filing of a process of court, makes a record of it. *Lill.* 212.

FINDING, any person finding any thing, has a special property therein, but he is answerable to the person in whom is the general property, but has a right against every person but the loser. The finder is not answerable for a mere nonfeasance or neglect; yet if he make gain of, or abuse, or spoil the things he finds, he shall be answerable.

If bank-bills, tickets, &c. stolen or lost, are paid to or delivered to another, without consideration, an action lies against any one in whose hands they are found; and the law seems to be the same, though a consideration were given, if the party had previous notice of their being lost or stolen. *Str.* 505.

But the property of goods found or stolen, may be changed by sale for a valuable consideration, and without notice, in a *market overt*, and the party purchasing them obtains a title to them, against the original owner.

FINE, a *fine* is sometimes said to be a feoffment of record, though it might with more accuracy, be called an acknowledgement of a feoffment on record: by which it is to be understood, that it hath at least, the same force and effect with a feoffment, in the conveying and assuring of lands; though it is one of those methods of transferring estates of freehold by the common law, in which livery of seisin is not necessary to be actually given · the supposition and acknowledgment thereof in a court of record, however fictitious, inducing an equal notoriety. But more particularly, a fine may be described to be, an amicable composition or agreement of a suit, either actual or fictitious, by leave of the king or his justices; whereby the lands in question become, or are acknowledged to be, the right of one of the parties. In its original, it was founded on an actual suit commenced at law, for the recovery of the possession thus gained by such composition, and was found to be so sure and effectual, that fictitious actions were, and continue to be, every day commenced, for the sake of obtaining the same security. 2 *Black.* 349.

Of the several kinds of fines. Fines are of four kinds, *first*, that which in law French is called a fine *sur cognizance de droit come ceo q'il a de son done*; or a fine upon acknowledgment of the right of the cognizee, as that which he hath of the gift of the cognizor.

 This

This is the best and surest kind of fine, for thereby the deforciant, in order to keep his covenant with the plaintiff of conveying to him the lands in question, and at the same time to avoid the formality of an actual feoffment and livery, acknowledges in a court a former feoffment, or gift in possession, to have been made by him to the plaintiff. This fine is therefore said to be a feoffment of record; the livery thus acknowledged in court, being equivalent to an actual livery; so that this assurance is rather a confession of a former conveyance, than a conveyance now originally made; for the deforciant or cognizor, acknowledges the right to be in the plaintiff or cognizee, as that which he hath *de son done*, of the proper gift of himself the cognizor.

Secondly, a fine, *sur cognizance de droit tantum*, or upon acknowledgment of the right merely, not with the circumstance of a preceding gift from the cognizor. This is commonly used to pass a reversionary interest which is in the cognizor; for such reversions, there can be no feoffment or donation with livery supposed; as the possession during the particular estate, belongs to a third person. *Moor.* 269.

Thirdly, a fine *sur concessit*, or upon grant, is, where the cognizor, in order to make an end of disputes, though he acknowledges no precedent right, yet grants to the cognizee an estate *de novo*, usually for life or years, by way of supposed composition; and this may be done reserving a rent, or the like; for it operates as a new grant.

Fourthly, a fine *sur done, grant, et render*; which is a double fine, being in a manner two fines, comprehending the fine *sur cognizance de droit come ceo, &c.* and the fine *sur concessit*; and may be used to create particular limitations of estate. In this species of fine, the cognizee, after the right is acknowledged to be in him, grants back again, or renders to the cognizor, or perhaps to a stranger, some other estate in the premises. But in general the first species of fine, *sur cognizance de droit come ceo*, &c. is more used, as it conveys a clear and absolute freehold, and gives the cognizee a seisin in law, without an actual livery; and is therefore called a fine *executed*, whereas the others are but *executory*. 2 *Black.* 352.

Operation of a fine levied. The force and effect of a fine principally depend on the common law, and the two statutes 4 H. VII.

c. 24

c. 24. and 32 H. VIII. c. 36. the ancient common law, with respect to this point, is forcibly declared by 18 Ed. I. c. 4. The fine is so high a bar, and of so great force, and of a nature so powerful in itself, that it precludes not only those which are parties and privies to the fine, and their heirs, but all other persons whatsoever who are of full age, out of prison, of sound memory, and within the four seas, on the day of the fine levied, unless they put in their claim within a year and a day, and by 4 H. VII. c. 241. five years after proclamation made.

A fine extends to *parties, privies,* and *strangers*; and the parties and privies are foreclosed by it *presently,* and the strangers *in future.* 2 *Inst.* 516.

The parties, are either the cognizors or cognizees; and these are immediately concluded by the fine, and barred of any latent right they might have, even though under the legal impediment of coverture. And indeed this is almost the only act that a *feme covert* is permitted by law to do (and that, because she is privately examined as to her voluntary consent, which removes the general suspicion of compulsion by her husband), it is therefore the usual, and almost the only safe method, whereby she can join in the sale, settlement, or incumbrance, of any estate.

Privies to a fine, are such as are any way related to the parties who levy the fine, and claim under them by any right of blood, or other right of representation: such as are the heirs general of the cognizor, the issue in tail, the vendee, the devise, and all others who must make title by the persons who levied the fine, 2 *Black.* 355.

Strangers to a fine, are all other persons in the world, except only *parties* and *privies*; whose right is bound unless they make claim within five years after proclamation made, except *femes coverts* (not being parties to the fine) infants, prisoners, persons beyond the seas, and such as are not of sound mind; who have five years allowed to them aud their heirs, after such impediment removed.

Persons also, that have not a present, but a future interest only, as in remainder or reversion, have five years allowed to claim in, from the time that such right accrues. And if within that time they neglect to claim, or if they do not conformably to the statute 4 Anne. c. 16. bring an action to try the right, within one

one year after making such claim, and prosecute the same with effect, all persons whatsoever, are barred of whatever right they may have, by force of the statute of non claim. *Id.*

And the courts of law will not suffer a fine to be impeached (when once levied) on account of any defect of understanding, or even lunacy or idiocy, of the cognizor. 12 *Co.* 124.

But in order to make a fine of any avail, it is necessary that the parties have some *interest* in the lands to be affected by it; otherwise two strangers, by confederacy, might defray the owners, by levying fines of their lands.

For if the attempt be discovered, they can be no sufferers as to the estate in question, but must only remain in *statu quo*; whereas if a tenant for life levy a fine, it is an absolute forfeiture of his estate to the remainder man or reversioner, if claimed in proper time. It is not therefore to be supposed that such tenants will often run so great a hazard; but if they do, and the claim is not duly made within five years after their respective terms expire, the estate is for ever barred by it. *Co. Lit.* 251.

Regularly a fine may be levied of any thing, whereof *a præcipe quod reddat,* or *faciat* lies, as the writ of customs and services: or whereof *a præcipe quod permittant,* as to have common, a way, &c. or to be short, where *a præcipe quod teneat* doth lie, as the writ of covenant to levy a fine, and the like. 2 *Inst.* 513.

Fines are now levied in the court of common pleas at *Westminster,* on account of the solemnity thereof, ordained by 18 Ed. I. *st.* 4; before which time, they were sometimes levied in the *exchequer,* in the *county courts, courts baron, &c.* They may be acknowledged before the lord chief justice of the *common pleas,* as well in as out of court; and two of the justices of the same court have power to take them in open court · also justices of assise may do it by the general words of their patent or commission; but they do not usually certify them, without a special writ of *dedimus potestatem.* 2 *Inst.* 512.

The chief justice of *common pleas,* may, by the prerogative of his place, take cognizance of fines in any place out of the court; and certify the same without any *dedimus potestatem.* But the chief justice of England cannot, nor any of the justices, except the chief justice of the common pleas, who hath this special authority by custom and not by statute. 9 *Co. Read. For further*

information

information respecting the levying of fines, &c. see Impey's C. B. Practice.

FINES FOR ALIENATIONS, were fines paid to the king, by his tenants in chief, for permission to alien their lands, according to 1 Ed. III. c. 12. But these are taken away by stat. 12 C. II. c. 24, abolishing all tenures but free and common soccage.

FINES FOR OFFENCES, originally all punishments were corporal; but after the use of money, when the profits of the courts arose from the money paid out of the civil causes, and the fines and confiscations in criminal ones, the commutation of punishments was allowed of, and the corporal punishment which was only *in terrorem*, changed into the pecuniary, whereby they found their own advantage. This begat the distinction between the greater and the less offences; for in the *crimina majora* there was at least a fine to the king, which was levied by a *capiatur*; but upon the less offences there was only an amercement, which was affeered, and for which a *distringas*, or action of debt only lay. 2 *Bac. Abr.* 502.

By the bill of rights 1 W. st. 2. c. 2. excessive fines ought not to be imposed; and all grants and promises of fines and forfeitures of particular persons, before conviction, are declared to be illegal and void. 4 *Black.* 379.

All courts of record, may fine and imprison an offender, if the nature of the offence be such as deserves such punishment. 8 *Co.* 39.

But no court, unless of record, can fine or imprison. 11 *Co.* 43. And all courts of law that have power given them to fine and imprison, are thereby made courts of record. 1 *Salk.* 200.

The sheriff in his torn, may impose a fine on all such as are guilty of any contempt in the face of the court, and may also impose what reasonable fine he shall think fitting, upon a suitor refusing to be sworn, or upon a bailiff refusing to make a panel, &c. or upon a tithing-man neglecting to make his presentment, or upon one of the jury refusing to present the articles wherewith they are charged, or upon a person duly chosen constable, refusing to be sworn. 2 *Inst.* 142.

Also the steward of a court leet, may by recognizance bind any person to the peace who shall make an affray in his presence, fitting

ting the court, or may commit him to ward, either for want of sureties, or by way of punishment, without demanding any sureties of him; in which case he may afterwards impose a fine according to his discretion. F. N. B. 82.

Also the sheriff in his torn, and the steward of a court leet, have a discretionary power, either to award a fine or amercement for contempt of the court; for a suitor's refusing to be sworn, &c. and the steward of a court leet may either amerce or fine an offender, upon an indictment for an offence not capital, within his jurisdiction, without any farther proceeding or trial; especially if the crime were any way enormous, as an affray accompanied with wounding. *Kitchin.* 43, 51.

Some courts cannot fine or imprison, but amerce, as the county, hundred courts, &c. 11 *Co.* 43.

But some courts can neither fine, imprison, or amerce; as ecclesiastical courts held before the ordinary, archdeacon, &c. or their commissaries, and such who proceed according to the canon or civil law. 11 *Co* 44.

A *fine* may be mitigated the same term it was set, being under the power of the court during that time; but not afterwards. *L. Raym.*, 376. And fines assessed in court by judgment upon an information, cannot be afterwards mitigated. *Cro. Car.* 251. If a fine certain is imposed by statute on any conviction, the court cannot mitigate it; but if the party come in before conviction, and submit to the court, they may assess a less fine; for he is not convicted, and perhaps never might. The court of exchequer may mitigate a fine certain, because it is a court of equity, and they have a privy seal for it. 3 *Salk.* 33.

FIRDWITE, a penalty imposed on military tenants for their defaults in not appearing in arms, or coming to an expedition.

FIRES and FIRECOCKS, by 14 G. III. c. 78, churchwardens in London, and within the bills of mortality, are to fix firecocks, &c. at proper distances in streets, and keep a large engine and hand engine for extinguishing fire, under the penalty of *ten pounds.* And to prevent fires, workmen in the city of London, &c. must erect party walls between buildings, of brick or stone of a certain thickness, &c. under penalties therein mentioned.

On the breaking out of any fire, all the constables and beadles, shall repair to the place with their staves, and be assisting in putting

ting it out, and causing people to work. No action shall be had against any person in whose house or chamber a fire shall accidentally begin.

FIRE BOTE, an allowance of fuel or estovers, to maintain competent *firing* for the use of the tenants: which by the common law, any man may take out of the lands granted to him.

FIRE ORDEAL. See *Ordeal.*

FIREWORKS. It is not lawful for any person, to make or cause to be made, or sell or expose to sale, any squibs, rockets, serpents, or other fireworks, or any cases, moulds, or other implements for making the same; or to permit the same to be cast or fired from his house or other place thereto belonging, into any public street or road; or to throw or fire, or be aiding in throwing and firing the same, in any public street, house, shop, river, or highway; and every such offence shall be adjudged a common nuisance. 9 & 10 W. c. 7.

FIRST FRUITS AND TENTHS. *First fruits* are the profits of every spiritual living, for one year, and *tenths*, are the tenth part of the yearly value of such living, given anciently to the pope through all *Christendom*; but by stat 26 H. VIII. c. 3. translated to the king here in *England*, for the ordering whereof there was a court erected, 32 H. VIII. c. 45, but again dissolved *anno primo Mariæ*. Sess. 2. c. 10. And since that time, though those profits be reduced again to the crown, by the stat. I. Eliz. c. 4, yet was the court never restored, but all matters therein wont to be handled, mere transferred to the exchequer.

By stat. 26 H. VIII. the lord chancellor, bishops, &c. are empowered to examine into the value of every ecclesiastical benefice and preferment in their several dioceses; and every clergyman entered on his living, before the first fruits are paid or compounded for, is to forfeit double value. But stat. 1 Eliz. c. 4, ordains, that if an incumbent on a benefice do not live half a year, or is ousted before the year expire, his executors are to pay only a fourth part of the first fruits; and if he live the year and then die, or be ousted in six months after, but half the first fruits shall be paid; if a year and a half, three quarters of them; and if two years, then the whole; not otherwise. The archbishops and bishops, have four years allowed for the payment, and shall pay one quarter every year, if they live so long upon the bishopric:

 other

other dignitaries in the church, pay theirs in the same manner, as rectors and vicars.

By 27 H. VIII. c. 8. no tenths are to be paid for the first year, as then the first fruits are due; and by several statutes of *Anne*, if a benefice be under *fifty pounds per annum*, clear yearly value, it shall be discharged of the payment of *first fruits* and *tenths*.

The queen also restored to the church, what at first had been thus indirectly taken from it, by remitting the tenths and first fruits entirely but by applying these superfluities of the larger benefices, to make up the deficiencies of the smaller; for this purpose she granted a charter, whereby all the revenue of the first fruits and tenths is vested in trustees for ever, to form a perpetual fund for the augmentation of poor livings under 50l. a year. This is usually called *queen Anne's bounty*, which has been still further regulated by subsequent statutes: though it is to be lamented that the number of such poor livings is so great, that this bounty extensive as it is, will be slow, and almost imperceptible in its operation; the number of livings under 50l. certified by the bishops, at the commencement of the undertaking, being 5597, the revenues of which, on a general average, did not exceed 23l. *per annum*. *Black*. 285, 286.

FISH. Any person may erect a fish pond without licence; because it is a matter of profit, and for the increase of victuals. 2 *Inst*. 199.

Concerning the right and property of fish, it has been held, that where the lord of the manor has the soil on both sides of the river, it is good evidence that he has the right of fishing; but where the river ebbs and flows, and is an arm of the sea, there it is common to all, and he who claims a privilege to himself must prove it. In the *Severn*, the soil belongs to the owners of the land, on each side; and the soil of the river *Thames*, is in the king, &c. but the fishing is common to all. 1 *Mod*. 105.

Any person who shall unlawfully break, cut, or destroy, any head or dam of a fish pond, or wrongfully fish therein, with intent to take or kill fish, shall on conviction at the suit of the king, or of the party, at the assizes or sessions, be imprisoned three months, and pay treble damages, and after the expiration of the three months, shall find sureties for his good abearing for seven years, or remain in prison till he doth. 5 Eliz. c. 21.

If

If any person shall enter into any park or paddock, fenced in and enclosed, or into any garden, orchard, or yard, adjoining or belonging to any dwelling house, in or through which park, or paddock, garden, orchard, or yard, any stream of water shall run, or wherein shall be any river, stream, pond, pool, moat, stew, or other water, and by any means or device whatsoever, shall steal, take, kill, or destroy, any fish bred or kept therein, without the consent of the owner thereof, or shall be aiding therein, or shall receive or buy any such fish, knowing them to be so stolen or taken as aforesaid, and shall be convicted thereof at the assizes, within six calender months after the offence shall be committed, he shall be transported for seven years. And any offender, surrendering himself to a justice, or being apprehended or in custody for such offence, or on any other account, who shall make confession thereof, and a true discovery on oath of his accomplice or accomplices, so as such accomplice may be apprehended, and shall on trial give evidence, so as to convict such accomplice, shall be discharged of the offence, so by him confessed.

And if any person shall take, kill, or destroy, or attempt to take, kill, or destroy, any fish in any river, or stream, pond, pool, or other water, (not in any park or paddock, or in any garden, orchard, or yard, adjoining or belonging to any dwelling house, but in any other inclosed ground, being private property) he shall, on conviction before one justice, on the oath of one witness, forfeit 5l. to the owner of the fishery of such river, pond, or other water, and such justice, on complaint upon oath, may issue his warrant to bring the person complained of before him; and if he shall be convicted before such justice, or any other of the county or place, he shall immediately pay the said penalty of 5l. to such justice, for the use of the person, as the same is appointed to be paid unto; and in default thereof, shall be committed by such justice to the house of correction, for any time not exceeding six months, unless the forfeiture shall be sooner paid: or such owner of the fishery may, within six calender months after the offence, bring an action for the penalty in any of the courts of record at *Westminster*. 5 G. III. c. 14.

FISHERMEN. There shall be a master, wardens, and assistants of the fishmongers company in *London*, chosen yearly, at the next court of the lord mayor and aldermen after the 10th of June, who are constituted a court of assistants; and they shall meet once a month at their common hall, to regulate abuses in fishery, register the names of fishermen, and mark their boats, &c.

FISHING, *right of.* Fishery in navigable rivers, or arms of the sea, is common and public; it *prima facie* belongs to the crown, and the presumption is against any exclusive right; yet an exclusive right may be prescribed for; but the proof lies on the claimers of it. In private rivers not navigable, it belongs to the lords on each side. *Bur.* 2184.

FISH ROYAL, these are whale and sturgeon, which the king is entitled to, when either are thrown on shore, or caught near the coasts. *Plowd.* 315.

FLEET, a well known prison in *London.* To this prison none are usually committed, but for contempt of the king and his laws, or upon absolute command of the king, or some of his courts. Or lastly, upon debt, when men are unable or unwilling to satisfy their creditors.

FLIGHT, is evading the course of justice, by a man's voluntarily withdrawing himself. On an accusation of treason, or felony, or even petit larceny, if the jury find that the party fled for the same, he shall forfeit his goods and chattels, although he be acquitted of the offence; for the very flight itself is an offence, carrying with it a strong presumption of guilt, and is at least an endeavour to elude and stifle the course of justice prescribed by the law. But now the jury very seldom find the flight; such forfeiture being looked upon, since the vast increase of personal property, as too large a penalty for an offence, to which a man is prompted by the natural love of liberty. 4 *Black.* 387.

FLOTSAM, JETSAM, and LAGAN. *Flotsam,* is when a ship is sunk or cast away, and the goods float on the sea; *jetsam,* is when a ship is in danger of being sunk, and to lighten the ship the goods are cast into the sea, and the ship notwithstanding perisheth; and *lagan* is, when the goods so cast into the sea, are so heavy that they sink to the bottom, and therefore the mariners fasten to them a buoy or cork, or such other thing that will not sink, to enable them to find them again. 5 *Rep.* 106. b. The king shall have *flotsam, jetsam,* and *lagan,* when the ship is lost, and the owner of the goods are not known; but not otherwise. F. N.

F. N. B. 122, where the proprietors of the goods may be known, they have a year and a day to claim *flotsam*. 1 *Keb*. 657.

FOLKLAND, was such as was held by no assurance in writing, but distributed among the common *folk*, or people, at the pleasure of the lord, and resumed at his discretion; and was no other than villenage.

FOLCMOTE or FOLKMOTE, was a common council of the inhabitants of a city, town, or borough, convened at the *moot* hall, or house. When this great assembly is made in a city, it may be called a *burgemote*; when in the county a *shiregemote*.

FORCE, in our common law, is most usually applied in its worst sense, signifying unlawful violence. *Force*, is either *simple* or *compound*; *simple force* is that which is so committed, that it is accompanied by no other crime; as if one by force shall enter into another man's possession, without doing any other unlawful act: *mixed* or *compound force*, is that violence which is committed with such a fact, as of itself only is criminal: as if one by force enter into another man's possession, and kill a man, or ravish a woman there, &c.

All force is against law; and it is lawful to repel force by force. 1 *Inst*. 267.

Where a crime in itself capital, is endeavoured to be committed by force, it is lawful to repel that force, by the death of the party attempting. 4 *Black*. 181.

FORCIBLE ENTRY AND DETAINER. *Forcible entry*, is a violent actual entry into a house or land, &c, or taking a distress of any person, weaponed, whether he offer violence or fear of hurt to any there, or furiously drive any out of the possession thereof. *West Symbol*. *p*. 2.

Where one or more persons, armed with unusual weapons, violently enter into the house or land of another; or where they do not enter violently, if they forcibly put another out of his possession; or if one enter another's house, without his consent, although the doors be open, &c. these are all forcible entries punishable by the law. *Co. Lit*. 257. So when a tenant keeps possession of the land at the end of his term against the landlord, it is a forcible detainer. 1 *Haw*. 145.

If any person be put out or disseised of any lands and tenements in a forcible manner, or put out peaceably, and after holden out with

with strong hand, the party grieved shall have *assize of novel disseisin,* or writ of trespass against the disseisor; and if he recover (or if any alienation be made to defraud the possessor of his right, which is also declared by the statute to be void) he shall have *treble damages,* and the defendant shall also make fine and ransom to the king. 8 H. VI. c. 9.

But as this action is at the suit of the party, and only for the right, it lies only where the entry for the defendant was not lawful; for though a man enter with force, where his entry is lawful, he shall not be punished by way of action; but he may be indicted by the statute, for the indictment is for the force and for the king; and he shall make fine to the king, be his right ever so good. *Dalt.* c. 129.

He shall recover treble damages, as well for the mesne occupation, as for the first entry; and though he shall recover treble damages, he shall recover costs which shall be trebled also; for the word *damages,* includes costs of suit. 1 *Inst.* 257.

An indictment will lie at common law for a forcible entry, though generally brought on the statutes; but it must shew on the face of it sufficient actual force. 3 *Bur.* 1702.

If the party grieved will lose the benefit of his treble damages and costs, he may have the assistance of the justices at the general sessions, by way of indictment on the statute 8 H. VI. which being found there, he shall be restored to his possession, by a writ of restitution granted out of the same court to the sheriff. *Dalt.* c. 129.

Forcible entry and detainer, is also punishable under the statute, by one justice of peace, and by *certiorari.* *Dalt.* c. 44.

FORCIBLE MARRIAGE. If any person shall take away any woman having lands or goods, or that is heir apparent to her ancestor, by force and against her will, and afterwards she be married to him, or to another by his procurement, or defiled; he, and also the procurers, and receivers of such a woman, shall be adjudged principal felons. And by 39 Eliz. c. 9, the benefit of clergy is taken away from the principals, procurers, and accessaries before. And by 4 and 5 P. et M. c. 8, if any person shall take or convey away any unmarried woman, under the age of sixteen (though not attended with force), he shall be imprisoned two years, or fined, at the discretion of the court; and if he deflower

flower her, or contract matrimony with her without the consent of her parent or guardian, he shall be imprisoned five years, or fined in like manner. And the marriage of any person under the age of twenty-one, by *licence*, without such consent, is void.

FORECLOSED, barred, shut out, or excluded for ever; as the barring the equity of redemption on mortgages. See *Mortgage*.

FOREIGN COURTS, upon a principle of the law of nations, every state being free, independent, and uncontroulable, the sentence of any foreign court of competent jurisdiction, is not to be called in question, but is admitted as evidence of the fact upon which it is founded. If however, in such sentence any foreign jurisdiction should state the evidence, upon which its sentence or device is founded, subsequent evidence may be admitted to disprove such evidence, and consequently the sentence or decree which is a deduction from it. But where it is peremptorily given as a sentence, it is conclusive evidence, which the *English* courts will not allow to be questioned.

FOREIGNERS, are persons subject to a foreign state to which they owe an allegiance, and although made free denizens or naturalized in Great Britain, they are nevertheless expressly disabled by the act of settlement from bearing offices in the government, from being members of the privy council, or members of parliament. See *Alien*.

FOREIGN OPPOSER, or APPOSER, an officer in the exchequer, to whom all sheriffs, after they are *apposed* of their sums out of the pipe-office, repair to be apposed by him of their green wax. He examines the sheriff's estreats with the record, and and *apposeth* the sheriff, what he says to every particular sum therein.

FOREIGN PLANTATIONS, a writ of error lies here upon any of their judgments in foreign plantations, or in any dominions belonging to England. *Vaugh*. 402.

FOREIGN PLEA, a *foreign plea* is, where the action is carried out of the county where it is laid, and is to be sworn, which a plea to the jurisdiction is not. *Carth*. 402.

FOREIGN SERVICE, is that whereby a mesne lord holds over of another, without the compass of his own fee. Or that which

which a tenant performs either to his own lord, or to the lord paramount out of the fee. *Bracton, lib.* 2. *c.* 16.

FOREIGN STATE, is the dominion of a foreign power. Thus, if any foreign subject purchase goods in London, and then depart privately to his own country, the owner of the goods may have a certificate from the Lord Mayor of London, on an affidavit being made of the sale and delivery of the goods, upon which the proper court in that state, will execute a legal process upon the party. At the instance of an ambassador also or consul, any criminal flying from justice to any foreign state, may be delivered up to the laws of the country where the crime was committed. Where any contract is made abroad, if the party be resident in England, it may be recovered by the English courts.

FOREJUDGER, a judgment, whereby a man is deprived, or put out of the thing in question.

FOREJUDGED THE COURT, is when an officer or attorney of the *court*, is expelled the same for some offence, or for not appearing to an action by bill filed against him; and in the latter he is not to be readmitted till he shall appear. 2 H. IV. c. 8. he shall lose his office and be *forejudged the court*.

FORESTS, are waste grounds belonging to the king, replenished with all manner of beasts of chace or venery, which are under the king's protection, for the sake of his royal recreation and delight; and to that end, and for preservation of the king's game, there are particular laws, privileges, courts and officers belonging to the king's forests. 1 *Black.* 379.

The forest courts are, the courts of *attachments*, of *regard*, of *Swainmote*, and of *justice seat*.

The court of *attachments*, is to be held before the verderers of the forest, once in every forty days, to enquire of all offenders against the king's deer, or covert for the same, who may be attached by their bodies, if found in the very act of transgression, otherwise by their goods; and in this court, the foresters are to bring in their attachments or presentments of vert and venison; and the verderers are to receive the same, and to inroll them, and to certify them under their seals, to the court of *justice seat*, or *Swainmote*; for this court can only inquire of but not convict offenders.

The

The court of *regard*, or survey of dogs, is to be holden every third year, for the lawing or expeditating of mastiffs, which is done by cutting off the claws of the fore-feet, to prevent them from running after deer. No other dogs but mastiffs, were permitted to be kept within the king's forests, it being supposed that the keeping of these, and these only, was necessary for the defence of a man's house.

The court of *Swainmote*, is to be holden before the verderers as judges, by the steward of the swainmote, thrice in every year, the swains or freeholders within the forest composing the jury.

The jurisdiction of this court, is, to enquire into the oppressions and grievances committed by the officers of the forest, and to receive and try presentments, certified from the court of *attachments*, against the offenders in vert and venison. And this court may not only enquire, but convict also; which conviction shall be certified to the court of *justice seat*; under the seals of the jury; for this court cannot proceed to judgment.

The court of *justice seat*, is the principal court, which is held before the chief justice in *eyre*, or chief itinerant judge, or his deputy, to hear and determine all trespasses within the forest, and all claims of franchises, liberties, and privileges, and all pleas and causes whatsoever, therein arising. It may also proceed to try presentments made in the inferior courts of the forest, and to give judgment upon the convictions that have been made in the swainmote courts. It may be held every third year. This court may fine and imprison, it being a court of record. And a writ of error lies to the court of king's-bench. 1 *Black.* 239. 2 *Black.* 38. 3 *Black.* 71.

But the forest laws have long ago ceased to be put in execution. 1 *Black* 289.

FORESTALLING, is the buying or bargaining for any corn, cattle, or other merchandize, by the way, before it comes to any market or fair, to be sold; or by the way, as it comes from beyond the seas, or otherwise, towards any city, port, haven, or creek af this realm, to the intent to sell the same again at a higher price.

At the common law, all endeavours to enhance the common price of any merchandize, and all practices which have an apparent tendency thereto, whether by spreading false rumours, or by by purchasing things in a market before the accustomed hour, or by buying and selling again the same thing in the same market, or by any other such like devices, are highly criminal, and punishable by fine and imprisonment. 1 *Haw.* 234.

Several statutes, have from time to time, been made against these offences in general, which were repealed by 12 Geo. III. c. 71.

But though these offences are no longer combated by the statutes, they are still punishable upon indictment at the common law, by fine and imprisonment.

FORFEITURE, is a punishment annexed by law, to some illegal act or negligence in the owner of lands, tenements, or hereditaments; whereby he loses all his interest therein, and they go to the party injured, as a recompense for the wrong which either he alone, or the public together with him have sustained. 2 *Black.* 267.

The offences which induce a forfeiture of lands and tenements, are principally the following: *treason, felony, misprision of treason, præmunire, drawing a weapon on a judge*; or *striking any one* in the presence of the king's court of justice, and *popish recusancy*, or non-observance of certain laws enacted in restraint of papists.

By the common law, all lands of inheritance whereof the offender is seised in his own right, and also all rights of entry to lands in the hands of a wrong doer, are forfeited to the king on an attainder of high treason, although the lands are holden of another; for there is an exception in the oath of fealty, which saves the tenants allegiance to the king; so that if he forfeits his allegiance, even the lands he held of another lord, are forfeited to the king, for the lord himself cannot give of lands but upon that condition. *Co. Lit.* 8.

Also upon an attainder of petit treason or felony, all lands of inheritance, whereof the offender is seised in his own right, as also all rights of entry to lands in the hands of a wrong doer, are forfeited to the lord of whom they are immediately holden; for this by the feudal law was deemed a breach of the tenant's oath of fealty in the highest manner; his body with which he had engaged to serve the lord being forfeited to the king, and thereby his blood corrupted, so that no person could represent him; and all

all personal estates, whether they are in action or possession, which the party has, or is entitled unto, in his own right, and not as executor or administrator, to another, are liable to such forfeiture in the following cases:

1st. Upon a conviction of treason or felony.

But the lord cannot enter into the lands, holden of him upon an escheat for petit treason or felony, without a special grant, till it appear by due process, that the king hath had his prerogative of the year day and waste. *Stamf.* P. C. 191.

As to forfeiture of goods and chattels, it seems agreed that all things whatsoever, which are comprehended under the notion of a personal estate are liable to such forfeiture.

2nd. Upon a flight found before the coroner, on view of a dead body.

3d. Upon an acquittal or a capital felony, if the party be found to have fled. 2 *Haw.* 450.

4th. If a person indicted of petit larceny and acquitted, be found to have fled for it, he forfeits his goods as in cases of grand larceny. 2 *Haw.* 451. But the party may in all cases, except that of the coroner's inquest, traverse the finding of the flight: and it seems agreed, that the particulars of the goods found to be forfeited, may also be traversed.

5th. Upon a presentment by the oaths of twelve men, that a person arrested for treason or felony, fled from, or resisted those who had him in custody, and was killed by them in the pursuit or scuffle. *Id.*

6th. If a felon waive, that is leave any goods in his flight from those who either pursue him, or are apprehended by him so to do, he forfeits them, whether they are his own goods, or goods stolen by him; and at common law, if the owner did not pursue and appeal the felon, he lost the goods for ever: but by 21 H. VIII. c. 11. for encouraging the prosecution of felons, it is provided, that if the party came in as evidence on the indictment, and attaint the felon, he shall have a writ of restitution. 4 *Inst.* 134.

7th. If a man be *felo de se,* he forfeits his goods and chattels. 5 *Co.* 109.

8th. A convict within clergy forfeits all his goods, though he

be

be burnt in the hand; yet thereby he becomes capable of purchasing other goods. But, on burning in the hand, he ought to be immediately restored to the possession of his lands. 2 H. H. 388. 389,

The forfeiture upon an attainder of treason or felony shall have relation to the time of the offence, for the avoiding all subsequent alienation of the lands; but to the time of conviction, or *fugam fecit found*, &c. only as to chattels, unless the party were killed in flying from, or resisting those who had arrested him; in which case it is said, that the forfeiture shall relate to the time of the offence. *Plowd.* 488. See *Corruption of Blood.*

FORFEITURE IN CIVIL CASES, a forfeiture of copyhold by felling timber, was relieved in equity; but the lord-keeper declared, that in case of a wilful forfeiture he would not relieve. *Chan. Cas.* 96.

In case of a forfeiture, equity can relieve, where they can give satisfaction. 1 *Salk.* 156.

FORFEITURE OF MARRIAGE, a writ which anciently lay against him, who, by holding knights service, and being under age, and unmarried, refused her whom the lord offered him without his disparagement, and married another. F. N. B. 141.

FORGERY, is where a person counterfeits the signature of another, with intent to defraud; which by the law of England is made a capital felony.

A receipt to a cash memorandum, is not a receipt on acquittance for the payment of money within 2 Geo. II. c. 25. against forgery.

Forgery may be committed by making a mark in the name of another person.

It may also be committed in the name of a person who never had existence.

And it may be committed of an instrument, though such an instrument as the one forged does not exist either in law or fact.

Indorsing a real bill of exchange, with a fictitious name; is forgery; although the use of a fictitious name, was not essential to the negociation.

A forged bank-note (although the word *pounds* is omitted in the body of it), and there is no water-mark in the paper, is a counterfeit note for the payment of money.

Altering

Altering an entry of money received, made by a cashier of the bank, in the bank-book of a person keeping cash there, by prefixing a figure to increase the amount of the sum received, is forging a receipt for money.

A receipt indorsed on a bill of exchange in a fictitious name, is forgery, although such name does not purport to be the name of any particular person.

If a person, who has for many years been known by a name, which was not his own, and afterwards assume his real name, and in that name draw a bill of exchange, he will not be guilty of forgery, although such bill were drawn for fraudulent purposes.

If any person shall falsely make, forge, or counterfeit, or cause or procure to be falsely made, forged, or counterfeited, or willingly aid or assist in the false making or counterfeiting any deed, will, bond, writing, obligatory, bill of exchange, promisory note for payment of money, acquittance, or receipt, either for money or goods, with intent to defraud any person; or shall utter or publish the same as true, knowing the same to be false, forged, or counterfeited, he shall be guilty of felony without benefit of clergy; but not to work corruption of blood, or disherison of heirs. 2 Geo. II. c. 25.

Forging or imitating stamps to defraud the revenue, is forgery by the several stamp acts: and the *receiving* them is made single felony, punishable with seven years transportation. 12 Geo. III. c. 48.

FORISFAMILIARI, a son is properly said *forisfamiliari* when he accepts of his father's part of his lands, and is contented with it in the life time of his father, so that he cannot claim any more.

FORM, is required in law proceedings, otherwise the law would be no art; but it ought not to be used to ensnare or entrap. *Hob.* 232.

The formal part of the law, or method of proceeding, cannot be altered but by parliament: for if once those outworks were demolished, there would be an inlet to all manner of innovation, in the body of the law itself, 1 *Black*. 142.

FORMA PAUPERIS, is when any person has cause of suit, and is so poor that he cannot support the usual charges of suing at law, or in equity. In this case, upon his making oath that he is not worth five pounds his debts being paid, and bringing a certificate from some lawyer, that he has just cause of suit, the judge admits him to sue *in forma pauperis,* that is without paying fees to counsellor, attornies, or clerk: and he shall have original writs and subpœnas gratis. 11 H. VII. c. 12.

And he shall when plaintiff, be excused from costs, but shall suffer other punishment at the discretion of the judge. And it was formerly usual to give such paupers, if nonsuited, their election either to be whipped, or pay the costs; though the practice is now disused. 3 *Black.* 400.

It seems agreed, that a pauper may recover costs, though he pay none; for although the counsel and clerks are bound to give their labour to *him,* yet they are not bound to give it to his antagonist. *Id.*

FORMEDON, a real action which lies for the issue in tail after after the death of the ancestor, or for him in remainder or reversion after the estate tail determined, and is called *formedon,* because the writ comprehends the form of the gift. *Co. Lit.* 326.

It is in the nature of a writ of right, and is the highest action that tenant in tail can have; for he cannot have an absolute writ of right, which is confined only to such as claim in fee simple; and for that reason this writ of *formedon* was granted him by the statute *de donis.* 13 Ed. I. c. 1. *Booth.* 139.

This writ is distinguished into three species; in the *descendar,* in the *remainder,* and in the *reverter.*

A writ of *formedon in the descender* lies, where a gift in tail is made, and the tenant in tail aliens the land intailed, or is disseised of them and dies; in this case the heir in tail shall have this writ of *formedon in the descender,* to recover these lands so given in tail, against him who is then the actual tenant of the freehold.

A formedon in the remainder lies, where one giveth lands to another for life or in tail, with remainder to a third person in tail or in fee; and he who hath the particular estate dieth without issue inheritable, and a stranger intrudes upon him in the remainder, and keeps him out of possession; in this case, the remainder man shall have this writ of *formedon in the remainder.*

A formedon in the reverter lies, where there is a gift in tail, and

and afterwards by the death of the tenant in tail without issue of his body, the reversion falls in upon the donor, his heirs, or assigns; in such case, the reversioner shall have this writ to recover the lands. 3 *Black.* 191.

But these writs are now seldom brought, except in some special cases, where it cannot be avoided; the trial of titles by *ejectment*, is now the usual method, and is done with much less trouble and expence.

FORMER ACTION, in some cases a good plea to the bringing a new action.

The general rule is, that the party shall not be vexed twice for the same cause of action; but then it must appear, that the court first possessed of the cause, had jurisdiction; and nothing shall be intended to be within the jurisdiction of an inferior court, but what is averred so to be. *Gibb.* 314.

FORNICATION, the act of incontinency in single persons; for if either party be married, it is adultery; the spiritual court hath the proper cognizance of this offence; but formerly the courts leet had power to enquire of and punish fornication and adultery; in which courts the king had a fine assessed on the offenders, as appears by the book of Domesday. 2 *Inst.* 488.

FORPRISE, an exception or reservation.

FOOTGELD, or FOUTGELD, an amereement for not cutting out the balls of great dogs feet in the forest.

To be quit of *footgeld*, is a privilege to keep dogs within the forest, without punishment or controul.

FRACTION, the law makes no fraction of a day; and therefore if a person die of a wound he received, the year and day shall be computed from the beginning of the day on which the wound was given, and not from the precise minute or hour. 1 *Haw.* P. C. 163.

FRANCHISE, is taken for a privilege or exemption from ordinary jurisdiction, and sometimes an immunity from tribute; it is either personal or real, that is, belonging to a person immediately, or else by means of this or that place, or court of immunity, whereof he is either chief or a member *Crompt. Jurisd.* 41.

FRANK-ALMOIN, signifies a tenure or title of lands and tenements bestowed upon God, that is given to such people as devote themselves to the service of God, for pure and perpetual alms; whence the feoffers or givers cannot demand any terrestrial service, so long as the lands, &c. remain in the hands of the feoffees. F. N. B. 211.

These donations in *frank-almoine,* are now out of use, as none but the king can make them; but they are expressly excepted by the stat. 12 C. II. c. 24. abolishing tenures, and therefore subsist in many instances at the present day. 2 *Black.* 101.

FRANK BANK. See *Free Bench.*

FRANK CHASE, is a liberty of *free chase,* whereby all men having lands within that compass, are prohibited to cut down any wood, &c. without the view of the forester, though it be in his own demesnes. *Cromp. Jurisd.* 187.

FRANK FEE, that which is in the hands of the king, or lord of any manor, being ancient demesne of the crown, is called a *frank fee,* and that which is in the hands of the tenant is ancient demesne only: whence that seems to be *frank fee,* which a man holds at the common law to himself and his heirs, and not by such service as is required in ancient demesne, according to the custom of the manor. *Reg. Orig.* 12.

FRANK FIRM, lands or tenements, wherein the nature of fee, is changed by feoffment out of knight-service, for several yearly services; and whence neither, homage, worship, marriage, nor relief, may be demanded, nor any other service not contained in the feoffment. *Britt.* c. 66.

FRANK FOLD, is where the lord hath the benefit of folding his tenant's sheep within his manor, for manuring his land. *Keil. Rep.* 198.

FRANK LAW, the benefit of the common law of the land.

FRANK MARRIAGE, is a tenure in tail special, whereby the donees shall have the land to them and the heirs of their bodies, and shall do fealty to the donor, till the fourth degree.

FRANK PLEDGE, a *pledge* or surety for the behaviour of freemen, by a certain number of neighbours becoming bound for each other, to see each man of their pledge forthcoming at all times, to answer the transgression committed by any gone away: so that whosoever offended, it was forthwith enquired in what pledge he was, and those of that pledge, either produced him within thirty-one days, or satisfied for his offence.

FRANK

FRANK TENEMENT, a possession of freehold lands and tenements.

FRATERNITY, many persons united together in respect of mystery and business into a company, but their laws and ordinances cannot bind strangers, for they have not a local power of government. 1 *Salk.* 193.

FRATRIAGIUM. The inheritance of younger brothers, for whatever they possess of the father's estate, they possess *in ratione fratriagii*, and are to do homage to the elder brother for it, because he is bound to do homage for the whole to the superior lord. *Bract. lib.* 2. c. 5.

FRAUD. All deceitful practices in defrauding or endeavouring to defraud another of his own right, by means of some artful device, contrary to the plain rules of common honesty, are condemned by the common law, and punishable according to the heinousness of the offence. *Co. Lit.* b. 3.

The distinction laid down, as proper to be attended to in all cases of this kind, is this, that in such impositions or deceits, where common prudence might guard persons from the offence, it is not indictable, but the party is left to his civil remedy; but where false weights or measures are used, or false tokens produced, or such measures taken to defraud or deceive, as people cannot by any ordinary care or prudence be guarded against, there it is an offence indictable. *Burr.* 1120.

Persons convicted of obtaining money or goods by false pretences, or sending threatening letters to extort money or goods, may be punished by fine and imprisonment, or by pillory, whipping, or transportation. 30 G. II. c. 24.

FREE BENCH, is the widow's share of her husband's copyhold or customary lands, in the nature of dower, which is variable according to the customs in different places. In some manors it is one third, sometimes half, sometimes the whole, during her widowhood, of all the copyhold or customary land, which her husband died possessed of. In some places by custom she holds them only during her *chaste* viduity.

FREE CHAPEL, is so called, from its being free or exempt from the jurisdiction of the ordinary. Most of the *free chapels*, were built upon the manors and ancient demesnes of the crown, whilst in the king's hands, for the use of himself and his retinue when he came to reside there. And when the crown parted with these estates, the chapels went along with them, and retained their first freedom. *Black.*

These chapels are visitable by the king, and not by the ordinary; which office of visitation is executed for the king by the lord chancellor. See *Chapels.*

FREEHOLD, may be in *deed* or in *law*. A freehold *in deed*, is actual seisin of lands or tenements in fee-simple, fee-tail, or for life. A freehold *in law*, is a right to such lands or tenements before entry or seizure.

So there is a *seisin in deed*, and a *seisin in law*: a seisin in *deed*, is when a corporal possession is taken; and a seisin in *law*, is where lands descend before entry, or where something is done which amounts in law to an actual seisin. 1 *Inst.* 31.

Tenant in fee-simple, or fee-tail for life, it said to have a freehold, so called, because it distinguishes it from terms of years, chattels upon uncertain interests, lands in villenage, or customary or copyhold lands. 1 *Inst.* 43.

A freehold cannot be conveyed to pass *in futuro*, for then there would be want of a tenant against whom to bring a *præcipe*, and therefore, notwithstanding such conveyance, the freehold continues in the vendor: but if livery of seisin be afterwards given, the freehold from thence passes to the vendee. 2 *Wils.* 165.

A man is said to be *seised* of freehold, but to be *possessed* of other estates, as of copyhold lands, leases for years, or goods and chattels. See *Estate* and *Fee-simple.*

FREEHOLDERS, such as hold any freehold estate.

FREEMAN, is a term applied to certain members of a corporate city or town, who have either purchased their freedom, or acquired it by serving an apprenticeship, &c.

FREIGHT, is the consideration money agreed to be paid for the use or hire of a ship, or in a larger sense, the burthen of such ship.

The freight is most frequently determined for the whole voyage, without respect to time; sometimes it depends on time; in the former case it is either fixed at a certain sum for the whole cargo, or so much per ton, barrel, bulk, or other weight or measure, or so much *per cent* on the value of the cargo.

If a certain sum be agreed on for the freight of the ship, it must

must all be paid, although the ship when measured should prove less, unless the burthen be warranted. If the ship be freighted for transporting cattle or slaves at so much per head, and some of them die on the passage, freight is only due for such as are delivered alive; if for lading them, it is due for all put on board.

When a whole ship is freighted, if the master suffer any goods besides those of the freight to be put on board, he is liable for damages.

If the voyage be compleated according to the agreement, without any accident, the master has a right to demand the freight, before the delivery of the goods; but if such delivery is prevented by negligence, or accidents, the parties will be reciprocally responsible in the following manner.

If the merchant should not load the ship within the time agreed on, the master may engage with another and recover damages.

If the merchant recal the ship after she is laden, and sailed, he must pay the whole freight; but if he unload before the ship has actually sailed, he will in such case only be responsible for damages.

If the merchant load goods which are not lawful to export, and the ship be prevented from proceeding on that account, he must nevertheless pay the freight.

If the master be not ready to proceed on the voyage at the time stipulated, the merchant may load the whole or part of the cargo on board another ship, and recover damages, but any real casualties will release the master from all damages.

If an embargo be laid on the ship before she sail, the charter party is dissolved, and the merchant pays the expence of loading and unloading; but if the embargo be only for a short limited time, the voyage shall be performed when it expires; and neither party is liable for damages.

If the master sail to any other port than that agreed on, without necessity, he must sail to the port agreed on at his own expence, and is also liable for any damages in consequence thereof.

If a ship be taken by the enemy, and retaken or ransomed, the charter party continues in force.

If the master transfer the goods from his own ship to another, without necessity, and they perish, he is responsible for the full value,

value, and all charges; but if his own ship be in imminent danger, the goods may be put on board another ship at the risk of the owner.

If a ship be freighted out and home, and a sum agreed on for the whole voyage, nothing becomes due until the return of such ship.

If a certain sum be specified for the homeward voyage, it is due, although the correspondent abroad, should have no goods to send home.

A ship was freighted to a particular port and home, a particular freight agreed upon for the homeward voyage, with an option reserved for the correspondent to decline it, unless the ship arrived before a certain day. The master did not go to the port agreed on, and therefore became liable to damages; the obligation being absolute on his part, and conditional only on the part of the freighter.

If the goods be damaged without fault of the ship or master, the owner is not obliged to receive them and pay the freight, but he must either receive or abandon the whole; he cannot receive those that are not damaged, and reject the others.

If the goods be damaged through the insufficiency of the ship, the master is liable for the same; but if it be owing to stress of weather, he is not accountable.

If part of the goods be thrown overboard, or taken by the enemy, the part delivered pays freight.

The master is accountable for all the goods received on board by himself and mariners, unless they perish by the act of God, or the king's enemies.

The master is not liable for leakage of liquors, nor accountable for contents of packages, unless packed in his presence.

FRESH FORCE, a force done within forty days. If a man be disseised of any lands or tenements, within any city or borough, or deforced from them after the death of his ancestor, to whom he is heir, or after the death of his tenant for life, or in tail; he may, within forty days after his title accrued, have a bill out of chancery to the mayor, &c.

FRESH SUIT, is such a ready and earnest following of an offender, as never ceases from the time, of the offence being committed or discovered, until he be apprehended. And the effect

of

of this in the pursuit of a felon, is, that the party pursuing shall have his goods again, whereas otherwise, they are forfeited to the king. *Standf.* Pl. Cor. lib. 3, c. 10.

It seems to have been anciently holden, that to make a fresh suit, the party ought to have raised a hue and cry with all convenient speed, and also to have taken the offender; but at this day it seems to be settled, that if the party have not been guilty of gross neglect, but hath used all reasonable care and diligence in enquiring after, pursuing, and apprehending, the felon, he ought to be allowed to have made sufficient fresh suit, whether any hue and cry were levied or not, and whether such offender were taken by means of such pursuit, or without any assistance from it. 2 *Haw.* 169.

FRUIT. Every person who shall bark any fruit tree, shall forfeit to the party grieved, treble damages, by action at the common law; and also 10l. to the king. 37 H. VIII. c. 6.

Every person who shall rob any orchard or garden, or dig or pull up any fruit trees, with intent to take the same away (the same not being felony by the laws of this realm), shall, on conviction, before one justice, give to the party such satisfaction for damages, as such justice shall appoint; and in default of payment to be whipped. 43 Eliz. c. 7.

And with respect to what shall be deemed *felony* by the laws of this realm, the distinction seems to be, that if they be any way annexed to the freehold, as trees growing, or apples growing upon the trees, then the taking and carrying them away is not felony, but trespass only, for a man cannot steal part of a freehold; but if they be severed from the freehold, as wood cut, or apples gathered from the trees, then the taking of them is not a trespass only, but felony. *Id.*

Fine and imprisonment may be inflicted on persons destroying fruit trees. 1 *G.* I. c. 48.

Robbing orchards or gardens of fruit growing therein, may be punished by fine, whipping, &c.

FUEL. All faggots made for sale, shall contain in compass, besides the knot of the bond, twenty-four inches of assize; and every faggot stick within the bond, shall contain full three feet of assize, except only one stick to be but one foot long, to stop or harden the binding. 43 Eliz. c. 14.

All

All billets (except those made of beech) that lie exposed in the public places, where they are usually bought or sold, shall be assized and cut as directed by 9 Anne. c. 15.

FUGAM FECIT, is where it is found by inquisition, that a person fled for treason or felony; as to which it is agreed, that wheresoever a person found guilty by such inquest, either as a principal, or as an accessary before the fact, is found also to have fled for the same, he forfeits his goods absolutely, and the issues of his lands, till he be pardoned or acquitted.

But wherever the indictment against a man is insufficient, the finding a *fugam fecit,* will not hurt him; and that in all cases, the particulars of the goods found to be forfeited, may be traversed. 2 *Haw.* 450.

FUGITIVE'S GOODS, are the proper goods of him that flies, which after the flight lawfully found, belong to the king, or lord of the manor. 5 *Co. Rep.* 109. See *Felon's Goods.*

FUNERAL EXPENCES, are allowed previous to all other debts and charges; but if the executor or administrator be extravagant, it is a species of devastation or waste of the substance of the deceased, and shall only be prejudicial to himself, and not to the creditors or legatees of the deceased. 2 *Black.* 508.

But in strictness, no funeral expences are allowable against a creditor, except for the shroud, coffin, ringing the bell, parson, clerk, grave-digger, and bearers' fees, but not for pall or ornaments. 1 *Salk.* 190.

And in general it is said, that no more than 40s. in the whole for funeral expences, shall be allowed against creditors. 3 *Atk.* 249.

FURBOTE, FYRBOTE, FIREBOTE, a liberty granted by the lord to his servant, to take underwood for fire.

FURCA, in ancient privileges, signified a jurisdiction of punishing felons, viz. the men with hanging, the women with drowning.

FURCAM ET FLAGELLUM, the meanest servile tenure, when the bondman was at the disposal of his lord, for life and limb.

FURIGELDUM, a fine paid for theft.

FURTA, a privilege derived from the king, as prime lord, to

try,

try, condemn, and execute thieves and felons within certain bounds.

FYRTHWITE, a fine for deserting the army.

G.

GAFOLD GYLD, signifies the payment or rendering of tribute or custom.

GAFOL-LAND, land liable to tribute or tax.

GAGE, to give security that a thing shall be delivered: for if he who distrained, being sued, hath not delivered the cattle that were distrained, then he shall not only avow the distress, but *gage* deliverance, that is, put in sureties that he will deliver the cattle distrained. F. N. B 74.

GAINAGE, signifies the draft oxen, horses, wain, plough, and furniture, for carrying on the work of tillage by the baser sort of sokemen and villains; and sometimes the land itself, or the profit raised by cultivating it. *Bract. Lib.* 1. c. 9.

GAME. It is a maxim of the common law, that goods of which no person can claim any property, belong to the king by his prerogative. Hence those animals *feræ naturæ,* which come under the denomination of *game,* are styled in our laws his majesty's game; and that which he has he may grant to another; in consequence of which another may prescribe to have the same, within such a precinct or lordship. And hence originated the right of lords of manors, or others, to the *game* within their respective liberties.

As the sole right of taking and destroying game belongs exclusively to the king, as such he may authorize the only persons who can acquire any property, however fugitive and transitory, in the animals coming under that denomination.

For the preservation of these species of animals, for the recreation and amusement of persons of fortune, to whom the king with the advice and assent of parliament, has granted the same, and to prevent persons of inferior rank from misemploying their time, the following acts of parliament have been made. The common people are not injured by these restrictions, no right being taken from

from them which they ever enjoyed; but privileges are granted to those who have certain qualifications therein mentioned, which, before rested solely in the king. 2 *Bac. Abr*. 612.

For the sake of perspicuity we have arranged the different acts of parliament in alphabetical order.

Certificates, to be dated the day of the month when issued, and shall be in force till the first of July following and no longer; and if any clerk of the peace, his deputy, or steward, clerk, &c. issue certificates otherwise than directed, to forfeit 20l. 25 G. III. *Sess*. 2.

No person to destroy game until he has delivered an account of his name and place of abode to the clerk of the peace, or his deputy, or to the sheriff, or steward clerk of the county, riding, shire, stewartry or place where such person shall reside, and annually take out a certificate thereof, which must have a stamp duty of *three pounds three shillings*. 25 G. III. *Sess*. 2.

Any person counterfeiting or forging any seal or stamp directed to be used by this act, with intent to defraud the revenue, or shall utter or sell such counterfeit, on conviction thereof shall be adjudged a felon, and shall suffer death without benefit of clergy; and all provisions of former acts relative to stamp duties, to be in force in executing this act. 25 G. III. *Sess*. 2.

Every qualified person, shooting at, killing, taking, or shooting, any pheasant, partridge, heath-fowl, or black game, or any grouse or red game, or any other game, or killing, taking, or destroying, any hare, with any greyhound, hound, pointer, spaniel, setting dog, or other dog, without having obtained such certificate, shall forfeit the sum of 20l. *Id*.

Clerks of the peace or their deputies, or the sheriff, or steward clerks, in their respective counties, ridings, shires, stewartries, or places, shall on or before November 1, 1785, or sooner if required by the commissioners of his majesty's stamp duties, transmit to the head office of stamps in London, a correct list in alphabetical order, of the certificates by them issued between the 25th day of March, in the year 1785, and the first of October in the same year; and shall also in every subsequent year, on or before the first of August in each year, make out and transmit to the stamp-office in London, correct alphabetical lists of the certificates so granted by them, distinguishing the duties paid on each respec-

 tive

tive certificate so issued, and on delivery thereof, the receiver general of the stamp duties shall pay to the clerk of the peace, &c. for the same, one halfpenny a name; and in case of neglect or refusal, or not inserting, a full, true, and perfect account, he shall forfeit 20l. *Id.*

Lists may be inspected at the stamp-office for 1s. each search; *id.* which lists shall once or oftener in every year, be inserted in the newspapers in each respective county.

If any qualified person, or one having a deputation, shall be found in pursuit of game, with gun, dog, or net, or other engine for the destruction of game, or taking or killing thereof, and shall be required to shew his certificate, by the lord or lady of the manor, or proprietor of the land whereon such person shall be using such gun, &c. or by any duly appointed game-keeper, or by any qualified, or certified person, or by any officer of the stamps, properly authorized by the commissioners, he shall produce his certificate: and if such person shall refuse, upon the production of the certificate of the person requiring the same, to shew the certificate granted to him for the like purpose; or in case of not having such certificate to produce, shall refuse to tell his christian and surname, and his place of residence, and the name of the county, where his certificate was issued, or shall give in any false or fictitious name, he shall forfeit 50l. *Id.*

Certificates do not authorize any person to shoot at, kill, take, or destroy, any game at any time that is prohibited by law, nor give any person a right to shoot at, &c. unless he be duly qualified by law *Id.*

No certificate obtained under any deputation, shall be pleaded or given in evidence, where any person shall shoot at, &c. any game out of the manors or lands for which it was given. The royal family are exempted from taking out certificates for themselves or their deputies. *Id.*

Conies. Destroying conies, transportation. 5 G. III. c. 14.

Robbing warrens, felony without clergy. 9 G. I. s. 22.

Killing them in the night, or endeavouring to kill them, fine of 10s. or commitment. 22 & 23 Car. II. c. 25.

Unqualified person using gun to kill them, same may be seized. 3 Jac. I. c. 13.

Deer. Stalking deer without leave 10l. 19 H. VII. c. 11.

Hunting or killing them 10l. costs, and sureties for good behaviour. 5 Eliz. c. 21.

Buck stalls or engines kept by unqualified persons may be seized. 3 Jac. I. c. 13.

Selling or buying them to sell again, 40l. 3 Jac. I. c. 27.

Coursing or killing them without consent, 20l. 13 Car. II. c. 10.

Hunting, taking, killing, or wounding, 30l. or transportation. 3 W. III. c. 10. 5 G. I. c. 15. 9 G. I. c. 22. 10 G. II. c. 32.

Destroying pales or walls of inclosed grounds, without consent, 30l. 5 G. I. c. 15.

Keeper of parks privately killing or taking them, 50l. 5 G. I. c. 15.

Robbing places where kept, felony without clergy. 9 G. I c. 22.

Game-keepers. All lords of manors or other royalties may appoint game-keepers, and empower them to kill game. 22 & 23 Car. II. c. 25.

But if game-keeper dispose of the game without the lord's consent, he shall be committed for three months, and kept to hard labour. 5 Anne c. 14.

But no lord shall make above one game-keeper within one manor, with power to kill game, and his name shall be entered with the clerk of the peace; certificate whereof shall be granted by clerk of the peace on payment of 10s. 6d. Unqualified game-keeper killing or selling hare, pheasant, partridge, moor, heath-game, or grouse, he shall forfeit 5l. by distress, or commitment for three months, for the first offence, and every other four. 9 Anne. c. 21.

No lord shall appoint unqualified game-keeper, or one who is not *bona fide* servant to such lord, or immediately employed and appointed to take and kill game for the sole use of the lord; other persons under colour of authority for taking and killing game, or keeping any dogs or engines whatsoever for that purpose, shall forfeit 5l. in like manner. 3 G. I. c. 11.

Every deputation of a game-keeper to be registered with clerk of the peace, or in the sheriff's or steward's court books of the county, &c. where the lands lie, and annually take out certificate thereof, stamped with an half-guinea stamp. 25 G. III. *Sess.* 2.

Every

Every game-keeper from and after the passing of this act, who shall deliver his name and place of abode as aforesaid, and require a certificate, shall be annually entitled thereto, stamped as before directed from clerk of the peace or his deputy, sheriff, or steward, clerk, &c. to the effect of the form in the act set forth. *Id.*

Clerk of the peace, &c. after signing certificate, shall issue the same stamped, to the person registering the deputation, on requiring the same, for which he may receive *one shilling*. *Id.*

If any person to whom any deputation or appointment of a game-keeper shall have been, or at any time thereafter shall be granted, by any lord or lady of a manor, &c. shall for the space of twenty days after the deputation or appointment shall be granted, neglect or refuse to register the same, and take out a certificate as aforesaid, shall forfeit and pay the sum of 20l. to be applied as the law directs. *Id.*

Neglect, or refusal of issuing certificates, incurs a forfeiture of 20l. recoverable in the courts of Westminster, court of session, of justiciar, or exchequer in Scotland, by action of debt or information, for the use of the plaintiff with double costs of suit. *Id.*

Clerk of the peace, &c. may issue his certificate, to any game-keeper first appointed in any year after 1st of July in that year. *Id.*

If any lord or lady of a manor, or proprietor of land, shall make any new appointment of a game-keeper, and shall register the deputation with the clerk of the peace, &c. and shall obtain a new certificate thereon, the first shall be void; and any person acting under the same, after notice, shall be liable to all the penalties of the game-laws, and those against unqualified persons. *Id.*

Hares. Every person tracing or coursing hares in the snow shall be committed for one year, 31 Eliz. c. 5. unless he pay to the churchwardens, for the use of the poor, 20 shillings for every hare, or become bound by recognizances, with two sureties in *twenty pounds* a piece, not to offend again: and every person taking or destroying hares with any sort of engine, shall forfeit for every hare, 20s. in like manner. 1 *Jac.* I. c. 27. Persons found using engines liable to the punishment inflicted, as above, by 31 Eliz. c. 5. Unqualified persons keeping or using shooting-dogs, or engine to kill or destroy hares, shall forfeit 5l. to the informer, with double costs, 2 Geo. III. c. 19. by distress, or committed for three months for the first offence, and for every other four. 5 Anne. c. 14. Taking or killing hares in the night-time forfeit 5l. 9 Anne. c. 25. the whole to the informer with double costs. 2 Geo. III. c. 19. Killing, or taking with gun, dog, or engine, hare in the night, between the hours of seven at night, and six in the morning, from Oct. 12 to Feb. 12, and between the hours of nine at night and four in the morning, from Feb. 12, to Oct. 12, or in the day-time upon Sunday or Christmas-day, to forfeit not less than 10l. nor more than 20l. for the first offence; nor less than 20l. nor more than 30l. for the second offence; and 50l. for the third offence, with costs and charges; and, upon neglect or refusal, be committed for six or twelve calendar months, and may be publicly whipped: final appeal to the quarter-sessions. 13 Geo. III. c. 80. Persons armed and disguised stealing them, felony without clergy. Geo. I. c. 22. Higler, chapman, carrier, inn-keeper, victualler, or alehouse-keeper, having in his custody, or buying, selling, or offering to sale, any hare, unless sent up by some person qualified (or any person selling, exposing or offering for sale hares, &c. 28 Geo. II. c. 22.) shall forfeit for every hare 5l. the whole to the informer. 2 Geo. III. c. 92.

Heath-fowl, for preserving heath-cocks or polts, no person whatsoever, on any waste, shall presume to burn, between Feb. 2 and June 24, any grig, ling, heath, furze, goss, or fern, on pain of commitment for a month, or ten days, to be whipped and kept to hard labour. 4 & 5 W. & M. c. 23. Shooting heath-cocks, grouse, or moor-game, contrary to 1 Jac. I. c. 27. and killing any of them in the night, or using gun, dog, or engine, with such intent, contrary to 9 Anne, c. 25. and 13 Geo. III. c. 80. and carriers and others having such in their possession, contrary to 9 Anne. c. 14. are all liable to the same penalties, and recoverable in the same manner as those offences are subjected to shooting, &c. hares.

Partridges, taking partridges by nets or other engines, upon anothers freehold, without special leave of the owner of the same, penalty 10l. half to him who shall sue, and half to the owner or possessioner. 11 H. VII. c. 17. Shooting, &c. at partridges, with gun or bow, or taking them, &c. with dogs or nets, by 7 Jac

Jac. I. c. 11. or taking their eggs out of their nest, liable as persons shooting, &c. at hares, and also 20s. for every bird or egg. Selling, or buying to sell again, a partridge (except reared and brought up in houses, or from beyond sea) forfeit for every partridge 10s. half to him who will sue, and half to the informer. 1 Jac. I. c. 27. Taking, killing, or destroying partridges in the night, forfeits for every partridge 10s. half to him who will sue and half to the lord of the manor, unless he licence, or cause the said taking or killing, in which case his half shall go to the poor, recoverable by churchwarden; and if not paid in ten days, to be imprisoned for one month; and moreover shall give bond to the justice, with good sureties, not to offend again for two years, 23 Eliz. c. 10. To kill a partridge in the night, penalty 5l. 9 Anne. c. 25. The whole whereof is given to the informer, 2 Geo. III. c. 19. and may be recovered within three months. 5 Anne. c. 14. before a justice of peace, or within six months, by action in the courts of record at Westminster, 9 Anne c. 25. with double costs. 2 Geo. III. c. 19. Keeping or using any greyhounds, setting dogs, or any engine for destroying partridges, penalty 5l. to be levied and recovered as the like penalty for killing hares. Penalties for using gun, dog, snare, net, or other engine, with intent to take or destroy partridges in the night, or on Sunday, or Christmas-day, same as using them against hares; by 13 Geo. III. c. 80. Carriers and others having partridges in their possession, liable to the same forfeitures, and penalties as having hares; and the same law against shooting them as for shooting hares.

Pheasants. All the laws respecting the penalties and recovery of them, for taking them by nets, snares, or other engines, without licence of the owner, by 11 H. VIII. c. 17. and for shooting or destroying them with dogs or snares, &c. by 7 Jac. I. c. 11. or taking their eggs by 1 Jac. I. c. 27. and for selling, and buying them to sell again, by last cited act (except that the penalty for a pheasant is 20s.) and for destroying them in the night (except as aforesaid) by 23 Eliz. c. 10. 9 Anne. c. 25. and 13 Geo. III. c. 80. and for keeping or using sporting dogs or engines for destroying them on Sunday or Christmas-day, by 13 Geo. III. c. 80. and for carriers and others having them in their possession; all these laws are *mutatis mutandis, verbatim,* the same as those respecting *partridges.*

Prosecutions. Any one prosecuted for any thing done in pursuance of this act, may plead the general issue, and give the special matter in evidence for his defence; and if upon trial, verdict pass for the defendant, or plaintiff become nonsuited, defendant shall have treble costs of plaintiff. 25 Geo. III. sess. 2. s. 28.

Qualifications, for killing game, are 1. having a freehold estate of 100l. per annum, 22 & 23 Car. II. c. 25. 2. A leasehold estate for 99 years, of 150l per annum. 3. The eldest son or heir apparent to an esquire, or person of superior degree. 4. The owner or keeper of a forest, park, chace, or warren. Unqualified person, keeping dogs or engines, to destroy game to forfeit 5l. 5 Anne. c. 14.

No person (other than the king's son) unless he have lands of freehold to the value of five marks a year, shall have any game of swans, on pain of forfeiting them, half to the king, and half to any person, so qualified, who shall seize the same. 22 Ed. IV. c. 6.

Any gentleman or other that may dispend 40s. a year freehold, may hunt and take wild fowls with their spaniels only, without using a net or other engine, except the long bow. 25 H. VIII. c. 11. From persons not having lands of 40s. a year, or not worth in goods 200l. using gun, or bow to kill deer, any person having 100l. may seize the same to his use. 3. Jac. I. c. 13.

Every person qualified to kill game, shall previous to his shooting at, killing, or destroying any game, take out a certificate. See *Certificate.*

Sporting Seasons. The time for sporting in the day, is from one hour before sun rising, until one hour after sun setting. 10 Geo. III. c. 19.

For Bustards. The sporting season is, from December 1st to March 1st.

For Grouse, or red grouse, from August 11 to December 10.

Hares may be killed all the year, under the restriction, in 10 Geo. III. c. 19.

Heath-fowl, or black game, from August 20 to December 20.

Partridges

Partridges, from September 1 to February 12.

Pheasants, from October 1 to February 1.

Widgeons, wild ducks, wild geese, wild fowls, at any time but in June, July, August, and September.

Summary Proceedings, from and after March 1, 1785, in all cases where the penalty by this act, doth not exceed 20l. justice of peace shall, upon information or complaint, summon the party and witnesses to appear, and proceed to hear and determine the matter in a summary way, and upon due proof by confession, or upon the oath of one witness, give judgment for the forfeiture; and issue his warrant for levying the same on the offenders goods, and to sell them, if not redeemed within six days, rendering to the party the overplus; and if his goods be insufficient to answer the penalty, shall commit the offender to prison, there to be for six calendar months, unless the penalty be sooner paid; and if the party be aggrieved by the judgment, he may, upon giving security amounting to the value of the forfeitures, with the costs of the affirmance, appeal to the next general quarter-sessions, when it is to be heard and finally determined; and in case the judgment be affirmed, the sessions may award such costs, incurred by the appeal, as to themselves shall seem meet. 25 Geo. III. sess. 2.

Witnesses neglecting or refusing to appear, without reasonable excuse, to be allowed of by the justice, shall respectively forfeit for every offence 10l. to be levied and paid as other penalties by this act. *Id.*

Justice to cause conviction to be made out, to the effect of the form set forth in the act. *Id.*

Justice may mitigate penalties as he thinks fit, so that reasonable costs and charges of the officers, and informers, for discovery and prosecution, be always allowed, over and above mitigation, and so as the same does not reduce the penalties to less than a moiety, over and above the costs and charges, any thing therein contained to the contrary notwithstanding; and no such conviction shall be removeable by *certiorari* into any court whatsoever.

No offender against this act to be imprisoned more than three months. *Id.*

The

The duties to be paid to the receiver-general of the stamp-duties, and by him paid into the exchequer. *Id.*

Swans, it is felony to take any swans that be lawfully marked, though they be at large; and so it is unmarked swans, if they be domestical or tame, so long as they keep within a man's manor, or within his private river, or if they happen to escape from them, and are pursued and taken, and brought back again; but if they be abroad, and attain their natural liberty, then the property of them is lost, and so long felony cannot be committed by taking them. *Burn's Just. tit. Game.*

Wild fowl, same laws against shooting wild fowl as for shooting hares, by 1 *Jac.* I. c. 27.

GAMING, from the destructive and pernicious consequences, which must necessarily attend excessive gaming, both the courts of law and equity have shewn their abhorrence of it; but the playing at cards and dice, &c. when practised innocently and as a recreation, the better to fit a person for business, is not at all unlawful, nor punishable as any offence whatsoever. 2 *Vent.* 175.

And as the gaming in the manner as has been mentioned, may be lawful, yet if a person be guilty of cheating, as by playing with false cards, dice, &c. he may be indicted for it at common law, and fined and imprisoned according to the circumstances of the case, and heinousness of the offence. 2 *Bac. Abr.* 620.

Also all common gaming-house, are nuisances in the eye of the law, not only because they are great temptations to idleness, but also because they are apt to draw together great numbers of disorderly persons, which cannot but be very inconvenient to the neighbourhood. 1 *Haw.* 198.

It was therefore by 16 Car. II. c. 7. enacted, that if any person of what degree soever, shall by any fraud, unlawful device, or other ill practice, in playing at cards, dice, tables, tennis, bowls, skittles, shuffle-board, or by cock-fightings, horse-races, dog-matches, foot-races, or other pastimes, game or games whatsoever, or bearing a share or part in the stakes, or by betting on both sides of such as shall play, act, ride, or run as aforesaid, win or obtain to himself any sum of money or other valuable things, he shall forfeit treble the value; half to the king, and half to the party grieved, or who shall lose the money or thing so won or obtained, (provided

(provided he shall sue in six months) otherwise to any other person who shall sue in one year next after the said six months, by action of debt, bill, plaint, or information, in any of the courts of record at *Westminster*, with treble costs.

And by 9 Anne. c. 14. it is further enacted, that if any person do or shall, by any fraud or shift, cosenage, circumvention, deceit, or unlawful device, or ill practice whatsoever, in playing at or with cards, dice, or any of the games aforesaid, or in or by bearing a share or part in the stakes, wagers, or adventures, or in or by betting on the sides or hands of such as do or shall play as aforesaid, win, obtain, or acquire, to himself or themselves, or to any other or others, any sum or sums of money, or other valuable thing or things whatsoever, or shall at any time or setting, win of any more person or persons whatsoever, above the sum of *ten pounds*; that then, every porson or persons so winning by such ill practice as aforesaid, or winning at any one time or sitting, above the said sum or value of *ten pounds*; and being convicted of any of the said offences, upon an indictment or information to be exhibited against him or them for that purpose, shall forfeit five times the value of the sum or sums of money, or other things so won as aforesaid; and in case of such ill practice as aforesaid, shall be deemed infamous, and shall suffer such corporal punishment, as in case of wilful perjury; and such penalty to be recovered by such person or persons as shall sue for the same by such action as aforesaid. *Id.*

And any person who shall at any time or sitting, by playing at cards, dice, tables, or other game or games whatsoever, or by betting on the sides of such as do play, *lose* to any one or more persons so playing or betting, in the whole, the sum or value of *ten pounds*, and shall pay or deliver the same, or any part thereof, the person so losing and paying, or delivering the same, shall be at liberty within three months then next, to sue for and recover the same, with costs, in any court of record; and if he shall not sue in three months, it shall be lawful for any person to sue for and recover the same, and treble value, with costs, half to the person who will sue for the same, and half to the poor of the parish where the offence shall be committed. *Id.*

And every person who shall be liable to be sued for the same, shall be obliged to answer on oath such bill as shall be preferred against

against him, for discovering the sum of money or thing so won. *Id.*

If any person shall play at cards, dice, tables, tennis, bowls, skittles, shuffle-board, or any other pastime, game or games whatsoever, other than with and for ready money, or shall bet on the sides of such as shall play, or shall lose any sum or other thing exceeding 100l. at any one time or meeting, upon ticket, or credit, or otherwise, and shall not pay down the same when he shall so lose it, he shall not in such case be bound to make it good, but the contract, or contracts for the same, and for every part thereof, and all assurances and securities for the same shall be void and of no effect; and the winner shall forfeit treble value, of all such sums or other things as he shall so win above 100*l.* half to the king, and half to him who shall sue, within one year, in any of the courts of record at *Westminster*, with treble costs. 16 Car. II. c. 7.

And all notes, bills, bonds, judgments, mortgages, or other securities or conveyances whatsoever, where the whole or any part of the consideration of such securities and conveyances shall be for money or other valuable things won by gaming, or playing at cards, dice, tables, tennis, bowls, or other game or games whatsoever; or by betting on the sides of such as do game at any of the games aforesaid; or for the reimbursing or repaying of any money knowingly lent or advanced at the time and place of such play, to any person or persons so gaming or betting as aforesaid, or that shall, during such play so play or bet, shall be utterly void, frustrate and of none effect. And where such securities shall be of lands, tenements, or hereditaments, or such as incumber and affect the same; they shall enure and be to the sole use and benefit of, and devolve upon such person as should or might have such lands, in case the said grantor, or person so incumbering the same had been dead: and all grants or conveyances to hinder them from devolving on such person *shall be deemed fraudulent and void.* 9 Anne. c. 14.

If any person shall win at play, or by betting, *at any one time*, the sum or value of *ten pounds*, or within the space of twenty-four hours, the sum or value of *twenty pounds*, he shall be liable to be indicted for such offence in six months, either in the king's-bench, or at the assizes; and being convicted, shall be fined five times

times the value of the sum won or lost; which after such charges as the court shall judge reasonable, allowed thereout to the prosecutor and evidence; shall go to the poor.

And if one offender shall discover another, so that he be convicted, the discoverer shall be discharged from all penalties on account of such offence, if not before convicted thereof, and shall be admitted as an evidence to prove the same. 18 Geo. III. c. 34.

Any two justices may cause to come or to be brought before them, every person whom they shall have just cause to suspect to have no visible estate, profession, or calling to maintain themselves by, but do for the most part support themselves by gaming; and if such person do not make it appear to the said justices, that the principal part of his expences is not maintained by gaming, they shall require of him sufficient securities for his good behaviour for the space of twelve months; and in default of his finding such securities shall commit him to the common goal till he shall find such securities as aforesaid.

And if he shall, during the time for which he shall be bound, at *any one time or sitting*, play or bet for any sum or sums of money, or other thing or things, exceeding in the whole the value of 20s. such playing shall be deemed a forfeiture of the recognizance.

In order toprevent such quarrels as may happen on account of gaming; if any person shall assault and beat, or challenge to fight, any other person whatsoever, on account of any money won by gaming, playing, or betting, at any one of the games aforesaid, he shall on conviction thereof by information or indictment, forfeit to the king, all his goods, chattels, and personal estate whatsoever, and shall also suffer imprisonment without bail or mainprize, in the common goal of the county where the conviction shall be had, during the term of *two years*. 9 Anne. c. 14.

If any person who shall be licensed to sell any sorts of liquors, or who shall sell, or suffer the same to be sold, in his house, outhouse, ground, or apartment thereto belonging, *shall knowingly suffer* any gaming with cards, dice, draughts, shuffle-boards, mississipi, or billiard-tables, skittles, nine-pins, or with any other implement of gaming in his house, outhouse, ground, or apartment thereto belonging, by any journeymen, labourers, servants, or or apprentices; and shall be convicted thereof on confession, or oath of one witness, before one justice, within six days after the offence committed, he shall forfeit for the first offence 40s. and for every other offence 10l. by distress, by warrant of such justice, three-fourths to the churchwardens for the use of the poor, and one-fourth to the informers. 30 Geo. I. c. 24.

GANG DAYS, days for perambulation of the boundaries of parishes.

GARBLING. The office of garbling spices, &c. with all the fees and profits thereof, is granted to the mayor and citizens of London; and all spices and drugs are to be cleansed and garbled before sold, on pain of forfeiting the same, or the value.

GARNISHEE, the party in whose hands money is attached, within the liberties of the city of London, so used in the sheriff of London's court, because he has had garnishment or warning not to pay the money, but to appear and answer to the plaintiff creditor's suit.

GARNISHMENT, a warning given to one for his appearance, for the better furnishing of the cause and court.

GARTER, the ensign of a noble order of knights, called *Knights of the Garter*, or *Saint George*, which is superior to all others.

This order consists of twenty-six distinguished persons, of whom the king of England is the sovereign, and the rest are either nobles of the realm, or princes of foreign countries, friends and allies of this kingdom.

GABEL, tribute, toll, custom, yearly rent, payment, or revenue.

GABELET, an ancient and special kind of *cessavil* used in *Kent*, where the custom of *gavel kind* continues, whereby the tenant shall forfeit his lands and tenement to the lord, of whom he holds, if he withdraw from him his rent and services.

GAVELKIND, of the many opinions concerning the original of this custom, the most probable seems to be, that it was first introduced by the *Roman* clergy, and therefore propagated more extensively in *Kent*, because there the Christian religion was first propagated. This tenure is reckoned by the best antiquaries, to be the same with the Saxon *Bockland*, which was allodial, and exempt from the feudal service. 2 *Bac. Abr.* 637.

Gavelkind is a tenure or custom annexed and belonging to

2 lands

lands in *Kent*, whereby the lands of the father are equally divided at his death among all his sons; and in more ancient times still, amongst all the children male and female. But now all or most of these lands both in *Kent* and *Wales*, are by several acts of parliament *disgavelled*, and made descendible according to the common laws.

One property of *gavelkind*, was, that it did not escheat in case of an attainder and execution for felony.

GAUGER, is an officer appointed in different parts of the kingdom, to ascertain the contents of exciseable commodities.

The commissioners or sub-commissioners, in their respective circuits and divisions, may constitute under their hand and seals as many gaugers as are needful. 12 Car. II. c. 24.

GAZETTE, the only authentic paper published by royal authority. Dissolution of partnerships, commissions of bankruptcy, legal notices by advertisement, proclamations relative to the shutting up the ports, quarantine, embargoes, suspension or continuation of bounties, are all inserted in the *gazette*, which is considered as legal notice to all those whom it concerns.

GOAL, *goals* are of such universal concern to the public, that none can be erected by any less authority than an act of parliament. 2 *Inst.* 705.

All prisons and goals belong to the king, although a subject may have the custody or keeping of them. 2 *Inst.* 100.

The justices of the peace at their general quarter-sessions, or the major part of them, provided that such major part shall not be less than seven, upon presentment made by the grand jury at the assizes, of the insufficiency, inconveniency, or want of repair of the goal, may contract for the building, repairing, or enlarging the same, together with the yards, courts, and outlets thereof, and adding such other building, and making such conveniences as shall be thought requisite; or for erecting any new goal within any distance not exceeding two miles from the scite, and in that case for selling the old goal and the scite thereof, and also the materials of the old goal; the contractors giving security to the clerk of the peace for the performance of the contract. 24 Geo. III. c. 54.

The expence of building, rebuilding, repairing, or enlarging such goals, and such other necessary incidental expences as aforesaid, shall be paid out of the county rate; and when the account of such expence, shall exceed half the amount of the ordinary annual assessment for the county rate (to be computed at a medium for the last preceding five years), the justices in sessions may borrow in mortgage of the said rates, any sum not less than 50l. nor exceeding 100l. and may order the growing interest and so much of the principal sum as shall be equal at least, to such interest, to be paid off yearly, till the whole thereof shall be discharged, and an account thereof shall be kept in a book provided for that purpose; and such book shall be delivered into court at every quarter-sessions, to be inspected by the justices, who shall make such orders relating thereto as to them shall seem meet. Provided that the whole sum of money borrowed, be fully paid within fourteen years from the time of borrowing it. *Id.*

As there are several persons confined in the county and city goals, under sentence and orders made by one or more justices at their sessions, or otherwise, upon conviction in a summary way without the intervention of a jury; it is therefore by 24 Geo. III. c. 56. enacted, that any judge of assize, or two justices, within whose jurisdiction such goal is situate, may remove such persons to any house of correction within the same jurisdiction, there to be confined, and to remain in execution of such sentence or order.

For the relief of prisoners in goals, justices of the peace in sessions have power to tax every parish in the county, not exceeding 6s. 8d. per week, leviable by constables, and distributed by collectors, &c. 12 Car. II. c. 29.

But it is observed by *Lord Coke,* that the goaler cannot refuse the prisoner victuals, for he ought not to suffer him to die for want of sustenance. 1 *Inst.* 295.

If any subject of this realm shall be committed to any prison, for any criminal, or supposed criminal matter, he shall not be removed from thence, unless it be by *habeas corpus,* or some other legal writ; or where he is removed from one prison or place to another, within the same county, in order to his trial or discharge; or in case of sudden fire, or infection, or other necessity; on pain that the person signing any warrant for such removal, and he who executes

executes the same, shall forfeit to the party grieved 100l. for the first offence, and 200l. for the second, &c.

GOAL, or PRISON BREAKING, at the common law was felony, for whatever cause the party was imprisoned; but by 1 Ed. II. st. 2. the severity of the common law is mitigated which enacts, that no person shall have judgment of life or member, for breaking prison, unless committed for some capital offence; so that, unless the commitment be for treason or felony, the breaking of prison is not felony, but is otherwise punishable as a misdemeanor only, by fine and imprisonment. 4 *Black.* 130.

Any place whatever, wherein a person under a lawful arrest for a supposed crime, is restrained of his liberty, whether in the stocks or street, or in the common goal, or the house of a constable, or a private person, is a prison in this respect, for a prison is nothing else but a restraint of liberty; and therefore this extends as well to a prison in law, as to a prison in deed. 2 *Inst.* 589.

He that breaks prison, may be proceeded against for such a crime, before he be convicted of the crime for which he is committed; because the breach of prison is a distinct independant offence; but the sheriff's return of a breach of prison, is not a sufficient ground to arraign a man without an indictment. 2 *Haw.* 197.

It is not sufficient to indict a man generally for having feloniously broken prison; but the case must be set forth specially, that it may appear that he was lawfully in prison, and for a capital offence. 2 *Inst.* 591. *Hale's* P. C. 109.

GOALER, besides the duties enjoined goalers by act of parliament, and the abuses for which by statute they are punishable, the common law subjects them to fine and imprisonment, as also to the forfeiture of their offices, for gross and palpable abuses in the execution of their offices. 2 *Inst.* 381.

Also goalers are punishable by attachment, as all other officers are, by the courts to which they more immediately belong, for any gross misbehaviour in their offices, or contempt of the rules of such courts, and punishable by any other courts for disobeying writs of *habeas corpus* awarded by such courts, and not bringing up the prisoner at the day prefixed by such writs. 2 *Haw.* 151.

If the goaler, by keeping the prisoner more strictly than he ought, occasion the prisoner's death, this is felony in the goaler by the common law. Therefore if a prisoner die in goal, the coroner ought to sit upon him; and if the death were occasioned by cruel and oppressive usage on the part of the goaler, or any officer of his, it will be deemed wilful murder in the person guilty of such duress. 3 *Inst.* 91.

But if a criminal endeavouring to break goal, assault the goaler, he may be lawfully killed by him in the affray. *Jenk.* 93. 1 *Haw.* 71.

A goaler is considered as an officer relating to the administration of justice, and is under the same special protection of the law, that other ministers of justice are. If a person threaten him for keeping a prisoner in safe custody, he may be indicted, and fined and imprisoned for it. 2 *Rol. Abr.* 71.

If in the necessary discharge of his duty he should meet with resistance, whether from prisoners in civil or criminal suits, or from others in behalf of such prisoners, he is not obliged to retreat as far as he can with safety, but may freely and without retreating, repel force with force: and if the party so resisting, happen to be killed, this will be justifiable homicide in the goaler, or his officer, or any person coming in aid of him. On the other hand, if the goaler, or his officer or any person in aid of him, should fall in the conflict, this will amount to wilful murder in all persons joining in such resistance; for it is homicide in defiance of the justice of the kingdom. *Fost.* 321.

The justices in their sessions, or in any special adjournment held for such express purpose, may, if they shall think it necessary or proper, appoint salaries or allowances to goalers, in lieu of the profits derived from the sale of liquors, as to them shall seem meet, and order the same to be paid out of the county rate, by a certificate of such allowance being signed by the chairman of the sessions: but no chairman shall sign such certificate, unless notice of such intended application, signed by the clerk of the peace, have been given fourteen days at least, before the holding of such session, or adjournment thereof, by two several advertisements, in some newspaper, which shall be printed and circulated in such county. 24 Geo. III. c. 54.

It seems clearly agreed, that a goaler by suffering voluntary escapes

escapes, by abusing his prisoners, by extorting unreasonable fees from them, or by detaining them in goal after they have been legally discharged, and paid their just fees, forfeits his office; for that in the grant of every office it is implied, that the grantee execute it faithfully and diligently. *Co. Lit.* 233.

GOAL DELIVERY, by the law of the land, that men might not be long detained in prison, but might receive full and speedy justice, commissions of goal delivery are issued out, directed to two of the judges, and the clerk of assize associate; by virtue of which commission, they have power to try every prisoner in the goal, committed for any offence whatsoever.

GELD, a fine or compensation for an offence.

GEMOTE, an assembly.

GENERAL ISSUE, is that which traverses and denies at once, the whole declaration, without offering any *special matter* whereby to evade: and it is called the general issue, because, by importing an absolute and general denial of what is alledged in the declaration, it amounts at once to an issue; that is, a fact affirmed on one side, and denied on the other. 3 *Black.* 305.

GENEROSA, seems of late to be a good addition; for if a gentlewoman be named *Spinster* in any original writ, appeal, or indictment, she may abate, and quash the same. 2 *Inst.* 668.

GENTLEMAN, according to *Sir Edward Coke*, is one who bears coat-armour, the grant of which adds gentility to a man's family. 2 *Inst.* 667.

GIFT, a transferring the property in a thing from one to another without a valuable consideration; for to transfer any thing upon a valuable consideration, is a contract or sale: he who gives any thing is called the *donor*; and he to whom is given is called the *donee*.

By the common law, all chattels real or personal may be granted or given, without deed, except in some special cases; and a free gift is good without a consideration, if not to defraud creditors. *Park.* 57.

But no leases, estates, or interests, either of freehold, or term of years, or any uncertain interest, not being copyhold or customary interest, of, in, to, or out of, any messuages, manors, lands, tenements, or hereditaments, shall at any time, be assigned, granted, or surrendered, unless it be by deed or not in writing

 signed

signed by the party so assigning, granting, or surrendering the same, or their agents thereunto lawfully authorized by writing, or by act and operation of law. 29 Car. II. c. 3.

A gift of any thing without a consideration, is good: but it is revocable before delivery to the donee, of the thing given. *Jenk.* 109. *pl.* 9.

GILD, is a compensation or fine for a fault.

GILD MERCHANT, was a certain privilege or liberty granted to *merchants,* whereby they were enabled among other things, to hold certain pleas of land within their own precincts; such as the *gild merchant* granted by king *John* to the burgesses of *Nottingham.*

GIST of action, is the cause for which the action *lieth*; the ground and foundation thereof, without which it is not maintainable.

GLASS, by several statutes, regulations are made for making, importing, and exporting glass, which is to be under the management of the officers of the customs and excise. See *Complete Abridgement of the Excise Laws.*

GLEANING, it hath been said, that by the common law and custom of *England,* the poor are allowed to enter and glean upon another ground after the harvest, without being guilty of trespass; and that this humane provision seem borrowed from the mosaical law. 3 *Black.* 212.

But it is now positively settled, by a solemn judgment of the court of common pleas, that a right to glean in the harvest field, cannot be claimed by any person at common law: neither have the poor of a parish, legally settled such a right. 1 H. *Black. Rep.* 51..63.

GLEBE, GLEBELAND, is a portion of land, meadow, or pasture, belonging to, or parcel of the parsonage or vicarage, over and above the tithes. *Godolph. Rep.* 409.

Glebe lands in the hands of the parson, shall not pay tithes to the vicar; nor being in the hands of the vicar, shall they pay tithe to the parson. *Deggs. Pars. Couns.* c. 2.

By stat. 28 H. VIII. c. 11, every successor on a month's warning, after induction, shall have the mansion house, and the glebe belonging thereto, not sown at the time of the predecessor's death.

He that is instituted, may enter into the glebe land before induction, and has right to have it against any strangers. *Roll. R.* 192.

GOOD ABEARING, an exact carriage or behaviour of a subject to the king and his liege people, to which men of evil course of life, or loose demeanour, are sometimes bound.

GOOD BEHAVIOUR, surety for the good behaviour, is the bail or pledge for any person, that he shall do or perform such a thing; as surety for the *peace*, is the acknowledging a recognizance or bond to the king, taken by a competent judge of record, for keeping the king's peace. *Dalt.* c. 116.

A binding to the good behaviour, is not by way of punishment; but it is to shew, that when a man has broken the good behaviour, he is not to be trusted. 12 *Mod.* 566.

Justices of peace may chastise rioters, barretors, and other offenders, and also imprison and punish them according to law, and by discretion and good advisement; and also bind persons of evil fame to the *good behaviour, &c.* 34 Ed. III. c. 1.

This statute being penned in such general words, seems in a great measure to have left it to the discretion of justices of the peace, to determine what persons should be bound to their good behaviour, and consequently seems to empower them, not only to bind over those, who seem to be notoriously troublesome, and likely to break the peace, as Eves-droppers, &c. but also those who are publicly scandalous, or contemners of justice, &c. as haunters of bawdy-houses, or keepers of lewd women in their own houses, common drunkards, or those who sleep in the day, and go abroad in the night, or such as keep suspicious company, or such as are generally suspected as robbers, or such as speak contemptuous words of inferior magistrates, as justices of peace, mayors, &c. not being in the actual execution of their offices; or of inferior officers of justice, as constables, &c. being in the actual execution of their office; but it seems that rash, quarrelsome, or unmannerly words, spoken by one private person to another, unless they directly tend to a breach of the peace, are not sufficient cause to bind a man to his good behaviour. 1 *Haw.* 153.

GOVERNMENT, an orderly power constituted for the public good, to maintain order, distribute justice, &c.

Government, may be reduced to three kinds: the government of one

one, the government of the *many*, or the mixture of the two, which makes a third. The first is termed absolute monarchy; the second republican; and the third mixed monarchy. But the experience of past times has taught us, that a mixed monarchy is that, which unites the advantages wished to be attained in the most complete manner of any.

GRAND DAYS, are those days in every term, which are solemnly kept in the inns of court and chancery, such as *Ascension Day*, &c.

GRAND DISTRESS, a writ which lies in two cases, either when the tenant or defendant is attached, and so returned, and appears not but makes default, then a *grand distress* is to be awarded; or else when the tenant or defendant hath once appeared, and after makes default, then this writ lies by the common law, in lieu of a *petit cape*.

GRAND JURY, the sheriff of every county is bound to return, to every commission of oyer and terminer and of goal delivery, and to every session of the peace, twenty-four good and lawful men of the county, some out of every hundred, to inquire, present, do, and execute, all those things, which on the part of our lord the king, shall then and there be commanded them. They ought to be freeholders; but to what amount is not limited by law. Upon their appearance, they are sworn upon the grand jury, to the amount of twelve at the least, and not more than twenty-three, that twelve may be a majority.

They are not only to hear evidence on behalf of the prosecution; for the finding of an indictment is only in the nature of an enquiry or accusation, which is afterwards to be tried and determined; and the *grand jury* are only to enquire, upon their oaths, whether there be sufficient cause, to call upon the party to answer it. 4 *Black*. 302. & 303.

GRAND SERJEANTRY, is when a person holdeth his lands of the king by such services as he ought to do in person; as to carry the king's banner, or his lance, or to carry his sword before him at his coronation, or to do other like services; and it is called *grand serjeantry*, because it is a greater and more worthy service, than the service in the common tenure of soccage. *Lit*. 153.

GRAND LARCENY, See *Larceny*.

GRANT,

GRANT, a gift in writing of such a thing, as cannot aptly be passed or conveyed by word only.

A *grant* is the regular method, by the common law, of transferring the property of *incorporeal* hereditaments, or such things whereof no livery of seisin can be had. For which reason all *corporeal* hereditaments, as lands and houses, are said to be in *livery*; and the others as advowsons, commons, services, rents, reversions, and such like lie *in grant*. He that granteth, is termed the grantor; and he to whom the grant is made, is termed the grantee. A grant differs from a gift in this; that *gifts* are always gratuitous, *grants*, are upon some consideration or equivalent. 2 *Black*. 440.

GREENCLOTH, of the king's household, so termed from the green cloth on the table; it is a court of justice composed of the lord-steward, treasurer of the household, comptroller, and other officers, to whom is committed the government and management of the king's court, and the keeping of the peace within the verge.

GREEN-WAX, signifies the estreats of fines, issues, and amercements in the exchequer, under the seal of that court made in *green-wax*, to be levied in the county.

GUARDIAN, a guardian is one appointed by the wisdom and policy of the law, to take care of a person and his affairs, who by reason of his imbecility and want of understanding is incapable of acting for his own interest; and it seems by our law, that his office originally was to instruct the ward in the arts of war, as well as those of husbandry and tillage, that when he came of age he might be the better able to perform those services to his lord, whereby he held his own land. 2 *Bac. Abr*. 672.

There are several kinds of guardians, as, *guardian by nature, guardian by the common law, guardian by statute, guardian by custom, guardian in chivalry, guardian in socage*, and *guardian by appointment of the Lord Chancellor*.

Guardian by nature, is the father or mother; and here it should be observed, that by the common law every father hath a right of guardianship of the body of his son and heir, until he attain to the age of twenty-one years. *Co. Lit*. 84.

This guardianship extends no further than the custody of the infant's person. 1 *Inst*. 84.

It

It yields as to the custody of the person, to guardianship in soccage, where the title to both guardianships concur in the same individuals. 1 *Inst.* 88. *b.*

But guardianship in soccage ending at 14, it seems that after that age, the father or other ancestor, having a like title to both guardianships, becomes guardian by nature till the infant's age of 21. *Carth.* 384.

Lastly the father may disappoint the mother, and other ancestors, of the guardianship by nature, by appointing a testamentary guardian under the statutes 4 & 5. P. et. M. and 12 Car. II.

Guardian by nature, hath only the care of the person and education of the infant, and hath nothing to do with his lands merely in virtue of his office; for such guardian may be, though the infant have no lands at all, which a guardian in soccage cannot. *Co. Lit.* 88.

Guardian by the common law. If a tenant in soccage die, his heir being under fourteen, whether he be his issue or cousin, male or female, the next of blood to the heir, to whom the inheritance cannot descend, shall be guardian of his body and land till his age of fourteen; and although the nature of socage tenure be in some measure changed from what it originally was, yet it is still called socage tenure, and the guardian in socage is still only where lands of that kind, as most of the lands in England now are, descend to the heir within age; and though the heir after fourteen may choose his own guardian, who shall continue till he is twenty-one, yet as well the guardian before fourteen, as he whom the infant shall think fit to choose after fourteen, are both of the same nature, and have the same office and employment assigned to them by the law, without any intervention or direction of the infant himself; for they were therefore appointed, because the infant in regard of his minority, was supposed incapable of managing himself and his estate, and consequently derive their authority not from the infant, but from the law; and that is the reason they transact all affairs in their own name, and not in the name of the infant, as they would be obliged to do, if their authority were derived from him. *Co. Lit.* 87.

Hence the law has invested them, not with a bare authority only, but also with an interest till the guardianship ceases; and to prevent their abuse of this authority and interest, the law has made

made them accountable to the infant, either when he comes to the age of fourteen years, or at any time after, as he thinks fit; and therefore are not to have any thing to their own use, as the guardian in chivalry had. *Co Lit.* 90. *a.*

Guardian by statute, by the common law, no person could appoint a guardian, because the law had appointed one, whether the father were tenant by knight service, or in socage. 3 *Co.* 37.

The first statute that gave the father a power of appointing, was the 4 & 5 P. & M. c. 8. which provides under severe penalties, such as fine and imprisonment for years, that no one shall take away any maid or woman child unmarried, being within the age of sixteen years, out of or from the possession, custody, or governance, and against the will of the father of such maid or woman child, or of such person or persons to whom the father of such maid or woman child, by his last will and testament, or by any other act in his life time, hath or shall appoint, assign, bequeath, give, or grant the order, keeping, education and governance of such maid or woman child. 1 *Sid.* 362.

In the construction of this statute, the following opinion has been holden.

That a testamentary guardian, or one formed according to this statute, comes in *loco parentis*, and is the same in office and interest with a guardian in socage, and differs only as to the *modus habendi*, or in a few particular circumstances; as first that it may be held for a longer time, viz. till the heir attain the age of twenty-one, where before it was but fourteen; secondly it may be by other persons held, for before it was the next of kindred not inheritable, could have it; and now who the father names shall have it. *Vaugh.* 178.

Guardian by custom. By the custom of the city of *London*, the custody and guardianship of orphans under age, unmarried, belongs to the city. 2 *Bac Abr.* 675.

By the custom of *Kent*, where any tenant died, his heir within age, the lord of the manor might and did commit the guardianship to the next relation within the court of justice, in whose jurisdiction the land was; but the lord was bound on all occasions to call him to account; and if he did not see that the accounts were fair, the lord himself was bound to answer it. This province the

the lord chancellor hath taken from inferior courts, only in *Kent*, where these customs are continued.

Guardian in Chivalry, by the common law, if tenant by knight-service had died, his heir male being under the age of twenty-one years, the lord shall have the land holden of him, till such heir had arrived at that age, because till then he was not intended to be able to do such service; and such lord, had likewise the custody of the body of the infant, to bring him up, and inure him to martial discipline, and was therefore called guardian in chivalry. *Co. Lit.* 74.

Guardian in Socage. Guardians in socage are also called guardians by the common law. Wardship is incident to tenure in socage, but of a nature very different from that which was formerly incident to knight-service: for if the inheritance descend to an infant under fourteen, the wardship of him does not, nor ever did belong to the lord of the fee; because in this tenure, no military or other personal service being required, there was no occasion for the lord to take the profits in order to provide a proper substitute for his infant tenant. *Co. Lit.* 84.

Guardian by appointment of the Lord Chancellor. It is not easy to state how this jurisdiction was acquired; it is certainly of no very ancient date, though now indisputable: for it is clearly agreed, that the king as *pater patriæ*, is universal guardian of all infants, idiots, and lunatics, who cannot take care of themselves; and as this care cannot be exercised otherwise than by appointing them proper curators or committees, it seems also agreed, that the king may as he has done, delegate the authority to his chancellor; and that therefore at this day, the court of chancery is the only propert court, that hath jurisdiction in appointing and removing guardians, and in preventing them and others, from abusing their persons or estates. 2 *Inst.* 14.

And as the court of chancery is now vested with this authority, hence in every day's practice we find that court determining, as to the right of guardianship, who is the next of kin, and who the most proper guardian; as also orders are made by that court on petition or motion, for the provision of infants during any dispute therein; as likewise guardians removed or compelled to give security; they and others punished for abuses committed on infants, and

2

and effectual care taken to prevent any abuses intended them in their persons or estates; all such wrongs and injuries being reckoned a contempt of that court, that hath by an established jurisdiction, the protection of all persons under natural disabilities. 2 *Mod.* 177.

GUARDIAN OF THE CINQUE PORTS, a principal magistrate who hath the jurisdiction of those havens in the east part of England, which are called the *Cinque Ports*. See *Cinque Ports*.

GUARDIAN OF THE SPIRITUALTIES, is he to whom the spiritual jurisdiction of any diocese is committed, during the vacancy of the see. The archbishop is guardian of the spiritualties, on the vacancy of any see within his province; but when the archiepiscopal see is vacant, the dean and chapter of the archbishop's diocese are guardians of the spiritualties.

GUEST, a lodger or stranger in an inn, &c. action lies against an innkeeper refusing a guest lodging, &c.

GUILD, a fraternity or company.

GUILD-RENTS, rents payable to the crown by any guild or fraternity, or such rents as formerly belonged to religious *guilds*, and came to the crown at the general dissolution ordered by sale by 22 Car. II. c. 6.

GUNPOWDER AND COMBUSTIBLES. No person shall make gunpowder but in the regular manufactories established at the time of making the stat. 12 Geo. III. c. 61. or licensed by the sessions, pursuant to certain provisions, under forfeiture of the gunpowder and 2s. per lb. nor are pestle mills to be used under a similar penalty.

Only 40 lbs. of powder to be made at one time under one pair of stones, except Battle-powder, made at Battle and elsewhere in Sussex.

Not more than 40 cwt. to be dried at one time in one stove; and the quantity only required for immediate use to be kept in or near the place of making, except in brick or stone magazines, 50 yards at least from the mill.

Not more than 25 barrels to be carried in any land carriage, nor more than 200 barrels by water, unless going by sea or coastwise, each barrel not to contain more than 100 lbs.

No dealer to keep more than 200 lbs. of powder, nor any person not a dealer, more than 50lb. in the cities of London or Westminster,

minster, or within three miles thereof, or within any other city, borough, or market-town, or one mile thereof, or within two miles of the king's palaces or magazines, or half a mile of any parish-church, on pain of forfeiture, and 2s. per lb. except in licensed mills, or to the amount of 300lbs. for the use of collieries, within 200 yards of them.

GYPSIES. See *Egyptians*.

H.

HABEAS CORPORA, a writ which lies for the bringing in of a jury, or so many of them as refuse to come upon the *venire facias*, for the trial of a cause brought to issue.

HABEAS CORPUS, a writ, which a man indicted of a trespass before justices of the peace, or in a court of franchise, and being apprehended for the same, may have out of the king's-bench, to remove himself thither at his own costs, and to answer the cause there.

This is the most celebrated writ in the English law. Of this there are various kinds made use of by the courts at *Westminster*, for removing prisoners from one court into another, for the more easy administration of justice.

The most efficacious of which writs, in all manner of illegal confinement, is that of *habeas corpus ad subjiciendum*, which is the subject's *writ of right*, in cases where he is aggrieved by illegal imprisonment, or any unwarrantable exercise of power.

This writ is founded upon common law, and has been secured by various statutes, of which the last and most efficacious, was the 31st Car. II. c.2. which is emphatically termed the *habeas act*. This act may justly be deemed a second *magna charta*.

By this important statute it is enacted, that on complaint in writing, by or on behalf of any person committed and charged with any crime (unless committed for felony or treason expressed in the warrant, or as accessary, or on suspicion of being accessary before the fact to any petit treason or felony plainly expressed in the warrant, or unless he be convicted or charged in execution by legal process). The lord chancellor, or any other, of the twelve

twelve judges in vacation, upon viewing a copy of the warrant, or affidavit that the copy is denied, shall (unless the party have neglected for two terms to apply to any court for his enlargement) award an *habeas corpus* for such prisoner, returnable immediately before himself or any other of the judges, and upon return made, shall discharge the party, if bailable, upon giving security to appear, and answer to the accusation in the proper court of judicature.

That such writs shall be indorsed, as granted in pursuance of this act, and signed by the person awarding them.

That the writ shall be returned, and the prisoner brought up within a limited time, according to the distance, not exceeding in any case 20 days.

That the officers and keepers neglecting to make due returns, or not delivering to the prisoner or his agent, within six hours after demand, a copy of the warrant of commitment, or shifting the custody of a prisoner from one to another, without sufficient reason or authority (specified in the act), shall, for the first offence forfeit 100l. and for the second offence 200l. to the party grieved, and be disabled to hold his office.

That no person, once delivered by *habeas corpus*, shall be recommitted for the same offence, on penalty of 500l.

That every person committing treason or felony, shall if he require it, the first week of the next term, or the first day of the sessions of *oyer and terminer*, be indicted in that term or session, or else be admitted to bail, unless the king's witnesses cannot be produced at that time; and if acquitted, or if not indicted and tried in the second term or session, he shall be discharged from his imprisonment for such imputed offence: but no person, after the assize shall be open for the county in which he is detained, shall be removed by *habeas corpus* till after the assizes are ended, but shall be left to the justice of the judges of assize.

That any such prisoner may move for and obtain his *habeas corpus*, as well out of the chancery or exchequer, as out of the king's-bench or common-pleas; and the lord chancellor, or judges denying the same, on sight of the warrant or oath that the same is refused, forfeit severally to the party grieved, the sum of 500l.

That this writ of *habeas corpus*, shall run into the counties Pala-

 tine,

time, cinque ports, and other privileged places, and the islands of Jersey, Guernsey, &c.

That no inhabitants of England (except persons contracting, or convicts praying to be transported, or having committed some capital offence in the place to which they are sent) shall be sent prisoners to Scotland, Ireland, Jersey, Guernsey, or any places beyond the seas, within or without the king's dominions, on pain that the party committing, his advisers, aiders, and assistants, shall forfeit to the party grieved a sum not less than 500l. to be recovered with treble costs, shall be disabled to bear any office of trust or profit, shall incur the penalties of *præmunire*, and shall be incapable of the king's pardon.

The writ of *habeas corpus* being an high prerogative writ, issuing out of the king's-bench or common-pleas, not only in term but in vacation, by a fiat from the chief justice, or any other judge, and running into all parts of the king's dominions; if issuing in vacation, it is usually returnable before the judge himself who awarded it, and he proceeds by himself thereon, unless the term should intervene, when it may be returned in court.

To obtain this writ, application must be made to the court by motion, as in the case of all other prerogative writs.

This writ may also be obtained to remove every unjust restraint or personal freedom in private life, though imposed by an husband, or a father; but when women or infants are brought up by *habeas corpus*, the court will set them free from an unmerited or unreasonable confinement, and will leave them at liberty to choose where they will go.

Thus, the *habeas corpus ad subjiciendum*, is that which issues in criminal cases, and is therefore deemed a prerogative writ, which the king may issue to any place, as he has a right to be informed of the state and condition of the prisoner, and for what reason he is confined. And it is therefore also, in regard to the subject, deemed his writ of right, that is, such a one as he is entitled to *ex debito justiciæ*, being in nature of writ of error to examine the legality of the commitment, and commanding the day, the caption, and cause of detention to be returned. 2 *Inst.* 55. 4 *Inst.* 182. 2 *Roll. Abr.* 69.

The *habeas corpus ad faciendum et recipiendum* issues only in civil cases, and lies where a person is sued, and in goal, in some inferior interior jurisdiction, and is willing to have the cause determined in some superior court, which hath jurisdiction over the matter; in this case the body is to be removed by *habeas corpus*, but the proceedings must be removed by *certiorari*. 3 *Bac. Abr.* 2.

This writ suspends the power of the court below; so that if they proceed after, the proceedings are void, and *coram non judice*. 1 *Salk.* 352.

By this writ, the proceedings in the inferior court are at an end, for the person of the defendant being removed to the superior court, they have lost their jurisdiction over him, and all the proceedings in the superior court are *de novo*, and bail *de novo* must be put in, in the superior court. *Skin.* 244.

Habeas corpus ad respondendum, is where a man hath a cause of action against one who is confined by the process of some inferior court; in which case, this writ is granted to remove the prisoner to *answer* this new action in the court above. *Dyer.* 197.

Habeas corpus ad deliberandum et recipiendum, is a writ which lies to remove a person to the proper place or county, where he committed some criminal offence. 3 *Bac. Abr.* 2.

Habeas corpus ad satisfaciendum, lies after a judgment; and on this writ, the attorney for the plaintiff must indorse the number roll of the judgment, on the back of the writ.

Habeas corpus upon a *cepi*, lies where the party is taken in execution in the court below.

Habeas corpus ad testificandum, lies to remove a person in confinement, in order to give his testimony in a cause depending.

HABENDUM, in a deed, is to determine what estate or interest is granted by the deed, the certainty thereof, for what time, and to what use. It sometimes qualifies the estate, so that the general implication thereof, which by construction of law, passeth in the premises, may by the *habendum* be controlled: in which case the *habendum* may lessen or enlarge the estate, but not totally contradict or be repugnant to it. As if a grant be to one and the heirs of his body, to leave to him and his heirs for ever, here he hath an estate tail by the grant, and by the *habendum* he hath a fee simple expectant thereon. But if it had been in the premises to him and his heirs, to have for life, the *ha-*

habendum would be utterly void; for an estate of inheritance is vested in him before the *habendum* comes, and shall not afterwards be taken away, or divested by it. 2 *Black.* 298.

The *habendum* cannot pass any thing that is not expressly mentioned, or contained by implication in the premises of the deed; because the premises being part of the deed by which the thing is granted, and consequently that makes the gift; it follows that the *habendum*, which only limits the certainty and extent of the estate in the thing given, cannot increase or multiply the gift, because it were absurd to say, that the grantee shall hold a thing which was never given him. 2 *Roll. Abr.* 65. See *Deed.*

HABERE FACIAS SEISINAM, a writ of execution directed to the sheriff, commanding him to give to the plaintiff possession of a freehold: if it be a chattel interest, and not a freehold, then the writ is entitled *habere facias possessionem.* 3 *Black.* 412.

In the execution of these writs, the sheriff, if needful, may take with him the power of the county, and may justify breaking open doors, if the possession be not quietly delivered; but if it be peacefully delivered up, the yielding of a twig, a turf, or the ring of a door in the name of seisin is sufficient. *Id.*

HABERE FACIAS VISUM, a writ that lies in divers cases in real actions, as in dower, formedon, &c. where view is required to be taken of the lands or tenements in question.

HALF-SEAL, is used in chancery for the sealing of commissions to *delegates*, appointed upon any appeal, either in ecclesiastical or marine causes.

HALLAGE, a fee due for cloths brought for sale to Blackwell-hall in London. Also the toll due to the lord of a fair or market, for such commodities as are vended in the common-hall of the place. 6 *Rep.* 62.

HALMOTE or HALIMOTE, is what is now called a court-room, because it was a meeting of the tenants of one hall or manor.

HALYMOTE, an holy or ecclesiastical court; but there is a court held in London by this name, before the lord mayor and sheriffs for regulating the bakers, and was formerly held on the *Sunday* next before *St. Thomas's day*, and therefore called the *halymote*, or holy court.

HAMLET, HAMEL, and HAMPSEL, are diminutives of *Ham* which signifies habitation.

HAMSOKEN, is used in Scotland for the crime of him that violently, and contrary to the king's peace, assaults a man in his own house, which is punishable equally with ravishing a woman.

HANAPER OFFICE, in the court of chancery, is that out of which issue all original writs that pass under the great seal, and all commissions of charitable uses, sewers, bankrupts, idiocy, lunacy, and such like. These writs, relating to the business of the subject, and the returns to them, were originally kept in a *hamper*, in *hanaperio*; the other writs, relating to such matters wherein the crown is immediately or mediately concerned, were preserved in a little sack or bag, *in parva baga*; and thence hath arisen the distinction of the *hanaper office*, and *petty bag office*; both of which belong to the common law court in chancery. 3 *Black*. 48.

HARES. See *Game*.

HARIOT. See *Heriot*

HARRIERS. See *Dogs*.

HARBOUR, a port or haven for the security of shipping. Various statutes have been made fot the improvement and protection of harbours, and inflicting penalties upon persons guilty of nuisances, by throwing ballast or otherwise obstructing them.

HAWKERS AND PEDLARS, are such dealers or itinerary petty chapmen, who travel to different fairs or towns with goods or wares, and are placed under the controul of commissioners, by whom they are licensed for that purpose pursuant to Stat. 8 & 9 W. III. c. 25. and 29 Geo. III. c. 26.

Traders in linen and woollen manufactories sending their goods to markets and fairs, and selling them by wholesale; manufacturers selling their own manufactures, and makers and sellers of *English* bone-lace going from house to house, &c. are excepted out of the acts, and not to be taken as hawkers.

HAWKS, hawking or falconry seems now entirely disused, and has long been declining, if a judgment may be formed from the statute on that subject; for formerly if a man stole a hawk, it should be done of him as of a thief that stole a horse or other thing,

thing, that is, he should be guilty of felony, but should have his clergy. 3 *Inst.* 98.

And if any manner of person should hawk in another man's corn after it were eared, and before it were shocked, and be thereof convicted at the assizes, sessions, or leet, he should forfeit 40s. to the owner, and if not paid within ten days, he should be imprisoned for a month. 23 Eliz. c. 10.

HAY AND STRAW. See 35 Geo. III.

HAY-BOTE, signifies either a fine or recompense for hedge-breaking; or a right to take wood necessary for making hedges, either by tenant for life or for years, though not expressed in the grant or lease.

HEADBORROW, or HEADBOROUGH, the chief of the frank pledge, and him that had the principal government of them within his own pledge. And as he was called *head-borrow*, so was he called *burrow-head*, *bursholder*, *third-borrow*, *tithing man*, *chief-pledge*, or *borrow-elder*, according to the diversity of terms in several places. The same officer is now occasionally called a constable. The headborough was the chief of the ten pledges, the other nine were called, *hardboroughs*, or inferior pledges. See *Deciner*, and *Frankpledge*.

HEARSAY, is generally not to be admitted as evidence; for no evidence is to be allowed but what is upon oath; for if the first speech were without oath, another oath that there was such speech, makes it no more than a bare speaking, and so of no value in a court of justice; and besides, the adverse party had no opportunity of a cross-examination; and if the witness be living, what he has been heard to say is not the best evidence that the nature of the thing will admit. But in some cases, hearsay evidence is allowed to be admissible; as to prove who was a man's grandfather, when he married, what children he had, and the like; of which it is not reasonable to presume that there is better evidence. So in questions of prescription, it is allowed to give hearsay evidence, in order to prove general reputation; as where the issue was of a right to a way over the plaintiff's close, the defendant was admitted to give evidence of a conversation between persons not interested, then dead, wherein the right to the way was agreed. *Theory of Evid.* III. See *Evidence*.

HEDGE-

HEDGE-BOTE, necessary stuff for making hedges, which the lessee for years, &c. may of common right take in his ground leased.

HEDGE-BREAKERS, by 43 Eliz. c. 7. shall pay such damages as a justice of the peace shall think fit; and on non-payment shall be whipped. And 15 Car. II. c. 6. the constable may apprehend a person suspected, and by warrant of a justice, may search his houses and other places; and if any hedge-wood shall be found, and he shall not give a good account how he came by the same, he shall be adjudged the stealer thereof.

HEIR, is he to whom lands, tenements, or hereditaments, by the act of god and right of blood, do descend of some estate of inheritance. *Co. Lit.* 7. *b.*

Heir apparent. Here we must observe, that no person can be heir until the death of his ancestor; yet in common parlance, he who stands nearest in degree of kindred to the ancestor, is called even in his life time, *heir apparent.* *Co. Lit.* 8. *n.*

Also the law takes notice of an *heir apparent,* so far as to allow the father to bring an action of trespass for taking away his son and heir, the father being guardian by nature to his son, where any lands descended to him. *Co. Lit* 37.

Heir general, the *heir general,* or heir at common law, is he who after his father's or ancestor's death hath a right to, and is introduced into all his land, tenements, and hereditaments; but he must be of the whole blood, not a bastard, alien, &c.

None but the heir general, according to the course of the common law, can be heir to a warranty, or sue an appeal of the death of his ancestor. *Co. Lit.* 14.

Customary heir, a custom in particular places varying the rules of descent at common law is good; such is the custom of gavel-kind, by which all the sons shall inherit, and make but one heir to their ancestor; but the general custom of gavel-kind lands extends to sons only, but a special custom, that if one brother die without issue, all his brothers may inherit, is good. *Co. Lit.* 140 *a.*

To prevent the wrong and injury to creditors by the alienation of the lands descended, &c. by 3 & 4 W. & M. c. 14. it is enacted, that in all cases, where any heir at law shall be liable to pay the debt of his ancestor, in regard of any lands, tenements, or or hereditaments descending to him, and shall sell, alien, and make over the same before any action brought or process sued out against him, that such heir at law shall be answerable for such debt or debts in action or actions of debt to the value of the said land so by him sold, alienated, or made over; in which case all creditors shall be preferred, as in actions against executors and administrators, and such execution shall be taken out upon any judgment or judgments so obtained against such heirs, to the value of the said land, as if the same were his own proper debts; saving that the lands, tenements, and hereditaments *bona fide* aliened before the action brought, shall not be liable to such execution.

Provided, that where any action of debt upon any specialty, is brought against any heir, he may plead *riens per descent* at the time of the original writ brought, or the bill filed against him; any thing therein contained to the contrary notwithstanding. And the plaintiff in such action may reply, that he had lands, tenements, or hereditaments from his ancestor before the original writ brought, or the bill filed; and if upon issue joined thereupon, it be found for the plaintiff, the jury shall inquire of the value of the lands, tenements, or hereditaments so descended, and thereupon judgment shall be given, and execution shall be awarded as aforesaid; but if judgment be given against such heir, by confession of the action with confes-ing the assets descended, or upon demurrer, or *nihil dixit*, it shall be for the debt and damages, without any writ to enquire of the lands, tenements, or hereditaments so descended.

Before this statute, if the ancestor had devised away the lands, a creditor by specialty had no remedy, either against the heir or devisee. *Abr. Eq.* 149.

But by the said statute, it is enacted that all wills and testaments, limitations, dispositions, or appointments, of or concerning any manors, messuages, lands, tenements, or hereditaments, or of any rent, profit, term, or charge out of the same, whereof any person at the time of his decease, shall be seized in fee simple, possession, reversion, or remainder, or have power to dispose of the same by his last will and testament, shall be deemed and taken, only against such creditor as aforesaid, his heirs, successors, executors, administrators and assigns and every of them, to

be

be fraudulent, and clearly, absolutely, and utterly void, frustrate, and of none effect; any pretence, colour, feigned, or presumed consideration, or any other matter or thing to the contrary notwithstanding.

And for the means, that such creditors may be enabled to recover their said debts, it is farther enacted, that in the cases beforementioned, every such creditor shall and may maintain his action of debt, upon his said bonds and specialties, against the heir at law of such obligor, and such devisee and devisees jointly, by virtue of this act; and such devisee and devisees, shall be liable and chargeable for a false plea by him or them pleaded, in the same manner as any heir, should have been for false plea by him pleaded, or for not confessing the lands or tenements to him descended.

Provided, that where there hath been or shall be any limitation or appointment, devise or disposition, of any manors, messuages, lands, tenements, or hereditaments, for the raising or payment of any real or just debt, or any portion, sum or sums of money, for any child or children of any person, other than the heir at law, in pursuance of any marriage contract or agreement in writing *bona fide* made before such marriage; the same and every of them shall be in full force, and the same manors, &c. may be holden and enjoyed by every such person, his heirs, executors, administrators, and assigns, for whom the said limitation, appointment, devise, or disposition was made, and by his trustee, his heirs, executors, administrators, and assigns, for such estate or interest, as shall be so limited or appointed, devised, or disposed, until such debt or debts, portion, or portions, shall be raised, paid, and satisfied; any thing contained in this act to the contrary notwithstanding.

And it is further enacted by the said statute, that all and every devisee and devisees made liable by this act, shall be liable and chargeable in the same manner as the heir at law, by force of this act, notwithstanding the lands, tenements, and hereditaments to him or them devised, shall be aliened before the action brought.

In the construction of this statute it hath been holden, that though a man is prevented thereby from defeating his creditors by will

will, that yet any settlement or disposition he shall make in his life-time of his lands, whether voluntary or not, will be good against bond creditors; for that was not provided against by the statute, which only took care to secure such creditors from any imposition, which might be supposed in a man's last sickness; but if he gave away his estate in his life time, this prevented the descent of so much to the heir, and consequently took away their remedy against him, who was only liable in respect of the lands descended; and as a bond is no lien whatsoever on the lands in the hands of the obligor, much less can it be so, when they are given away to a stranger. *Abr. Eq.* 149.

HEIRESS, is a female heir to a person having an estate of inheritance of lands. If there be more than one, they are called *co-heiresses*, or rather in legal expression, *co-heirs*. The offence of stealing an heiress is founded on the statute 3 H. VII. c. 2. which enacts, that if any man shall, for lucre, take any woman, being maid, widow, or wife, and having substance either in goods or lands, or being heir apparent to her ancestor, contrary to her will, and afterwards she be married to such misdoer, or by his consent to another, or defiled; he, his procurors, and abbettors, and such as knowingly receive such woman, shall be deemed principal felons: and by 39 Eliz. c. 9. the benefit of clergy is taken away from principals, procurors, and accessaries before. And it is not material, whether a woman so taken, contrary to her will be at last married or defiled, with her own consent or not, if she were under the force at the time.

HEIR-LOOMS, are such goods and personal chattels, as contrary to the nature of chattels, shall go by special custom to the heir, along with the inheritance, and not the executor of the last proprietor.

HEMP AND FLAX, no hemp or flax is to be watered in any river, running water, stream, brook, or pond, where beasts are used to be watered, but only in their several ponds for that purpose, on pain of 20s. 33 H. VIII. c. 17.

Any persons may in any place, corporate town, privileged or unprivileged, set up manufactories of hemp or flax; and persons coming from abroad, using the trade of hemp or flax-dressing, and of making thread, weaving cloth made of hemp or flax, or

making

making tapestry hangings, twine or nets for fishery, cordage, &c. after three years, shall have the privileges of natural born subjects. 15 Car. II. c. 15.

HERALD, is an officer at arms, whose business is to denounce war, proclaim peace, or be otherwise employed by the king in martial messages or other business.

They are the judges and examiners of gentlemen's coats of arms, and preservers of genealogies; and they marshall all solemnities at the coronation of princes, and funerals of great persons.

Their office in adjusting armorial ensigns, and preserving genealogies, is now but little attended to; so much falsity and confusion having crept into their records, that though formerly some credit hath been paid to their testimony, yet now even their common seal will not be received as evidence in any court of justice. But their original visitation books, compiled when progresses were solemnly and regularly made into every part of the kingdom, to enquire into the state of families, and to register such marriages and descents as were verified to them upon oath, are allowed to be good evidence of pedigrees. It were to be wished, that this practice of visitation at certain periods were revived; for the failure of *inquisitions post mortem*, by the abolition of military tenures, combined with the negligence of the heralds in omitting their usual progresses, hath rendered the proof of a modern descent, for the recovery of an estate, or succession to a title of honour, more difficult than that of an ancient. This will indeed be remedied for the future, with respect to claims of peerage, by a standing order of the house of lords, 11 May 1767, directing the heralds to take exact accounts, and preserve regular entries, of all peers and peeresses of England, and their respective descendants; and that an exact pedigree of each peer and his family, shall on the day of his first admission, be delivered to the house by *garter*, principal king at arms. But the general inconvenience, affecting more private successions, still continues without a remedy. 3 *Black.* 105.

HERBAGE, is most generally used for a liberty that a man hath to feed his cattle in another man's ground, as in the forest.

HEREDITAMENTS, all such things immoveable, whether corporeal or incorporeal, as a man may leave to him and his heirs, by way of inheritance: or not being otherwise devised, do naturally descend to him who is next heir of blood, and fall not within the compass of an executor or administrator, as chattels do. It is a word of large extent, and much used in conveyances; for by the grant of *hereditaments*, isles, seignories, manors, houses, and lands of all sorts, charters, rents, services, advowsons, commons, and whatever may be inherited, will pass. *Co. Lit.* 6.

Hereditaments, are of two kinds, *corporeal* and *incorporeal*. *Corporeal hereditaments*, consist wholly of substantial and permanent objects, all which may be comprehended under the general denomination of land only: for land comprehends in its legal signification, any ground, soil, or earth whatsoever, as arable, meadows, pastures, woods, moors, waters, marshes, furzes, and heath. 1 *Inst.* 4.

Incorporeal hereditaments, are not the object of sensation, neither can they be seen or handled, are creatures of the mind, and exist only in contemplation: they are principally of ten sorts, viz. advowsons, tithes, commons, ways, offices, dignities, franchises, corodies or presents, and rents. *Black.*

HERESY, among protestants, is said to be a false opinion, repugnant to some point of doctrine clearly revealed in scripture, and either absolutely essential to the Christian faith, or at least of most high importance. 1 *Haw.* 3.

All old statutes, that give a power to arrest or imprison persons for heresy, or introduced any forfeiture on that account, are repealed; yet by the common law, an obstinate heretic being excommunicated, is still liable to be imprisoned by force of the writ, *de excommunicato capiendo*, till he make satisfaction to the church. 1 *Haw.* 5.

And if any person having been educated in, or having made profession of the Christian religion within this realm, shall be convicted in any of the courts at Westminster, or at the assizes, of denying any of the persons in the holy trinity to be God, or maintaining that there are more Gods than one, or of denying the truth of the Christian religion, or the divine authority of the holy scriptures, he shall for the first offence, be adjudged incapable of any office, and for the second shall be disabled to sue any action, or to be guardian, executor, or administrator, or take by any legacy

or

deed of gift, or to bear any office civil or military, or benefice ecclesiastical, for ever, and shall also suffer imprisonment for three years, without bail or mainprize, from the time of such conviction.

HERIOT, signifies a tribute given to the lord, for his better preparation towards war. And by the laws of *Canute*, it appears, that at the death of the great men of this nation, so many horses and arms were to be paid for, as they were in their respective lifetimes obliged to keep for the king's service.

A heriot was first paid in arms and horses; it is now by custom sometimes the best live beast which the tenant dies possessed of, sometimes the best inanimate good, under which a jewel or piece of plate may be included. 2 *Black.* 422.

As to the several kinds of heriots, some are due by custom, some by tenure, and by reservation on deeds executed within time of memory; those due by custom are the most frequent, and arose by the contract or agreement of the lord and tenant, in consideration of some benefit or advantage accruing to the tenant, and for which an heriot, as the best beast, best piece of household-furniture, &c. became due, and belonged to the lord either on the death or alienation of the tenant, and which the lord may seize, either within the manor or without, at his election. *Dyer.* 199. *b.*

It hath been solemnly adjudged, that for an heriot service, or for an heriot reserved by way of tenure, the lord may either *seize or distrain*; for when the tenant agrees that the lord shall on his death have the best beast, &c. the lord hath his election which beast he will take, and by seizing thereof reduces that to his possession, wherein he had a property at the death of the tenant, without the concurring act of any other person; and it is not like the case where the tenant receives 20*s.* or a robe, for there the lessee has his election which he will pay, and being to do the first act, the lord cannot seize, but must distrain. *Plowd.* 96.

If the tenure be by rent and heriot service, viz. to have the best beast after the death of the tenant, and the lord distrain for the heriot, he need not in his avowry shew which was the best beast that he was entitled to, nor of what value it was; for the tenant might have esloined the cattle, and thereby it might have been impossible for the lord to know which was the best beast;

 and

and the tenant at his peril is to render the best beast, or sufficient recompence. *Cro. Car.* 260.

Upon the whole, the custom of the manor is the law of it, in all such like cases.

HERRINGS, it is unlawful to buy or sell herrings at sea, before the fishermen come into the haven, and the cable of the ship be drawn to the land. 31 Ed. III. c. 2.

No herrings shall be sold in any vessel but where the barrel contains 32 gallons, and half barrel and firkin accordingly; and they must be well packed, of one time's packing and salting, and be as good in the middle as at the ends; on pain of forfeiting 3s. 4d. a barrel.

Vessels for herrings are to be marked with the quantity and place where packed: and packers are to be appointed and sworn in all fishing ports, and under the penalty of 100l.

HIDE OF LAND, is said to be one hundred and twenty acres; but according to *Sir Edward Coke*, a knight's fee, a hide or plough land, a yard land, or an oxgang of land, do not contain any certain number of acres.

HIGHWAY, a public passage for the king's people; whence it is called the *king's highway*. It seems that anciently there were but four highways in England, which were free and common to all the king's subjects, and through which they might pass without any toll, unless there were a particular consideration for it; all others which we have at this day, are supposed to have been made through the grounds of private persons, on writs of *ad quod dammum*, &c. which being an injury to the owner of the soil, it is said they may prescribe for toll, without any special consideration. 3 *Bac. Abr.* 54.

There are three kinds of ways, a foot-way, a pack and prime way, which is both an horse and foot-way, and a cart-way, which contains the other two. 1 *Inst.* 56.

But notwithstanding these distinctions, it seems that any of the said ways which is common to all the king's subjects; whether it lead directly to a market-town, or only from town to town, may properly be called an highway: and that any such cart-way may be called the king's highway: that a river common to all men may also be called an highway; and that nuisances in any of the said ways are punishable by indictment; otherwise they would

would not be punished at all: for they are not actionable unless they cause a special damage to some particular person; because if such action would lie, a multiplicity of suits would ensue. 2 *Durnf. & East.*

But it seems that a way to a parish-church, or to the common field of a town, or to a village, which terminates there, may be called a private way, because it belongs not to all the king's subjects, but only to the particular inhabitants of such parish, house, or village, each of which as it seems, may have an action for a nuisance therein. 1 *Haw.* 201.

If passengers have used time out of mind, where the roads are bad, to go by outlets on the land adjoining to an highway in an open field, such outlets are parcel of the highway; and therefore if they be sown with corn, and the track foundrous, the king's subjects may go upon the corn. 1 *Roll. Abr.* 390.

If a way which a man has, become impassable or very bad, by the owner of the land tearing it up with his carts, by which means it is filled with water; yet he who has the way, cannot dig the ground to let out the water, for he has no interest in the soil. But he may bring his action against the owner of the land for spoiling the way. *Godb.* 52.

Where a private way is spoiled by those who have a right to pass thereon, and not through the default of the owner of the land, it seems that they who have the use and benefit of the way, ought to repair it, and not the owner of the soil, unless he be bound thereto by custom or special government. 2 *Burn.* 483.

Repairing highways, it seems agreed that by the common law, the general charge of repairing all highways, lies on the occupiers of the lands in the parish wherein they are. But it is said that the tenants of the lands adjoining are bound to scour their ditches. 1 *Roll. Abr.* 39.

Particular persons may be burdened with the general charge of repairing an highway, in two cases: in respect of an inclosure, or by prescription. As where the owner of lands not inclosed, next adjoining to the highway, incloses his lands on both sides thereof; in which case he is bound to make a perfect good way, and shall not be excused for making it as good as it was at the time of the inclosure, if it were then any way defective; because, before the inclosure, when the way was bad, the people for their better passage, went over the fields adjoining, out of the common track, a liberty which the inclosure has deprived them of.

And particular persons may be bound to repair an highway by prescription; and it is said that a corporation aggregate, may be compelled to do it by force of a general prescription, that it ought and has used to do it, without shewing that it used to do so in respect of the tenure of certain lands, or for other consideration; because such a corporation, in judgment of law, never dies, and therefore if it were ever bound to such duty, it must continue to be always so; neither is it any plea, that such a corporation has always done it out of charity, for what it has always done, it shall be presumed to have been always bound to do. But it is said that such a general prescription is not sufficient to charge a private person, because no man is bound to do a thing which his ancestors have done, unless it be for some special reason; as having lands descended to him holden by such service, &c. 1 *Haw*. 202. 203.

It seems certain in all cases, whether a private person be bound to repair an highway by inclosure or prescription, that the parish cannot take the advantage of it on the general issue, but must plead it specially; and that therefore, if to an indictment against the parish for not repairing an highway, they plead not guilty, this shall be intended only that the ways are in repair, but does not go to the right of reparation. 1 *Mod*. 112.

At common law, it it is said that all the county ought to make good the reparations of an highway, where no particular persons are bound to do it; by reason the whole county have their ease and passage by the said way. *Co. Rep*. 13.

By the ancient common law, villages are to repair their highways, and may be punished for their decay; and if any do injury or straighten the highway, he is punishable in the king's-bench, or before the justices of peace, in the court leet, &c. *Cromp. Jurisd*. 76.

Destroying any public turnpike-gate, or the rails or fences thereto belonging, subjects the offender to hard labour for three months, and to be publicly whipped. 1 Geo. II. c. 19.

On conviction at the assizes, the offender may be transported for seven years. And on a second offence, or on demolishing any turnpike-house, he shall be guilty of felony, and transported for seven

seven years. But in both these cases the prosecution must be within six months; and on the convict's returning from transportation, he shall suffer death. 5 G. II. c. 33.

Every justice of the peace, by the statute, upon his own view, or on oath made to him by the surveyor, may make presentment of roads being out of repair; and thereupon like process shall be issued as upon indictment.

HIGHWAYMEN. A reward of 40l. is given for the apprehending and taking of an highwayman, to be paid within a month after conviction, by the sheriff of the county, &c. 4 & 5 W. & M. c. 8. See *Felony*.

HIRING AND BORROWING, are contracts by which a qualified property may be transferred to the hirer, or borrower; in which there is only this difference, that *hiring*, is always for a price, a stipend, or additional recompence; *borrowing* is merely gratuitous. But the law in both cases is the same. They are both contracts, whereby the possession and a transient property is transferred for a particular time or use, on condition or agreement to restore the goods so hired or borrowed, as soon as the time is expired, or use performed; together with the price or stipend, in case of hiring, either expressly agreed on by the parties, or left to be implied by law, according to the value of the service. 2 *Black.* 454.

HOLDING OVER, is keeping possession of the land after the expiration of the term.

If any person shall hold over after the determination of any term for life or years, and after demand made, and notice in writing given for delivering possession, he shall pay double the yearly value, to be recovered by action of debt. 4 G. II. c. 28.

And if any person shall hold over, after himself hath given notice (either verbal or in writing) to quit, he shall pay double rent; to be recovered in like manner as the single rent. 11 G. II. c. 19.

HOLDING OVER A TERM, &c. Lands being devised to one till 800l. raised; if the heir at law, or he in reversion or remainder, in case of lease or limitation of a life, enter on him to whom the lands are devised or limited, and expel him, it is in the election of him so expelled, either to bring his action and recover the mean profits which shall be accounted parcel of the sum, or or he may re-enter and hold over till he shall levy the entire sum, not accounting the time of his expulsion. But otherwise, if the expulsion were by a stranger. 4 *Rep.* 82.

HOLIDAYS, or days of rest, are certain days on which religious festivals were formerly held, and upon which labour or business are prohibited. Thus Sunday, Good-Friday, and Christmas-day, are days expressly constituted holidays by statute: there are also certain days which are kept by the public offices as holidays.

A bill of exchange, if falling due on Sunday, is payable on Saturday; and if in case where Christmas-day fell upon a Saturday, and the bill become thus payable, it has never been legally determined whether such bill is demandable upon the Friday, which contrary to the custom of merchants, is allowing only *one* day of grace; or on the Monday following, which is allowing five, although the former mode is the usual practice.

Where bills of exchange and promissory notes become payable on Good-friday, the same shall be payable on the day before, and the holders thereof may protest the same for nonpayment on such preceding day. 40 G. III. c, 42.

HOMAGE, in the original, grants of lands and tenements by way of fee, the lord did not only tie his tenants to certain services, but also took a submission, with promise and oath, to be true and loyal to him as their lord and benefactor. This submission was and is called *homage*.

HOMAGE ANCESTREL, is where a man and his *ancestors*, time out of mind, held their land of their lord and his *ancestors*, by *homage*; and if such lord have received *homage*, he is bound to acquit the tenant against all other lords above him of all service; and if the tenant have done *homage* to his lord, and be impleaded, and vouch the lord to warranty, the lord is bound to warrant him; and if the tenant lose, he shall recover in value against the lord so much of the lands as he had at the time of the voucher, or any time after.

HOMAGE JURY, a jury in a court baron, consisting of tenants that do homage to the lord of the fee; and there by the feudists are called *pares curiæ:* they inquire and make presentments of defaults and deaths of tenants, admittances, and surrenders in the lord's court, &c.

HOMAGIO

HOMAGIO RESPECTUANDO, a writ directed to the escheator; commanding him to deliver seisin of lands to the heir that is of full age, notwithstanding his *homage* not done, which ought to be performed before the heir have livery, or his lands; except there shall fall out some reasonable cause to hinder it. F. N. B. 269.

HOMAGIUM REDDERE, to renounce *homage*, when the vassal made a solemn declaration of disowning and defying his lord. For which there was a set form and method prescribed by the feudatory laws.

HOMESOKEN. The privilege or freedom which every man hath in his house; and he who invades that freedom is properly said *facire homesoken*. This was probably what we now call *burglary*, which is a crime of a very heinous nature, because it is not only a breach of the king's peace, but a breach of that liberty which a man hath in his house; which, as is commonly said should be his castle, and therefore ought not to be invaded. *Bracton. Lib.* 8.

HOMICIDE, properly so called, is the killing of a man by a man. Of this there are several species, as *homicide by self-defence, homicide by misadventure, justifiable homicide, manslaughter, chance medley*, and *murder*.

Homicide by self-defence. Homicide *se defendendo*, or in a man's own defence, seems to be, where one has no other possible means of preserving his life from one who combats with him on a sudden quarrel, and kills the person by whom he is reduced to such inevitable necessity. 1 *Haw*. 75.

And not only he who on an assault retreats to a wall, or some such strait, beyond which he can go no farther, before he kills the other, is judged by the law to act upon unavoidable necessity; but also he, who being assaulted in such a manner, and in such a place, that he cannot go back without manifestly endangering his life, kills the other without retreating at all. *Id*.

And though a person who retreats from an assault to the wall, should give the other wounds in his retreat, yet if he give him no mortal wound till he get thither, and then kill him, he is guilty of homicide *se defendendo* only. *Id*.

But if the mortal wound were given first, then it is manslaughter. *Hale's Pl*. 42.

Homicide

Homicide by misadveuture, is where a man in doing a lawful act, without any intent of hurt, unfortunately chances to kill another; as where a labourer being at work with an hatchet, the head thereof flies off, and kills one who stands by. 1 *Haw.* 73.

It seems clear, that neither homicide by *misadventure,* nor homicide *se defendendo,* are felonious, because they are not accompanied with a felonious intent, which is necessary in every felony. 1 *Haw.* 29.

Justifiable homicide. To make homicide justifiable, it must be owing to some unavoidable necessity, to which a person who kills another must be reduced, without any manner of fault in himself.

And there must be no malice coloured under pretence of necessity; for wherever a person who kills another, acts in truth upon malice, and takes occasion upon the appearance of necessity to execute his own private revenge, he is guilty of murder. 1 *Haw.* 69.

But if a woman kill him who assaulteth to ravish her, it is no felony: or if a man come to burn my house, and I go out thereof and kill him, it is no felony. *Id.* 39.

If any evil-disposed person, shall attempt feloniously to rob or murder any person in any dwelling-house, or highway, or feloniously attempt to break any dwelling-house in the night time, and shall happen to be slain in such felonious attempt, the slayer shall be discharged, and shall forfeit no lands, nor goods. 24 H. VIII. c. 5.

Justifiable homicide of a public nature, is such as is occasioned by the due execution or advancement of public justice, with regard to which it must be observed.

1. That the judgment, by virtue whereof any person is put to death, must be given by one who has jurisdiction in the cause; for otherwise both judge and officer may be guilty of felony.

2. The execution must be pursuant to, and warranted by the judgment, otherwise it is without authority; and consequently, if a sheriff shall behead a man, when it is no part of the sentence to cut off the head, he is guilty of felony. 1 *Haw.* 70.

Manslaughter. Homicide against the life of another, is either *with* or *without* malice; that which is without malice is called manslaughter, or sometimes chaunce medley, by which is understood

stood such killing as happens either on a sudden quarrel, or in the commission of an unlawful act, without any deliberate intention of doing any mischief at all. 3 *Inst.* 56.

Hence it follows, that there can be no accessaries to this offence before the fact, because it must be done without premeditation; but there may be accessaries after the fact. *Id.*

The only difference between murder and manslaughter, is, that murder is upon *malice aforethought*, and manslaughter upon a *sudden occasion*, as if two meet together, and striving for the wall, the one kills the other, this is manslaughter and felony. And so it is if they had, ou that sudden occasion, gone into the field and fought, and the one had killed the other, this had been but manslaughter, and no murder; because all that followed was but a continuance of the first sudden occasion, and the blood was never cooled till the blow was given. 3 *Inst.* 55.

Chance or *chaunce medley.* Authors of the first authority disagree about the application of this word: by some it is applied to homicide by misadventure, by others to manslaughter. The original meaning of the word seems to favour the former opinion, as it signifies a sudden or casual meddling or contention; but homicide by misadventure supposes no previous meddling or falling out.

Murder, is the highest crime against the law of nature, that a man is capable of committing.

Murder is when a man of sound memory, and at the age of discretion, unlawfully killeth another person under the king's peace with malice aforethought, either expressed by the party, or implied by the law, so as the party wounded or hurt, die of the wound or hurt within a year and a day. 3 *Inst.* 47.

And the whole day on which the hurt was done, shall be reckoned the first. 1 *Haw.* 79.

By *malice expressed,* is meant a deliberate intention of doing any bodily harm to another, whereunto by law a person is not authorized.

And the evidences of such malice, must arise from external circumstances discovering that inward intention; as lying in wait, menacings antecedent, former grudges, deliberate compassings, and the like, which are various, according to the variety of circumstances. 1 H. H. 451.

Malice

Malice implied, is where a person voluntary kills another, without any provocation; for in this case the law presumes it to be *malicious,* and that he is a public enemy of mankind. 1 H. H. 455.

In general any formed design of doing mischief may be called malice; and therefore not such killing only as proceeds from premeditated hatred or revenge against the person killed, but also in many other cases, such as is accompanied with circumstances which shew the heart to be perversely wicked, is judged to be of malice prepense, or aforethought, and consequently murder. 2 *Haw.* 80.

If a man kill another, it shall be intended *prima facie* that he did it maliciously, unless he can make the contrary appear, by shewing that he did it on a sudden provocation or the like. 1 *Haw.* 82.

When the law makes use of the term *malice aforethought,* as descriptive of the crime of murder, it must not be understood in that narrow restrained sense, to which the modern use of the word malice is apt to lead one, *a principle of malevolence to particulars*; for the law by the term *malice,* in this instance means, that the fact has been attended with such circumstances, as are the ordinary symptoms of a wicked heart, regardless of social duty, and fatally bent upon mischief. *Fost.* 256.

The law so far abhors all dueling in cold blood, that not only the principal who actually kills the other, but also his seconds are guilty of murder, whether they fought or not; and it is holden that the seconds of the person killed, are also equally guilty, in respect to that countenance which they give to their principals in the execution of their purpose, by accompanying them therein, and being ready to bear a part with them. 1 *Haw.* 82.

Also it seems agreed, that no breach of a man's word or promise, no trespass either to land or goods, no affront by bare words or gestures, however false or malicious it may be, and aggravated with the most provoking circumstances, will excuse him from being guilty of murder, who is so far transported thereby, as immediately to attack the person who offends, in such a manner as manifestly endangers his life, without giving him time to put himself upon his guard, if he kill him in pursuance of such assault, whether the person slain did at all fight in his defence or not. *Id.*

Self-murder. See *Felo de se.*

HOMINE REPLEGIANDO, a writ to bail a man out of prison. When one conveys away secretly, or keeps in his custody another man against his will; then upon oath made thereof, and a petition to the lord chancellor, he will grant a writ of *replegiari facias*, with an *alias*, and *pluries*, upon which the sheriff returns an *elongatus* and thereupon issues a *capias in withernam*, made by the filager, and when he is thereupon taken, the sheriff cannot take bail for him: but the court where the writ is returnable may, if they think fit, grant an *habeas corpus* to the sheriff to bring him into court, and bail him, or else remand him.

HOMINES, a sort of feudatory tenants, who claimed a privilege of having their causes and persons tried only in the court of their lord.

HOND-HABEND, signifies a circumstance of manifest theft, as when a person is apprehended with the *mainour* or *mainover*, that is, the thing stolen in his hand.

HONOUR, is used especially for the more noble sort of *seigniories* on which other inferior lordships or manors depend, by performance of some customs or services to those who are lords of them. Before the stat. 18 Ed. I. the king's greater barons, who had a large extent of territory holden under the crown, frequently granted out smaller manors to inferior persons to be holden of themselves; which do therefore now continue to be held under a superior lord, who is called in such cases the lord *paramount* over all these manors; and his seigniory is frequently termed an *honour*, not a *manor*, especially if it hath belonged to an ancient feudal baron, or hath been at any time in the hands of the crown. 2 *Black.* 91.

When the king grants an *honour* with appurtenances, it is superior to a manor with appurtenances; for to an *honour*, by common intendment, appertain franchises, and by reason of those liberties and franchises, it is called an *honour*. *Roll.* 151.

HONOUR COURTS. There is a court of honour of earl marshal of England, &c. which determines disputes concerning precedency and points of honour. See *Court of Chivalry.*

HONOURARY SERVICES, are such as are incident to *grand serjeantry*, and annexed commonly to some honour.

HOPS, by several statutes, regulations are made for the curing of hops, &c. which are placed under the inspection of the officers of excise. See *Complete Abridg. Excise Laws.*

HORNEGELD, a tax within a forest to be paid for *horned* beasts.

HORS DE SON FEE, an exception to avoid an action brought for rent issuing out of certain lands, by him that pretends to be the lord, or for some customs and services; for if the defendant can prove the land to be *without the compass of his fee,* the action fails.

HORSEDEALERS. Every person exercising the trade or business of an horsedealer, must take out a licence from the stamp office, for which he shall pay annually, if within London, Westminster, the bills of mortality, the parish of St. Pancras, or the borough of Southwark, 20l. elsewhere 10l.

The commissioners are to grant licenses to horse-dealers for not exceeding one year; and every licence shall cease on Sept. 29, then in the year for which the same shall be issued, and commence from the date; and every licence taken out for any year subsequent to the year in which the same shall be issued, shall commence from Sept. 29 then next ensuing, and continue to Sept. 29 following; and a fresh licence is to be taken out ten days at least before the expiration of the year.

One licence is sufficient for partners, and the licence is confined to the place mentioned therein.

But no licences to be granted to horsedealers, unless they declare they seek their living by buying and selling horses, and add the name of the place where the said business is carried on. 29 G. III. c. 49.

Horse-dealers so licenced, shall cause the words *licenced to deal in horses,* to be painted or written in large and legible characters, either on a sign hung out, or on some visible place in the front of their house, gate-way, or stables; and if they shall sell any horse, without fixing such token, they shall forfeit 10l. to be recovered by action; half to the king, and half to the informer. 36 G. III. c. 17.

Horse-dealers who shall after Jan. 1, 1796, carry on the said business without having obtained a licence under this act, shall be liable to be assessed the duties on riding horses, and shall deliver lists thereof as other persons.

HORSES.

HORSES. It shall be lawful for any person, native, or foreigner, at any time to ship, lade, and transport by way of merchandize, horses into any parts beyond the seas, in amity with his majesty, paying for each horse, mare, or gelding, 5s. and no more.

No person convicted for feloniously stealing, a *horse, gelding*, or *mare*, shall have the privilege of clergy. 1 Ed. VI. c. 12.

And not only all accessaries before such felony done, but also all accessaries after such felony, shall be deprived and put from all benefit of their clergy, as the principal, by statute heretofore made, is or ought to be.

If an horse be stolen out of the stable, or other curtilage of a dwelling-house, in the night time, it falls under the denomination of *burglary*; if in the day time, it falls under the denomination of *larceny from the house*: and in either case there is a reward of 40l. for convicting an offender, and the prosecutor is entitled to a certificate, which will exempt him from all parish and ward offices in the parish and ward where the burglary, or larceny is committed, and which may be once assigned over, and will give the same exemption to the assignee, as to the original proprietor. *Burn's Just.* 621.

If an unsound horse be sold at the *price of a sound horse*, though not absolutely *warranted* to be sound, the seller sins against the law of morality, and the law of the land; but if he acknowledge him not to be sound, and sell him greatly under the value of a sound horse, as if he dispose of him for 25l. when he would have been worth 50l. if sound, such sale may be considered as fair and legal.

If a horse which is warranted sound at the time of sale, be proved to have been *at that time* unsound, it is not necessary that he should be returned to the seller. *No length of time* elapsed after the sale will alter the nature of a contract originally false. Neither is notice necessary to be given: though the not giving notice will be a strong presumption against the buyer, that the horse at the time of sale had not the defect complained of, and will make the proof on his part much more difficult. The bargain is compleat, and if it be fraudulent on the part of the seller, he will be liable to the buyer in damages, without either a return or notice.

If on account of an horse warranted sound, the buyer shall sell

 him

him again at a loss, an action might *perhaps* be maintained against the original seller, to recover the difference of the price. 1 *Hen. Black.* 17.

Slaughtering horses, great abuses having arisen, and many horses having been stolen, from the facility and safety of disposing of them to those who kept slaughterhouses for horses, some regulations and restrictions seemed absolutely necessary. It was no uncommon thing for horses of great value to be sold for the purpose of making food for dogs; the thief rather choosing to receive twenty shillings for a stolen horse, without fear or danger of detection, than venture to dispose of him publicly, though he might possibly have found a purchaser who would have given as many pounds for him. These considerations induced the legislature to pass the act of 26 G. III. c. 71, for regulating these slaughter-houses.

Killing or maiming horses, where any person shall *in the night-time,* maliciously, unlawfully, and willingly kill, or destroy any *horses, sheep, or other cattle* of any person, every such offence shall be adjudged felony, and the offender shall suffer as in the case of felony. 22 & 23 Car. II. c. 7.

Offenders may be transported for seven years, either at the assizes, or at the sessions, by three justices of the peace; one to be of the quorum.

By the 9 G. I. c. 22, commonly called the black act, it is enacted, that if any person shall unlawfully and maliciously kill, maim, or wound any cattle, every person so offending, being thereof lawfully convicted, in any county of England, shall be adjudged guilty of felony, and shall suffer death, as in cases of felony, without benefit of clergy.

But not to work corruption of blood, loss of dower, nor forfeiture of lands or goods.

Prosecution upon this statute, shall or may be commenced, within three years from the time of the offence committed, but not after.

If an horse, or other goods, be delivered to an inn-keeper or his servants, he is bound to keep them safely, and restore them when his guest leaves the house. 2 *Black.* 451.

If an horse be delivered to an agisting farmer, for the purpose of depasturing in his meadows, he is answerable for the loss of the horse,

horse, if it be occasioned by the ordinary neglect of himself or his servants. *Jones on Bailm.* 91.

If a man ride to an inn, where his horse has eat, the host may *detain the horse,* till he be satisfied for the eating, and without making any demand. 14 *Vin. Abr.* 437.

But an horse committed to an inn-keeper, can only be detained for his own meat, and not for that of his guest, or any other horse; for the chattels in such case, are only in the custody of the law for the debt which arises from the thing itself, and not for any other debt due from the same party. 2 *Rol. Abr.* 85.

By the custom of *London* and *Exeter,* if a man commit an horse to an inn-keeper, if he eat out his price, the inn-keeper may take him as his own, upon the reasonable appraisement of four of his neighbours; which was it seems a custom, arising from the abundance of traffic with strangers, that could not be known so as to be charged with an action.

But it hath been holden though an inn-keeper in London, may, after long keeping, have the horse appraised and sell him, yet, when he has in such case had him appraised, he cannot justify the taking him to himself, at the price he was appraised at. *Vin. Abr.* 233.

HOVERING, ships of 50 tons, laden with customable or prohibited goods, hovering on the coasts of this kingdom, within the limits of any port (and not proceeding from foreign parts) may be entered by officers of the customs, who are to take an account of the lading, and to demand and take a security from the master, by his bond to his majesty, in such sum of money as shall be treble the value of such foreign goods then on board; that such ship shall proceed (as soon as wind and weather, and the condition of the ship will permit) on her voyage to foreign parts, and shall land the goods in some foreign port; the master refusing to enter into such bond, on demand, or who having given bond, shall not proceed on such voyage (unless otherwise suffered to make a longer stay by the collector, or other principal officer of such port where the vessel shall be, not exceeding twenty days); in either of the said cases, all the foreign goods on board, may be taken out by the customhouse-officers, by direction of the collector, and properly secured; and if they are customable the duties shall be paid; and if prohibited they shall be forfeited.

 The

The officers of the customs may prosecute the same, as also the ship, if liable to condemnation. 3 G. III. c. 21.

Commanders of men of war, and customhouse-officers, may compel ships of fifty tons, or under, hovering within two leagues of shore, to come into port. 6 G. I. c. 21.

If any ship or vessel shall be found at anchor, or hovering within eight leagues of the coast (except between the north foreland and Beachy Head) unless by distress of weather, having on board foreign spirits, in any vessel or cask which shall not contain sixty gallons at least, or any wine in casks (provided such vessel have wine on board) shall not exceed sixty tons burthen, or six pounds weight of tea, or twenty pounds weight of coffee or any goods whatever liable to forfeiture upon importation, that such goods with the ship and furniture, shall be forfeited; spirits for the use of seamen, not exceeding two gallons per man, excepted. 42 G. III. c. 82.

HOUSAGE, a kind of fee paid for housing goods, by a carrier, or at a wharf or quay.

HOUSE. Every man's house is as his castle, as well to defend him against injuries as for his repose.

Upon recovery in any real action or ejectment, the sheriff may break the house and deliver seisin, &c. to the plaintiff, the writ being *habere facias seisinam*, or *possessionem*; and after judgment it is not the house of the defendant in right and judgment of the law.

In all cases where the king is party, the sheriff, if no door be open, may break the parties house to take him, or to execute other process of the king, if he cannot otherwise enter; but he ought first to signify the cause of his coming, and request the door to be opened; and this appears by the statute *Westm.* 1, 17, which is only in affirmance of the common law; and without default in the owner, the law will not suffer an house to be broken.

In all cases where the door is open, the sheriff may enter and make execution at the suit of any subject, either of body or goods; but otherwise where the door is shut, there he cannot break it to execute process at the suit of a subject.

Though an house be a castle for the owner himself and his family, and his own goods, &c. yet it is no protection for a stranger flying thither, or the goods of such a one, to prevent lawful execution;

cution; and therefore in such case, after request to enter, and denial, the sheriff may break the house. 5 *Rep.* 91.

If a person authorized to arrest another who is sheltered in an house, be denied quietly to enter into it, in order to take him; it seems generally to be agreed, that he may justify the breaking open the doors upon a *capias* from the king's bench or chancery, to compel a man to find sureties for the peace or good behaviour, or even upon a warrant from a justice of the peace for such purpose.

So where one known to have committed treason, is pursued either with or without a warrant, by a constable or private person.

So where an affray is made in an house in the view or hearing of a constable; or where those who have made an affray in his presence fly to an house, and are immediately pursued by him, and he is not suffered to enter in order to suppress the affray, in the first case, or to apprehend the affrayers in either case. 2 *Haw.* 86, 87.

A man ought so to use his house, as not to damnify his neighbour: and a man may compel another to repair his house, in several cases by the writ *de domo reparanda.* 1 *Salk.* 360.

If a man build his house so close to mine, that his roof overhangs my roof, and throws the water of his roof upon mine, this is a nuisance for which an action will lie.

But depriving one of a mere matter of pleasure, as of a fine prospect, by building a wall or the like; this, as it abridges nothing really convenient or necessary, is no injury to the sufferer, and is therefore not an actionable nuisance. 3 *Black.* 217.

HOUSE-BOTE, *estovers,* or an allowance of necessary timber out of the lord's wood, for the repairing and support of an house or tenement. And this belongs of common right, to any lessee for years or life; but if he take more than is needful, he may be punished by an action of waste.

HOUSE-BREAKING. See *Burglary.*

HOUSE-BURNING. See *Arson.*

HUE AND CRY, is the ancient common law process after felons, and such as have dangerously wounded any person, or assaulted any one with intent to rob him. And it hath received great countenance and authority by several acts of parliament. In

In any of which cases, the party grieved, or any other, may resort to the constable of the vill; and, 1. give him such reasonable assurance thereof, as the nature of the case will bear; 2. if he know the name of him that did it, he must tell the constable the same; 3. if he know it not, but can describe him, he must describe him, his person, or his habit, or his horse, or such circumstances as he knows, which may conduce to the discovery; 4. if the thing be done in the night, so that he knows none of these circumstances, he must mention the number of persons, or the way they took; 5. if none of all these can be discovered, as where a robbery, or burglary, or other felony is committed in the night, yet they are to acquaint the constable with the fact, and desire him to search his town for suspected persons, and to make hue and cry after such as may probably be suspected, as being persons vagrant in the same night; for many circumstances may happen to be useful for discovering a malefactor, which cannot at first be found out.

For the levying of hue and cry, although it is a good course to have a justice's warrant, where time will permit, in order to prevent causeless hue and cry; yet it is not necessary, nor always convenient, for the felon may escape before the warrant be obtained. And upon hue and cry levied against any person, or where any hue and cry comes to a constable, whether the person be certain or uncertain, the constable may search suspected places within his vill, for the apprehending of the felon. And if the person, against whom the hue and cry is raised, be not found in the constablewick, then the constable, and also every officer to whom the hue and cry shall afterwards come, ought to give notice to every town round about him, and to one next town only; and so from one constable to another, until the offender be found, or till they come to the sea-side. And this was the law before the conquest.

And in such cases it is needful to give notice in writing, to the pursuers, of the thing stolen, and of the colour and marks thereof, as also to describe the person of the felon, his apparel, horse, or the like, and which way he is gone, if it may be: but if the person that did the fact, be neither known, nor describable by his person, cloaths, or the like, yet such an hue and cry is good, and must

must be pursued, though no person certain can be named or described. 2 H. H. 100. 103.

HUNDRED. In the time of king *Alfred*, the kingdom was in gross, and then divided into counties and hundreds, and all persons came within one hundred or other.

By stat. 2 Ed. III. c. 12. it was enacted, that all hundreds and wapentakes granted by the king, shall be annexed to the county and not severed.

And by 14 Ed. III. c. 9. that all should be annexed, and the sheriff should have power to put in bailiffs, for which he will answer, and no more should be granted for the future.

Hundreds are not answerable to persons who are robbed travelling on a *Sunday*. 29 Car. II. c. 7.

Hundreds are liable to penalty on exportation of wool. 7 & 8 W. III. c. 28.

Hundreds are liable to damages sustained by pulling down buildings. 1 G. I. c. 5.

Hundreds are liable for damages, by killing cattle, cutting down trees, burning houses, &c. 9 G. I. c. 22, and 29 G. II. c. 36.

Hundreds are liable for damages incurred by destroying turnpikes, or works on navigable rivers. 8 G. II. c. 20.

By cutting hop binds. 10 G. II. c. 32. By destroying corn to prevent exportation, 11 G. II. c. 22. By wounding officers of the customs. 19 G. II. c. 34, or by destroying wood, &c. 29 G. II. c. 36.

All monies recovered against the hundred to be levied by a rate. 22 G. II. c. 46.

HUNDREDORS, men impanelled, or fit to be impanelled on a jury upon a controversy, dwelling in the *hundred* where the land in question lies. Hundredor signifies also him that hath the jurisdiction of an *hundred*, and holds the *hundred court*.

HUNDRED-LAGH, the *hundred* court, from which all the officers of the king's forests were exempted by the charter of king *Canute*.

HUNTING. See *Dogs*, and *Game*.

HUSBAND AND WIFE, usually termed *baron and feme*, are one person in law: that is, the very being or legal existence of the woman, is suspended during the marriage; or at least is incorporated

corporated and consolidated into that of the husband, under whose wing, protection and cover he performs every thing: she is therefore called in our law French, a *feme covert,* that is, under the protection and influence of her husband, her *baron,* or lord; and her condition during her marriage is called her *coverture.*

A man cannot grant lands to his wife during the coverture, nor any estate or interest to her, nor enter into covenant with her. But he may by his deed covenant with others for her use, as for her jointure, or the like; and he may give to her by devise or will, because the devise or will, doth not take effect till after his death. 1 *Inst.* 112.

All deeds executed by the wife, and acts done by her during her coverture, are void; except it be a fine, or the like matter of record, in which case she must be solely and secretly examined, that it may be known whether or no her act be voluntary. *Black.* 444.

A wife is so much favoured in respect of that power and authority which her husband has over her, that she shall not suffer any punishment for committing a bare theft in company with, or by coercion of her husband.

But if she commit a theft of her own voluntary act, or by the bare command of her husband, or be guilty of treason, murder, or robbery, in company with, or by coercion of her husband, she is punishable as much as if she were sole; because of the odiousness and dangerous consequence of these crimes. 1 *Haw.* 2.

By marriage, the husband hath power over his wife's person; and the courts of law still permit an husband to restrain a wife of her liberty, in case of any gross misbehaviour. But if he threaten to kill her, &c. she may make him find surety of the peace, by suing a writ of *supplicavit* out of chancery, or by preferring articles of the peace against him, in the court of king's-bench, or she may apply to the spiritual court for a divorce *propter sævitatem.*

The husband by marriage obtains a *freehold* in right of his wife, if he takes a woman to wife that is seized of a freehold; and he may make a lease thereof for twenty-one years or three lives, if it be made according to the statute. 32 H. VIII. c. 28.

The husband also gains a *chattel real,* as a term for years, to dispose of if he please, by grant or lease in her life time, or by surviving

surviving her: otherwise it remains with the wife. And upon execution for the husband's debt, the sheriff may sell the term during the life of the wife. 1 *Inst.* 351.

The husband also by the marriage, hath an absolute gift of all *chattels personal* in possession of the wife in her own right, whether he survives her not. But if these chattels personal are *choses in action*; that is, things to be sued for by action, as debts by obligation, contract, or the like, the husband shall not have them, unless he and his wife recover them. 1 *Inst.* 351.

By custom in *London*, a wife may carry on a separate trade; and as such, is liable to the statutes of bankruptcy, with respect to the goods in such separate trade, with which the husband cannot intermeddle. *Burr.* 1776.

If the wife be indebted before marriage, the husband is bound afterwards to pay the debt, living the wife; for he has adopted her and her circumstances together. 1 *Black.* 143.

But if the wife die, the husband shall not be charged for the debt of his wife after her death; if the creditor of the wife do not get judgment during the coverture. 9 *Co.* 72.

The husband is bound to provide his wife necessaries; and if she contract for them, he is obliged to pay for the same; but for any thing besides necessaries he is not chargeable.

And also if a wife elope, and live with another man, the husband is not chargeable even for necessaries; at least if the person who furnish them be sufficiently apprized of her elopement. 1 *Black.* 442.

A man having issue by his wife born alive, shall be tenant by the courtesy of all the lands in fee simple, or fee tail general, of which she shall die seized. *Litt.* 52.

And after her death, he shall have all *chattels real*: as the term of the wife, or a lease for years of the wife, and all other chattels in possession, and also, all such as are of a *mixed nature* (partly in possession and partly in action), as rents in arrear, incurred before the marriage or after: but things merely *in action*, as of a bond or obligation to the wife, he can only claim them as administrator to his wife, if he survive her. *Wood. b.* 1. *c.* 6.

If the wife survive the husband, she shall have for her dower, the third part of all his freehold lands: so she shall have her term for years again, if he have not altered the property during

his

his life: so also she shall have again all other chattels real and mixed: and so things in action, as debts, shall remain to her, if they were not received during the marriage. *Id.*

But if she elope from her husband, and go away with her adulterer, she shall lose her dower; unless her husband had willingly, without coercion ecclesiastical, been reconciled to her, and permitted her to cohabit with him. 1 *Inst.* 32.

HUSTINGS, this court is held before the lord mayor and aldermen of *London*. Error or attaint lies there, of a judgment or false verdict in the sheriff's court. Other cities and towns, as York, Lincoln, &c. also have had a court of the same name. See *Court of Hustings*.

HYPOTHECATE, to *hypothecate* a ship, is to pawn the same for necessaries; and a master may hypothecate either ship or goods for relief when in distress at sea; for he represents the traders as well as owners; and in whose hands soever a ship or goods hypothecated, come, they are liable. 1 *Salk.* 34.

I.

JACTITATION OF MARRIAGE, is when one of the party boasts, or gives out, that he or she is married to the other, whereby a common reputation of their matrimony may ensue. On this ground the party injured may libel the other in the spiritual court: and unless the defendant undertake, and make out a proof of the actual marriage, he or she is enjoined perpetual silence on that head. 3 *Black.* 93.

IDENTITATE NOMINIS, is a writ that lies for him, who upon a *capias* or *exigent* is arrested in a personal action, and committed to prison for another man of the same name; in such case he may have this writ directed to the sheriff, which is in the nature of a commission to inquire, whether he be the same person against whom the action was brought; and if not then to discharge him. *Reg. Orig.* 194.

IDENTITY OF THE PERSON, is when the defendant in a criminal cause, pleads that he is not the same person that was attainted; in which case, a jury shall be impanelled to inquire concernin cerning the identity of the person. And this shall be done immediately, and no time allowed to the prisoner to make his defence, or produce his witnesses, unless he will make oath that he is not the person attainted. 4 *Black.* 396.

IDEOTS, an ideot is a fool or madman from his nativity, and one who never has any lucid intervals; therefore the king has the protection of him and his estate, during his life, without rendering any account; because it cannot be presumed that he will ever be capable of taking care of himself or his affairs.

By the old common law, there is a writ *de ideota inquirendo*, directed to the sheriff, to inquire by a jury, whether the party be an ideot or not; and if they find him a perfect ideot, the profits of his lands and the custody of his person, belong to the king according to the stat. 17 Ed. II. c. 9. by which it is enacted, that the king shall have the custody of the lands of natural fools, taking the profits of them without waste or destruction, and shall find them necessaries of whose fee soever the land shall be holden. And after the death of such ideots, he shall render it to the right heir, so that such ideots shall not aliene, nor their heirs be disinherited. But it seldom happens, that a jury finds a man an ideot from his nativity; but only *non compos mentis* from some particular time; which has an operation very different in point of law: for in this case, he comes under the denomination of a *lunatic*; in which respect, the king shall not have the profits of his lands, but is accountable for the same to the lunatic when he comes to his right mind, or otherwise to his executors or administrators. 1 *Black.* 303.

It seems to be agreed at this day, that the king as *parens patriæ*, hath the protection of all his subjects; and that in a more peculiar manner he is to take care of all those, who by reason of their imbecility and want of understanding, are incapable of taking care of themselves. *Staundf. Prerog.* c. 9. f. 53.

But though a lunatic is by commission to be under the care of the public, and such committee is to be appointed for him by the lord chancellor, whose acts are subject to the correction and controul of the court of chancery; yet such an one, whether so appointed, or whether he of his own head take upon him the care and management of the estate of a lunatic, is but in nature of a bailiff or trustee for him, and accountable to him, his executors, or administrators, 4 *Co* 127.

And as the committees of a lunatic have no interest, but an estate during pleasure, it has been ruled, that they cannot make leases, nor any ways incumber the lunatic's estate, without a special order from the court of chancery, where the profits are not sufficient to maintain the lunatic. 1 *Vern.* 262.

In case of a lunatic's recovery, he must petition the chancellor to supersede the commission; upon the hearing of which, the lunatic must attend in person, that he may be inspected by the chancellor; it is also usual for the physician to attend, and to make an affidavit that the lunatic is perfectly recovered. *Fonblanque Treat. Eq. c.* 2. *s.* 3.

An ideot, or person *non compos*, may inherit, because the law in compassion to their natural infirmities, presumes them capable of property. *Co. Litt.* 2.

Also an ideot or person of non sane memory, may purchase, because it is intended for their benefit; and if after recovery of their memory they agree thereto, they cannot avoid it; but if they die during their lunacy, their heirs may avoid it, for they shall not be subject to the contracts of persons who want capacity to contract; so if after their memory recovered, the lunatic, or person *non compos*, die without agreement to the purchase, their heirs may avoid it. *Co. Litt.* 2.

If an ideot or lunatic marry, and die, his wife shall be endowed; for this works no forfeiture, and the king has only custody of the inheritance in one case, and the power of providing for him and his family in the other; but in both cases the freehold and inheritance is in the ideot or lunatic; and therefore if lands descend to an ideot or lunatic after marriage, and the king, on office found, takes those lands into his custody, or grants them over to another as committee in the usual manner; yet this seems no reason why the husband should not be tenant by the courtesy, or the wife endowed, since their title does not begin to any purpose till the death of the husband or wife, when the king's title is at an end. *Co. Litt.* 31.

It is laid down as a general rule, that ideots and lunatics, being by reason of their natural disabilities incapable of judging between

tween good and evil, are punishable by no criminal prosecution whatsoever. 1 *Haw.* 2.

And therefore a person who loses his memory by sickness, infirmity, or accident, and kills himself is no *felo de se.* 3 *Inst.* 54.

And as a person *non compos* cannot be a *felo de se* by killing himself, so neither can he be guilty of homicide in killing another, nor of petit treason; also if one committed for a capital offence become *non compos* before conviction, he shall not be arraigned; and if after conviction, he shall not be executed. 1 H. H. 30.

We must distinguish between acts done by ideots and lunatics *in pais*, and in a court of record; that as to those solemnly acknowledged in a court of record, as fines and recoveries, and the uses declared on them, they are good, and can neither be avoided by themselves, nor their representatives, for it is to be presumed, that had they been under these disabilities, the judges would not have admitted them to make those acknowledgments. 4 *Co.* 124.

Therefore if a person *non compos* acknowledge a fine, it shall stand against him and his heirs; for though the judges ought not to admit of a fine from a madman under that disability, yet when it is once received, it shall never be reversed, because the record and judgment of the court being the highest evidence that can be, the law presumes the conusor at that time capable of contracting; and therefore the credit of it is not to be contested, nor the record avoided by any averment against the truth of it. 2 *Inst.* 483.

And to acts done by them *in pais*, they are distinguished into void and voidable, though as to themselves they are regularly unavoidable, because no man is allowed to disable himself, for the insecurity that may arise in contracts from counterfeited madness and folly; besides, if the excuse were real, it would be repugnant that the party should know or remember what he did; but their heirs and executors may avoid such acts *in pais*, by pleading the disability; because if they can prove it, it must be presumed real, since no body can be thought to counterfeit it, when he can expect no benefit from it himself. 4 *Co.* 124.

There are frequent instances in equity, where not only ideots and lunatics, who come within the protection of the law, but also persons of weak understandings have been relieved, when they appeared to have been imposed upon in their dealings, and unreasonable purchases, and securities obtained from them set aside in their favour. 1 *Chan. Ca.* 113.

Ideots and lunatics, during their lunacy, are incapable of making any will or testament; as are also persons grown childish by reason of extreme old age; so one actually drunk, if he be so drunk as to have lost the use of his reason: but though a person who wants understanding cannot make a will, yet the rule herein is not to be taken from his not being able to measure an ell of cloth, tell twenty or the like, but whether he have sense enough to dispose of his estate with understanding. *Swinb.* 71.

When an ideot sues or defends, he shall not appear by guardian, *prochein amy*, or attorney, but he must be ever in proper person. *Co. Litt.* 135. *b.*

But otherwise of him who becomes *non compos mentis*; for he shall appear by guardian if within age, or by attorney if of full age. 4 *Co.* 124.

IDEOTA INQUIRENDO VEL EXAMINANDO. See *Ideots.*

JETSAM, any thing thrown out of a ship, being in the danger of wreck, and by the waves driven to the shore. See *Flotsam.*

JEWS. Here in England in former times, the Jews and all their goods belonged to the chief lord where they lived; and he had such an absolute property in them, that he might sell them; for they had not liberty to remove to another lord without leave. They were distinguished from the Christians in their lives, and at their deaths; for they had proper judges and courts, where their causes were decided.

By stat. Ed. I. the Jews to the number of 15,000 were banished out of *England*; and never returned, till Oliver Cromwell re-admitted them.

Whenever any Jew shall present himself, to take the oath of abjuration, in pursuance of the 10 Geo. III. c. 10. the words *upon the true faith of a Christian*, shall be omitted out of the said oath in administering it to such persons; and the taking the said oath by persons professing the Jewish religion, without the said words, in like manner as Jews are admitted to give evidence in in courts of justice, shall be deemed a sufficient taking of the abjuration oath.

By 26 Geo. II. c. 26. bills in parliament were permitted for naturalizing Jews, but this was repealed by 27 Geo. II. c. 1.

IGNORAMUS, were formerly indorsed by the grand jury on the back of a bill, for which they did not find sufficient evidence; but now, since the proceedings were in *English*, they indorse *no bill*, or *not a true bill*, or which is the better way, *not found*. 4 *Black*. 305.

IGNORANCE, which is want of knowledge of the law, shall not excuse any man from the penalty of it: and every person is bound at his peril to take notice what the law of the realm is; and ignorance of it, though it be invincible, where a man offering that he hath done all that in him lies, will not excuse him.

But though ignorance of the law excuseth not, ignorance of the fact doth; as if a person buy an horse or other thing in open market, of one that had no property therein, and not knowing but he had right; in that case he hath good title, and the ignorance shall excuse him. But if the party bought the horse out of the market, or the seller had no right, the buying in open market would not have excused. 5 *Rep*. 83.

And an infant at the age of discretion shall be punished for crimes, though he be ignorant of the law; but infants of tender age have ignorance by *nature* to excuse them; and so persons *non compos*, have ignorance by the hand of God. *Stud. Com*. 83.

ILLEVIABLE, that may or cannot be levied, and therefore *nihil* is a word set upon a debt illeviable.

IMPANEL, to impanel a jury, is to enter into a parchment schedule by the sheriff, the names of the jury summoned to appear, for the performance of such public service as juries are employed in.

IMPARLANCE, is a petition in court, for a day to consider or advise what answer the defendant shall make to the action of the plaintiff; being a continuance of the cause till another day, or a larger time given by the court, which is generally till the next term.

Formerly the defendant in all cases, had an imparlance to the term next after the return of the process, except the proceedings were by original, or for or against attornies or other privileged persons, or against prisoners in the custody of the marshal; in which cases the defendant was bound to plead without any imparlance, and the same term the declaration was delivered (if delivered four days before the end of the term) and except the proceedings were by *habeas corpus*, or the process were returnable the first return of Easter or Michaelmas term, and the action laid in London or Middlesex; and in which last cases, if the declaration were delivered before the essoin day of *Cras. Ani*, the defendant was to plead two days before the essoin day of the subsequent term. *Mich*. 5 Anne.

But now by a rule made in Trinity term 5 & 6 Geo. II. upon all process to be sued out of this court, returnable the first or second return of any term, if the plaintiff declare in London or Middlesex, and the defendant live within twenty miles of London, the declaration shall be delivered with notice to plead within eight days after the delivery, and the defendant shall plead within the said eight days without any imparlance; and in default of pleading in either of these cases, judgment may be entered. In both these cases the declaration must be delivered at least four days before the end of the term, exclusive of the day of delivery, otherwise the defendant will be entitled to an imparlance.

The defendant may imparl if he amend his declaration; otherwise if he accept of costs; for by such amendment it shall be accounted as a new declaration; but if the defendant accept of costs for such amendment, it is intended that he is satisfied for what he is prejudiced by the amendment, and therefore it is reason he should plead to the declaration so amended, and not imparl. L. P. R. 34.

IMPEACHMENT, is the accusation and prosecution of a person in parliament, for treason, or other crime and misdemeanor. An impeachment before the lords by the commons of Great Britain, is a presentment to the most high and supreme court of criminal jurisdiction, by the most solemn grand inquest of the whole kingdom. A commoner cannot be impeached before the lords for any capital offence, but only for high misdemeanors; but a peer may be impeached for any crime. The articles of impeachment are a kind of bills of indictment, found by the house of commons, and afterwards tried by the lords, who are, in cases of misdemeanors,

misdemeanors, considered not only as their own peers, but as the peers of the whole nation. By stat. 12 & 13 W. c. 2. no pardon under the great seal, shall be pleadable to an impeachment by the commons in parliament. 4 *Black.* 259.

IMPEACHMENT OF WASTE, signifies a restraint from committing of waste upon lands and tenements: and therefore he that hath a lease without impeachment of waste, hath by that a property or interest given him in the houses and trees, and may make waste in them without being impeached for it, that is, without being questioned, or demanded any recompense for the waste done. 11 *Rep.* 82.

IMPEDIMENTS IN LAW, persons under impediments are those within age, under coverture, *non compos mentis,* in prison, or beyond seas; who by a saving in our laws, have time to claim and prosecute the right, after the impediments removed, in case of fines levied, &c.

IMPLEAD, to sue or prosecute by course of law.

IMPLICATION, is where the law implies something that is not declared between parties in their deeds and agreements; and when our law gives any thing to a man, it gives implicitly whatsoever is necessary for enjoying the same. 4 *Black.* 200.

An implied contract is such, where the terms of agreement are not expressly set forth in words, but are such as reason and justice dictate, and which therefore the law presumes that every man undertakes to perform. *Id.*

An implication cannot be intended by deed, unless there are apt words, but otherwise in a will. *Brownl.* 153.

IMPOSSIBILITY, a thing impossible in law, is all one with a thing impossible in nature: and if any thing in a bond or deed be impossible to be done, such deed, &c. is void. Yet where the condition of a bond becomes impossible by the act of God, in such case it is held, the obligor ought to do all in his power towards a performance; as when a man is bound to enfeoff the obligee and his heirs, and the obligee dies, the obligor must enfeoff his heirs. 2 *Ca. Rep.* 74.

IMPOST, a duty on the importation of an article into a state or kingdom. It may in some degree be distinguished from custom, because custom is rather that profit which the prince makes of wares shipped out; yet they are frequently confounded.

IMPOTENCY,

IMPOTENCY, in the ecclesiastical law, signifies an inability of generation, or propagating the species, which is a cause of divorce *a vinculo matrimonii*, as being merely void, and therefore needs only a sentence declaratory of its being so.

IMPRESSING MEN. The power of impressing seamen for the sea service, by the king's commission, has been a matter of some dispute, and submitted to with great reluctance, though it hath very clearly and learnedly been shewn by *Sir Michael Forster*, that the practice of impressing, and granting power to the admiralty for that purpose, is of very ancient date, and hath been uniformly continued, by a regular series of precedents, to the present time, whence he concludes it to be part of the common law. The difficulty arises from hence, that no statute has expressly declared this power to be in the crown, though many of them very strongly imply it. The stat. 2 R. II. c. 4. speaks of mariners being arrested and retained for the king's service, as of a thing well known and practised without dispute; and provides a remedy against the running away.

By stat. 2 & 3 P. & M. c. 16. if any waterman who uses the river Thames, shall hide himself during the execution of any commission for pressing for the king's service he is liable to heavy penalties.

By stat 5 Eliz. c. .6 no fisherman shall be taken by the queen's commission to serve as a mariner; but the commission shall be first brought to two justices of the peace, inhabiting near the sea-coast where the mariners are to be taken, to the intent that the justices may choose out, and return such a number of able bodied men as in the commission are contained to serve her majesty.

And by stat. 7 & 8 W. c. 21. 2 Anne. c. 6. 4 & 5 Anne. c. 19. 13 G. II. c. 17. especial protection are allowed to seamen in particular circumstances, to prevent them from being impressed. All which do most evidently imply a power of impressing to reside somewhere; and if any where, it must, from the spirit of our constitution, as well as from the frequent mention of the king's commission, reside in the crown alone. 1 *Black.* 419.

IMPRISONMENT, is the restraint of a man's liberty under the custody of another; and extends not only to a goal, but an house, stocks, or where a man is held in the street, or any other place;

place; for, in all these cases, the party so restrained is said to be a prisoner, so long as he hath not his liberty freely to go about his business, as at other times.

None shall be imprisoned but by the lawful judgment of his peer, or by the law of the land. M. C.

IMPROPRIATION, is properly so called, when a benefice ecclesiastical is in the hands of a layman; and *appropriation* when in the hands of a bishop, college, or religious house, though sometimes these terms are confounded. It is said there are three thousand eight hundred and forty-five impropriations in England.

IN AUTER DROIT, in another's right, as where executors or administrators sue for a debt or duty, &c. of the testator or intestate.

INCENDIARY. See *Arson*.

INCEPTION, the same person is patron and incumbent, and he devises the next avoidance; it was objected that by his death the church is void, and then the presentation is a *chose in action*, and not grantable, and the devise takes not effect till after the death of the devisor, and therefore void; but held a good devise, because it has inception in his life. *Col. Rep.* 214.

INCEST, is the carnal knowledge of persons within the Levitical degrees of kindred. These by our law, are totally prohibited to marry with each other; and sentence of divorce in such case, is only declaratory of the illegality of the marriage, for the marriage itself is void *ab initio*.

INCIDENT, signifies a thing necessarily depending upon another as more principal. For example, a court baron is so incident to a manor, and a court of pye-powder to a fair, that they cannot be severed by grant; for if a manor or fair be granted, these courts cannot be severed. *Co. Litt.* 151.

INCLOSURES, any person who shall wilfully or maliciously demolish, pull down, or otherwise destroy or damage, any fence raised or made for dividing or inclosing any common, waste, or other lands, in pursuance of any act of parliament, or shall cause or procure the same to be done, shall be guilty of felony, and transported for seven years. Prosecution to be commenced in eighteen months after the offence committed.

INCORPORATION, power of. To the erection of any corporation,

poration, the king's consent is necessary, either impliedly, or expressly given; the king's implied consent, is to be found in corporations which exist by force of the common law, to which our former kings are supposed to have given their concurrence; of this sort are all bishops, parsons, vicars, churchwardens, and some others, who by common law have ever been held to have been corporations by virtue of their office.

Another method of implied consent, is with regard to all corporations by prescription; such as the city of London, and many others, which have existed as corporations for time immemorial; for though the members thereof can shew no legal charter of incorporation, yet in cases of such high antiquity, the law presumes there once was one, and that by variety of accidents which a length of time may produce, the charter is lost or destroyed. The methods by which the king's consent is expressly given, are either by act of parliament or charter; but the immediate creative act, is usually performed by the king alone, in virtue of his royal prerogative. 1 *Black.* 472.

INCUMBENT, a clerk diligently resident on his benefice with cure: and called incumbent of that church, because he does or ought to apply himself sedulously to discharge the duty of his cure. *Co. Litt.* 119.

INDEBITATUS ASSUMPSIT, is used in declarations and law proceedings, where one is indebted unto another in any certain sum; and the law creates it: it is also an action thereupon. *Pract. Attorn.*

And it has been held, that the action upon *indebitatus assumpsit* lies in no case, but where debt will lie for the same thing. 1 *Salk.* 23.

INDECIMABLE, not tithable, or ought not to pay any tithe. 2 *Inst.* 490.

INDEFEISABLE, that cannot be defeated, undone, or made void; as *a good and indefeisable estate, &c.*

INDEMNITY, when a church is appropriate to any abbey or college, then the archdeacon for ever loses his induction money; in recompense whereof, he shall have yearly out of the church *twenty-two pence* or *two shillings*, more or less for a yearly pension, as it is agreed at the time of appropriating: and his payments are called pensions or indemnities.

Indemnity,

Indemnity, is also an agreement to save harmless from all damage or danger that may result from any particular transaction: thus, insuring any person against a risk, perils of the sea, or fire, is termed a contract of indemnity against these risks respectively.

Acts of indemnity are passed every session of parliament, for the relief of those who have neglected to take the necessary oaths, &c. required to qualify them for their respective offices.

INDENTURE, is a writing, containing a conveyance between two or more, indented or cut unevenly, or in and out, on the top or side, answerable to another writing that likewise comprehends the same words. Formerly when deeds were more concise than at present, it was usual to write both parts on the same piece of parchment, with some words or letters written between them, through which the parchment was cut, either in a straight or indented line, in such a manner as to leave half the word on one part, and half on the other: and this custom is still preserved in making out the indentures of a fine. But at last, indenting only hath come into use, without cutting through any letters at all; and it seems at present to serve for little other purpose, than to give name to the species of the deed. 2 *Black* 294.

INDICTMENT, is a written accusation of one or more persons, of a crime or misdemeanor, preferred to, and presented on oath by, a grand jury. 4 *Black*. 302.

An indictment may be found on the oath of one witness only, unless it be for high treason, which requires two witnesses. And unless in any instance it is otherwise specially directed by acts of parliament. 2 *Haw*.

The sheriff of every county is bound to return to every session of the peace, and every commission of *oyer and terminer*, and of *general goal delivery*, twenty-four good and lawful men, of the county, some out of every hundred, *to enquire, present, do, and execute all those things which on the part of our lord the king, shall then and there be commanded therein*. As many as appear upon this panel are sworn of the grand jury, to the amount of twelve, at the least, and not more than twenty-three, that twelve may be a majority. This grand jury is previously instructed in the articles of their enquiry, by a charge from the judge on the bench. They then withdraw from court to sit and receive indictments, which are preferred to them in the name of the king, but at the suit

suit of any private prosecutor; and they are only to hear evidence on behalf of the prosecution: for the finding an indictment is only in the nature of an enquiry or accusation, which is afterwards to be tried and determined; and the grand jury are only to enquire upon their oaths whether there be sufficient cause to call upon the party to answer it.

It seems generally agreed, that the grand jury may not find part of an indictment true, and part false; but must either find a true bill, or *ignoramus*, for the whole; and if they take upon them to find it specially, or conditionally, or to be true for part only, and not for the rest, the whole is void, and the party cannot be tried upon it, but ought to be indicted anew. 2 *Haw.* 210.

All capital crimes whatsoever, and all kinds of inferior crimes which are of a public nature, as misprisions, contempts, disturbances of the peace, oppressions, and all other misdemeanors whatsoever of a *public* evil example, against the common law, may be indicted, but no injuries of a private nature, unless they in some degree concern the king.

And generally where a statute prohibits a matter of public grievance to the liberties and security of a subject, or commands a matter of public convenience, as the repairing of the common streets of the town, &c. every disobedience of such statute is punishable, not only at the suit of the party grieved, but also by way of indictment, for contempt of the statute, unless such method of proceeding shall manifestly appear to be excluded by it. Yet if the party offending, have been fined in an action brought by the party (as it is said he may in every action for doing a thing prohibited by statute); such fine is, a good bar to the indictment, because by the fine the end of the statute is satisfied; otherwise he would be liable to a second fine for the same offence. 2 *Inst.* 55.

If several offenders commit the same offence, though in law they are several offences in relation to the several offenders, yet they may be joined in one indictment; as if several commit a robbery, or burglary, or murder. 2 H. H. 173.

No indictment for high treason, or misprision thereof (except indictments for counterfeiting the king's coin, seal, sign or signet), nor any process or return thereupon, shall be quashed for mis-reciting, mis-spelling, mis-spelling, false or improper Latin, unless exception concerning the same be taken and made in the respective court where the trial shall be, by the prisoner or his counsel assigned, before any evidence given in open court on such indictment; nor shall any such mis-reciting, mis-spelling, false, or improper Latin, after conviction on such indictment, be any cause or stay, or arrest of judgment; but nevertheless any judgment on such indictment shall be liable to be reversed on writ of error, as formerly.

An indictment accusing a man in general terms, without ascertaining the particular fact laid to his charge, is insufficient; for no one can know what defence to make to a charge which is uncertain, nor can plead it in bar or abatement of a subsequent prosecution; neither can it appear, that the facts given in evidence against a defendant on such a general accusation, are the same of which the indictors have accused him; nor can it judiciously appear to the court what punishment is proper for an offence so loosely expressed. 2 *Haw*. 266.

It is therefore best to lay all the facts in the indictment as near to the truth as possible; and not to say, in an indictment for a small assault (for instance) wherein the person assaulted received little or no bodily hurt, that such a one, with swords, staves, and pistols, beat, bruised, and wounded him, so that his life was greatly despaired of; nor to say in an indictment for an highway being obstructed, that the king's subjects cannot go thereon, without manifest danger of their lives, and the like. Which kind of words not being necessary, may stagger an honest man upon his oath, to find the fact as so laid.

No indictment can be good, without expressly shewing some place wherein the offence was committed, which must appear to have been within jurisdiction of the court. 2 *Haw*. 236.

There are several emphatical words of art, which the law has appropriated for the description of an offence, which no circumlocution will supply; as *feloniously*, in the indictment of any felony; *burglariously* in an indictment of burglary, and the like. 2 H. H. 184.

An indictment on the black act for shooting at any person, must charge that the offence was done *wilfully* and *maliciously*.

By 10 & 11 W. c. 23, it is enacted, that no clerk of assize, clerk of the peace, or other person, shall take any money of any person bound over to give evidence against a traitor or felon for the discharge of his recognizance, nor take more than 2s. for drawing any bill of indictment against any such felon, on pain of 5l. to the party grieved, with full costs: And if he shall draw a defective bill, he shall draw a new one *gratis*, on the like penalty.

With respect to drawing indictments for other misdemeanours, not being treason or felony, no fee is limited by the statute, the same therefore depends on the custom and ancient usage.

Every person charged with any felony or other crime, who shall on his trial be acquitted, or against whom no indictment shall be found by the grand jury, or who shall be discharged by proclamation for want of prosecution, shall be immediately set at large in open court, without payment of any fee to the sheriff or goaler; but in lieu thereof, the treasurer, on a certificate signed by one of the judges or justices before whom such prisoner shall have been discharged, shall pay out of the general rate of the county or district, such sum as has been usually paid, not exceeding 13s. 4d.

But an action cannot be brought by the person acquitted against the prosecutor of the indictment, without obtaining a copy of the record of his indictment, and acquittal; which in prosecutions for felony, it is not usual to grant, if there be the least probable cause to found such prosecution upon. For it would be a very great discouragement to the public justice of the kingdom, if prosecutors who had a tolerable ground of suspicion, were liable to be sued at law whenever their indictments miscarried. But an action on the case for a malicious prosecution, may be founded on such an indictment whereon no acquittal can be, as if it be rejected by the grand jury, or be *coram non judice*, or be insufficiently drawn; for it is not the danger of the plaintiff, but the scandal, vexation, and expence, upon which this action is founded. However, any probable cause for preferring it, is sufficient to justify the defendant, provided it do not appear, that the prosecution was malicious. 3 *Black*. 126.

INDORSEMENT, signifies any thing written upon the back of a deed or other instrument.

On sealing of a bond, the condition of the bond may be indorsed, and then the bond and indorsement shall both stand together.

In order to the executing a justice of the peace's warrant in another county, it must be indorsed by some justice in such other county, which is commonly called backing the warrant.

It is customary also to indorse the receipt of the consideration money upon a deed; or an assignment of a lease may sometimes be made by indorsement.

Indorsement, is also that act, by which the holder of a bill of exchange, or promissory note payable to order, transfers such instrument, and his interest therein, to some other person, who is then termed the *indorsee*, and who, by such transfer and assignment renders himself responsible for presenting such instruments and using all due diligence to obtain payment of the acceptor or maker.

INDUCEMENT, what is alledged as a motive or incitement to a thing; and is used specially in many cases; as, there is an inducement in actions, to a traverse in pleadings, a fact or offence committed &c.

Inducements to actions need not have so much certainty as in other cases: a general *indebitatus* is not sufficient where it is the ground of the action; but where it is the inducement to the action, as in consideration of forbearing a debt till such a day (for that the parties are agreed upon the debt), this being but a collateral promise, is good without shewing how due. 2 *Mod.* 70.

An *inducement* to a traverse must be such matter, as is good and justifiable in law.

There is an *inducement* to a justification, when what is alledged against it, is not the substance of the plea. *Moor.* 847.

INDUCTION, is the giving a clerk instituted to a benefice, the actual possession of the temporalities thereof, in the nature of livery of seisin. It is performed by a mandate from the bishop to the archdeacon, who commonly issues out a precept to some other clergyman to perform it for them. Which being done, the clergyman who inducts him, indorses a certificate of his induction on the archdeacon's mandate, and they who were present testify the same under their hands. And by this the person inducted, is in full and complete possession of all the temporalities of his church.

IN ESSE. There is this difference between things *in esse*, and things *in posse*, or potentia; a thing apparent and visible, is *in esse*, that is, has a real being *eo instanti*, whereas the other is casual, and but a possibility. As a child before he is born, or even conceived, is a thing *in posse*, or which may be; after he is born, he is said to be *in esse*, or actual being.

INFAMY, which extends to forgery, perjury, gross cheats, &c. disables a man to be a witness or a juror; but a pardon of crimes restores a person's credit to make him a good evidence. 2 *Haw*. 432.

INFANT, from the observations daily made on the actions of infants, as to their arriving at discretion, the laws and customs of every country have fixed upon particular periods, on which they are presumed capable of acting with reason and discretion; in our law, the full age of man or woman is twenty-one years. 3 *Bac. Abr*. 118.

The ages of male and female are different for different purposes: a male at twelve years of age may take the oath of allegiance; at fourteen, is of years of discretion, and therefore may consent or disagree to marriage, may chuse his guardian, and if his discretion be actually proved, may make his testament of his personal estate; at seventeen may be a procurator or an executor; and at twenty-one, is at his own disposal, and may alien his lands, goods, and chattels. A female at seven years of age may be betrothed or given in marriage; at nine, is intitled to dower; and at 12, is of years of maturity, and therefore may consent or disagree to marriage, and if proved to have sufficient discretion, may bequeath her personal estate; at 14, is at years of legal discretion, and may chuse a guardian; at seventeen may be executrix; and at twenty-one, may dispose of herself and her lands. 1 *Black*. 463.

An *infant* is capable of inheriting, for the law presumes him capable of property; also an infant may purchase, because it is intended for his benefit, and the freehold is in him till he disagree thereto, because an agreement is presumed, it being for his benefit, and because the freehold cannot be in the grantor contrary to his own act, nor can be in obeyance, for then a stranger would not know against whom to demand his right: and if at his full age, the infant agree to the purchase, he cannot afterwards avoid it; but if he die during his minority, his heirs may avoid it; for they shall not be bound by the contracts of a person, who wanted capacity to contract. *Co. Litt*. 2.

As

As to *infants* being witnesses, there seems to be no fixed time at which children are excluded from giving evidence: but it will depend in a great measure on the sense and understanding of the children, as it shall appear on examination in court. *Bull.* N. P. 293.

And where they are admitted, concurrent testimony seems peculiarly desirable. 4 *Black.* 214.

An *infant* is not bound by his contract to deliver a thing, so if one deliver goods to an infant upon a contract, &c. knowing him to be an infant, he shall not be chargeable in trover and conversion, or any other action for them; for the infant is not capable of any contract but for necessaries, therefore such delivery is a gift to the infant; but if an infant without any contract, wilfully take away the goods of another, trover lies against him; also it is said, that if he take the goods under pretence that he is of full age, trover lies, because it is a wilful and fraudulent trespass. 1 *Sid.* 129.

Infants are disabled to contract for any thing but necessaries for their person, suitable to their degree and quality, and what is necessary must be left to the jury. *Co. Litt.* 172.

An *infant* knowing of a fraud, shall be as much bound as if of age. 13 *Vin. Abr.* 536.

But it is held that this rule is confined to such acts only as are voidable, and that a warrant of attorney given by an infant being absolutely void, the court will not confirm it, though the infant appeared to have given it knowing it was not good, and for the purpose of collusion.

As to acts of infants being void, or only voidable, there is a diversity between an actual delivery of the thing contracted for, and a bare agreement to deliver it; the first is voidable, but the last absolutely void.

As necessaries for an infant's wife, are necessaries for him, he is chargeable for them, unless provided before marriage; in which case he is not answerable, though she wore them afterward. 1 *Str.* 168.

An *infant* is also liable for the nursing of his lawful child.

Where goods are furnished to the son, he is himself liable if they be necessaries. If tradesmen deal with him, and he undertakes to pay them, they must resort to him for payment; but if

 they

they furnished the infant on the credit of his father, the father only is liable. 2 *Esp.* 471.

With respect to education, &c. infants may be charged, where the credit was given *bona fide* to them. But where the infant is under the parent's power, and living in the house with them, he shall not be liable even for necessaries. 2 *Black. Rep.* 1325.

If a taylor trust a young man under age for cloaths to an extravagant degree, he cannot recover; and he is bound to know whether he deals at the same time with any other taylor. 1 *Esp. Rep.* 212.

If one lend money to an infant to pay a debt for necessaries, and he do pay it, although he is not bound in law, it is said he is in equity; but, if the infant mis-apply the money, it is at the peril of the lender.

A promissory note given by an infant for board and lodging, and for teaching him a trade, is valid, and will support an action for the money. 1 T. R. 41.

And debts contracted during infancy, are good considerations to support a promise made to them when a person is of full age; but the promise must be express.

A bond without a penalty for necessaries will bind an infant, but not a bond with a penalty. *Esp. Rep.* 164.

Legacies to infants cannot be paid either to them or their parents.

An infant cannot be a juror, neither can he be an attorney, bailiff, factor, or receiver. *Co. Lit.* 172.

By the custom of London, an infant unmarried, and above the age of 14, if under 21, may bind himself apprentice to a freeman of London, by indenture with proper covenants, which covenants by the custom of London, will be as binding as if of age.

If an infant draw a bill of exchange, yet he shall not be liable on the custom of merchants; but he may plead infancy in the same manner as he may to any other contract.

An infant cannot be sued but under the protection and joining the name of his guardian; but he may sue either by his guardian or his next friend who is not his guardian. *Co. Lit.* 135.

An action on an account stated will not lie against an infant, though it be for necessaries. *Co. Lit.* 172.

INFINITY

INFINITY OF ACTIONS. The lord of the soil may have a special action against him who shall dig soil in the king's highway. But one subject cannot have his action against another for common nuisances; for if he might, then every man would have it, and so the actions would be infinite, &c. 2 *Inst.* 56.

IN FORMA PAUPERIS. When any man who has a just cause of suit either in chancery, or any of the courts of common law, will come before the lord-keeper, master of the rolls, either of the chief justices, or chief baron, and make oath, that he is not worth five pounds, his debts paid; either of the said judges will, in his own proper court, admit him to sue *in forma pauperis*, and he shall have counsel, clerk or attorney assigned him to do his business, without paying any fees.

INFORMATION. An information may be defined an accusation or complaint exhibited against a person for some criminal offence, either immediately against the king or against a private person; which, from its enormity or dangerous tendency, the public good requires should be restrained and punished. It differs principally from an indictment in this, that an indictment is an accusation found by the oath of twelve men, but an information, is only the allegation of the officer who exhibits it. 3 *Bac. Abr.* 164.

Informations are of two kinds: first, those which are partly at the suit of the king, and partly at the suit of a subject; and secondly, such as are only in the name of the king: the former are usually brought upon penal statutes, which inflict a penalty on conviction of the offender, one part to the use of the king, and another to the use of the informer, and are a sort of *qui tam*, or popular actions, only carried on by a criminal instead of a civil process.

Informations that are exhibited in the name of the king alone, are also of two kinds; first, those which are truly and properly his own suits, and filed *ex officio* by his own immediate officer, the attorney-general; secondly, those in which, though the king is the nominal prosecutor, yet it is at the relation of some private person, or common informer; and they are filed by the master of the crown office, under the express direction of the court. The objects of the king's own prosecutions, filed *ex officio* by the attorney-general, are properly such enormous misdemeanours, as peculiarly

peculiarly tend to disturb or endanger the government. The objects of the other species of informations, filed by the master of the crown-office, upon the complaint or relation of a private subject, are any gross and notorious misdemeanours, riots, batteries, libels, or other immoralities, of an atrocious kind, not peculiarly tending to disturb the government, but which on account of their magnitude, or pernicious example, deserve the most public animadversion. And when an information is filed either thus, or by the attorney-general *ex officio*, it must be tried by a petit jury of the county where the offence arises; after which, if the defendant be found guilty, he must resort to the court of king's bench for his punishment. 4 *Black.* 308.

If a *common* informer shall willingly, delay his suit, or discontinue or be nonsuit, or shall have a verdict or judgment against him, he shall pay costs to the defendant. 18 Eliz. c. 5.

And in the court of king's bench, particularly, if the defendant shall appear and plead to issue, and the prosecutor shall not at his own costs, within a year after issue joined, procure the same to be tried; or if a verdict pass for the defendant, or the informer procure a *noli prosequi* to be entered, the said court of king's bench may award the defendant his costs, unless the judge shall certify that there was a reasonable cause for exhibiting such information, and if the informer shall not, in three months after such costs taxed, and demand made, pay the same, the defendant shall have the benefit of the recognizance above mentioned, to compel him thereunto. 4 and 5 W. c. 18.

INFORMATUS NON SUM, is a formal answer made of course by an attorney who is authorized by his client to let judgment pass in that form against him. It is commonly used in warrants of attorney, given for the express purpose of confessing judgment.

INFORMER, one who informs against or prosecutes in any of the king's courts, those who offend against any law or penal statute.

INGRESS, EGRESS, AND REGRESS, words in leases of lands, to signify a free entry into, going out of, and returning from some part of the lands let; as to get in a crop of corn, &c. after the term expired.

INGRESSU, a writ of entry, whereby a man seeks entry into lands

lands or tenements; it lies in many cases, and hath many several forms.

INGRESSUS, the relief which the heir or successor at full age paid to the prime lord, for entering upon the fee or lands which were fallen by the death or forfeiture of the former feudatory.

IN GROSS, is that which belongs to the person of the lord, and not to any manor, lands, &c. as villain in gross, advowson in gross, &c. *Co. Lit.* 120.

INGROSSER. See *Forestalling*.

INGROSSING OF A FINE, is making the indentures by the *chirographer*, and the delivery of them to the party unto whom the cognizance is made.

INHABITANT, a dweller or householder in any place; as, inhabitants in a vill, are the householders in the vill. 2 *Inst.* 702.

But the word inhabitant does not extend to lodgers, servants, or the like, but to householders only. 2 *Inst.* 702.

INHERITANCE, is a perpetuity in lands or tenements, to a man and his heirs; and the word inheritance is not only intended where a man hath lands or tenements by descent, but also every fee-simple, or fee-tail, which a person hath by purchase, may be said to be an inheritance, because his heirs may inherit it. *Lit.* s. 9.

Inheritances are *corporeal* or *incorporeal*. *Corporeal* inheritances, relate to houses and lands, which may be touched or handled; and *incorporeal* hereditaments, are rights issuing out of, annexed to, or exercised with corporeal inheritances; as advowsons, tithes, annuities, offices, commons, franchises, privileges, and services. 1 *Inst.* 49.

There are several rules of inheritances of lands, according to which estates are transmitted from ancestor to heir, viz. 1. that inheritances shall lineally descend to the issue of the person last actually seized, *in infinitum*, but shall never lineally ascend. 2. The male issue shall be admitted before the female. 3. Where there are two or more males in equal degree, the eldest only shall inherit; but the females altogether. 4. The lineal descendants *in infinitum*, of any person deceased, shall represent their ancestor; that is, shall stand in the same place as the person himself would have done had he been living: thus the child, grand-child, or or great grand-child (either male or female), of the eldest son, succeeds before the younger son, and so *in infinitum*. 5. On failure of issue of the person last seized, the inheritance shall descend to the blood of the first purchaser. 6. The collateral heir of the person last seized, must be his next collateral kinsman of the whole blood. 7. In collateral inheritances, the male stocks shall be preferred to the female, unless where lands are descended from a female: thus the relations on the father's side are admitted *in infinitum*, before those on the mother's side are admitted at all; and the relations of the father's father; before those of the father's mother, and so on. 2 *Black*. c. 14.

INHIBITION, a writ to inhibit or forbid a judge from farther proceedings in the cause depending before him. F. N. B. 39.

INJUNCTION, an injunction is a prohibitory writ, restraining a person from committing or doing a thing which appears to be against equity and conscience. 3 *Bac. Abr*. 172.

An injunction is usually granted for the purpose of preserving property in dispute pending a suit; as to restrain the defendant from proceedings at the common law against the plaintiff, or from committing waste, or doing any injurious act. *Milf. Treat. Chan. Plead*.

Injunctions issue out of the courts of equity in several instances; the most usual injunction is to stay proceedings at law; as if one man bring an action at law against another, and a bill be brought to be relieved either against a penalty, or to stay proceedings at law, or some equitable circumstances, of which the party cannot have the benefit at law. In such case the plaintiff in equity, may move for an injunction either upon an attachment, or praying a *dedimus*, or praying a farther time to answer; for it being suggested in the bill, that the suit is against conscience, if the defendant be in contempt for not answering or pray time to answer, it is contrary to conscience to proceed at law in the mean time; and therefore an injunction is granted of course; but this injunction only stays execution touching the matter in question, and there is always a clause giving liberty to call for a plea, to proceed to trial, and for want of it, to obtain judgment; but execution is stayed till answer, or farther order. 3 *Bac. Abr*. 173.

When a bill in chancery is filed in the office of the six clerks, if if an injunction be prayed therein, it may be had, at various stages of the cause, according to the circumstances of the case. If the bill be to stay execution upon an oppressive judgment, and the defendant do not put in his answer within the time allowed by the rules of the court, an injunction will issue of course; and when the answer comes in, the injunction can only be continued upon a sufficient ground appearing from the answer itself. But if an injunction be wanted to stay waste, or other injuries of an equally unjust nature, then upon the filing of the bill, and a proper case supported by affidavits, the court will grant an injunction immediately; to continue till the defendant have put in his answer, and till the court shall make some further order concerning it: and when the answer comes in whether it shall then be dissolved, or continued till the hearing of the cause; is determined by the court upon argument, drawn from considering the answer and affidavits together. 3 *Black.* 443.

The methods of dissolving injunctions are various; when the answer comes in, and the party hath cleared his contempt by paying the costs of the attachment, if there is one, he obtains an order to dissolve *nisi*, and serves it on the plaintiff's clerk in court; this order takes notice of the defendant's having fully answered the bill, and thereby denied the whole equity thereof, and being regularly served, the plaintiff must shew cause at the day, or the defendant's counsel, where there is no probability of shewing cause, may move to make the order absolute, unless cause, sitting the court. 3 *Bac. Abr.* 177.

If the plaintiff who hath an injunction die pending the suit, in strictness the whole proceedings are abated, and the injunction with them; but even in this case the party shall not take out execution without special leave of the court; he must move the court for the plaintiff to revive his suit within a limited time, or the injunction to stand dissolved; and as this is never denied, so if the suit be not revived, the party takes out execution. There are some instances where a plaintiff may move to revive his injunction; but as that rarely happens, so it is rarely granted, especially where the injunction hath been before dissolved: but where a bill is dismissed, the injunction and every thing else is gone, and execution may be taken out the next day. 3 *Bac. Abr.* 178.

INJURY, a wrong or damage to a man's person or goods. The

law will suffer a private injury rather than a public evil; and the act of God or of the law, doth injury to none. 4 *Rep.* 124.

INLAND BILLS. See *Bills of Exchange.*

INMATE, is one who is admitted to dwell in the same house with another person. Inmates by 31 Eliz. c. 7, were prohibited to be in cottages, but by 15 G. III. c. 32 the said statute of Eliz. was repealed; setting forth that the same had laid the industrious poor under great difficulties to procure habitations, and tended very much to lessen population.

INNS AND INNKEEPERS, common inns were instituted for passengers, and the duty of inn-keepers extends chiefly to the entertaining and harbouring of travellers, finding them victuals and lodgings, and securing the goods and effects of their guests; and therefore if one who keeps a common inn refuse either to receive a traveller as a guest into his house, or to find him victuals or lodging, upon his tendering a reasonable price for the same, he is not only liable to render the damages for the injury in an action on the case, at the suit of the party grieved, but also may be indicted and fined at the suit of the king. *Dyer.* 158.

In return for such responsibility, the law allows him to retain the horse of his guest until paid for his keep; but he cannot retain such horse for the bill of the owner, although he may retain his goods for such bill; neither can he detain one horse for the food of another. 1 *Bulst.* 207, 217.

An inn-keeper, however, is not bound to receive the horse, unless the master lodge there also. 2 *Brown.* 254.

Neither is a landlord bound to furnish provisions unless paid beforehand. 9 *Co.* 87.

If an inn-keeper make out unreasonable bills, he may be indicted for extortion; and if either he or any of his servants knowingly sell bad wine or bad provisions, they will be responsible in an action of deceit.

Any person may set up a new inn, unless it be inconvenient to the public, in respect of its situation, or to its increasing the number of inns, not only to the prejudice of the public, but also to the hindrance and prejudice of other ancient and well-governed inns: for the keeping of an inn is no franchise, but a lawful trade, open to every subject, and therefore there is no need of any licence from the king for that purpose. 2 *Roll. Abr.* 84.

An

An innkeeper is distinguished from other trades, in that he cannot be a bankrupt; for though he buys provisions to be spent in his house, yet he does not properly sell them, but utter them at such rates as he thinks reasonable, and the attendance of his servants, furniture of his house, &c. are to be considered; and the statutes of bankruptcy only mention merchants that use to buy and sell in gross, or buy retail, and such as get their living by buying and selling; but the contracts with innkeepers are not for any commodities in specie, but they are contracts for house-room, trouble, attendance, lodging, and necessaries, and therefore cannot come within the design of such words, since there is no trade carried on by buying and bartering commodities. 1 *Jones*. 437.

But where an innkeeper is a chapman also and buys and sells, he may on that account be a bankrupt, though not barely as an innkeeper, and this has been frequently seen. 7 *Vin. Abr*. 57.

Innkeepers are clearly chargeable for the goods of guests stolen or lost out of their inns, and this without any contract or agreement for that purpose; for the law makes them liable in respect of the reward, as also in respect of their being places appointed and allowed of by law, for the benefit and security of traders and travellers. *Dyer*. 266.

But if a person come to an innkeeper, and desire to be entertained by him, which the innkeeper refuses, because his house is already full; whereupon the party says he will shift among the rest of his guests, and there he is robbed, the host shall not be charged. *Dyer*. 158.

If a man come to a common inn to harbour, and desire that his horse may be put to grass, and the host put him to grass accordingly, and the horse is stolen, the host shall not be charged; because by law the host is not bound to answer for any thing out of his inn, but only for those things that are *infra hospitium*. 8 *Co*. 32 b.

Innkeepers may detain the person of the guest who eats, or the horse which eats, till payment, and this he may do without any agreement for that purpose; for men that get their livelihood by entertainment of others, cannot annex such disobliging conditions that they should retain the party's property in case of non-payment, nor make such disadvantageous and impudent a supposition, that they shall not be paid: and therefore the law annexed such a condition without the agreement of the parties. *Roll. Abr.* 85.

By the custom of *London* and *Exeter*, if a man commit an horse to an hostler, and he eat out the price of his head, the hostler may take him as his own, upon the reasonable appraisement of four of his neighbours; but the innkeeper hath no power to sell the horse, by the general custom of the whole kingdom. *Moor.* 876. 3. *Bulst* 271.

But it has been held that though an innkeeper in London, may after long keeping, have the horse appraised and sell him; yet when he has in such case had him appraised, he cannot justify the taking him to himself, at the price it was appraised at. 1 *Vin. Abr.* 233.

INNS OF COURT, are so called, because the students therein study the law, to enable them to practice in the courts at Westminster, or elsewhere; and also because they use all other gentle exercises, as may render them better qualified to serve the king in his court. *Fortesq.* c. 49.

INNUENDO, is a word used in declarations and law pleadings, to ascertain a person or thing which was named before; as to say he, (innuendo the plaintiff) did so and so, when there was mention before of another person.

Innuendo, may serve for an explanation, where there is precedent matter, but never for a new charge; it may apply what is already expressed, but cannot add or enlarge the importance of it. 2 *Salk.* 513.

INQUEST, an inquisition by jurors, or a jury, which is the most usual trial of all causes both civil and criminal within this realm, for causes civil, after proof is made on either side, of so much as each party thinks good for himself; if the fact be in doubt, it is referred to the discretion of twelve indifferent men, impanelled by the sheriff for that purpose, and as they bring in their verdict, so judgment passes. See *Jury*.

INQUISITION, a manner of proceeding by way of search or examination, and used in the king's behalf on temporal causes and process; in which sense it is confounded with office. *Staundf. Prærog.* 51.

This inquisition is upon an outlawry found, in case of treason and felony committed; upon a *felo de se*, &c. to entitle the king

to

to a forfeiture of lands and goods; and there is no such nicety required in an inquisition as in pleading: because an inquisition is only to inform the court how process shall issue for the king, whose title accrues by the attainder, and not by the inquisition; and yet in cases of the king and a common person, inquisitors have been held void for incertainty. *Lane.* 39.

Some of the inquisitions are in themselves convictions, and cannot afterwards be traversed or denied; and therefore the inquest ought to hear all that can be alledged on both sides: of this nature are all inquisitions of *felo de se*; of flight in persons accused of felony; of deodands and the like; and presentment of petty offences in the sheriff's torn or court leet, whereupon the presiding officer may set a fine. Other inquisitions may be afterwards traversed and examined; as particularly the coroner's inquisition of the death of a man; for in such cases, the offender may be arraigned upon the inquisition, and dispute the truth of it. 4 *Black.* 301.

INQUISITORS, are sheriffs, coroners *super visum corporis*, or the like, who have power to enquire into certain causes.

INROLLMENT, is the registering, recording, or entering in the rolls of the chancery, king's-bench, common-pleas, or exchequer, or by the clerk of the peace in the records of the quarter-sessions, of any lawful act; a statute or recognizance acknowledged, a deed of bargain and sale of lands, and the like: but the inrolling a deed doth not make it a record, though it thereby becomes a deed recorded; for there is a difference between a matter of record, and a thing recorded to be kept in memory; a record being the entry in parchment of judicial matters controverted in a court of record, and whereof the court takes notice whereas an inrollment of a deed, is a private act of the parties concerned, of which the court takes no cognizance at the time of doing it, although the court permits it. 2 *Lill. Abr.* c. 9.

By stat. 27 H. VIII. c. 16. no lands shall pass, whereby any estate of inheritance or freehold shall take effect, or any use thereof be made, by reason only of any bargain and sale thereof, except the bargain and sale be made by writing indented, sealed, and within six months inrolled in one of the king's courts of record at Westminster; or else within the county where the lands lie, before the clerk of the peace, and one or more justices.

But by 5 Eliz. c. 26. in the counties palatine, they may be inrolled at the respective courts there, or at the assizes.

Every deed before it is inrolled, is to be acknowledged to be the deed of the party, before a master of chancery, or a judge of the court wherein it is inrolled; which is the officer's warrant for inrolling the same; and the inrollment of a deed, if it be acknowledged by the grantor, it will be a good proof of the deed itself upon trial. 2 *Lill. Abr.* 69.

But a deed may be inrolled without the examination of the party himself; for it is sufficient if oath be made of the execution. If two are parties, and the deed be acknowledged by one, the other is bound by it. And if a man live abroad, and would pass lands here in England, a nominal person may be joined with him in the deed, who may acknowledge it here, and it will be binding. 1 *Salk.* 389.

INSIMUL COMPUTASSENT, is a writ that lies upon a stated account between two merchants or other persons; in which case the law implies, that he against whom the balance appears hath engaged to pay it to the other, though there be not any actual promise: and from this implication, it is frequent for actions on the case to be brought, declaring that the plaintiff and defendant had settled their accounts together, *insimul computassent*, and that the defendant engaged to pay to the plaintiff the balance, but hath since neglected to do it: if no account have been made up, then the legal remedy is by bringing a writ of account, *de computo*, commanding the defendant to render a just account to the plaintiff, or shew to the court good cause to the contrary. 3 *Black.* 162.

INSOLVENT, till of late the chancery would not put out an insolvent trustee, for that he was intrusted by the donor.

An insolvent person made an executor cannot be put out by the ordinary; for he is intrusted by the testator. *Comb.* 185.

But chancery granted an injunction against him, not to intermeddle with the assets any farther than to satisfy the legacy given to himself; for in equity he is but a trustee for other legatees (infants), and when a trustee is insolvent, the court of chancery will compel him to give security before he shall enter upon the trust. *Carth.* 458.

INSOLVENT DEBTORS, insolvent acts, are statues passed

fur

for the purpose of releasing from prison, and sometimes their debts, persons whose transactions have not been of such a nature as would subject them to the bankrupt laws. Their discharge is usually from all suits and imprisonment, upon delivering up all their estates and effects, real and personal, for the benefit of their creditors.

By the last act 41 Geo. III. c. 4. it extended to persons in custody on the 1st day of March 1801, whose debts did not exceed the sum of 1500l. but this act does not discharge the future effects of the debtor.

By the 6th section, persons under bail on or before the said 1st day of March 1801, were considered as in custody, and entitled to all benefits.

INSTANT, an instant is not to be considered in law as in logic, as a point of time; but in our law, things which are to be done in an instant, have in consideration of law, a priority of time in them; as lessee for life makes a lease for years, they both surrender to him in reversion, though it is made in an instant, yet it shall be understood to have degrees, *silicet*, the surrender of the lessee for years to tenant for life, and then the surrender of tenant for life. *3 Sec.* 247.

INSTITUTION, institution to a benefice, is that whereby the ordinary commits the cure of souls to the parson presented, as by induction he obtains a temporal right to the profits of the living. Previous to the institution, the oath against simony, the oaths of allegiance and supremacy, are to be taken, and if it be a vicarage, the oath of residence. They are also to subscribe the thirty-nine articles, and the articles concerning the king's supremacy, and the book of common prayer.

INSUPER, a word used by the auditors in their accounts in the exchequer, when they say so much remains *insuper* to such an account, that is, so much remains due upon such account.

INSURANCE *marine*. Insurance is a contract of indemnity, whereby the party, in consideration of a stipulated sum, undertakes to indemnify the other against certain specific perils or risks to which he is exposed, or against the occurrence of such events.

The party who takes on himself the risk is called the *insurer*, the party protected by the insurance is called the *insured*; the

 sum

sum paid to the insurer as the price of this risk, is called the *premium*; and the written instrument, in which the contract is set forth and reduced into form, is called a *policy of insurance.*

The aim and intention of insurance of every species, whether against risk at sea, fire, or on lives, is to subdivide casual calamity, so far as it relates to loss in value, and may be measured by money. By this means merchants and individuals insuring, in consequence of submitting to pay a small sum certain on all hazardous transactions, are secure of indemnity or reimbursement in case of loss. From this invention, the most beneficial consequences arise, as pecuniary loss, when subdivided to a certain degree, ceases to deserve the name of calamity. Such is the advantage to the insured; the insurers, on the other hand, who undertake the risk for a small certain gain, are divided into two classes: they are either wealthy joint-stock companies, running a great number of heavy risks, the certain income on the whole compensating the chance of loss on any individual transactions, or they consist of individuals, who by running a great number of small risks, calculate, that on the whole, the chance is in their favour.

Marine insurance is made for the protection of persons having an interest in ships or goods on board, from the loss or damage which may happen from the perils of the sea, during a certain voyage, or for a fixed period of time.

Of parties to the contract; in this country all persons, whether British subjects or aliens, may in general be insured; the only exception is in the case of an alien enemy.

An alien enemy cannot maintain an action on a policy on goods, though they were shipped before the war commenced: nor can an agent of such insured maintain the action, though he be a creditor of the insured for more than the sum insured. 6 T. R. 23.

At common law, any man or company of men might have been insurers: and individuals, upon their own separate account, have still the same right; but commerce having suffered considerably by persons in insolvent circumstances underwriting policies of insurance, it was thought expedient to establish two companies for the purpose of making marine insurances, with sufficient funds to answer all demands on their policies; still however, leaving the merchants

merchants to the option of insuring with individual underwriters when they thought proper. To this end the stat. 6 Geo. I. c. 18. authorized the king to grant charters to two distinct companies or corporations, called the Royal Exchange Assurance, and London Assurance; for the insurance of ships, goods, and merchandizes at sea, or going to sea, and for lending money on bottomry. They are invested with all the powers usually granted to corporations, and the privilege of purchasing lands to the amount of 1000l. per annum each, to provide a sufficient capital to insure all demands on their policies. All other companies, are restrained from insuring ships and goods at sea, or lending money on bottomry. And all policies made by any other corporation shall be void, and the sums underwritten forfeited, and all bottomry bonds deemed usurious; but the right of individual insurers continues as before the act.

Contracts made in derogation of the rights of the insurance companies, are illegal and void. 2 H. *Black.* 379.

Subjects of insurance; ships, freight, goods, and merchandizes, &c. are the proper subjects of marine insurance; and there are certain articles which from motives of public policy, cannot be legally insured in this country, and others which can only be insured under particular restrictions.

Insurable interests. Insurance being a contract of indemnity from loss or damage, arising upon an uncertain event, there cannot be an indemnity without a loss, nor a loss without an interest; a policy therefore, without interest, is not an insurance, but a mere wager.

Different persons, having each a qualified property in goods, may insure them to the full value. 2 T. R. 188.

A reasonable expectation of profit, or a well-founded expectation of a future interest in the thing insured, is an insurable interest.

Wager policy. This is usually conceived in the terms, *interest or no interest,* or, *without further proof of interest than the policy,* to preclude all enquiry into the interest of the insured; and as a consequence of the insured's having no interest in the pretended subject of the policy, it follows, that the insurer cannot be liable for any partial loss.

A partial loss is not an event sufficiently defined and accurate to be the criterion of a wager, and nothing but that sort of misfortune which is considered as amounting to total loss can decide it. The parties mean to play for the whole stake, and when the underwriter pays a loss, he cannot, as in the case of an insurance upon interest, claim any benefit from what may have been saved. To preclude all claim of that sort the words, *free of average and without benefit of salvage,* are always introduced into wager policies.

Re-insurance. A policy of insurance being once signed, the underwriters are bound by the terms of it, nor can they be released from their contract without the consent of the insured. But an underwriter may shift it, or part of it from himself to insurers, by causing a re-insurance to be made on the same risk, and the new insurers will be responsible to him in case of loss, to the amount of the re-insurance. But the re-insurer is only responsible to the original insurer, and *not to* the original insured.

Thus stands the law on this subject in most of the states of Europe; but in England, by the 19 Geo. II. c. 37. re-insurances are prohibited except in case of the insolvency or death of the original insurer. This has been held to extend not only to British, but also to foreign ships. 2 T. R. 161.

Double insurance, is where the insured makes two insurances on the same risk and the same interest. A double insurance, though it be made with a view to a double satisfaction in case of loss, and is therefore in the nature of a wager, is not void. The two policies are considered as making but one insurance; they are good to the extent of the value of the effects put in risk; but the insured shall not be permitted to recover a double satisfaction. He may sue the underwriters on both the policies; but he can only recover the real amount of his loss, to which all the underwriters shall contribute in proportion to their several subscriptions; and therefore if he should content himself with suing only on one of the policies, the underwriters on that policy may recover a rateable contribution from those on the other. N. P. *Aft East.* 17 Geo. III.

Of the voyage. It may be laid down as a general rule, that no insurance can be legally made upon any voyage undertaken contrary to the laws of this kingdom, or to those of its dependencies, or to the law of nations, and it is immaterial whether the

insurer

insurer was or was not informed that the voyage was illegal. An insurance therefore, upon a voyage undertaken contrary to the navigation law, is void.

Risks against which insurances may be made. Insurances may be made against all the risks or perils which are incident to sea voyages, subject however to certain exceptions founded in public policy and the interests of humanity, which require, that in certain cases men shall not be permitted to protect themselves against some particular perils of insurance. But an insurer cannot make himself answerable for a loss, proceeding from the fault of the insured. No insurance can be made, even against the perils of the sea, upon illegal commerce.

In order to confine insurances against real and important losses arising from the perils of the sea, and to obviate disputes respecting losses from the perishable quality of the goods insured, and all trivial subjects of litigation, it appears to be the general law of all states, that the insurer shall not be liable for any average loss, unless it exceed *one* per cent, independent of which a clause has been introduced into the policies of most countries, by which it is stipulated that the insurer shall not be liable for any partial loss under a given rate per cent. In England it is now constantly stipulated in all policies, that upon certain enumerated articles, the insurer shall not be answerable for any partial loss whatever, that upon certain others, liable to partial injuries, but less difficult to be preserved at sea, he shall only be liable for partial losses above five per cent; and that as to all other goods, and also the ship and freight, he shall only be liable for partial losses above three per cent. This change was first introduced in 1749, to save the necessity of adapting the premium to the nature of the commodity. But the insurer is liable for the losses, however small, called general average, and losses occasioned by the stranding of the ship.

The meaning of the memorandum in the common policies, used in London by private underwriters, is, that in no case the insurer shall be liable for any partial loss on the articles enumerated, unless it be a general average, or the ship stranded; and he shall be liable for no other loss, though it be of a nature to which any other commodity is equally liable. A loss by stranding must be an an immediate, not a remote consequence of the stranding, to be within the memorandum.

Commencement and continuance of the risk. In England the commencement of the risk on the ship varies in almost every case. In outward-bound voyages, it is generally made to commence from her beginning to load at her port of departure.

Sometimes privateers on a cruise, ships engaged in the coasting-trade, or in short voyages, are insured for a limited period of time; and in such case the risk commences and ends with the term, wherever the ship may then happen to be.

If a ship be insured *from* the port of London to any other port, and before she breaks ground an accident happen to her, the insurers are not answerable, for the risk does not commence till she sets sail on her departure from the port of London. But if the insurance be *at and from* the port of London the insurers are liable to any accident that may happen to her from the time of subscribing the policy.

When a ship expected to arrive at a certain place abroad, is insured *at and from* that place, or from her arrival there; the risk begins from the first moment of her arrival at the place specified, and the words *first arrival* are implied, and always understood, in policies so worded. The risk in such cases continues there as long as the ship is preparing for the voyage insured; but if all thought of the voyage be laid aside, and the ship be suffered to lay there for a length of time with the owner's privity, the insurers are not liable.

In English policies, it is usually made to continue only, *until the ship hath moored at anchor 24 hours in good safety*; and on such policies the insurer is liable for no loss after that time.

Duration of the risk; to charge the insurer it is not enough that a loss has happened at sea, it must appear to have happened in the course of the voyage, and during the continuance of the risk insured. Upon goods, the risk does not commence until they are actually on board the ship, and therefore the insurer is not answerable for any loss or damage which may happen to them while they are on the passage to the ship; and in general the risk on goods continues no longer than while they are on board the ship mentioned in the policy, and that if they be removed from on board

board that ship and landed, or put on board another ship without the consent of the insurers, the contract is at an end.

Of the policy. A policy of insurance is the name given to the instrument by which the contract of insurance is effected and reduced into form, and it is not, like most contracts, signed by both parties, but only by the insurer. As the premium, which is the consideration of the promise made by the insurer, is paid, or supposed to be paid, at the time the policy is subscribed, the contract contains nothing in nature of a counter-promise to be performed by the insured; in general therefore, it contains only the contract on the part of the insurers.

Policies, with reference to the reality of the interest of the insured, are distinguished into *interest* and *wager* policies; with reference to the amount of the interest, they are distinguished into *open* and *valued.*

An interest policy, is where the insured has a real, substantial, assignable interest in the thing insured, in which case only it is a contract of indemnity.

A wager policy, is a pretended insurance, founded on an ideal risk, where the insured has no interest in the thing insured, and can therefore sustain no loss by the occurrence of any of the misfortunes insured against. Insurances of this sort, are usually expressed by the words *interest or no interest,* or *without further proof of interest than the policy,* or *without benefit of salvage to the insurer.*

An open policy, is where the amount of the insured is not fixed by the policy, but is left to be ascertained by the insured in case a loss should happen.

A valued policy, is where a value has been set on the ship or goods insured, and the value is inserted in the policy in the nature of liquidated damages, to save the necessity of proving it in case of total loss; for by allowing the value to be thus inserted in the policy, the insurer agrees that it shall be taken as there stated. This value is or ought to be the real value of the ship, or the prime cost of the goods at the time of effecting the policy.

By whom the policy may be effected. The business of negociating insurances with the underwriters, and of getting policies effected, is usually transacted by brokers, who make this branch of business their profession. To the broker the merchant looks for the

the regularity of the contract. To him also the underwriters look for a fair and candid disclosure of all material circumstances affecting the risk, and for the payment of their premiums.

But though the underwriter looks to the broker for his premium, and though the broker in his account with the underwriter, takes credit for the loss and return of premiums which he is authorized to receive from the underwriter, yet such losses are not to be looked upon as debt from the underwriter to the broker.

The form and requisites of the policy. From the nature and object of the contract, courts of justice have always construed it according to the intention of the parties, so as that the indemnity of the insured, and the advancement of trade, which are the great objects of insurance, may be attained.

When a clause is clear in itself, it ought to be understood literally; but when clauses are obscure, the best and only mode of fixing their meaning, is by the rules of the common law.

Voyage how to be described in the policy. Every fact and circumstance relating to the contract of insurance, must be stated with the most scrupulous regard to truth. The voyage insured must therefore be truly and accurately described in the policy; namely, the time and place at which the risk is to begin; the place of the ship's departure; the place of her destination; and the time when the risk shall end; whether on goods or on the ship. If a blank be left for the place either of the ship's departure or destination, the policy will be void for the uncertainty.

Date and subscription of the policy. The sum insured is generally placed after the signature in the underwriter's handwriting, and in words at length. But it is not indispensably necessary, that the sum shall be specified in the policy. An insurer may bind himself to pay the value of the effects insured, or a given proportion of it, without fixing that value in the policy.

There are few instruments to which the true date is more necessary. This date, when compared with the dates of facts connected with the transaction, serves to discover whether there be reason to suspect any fraudulent concealment at the time.

The date is not inserted in the body of the policy; for as each subscription to a policy, makes a distinct contract, each underwriter sets down the day, month, and year of his subscription.

The

The last requisite of a policy is that it be duly stamped. See *Stamps.*

When a policy may be altered. Though a policy of insurance, being a contract of indemnity, and being only considered as a simple contract, must always be construed, as nearly as possible, according to the intention of the parties, and not according to the strict and literal meaning of the words; the general form of the policy, which has been for many ages nearly the same, is never altered but with the utmost precaution, and upon very great consideration; and therefore when once a policy is filled up and underwritten, no alteration can be made in it, but by the consent of all parties, or by the authority of a court of equity, or perhaps a court of law, and then only in a case where something has by mistake or fraud, been inserted or omitted, contrary to the manifest intention and the real agreement of the parties; and a very clear case of this sort must be made out by unquestionable testimony, to warrant such alteration. But where such a case is made out, the court will direct the alteration to be made even after a loss has happened. 1 *Atk.* 545.

Of warranty. A warranty is a stipulation or agreement on the part of the insured, in nature of a condition precedent. It may be either *affirmative,* as where the insured undertakes for the truth of some private allegation, as that the thing insured is neutral property, that the ship is of such a force, that she sailed or was well on such a day, &c. or it may be *promissory,* as where the insured undertakes to perform some executory stipulations; as that a ship shall sail on or before some given day, that she shall depart with convoy, that she shall be manned with such a complement of men, &c.

Warranties are either *express* or *implied.* An *express warranty* is a particular stipulation introduced into the written contract by the agreement of the parties; as that the thing insured is neutral property, that the ship shall sail by a given day, that she shall depart with convoy, &c.

An implied warranty, is that which reasonably results from the nature of the contract, as that the ship shall be sea-worthy when she sails on the voyage insured, that she shall be navigated with reasonable skill and care, that the voyage is lawful, and shall be performed according to law, and in the usual course and without deviation, &c.

Warranty to sail with convoy. Another species of warranty often inserted in policies in time of war, is to sail or depart with convoy. This like other warranties, must be strictly performed; and if the ship depart without convoy, from whatever cause, the policy becomes void, and the insurer shall not be answerable even for the peril of the seas.

There are five things essential to a sailing with convoy: 1. It must be with the regular convoy appointed by government. 2. It must be from the place of rendezvous appointed by government. 3. It must be a convoy for the voyage. 4. The ship insured must have sailing instructions. 5. She must depart and continue with the convoy till the end of the voyage unless separated by necessity.

Warranty of neutrality. As the premium is meant to be proportioned to the nature of the risk, and as the general words of the policy, unless restrained or qualified by some special stipulation, subject the insurer to every loss by capture, it is of great importance in time of war, between maritime states, to ascertain whether the ship or goods meant to be insured, be liable to capture as belonging to either of the belligerent powers. If the insured profess to be the subject of a neutral state, and mean to be insured as such, the insurer requires him to warrant the ship or goods to be neutral property. This is done by inserting in the policy either the words, *warranted neutral,* or *warranted neutral property*; and sometimes the warranty is, that they belong to the subjects of some particular neutral state.

Neutral property, in the sense of which that expression must be understood in this warranty, is, that which belongs to the subjects of a state in amity with the belligerent powers.

The documents requisite for neutral ships are: 1. The passport. This is a permission from the neutral state to the captain or master of the ship to proceed on the voyage proposed, and usually contains his name and residence, the name, description, and destination of the ship, with such other matters as the practice of the place requires. This document is indispensably necessary for the safety of every neutral ship.

2. The

2. The sea-letter or sea-brief, which specifies the nature and quantity of the cargo, the place from whence it comes, and its destination. This paper is not so necessary as the passport, because the former in most particulars supplies its place.

3. The proofs of property, which ought to shew that the ship really belongs to the subjects of a neutral state. If she appear to either belligerent, to have been built in the enemy's country, proof is generally required that she was purchased by the neutral before captured, and legally condemned since the declaration of war; and in the latter case the bill of sale, properly authenticated, ought to be produced.

4. The muster roll, containing the name, age, quality, place of residence, and above all the place of birth, of every person of the ship's company.

5. The charty party.

6. The bill of lading, by which the captain acknowledges the receipt of the goods specified therein, and promises to deliver them to his consignee or his order.

7. The invoices, which contain the particulars and prices of each parcel of goods, with the amount of the freight, duties and other charges thereon, which are usually transmitted from the shippers to their factors or consignees. These invoices prove by whom the goods were shipped, and to whom consigned.

8. The log-book, or ship's journal, which contains an account of the ship's course with a short history of every occurrence during the voyage.

9. The bill of health, which is a certificate, properly authenticated, that the ship comes from a place where no contagious distemper prevails, and that none of the crew at the time of her departure were infected with any such distemper.

Upon this subject of the ship's documents, it is to be observed, that though by the law of nations the want of some of these papers, may be taken as strong presumptive evidence; yet the want of none of them amounts to conclusive evidence against the ship's neutrality.

Representations. Good faith should preside in all transactions of commerce, and in none more than in those of insurance. In this contract each party is bound to conduct himself towards the other, not only with integrity but with the most unreserved openness

ness and candour, and they ought mutually to disclose to each other every circumstance, which can in any degree affect the risk.

A representation in insurance is denoted to be a collateral statement, either by parole or in writing, of such facts or circumstances relative to the proposed adventure, and not inserted in policy, as are necessary for the information of the insurer, to enable him to form a just estimate of the risk. Such representations are often the principal inducements to the contract, and afford the best ground on which the premium can be calculated.

A misrepresentation in a material point avoids the contract; and the insured cannot recover on the policy for loss arising from a cause unconnected with the fact misrepresented. So if it be made without knowing whether it be true or false, or even if the person making it, believe it to be true; but if he only give it as his belief, without knowing the contrary, it will not affect the contract.

Concealment consists in a fraudulent suppression of any fact or circumstance material to the risk. This, like every other fraud, avoids the contract *ab initio*, upon principles of natural justice; for as the facts on which the risk must be estimated, lie generally within the knowledge of the insured or his agent, the underwriter must in most cases rely on him for all the necessary information o enable him to decide upon what terms he will take upon himself the proposed risk; and he computes the premium, and enters into the contract, in the confidence that the insured, being fully informed of all circumstances relating to the intended voyage, has dealt fairly with him, and has kept back nothing which it might be material for him to know.

But it is not merely on the ground of fraud that a concealment avoids the contract; even an innocent concealment if material, will avoid the policy; the insurer should therefore not conceal any necessary information, but disclose all material circumstances; for a concealment is to be considered not with reference to the event, but to its effect at the time of making the contract.

Sea worthiness; in every insurance, whether of ship or goods, there is an implied warranty of the sea worthiness of the ship, that is to say, that she shall be *tight, staunch, and strong, properly manned, and provided with all necessary stores*, and in every other respect fit for the voyage.

Where

Where a ship is lost, or is in the course of the voyage condemned as incapable of proceeding to the place of her destination, and this cannot be ascribed to stress of weather or any accident, the presumption is, that she was not sea worthy, in so far as to throw the proof that she was sea worthy, on the insured.

A ship must not only be perfect in herself, but must from the nature of her structure, be capable of performing the voyage on which the insurance is made, otherwise she is not tight, staunch, and strong, according to the tenor of the charter-party; and it is also required that there shall be good and sufficient evidence of this, and also that the insured shall bring forward all the evidence he has, of the condition of the ship at the time she sailed, and when the loss happened, or she was condemned or unfit to proceed on her voyage. If on the other hand, the loss or disability of the ship may be fairly ascribed to sea damage, the proof of the un-sea-worthiness lies on the insurers.

Deviation, is a voluntary departure, without reasonable cause, from the regular course of the voyage insured. From the moment this happens the contract becomes void. The course of the voyage does not mean the nearest possible way, but the usual and regular course. Accordingly, stopping at certain places on the voyage is no deviation, if it be customary so to do; but such usage can only be supported by long and regular practice.

Loss is the injury or damage sustained by the insured in consequence of one or more of the accidents or misfortunes against which the insurer, in consideration of the premium, has undertaken to indemnify the insured, and which perils are all distinctly enumerated in the policy.

Loss is either *total* or *partial*. The term *total loss* means not only the total destruction of, but also such damage to the thing insured, as renders it of little or no value to the insured, although it may specifically remain. Thus a loss is said to be total, if, in consequence of the misfortune that has happened, the voyage be lost or not worth pursuing, and the projected adventure frustrated; or if the value of what is saved be less than the freight, &c.

A partial loss is any thing short of a total loss. Thus if a ship insured for a particular voyage arrive at her port of destination, and there remain twenty-four hours, moored in safety, or if she be insured for a term, and survive the term, no injury which she could have sustained during the voyage in one case, or during the term in the other, however great can amount to a total loss. So in the case of an insurance on goods, the insurer contracts that they shall arrive safe at the port of delivery. If they specifically remain, and are landed at the port of delivery, however damaged in the voyage, the injury will only amount to a partial loss; being of the nature of those losses which are the subject of average contributions. Partial losses are sometimes stiled average losses.

Losses by perils of the sea. These are generally understood to be such accidents or misfortunes as proceed from sea damage; that is to say such as arise from stress of weather, winds, waves, lightning, tempests, rocks, sand, &c. This sort of loss may happen by the ship's foundering at sea; and then it must in most cases, be a total loss. It may be by stranding, either accidental, where the ship is driven on shore by the winds and waves; or voluntary, when she is run on shore, either to preserve her from a worse fate, or with a fraudulent purpose. If the stranding be followed by shipwreck, then it becomes a total loss; if she is got off and rendered fit to continue the voyage, it is a partial and general average loss. It may also happen from the ship striking on a sunken rock, which may occasion the springing a leak, or absolute shipwreck.

If a ship be not heard of for a reasonable time, she shall be presumed to have foundered at sea, and the insured has a right to recover as such, from the underwriters. *Park.* 63.

A loss by fire which is merely accidental, and not imputable to the master or mariners, is undoubtedly within the policy. If a ship be burnt by order of the state where she happens to be, to prevent infection, this also has been held a loss within the policy.

If a ship be attacked by an enemy, and the captain, unable to defend her, leave and set fire to her to prevent her from falling into the enemy's hands, the insurer is said to be liable.

Capture is where a ship is taken by an enemy in war, or by way of reprisals, or by a pirate. Capture may be with an intent to possess the ship and cargo, or only to seize the goods on board as contraband: the former is a capture, the latter only an arrest or detention. Every capture, whether lawful or unlawful, is within

within the policy; provided the words of the policy be sufficiently comprehensive. Where the ship is re-captured before abandonment, it is a partial loss; and the insurer is bound to pay the salvage, and other necessary expences the insured may have incurred to recover his property. In general wherever a ship is taken by the enemy, the insured may abandon and demand as for a total loss: but he is not bound to abandon; if he do, the insurer, in case of re-capture, will stand in his place, and is liable for all fair charges occasioned by the capture.

Loss by detention of princes, &c. There is an obvious difference between this and capture; the object of the one is prize, that of the other detention; with a design to restore the ship or goods detained, or pay the value to the owner: and though neither of these should be done, still it must be considered as the arrest of princes, the character of any action depending on the original design with which it was done. An arrest of princes may be at sea, as well as in port, if it be done from public necessity, and not with a view to plunder.

Loss by barratry. Barratry is any species of fraud committed by the master or mariners, whereby the owners sustain an injury; as by running away with the ship, wilfully carrying her out of her course, sinking or deserting her, embezzling the cargo, smuggling, or any other offence, whereby the ship or cargo may be subjected to arrest, detention, loss, or forfeiture. No fault of the master or mariners amounts to barratry, unless it proceed from an intention to defraud the owners; therefore a deviation, if made through ignorance, unskilfulness, or any motive which is not fraudulent, although it will avoid the policy, does not amount to barratry.

Loss by average contributions. The goods on board are in proportion to their respective interests, towards any particular loss or expence incurred for the general safety of the ship or cargo, so that the particular loser may not be a greater sufferer than the other owners of the goods. Thus, where the goods of a particular merchant are thrown overboard to lighten the ship; where the masts. cables, anchors, or other furniture of the ship are cut away or destroyed for the safety of the whole; in these and similar cases, the loss is the proper subject of a general contribution, and ought to be rateably borne by the owners of the ship, freight, and cargo, so that the loss may fall proportionably on all.

As

As to the articles liable to contribute, the rule is, that the ship, freight, and every thing remaining of the cargo, is subject to this charge; therefore money, plate, and jewels, are as much liable as more heavy and bulky goods. But the persons on board, their wearing apparel, and the jewels belonging to it, shall not contribute; neither are seamen's wages liable to contribute.

Loss by expence of salvage. At common law, the party has a lien on every thing saved, till payment of salvage; but the regulations now principally in force, are ascertained by the statutes 12 Anne, c. 18: 26 G. II c. 19: 33 G. III. c. 66.

The insured need not in his action declare for salvage, but may recover under a declaration, for the loss which occasioned it, and the damage which the goods have sustained. In case of neutral ships captured by the enemy, and re-taken by British men of war, or privateers, the court of admiralty has a discretionary power of adjusting the salvage. Before an action will lie for a loss by payment of salvage, the amount must be ascertained by decision of the court of admiralty.

Abandonment. The insured may abandon in every case, where, in consequence of any of the perils insured against, the voyage is lost, or not worth pursuing; where the thing insured is so damaged as to be of little or no value to the owner, where the salvage is immoderate, where what is saved is of less value than the freight, or where further expence is necessary, and the insurer will not undertake to pay that expence, &c.

Shipwreck is generally a total loss. What may be saved of the ship or cargo is so uncertain, that the law cannot distinguish this from the loss of the whole. The wreck of a ship may remain, but the ship be lost. A thing is said to be destroyed, when it is so broken, disjointed, or otherwise injured, that it no longer exists in its original nature and essence. So goods may remain; but if no ship can be procured in a reasonable time, to carry them to the place of their destination, the voyage is lost. But a mere stranding of the ship is not of itself a total loss; it is only where the stranding is followed by shipwreck, or the ship is otherwise incapable of prosecuting her voyage.

Adjustment of loss. In settling the amount of the indemnity which the insured is entitled to, and fixing the proportion to be paid by each underwriter, the general rule is, that the contract of insurance

insurance should not be lucrative to the insured, nor enable him to make a profit out of the loss of another, and he is entitled only to a fair indemnity, according to the damage sustained and the sum insured.

Return of premium. The premium is to be returned in all cases where the contract is void for want of interest; which may be either total, as where the insured has nothing on board the ship; or partial where he has some interest, but to the amount in the policy; and it is a general rule, that wherever insurance is made through mistake, misinformation, or other innocent cause, without interest, or for more than the real interest, there shall be a return of premium.

If by several policies, made without fraud, the sum insured exceed the value of the effects, the several policies in effect make but one insurance, and will be good to the extent of the true interest of the insured; and in case of loss, all the underwriters on the several policies shall pay according to their respective subscriptions; and in like manner all will be entitled to a return of premium for the sum insured above the value of the effects, in proportion to their respective quotas. On a wager policy, the insured cannot recover back the premium, at least after the risk is run. This policy is void, as being without interest, but both parties being guilty of a breach of the stat. 19 G. II. c. 37, the rule, that where both parties are equally criminal the possessor has the advantage, applies, and the insured cannot recover back the premium.

Insurance upon life, is a contract, by which the underwriter for a certain sum, proportioned to the age, health, and profession of the person whose life is the object of the insurance, engages that the person shall not die within the time limited in the policy; or, if he do, that he the underwriter will pay a sum of money to the person in whose favour the policy is granted. *Parke.* c. 22.

Insurance against fire, is a contract by which the insurer undertakes, in consideration of a premium, to indemnify the insured against all losses, which he may sustain in his house or goods, by means of fire, within the time limited in the policy.

INTENDMENT OF LAW. The understanding, intention, and true meaning of law. 1 *Inst.* 78.

The

The law presumes that every one will act for his best advantage; and therefore credits the party, in whatsoever is to his own prejudice.

In every agreement the intent is the chief thing that is to be considered; and if by the act of God, or other means not arising from the party himself, the agreement be not performed according to the words, yet the party shall perform it as near the intent as he may.

INTERCOMMONING, is where the commons of two manors lie together, and the inhabitant of both have time out of mind, depastured their cattle promiscuously in each.

INTERDICTION, is an ecclesiastical censure, prohibiting the administration of divine ceremonies.

But this censure hath been long disused; and nothing of it appears in the laws of church or state since the reformation.

INTEREST, is usually taken for a term, or chattel real, and more particularly for a future term.

A mortgage is an interest in land, and on nonpayment, the estate is absolute in law, and his interest is good in equity to entitle him to receive and enjoy the profits till redemption or satisfaction, and on a foreclosure, has the absolute estate both in law and equity. 9 *Mod.* 196.

INTEREST *of money*, is the premium paid for the use of a sum, and is by law in this country, limited to *five per cent. per annum.*

The laws relative to interest are extremely strict, and many different opinions have been formed on the subject. Thus the sum of 1000l. borrowed for twelve months, on good security, may be well enough paid for with 50l. and it may be difficult in general to employ it, so as to be able to reap advantage by paying more; but the sum of 20l. borrowed for one month, can never be adequately paid for by 1s. 8d.

The law as it now stands, forbids under an heavy penalty, a greater sum to be paid; and the person who would take 3s. 4d. for the loan of 20l. for the period last mentioned, would incur that penalty as indisputably as if he had committed an extortion to a great amount.

The nature of things, however, which is paramount to the regulations of men, has so ordered it, that a loan of a small sum, for a short a short time, may be as imperiously wanted as a larger one, and it may be, proportionably considered, employed to much greater advantage: the law in this case then, prohibits a transaction which would be beneficial to both parties, and which in its nature, is just as fair as any of the large transactions which it does allow of.

Where an estate is devised for payment of debts, chancery will not allow interest for book debts. *Ch. Rep.* 94.

In case of a vested legacy, due immediately, and charged on land, or money in the funds, which yield an immediate profit, interest shall be payable thereon from the testator's death; but if charged only on the personal estate, which cannot be immediately got in, it shall carry interest only from the end of the year after the death of the testator. 2 *Perc. Wms.* 26, 27.

Where lands are charged with payment of a sum in gross, they are also chargeable in equity with payment of interest for such sum. *Fin. Rep.* 286.

INTEREST COMPOUND, or *interest upon interest*, is as the latter designation expresses, when the interest instead of being paid, is added to the capital sum, and becomes an increased capital. This is not allowed by law, though it can be practised without infringing any statute, by renewing the bond or instrument, and comprising the whole in it, or by lending the interest separately.

INTERLOCUTORY JUDGMENTS, are such as are given in the middle of a cause, upon some plea, proceeding, or default; which is only intermediate, and doth not finally determine, or complete the suit. 3 *Black.* 295.

INTELOCATORY ORDER, is that which does not decide the cause, but only settles some intervening matter relative to the cause; as where an order is made, by motion of chancery, for the plaintiff to have an injunction to quiet his possession, till the hearing of the cause.

INTERROGATORIES, are questions exhibited in writing to be asked witnesses or contemners, to be examined.

Those interrogatories are in the nature of a charge or accusation; and if any of them be improper, the defendant may refuse to answer it, and move the court to have it struck out. *Str.* 444.

INTERTIARI,

INTERTIARI, to sequester or put in a third hand, as when any thing is stolen, and sold to another, and afterwards demanded by the right owner of him in whose possession it is found; it was usual to sequester the thing to a third person, who was to keep it till the buyer produced the seller, and so on to the thief.

INTESTATES. There are two kinds of *intestates*; one that makes no will at all; and another that makes a will, and nominates executors, but they refuse; in which case he dies an *intestate*, and the ordinary commits administration. 2 *Par. Inst.* 397.

The ordinary by special acts of parliament, is required to grant administration of the effects of the deceased to the widow or next of kin, who shall first pay the debts of the deceased, and then distribute the surplus amongst the kindred, in the manner and according to the proportions directed by 22 and 23 Car. II. c. 10.

INTRUSION, is when the ancestor dies seised of any estate of inheritance, expectant upon an estate for life; and then tenant for life dies, between whose death, and the entry of the heir, a stranger intrudes.

INTRUSION DE GARD, a writ that lies where the infant within age, entered into his lands, and held his lord out.

INVENTIONES, treasure trove, money or goods found by any person, and not challenged by the owner, which therefore by the common law was due to the king, who granted the privilege to some particular subjects.

INVENTORY, a catalogue or schedule regularly made out, of persons, goods, and chattels, after death, previous to a sale or transfer of the property.

An inventory after decease ought to contain an appraisement of the value by indifferent persons. In cases such as previous to a sale, the inventory is only intended to certify the existence of the articles contained in it.

IN VENTRE SA MERE, is where a woman is with child at the time of her husband's death; which child if he had been born, would be heir to the land of the husband. And the law hath consideration of such child, on account of the apparent expectation of his birth. For a devise to an infant *in ventre sa mere*, is good, by way of future executory devise. And where a daughter comes into land by descent, the son born after, shall oust her and have the land.

INVEST, signifies to give possession; we use likewise to *invest* the tenants, by delivering them a verge or rod in their hands, and ministering them an oath which is called *investing*.

INVESTITURE, is the giving possession of lands by actual seisin. The ancient feudal investiture was, where the vassal on descent of lands, was admitted in the lord's court, and there received his seisin, in the nature of a renewal of his ancestor's grant, in the presence of the rest of the tenants: but in after times, entering on any part of the lands, or other notorious possession, was admitted to be equivalent to the formal grant of seisin and investiture. 2 *Black.* 209.

The manner of grant was by words of pure donation, *have given and granted*: which are still the operative words in our modern infeodations or deeds of feoffment. This was perfected by the ceremony of corporal investiture, or open and notorious delivery of possession in the presence of the other vassals.

But a corporal investiture being sometimes inconvenient, a symbolical delivery of possession was in many cases anciently allowed of; by transferring something near at hand, in the presence of credible witnesses, which by agreement should serve to represent the very thing designed to be conveyed; and an occupancy of this sign or symbol, was permitted as equivalent to the occupancy of the land itself. And to this day, the conveyance of many of our copyhold estates is made from the seller to the lord, or his steward, by delivering of a rod or verge, and then from the lord to the purchaser, by a re-delivery of the same, in the presence of a jury of tenants. 2 *Black.* 313.

INVOICE, an account in writing of the particulars of goods or merchandize sent by any one conveyance or at one time, and transmitted from one person in trade to another: or a particular, of the value, custom, and charges of any goods sent by a merchant in another man's ship, and consigned to a factor or correspondent in another country.

JOINDER IN ACTION, is the coupling or joining of two in a suit or action against another.

JOINDER OF ISSUE, an issue of fact, is where the fact only, and not the law, is disputed. And when he that denies or traverses the fact pleaded by his antagonist, has tendered the issue, thus, *and this he prays may be inquired of by the country*, or, *and of this he puts himself upon the country*, it may be immediately subjoined by the other party, *and the said A. B. doth the like*; which done, the issue is said to be joined; both parties having agreed to rest the fate of the cause upon the truth of the fact in question. 3 *Black.* 315.

JOINT ACTIONS, in personal actions, several wrongs may be joined in one writ; but actions founded upon a tort, and a contract cannot be joined, for they require different pleas and different process. 1 *Vent.* 336.

JOINT AND SEVERAL, an interest cannot be granted jointly and severally; as if a man grant the next advowson, or make a lease for years, to two jointly and severally; these words (*severally*, are void, and they are joint tenants. 5 *Rep.* 19.

JOINT FINES, if a whole vill is to be fined, a joint fine may be laid, and it will be good for the necessity of it; but in other cases, fines for offences are to be severally imposed on each particular offender, and not jointly upon all of them. 1 *Rol. Rep.* 33.

JOINT LIVES, lease for years to husband and wife, if they or any issue of their bodies should so long live, has been adjudged so long as either the husband, wife, or any of their issue should live; and not only so long as the husband and wife, &c. should jointly live. *Moor.* 539.

JOINT TENANTS, are those that come to, and hold lands or tenements by one title *pro indiviso*, or without partition.

These are distinguished from sole or several *tenants*, from *parceners*, and from *tenants* in common: and they must jointly implead, and jointly be impleaded by others, which properly is common between them and coparceners; but joint tenants have a sole quality of survivorship, which coparceners have not; for if there be two or three *joint tenants*, and one hath issue and dies, then he or those *joint tenants* that survive, shall have the whole by survivorship. *Cowel.*

The creation of an estate in joint tenancy depends on the wording of the deed or devise, by which the tenant claims title; for this estate can only arise by purchase or grant, that is, by the act of the parties; and never by the mere act of law. Now if

4 any

any estate be given to a plurality of persons, without adding any restrictive, exclusive, or explanatory words, as if an estate be granted to A. and B. and their heirs, this makes them immediately joint tenants in fee of the lands; for the law interprets the grant, so as to make all parts of it take effect, which can only be done by creating an equal estate in them both. As therefore the grantor has thus united their names, the law gives them a thorough union in all other respects. 2 *Black.* 180.

If there be two joint tenants, and one release the other, this passeth a fee without the word *heirs*, because it refers to the whole fee, which they jointly took, and are possessed of by force of the first conveyance; but the tenants in common cannot release to each other, for a release supposeth the party to have the thing in demand, but tenants in common have several distinct freeholds, which they cannot transfer otherwise than as persons who are sole seized. *Co. Lit.* 9.

Although joint tenants are seised *per mie et per tout,* yet to divers purposes each of them hath but a right to a moiety; as to enfeoff, give, or demise, or to forfeit or lose by default in a *præcipe*; and therefore where there are two or more joint tenants, and they all join in a feoffment, or each of them in judgment gives but his part. *Co Lit,* 186.

The right of survivorship shall take place immediately upon the death of the joint tenant, whether it be a natural or civil death; as if there be two joint tenants, and one of them enters into religion, the survivor shall have the whole. *Co. Lit.* 181.

At common law, joint tenants in common were not compellable to make partition, except by the custom of some cities and boroughs. *Co. Lit.* 187.

But now joint tenants may make partition; the one party may compel the other to make partition, which must be by deed: That is to say, all the parties must by deed actually convey and assure to each other the several estates, which they are to take and enjoy severally and separately. 2 *Black.* 324.

Joint tenants being seised *per mie et per tout,* and deriving by one and the same title, must jointly implead, and be jointly impleaded with others. *Co. Lit.* 180.

If one joint tenant refuse to join in action, he may be summoned and severed; but herein it is to be observed, that if the

 person

person severed die, the writ abates, because the survivor then goes for the whole, which he cannot do on that writ, where on the summons and severance he went only for a moiety before, for the writ cannot have a double effect, to wit, for a moiety in case of summons and severance, and for the whole in case of survivorship. *Co. Lit.* 188.

But in personal and mixed actions where there is summons and severance, and yet after such summons and severance the plaintiff goes on for the whole, there if one of them die, yet the writ shall not abate, because they go on for the whole after summons and severance; and if they were to have a new writ, it would only give the court authority to go on for the whole. *Co. Lit.* 197.

JOINTURE, a jointure strictly speaking, signifies a joint estate, limited to both husband and wife; but in common acceptation, it extends also to a sole estate, limited to the wife only, and may be thus defined, viz. a competent livelihood of freehold for the wife of lands and tenements, to take effect, in profit or possession, presently after the death of the husband; for the life of the wife at least. 2 *Black.* 137.

By the statute of the 27 H. VIII. c. 10. if a jointure be made to the wife, it is a bar of her dower, so as she shall not have both jointure and dower. And to the making of a perfect jointure within that statute six things are observed: 1. Her jointure is to take effect presently after her husband's decease. 2. It must be for the term of her own life, or greater estate. 3. It should be made to herself. 4. It must be made in satisfaction of her whole dower, and not of part of her dower. 5. It must either be expressed or averred to be in satisfaction of her dower. 6. It should be made during the coverture. 1 *Inst.* 32.

The estate must take effect presently after her husband's decease; therefore if an estate be made to the husband for life, remainder to another person for life, remainder to the wife for her jointure, this is no good jointure, for it is not within the words or intent of the statute; for the statute designed nothing as a satisfaction for dower, but that which came in the same place, and is of the same use to the wife, and though the other person die during the life of the husband, yet this is not good; for every interest not equiva-

lent

lent to dower not being within the statute, is a void limitation to deprive the wife of her dower. 4 *Co.* 3.

The estate must be for term of the wife's life, or a greater estate; therefore if an estate be made for the life or lives of many others, this is no good jointure; for if she survive such lives, as she may, then it would be no competent provision during her life, as every jointure within the statute ought to be. *Co. Lit.* 36.

The estate should be made to herself; but as the intention of the statute was to secure the wife a competent provision, and also to exclude her from claiming dower, and likewise her settlement, it seems that a provision or settlement on the wife, though by way of *trust*, if in other respects it answer the intention of the statute, will be inforced in a court of equity.

The estate must be in satisfaction of the whole dower; the reason hereof is, that if it be made in satisfaction of part only, it is uncertain for what part it is in satisfaction of her dower, and therefore void in the whole. *Co. Litt.* 36.

The estate must be expressed or averred to be in satisfaction of her dower. Lord Coke says, that it must be expressed or averred to be in satisfaction of her dower; but *quære*, for this does not seem requisite either within the words or intention of the statute. *Co. Litt.* 36.

It should be made during the coverture; this the very words of the act of parliament require, and therefore if a jointure be made to a woman during her coverture in satisfaction of dower, she may wave it after her husband's death; but if she enter and agree thereto, she is concluded; for though a woman is not bound by any act when she is not at her own disposal, yet if she agree to it when she is at liberty, it is her own act, and she cannot avoid it. *Co. Lit.* 36. 4 *Co.* 3.

JOINTRESS, a woman who hath an estate settled on her by her husband, to hold during her life, if she survive him.

A jointure hath a great advantage over dower in one respect: the *jointress* may enter without any formal process; whereas no small trouble, and a very tedious method of proceeding, is necessory to compel a legal assignment of dower. 2 *Black.* 139.

JOURNEYMAN. See *Master and Servant.*

JOURNEY'S ACCOMPTS, a term in our old law to be thus understood: if a writ abated without the default of the plaintiff or demandant, but merely by default of the clerk, or sheriff, the plaintiff might purchase a new writ, which if purchased by *journey's accompts*, that is within as little time as possible after the abatement of the first writ, (and the space of fifteen days has been held a convenient time for the purchase of it) then this second writ shall be a continuance of the first. *Co. Rep.* 6. *fol* 9.

This doctrine is now of little use, it being customary to enter a judgment that the writ be quashed, and then to sue forth another.

IPSO FACTO, a termed used to signify the instant any thing is done, as, the church is made void for not reading the articles; adjudged, that there needs no deprivation, but it becomes *ipso facto* void, presently by not reading the articles. *Cro. Eliz.* 679.

IRELAND, by statutes 39 and 40 Geo. III. c. 67. the kingdoms of Great Britain and *Ireland*, shall, upon the first day of Jan. 1801, and for ever after, be united by the name of *the united kingdom of Great Britain and Ireland*; and that the royal stile and titles appertaining to the imperial crown of the said united kingdom and its dependencies; and also the ensigns, armorial flags and banners thereof, shall be such as his majesty, by his royal proclamation under the great seal of the united kingdom, shall be pleased to appoint.

Where a debt is contracted in England, and a bond is taken for it in Ireland, it shall carry Irish interest; for it must be considered as referable to the place where it is made: but if it were a simple contract debt only, it ought to carry English interest, the variation of place in this case making no difference. 2 *Atk.* 382.

IRONY, in libels, makes them as properly libels as what is expressed in direct terms. 1 *Haw.* 193.

IRREGULARITY, in the cannon law signifies any impediment, which hinders a man from taking holy orders; as if he be base born, notoriously defamed of any crime, &c.

IRREPLEVIABLE or IRREPLEVISABLE, that neither may nor ought to be replevied or delivered upon sureties.

ISSUE, hath many significations in law; sometimes being used for the children begotten between a man and his wife; sometimes for profit growing from amercements or *fines*; and sometimes for profits of lands or tenements; sometimes for that point of matter depending

depending in a suit, when, in the course of pleading, the parties in the cause affirm a thing on one side and deny it on the other, they are then said to be at issue; all their debates being at last contracted into a single point, which must be determined either in favour of the plaintiff or defendant. 3 *Black.* 313.

ISSUE ON SHERIFFS, are for neglects and defaults, by amercement and fine to the king, levied out of the issues and profits of the lands; and double and treble issues may be laid on a sheriff for not returning writs, &c. but they may be taken off before estreated into the exchequer by rule of court, on good reason shewn. 2 *Lil. Abr.* 89.

ITINERANT, those were anciently called *justices itinerant,* who were sent with a commission into divers counties to hear such causes specially, as were termed pleas of the crown, and the journeys themselves were called *itera.*

JUDGE. The judges are the chief magistrates in the law, to try civil and criminal causes. Of these there are twelve in England, viz. the lords chief justices of the courts of king's-bench, and common-pleas; the lord chief baron of the exchequer; the three puisne or inferior judges of the two former courts, and the three *puisne* barons of the latter.

By stat. 1 Geo. III. c. 23. the judges are to continue in their offices during their good behaviour, notwithstanding any demise of the crown (which was formerly held immediately to vacate their seats) and their full salaries are absolutely secured to them during the continuance of their commissions, by which means the judges are rendered completely independent of the king, his ministers, or his successors.

A judge at his creation takes an oath, that he will serve the king, and indifferently administer justice to all men, without respect of persons, take no bribe, give no counsel where he is a party, nor deny right to any, thought he king or any other, by letters, or by expressed words, command the contrary, &c. and in default of duty, be to answerable to the king in body, land, and goods.

Where a judge has an interest, neither he nor his deputy can determine a cause, or sit in court, and if he do, a prohibition lies. *Hardw.* 503.

Judges

Judges are punishable for wilful offences, against the duty of their situations; instances of which happily live only in remembrance. There are ancient precedents of judges, who were fined when they transgressed the laws, though commanded by warrants from the king.

Judge is not answerable to the king, or the party, for mistakes or errors of his judgment, in a matter of which he has jurisdiction. 1 *Salk.* 397.

JUDGMENT. The opinion of the judges is so called, and is the very voice and final doom of the law; and therefore is always taken for unquestionable truth; or it is the sentence of the law pronounced by the court, upon the matter contained in the record.

Judgments are of four sorts, *viz.* 1. Where the facts are confessed by the parties, and the law determined by the court, which is termed judgment by demurrer.

2. Where the law is admitted by the parties, and the facts only are disputed, as in judgment upon a demurrer.

3. Where both the fact and the law arising thereon, are admitted by the defendant, as in case of judgment by confession or default.

4. Where the plaintiff is convinced that fact or law, or both, are insufficient to support his action, and therefore abandons or withdraws his prosecution, as in case of judgment upon a nonsuit or retraxit. See *Warrant of Attorney.*

Judgments are either *interlocutory* or *final.*

Interlocutory judgments are such as are given in the middle of a cause, upon some plea, proceeding, or default, which is only intermediate, and doth not finally determine or complete the suit; as upon dilatory pleas, when the judgment in many cases is, that the defendant shall answer over; that is, put in a more substantial plea.

Final judgments, are such as at once put an end to the action, by declaring that the plaintiff hath either entitled himself, or hath not, to recover the remedy he sues for. 3 *Black.* 398.

For further information respecting, signing, entering, and setting aside judgments, see *Impey's B. R. and C. B. Practice.*

JUDGMENT IN CRIMINAL CASES, are of two kinds,

1. Such

1. such as are fixed and stated, and always the same for the species of crimes. 2. Such as are discretionary and variable, according to the different circumstances of each case. 2 *Haw.* 444.

JUDICATORES TERRARUM, persons in the county palatine of *Chester,* who on a writ of error out of chancery are to consider of the judgment given there, and reform it; and if they do not, and it be found erroneous, they forfeit 100l. to the king by the custom. *Dyer.* 348.

JUDICIAL, DECISIONS, OPINIONS, or DETERMINATIONS, as far as they refer to the laws of this kingdom, are for the matter of them of three kinds.

1. They are either such as have their reasons singly in the laws and customs of this kingdom; as who shall succeed as heir to the ancestor; what is the ceremony requisite for passing a freehold; what estate, and how much the wife shall have for her dower; and many such matters, wherein the ancient and expressed laws of the kingdom give an express decision, and the judge seems only the instrument to pronounce it; and in those things the law or custom of the realm is the only rule and measure to judge by, and in reference to those matters, the decision of courts are the conservatories and evidences of those laws. Or,

2. They are such decisions, as by way of deduction and illation upon those laws, are formed or deduced; as for the purpose, whether of an estate thus or thus limited, the wife shall be endowed? whether if thus or thus limited, the heir may be barred? and many more of the like complicated questions. And herein the rule of decision is, first, the common law and custom of the realm, which is the great *substratum* to be maintained; and then authorities of decisions of former times in the same or like cases; and then the reason of the thing itself.

3. They are such as seem to have no other guide but the common reason of the thing, unless the same point has been formerly decided, as in the exposition of the intention of clauses in deeds, wills, covenants, &c. where the very sense of the words, and their positions and relations, give a rational account of the meaning of the parties, and in such cases the judge does much better herein, than what a bare grammarian or logician, or other prudent men could; for in many cases there have been former resolutions,

resolutions, either in print, or agreeing in reason or analogy with the case in question; or perhaps also the clause to be expounded, is mingled with some term or clauses that require the knowledge of the law to help out with the construction or exposition; both which often happen in the same case, and therefore it requires the knowledge of the law, to render and expound such clauses and sentences; and doubtless a good common lawyer is the best expositor of such clause, &c. *Hale's Hist. Com. Law.*

JUDICIUM DEI. See *Ordeal.*

JURATS, officers in the nature of aldermen, for the government of their several corporations, as the mayor and jurats of *Maidstone*, &c.

JURISDICTION, an authority of power given, which a man hath to do justice in causes of complaint made before him, of which there are two kinds: the one which a man hath by reason of his fee; the other is a *jurisdiction* given by the prince to a bailiff. 4 *Inst.*

JURIS UTRUM, a writ which lies for the incumbent, whose predecessor hath alienated his lands and tenements.

JURY, a certain number of persons sworn to enquire of and try some matter of fact, and to declare the truth upon such evidence as shall be laid before them.

The jury are sworn judges upon all evidence in any matter of fact.

Juries may be divided into two kinds, common and special. Resort is generally had to the latter in commercial cases, which involve some difficulties relative to mercantile regulations, and are best decided by a special jury of merchants.

A common jury is such as is returned by the sheriff, according to the directions of the stat. 3 G. II. c. 25, which appoints that the sheriff's officer shall not return a separate pannel for every separate cause, but one and the same pannel for every cause to be tried at the same assizes, containing not less than forty-eight, nor more than seventy-two jurors; and their names being written on tickets, shall be put into a box or glass, and when each clause is called, twelve of those persons, whose names shall be first drawn out of the box, shall be sworn upon a jury, unless absent, challenged, or excused.

When a sufficient number of persons are impannelled, they are then

then separately sworn well and truly to try the issue between the parties, and true verdict give according to the evidence.

Special juries: these were originally introduced in trials at bar, when the causes were of too great nicety for the discussion of ordinary freeholders. To obtain a special jury, a motion is made in court, and a rule is granted thereupon, for the sheriff to attend the master, prothonotary, or other proper officer, with his freeholders' book, and the officer is to take indifferently forty-eight of the principal freeholders, in the presence of the attornies on both sides, who are each of them to strike off twelve, and the remaining twenty-four are returned upon the pannel.

Jurors are punishable for sending for, or receiving instructions from either of the parties, concerning the matter in question.

Where more than one of the persons returned on a jury shall appear, but not a sufficient number to make an inquest, and some of the others come within view of the court, or into the town where the court is holden, but refuse to come into the court to be sworn; on proof thereof, the court may at the prayer of the party, order the jurors who appeared, to inquire into the yearly value of such defaulter's lands, and after such enquiry made, either summon them to 'appear on pain of forfeiting such sum as their lands have been found to be worth by the year, or some less sum, or impose a fine of the like sum upon them, without any farther proceeding. But it seems that such juror shall be liable to lose his issues only for such default, and not the yearly value of his lands, unless the party pray it: but a juror who has actually appeared, and afterwards makes default, is said to be subject to such forfeiture of the yearly value of his lands, whether the party pray it or not; because his contempt appears to the court by its own record; yet even in this case, the court in discretion will sometimes only impose a small fine. Also it seems, that a juror who makes default without ever coming into the town wherein the court is holden, is liable only to hold his issues, or to be amerced, but not to be fined. 2 *Haw*. 146.

And in causes of *nisi prius*, every person whose name shall be drawn, and who shall not appear after being openly called three times, shall on oath made of his having been lawfully summoned, forfeit a sum not exceeding 5l. nor less than 40s. unless some reasonable

sonable cause of absence be proved, by oath or affidavit, to the satisfaction of the judge. 3 G. III. c. 25.

If any juror shall take of either party to give his verdict, he shall, on conviction by bill or plaint, before the court where the verdict shall pass, forfeit ten times as much as he has taken; half to the king, and half to him who shall sue. 5, 34, and 38 Ed. III. c. 10, 8, and 12.

A man who shall assault or threaten a juror for giving a verdict against him, is highly punishable by fine and imprisonment; and if he strike him in the court, in the presence of the judge of assize, he shall lose his hand and his goods, and the profits of his lands during life, and suffer perpetual imprisonment. 1 *Haw.* 57.

JUS ACCRESCENDI, the right of survivorship between joint tenants.

JUS CORONÆ, the right of the crown is part of the law of England, though it differs in many things from the general law, relating to the subject.

JUS GENTIUM, the law by which society in general and nations are governed. See *Law of Nations.*

JUS HÆREDITATIS. The right of inheritance. See *Heir.*

JUS PATRONATUS, the right of presenting a clerk to a benefice.

JUSTICE and right shall not be sold, denied, or delayed. M. C.

JUSTICE, signifies him who is deputed by the king to do right by way of judgment.

JUSTICES IN EYRE in ancient times, were sent with commission into several countries to hear such causes especially, as were termed *pleas of the crown.* And this was done for the ease of the people, who must otherwise have been hurried to the king's bench, if the case were too high for the county-court: they differed from the justices of *oyer and terminer,* because they were sent upon one or for special causes and to one place; whereas the *justices in eyre* were sent through the province and counties of the land, with more indefinite and general commissions.

JUSTICES OF GOAL DELIVERY, such as one sent with

commission

commission to hear and determine all causes appertaining to such as for any offence are cast into the goal.

JUSTICES OF NISI PRIUS, are the same with *justices of assize*, for it is a common adjournment of a cause, to put it off to such a day, *nisi prius justiciarii venerint ad eas partes ad capiendas assisas*; and upon this clause of adjournment, they are called *justices of nisi prius*, as well as justices of assize, by reason of the writ or action they have to deal in.

JUSTICES OF OYER AND TERMINER, as the justices of *assize* and *nisi prius*, are appointed to try civil causes, so are the justices of *oyer and terminer*, and *goal delivery*, to try indictments for all crimes all over the kingdom; at what are generally denominated the circuits or assizes, and the towns where they come to execute their commission, are called the assize towns, and are generally the county towns. 4 *Black.* 269.

JUSTICES OF THE PAVILION, are certain judges of a *pie powder court*, of a most transcendent jurisdiction, held under the bishop of Winchester at a fair on St. Giles's Hill, near that city, by virtue of letters patent granted by Richard II. and Edward IV.

JUSTICES OF THE PEACE, are persons appointed by the king's commission, to attend to the peace of the county where they dwell. They were called *guardians of the peace*, till the thirty sixth year of Ed. III. c. 12, where they are called *justices*.

A justice of the peace must before he acts, take the oath of office, which is usually done before some persons in the country, by virtue of a *dedimus protestatem* out of chancery.

Sheriffs, coroners, attorneys, and proctors, may not act as justices of the peace.

The power, office, and duty of this magistrate, extends to an almost infinite number of instances, specified in some hundreds of acts of parliament, and every year accumulating.

The commission of the peace doth not determine by the demise of the king, nor until six months after, unless sooner determined by the successor: but before his demise, the king may determine it, or may put out any particular person; which is most commonly done by a new commission, leaving out such persons' name.

Justices of the peace can only be appointed by the king's special commission, and such commission must be in his name; but it is not requisite that there should be a special suit or application to, or warrant from the king for the granting thereof, which is only requisite for such as are of a particular nature; as constituting the mayor of such a town and his successors perpetual justices of the peace within their liberties, &c. which commissions are neither revocable by the king, nor determinable by his demise, as the common commission of the peace is, which is made of course by the lord chancellor according to his discretion. 1 *Lev.* 219.

The form of the commission of the peace, as it is at this day, was according to *Hawkins*, settled by the judges about the 23 Eliz. 4 *Inst.* 471.

Jurisdiction. It seems now to be settled, that justices of the peace have no power to hear and determine felonies, unless they are authorized so to do by the express words of their commissions; and that their jurisdictions to hear and determine murder, manslaughter, and other felonies and trespasses, is by force of the word *assignavimus* in their commission, which gives them or two of them, whereof one is of the *quorum*, power to hear and determine felonies, &c. 2 *Haw.* P. C. 38.

And hence it hath been lately adjudged, that the caption of an indictment of trespass before justices of the peace, without adding *nec non ad diversas felonias &c. assignat'*, is naught. *Trin.* 7 G. I. *in B. R.*

But though justices of the peace by force of their commission have authority to hear and determine murder and manslaughter, yet they seldom exercise a jurisdiction herein, or in any other offences in which clergy is taken away, for two reasons.

1. By reason of the monition and clause in their commission, viz. in cases of difficulty to expect the presence of the justices of assize.

2. By reason of the direction of the statute of 1 & 2 P. & M. c. 13, which directs justices of the peace in case of manslaughter and other felonies, to take the examination of the prisoner, and the information of the fact, and put the same in writing, and then to bail the prisoner if there be cause, and to certify the same with the bail, at the next general goal delivery; and therefore in cases of great moment they bind over the prosecutors, and bail the party if bailable to the next general goal delivery; but in smaller matters

matters, as petty larceny; and in some cases they bind over to the sessions, but this is only in point of discretion and convenience, not because they have not jurisdiction of the crime.

As to inferior offences, the jurisdiction herein given to justices of the peace by particular statutes, is so various, and extends to such a multiplicity of cases, that it were endless to endeavour to enumerate them; also they have as justices of the peace a very ample jurisdiction in all matters concerning the peace. *6 Mod.* 128.

And therefore it hath been held, that not only assaults and batteries, but libels, barratry, and common night-walking, and haunting bawdy-houses, and such like offences, which have a direct tendency to cause breaches of the peace, are cognizable by justices of the peace, as trespasses within the proper and natural meaning of the word. 1 *Lev.* 139.

Qualifications, on renewing the commission of the peace (which generally happens when any person is newly brought into the same) a writ of *dedimus potestatem* is issued out of chancery to take the oath of him who is newly inserted, which is usually in a schedule annexed; and to certify the same into that court at such a day as the writ commands. Unto which oath are usually annexed the oaths of allegiance and supremacy. *Lamb.* 53.

Duty. Justices of the peace are to hold their sessions four times in the year, viz. the first week after *Michaelmas*, the *Epiphany*, *Easter*, and *St. Thomas*. They are justices of record, for none but justices of record can take a recognizance of the peace. Every justice of the peace hath a separate power, and may do all acts concerning his office apart and by himself; and even may commit a fellow justice upon treason, felony, or breach of the peace: and this is the ancient power which conservators of the peace had at common law. By several statutes, justices may act in many cases where their commission does not reach; the statutes themselves being a sufficient commission. *Wood. Inst.* 79, 80.

Justices of the peace are authorized to do all things appertaining to their office, so far as they relate to the laws for the relief, maintenance, and settlement of the poor; for passing and punishing vagrants; for repair of the highways; or to any other laws concerning parochial taxes, levies, or rates; notwithstanding they are rated or chargeable with the rates, within any place affected

 by

by such their acts. Provided that this shall not empower any justice for any county at large, to act in the determination of any appeal to the quarter sessions of such county, from any order, matter, or thing, relating to any such parish, township, or place, where such justice is so charged or chargeable. 16 G. II. c. 18.

The power of justices is ministerial, when they are commanded to do any thing by a superior authority, as the court of B. R. &c. In all other cases they act as judges; but they must proceed according to their commission, &c. Where a statute requires an act to be done by two justices, it is an established rule, that if the act be of a judicial nature, or the result of discretion, the two justices must be present to concern and join in it, otherwise it will be void; as in the orders of removal and filiation, the appointment of overseers, and the allowance of the indenture of a parish apprentice; but where the act is merely ministerial, they may act separately, as in the allowance of a poor-rate. This is the only act of two justices which has been construed to be ministerial; and the propriety of this construction has been justly questioned. 4 *Durnf. & East.* 386.

If a justice of peace do not observe the form of proceeding directed by a statute, it is *coram non judice,* and void; but if he act according to the direction of the statutes, neither the justices in sessions, nor B. R. can reverse what he has done. *Jones* 170.

Where a justice shall exceed his authority in granting a warrant, the officer must execute it, and he is indemnified for so doing; but if it be in a case wherein he has no jurisdiction, or in a matter whereof he has no cognizance, the officer ought not to execute such warrant; for the officer is bound to take notice of the authority and jurisdiction of the justice. 10 *Co.* 76.

Justices acting improperly. If a justice of the peace will not, on complaint to him made, execute his office, or if he shall misbehave in his office, the party grieved may move the court of king's bench for an information, and afterwards may apply to the court of chancery to put him out of the commission.

But the most usual way of compelling justices to execute their office, in any case, is by writ of *mandamus* out of the court of king's bench.

Where the plaintiff in an action against a justice, shall obtain a verdict,

verdict, and the judge shall in open court certify on the back of the record, that the injury for which such action was brought, was wilfully and maliciously committed, the plaintiff shall have double costs. 24 G. II. c 44.

And if a justice of peace act improperly, knowingly, information shall be granted. 27 G. III.

No justice shall be liable to be punished both ways, that is, criminally, and civilly; but before the court will grant an information, they will require the party to relinquish his civil action, if any such be commenced. And even in the case of an indictment, and though the indictment be actually found, the attorney general on application made to him, will grant a *noli prosequi* upon such indictment, if it appear to him that the prosecutor is determined to carry on a civil action at the same time. *Bur.* 719.

If any action shall be brought against a justice for any thing done by virtue of his office, he may plead the general issue, and give the special matter in evidence; and if he recover, he shall have double costs. 7 *Jac.* c. 5.

Such action shall not be laid but in the county where the fact was committed. 21 *Jac.* c. 12.

And no suit shall be commenced against a justice of the peace till after one month's notice.

And unless it is proved upon the trial, that such notice was given, the justice shall have a verdict and costs.

And no action shall be brought against any constable or other officer, or any person acting by his order and in his aid, for any thing done in obedience to the warrant of a justice, till demand hath been made, or left at the usual place of his abode, by the party or by his attorney, in writing, signed by the party demanding the same, of the perusal and copy of such warrant, and the same has been refused or neglected for six days after such demand.

And no action shall be brought against any justice for any thing done in the execution of his office, unless commenced within six months after the act committed. 24 G. II. c. 44.

JUSTICES OF PEACE WITHIN LIBERTIES, are such in cities and other corporate towns, as those others of the counties, and their authority or power is the same within their several precincts.

JUSTICES OF TRAILE-BASTON, were a kind of justices

appointed by king Edward the First, on account of the great disorders grown in the realm, during his absence in the Scotch and French wars. Their office was to make inquisition through the realm, by the verdict of substantial juries, upon all officers, as mayors, sheriffs, bailiffs, escheators, and others, touching extortion, bribery, and other such grievances; as intrusions into other men's lands, barretors, and breakers of the peace, with divers other offenders; by means of which inquisitions, many were punished by death, many by ransom, and the rest flying the realm, the land was quieted, and the king gained great riches towards the support of his wars.

JUSTICIAR or JUSTICIER, a judge, justice, or justicier. The whole jurisdiction which is now distributed among the several courts of Westminster-hall, seems in the first reigns after the conquest, to have been lodged in one court, commonly called the king's court, where justice is said to have been administered sometimes by the king himself in person, and sometimes by the high *justicier*, who was an officer of very great authority, and in the king's absence beyond sea, governed the realm as viceroy. 2*Haw.* 6.

JUSTICE SEAT, is the highest court of the forest, being always holden before the chief *justice in eyre*, or chief itinerant judge, or his deputy, to hear and determine all trespasses within the forest, and all claims of franchises, liberties, and privileges, and all pleas and causes whatsoever, therein arising. It may also proceed to try presentments made in the inferior courts of the forest, and give judgment upon the convictions that have been made in the swainemote courts. It may be held every third year. This court may fine and imprison, being a court of record: and a writ of error lies to the court of king's bench. 2 *Black.* 72.

JUSTICIES is a writ directed to the sheriff to do justice in a plea of trespass *vi et armis*, or of any sum above 40s. in the county court; of which he hath no cognizance by ordinary power. It is in the nature of a commission to the sheriff; and is not returnable. 4 *Inst.* 266.

JUSTIFIABLE HOMICIDE. See *Homicide*.

JUSTIFICATION, is an affirming or shewing good reason in court, why one does such a thing as he is called to answer; as to justify in a cause of a replevin.

K.

KEELAGE, a privilege to demand money for the bottom of ships resting in a port or harbour.

KEEPER OF THE FOREST, also called chief warden of the forest, who hath the principal government of all things therein, and the check of all officers belonging to the same.

KEEPER OF THE GREAT SEAL, is a lord by virtue of his exalted office, and stiled the lord keeper of the great seal of England; he is one of the king's privy council; through whose hands pass all charters, commissions, and grants of the king under the great seal; without which seal, all such instruments by law are of no force. For the king is in the interpretation of law a corporation, and passeth nothing firmly but under the said seal, which is as the public faith of the kingdom, in the high esteem and reputation justly attributed thereto. This lord keeper, by the statute 5 Eliz. c. 18, hath the same place, authority, pre-eminence, jurisdiction, execution of laws, and all other customs, commodities, and advantages, as hath the lord chancellor of England for the time being. He is constituted by the delivery of the *great seal* to him, taking his oath. *Co.* 4. See *Chancery*.

KEEPER OF THE PRIVY SEAL, is a lord by virtue of his office, through whose hands pass all charters signed by the king before they come to the great seal. He is of the king's privy council, and was anciently called *clerk of the privy seal*.

KEY or QUAY, a wharf to land or ship goods or wares at.

KEYUS, KEYS, a guardian, warden, or keeper. In the Isle of Man, the twenty-four chief commoners, who are considered as conservators of the liberties of the people, are called *keys* of the island.

KIDNAPPING, is the forcible taking and carrying away a man, woman, or child, from their own country, and sending them to another. This is an offence at common law, and punishable by fine, imprisonment, and pillory.

By stat. 11 and 12 W. III. c. 7, if any captain of a merchant vessel shall during his being abroad force any person on shore, and wilfully

wilfully leave him behind, or refuse to bring home all such men as he carried out, if able and desirous to return, he shall suffer three months imprisonment.

Exclusive of the above punishment for this as a criminal offence, the party may recover upon an action for compensation in damages for the civil injury.

KILLING a man at *sea*, by a shot fired from a gun on *land* is properly triable at the admiralty session. See *Homicide*.

KINDRED. See *Descent*.

KING, signifies him who hath the highest power, and absolute rule over the whole land; and therefore the king is in intendment of law, cleared of those defects which common persons are subject to; for he is always supposed to be of full age, though never so young. He is taken as not subject to death, but is a corporation in himself. He is *supra legem* by his absolute power. And though for the better and more equal course in making laws, he admits the three estates, that is lords spiritual, lords temporal, and the commons, into council; yet this derogates not from his power; for whatever they act, he by his negative voice may quash. He pardoneth life and limb to offenders against the crown and dignity, except such as he bindeth himself by oath not to forgive. He may alter or suspend any particular law that seems hurtful to the public.

The law ascribes to his majesty, in his political capacity, an absolute immortality. The king never dies. For immediately on the decease of the reigning prince in his natural capacity, his imperial dignity, by act of law, without any *interregnum* or interval, is vested at once in his heir, who is *eo instanti* king to all intents and purposes. And so tender is the law of supposing even a possibility of his death, that his natural dissolution is generally called his *demise*; an expression signifying merely a transfer of property. *Plowd.* 177.

By the articles of the union of the two kingdoms of England and Scotland, all papists, and persons marrying papists, are for ever excluded from the imperial crown of Great-Britain; and in such case, the crown shall descend to such person being a protestant, as should have inherited the same, in case such papist, or person marrying a papist, were naturally dead. 5 Anne. c. 8.

KING'S BENCH. The king's bench is the supreme court of common

common law in the kingdom; and is so called, because the king used to sit there in person: it consists of a chief justice, and three puisne justices, who are by their office, the sovereign conservators of the peace, and supreme coroners of the land.

This court has a peculiar jurisdiction, not only over all capital offences, but also over all other misdemeanours of a public nature, tending either to a breach of the peace, or to oppression, or faction, or any manner of misgovernment. It has a discretionary power of inflicting exemplary punishment on offenders, either by fine, imprisonment, or other infamous punishment, as the nature of the crime, considered in all its circumstances, shall require.

The jurisdiction of this court is so transcendant, that it keeps all inferior jurisdictions within the bounds of their authority; and it may either remove their proceedings to be determined here, or prohibit their progress below: it superintends all civil corporations in the kingdom; commands magistrates and others, to do what their duty requires, in every case where there is no specific remedy; protects the liberty of the subject, by speedy and summary interposition; takes cognizance both of criminal and civil causes; the former in what is called the crown side, or crown office; the latter in the plea side of the court.

This court has cognizance on the plea side, of all actions of trespass, or other injury alledged to be committed *vi et armis*; of actions for forgery of deeds, maintenance, conspiracy, deceit; and actions on the case which alledge any falsity or fraud.

In proceedings in this court, the defendant is arrested for a supposed trespass, which, in reality he has never committed; and being thus in the custody of the marshal of this court, the plaintiff is at liberty to proceed against him for any other personal injury, which surmise of being in the custody of the marshal, the defendant is not at liberty to dispute.

This court is likewise a court of appeal, into which may be removed, by writ of error, all determinations of the court of common pleas, and of all inferior courts of record in England.

KING'S BENCH PRISON. *King's Bench new rules. East.* 30 G. III. it is ordered by the court, that from and after the first day of trinity term next, the rule made in the sixth year of the reign of king George the first, and all other rules for establishing the

the rules of the king's bench prison, shall be and the same are hereby repealed. And it is further ordered, that from and after the said first day of trinity term next, the rules of the king's bench prison, shall be comprized within the bounds following, exclusive of the public houses hereinafter mentioned : that is to say, from *Great Cumber Court* in the parish of *St. George the Martyr*, in the county of *Surry*, along the north side of *Dirty-lane*, and *Melancholy-walk*, to *Blackfriar's-road*, along the western side of the said road to the *obelisk*, and from thence along the south-west side of the *London-road*, round the *direction-post* in the center of the roads, near the public house known by the sign of the *Elephant and Castle*, and from thence along the eastern side of *Newington causeway*, to *Great Cumber-court* aforesaid : and it is also ordered, that the new goal *Southwark*, and the highway, exclusive of the houses on each side of it, leading from the king's bench prison, to the said new goal, ſhall be within and part of the said rules. And it is lastly ordered, that all taverns, victualling-houses, ale-houses, and wine-vaults, and houses or places licenced to sell gin or other spirituous liquors shall be excluded out of and deemed no part of the said rules.

It is ordered, that from and after the first day of trinity term next, no prisoner in the king's bench prison, or within the rules thereof, shall have, or be entitled to have, day rules above three days in each term. And it is further ordered, that every such prisoner having a day rule, shall return within the walls or rules of the said prison, at or before nine o'clock in the evening of the day on which such rule shall be granted.

KING'S PALACE. The limits of the king's palace at Westminster, extend from Charing-cross, to Westminster-hall, and shall have such privileges as the ancient palaces. 28 H. VIII. c. 12.

KING'S SILVER, otherwise called a *post fine*, is a sum of money paid to the king, in the court of common pleas, for a licence granted to levy a fine of lands, tenements, or hereditaments; and this must be compounded for, at the rate of ten shillings for every five marks of lands; that is, three twentieth parts of the supposed annual value.

KNIGHT, originally signified a servant; but there is now but one instance where it is taken in that sense, and that is *knight of a shire*, *a shire*, who properly serves in parliament for such a county; but in all other instances, it signifies one who bears arms; who for his virtue and martial prowess, is by the king, or one having his authority, exalted above the rank of gentleman, to an higher step of dignity.

They were called *milites*, because they formed a part of the royal army, by virtue of their feudal tenures; one condition of which was, that every one who held a knight's fee, immediately under the crown (which in *Edward the Second's* time amounted to 20l. *per annum*) was obliged to be knighted. He was also to attend the king in his wars, or fine for his non-compliance. The execution of this prerogative, as an expedient to raise money in the reign of *Charles the First* gave great offence; though then warranted by law, and the recent example of queen *Elizabeth*: it was therefore abolished by 16 C. I. c. 20. Considerable fees accrued to the king on the performance of the ceremony. *Edward the Sixth*, and queen *Elizabeth*, had appointed commissioners to compound with the persons who had lands to the amount of 40l. a year, and who declined the honour and expence of knighthood. 1 *Black*. 404.

KNIGHTS BACHELORS, the most ancient, though the lowest order of knighthood. King *Alfred*, conferred this order on his son *Athelstan*. 1 *Black*. 404.

KNIGHTS BANERET. These knights are only made in the time of war; they are ranked next after the barons; and their precedence before the younger sons of viscounts, was confirmed by Jac. I in the tenth year of his reign. But to entitle them to this rank, they must be created by the king in person in the field, under the royal banners in time of open war; otherwise they rank after baronets. 1 *Black*. 403.

KNIGHTS OF THE BATH, they are so called from their bathing the night before their creation; this order was re-established by king *George* the First, in 1725; who erected the same into a regular military order for ever, by the name and title of *the Order of the Bath*, to consist of thirty-seven *knights* besides the sovereign.

They have each three honorary esquires, and now wear a red ribbon across their shoulders, have a prelate of the order (the bishop

shop of Rochester) several heralds and other officers. 1 *Black.* 404.

KNIGHTS OF THE CHAMBER, seem to be such knights bachelors as are made in time of peace, because usually *knighted* in the king's *chamber*, not in the field, as in time of war.

KNIGHT's COURT, a court baron, or honour court, held twice a year under the bishop of *Hereford*, at his palace; wherein those who are lords of manors, and their tenants, holding by knight's service of the honour of that bishopric, are suitors. If the suitor appear not at it, he pays 2s. *suit silver* for respite of homage.

KNIGHT'S FEE, is so much inheritance yearly, as is sufficient to maintain a *knight* with convenient revenue; which in Henry the Third's days was 15l. and in the time of *Edward the Second*, 20l.

KNIGHTS OF THE GARTER, an order of *knights* first created by king *Edward the Third*, after having obtained some signal victories, who, for furnishing of this honourable order, made choice out of his realm, and all christendom, of the best and most excellently renowned *knights* in virtue and honour, bestowing this dignity on them, and giving them a blue *garter*, decked with gold, pearl, and precious stones, and a buckle of gold to wear daily on the left leg only, a kirtle, crown, cloak, chaperon, a collar, and other stately and magnificent apparel, both of stuff and fashion. Of which he and his successors, kings of England, were ordained sovereigns, and the rest fellows and brethren to the number of twenty-six. This honourable society is a college or corporation having a common seal belonging to it, and consisting of a sovereign guardian, who is the king of England, who always governs this order by himself or his deputy; of twenty-five champions called *knights of the garter*, and fourteen secular canons who are priests, or must be within one year after their admission; thirteen vicars also priests; and twenty-six poor knights, that have no other sustenance, or means of living, but the allowance of this house, which is given them in respect to their daily prayer to the honour of God and St. George. There are also certain officers belonging to this order, viz. the prelate of the *garter*, which office is inherent to the bishop of *Winchester* for the time being; the chancellor of the *garter*; the register, who is always the dean of

Windsor; the principal king of arms, called *garter*, whose chief business is to manage and marshal their solemnities at their yearly feasts and installations, lastly the usher of the *garter*, who is also the usher of the *black rod*.

KNIGHTS' HOSPITALLERS, were an order of knights that had their names from an hospital erected at Jerusalem, for the use of the pilgrims coming to the holy land, and dedicated to *St. John* baptist. Being driven out of the holy land they retired to Rhodes, from whence also they were compelled to fly, and take up their abode at Malta, where they lately resided, (prior to the capture of that island by the French) and are therefore called *knights of Malta*.

KNIGHT MARSHAL, an officer of the king's house, having jurisdiction and cognizance of transgressions within the king's house, and verge of it; as also of contracts made within the same house, whereto one of the house is a party.

KNIGHT SERVICE, a tenure, where several lands were held of the king, which draw after it homage and service in war, escuage, ward, marriage, &c. but is taken away by stat. 12 Car. II. c. 24.

KNIGHTS OF THE SHIRE, were so called, because anciently they were to be real knights; and still the form of the writ runs, that they be knights girt with the sword. But now by several statutes, notable esquires may be chosen; and their qualification is to be determined according to the value of the estate, which is not to be less than 600l. a year. See *Election*.

KNIGHTS TEMPLARS, an order of knighthood instituted by pope *Gelasius*, in 1118, and so called, because they dwelt in a part of the building belonging to the temple at Jerusalem, not far from the sepulchre of our Lord. But this order is long since abolished.

KNIGHTS OF THE THISTLE and ST. PATRICK. See *Precedency*.

L.

LABEL, is a narrow strip of paper or parchment, affixed to a deed or writing to hold the seal belonging to it. Any paper annexed by way of addition or explication to any will or testament, is also called a *label* or codicil.

LABOURERS. See *Master and Servant.*

LACHES, signifies slackness or negligence; as when we say, there is a *laches* of entry, it means the same as to say, there is *lack* of entry.

LAGAN, at first was that right which the chief lord of the fee had to take goods, which were cast on shore by the violence of the sea; but afterwards it signified a right, which any one had to goods which were shipwrecked and floating in the sea. See *Flotsam.*

LAMPS. None but *British* oil shall be used for lamps in private houses, under the penalty of 40s. 8 Anne, c. 9.

The wilfully breaking or extinguishing any lamp, incurs the penalty of 20s. for each lamp or light destroyed or extinguished. 11 G. III. c. 49.

LAND, in a general and legal signification, comprehends any ground, soil, or earth; as meadows, pastures, woods, moors, waters, marsh, furze and heath: it includes also messuages, (that is houses), tofts, (that is, places were houses once stood), mills, castles, and other buildings; for in conveying the land, the buildings pass with it. 1 *Inst.* 4.

LAND-BOC, a charter or deed whereby lands or tenements were held.

LAND CARRIAGE, *outward,* all foreign goods sent by land carriage from one part of this kingdom to another, must be accompanied with certificates under the hand of the collector, customer, and comptroller of the port from whence they are sent, otherwise any officer of the customs may stop them till due proof be made that the duties have been paid. 6 G. I. c. 31.

LAND-CHEAP, an ancient customary fine, paid either in cattle or money at every alienation of *land* lying in some particular manor, or the liberty of some borough.

LANDLORD. See *Distress, Ejectment, Lease, Rent, Tenant.*

LAND-TAX, a tax imposed on land and personal property, by statutes annually passed for that purpose. This and the malt-tax are considered as annual taxes imposed on the subject.

The assessment or valuation of estates, made in 1692, though far from a perfect one, had this effect, that a supply of half a million sterling was equal to 1s. in the pound, of the value of the estates given in. And according to this valuation, from the year 1693 to the present time, the tand-tax has continued an annual charge upon the subject, above half the time at 4s. in the pound; sometimes at 3s. sometimes at 2s. twice at 1s. but without any total intermission. The method of raising it, is by charging a particular sum on each county, according to the valuation in 1692: and this sum is assessed upon individuals by commissioners appointed in the act.

LAND TENANT, he who actually possesses the *land*, or hath it in manual occupation.

LAPSE, the omission of a patron to present to a church, within six months after voidable; by which neglect, title is given to the ordinary to collate to such church. And, in such case, the patronage devolves from the patron to the bishop, from the bishop to the archbishop, and from the archbishop to the king.

A donative doth not go in lapse; but the ordinary may compel the patron by ecclesiastical censures to fill up the vacancy. But if the donative have been augmented by the governors of queen Anne's bounty, it will lapse in like manner as presentative livings.

LAPSED LEGACY, is where the legatee dies before the testator; or where a legacy is given upon a future contingency, and the legatee dies before the contingency happens. As if a legacy be given to a person when he attains the age of twenty-one years, and the legatee dies before that age; in this case, the legacy is a lost or lapsed legacy, and shall sink into the residuum of the personal estate. 2 *Black.* 613.

LARCENY, is the felonious and fraudulent taking away of the personal goods of another; which goods, if they are above the value of 12d. it is called *grand* larceny; if of that value or under, it is *petit* larceny: which two species are distinguished in their punishment, but not otherwise. 4 *Black.* 229.

The mind only makes the taking of another's goods to be felony, or a bare trespass only; but as the variety of circumstances is so great, and the complications thereof so mingled, it is impossible to prescribe all the circumstances evidencing a felonious intent, or the contrary: it must therefore be left to the due and attentive consideration of the judge and jury, wherein the best rule is, in doubtful matters, rather to incline to acquittal, than conviction. But in general it may be observed, that the ordinary discovery of a felonious intent, is, if the party do it secretly, or, being charged with the goods, deny it. 1 H. H. 509.

As all felony includes trespass, every indictment must have the words *feloniously took,* as well as *carried away*; whence it follows, that if the party be guilty of no trespass in taking the goods, he cannot be guilty of felony in carrying them away. 1 *Haw.* 89.

With respect to what shall be considered a sufficient carrying *away,* to constitute the offence of larceny; it seems that any the least removing of the thing taken, from the place where it was before, is sufficient for this purpose, though it be not quite carried off. 1 *Haw.* 93.

As grand larceny is a felonious and fraudulent taking of the mere personal goods of another above the value of 12d. so it is *petit larceny,* where the thing stolen is but of the value of 12d. or under. In the several other particulars abovementioned, petit larceny agrees with grand larceny. 1 *Haw.* 95.

In petit larceny there can be no accessaries either before or after. 1 H. H. 530.

Larceny from the person. If larceny from the person be done privily without his knowledge, by picking of pockets or otherwise, it is excluded from the benefit of clergy by 8 Eliz. c. 4 provided the thing stolen be above the value of 12d. 2 H. H. 336.

But if done openly and avowedly before his face, it is within the benefit of clergy. 1 *Haw.* 97.

Larceny from the house. Every person who shall be convicted of the feloniously taking away in the day-time, any money or goods of the value of 5s. in any dwelling-house, or out-house thereunto

thereunto belonging, and used to and with the same, though no person be therein, shall be guilty of felony without benefit of clergy. 39 Eliz. c. 15.

Receiving stolen goods. Any person who shall buy or receive any stolen goods, knowing them to be stolen; or shall receive, harbour, or conceal any felons or thieves, knowing them to be so, shall be deemed accessary to the felony; and being convicted on the testimony of one witness, shall suffer death as a felon convict. But he shall be entitled to his clergy. 5 Anne, c. 31.

Any person convicted of receiving or buying stolen goods, knowing them to be stolen, may be transported for fourteen years. 4 G. I. c. 11.

Where the principal felon is found guilty to the value of 10d. that is, of petit larceny only, the receiver, knowing the goods to have been stolen, cannot be transported for fourteen years, and ought not to be put upon his trial. For the acts which make receivers of stolen goods knowingly, accessaries to the felony, must be understood to make them accessaries in such cases only, where, by law an accessary may be; and there can be no accessary to petit larceny. *Fost.* 74.

Every person who shall apprehend any one guilty of breaking open houses in a felonious manner; or of privately and feloniously stealing, *goods, wares,* or *merchandizes,* of the value of 5s. in any *shop, warehouse, coach-house,* or *stable,* though it be not broken open, and though no person be therein to be put in fear, and shall prosecute him to conviction, shall have a certificate without fee, under the hand of the judge, certifying such conviction, and within what parish or place the felony was committed, and also that such felon was discovered and taken, or discovered or taken, by the person so discovering or apprehending; and if any dispute arise between several persons so discovering or apprehending, the judge shall appoint the certificate into so many shares, to be divided among the persons concerned, as to him shall seem just and reasonable. *Leache's Cro. Law.* 307. See *Burglary.*

LAST, in the marshes of East Kent, signifies a court held by twenty-four jurats, and summoned by the two bailiffs thereof, wherein they make orders, impose, and levy taxes, penalties, &c. for the preservation of the said marshes.

LAST HEIR, he to whom lands come by escheat for want of

 lawful

lawful heirs, that is, the lord of whom they held, in some cases, but in others, the king.

LATH, LATHE, or LETH, a large division of a county, sometimes containing three or more hundreds or wapentakes.

LATHREVE, an officer who formerly had authority over the *lath*, or *lathe*.

LATIN, formerly all law proceedings were in Latin, but by stat. 4 & 6 G. II. c. 26, and 14, all records and proceedings shall be in English.

LATITAT, a writ, whereby all men in personal actions are called originally to the king's bench. F. N. B. 78.

A latitat may be considered either as the commencement of the action, or only as a process to bring the defendant into court, at the election of the plaintiff. *Bul.* N. P. 151.

If it be stated as the commencement of the action to avoid a *tender*, the defendant may deny that the plaintiff had any cause of action at the time of suing it out. 1 *Wils.* 141.

Or if it be replied to a plea of the statute of limitations, the defendant, in order to maintain his plea, may aver the real time of suing it out, in opposition to the test. 2 *Burr.* 950. See *Impey's B. R.* and *C. B. Practice.*

LAW, in its most comprehensive sense, signifies a rule of action, whether animate or inanimate, rational or irrational. And it is a rule of action, which is prescribed by some superior, and which the inferior is bound to obey. 1 *Black.* 38.

LAW OF ENGLAND. The law of England consists of three parts, viz. 1. the common law. 2. Statutes or acts of parliament. 3. Particular customs.

The common law is derived from the English, Saxons, and Danes; and it is so called, from comprising general customs well known and observed throughout the nation; and is distinguished from written or statute law, as being of that antiquity that its origin cannot be easily traced. Customs being only matter of fact, and existing only in the memory of the people, and is neither made by charter or parliament: whose origin is therefore known, these being matters of record.

The statutes or acts of parliament. These are laws adapted by the legislature to particular exigencies, and prescribing regulations, for all the different varieties of civil intercourse. These statutes

statutes are in force as soon as enacted; and to these the people at large by their representatives are parties, and are bound to yield obedience to them.

Particular customs, which are peculiar to certain places, and which are observed as part of the common law, which is composed of these general and local customs, of principles and maxims, and certain particular laws; and the whole are collectively founded upon the laws of nature, of nations, and of religion.

These laws extend, more or less particularly, to all parts of the British empire; their objects are the safety and preservation of the *persons* and *properties* of individuals, from *civil injuries* and *criminal violence,* and promoting that general peace and harmony, upon which depend all the comforts and advantages of society.

LAW OF ARMS. See *Court of Chivalry.*

LAW-DAY, was properly any day in open court, and commonly used for the more solemn courts of a county or hundred.

LAW OF MARQUE, is where those are driven to make use of this law, and take the shipping or goods of that people of whom they have received wrong, and cannot get ordinary justice, when they can find them within their own bounds or precincts. See *Letters of Marque.*

LAW OF NATIONS, is a system of rules deducible by natural reason from the immutable principles of natural justice, and established by universal consent amongst the civilized inhabitants of the world, in order to decide all disputes, and to insure the observance of justice and good faith, in that intercourse which must frequently occur between them, and the individuals belonging to each; or they may depend upon mutual compacts, treaties, leagues, and agreements between the separate, free, and independant communities.

In the construction of these principles, there is no judge to resort to but the general law of nature and of reason, being the only law with which the contracting parties are all equally conversant, and to which they are all equally amenable.

Laws have properly their effect only in the country where and for which they have been enacted. However, 1. Those which relate to the state, and to the personal condition of the subjects, are acknowledged in foreign countries. 2. A foreigner, who is

plaintiff

plaintiff against a subject, must abide by the decisions of the law of the country in which he pleads. 3. When the validity of an act done in a foreign country is in question, it ought to be decided by the laws of that foreign country. 4. Sometimes the parties agree to the question being determined by particular laws of a foreign country. 5. A foreign law may have been received as a subsidiary law. 6. Foreigners, sometimes obtain the privilege of having their disputes with each other settled by the laws of their own country.

LAW PROCEEDINGS, of all kinds, are to be in the English language, except known abbreviations, and technical terms. 6 G. II. c. 14.

LAW SPIRITUAL, is the *ecclesiastical law,* allowed by our law, where it is not against the common law, nor against the statutes and customs of the realm. And regularly, according to such *ecclesiastical laws,* the ordinary and other ecclesiastical judges proceed in causes within their cognizance. *Co. Lit.* 344.

LEASE, is a conveyance of lands or tenements, in consideration of rent or other annual recompence made for life, for years, or at will, but always for a less time than the interest of the lessor in the premises; for if it were of the whole interest, it would be more properly an assignment.

In all leases there must be a lessor and lessee. He that demises or lets to farm, is the lessor; and he unto whom it is demised or let, is the lessee. *Wood.* b. 2. c. 3.

A lease may either be made in writing or by word of mouth, the former of which is the most usual; but by the statute of frauds, 29 Car. II. c. 3, all leases of lands, except leases not exceeding three years, must be made in writing, and signed by the parties themselves, or their agents duly authorized, otherwise they will operate only as leases at will.

If a lease be but for half a year, or a quarter, or less time, the lessee is respected as a tenant for years; a year being the shortest term of which the law in this case takes notice. *Lit. s.* 58.

To constitute a good lease, there must be a lessor not restrained from making such lease, a lessee capable of receiving it, and the interest demised, must be a demisable interest, and be sufficiently and properly described. If it be for years, it must have a certain commencement and determination, it is to have all the usual ceremonies,

ceremonies, as sealing, delivery, &c. and there must be an acceptance of the thing demised. 1 *Inst.* 46. See *Deed.*

LEASE AND RELEASE, a conveyance of the fee simple, right or interest, in lands, or tenements, which in law amounts to a feoffment. 1 *Inst.* 207.

It was invented to supply the place of livery of seisin, and is thus contrived; a lease, or rather bargain and sale, upon some pecuniary consideration, for one year, is made by the tenant of the freehold to the lessee or purchaser, which vests in the said purchaser the use of the term for a year; and then the statute of uses 27 H. VIII. c. 10. immediately transfers the uses into possession. He therefore being thus in possession, is capable of receiving a *release* of the freehold and reversion; and accordingly, the next day, a release is granted to him. 2 *Black.* 339.

LEATHER, by several statutes, regulations are made for the tanning and manufacturing of leather, *to which on account of their length we refer the reader,* viz. 27 H. VIII. c. 14. 18 Eliz. c. 9. 20 Car. II. c. 5. 1 Jac. I. c. 22. 27 Geo. III. c. 13. and 28 Geo. III. c. 37.

LECTURERS, in many churches in London and other places, are appointed as assistants to the rectors or vicars. They are usually chosen by the vestry, or principal inhabitants, and are generally the afternoon preachers.

LEET. See *Court Leet.*

LEGACY, is bequest of a sum of money, or any personal effects of a testator, and these are to be paid by his representative, after all the debts of the deceased are discharged as far as the assets will extend.

All the goods and chattels of the deceased, are by law vested in the representative, who is bound to see whether there be left a sufficient fund to pay the debts of the testator, which if it should prove inadequate, the pecuniary legacies must proportionately abate; a specific legacy however, is not to abate unless there be insufficient without it.

If the legatee die before the testator, such will in general be termed a lapsed legacy, and fall into the general fund; where however from the general import of the will, it can be collected that the testator intended such a vested legacy, it will in such case, go to the representative of the deceased legatee.

If

If a bequest be made to a person, *if* or *when*, he attains a certain age, the legacy will be lapsed, if he die before he attain that age; but if such legacy may be made payable at that age, and the legatee die before that age, such legacy will be vested in his representative.

If in the latter case, the testator devise interest to be paid in the mean time, it will nevertheless be a vested legacy.

Where a legacy is bequeathed over to another, in case the first legatee die under a certain age, or the like, the legacy will be payable, immediately on the death of the first legatee; and though such legacy be not bequeathed over, yet if it carry interest, the representative will become immediately entitled to it.

In case of a vested legacy due immediately, and charged on land, or money in the funds which yields an immediate profit, interest shall be payable from the death of the testator; but if it be charged on the personal estate only of the testator, which cannot be collected in, it will carry interest only from the end of the year, after the death of the testator.

If a bequest be for necessaries, and of small amount, the executor will be justified in advancing a part of the principal; but this should be done under very particular circumspection, as the executor may be compelled to pay the full legacy on the infant's attaining his majority, without deducting the sum previously advanced.

When all the debts and particular legacies are discharged, the residue or surplus must be paid to the residuary legatee, if any be so appointed in the will; but if there be none appointed or intended, it will go to the executor or next of kin.

When this residue does not go to the executor, it is to be distributed among the intestates next of kin, according to the statute of distributions, except the same is otherwise disposeable by particular customs, as those of London, York, &c. See *Executor*.

LEGEM FACERE, to make oath. *Legem haberc*, to be capable of giving evidence upon oath.

LE ROY LE VEUT, by these words the royal assent is signified by the clerk of the parliament to public bills; and to a private bill his answer is *soit fait comme il est desiré.*

LE ROY S'AVISERA, by these words to a bill presented to the

the king by his parliament, are understood his absolute, but civil denial of that *bill*: and the bill thereby becomes wholly nulled.

LESSOR AND LESSEE. See *Lease*.

LETTER, a servant of the post-office is within the penalty of 5 Geo. III. c. 25. which makes it a capital felony to secrete a letter containing any bank-note, though he have not taken the oath required by 9 Anne. c. 10.

But to secrete a letter containing *money*, is not an offence within the statutes concerning the servants of the post-office.

LETTER, *threatening*, all persons who shall *knowingly send or deliver* any letter or writing, with or without a name or names, threatening to accuse any person of any crime punishable by law, with death, transportation, pillory, or other *infamous* punishment, with a view or intent to extort or gain money, goods, wares, or merchandizes, from the person or persons so threatened to be accused, shall be deemed offenders against the law and the public peace; and the court before whom they shall be convicted, may order such offenders to be fined and imprisoned, or put in the pillory, or publicly whipped, or to be transported according to the laws made for the transportation of felons.

LETTER OF ATTORNEY, an instrument or deed whereby a person is authorized to act for another, either generally or in any specific transaction. A letter of attorney is, in its nature revocable, and its revocation, may also be either general, or special.

LETTERS CLOSE, are grants of the king, specially distinguished from *letters patent*, in that the letters close, being not of public concern, but directed to particular persons, are closed up and sealed.

LETTER OF CREDIT, is where a merchant or correspondent writes a letter to another, requesting him to credit the bearer with a certain sum of money.

LETTER OF LICENCE, is a written permission granted to a person under embarrassment, allowing him to conduct his affairs for a certain time without being molested. Such instrument will bind all the creditors by whom it is executed, and it generally contains certain stipulations to be observed by all parties.

LETTERS OF MARQUE, are extraordinary commissions, granted

granted to captains or merchants for reprisals, in order to make a reparation for those damages they have sustained, or the goods they have been deprived of by strangers at sea.

These appear to be always joined to those of reprize for the reparation of a private injury; but under a declared war, the former only are granted.

LETTERS PATENT, writings sealed with the great seal of *England*, whereby a man is authorized to do or enjoy any thing, which otherwise of himself he could not do.

LEVANT AND COUCHANT, cattle that have been so long in another man's ground, that they have lain down, and are arisen again to feed.

LEVARI FACIAS, a writ directed to the sheriff, for the levying a sum of money upon the lands and tenements of him that hath forfeited a recognizance.

LEVARI FACIAS DAMNA DE DISSEISITORIBUS, a writ directed to the sheriff, for the levying of damages wherein the *disseisor*, hath formerly been condemned to the disseisee.

LEVARI FACIAS RESIDUUM DEBITI, a writ directed to the sheriff, for levying the remnant of a debt upon lands and tenements, or chattels of the debtor, that hath in part satisfied before.

LEVARI FACIAS, QUANDO VICE COMITES RETURNAVIT QUOD NON HABUIT EMPTORES, a writ commanding the sheriff to sell the goods of the debtor, which he hath already taken, (and returned that he could not sell them) and as much more of the debtor's goods as will satisfy the whole debt.

LEVY, signifies to gather or collect.

LEWDNESS, is punishable not only with fine and imprisonment, but with all such infamous punishment as to the court in discretion shall seem proper, 1 *Haw.* 196.

LEX AMISSA, one who is infamous, perjured, or outlawed.

LEX APOSTATA, to do a thing contrary to law.

LEX TERRÆ, the law and custom of the land, distinguished by this name from *lex civilis*.

LIBEL, *a libel* is defined a malicious defamation of any person, especially a magistrate, expressed either in printing or writing, or by signs, pictures, &c. tending either to blacken the memory

mory of one who is dead, or the reputation of one who is alive, and thereby exposing him to public hatred, contempt, and ridicule. 2 *Haw*. 192.

With regard to libels in general, there are, as in many other cases, two remedies; one by indictment, or information; and the other by action. The former for a public offence; for as has been repeatedly remarked, every libel has a tendency to the breach of the peace, by provoking the person libelled to break it; which offence, we have seen, is the same in point of law, whether the matter contained be true or false; and therefore it is, that the defendant on an indictment for publishing a libel, is not allowed to alledge the truth of it by way of justification. But in the remedy by *action on the case*, which is to repair the party in damages for the injury done him, the defendant may, as for words spoken, justify the truth of the facts, and shew that the plaintiff has received no injury at all. The chief excellence therefore of a civil action for a libel, consists in this, that it not only affords a reparation for the injury sustained, but it is a full vindication of the innocence of the person traduced. 3 *Black*. 125.

LIBEL, in the ecclesiastical court, is the declaration or charge drawn up in writing, on the part of the plaintiff; to which the defendant is obliged to answer.

LIBERATE, a writ issuing out of chancery, to the treasurer, chamberlain, or barons of the exchequer, or clerk of the *hanaper*, &c. for the payment of any annual pension or other sums granted under the great seal.

Or sometimes to the sheriff for the delivery of any lands or goods taken upon forfeits of recognizance: it also lies to a goaler, for the delivery of a prisoner, that hath put in bail for his appearance.

LIBERAM LEGEM, in the ancient trial by *battel*, if either party became recreant, or yielded and submitted, he was condemned to lose his *liberam legem*, that is, to become infamous, and not to be accounted *liber et legalis homo*, and never after to be put upon a jury, or admitted as a witness in any cause. 3 *Black* 340.

LIBERTATIBUS ALLOCANDIS, a writ lying for a citizen, or burgess of any city or borough, who contrary to the liberties of the city or town whereof he is, is impleaded before the king's justices, or justices errant, or justices of the forest, &c. to have his privilege allowed. F. N. B. 229.

LIBERTATIBUS ERIGENDIS IN ITINERE, a writ whereby the king commands the justice in *eyre*, to admit of an attorney, for the defence of another man's liberty before them.

LIBERTIES AND FRANCHISES, are synonimous terms, and are defined a royal privilege, or branch of the king's prerogative, subsisting in the hands of a subject. 2 *Black.* 37.

LIBERTY, is a privilege held by grant or prescription, by which men enjoy some benefit beyond the ordinary subject; but in a more general signification, it is said to be, a power of doing whatever the law permits.

The absolute rights of every *Englishman* (which taken in a political and extensive sense, are usually called their liberties) as they are founded on nature and reason, so they are coeval with our form of government, though subject at times to fluctuate and change, their establishment, excellent as it is, being still human. At some times we have seen them depressed by overbearing and tyrannical princes; at others, so luxuriant as to bend even to anarchy, which is a worse state than tyranny itself. But the vigour of our free constitution, hath always delivered the nation from these embarrassments: and their fundamental articles have been from time to time asserted in parliament, as often as they were thought in danger. See *Magna Charta, Bill of Rights, and Act of Settlement.*

LIBRATA TERRÆ, contains four oxgangs of land, and every oxgang, 13 acres.

LICENTIA SURGENDI, the writ whereby the tenant essoined *de malo lecti,* obtains liberty to rise.

LIEN, a law term having two significations; viz. *personal lien,* such as bond, covenant, or contract; and *real lien,* a judgment or statute, recognizance, which oblige and effect the land.

LIEU, instead or in place of another thing.

LIEUTENANT, he who occupies the king's or any other person's place, or represents his person, as the lieutenant of Ireland.

LIFE, the life of every man is under the protection of the law. *Wood's Just.* 11.

LIFE ESTATES, or estates for life, are of two kinds; either such

such as are created by the act of the parties; or such as are created by the operation of law, as estates by curtesy or dower. 2 *Black.* 120.

Estates for life, created by deed or grant, are, where a lease is made of lands or tenements to a man, to hold for the term of his own life, or for that of another person, or for more lives than one; in any of which cases, he is called tenant for life: only when he holds the estate by the life of another, he is usually termed tenant *pur auter vie*, for another's life.

Estates for life, may be created not only by the express terms before mentioned, but also by a general grant, without defining or limiting any specific estate. 2 *Black.* 121.

If such persons, for whose life any estate shall be granted, shall absent themselves seven years, and no proof made of the lives of such persons; in any action commenced for the recovery of such tenements by the lessors or reversioners, the persons, upon whose lives such estate depended, shall be accounted as dead; and the judges shall direct the jury to give their verdict, as if the person absenting himself were dead. 19 Car. II. c. 6.

LIFE RENT, is a rent which a man receives either for term of life, or for sustentation of life.

LIGEANCE, is such a duty or fealty, as no man may owe or bear to more than one lord: and therefore it is chiefly used for that duty and allegiance, which every good subject owes to his *liege lord* the king.

LIGHTS, stopping lights of any house is a nuisance, for which an action will lie, if the house be an ancient house, and the lights ancient lights: but stopping a prospect is not, being only matter of delight, not of necessity; and a person may have either an assize of nuisance against the persons erecting any such nuisance, or he may stand on his own ground and abate it. 2 *Salk.* 247.

LIMITATION, a certain time prescribed by statute, within which an action must be brought. The time of limitation is two fold; first in writs, by divers acts of parliament; secondly to make a title to any inheritance, and that is by the common law.

Limitation on penal statutes. All actions, suits, bills, indictments,

ments, or informations, which shall be brought for any forfeiture upon any statute penal, made or to be made, whereby the forfeiture is or shall be limited to the *queen*, her heirs or successors only, shall be brought within *two years* after the offence committed, and not *after* two years; and that all actions, suits, bills, or informations, which shall be brought for any forfeiture upon any penal statute, made or to be made, except the statutes of tillage, the benefit and suit whereof is or shall be by the said statute limited to the *queen*, her heirs or successors, and to any other that shall prosecute in that behalf, shall be brought by any person that may lawfully sue for the same, within *one year* next after the offence committed; and in default of such pursuit, that then the same shall be brought for the *queen's* majesty, her heirs or successors, any time within the two years, after that year is ended: and it is provided, that where a shorter time is limited by any penal statute, the prosecution must be within that time. 31 Eliz. c. 5.

Limitation in regard to personal actions of assault and battery, and actions arising upon contract and trespass.

All actions of trespass, of assault, battery, wounding, imprisonment, or any of them, shall be commenced and sued *within four years* next after the cause of such actions or suits, and not after. 21 *Jac.* I. c. 16.

Actions of account, &c. All actions of trespass *quare clausum fregit*, all actions of trespass, detinue, trover, and replevin, all actions of account, and upon the case, (other than such accounts as concern the trade of merchandize, between merchant and merchant) all actions of debt grounded upon any lending, or contract without specialty, (that is not being by deed or under seal) all actions of debt for arrearages of rent, and all actions of assault, menace, battery, wounding, and imprisonment, shall be commenced within the time and limitation as followeth, and not after; that is to say, the said actions upon the case, (other than for slander) and the said actions for account, and the said actions for trespass, debt, detinue, and replevin, and the said action for trespass *quare clausum fregit, within six years*, after the cause of such action. 21 *Jac.* c. 16.

Exception in relation to infants. It hath been holden, that if an infant during his infancy, by his guardian bring an action, the defendant

defendant cannot plead the statute of limitation; although the cause of action accrued six years before, and the words of the statute are, that after his coming of age, &c.

Exception in relation to merchants accounts. As to this exception, it hath been matter of much controversy, whether it extends to all actions and accounts relating to merchants and merchandize, or to actions of account open and current only. But it is now settled, that accounts open and current only are within the statute; and that therefore, if an account be stated and settled between merchant and merchant, and a sum certain agreed to be due to one of them, if in such case, he to whom the money is due, do not bring his action within the limited time he is barred by the statute. *2 Mod.* 312.

Exception in relation to persons beyond sea; it seems to have been agreed, that the exception as to persons being beyond sea, extends only where the creditors or plaintiffs are so absent, and not to debtors or defendants, because the first only are mentioned in the statute; and this construction has the rather prevailed, because it was reputed the creditor's folly, that he did not file an original, and outlaw the debtor, which would have prevented the bar of the statutes.

Executor or administrator. If A receive money belonging to a person who afterwards died intestate, and to whom B takes out administration, and brings an action against A, to which he pleads the statute of limitations, and the plaintiff replies, and shews that administration was committed to him such a year, which was within six years, though six years are expired since the receipt of the money, yet not being so since the administration committed, the action is not barred by the statute. 1 *Salk.* 421.

Where a debt barred by the statute shall be revived. Any acknowledgment of the existence of the debt, however slight, will take it out of the statute, and the limitation will then run from that time: and where an expression is ambiguous, it shall be left to the consideration of the jury, whether it amounts or not, to such acknowledgment. 2 *Durnf. & East.* 760.

It is clearly agreed, that if after the *six years*, the debtor acknowledge the debt, and promise payment thereof, that this revives it, and brings it out of the statute: as if a debtor by promissory note, or simple contract, promise within six years of the action

tion brought, that he will pay the debt; though this was barred by the statute, yet it is revived by the promise; for as the note itself was at first but an evidence of the debt so that being barred the acknowledgment and promise is a new evidence of the debt, and being proved, will maintain an *assumpsit* for recovery of it. 1 *Salk.* 28.

LINSEED, may be imported duty free. 3 Geo. I. s. 38.

LITERARY PROPERTY. Authors have not by the common law, the sole and exclusive copy-right remaining in themselves or their assigns in perpetuity, after having printed and published their compositions. But by stat. 8 Anne. c. 19. it is secured to them for 14 years from the day of publishing; and after the end of 14 years, the sole right of printing or disposing of copies shall return to the authors, if then living for other 14 years. *Bur.* 2409. See *Books*.

When an author transfers all his right or interest in a publication to another, and happens to survive the first 14 years, the second term will result to his assignee, and not to himself.

LITIGIOUS, in a legal sense, is where a church is void, and two presentations are offered to the bishop upon the same avoidance; in which case the church is said to become litigious; and if nothing further is done by either party, the bishop may suspend the admission of either of the clerks, and suffer a lapse to incur 3 *Black.* 246.

LIVERY OF SEISIN, a delivery of possession of lands, tenements, or other corporeal thing (for of things incorporeal no livery of seisin may be) to one that has right, or a probability of right thereunto. See *Estate and Fee Simple*.

LIVERY AND OUSTER LE MAINE, is where by inquest before the escheator, it was found that nothing was held of the king: then he was immediately commanded by writ, to put from his hands, the lands taken into the king's hands.

LIVERY MEN OF LONDON, are chosen out of the freemen as assistants to the masters and wardens of the several companies in matters of council, and for their better internal regulations. If any liveryman refuse to take upon him the office, the lord mayor and aldermen may fine him in a certain sum, and bring an action of debt for the same. 1 *Mod. Rep.* 10.

LOCAL ACTION, is an action restrained to the proper county,

ty, in opposition to a *transitory* action, which may be laid in any county at the plaintiff's discretion. In local actions, where possession of land is to be recovered, or damages for an actual trespass, or for waste, or the like, affecting land, the plaintiff must lay his declaration, or declare his injury to have happened in the very county and place that it really did happen: but in transitory actions, for injuries that may happen any where, as debt, detinue, slander, and the like, the plaintiff may declare in what county he pleases, and then the trial must be in that county in which the declaration is laid; though if the defendant will make affidavit that the cause of action, if any, arose not in that, but in another county, the court will oblige the plaintiff to declare in the proper county. 3 *Black.* 294.

LOCKMAN, in the *Isle of Man*, the *lockman* is an officer to execute the orders of the governor or deemsters, much like our under-sheriff.

LONDON. See *Custom of London.*

LORD'S DAY, all persons not having a reasonable excuse, shall resort to their parish-church or chapel (or some congregation of religious worship allowed by the toleration act) on every Sunday, on pain of punishment by the censures of the church, and of forfeiting *one shilling* to the poor for every offence. To be levied by the churchwardens by distress, by warrant of one justice.

The hundred shall not be answerable for any robbery committed on the lord's day.

No person upon the lord's day, shall serve or execute any writ, process, warrant, order, judgment, or decree (except in cases of treason, felony, or breach of the peace), but the service thereof shall be void.

LORD HIGH ADMIRAL. See *Admiral.*

LORD OF A MANOR. See *Copyhold.*

LORD IN GROSS, he who is lord having no manor, as the king in respect of his crown.

LOTTERIES, are declared to be public nuisances; 5 Geo. I. c. 9. but for the public service of the government, *lotteries* are frequently established by particular statutes, and managed by special officers and persons appointed.

By stat. 42 Geo. III. c. 54. lottery-office keepers, are to pay

50l.

50l. for every licence in London, Edinburgh, and Dublin, or within 20 miles of either, and 10l. for every licence for every other office; and licensed persons shall deposit 30 tickets with the receiver-general of the stamp-duties, or licence to be void.

By stat. 22 Geo. III. c. 47. lottery-office keepers must take out a licence; and offices are to be open only from eight in the morning to eight in the evening, except the Saturday evening preceding the drawing. The sale of chances and shares of tickets, by persons not being proprietors thereof, are prohibited under penalty of 50l. and by 42 Geo. III. c. 119. all games or lotteries called *little goes*, are declared public nuisances, and all persons keeping any office or place for any game or lottery, not authorized by law, shall forfeit 500l. and be deemed rogues and vagabonds. The proprietor of a whole ticket may nevertheless insure it for its value only, with any licensed office for the whole time of drawing, from the time of insurance, under a *bona fide* agreement without a stamp.

LUNATIC. See *Ideot*.

M.

MAGISTRATE, a contemptuous carriage and behaviour to a magistrate is a breach of the *good behaviour*, and he to whom such affront is offered may bind him to the good behaviour, or if he have no sureties, commit him till he find some.

MAGNA ASSISA ELIGENDA, a writ directed to the sheriff, to summon four lawful knights before the justices of *assize*, there upon their oaths to choose twelve knights of the vicinage, &c. to pass upon the great assize, between a certain plaintiff and defendant.

MAGNA CHARTA. See *Charta Magna*.

MAIHEM or MAIM, signifies a corporal wound or hurt, by which a man loseth the use of any member.

By the old common law, castration was punished with death, and other members with the loss of member for member; but of latter days, maihem was punishable only by fine and imprisonment. 3 *Inst.* 62.

If

If a man attack another with an intent to murder him, and he does not murder the man, but only maim him, the offence is nevertheless within the statute 22 & 23 Car. II. c. 1 usually called the *Coventry Act*. 1 *Haw*. 112.

MAINOUR, denotes the thing which the thief takes away or steals: as to be taken with the *mainour*, is to be taken with the thing stolen about him.

MAINPERNABLE, bailable.

MAINPERNORS, those persons to whom a man is delivered out of custody or prison, and they become surety for him, either for appearance or satisfaction.

MAINPRISE, the taking or receiving a man into friendly custody, that otherwise is or might be committed to prison, upon security given for his forth coming at a day assigned. See *Bail Bond*.

MAINTENANCE, is the unlawful taking in hand, or upholding of a cause or person: this offence bears a nearer resemblance to barratry, being a person's intermeddling in the suit of another, by maintaining or assisting him with money, or otherwise, to prosecute or defend it.

A man may maintain the suit of his near kinsman, servant, or poor neighbour, out of charity or compassion, without being guilty of maintenance.

By the common law, persons guilty of maintenance, may be prosecuted by indictment, and be fined and imprisoned, or be compelled to make satisfaction by action, &c. and a court of record may commit a man for an act of *maintenance* done in the face of the court. 1 *Inst*. 368.

MAJORITY. The only method of determining the acts of many is by a majority; the major part of members of parliament enact laws, and the majority of electors choose members of parliament.

MALEFEASANCE, an evil act or transgression.

MALICE, a formed design of doing mischief to another. Malice is of two kinds; express or implied. Malice *express* is, where one with a sedate deliberate mind, doth kill another; which formed design is evidenced by external circumstances, discovering that inward intention; as lying in wait, antecedent menaces, for-

mer

mer grudges, and concerted schemes to do him some bodily harm. Malice *implied* is various; as where one voluntarily kills another without any provocation, or where one wilfully poisons another; in such like cases, the law implies malice, though no particular enmity can be proved. 4 *Black.* 198. See *Homicide.*

MALT. See *Excise.*

MALUM IN SE, an offence is said to be *malum in se*, or unlawful in itself, when it is either against the law of nature, or so far against the public good, as to be indictable at common law. 2 *Haw.* 389.

MAN *Isle of*, an island off the coast of *Cumberland*, *Westmoreland*, and *Lancashire*, in the channel which parts Ireland from England. This island was purchased of the last proprietor the Duke of Athol, under authority of stat. 5 Geo. III. c. 26. whereby the whole island, and all its dependencies (except the landed property of the Athol family, their manorial rights and emoluments, and the patronage of the bishopric and other ecclesiastical benefices) are unalienably vested in the crown, and subjected to the regulations of the British excise and customs. 1 *Black.* 105.

MANDAMUS, is a writ issuing in the king's name out of the court of king's-bench, and directed to any person, corporation, or inferior court of judicature, *commanding* to some particular thing therein specified, as appertaining to their office and duty.

A writ of *mandamus* is an high prerogative writ, of a most extensive remedial nature, and may be issued *in some cases*, where the injured party has also *another more tedious* method of redress, as in the case of admission or restitution to an office; but it issues *in all cases*, where the party hath a right to have any thing done, and hath no other specific means of compelling its performance. 3 *Black.* 100.

And this general jurisdiction and superintendancy of the king's-bench over all inferior courts to restrain them within their bounds, and to compel them to execute their jurisdiction, whether such jurisdiction arises from a modern charter, subsists by custom, or is created by act of parliament, yet being *in subsidium justiciæ*, has of late been exercised in a variety of instances.

Mandamus was also a writ that lay after the year and a day, (where in the mean time the writ called *diem clausit extremum* had not

not been sent out) to the escheator, commanding him to inquire of what lands holden by knight service the tenant died seised, &c. F. N. B. 561.

Mandamus, was also a writ to charge the sheriff, to take into the king's hands all the lands and tenements of the king's widow, who, against her oath formerly given, marries without the king's consent. *Reg.* 295.

MANDATE, a commandment judicial of the king, or his justices, to have any thing done for dispatch of justice.

MANOR, was a district of ground, held by lords or great personages, who kept in their own hands, so much land as was necessary for the use of their families, which were called *terræ dominicales*, or demesne lands, being occupied by the lord, or *dominus manerii*, and his servants. The other lands they distributed among their tenants, which the tenants held under divers service. The residue of the manor being uncultivated, was termed the lord's waste, and served for common of pasture to the lord and his tenants. All manors existing at this day must have existed as early as king Edward the First. 2 *Black.* 90. See *Court Baron*.

MANSLAUGHTER. See *Homicide*.

MANSTEALING. See *Kidnapping*.

MANUCAPTIO, a writ that lies for a man who being taken upon suspicion of felony, and offering sufficient bail for his appearence, cannot be admitted thereto by the sheriff, or other having power to let to mainprize. F. N. B. 149.

MANUMISSION, was the freeing a villain or slave from bondage: there were two kinds of *manumission*, one expressed, the other implied.

Manumission expressed, is when the lord makes a deed to his villain, to infranchise him by this *manumittere*.

Manumission implied, is when the lord makes an obligation for the payment of money to the bondman at a certain day, or sues him, when he might enter without suit; or grants him an annuity; or leases lands to him by deed, for years, or for life, and such like. *Cowel*.

MARCHERS, or LORDS MARCHERS, those noblemen who lived on the marches of Wales or Scotland, who anciently had their private laws like petty kings, but which were all abolished, by statute 27 H. VIII. c. 26.

MARCHES

MARCHES, the bounds and limits, between England and Wales, or England and Scotland.

MARITAGIO AMISSO PER DEFALTAM, a writ for the tenant in *frank marriage*, to recover lands, &c. whereof he is deforced by another.

MARITAGIUM, is the right which the lord of the fee, had to dispose of the daughters of his vassals in marriage after their decease: Others say, it was that profit which might accrue to the lord by the marriage of one under age, who held his lands of him by knight's service.

MARITAGIUM HABERE, to have the free disposal of an heiress in marriage, a favour granted by the kings of England, while they had the custody of all wards or heirs in minority.

MARKET, the establishment of public marts or places of buying and selling, with the tolls thereunto belonging, is enumerated as one of the king's prerogatives, and can only be set up by virtue of the king's grant, or by long and immemorial usage.

All sales and contracts, of any thing saleable in markets overt, shall not only be good as between the parties, but binding also upon all persons, having any property therein.

In London, every shop in which goods are exposed publicly to sale, is market overt for such things only, as the owner professes to trade in: Though if the sale be in a warehouse, and not publicly in the shop, the property is not altered. But if goods are stolen from one, and sold out of the market overt, the property is not altered, and the owner may take them wherever he finds them. 5 *Rep*. 83.

If a man buy his own goods in a market, the contract shall not bind him, unless the property had been previously altered by a former sale.

MARK OF GOODS, is used to ascertan their property or quality, &c. and if one man shall use the mark of another, with intent to do him damage, upon injury proved, an action on the case will lie. 2 *Cro*. 471.

MARQUE. See *Letters of Marque*.

MARQUIS, or MORQUESS, a title of honour next above an earl, and next under a duke.

MARRIAGE, is not only the lawful conjunction of man and wife,

wife, but also the interest of bestowing a ward or a widow in *marriage*.

Taking marriage in the light of a civil contract, the law treats it as it does all other contracts: allowing it to be good and valid in all cases where the parties, at the time of making it, were in the first place *willing* to contract; secondly, *able* to contract; and lastly, actually, *did* contract, in the proper forms and solemnities required by law. 1 *Black.* 433.

By several statutes, a penalty of 100l. is inflicted for marrying any persons without banns or licence. But by 26 G. II. c. 33, if any person shall solemnize matrimony without banns or licence, obtained from some persons having authority to grant the same, or in any other place than a church or chapel where banns hav been usually published, unless by special licence from the archbishop of Canterbury, he shall be guilty of felony, and transported for fourteen years, and the marriage shall be void.

MARSHAL OF ENGLAND. See *Court of Chivalry*.

MARSHAL OF THE KING'S BENCH, power of appointing the marshal of the king's bench, revested in the crown. 27 G. II. c. 2.

MARSHALSEA, *court*, is a court of record originally instituted to hear and determine causes between the servants of the king's household, and others within the verge; and hath jurisdiction of things within the verge of the court, and of pleas of trespass, where either party is of the king's family, and of all other actions personal, wherein both parties are the king's servants; but the court hath also power to try all personal actions, as debt, trespass, slander, trover, action on the case, &c. between party and party, the liberty whereof extends 12 miles about Whitehall.

The judges of this court are the steward of the king's household, and high marshal for the time being; the steward of the court or his deputy, is generally an eminent counsel.

If a cause of importance is brought in this court, it is generally removed into the court of king's bench, or common pleas, by an *habeas corpus cum causa*.

MASTERS AND SERVANTS. In London and other places, the mode of hiring is by what is commonly called a month's warning, or a month's wages; that is the parties agree to separate, on either of them giving to the other a month's notice for that purpose, or in lieu thereof, the party requiring the separation, to pay, or give up a month's wages.

But if the hiring of a servant be general, without any particular time specified, it will be construed to be an hiring for a year certain, and in this case, if the servant depart before the year, he forfeits all his wages. *Noy. Max.* 107.

And where a servant is hired for one year certain, and so from year to year, as long as both parties shall agree, and the servant enter upon a second year, he must serve out that year, and is not merely a servant at will after the first year.

If a woman servant marry, she must nevertheless serve out her term, and her husband cannot take her out of her master's service.

If a servant be disabled in his master's service by an injury received through another's default, the master may recover damages for loss of his service.

And also a master may not only maintain an action against any one who entices away his servant, but also against the servant; and if without any inticement, a servant leaves his master without just cause, an action will lie against another who retains him with a knowledge of such departure.

A master has a just right to expect and exact fidelity and obedience in all his lawful commands; and to enforce this, he may correct his servant in a reasonable manner, but this correction must be to enforce the just and lawful commands of the master. *Bul.* N. P. 18.

In defence of his master, a servant may justify assaulting another, and though death should ensue, it is not murder, in case of any unlawful attack upon his master's person or property.

Acts of the servant, are in many instances deemed acts of the master; for as it is by indulgence of law, that he can delegate the power of acting for him to another, it is just he should answer for such substitute, and that his acts being pursuant to the authority given him, should be deemed the acts of his master. 4 *Bac. Abr.* 583.

If a servant commit an act of trespass by command or encouragement of his master, the master will be answerable. But in so doing, his servant is not excused, as he is bound to obey the master in such things only as are honest and lawful.

If a servant of an innkeeper, rob his master's guest, the master is bound to make good the loss.

Also, if a waiter at an inn sell a man bad wine, by which his health is impaired, an action will go against the master; for his permitting him to sell it to any person, is deemed an implied general command. 1 *Black.* 430.

In like manner if a servant be frequently permitted to do a thing by the tacit consent of his master, the master will be liable, as such permission is equivalent to a general command.

If a servant be usually sent upon trust with any tradesman, and he takes goods in the name of his master upon his own account, the master must pay for them: and so likewise if he be sent sometimes on trust, and other times with money; for it is not possible for the tradesman to know when he comes by the order of his master, and when by his own authority, or when with and without money. 1 *Str.* 506.

But if a man usually deal with his tradesmen himself, or constantly pay them ready money, he is not answerable with what his servant may take up in his name, for in this case there is not as in the other, any implied order to trust him.

Or if the master never had any personal dealings with the tradesman, but the contracts have always been between the servant and the tradesman, and the master has regularly given his servant money for payment of every thing had on his account, the master shall not be charged. *Esp.* N. P. 115.

Or if a person forbid his tradesman to trust his servant on his account, and he continue to purchase upon credit, he is not liable.

The act of a servant, though he has quitted his master's service, has been held to be binding upon the master, by reason of the former credit given him on his master's account, and it not being known to the party trusting, that he was discharged. 4 *Bac. Abr.* 586.

The master is also answerable for any injury arising by the fault or neglect of his servant when executing his master's business. 6 T. R. 659, but if there be no neglect or default in the servant, the master is not liable. *Esp. Rep.* 533.

If a smith's servant lame a horse whilst shoeing him, or the servant of a surgeon make a wound worse, in both these cases an action for damages will lie against the master, and not against the servant. But the damage must be done whilst the servant is actually employed in his master's service, otherwise he is liable to answer for his own misbehaviour or neglect.

A master is likewise chargeable, if his servant cast any dirt, &c. out of the house into the common street, and so for any other nuisance occasioned by his servants, to the damage or annoyance of any individual, or the common nuisance of his majesty's people. *Lord Raym.* 264.

A servant is not answerable to his master for any loss which may happen without his wilful neglect, but if he be guilty of fraud or gross negligence, an action will lie against him by his master.

A master is not liable in trespass for the wilful act of his servant, as by driving his master's carriage against another, done without the direction or assent of his master, no person being in the carriage when the act was done. But he is liable to answer for any damage arising to another from the negligence or unskilfulness of his servant acting in his employ. *Mc'Manus,* v. *Crickitt. Mich.* 41 G. III.

MASTER OF CHANCERY. The masters in chancery are assistants to the lord chancellor and master of the rolls; of these there are some *ordinary*, and others *extraordinary*; the masters in *ordinary* are twelve in number; some of whom sit in court every day, during the term, and have refered to them interlocutory orders for stating accounts, and computing damages and the like; and they also administer oaths, take affidavits, and acknowledgments of deeds and recognizances: the masters-extraordinary, are appointed to act in the country, in the several counties of England, beyond ten miles distant from London; by taking affidavits, recognizances, acknowledgments of deeds, &c. for the ease of the suitors of the court.

MASTER OF THE COURT OF WARDS AND LIVERIES. This court was abolished by 12 Car. II. c. 24.

MASTER OF THE FACULTIES, an officer under the archbishop of Canterbury, who grants licences and dispensations.

MASTER OF THE ROLLS, is an assistant to the lord chancellor of England in the high court of chancery, and in his absence heareth causes there, and gives orders.

By stat. 23 G. II. c. 25. 1200l. *per annum*, is directed to be paid to the master of the rolls.

MASTER OF THE TEMPLE, notwithstanding the abolition of the order of the *templars*, the chief minister of the temple church, is still called master of the temple.

MAXIMS IN LAW. Maxims are the foundations of the law, and conclusions of reason; and therefore ought not to be impugned, but always to be admitted; but they may by reason be conferred and compared the one with the other, though they do not vary, or it may be discussed by reason, which thing is nearest the maxim, and the mean between the maxims, and which is not; but the maxims can never be impeached or impugned, but ought always to be observed, and held as firm principles and authorities of themselves. Pl. C. 27. b.

MAYOR, is the chief magistrate in a city or town corporate, who hath under him aldermen, common council, and officers of different kinds.

MEASURE, there shall be one measure through the realm. 9 H. VIII. c. 25. Bushels, gallons, and ells, shall be according to the standard and sealed. 25 Ed. III. c. 10.

MEDIETAS LINGUÆ, a jury or inquest impanelled, whereof the one half consists of natives or denizens, the other strangers; and is used in pleas, wherein the one party is a stranger, the other a denizen.

MEDIA ACQUIETANDO, a writ judicial, to distrain a lord for acquiring a mean lord for a rent which he formerly acknowledged in court not to belong to him.

MELIUS INQUIRENDO, a writ that lies for a second inquiry of what lands and tenements a man dieth seized, where partial dealing was suspected upon the writ *diem clausit extremum*.

MEMBERS OF PARLIAMENT. See *Election* and *Parliament*.

MEMORY, time of, is ascertained by our law, from the time of the transfretation of king Richard the First to the holy land; and any custom may be destroyed by evidence of its *non-existence* in any part of that long period to the present time. 2 *Black*. 31.

MERCHANT, every one who buys and sells, is not to be denominated a merchant, but only he who traffics in the way of commerce by importation or exportation, or otherwise in the way

 of

of emption, vendition, barter, permutation, or exchange, and who makes it his living to buy and sell.

MERCHENLAGE, is one of the three laws, out of which the conqueror framed our common laws with a mixture of those of Normandy, and was the law of the *Mersians*, when they governed the third part of this realm.

MERGER, is where a less estate in lands, &c. is drowned in the greater; as if the fee come to the tenant for years or life, the particular estates are merged in the fee; but an estate tail cannot be *merged* in an estate in fee; for no estate in tail can be extinct, by the accession of a greater estate to it. 2 *Co. Rep.* 60.

MESNE, he who is lord of a manor, and so hath tenants holding of him; yet himself holds of a superior lord. 15 *Vin Abr.*

MESNES PROCESS, is an intermediate process, which issues pending the suit, upon some collateral interlocutory matter, as to summon juries, witnesses, and the like; sometimes it is put in contradistinction to final process, or process of execution; and then it signifies all such process as intervenes between the beginning and end of a suit. 3 *Black.* 279.

MESSENGER OF THE EXCHEQUER, an officer in that court, of which there are four, who as pursuivants attend the lord treasurer, to carry his letters and precepts.

MESSUAGE, a dwelling house, with some adjacent land assigned to the use thereof.

MILES. See *Knight.*

MILITIA, the national soldiery, the standing army of the nation.

MILL. From and after July 1, 1796, every miller shall have in his mill, a true balance with proper weights; and every miller, in whose mill shall be found no balance or weights, shall forfeit not exceeding 20s.

Every person may require the miller to weigh, in his presence, the corn before it shall be ground, also after it shall be ground, and if he refuse, he shall forfeit not exceeding 40s.

Every miller, shall if required, deliver the whole produce of the corn, allowing for the waste in grinding, and toll, when toll is herein-after allowed to be taken, on pain to forfeit not exceeding 1s. per bushel and treble the value of the deficiency. Where toll is is allowed to be taken, it shall be deducted before the corn is put into the mill.

From and after June 1, 1796, no miller shall, under the penalty of 5l. take any part of the corn, or of the produce for toll, but in lieu thereof he shall be entitled to demand payment in money.

But where the party shall not have money to pay for grinding, the miller with his consent, may take such part of the corn, as will be equal to the money price, expressed in their table of prices for grinding. Also nothing in this clause shall extend to the ancient mills, called *soke mills*, or such others where the possessors are bound to grind for particular persons, or within particular districts, and to take a fixed toll.

From and after June 1, 1796, every miller shall put up in his mill, a table of the prices, or of the amount of toll at his mill, on pain of forfeiting not exceeding 20s.

MINES, by the old common law, if gold or silver be found in mines of base metal, the whole was said to be a royal mine, and belonged to the king; but by statutes 1 & 5 W. c. 30, and 6. no mine of copper, tin, iron, or lead, shall be deemed a royal mine, notwithstanding gold or silver may be extracted from them in any quantities.

Coal mines by name are rateable to the poor; but other mines are not. 43 Eliz. c. 2.

MINOR, one in his minority, or under age. See *Infant*.

MINUTE TITHES, small tithes, such as usually belong to the vicar, as of wool, lambs, pigs, butter, cheese, herbs, seeds, eggs, honey, wax, &c. 2 *Inst*. 649.

MISADVENTURE, when applied to homicide, is, where a man is doing a lawful act, without intent of hurt to another, and death casually ensues. 4 *Black*. 182. See *Homicide*.

MISDEMEANOUR, a crime or misdemeanour, is an act committed or omitted, in violation of a public law, either forbidding or commanding it.

MISE, is a customary gift or present which the people of Wales, give to every new king or prince of Wales, at their entrance into that principality.

MISFEASANCE, a misdeed or trespass.

MISNOMER, the using of one name for another.

Where a person is described so that he may not be certainly distinguished

distinguished and known from other persons, the omission, or in some cases the mistake of the name shall not avoid the grant. 11 *Rep.* 20.

If the christian name be wholly mistaken, this is regularly fatal to all legal instruments, as well declarations and pleadings, as grants and obligations.

The mistake of the surname does not vitiate, because there is no repugnancy that a person shall have different surnames; and therefore if a man enter into an obligation by a particular name he may be impleaded by the name in the deed, and his real name brought in by an *alias*, and then the name in the deed he cannot deny, because he is estopped to say any thing contrary to his own deed. 2 *Rol. Abr.* 146.

MISPRISION, is generally understood to be of all such high offences as are under the degree of capital, but bordering thereon, and it is said, that a misprision is contained in every treason and felony whatsoever; and, that if the king please, the offender may be proceeded against for the misprision only 4 *Black.* 119.

MIS-RECITAL, in deeds, is sometimes injurious, and sometimes not; if a thing be referred to time, place, and number, and that is mistaken, all is void.

MISTAKE. *Mistakes* in law proceedings are generally subversive of the whole cause or suit.

Any party who is injured through the negligence or mistake of the person employed by him, is intitled to an action, and will recover proportionate damages.

If money be paid by mistake, or upon a consideration which happens to fail, or if money be obtained by imposition (express or implied) or extortion, or oppression, or through any undue advantage taken of the plaintiff's situation, such money may be recovered back.

MITTENDO MANUSCRIPTUM PEDIS FINIS, a judicial writ, directed to the treasurer and chamberlains of the exchequer, to search and transmit the part of a fine acknowledged before the justices *in eyre*, into the common pleas.

MITTIMUS, a writ by which records are transferred from one court to another. This word is also used for the precept directed to a goaler, under the hand and seal of a justice of the peace, for the receiving and safe keeping a felon, or other offender, by him committed to goal.

MIXED

MIXED TITHES, are those of cheese, milk, &c. and of the young of beasts. *2 Inst. 649.*

MODERATA MISERICORDIA, a writ for him who is amerced in a court baron, or other court, being not of record, for any transgression or offence beyond the quality of a fault. It is directed to the lord of the court, or his bailiff, commanding them to take a *moderate amercement* of the party.

MODO ET FORMA, words of art in process and pleadings, and in answer of the defendant, whereby he denies himself to have done the thing laid to his charge, *modo et forma declarata.*

MODUS DECIMANDI, is when either land, a sum of money, or yearly pension is given to the person, &c. by composition, or custom, as satisfaction for his tithes in kind. *2 Inst.* 490.

MOIETY, the half of any thing.

MONASTERIES, were dissolved and given to the crown by stat. 31 H. VIII. c. 13.

MONEY, is a material representing a fixed and certain value, generally made of metal, struck with a peculiar mark, indicating its weight, fineness, and the value for which it passes.

No person is obliged to take in payment any money which is not lawful metal, that is, of silver and gold, except for sums under sixpence. *2 Inst.* 577.

But it was decided in hilary term, 1790, that bank notes are considered as money, and therefore a proper tender in payment.

MONOPOLY, is an allowance by the king, by his grant, commission, or otherwise, to any person, or persons, bodies politic, or corporate, or of or for the sole buying, selling, making, working, or using of any thing, whereby any person or persons, bodies politic or corporate, are sought to be restrained of any freedom or liberty they had before, or hindered in their lawful trade. 3*Inst.*181.

But it seems that the king's charter, impowering particular persons to trade to and from such place is void, so far as it gives such persons an exclusive right of trading, and debarring all others; and it seems now agreed, that nothing can exclude a subject from trade but an act of parliament. *Raym.* 489.

MONSTRANS DE DROIT, in a legal sense denotes a writ issuing out of chancery, for the subject to be restored to lands and tenements, which he shews to be his right, though by office found to be in the possession of another lately dead; by which office the king

king is entitled to a chattel, freehold, or inheritance in the said lands.

MONSTRANS DE FAITS OU RECORDS, the shewing of deeds or records is thus; in an action of debt brought upon an obligation after the plaintiff hath declared, he ought to shew his obligation, and so it is of records.

MONSTRAVERUNT, a writ which lies for the tenants in *ancient demesne,* being distrained for the payment of any toll to imposition, contrary to their liberty, which they do or should enjoy.

MOOR GAME. See *Game.*

MOOT, a term well understood in the inns of the court, to be the practice of arguing cases, which young students perform at appointed times, the better to enable them to support or defend their client's causes.

MORATUR, or DEMORATUR IN LEGE, whenever the counsel is of opinion, that the count or plea of the adverse party insufficient in law, then he *demurs,* or abides in law, and refers the same to the judgment of the court.

MORTGAGE, signifies a pawn of land or tenement, or any thing immoveable, laid or bound for money borrowed, to be the creditor's for ever, if the money be not paid at the day agreed upon; and the creditor holding land and tenement upon this bargain, is called tenant in mortgage. He who pledgeth this pawn or gage, is called the *mortgagor,* and he who taketh it, the *mortgagee.*

The last and best improvement of mortgages seems to be that in the mortgage deed of a term for years, or in the assignment thereof, the mortgagor should covenant for himself and his heirs, that if default be made in the payment of the money at the day, that then he and his heirs will, at the costs of the mortgagee and his heirs, convey the freehold and inheritance of the mortgaged lands to the mortgagee and his heirs, or to such person or persons (to prevent merger of the term) as he or they shall direct and appoint: for the reversion, after a term of fifty or a hundred years, being little worth, and yet the mortgagee for want thereof continuing but a termer, and subject to forfeiture, &c. and not capable of the privileges of a freeholder; therefore when the mortgagor cannot redeem the land, it is but reasonable the mortgagee should have

have the whole interest and inheritance of it, to dispose of it as absolute owner. 3 *Bac. Abr.* 633.

Although after breach of the condition, an absolute fee-simple is vested at common law in the mortgagee; yet a right of redemption being still inherent in the land, till the equity of redemption is foreclosed, the same right shall descend to, and is invested in such persons as have a right to the land, in case there had been no mortgage or incumbrance whatsoever; and as an equitable performance as effectually defeats the interests of the mortgagee, as the legal performance doth at common law, the condition still hanging over the estate, till the equity is totally foreclosed; on this foundation it hath been held, that a person who comes in under a voluntary conveyance, may redeem a mortgage; and though such right of redemption be inherent in the land, yet the party claiming the benefit of it, must not only set forth such right, but also shew that he is the person entitled to it. *Hard.* 465.

But if a mortgage be forfeited, and thereby the estate absolutely vested in the mortgagee at the common law, yet, a court of equity will consider the real value of the tenements compared with the sum borrowed. And if the estate be of greater value than the sum lent thereon, they will allow the mortgagor at any reasonable time, to recal or redeem the estate, paying to the mortagee his principal, interest, and costs. This reasonable advantage, allowed to the mortgagors, is called the equity of redemption. 2 *Black.* 159.

It is a rule established in equity, analagous to the statute of limitation, that after *twenty years* possession of the mortgagee, he shall not be disturbed, unless there be extraordinary circumstances; as in the case of femes *couvert*, infants, and the like. 3 *Atk.* 313.

MORTMAIN, signifies an alienation of lands and tenements, to any guild, corporation, or fraternity, and their successors, as bishops, parsons, vicars, &c. which may not be done without the king's licence, and the lord of the manor, or of the king alone, if it be immediately holden of him.

But in order to prevent any imposition in respect to the disposal of lands to charitable uses, which might arise in a testator's last hours, and in some measure from political principles to restrain devises in mortmain, or the too great accumulation of land in

hand

hands where it lies dead, and not subject to change possession, it is provided by stat. 9 G. II. c. 36, (called the statute of *mortmain*) that no manors, lands, tenements, rents, advowsons, or other hereditaments, corporeal, or incorporeal, whatsoever, nor any sum, or sums of money, goods, chattels, stocks in the public funds, securities for money, or other personal estate whatsoever, to be laid out or disposed of in the purchase of any lands, tenements, or hereditaments, *shall be given, limited, or appointed by will*, to any person or persons, bodies politic or corporate, or otherwise, for any estate or interest whatsoever, or any ways charged or incumbered by any person or persons whatsoever, in trust, or for the benefit of any charitable use whatsoever; but such gift shall be by deed indented, sealed and delivered in the presence of two or more credible witnesses, *twelve calendar months at least*, before the death of such donor, and be inrolled in the high court of chancery within six calendar months after execution, and the same to take effect immediately after the execution for the charitable use intended, and be without any power of revocation, reservation, or trust for benefit of the donor. And all gifts and appointments whatsoever, of any lands, tenements, or other hereditaments, or of any estate or interest therein, or of any charge or incumbrance, affecting or to affect any lands, tenements, or hereditaments, or any personal estate, to be laid out in the purchase of any lands, tenements, or hereditaments, or any estate, or interest therein, or of any charge or incumbrance affecting or to affect the same, to or in trust for any charitable use whatsoever, made in any other manner than is directed by this act, shall be absolutely null and void. But the two universities, their colleges, and the scholars upon the foundation of the colleges at Eaton, Westminster, and Winchester, are excepted out of this act; but with this proviso, that no college shall be at liberty to purchase more advowsons than are equal in number to one moiety of the fellows or students upon the respective foundations.

MORTUARY. See *Corse Present.*

MOSS-TROOPERS, a rebellious sort of people in the north of England, who lived by robbery and rapine, for whose suppression the statutes 4 Jac. I. c. 1: 7 Jac. I. c. 1: and 14 Car. II. c. 22, were enacted.

MOTION

MOTION IN COURT, is an occasional application by the party or his counsel, in order to obtain some rule or order of court, and is usually grounded upon an affidavit of the truth of the suggestion. 3 *Black.* 304.

MULIER in the common law is used for *melior,* and signifies the lawful issue born in wedlock (though begotten before), preferred before an elder brother born out of matrimony.

MULTÆ, or MULTURA EPISCOPI, a fine given to the king, that the bishop might have power to make his will and testament, and to have the probate of other men's, and the granting administrations. 2 *Inst.* 491.

MULTO FORTIORI, or A MINORI AD MAJUS, is an argument thus used; if it be so in a feoffment passing a new right, *much more* it is for the restitution of an ancient right, &c. *Co. Lit.* 253.

MURAGE, a toll or tribute to be levied for the building or repairing of public walls; it is due either by grant or prescription. 2 *Inst.* 222.

MURDER. See *Homicide.*

MUTE. If any person being arraigned on any indictment or appeal for felony, or on any indictment for piracy, shall upon such arraignment stand mute, or will not answer directly to the felony or piracy, he shall be convicted of the offence, and the court shall thereupon award judgment and execution, in the same manner as if he had been convicted by verdict or confession; and by such judgment shall have all the same consequences as a conviction by verdict or confession. 12 G. III. c. 20.

And the law is the same with respect to an arraignment for petit treason or larceny; for before this act, persons standing mute in either of these cases, were to have the like judgment as if they had confessed the indictment. 2 *Inst.* 177.

MUTUAL PROMISE, is where one man promises to pay money to another, and he in consideration thereof, promises to do a certain act, &c. &c. such promises must be binding, as well of one side as the other; and both made at the same time. 1 *Salk.* 21.

MUTUS ET SURDUS, a person dumb and deaf, and being tenant of a manor, the lord shall have the wardship and custody of him. But if a man be dumb and deaf, and have understanding, he may be grantor or grantee of lands, &c. 1 *Co. Inst.*

A prisoner deaf and dumb from his birth, may be arraigned for a capital offence, if intelligence can be conveyed to him by signs or symbols. *Leach's Cr. Law*. 97. See *Evidence*.

N.

NAME. See *Misnomer*.

NAMIUM VETITUM, an illegal taking the cattle of another, and driving them to an unlawful place, pretending damage done by them. In this case the owner may demand satisfaction for the injury, which is called *placitum de namio vetito*. 3 *Black*. 149.

NATIVI DE STIPITE, were villains or bondmen by birth or stock.

NATIVO HABENDO, a writ that lay to the sheriff, for a lord, whose villain claimed for his inheritance, run from him, for the apprehending and restoring him to his lord again.

NATURAL AFFECTION, is a good consideration in a deed. *Carth*. 138.

NATURALIZATION, is when an alien born, is made the king's natural subject.

Hereby an alien is put in the same state as if he had been born in the king's ligeance, except only, that he is incapable of being a member of the privy council, or parliament, and of holding any office or grant. No bill for a naturalization, can be received in either house of parliament, without such disabling clause in it; nor without a clause disabling the person from obtaining any immunity in trade thereby, in any foreign country, unless he shall have resided in Britain *seven* years next after the commencement of the session in which he is naturalized. Neither can any person be naturalized, or restored in blood, unless he have received the sacrament within one month before the bringing in of the bill, and unless he also take the oaths of allegiance and supremacy in the presence of the parliament. 1 *Black*. 374. See *Alien*.

NAVY, for the regulation of the officers and seamen belonging to the navy, see *Statutes*. 29 Car. II. c. 3: 22 G. II. c. 33, and 31 G. II. c. 10.

NE ADMITTAS, a writ that lies for the plaintiff, in a *quare impedit*,

pedit, or him who hath an action of *darrein presentment* depending in the common bench, and fears the bishop will admit the clerk of the defendant, during the suit between them; which writ must be sued within six calendar months after the avoidance, because after six months, the bishop may present by lapse.

NECESSITY. The law charges no man with default where the act is compulsory, and not voluntary, and where there is not a consent and election; and therefore if either there be an impossibility for a man to do otherwise, or so great a perturbation of the judgment and reason, as in presumption of law, man's nature cannot overcome, such necessity carries a privilege in itself.

Necessity is of three sorts; necessity of conservation of life, necessity of obedience, and necessity of the act of God, or of a stranger.

And *first*, of *conservation of life*: if a man steal viands to satisfy his present hunger, this is no felony nor larceny.

The *second* necessity is *of obedience*: and therefore where baron and feme commit a felony, the feme can neither be principal, nor accessary, because the law intends her to have no will in regard of the subjection and obedience she owes her husband.

The *third* necessity is of *the act of God, or of a stranger*; or if a man be particular tenant for years of an house, and it be overthrown, by thunder, lightning, and tempest, in this case, he is excused of wate. *Bac. Elem.* 25, 26, 27.

NE EXEAT REGNO, is a writ to restrain a person from going out of the kingdom without the king's licence.

Within the realm, the king may command the attendance and service of all his liegemen; but he cannot send any man out of the realm, or even upon the public service, except seamen and soldiers, the nature of whose employment necessarily implies an exception. 1 *Black.* 138.

This writ is now mostly used, where a suit is commenced in the court of chancery against a man, and he intending to defeat the other of his just demand, or to avoid the justice and equity of the court, is about to go beyond sea, or however, that the duty will be endangered if he go.

If the writ be granted on behalf of a subject, and the party taken, he either gives security by bond in such sum as is demanded, or he satisfies the court by answering (where the answer is not already

ready in) or by affidavit, that he intends not to go out of the realm, and gives such reasonable security as the court directs, and then he is discharged. P. R. C. 252.

NEGLIGENCE, is where a person neglects or omits to do a thing which he is obliged by law to do. Thus where one has goods of another to keep till such a time, and he hath a certain recompence or reward for the keeping, he shall stand charged for injury by negligence, &c.

NEGLIGENT ESCAPE. See *Escape*.

NE INJUSTE VERES, a writ that lies for a tenant that is distrained by his lord for other services than he ought to perform, and is a prohibition to the lord, commanding him not to distrain.

NEMINE CONTRADICENTE, words used to signify the unanimous consent of the members of the house of commons to a vote or resolution.

NEW TRIAL, formerly the only remedy for a reversal of a verdict unduly given, was by writ of *attaint*; but this course is now justly exploded, and a new trial is granted. 3 *Black*. 389.

A new trial ought only to be granted to obtain real justice, and not to gratify litigious passions. *Bur*. 11.

A new trial therefore, in many cases, may be absolutely necessary. But a new trial is not granted upon nice and formal objections, which do not go to the real merits. It is not granted where the scales of evidence hang nearly equal; for that which leans against the verdict, ought always very strongly to preponderate. 3 *Black*. 391.

NIENT COMPRISE, an exception taken to a petition, as unjust, because the thing desired, is not contained in the act or deed whereon the petition is grounded.

NIHIL, is a word which the sheriff answers, that is apposed concerning debts illeviable, and that are nothing worth by reason of the insufficiency of the parties from whom they are due.

NIHIL CAPIAT PER BREVE, is the judgment given against the plaintiff, either in bar of his action, or in abatement of his writ. *Co. Lit*. 363.

NIHIL DICIT, a failing to put in answer to the plea of the plaintiff by the day assigned, which if a man omit, judgment passes against him of course by *nihil dicit*, because he says nothing in his own defence, why it should not.

NISI

NISI PRIUS, a commission directed to the judges of assize, empowering them to try all questions of fact issuing out of the courts at Westminster that are then ready for trial by jury. The original of which name is this; all causes commenced in the courts of Westminster-hall, are by course of the courts, appointed to be tried on a day fixed in some Easter or Michaelmas term, by a jury returned from the county wherein the cause of action arises; but with this proviso, *nisi prius justiciarii ad assisas capiendas venerint*: that is, *unless before*, the day prefixed, the judges of assize come into the county in question, which they always do in the vacation preceding each Easter and Michaelmas term, and there try the cause. And then, upon the return of the verdict given by the jury, to the court above, the judges there give judgment for the party for whom the verdict is found. 3 *Black*. 59. See *Assizes*.

NOBILITY, the civil state of England, consists of the nobility and commonalty. The nobility are all those who are above the degree of knight, under which term is included that of a baronet; namely, dukes, marquisses, earls, viscounts and barons. 1 *Black*. 396

NOLLE PROSEQUI, is used where the plaintiff will proceed no farther in his action, and may be as well before as after a verdict, and is stronger against the plaintiff than a nonsuit, which is only a default in appearance; but this is a voluntary acknowledgment, that he hath no cause of action. *Impey's* B. R.

NOMINATION, is to be taken for a power that a man by virtue of a manor, or otherwise, hath to appoint a *clerk* to a *patron* of a benefice, by him to be prescribed to the ordinary.

NON-ABILITY, an exception taken against the plaintiff upon some cause why he cannot commence suit at law, as *præmunire*, *&c*.

NONAGE. See *Age* and *Infancy*.

NON ASSUMPSIT, a plea in personal actions, whereby a man denies any promise made, &c.

NON-CLAIM, where one person has a demand upon another, and does not enforce his claim within a reasonable time, he is precluded by law from bringing his action to enforce it; and where a creditor neglects to make his claim upon a bankrupt's estate within a certain period, he will not be let in afterwards, so as to disturb the dividend. See *Limitation*.

NON COMPOS MENTIS. See *Ideots.*

NON CUL', abbreviated from *non culpabilis,* is a plea of not guilty to any action of trespass or wrong in any civil suit, or to an indictment in a criminal matter.

NON EST FACTUM, is a plea where an action is brought upon a bond or any other deed, and the defendant denies it to be *his deed* whereon he is impleaded. In every case where the bond is void, the defendant may plead *non est factum*; but where a bond is voidable only, he must shew the special matter. 2 *Lil.* 226.

NON EST INVENTUS, the sheriff's return to a writ, when the defendant is not to be found in his bailiwick.

NON-FEASANCE, an *omission* of what ought to be done.

NON IMPLACITANDO ALIQUEM DE LIBERO TENEMENTO SIVE BREVI, a writ to inhibit bailiffs, &c. from distraining any man touching his freehold, without the king's writ.

NON-JURORS, persons refusing to take the oaths to government, and who are liable to certain penalties; and those who deny that oaths are unlawful, are for a third offence to abjure the realm, by stat. 13 & 14 Car. II. c. 1.

NON MOLESTANDO, a writ which lies for him who is *molested* contrary to the king's protection granted him.

NON OBSTANTE, was a clause frequent in the king's letters patent, granting a thing, *notwithstanding* any statute or act of parliament to the contrary; which assumed power, setting the prerogative above the laws, was effectually demolished by the bill of rights.

NON OMITTAS, PROPTER ALIQUAM LIBERTATEM, is a writ directed to the sheriff, where the bailiff of a liberty or franchise, who hath the return of writs, refuses or neglects to serve a process, for the sheriff to enter into the franchise, and execute the king's process himself or by his officer.

NON PLEVIN, by 9 Ed. III. c. 2, it was enacted, that none henceforth should lose his land because of *non plevin*; that is, when the land was not replevined in due time.

NON PONENDIS IN ASSISIS ET JURATIS, a writ for freeing and discharging persons from serving on assizes and juries; particularly by reason of their old age; but by 4 & 5 W. c. 24, no no such writ shall be granted, unless upon oath made, that the suggestions upon which it is granted are true.

NON PROS. If the plaintiff neglect to deliver a declaration for two terms after the defendant appears, or is guilty of other delays or defaults against the rules of law in any subsequent stage of the action, he is adjudged not to pursue his remedy as he ought; and thereupon a nonsuit or *non prosequitur*, is entered, and he is then said to be *non pros'd*. *3 Black.* 395.

NON RESIDENCE, is applied to those spiritual persons who are not resident, but absent themselves by the space of one month together, or two months at several times in one year, from their dignities or benefices, which is liable to the penalties, by the statute against non residence. 21 H. VIII, c. 13.

But chaplains to the king, or other great persons mentioned in this statute, may be non resident on their livings; for they are excused from residence whilst they attend those who retain them.

NON SANE MEMORY. See *Non compos Mentis.*

NON-SUIT, where a person has commenced an action, and at the trial fails in his evidence to support it, or has brought a wrong action. See *Calling the Plaintiff.*

There is this advantage attending a nonsuit, that the plaintiff, though he pay costs, may afterwards bring another action, for the same cause; which he cannot do, after a verdict against him. *Tidd's* K. B. *Practice.*

NON-TENURE, an exception to a count, by saying that he the defendant, holdeth not the land specified in the count.

NON-TERM, the time of vacation between term and term.

NORTHERN BORDERS. See *Black Mail* and *Moss Troopers.*

NOSE-SLITTING, if any person shall of malice aforethought, and by laying wait, slit the nose, or cut off a nose or lip, of any person with intent to disfigure him, he shall be guilty of felony without benefit of clergy. See *Maihem.*

NOT GUILTY, the general issue or plea of the defendant in any criminal action or prosecution; as also in an action of trespass, or upon the case for deceits and wrongs; but not on a promise or assumpsit. *Palm.* 393. See *Non Cul.*

NOTARY, is a person duly appointed to attest deeds and writings; he also protests and notes foreign and inland bills of exchange

change and promissory notes, translates languages, and attests the same, enters and extends ship's protests, &c.

NOTARIAL ACTS, are those acts in the civil law, which require to be done under the seal of a notary, and which are admitted as evidence in foreign courts.

NOTE OF A FINE, is a brief of a fine made by the *chirographer* before it is engrossed.

NOTES PROMISSORY. See *Bills of Exchange*.

NOTICE, is the making something known, that a man was or might be ignorant of before; and it produces divers effects; for by it the party that gives the same, shall have same benefit, which otherwise he should not have had: and by this means, the party to whom the notice is given, is made subject to some action or charge, that otherwise he had not been liable to, and his estate in danger of prejudice. *Co. Lit.* 309.

The plaintiff and defendant are both bound at their peril to take notice of the general rules of the practice of the court; but if there be a special particular rule of court made for the plaintiff, or for the defendant, he for whom the rule is made, ought to give *notice* of this rule to the other; or else he is not bound generally to take notice of it, nor shall be in contempt of the court, although he do not obey it. 2 L. P. R. 204.

NOVEL ASSIGNMENT, is an assignment of time, place, or the like, in an action of trespass, otherwise than as it was before in the writ assigned.

NUDE CONTRACT, a bare promise without any consideration, and therefore void.

NUL TIEL RECORD, the plea of a plaintiff, that there is no such record, on the defendant's alledging matter of record in bar of the plaintiff's action.

NUISANCE, signifies generally any thing that worketh hurt, inconvenience, or damage, to the property or person of another. Nuisances are of two kinds; *public*, or *private nuisances*, and either affect the public or the individual. The remedy for a nuisance is by action on the case for damages. Every continuance of a nuisance, is a fresh nuisance, and a fresh action will lie.

OATH,

O.

OATH, an affirmation or denial of any thing before one or more persons, who have the authority to administer the same, for the discovery and advancement of truth and right. See *Affidavit.*

OBLIGATION, a bond containing a penalty, with a condition annexed, either for payment of money, performance of covenants, or the like. This security is called a specialty. *Co. Lit.* 172. See *Bond* and *Deed.*

OBLIGOR, he who enters into an obligation, and *obligee* the person to whom it is entered into.

OCCUPANT, if a tenant for a term of another's life die, leaving *cestui que vie*; he who first enters shall hold the land during that other man's life; and he is in law called an *occupant,* because his title is by his first occupation; and so, if tenant for his own life, grant over his estate to another, if the grantee die, there shall be an *occupant.* *Co. Lit.* c. 6.

The law of *occupancy* is founded upon the law of nature; and is simply the taking possession of those things, which before belonged to nobody: and this is the true ground and foundation of all property.

OFFENCE, is any act committed against any law. *Offences* are either *capital,* or *not capital.* Capital offences are those for which an offender shall lose his life; not capital, where the offender may lose his lands and goods, be fined, or suffer corporal punishment, or both, but not loss of life.

High treason, petit treason, and felony, constitute capital offences; other offences, not capital, include the remaining part of criminal offences or pleas of the crown, and come under the denomination of misdemeanours.

OFFERINGS. Oblations and offerings partake of the nature of tithes, and all persons which by the laws of this realm ought to pay their offerings, shall yearly pay to the parson, vicar, proprietary, or their deputies, or farmers of the parishes where they dwell, at such four offering days as heretofore within the space of four years last past hath been accustomed, and in default thereof, shall

shall pay for the said offerings at *Easter* following. 2 & 3 Ed. VI. c. 13.

OFFERINGS OF THE KING, *offerings* made at the holy altar by the king and queen, are distributed among the poor by the dean of the chapel.

OFFICE, is that function, by virtue whereof a person hath some employment in the affairs of another.

An *office* is a right to exercise any public or private employment, and to take the fees and emoluments thereunto belonging, whether public as those of magistrates, or private as of bailiffs, receivers, &c.

The stat. 5 & 6 Ed. VI. c. 16, declares all securities given for the sale of offices unlawful. And if any person shall bargain or sell, or take any reward, or promise of reward, for any office, or the deputation of any office, concerning the revenue, or the keeping of the king's castles, or the administration and execution of justice, unless it be such an office as had been usually granted by the justices of the king's bench or common pleas, or by justices of assize, every such person shall not only forfeit his right to such office, or to the nomination thereof, but the person giving such reward, &c. shall be disabled to hold such office.

But it has been decided, that where an office is within the statute, and the salary certain, if the principal make a deputy, reserving by bond a less sum out of the salary, it is good; or, if the profits are uncertain, reserving a part as half the profits, it is good; for the fees still belong to the principal, in whose name they must be sued for. *Salk.* 466: but where a person so appointed, gives a bond to the principal to pay him a sum certain, without reference to the profits, this is void under the statute. *Salk.* 465.

To offer money to any officer of state, to procure the reversion of an office in the gift of the crown, is a misdemeanour at common law, and punishable by information; and even the attempt to induce him under the influence of a bribe, is criminal, though never carried into execution.

Any contract to procure the nomination to an office, not within the stat. 6 Ed. VI. is defective on the ground of public policy, and the money agreed to be given, is not recoverable.

OFFICIAL. By the ancient law, signifies him who is the minister

nister of or attendant upon a magistrate. In the canon law, it is especially taken for him to whom any bishop generally commits the charge of his spiritual jurisdiction, and n this sense there is one in every diocese called *officialis principalis*, whom the laws and statutes of this kingdom call *chancellor*. 3. H. 8. 15.

OFFICIARIIS NON FACIENDIS VEL AMOVENDIS, a writ directed to the magistrates of a corporation, willing them not to make such a man an officer, and to put him out of the office he hath, until inquiry be made of his manners, according to an inquisition formerly ordained.

OLERON LAWS, laws relating to maritime affairs, and so called because made when king Richard the First was at the Isle of *Oleron*, in *Aquitaine*.

OMISSIONS, in law proceedings, render them vicious and defective. See *Nonfeasance*.

ONERANDO PRO RATA PORTIONIS, a writ that lies for a joint tenant, or tenant in common, who is distrained for more rent than his proportion of the land comes to.

ONUS PROBANDI, the burden of proving any thing.

OPERATIO, one day's work performed by an inferior tenant to the lord; whence, those bound to perform servile labours for their landlords, are often called *operarii*.

OPPRESSION, in a private sense, is the trampling upon, or bearing down, on pretence of law, which is unjust: but where the law is known and clear, though it appear to be inequitable, the judges must determine according to that. *Vaugh.* 37.

OPTION, every bishop whether created, or translated, is bound immediately after confirmation, to make a legal conveyance to the archbishop, of the next avoidance of such dignity or benefice belonging to the fee, as the said archbishop shall choose, which is therefore called an *option*. See also *Election*.

ORDEAL, was anciently a form of trial for discovering innocence or guilt; and it was of two sorts; either *fire* ordeal, or *water* ordeal; the former being confined to persons of higher rank, the latter to the common people. Both these might be performed by deputy, but the principal was to answer for the success of the trial; the deputy only venturing some corporal pain, for hire, or perhaps for friendship. *Fire* ordeal, was performed either by taking up in the hand a piece of red hot iron, of one, two, or three

three pounds weight; or else by walking bare foot and blindfold, over nine red hot plough-shares, laid at unequal distances; and if the party escaped unhurt, he was adjudged innocent; if not, he was condemned as guilty. *Water* ordeal was performed, either by plunging the bare arm up to the elbow in boiling water, and escaping unhurt thereby, or by casting the person suspected into a river or pond of water; and if he floated therein, without any action of swimming, it was deemed an evidence of his guilt: but if he sunk he was acquitted. 4 *Black.* 340.

This trial by ordeal, was abolished by parliament *anno* 3 Hen. III.

ORDERS, are of several sorts, and by several courts, as of the *chancery, king's-bench, common-pleas,* and *exchequer,* for the particulars thereof we refer the reader, to *Mitford's Chancery, Impey's King's-Bench and Common-Pleas,* and *Fowler's Exchequer Practices.*

ORDERS or ORDINATION, no person shall be admitted to the holy order of deacon, under twenty-three years of age; nor to the order of priest, unless he be twenty-four complete; and none shall be ordained without a title. And he shall have a testimonial of his good behaviour. And the bishop shall examine him, and if he see cause, may refuse him. And before he is ordained, he shall take the oath of allegiance and supremacy before the ordinary, and subscribe the thirty-nine articles.

ORDINARY, in the civil law, signifies any judge that hath authority to take cognizance of causes in his own right, as he is a magistrate, and not by deputation; but in the common law, it is taken for him, who hath exempt and immediate jurisdiction in causes ecclesiastical. 2 *Inst.* 19.

ORGILD, a restitution made by the hundred, or county, of any wrong done by one who was in pledge. See *Frank Pledge.*

ORIGINAL, in the court of king's-bench, the usual original writ issued in the actions; as for action of trespass upon the case; and this court doth not issue originals in actions of debt, covenant, or account, &c. Whereas the court of common pleas proceeds by original in all kinds of actions: but to arrest and sue a party to outlawry, it is used in both courts. See *Impey's B. R. and C. B.*

ORPHAN,

ORPHAN, in the city of London, there is a court of record established for the care and government of orphans.

OVERSEERS OF THE POOR. The proper number of overseers of the poor for each parish, must be duly appointed, and sworn before two justices of the peace, one whereof must be of the quorum.

The overseers thus appointed, and taking on them the office, shall within fourteen days, receive the books of assessments, and of accounts from their predecessors, and what money and materials shall be in their hands, and reimburse them their arrears. 17 Geo. II. c. 38.

And shall take order from time to time, with the consent of two such justices as aforesaid, for setting to work the children of such parents who shall not by the said overseers, be thought able to keep or maintain them, and using no ordinary and daily trade of life to get their living by. 43 Eliz. c. 2.

By the 13 & 14 Car. II. it is enacted, that within forty days after any poor persons shall come to settle in any tenement under ten pounds a year, two justices may remove them to the place where they were last legally settled.

But by the 1 Jac. II. such forty days continuance shall not make a settlement, but from the time of delivering notice in writing; and by 3 W. it must be from the time of the publication of such notice in the church: but it has always been understood, that a person who is not removeable, need not give such notice; and that a person continuing forty days unremoveable, and a person not removed for forty days after such notice given and published, shall equally gain a settlement.

By the 17 Geo. II. c. 38. if any person shall be aggrieved by any thing done or omitted by the churchwardens and overseers, or by any of his majesty's justices of the peace, he may, giving reasonable notice to the churchwardens or overseers, appeal to the next general or quarter-sessions, where the same shall be heard, or finally determined; but if reasonable notice be not given, then they shall adjourn the appeal to the next quarter-sessions; and the court may award reasonable costs to either party, as they may do by 8 & 9 W. in case of appeals concerning settlements. See *Poor*.

OVERT ACT. In the case of treason in compassing or imagining the death of the king, this imagining must be manifested by some open act; otherwise being only an act of the mind, it cannot fall under any judicial cognizance. Bare words are held not to amount to an overt act, unless put into writing, in which case they are then held to be an overt act, as arguing a more deliberate intention. No evidence shall be admitted of any overt act, that is not expressly laid in the indictment. 7 W. c. 3.

OUSTED, put out, or removed.

OUSTER LE MAIN, denotes a judgment given for him that traversed or sued a *monstrans le droit*, and is indeed a delivery of lands out of the king's hands; for when it appears upon the matter discussed, that the king hath no right or title to the thing seized, then judgment shall be given in chancery, that the king's hands be amoved, and thereupon an *amoveas manum* shall be awarded to the escheator, which is as much as if the judgment were given, that the party shall have his land again. *Staundf. Prærog.* c. 24.

OUTLAWRY, is being put *out of the law*, or out of the king's protection. It is a punishment inflicted for a contempt in refusing to be amenable to the process of the higher courts. By outlawry in civil actions, a person is put out of the protection of the law, so that he is not only incapable of suing for the redress of injuries, but may be imprisoned, and forfeits all his goods and chattels, and the profits of his land; his personal chattels immediately upon the outlawry, and his chattels real, and the profits of his lands, when found by inquisition. 1 *Salk.* 395.

It seems that originally process of outlawry only lay in treason and felony, and was afterwards extended to trespass of an enormous nature; but the process of outlawry at this day lies in all appeals, and in all indictments of conspiracy and deceit, or other crimes of an higher nature than trespass *vi et armis*; but it lies not in an action, nor on an indictment on a statute, unless it be given by such statute either expressly, as in the case of a *præmunire*, or impliedly, as in cases made treason or felony by statute, or where a recovery is given by an action in which such process lay before, as in case of forcible entry. *Staundf.* 192.

Process of outlawry. The exigent must be sued in the county where the party *really* resides, for there all actions were originally laid; and because that outlawries were at first only for treason, felony,

felony, or very enormous trespasses, the process was to be executed at the *torn*, which is the sheriff's criminal court; and this held not only before the sheriff, but before the coroners, who were ancient conservators of the peace, being the best men in each county, to preside with the sheriff in his court, and who pronounced the outlawry in the county court on the parties being *quinto exactus*; and therefore anciently there was no occasion for any process to any other county than that in which the party actually resided. But the modern practice being different the reader is referred to *Tidd's Pract.* K. B.

Of the reversal of outlawries. There are two ways of reversing an outlawry; first, by a writ of error returnable *coram nobis*; secondly by motion founded on a plea, averment, or suggestion, of some matter apparent; as in respect of a *supesedeas*, omission of process, variance, or other matter apparent on the record.

OYER, a term anciently used for what is now called assizes.

OYER OF DEED, is when a man brings an action upon a deed, bond, &c. and the defendant appears and prays that he may hear the bond, &c. wherewith he is charged, and the same shall be allowed him. And he is not bound to plead till he has it, paying for the copy of it.

The time allowed for the plaintiff to give *oyer* of a deed, &c. to the plaintiff, is two days exclusive after it is demanded. *Carth.* 454. 2 *Durnf. & East.* 40.

OYER AND TERMINER, is a court held by virtue of the king's commission, to hear and determine all treasons, felonies, and misdemeanors. This commission is usually directed to two of the judges of the circuit, and several gentlemen of the county; but the judges only are of the quorum, so that the rest cannot act without them. See *Assizes.* 4 *Black* 269.

OYER DE RECORDO, is a petition made in court, that the judges for more satisfactory proof, will be pleased to hear or look upon any record. *Cowel.*

OYES, corrupted from the French oyez, *hear ye*, is an expression used by the crier of a court, in order to enjoin silence, when any proclamation is made. 4 *Black.* 340.

P.

PACKETS, packet-vessels are prohibited from exporting or importing goods under certain penalties.

PAIS, trial *per pais*, is trial by the country or a jury.

PALATINE COUNTIES, are those of *Chester*, *Durham*, and *Lancaster* See *Counties Palatine*.

PANEL, a little *pane*, an oblong piece of parchment, containing the names of the jurors, annexed to the writ of *venire facias*, and returned by the sheriff to the court from whence the process issued.

PANNAGE or PAWNAGE, the fruit of trees, as *acorns*, *crabs*, *nuts*, *mast of beech*, &c. which the swine feed upon in the woods.

PAPER. See *Excise*, and *Complete Abridgment of the Excise Laws*.

PAPISTS, persons professing the popish religion. By several statutes, if any English priest of the church of Rome, born in the dominions of the crown of England, came to England from beyond the seas, or tarried in England three days without conforming to the church, he was guilty of high treason; and they also incurred the guilt of high treason, who were reconciled to the see of Rome, or procured others to be reconciled to it. By these laws also, papists were disabled from giving their children any education in their own religion. If they educated their children at home, for maintaining the schoolmaster, if he did not repair to church, or was not allowed by the bishop of the diocese, they were liable to forfeit 10l. a month, and the schoolmaster was liable to the forfeiture of 40s. a day: if they sent their children for education abroad, they were liable to forfeit 100l. and the children so sent were incapable of inheriting, purchasing, or enjoying, any lands, profits, goods, debts, legacies, or sums of money: saying mass was punishable by a forfeiture of 200 marks; and hearing it by a forfeiture of 100l.

But during the present reign, the Roman Catholics have been in a great measure relieved from the odious and severe (if not unjust)

unjust) restrictions formerly imposed on them, by the statutes 18 Geo. III. c. 60. and 31 Geo. III. c. 22. to which, on account of their length and consequence, the reader is referred.

PAR. See *Exchange.*

PARAMOUNT, the supreme or highest lord of the fee. This seigniory of a *lord paramount,* is frequently termed an *honour,* and not a manor; especially, if it have belonged to an ancient feudal baron, or hath been at any time in the hands of the crown. 2 *Black.* 91.

PARAPHERNALIA, are the woman's apparel, jewels, and other things, which, in the life time of her husband, she wore as the ornaments of her person, to be allowed by the discretion of the court, according to the quality of her and her husband. The husband cannot devise such ornaments and jewels of his wife; though during his life, he hath power to dispose of them. But if she continue in the use of them till his death, she shall afterwards retain them against his executors and administrators, legatees, and all other persons, except creditors where there is a deficiency of assets. 2 *Black.* 436.

PARCELS. See *Portcrage.*

PARCENERS, persons holding lands in copartnership, and who may be compelled to make division. See *Coparceners.*

PARCHMENT. See *Stamps.*

PARCO FRACTO, a writ that lies against him who violently breaks a pound, and takes out beasts, which for some trespass done were legally impounded.

PARDON, is the remitting or forgiving a felony or other offence committed against the king.

Blackstone mentions the power of pardoning offences to be one of the greatest advantages of monarchy in general, above every other form of government; and which cannot subsist in democracies. Its utility and necessity are defended by him, on all those principles which do honour to human nature. See 4 *Black.* 396.

Pardons are either general or special; *general* as by act of parliament; of which, if they are without exceptions, the court must take notice *ex officio*; but if there are exceptions therein, the party must aver, that he is none of the persons excepted. 3 *Inst.* 233.

Special pardons, are either of course, as to persons convicted of manslaughter, or *se defendendo*, and by several statutes to those who shall discover their accomplices in several felonies; or of grace, which are by the king's charter, of which the court cannot take notice *ex officio*, but they must be pleaded. 3 *Inst.* 233.

A pardon may be *conditional*, that is the king may extend his mercy upon what terms he pleases; and may annex to his bounty a condition either precedent or subsequent, on the performance whereof, the validity of the pardon will depend; and this by the common law. 2 *Haw.* 37.

All pardons must be under the great seal. The effect of a pardon, is to make the offender a new man; to acquit him of all corporal penalties and forfeitures annexed to that offence, and to give him a new credit and capacity: but nothing but an act of parliament can restore or purify the blood after an attainder.

PARENTS AND CHILDREN, if parents run away, and leave their children at the charge of the parish, the churchwardens and overseers, by order of the justices, may seize the rents, goods, aud chattels of such parents, and dispose thereof towards their children's maintenance.

A parent may lawfully correct his child, being under age, in a reasonable manner: but the legal power of the father over the persons of his children, ceaseth at the age of twenty-one. 1 *Black.* 452. See *Father and Son.*

PARISH, signifies the precinct of a parish-church, and the particular charge of a secular priest. These districts are computed to be near ten thousand in number. 2 *Black.* 112.

PARISH CLERK, in every parish, the parson, vicar, &c. hath a parish-clerk under him, who is the lowest officer of the church. These were formerly clerks in orders, and their business at first was to officiate at the altar, for which they had a competent maintenance by offerings; but now they are laymen, and have certain fees with the parson, on christenings, marriages, burials, &c. besides wages for their maintenance.

PARISHIONER, an inhabitant of or belonging to any parish, *lawfully* settled therein.

Parishioners are a body politic to many purposes; as to vote at at a vestry if they pay scot and lot; and they have a sole right to raise taxes for their own relief, without the interposition of any superior court; may make bye-laws to mend the highways; and to make banks to keep out the sea, and for repairing the church, and making a bridge, &c. or any such thing for the public good.

PARK, a piece of ground inclosed, and stored with wild beasts of chase, which a man may have by prescription, or the king's grant.

By 16 Geo. III. c. 30. if any person shall pull down or destroy the pale or wall of a park, he shall forfeit 30l.

PARKBOTE, is to be quit of inclosing a *park*, or any part thereof.

PARLIAMENT, the parliament is the legislative branch of the supreme power of Great Britain, consisting of the king, the lords spiritual and temporal, and the knights, citizens, burgesses, representatives of the commons of the realm, in parliament assembled.

The power and jurisdiction of parliament, is so transcendent and absolute that it cannot be confined, either for causes or persons, within any bounds. 4 *Inst.* 36.

The house of commons is a denomination given to the lower house of parliament. In a free state, every man, who is supposed a free agent, ought to be in some measure his own governor; and therefore a branch at least of the legislative power should reside in the whole body of the people. In elections for representatives for Great Britain, anciently, all the people had votes; but king Henry VI. to avoid tumults, first appointed that none should vote for knights but such as were freeholders, did reside in the county, and had forty shillings yearly revenue. In so large a state as ours, therefore, it is very wisely contrived, that the people should do that by their representatives, which it is impracticable to perform in person; representatives chosen by a number of minute and separate districts, wherein all the voters are or may be easily distinguished. The counties are therefore represented by knights, elected by the proprietors of lands; the cities and boroughs are represented by citizens and burgesses, chosen by the mercantile, or supposed trading interest of the nation.

The

The peculiar laws and customs of the house of commons, relate principally to the raising of taxes, and the elections of members to serve in parliament.

The method of making laws is nearly the same in both houses. In the house of commons, in order to bring in the bill, if the relief sought be of a private nature, it is first necessary to prefer a petition; which must be presented by a member, and usually set forth a grievance required to be remedied. This petition, when founded on facts of a disputable nature, is referred to a committee of members, who examine the matter alledged, and accordingly report it to the house; and then, (or otherwise upon the mere petition), leave is given to bring in the bill. In *public* matters, the bill is brought in upon motion made to the house, without any petition.

If the bill begin in the house of lords, if of a *private* nature, it is referred to two judges, to make report.

After the second reading, the bill is said to be *committed*, that is, referred to a committee; which is selected by the house, in matters of small importance; or upon a bill of consequence, the house resolves itself into a committee of the whole house. A committee of the whole house, is composed of every member: and to form it, the speaker quits the chair, and may consequently sit and debate upon the merits of it as a private member, another member being appointed chairman for the time. In these committees the bill is usually debated clause by clause, amendments made, and sometimes it is intirely new modelled. Upon the third reading, further amendments are sometimes made; and if a new clause be added, it is done by tacking a separate piece of parchment on the bill which is called a rider. 1 *Black.* 182.

The royal assent may be given two ways; 1. in person, when the king comes to the house of peers, in his crown and royal robes, and sending for the commons to the bar, the titles of all the bills that have passed both houses are read; and the king's answer is declared by the clerk of the parliament. If the king consent to a public bill, the clerk usually declares, *le roy le veut*, the king wills it so to be; if to a private bill, *soit fait comme il est desiré*, be it as it is desired. If the king refuse his assent, it is in the gentle language of *le roy s'avisera*, the king will advise upon it. When a bill of supply is passed, it is carried up and presented

presented to the king by the speaker of the house of commons; and the royal assent is thus expressed, *le roy remercie ses loyal ujets, accepte leur benevolence, et aussi le veut*; the king thanks his loyal subjects, accepts their benevolence, and also wills it so to be. By the stat 33 H. VIII. c. 21. the king may give his assent by letters patent under his great seal, signed with his hand, and notified in his absence to both houses assembled together in the upper house. And when the bill has received the royal assent in either of these ways, it is then, and not before, a statute or act of parliament.

An act of parliament thus made, is the exercise of the highest authority that this kingdom acknowledges upon the earth. It hath power to bind every subject in the land, and the dominions thereunto belonging; nay even the king himself, if particularly named therein. And it cannot be altered, amended, dispensed with, suspended, or repealed, but in the same forms, and by the same authority of parliament.

Adjournment is no more than a continuance of the session from one day to another, as the word itself signifies; and this is done by the authority of each house separately every day, or for a longer period; but the adjournment of one house, is no adjournment of the other. 1 *Black.* 186.

Prorogation, is the continuance of the parliament from one sessions to another, as an adjournment is a continuation of the session from day to day. And this is done by the royal authority, expressed either by the lord chancellor, in his majesty's presence, or by commission from the crown, or frequently by proclamation, and by this, both houses are prorogued at the same time; it not being a prorogation of the house of lords or commons, but of the parliament. The session is never understood to be at an end, until a prorogation; though unless some act be passed, or some judgment given in parliament, it is in truth, no session at all. *Id.*

A dissolution is the civil death of the parliament; and this may be effected three ways; 1. by the king's will expressed either in person or representation; 2. by the demise of the crown; 3. by length of time.

By the king's will; for as the king has the sole right of convening the parliament, so also it is a branch of the royal prerogative, that

that he may, whenever he please, prorogue the parliament for a time, or put a final period to its existence.

By the demise of the crown, this dissolution formerly happened immediately upon the death of the reigning sovereign; but the calling a new parliament immediately on the inauguration of the successor being found inconvenient, and dangers being apprehended from having no parliament in being, in case of a disputed succession; it was enacted by statutes 7 & 8 W. III. c. 15 and 6 Anne. c. 7. that the parliament in being, shall continue for six months after the death of any king or queen, unless sooner prorogued or dissolved by the successor. That if the parliament be, at the time of the king's death, separated by adjournment or prorogation, it shall notwithstanding assemble immediately: and that if no parliament is then in being, the members of the last parliament, shall assemble and be again a parliament.

Lastly, a parliament may be dissolved or expire by *length of time*.

The utmost extent of time that the same parliament was allowed to sit by the stat. of 6 W. c. 3. was *three* years; after the expiration of which, reckoning from the return of the first summons, the parliament was to have no longer continuance. But by stat. 1 Geo. I. c. 38. in order, *professedly*, to prevent the great and continued expences of frequent elections, and the violent heats and animosities consequent thereupon, and for the peace and security of the government just then recovering from the late rebellion, this term was prolonged to *seven* years. So that as our constitution now stands, the parliament must expire, or die a natural death, at the end of every seventh year, if not sooner dissolved by the royal prerogative. See *Election*.

Parliament, the high court of; is the supreme court of the kingdom, not only for the making, but also for the execution of laws, by the trial of great and enormous offenders, whether lords or commoners, in the method of parliamentary impeachment. An impeachment before the lords, by the commons of Great Britain in parliament, is a prosecution of the already known and established law, and has been frequently put in practice; being a presentment to the most high and supreme court of criminal jurisdiction by the most solemn grand inquest of the whole kingdom. A commoner cannot, however, be impeached before the

the lords for any capital offence, but only for high misdemeanors; a peer may be impeached for any crime. And they usually, in case of an impeachment of a peer for treason, address the crown to appoint a lord high steward, for the greater dignity and regularity of their proceedings; which high steward was formerly elected by the peers themselves, though he was generally commissioned by the king; but it hath of late years been strenuously maintained, that the appointment of a high steward in such cases, is not indispensably necessary, but the house may proceed without one. The articles of impeachment, are a kind of bills of indictment, found by the house of commons, and afterwards tried by the lords; who are in cases of misdemeanors considered not only as their own peers, but as the peers of the whole nation.

PAROLE, a term signifying any thing done verbally or by word of mouth, in contradistinction to what is written; thus an agreement may be by parole. Evidence also, may be divided into parole evidence and written evidence. A parole release is good to discharge a debt by simple contract. 2 *Show.* 417. The holder of a bill of exchange, may authorize another to indorse his name upon it.

PAROLE ARREST, any justice of the peace may, by word of mouth, authorize any one to arrest another, who is guilty of a breach of the peace in his presence. *Dalt.* 117.

PAROLE DEMURRER, a privilege allowed an infant, who is sued concerning lands which came to him by descent; and the court thereupon will give judgment *quod loquela prædicta remaneat quosque*, the infant come to the age of twenty-one years.

PAROLE EVIDENCE. See *Evidence*.

PARRICIDE, is properly, he who kills his father, and may be applied to him who kills his mother.

PARSON, signifies the rector of a church. He is in himself a body corporate, in order to protect and defend the rights of the church by a perpetual succession. When a parson is instituted and inducted into a rectory, he is then, and not before, in full and complete possession. 1 *Black.* 391.

PARSONAGE, or *rectory*, is a spiritual living, composed of land, tithe, and other oblations of the people, separated or dedicated to God, in any congregation for the service of his church there,

there, and for the maintenance of the minister, to whose charge the same is committed.

PARTES FINIS NIHIL HABERUNT, an exception taken against a fine levied. 3 *Rep.* 88.

PARTIES, are those which are named in a deed or fine, as parties to it. See *Fine.*

PARTITION, is a dividing of lands descended by the common law or custom, among coheirs or parceners, where there are two at the least.

PARTNERS. See *Copartnership.*

PART-OWNERS, are partners interested and possessed of certain shares in a ship. Owners are tenants in common with each other; but one or more joint owners refusing to contribute their quota to the outfit of the vessel, cannot prevent her from going to sea against the consent of the majority of the owners, who, giving security in the admiralty, may freight the ship at their own exclusive risk, by which the smaller dissentient number of owners will be excluded at once from any share, either in the risk or in the profits.

PASCAL RENTS, rents or annual duties paid by the inferior clergy to the bishop or archdeacon, at their Easter visitation.

PASSAGE, in stat. 4 Ed. III. c. 7. this term is used for the hire a man pays for being transported by any sea or river. Various statutes of a local nature have been passed for regulating the passage of particular rivers. By a statute of Edward the Fourth, the passage from Kent to Calais is restrained to Dover.

PASSPORT, is a license for the safe passage of any person from one port to another.

PASTURE, is generally any place where cattle may feed. See *Common.*

PATENT. See *Letters Patent.*

PATRON, both in the canon and common law, signifies him that hath the gift of a benefice.

PAUPER. See *Forma Pauperis.*

PAWN-BROKERS, on account of the length of the acts on this subject, we are precluded partly by want of room, and the little interest they may be of to our readers, from going particularly into them, but refer to the last acts, viz. 39 & 40 Geo. III. c. 99.

PAYMENT,

PAYMENT, is the consideration or purchase-money for goods, and may be made by the buyer giving to the seller the price agreed upon, either by bill or note, or by money. Where a day certain is appointed for payment, the party bound, shall be allowed till the last moment of the day to pay it in, if it be an inland bill. 4 T. R. 173.

Payment of money before the day, is in law, payment at the day; for it cannot, in presumption of law, be any prejudice to him to whom the payment is made, to have his money before the time; and it appears by the party's receipt of it, that it is for his own advantage to receive it then. 5 *Co.* 117. See *Acquittance, Discharge, Release.*

PEACE, in law, signifies a quiet and harmless behaviour towards the king and his people.

The king, by his office and dignity royal, is the principal conservator of the peace within all his dominions; and may give authority to any other to see the peace kept, and to punish such as break it; hence it is usually called the king's peace. All the great officers of state, are generally conservators of the peace, throughout the kingdom, and may commit all breakers of it, or bind them in recognizance to keep it. Also the sheriff, coroner, constables, and tithingmen, are conservators of the peace within their own jurisdiction, and may apprehend all breakers of the peace, and commit them till they find sureties to keep the peace. 1 *Black.* 350.

PEACE-OFFICERS, actions against peace-officers made local. 21 Jac. I. c. 12.

PECULIAR, signifies a particular parish or church that hath jurisdiction within itself, for probate of wills, &c. exempt from the ordinary, and the bishop's court.

The *court of peculiars,* is that which deals in certain parishes, lying in several dioceses; which parishes are exempt from the jurisdiction of the bishops of those dioceses, and are peculiarly belonging to the archbishop of Canterbury, within whose province there are 57 such peculiars.

PEDLARS. See *Hawkers.*

PEERS, in our common law, are those who are impannelled in an inquest upon any man, for the convicting or clearing him of any offence, for which he is called in question; and the reason thereof is, because the course and custom of our nation is, to try every man in such a case by his equals, or *peers*.

PEERS OF THE REALM, are the nobility of the kingdom, and lords of parliament; who are divided into dukes, marquisses, earls, viscounts, and barons; and the reason why they are called peers, is, because notwithstanding there is a distinction of dignities in our nobility, yet in all public actions they are equal; as in their votes of parliament, and in passing upon the trial of any nobleman.

It seems clearly, that the right of peerage was originally territorial; that is, annexed to lands, houses, castles, and the like; the proprietors and possessors of which were, in right of those estates, allowed to be peers of the realm, and were summoned in parliament to do suit and service to their sovereign; and, when the land was alienated, the dignity passed with its appendant. Thus the bishops sit still in the house of lords in right of succession to certain ancient baronies annexed, or supposed to be annexed, to their episcopal lands.

But afterwards, as alienations grew frequent, the dignity of peerage was confined to the lineage of the party enobled, and instead of territorial, became personal. Actual proof of a tenure by barony became no longer necessary to constitute a lord of par liament; but the record of the writ of summons to him, or his ancestors, was admitted as a sufficient evidence of the tenure.

Peers are now created either by writ, or patent; for those who claim by prescription must suppose either a writ or patent made to their ancestors, though by length of time it may be lost. The *creation by writ* or the king's letter, is a summons to attend the house of peers, by the stile and title of that barony, which the king is pleased to confer; *that by patent*, is a royal grant to a subject of any dignity and degree of peerage. The creation *by writ*, is the more ancient way; but a man is not enobled thereby, unless he actually take his seat in the house of lords; and therefore the most usual, because the surest way, is to grant the dignity by patent, which ensures to a man and his heirs, according to the limitations thereof, though he never himself make use of it. 1 *Black*. 399.

In criminal cases, a nobleman is tried by his peers. Peers shall have the benefit of clergy for the first offence of felony, without

without being burned in the hand. 1 Ed. VI. c. 11. See *Parliament*, and *High Court of Parliament*.

PEERESS, as we have noblemen, so we have noblewomen, and these may be by creation, descent, or marriage.

PENAL LAWS or STATUTES, having been made on many occasions, to punish and deter offenders, they ought to be construed *strictly*, and not be extended by equity, but the words of them may be interpreted beneficially according to the intent of the legislators. 1 *Inst.* 54.

PENALTY, is a forfeiture inflicted for not complying with the regulations of certain acts of parliament: a penalty is also annexed to secure the performance of certain covenants in a deed, articles of agreement, copartnership, &c. In a bond also for payment of money, it is usual to annex a penalty in double the amount of the obligation. See *Bond*.

PENANCE, a punishment by which a penitent is obliged to give public satisfaction to the church for the scandal he hath given by evil example.

PENSION, no person having a pension from the crown, during pleasure, or for any term of years, is capable of being elected a member of the house of commons. 1 *Black.* 176.

To receive a pension from a foreign prince or state, without leave of the king, has been held to be criminal, because it may incline a man to prefer the interest of such foreign prince to that of his own country. 1 *Haw.* 58.

PENSIONS OF CHURCHES, certain sums of money paid to clergymen in lieu of tithes.

PENSIONS OF THE INNS OF COURT, are certain annual payments of each member to the house.

PEREMPTORY, a final and determinate act, without hope of renewing or altering.

PERJURY, is a crime committed when a lawful oath is administered, by any one who hath authority, to a person in any judicial proceeding, who swears wilfully, absolutely, and falsely, in a matter material to the issue or cause in question, by his own act, or by the subornation of others. To constitute perjury, it is essential that the oath be *wilfully* taken; that it be in a judicial proceeding, or some other public proceeding of a similar nature: the oath must be taken before persons lawfully authorized to administer it, and also by a person sworn to depose the truth; it must also be taken absolutely and directly, and upon something material to the point in issue.

It is not material whether the false oath were credited or not, or whether the party in whose prejudice it was taken, was in the event damaged by it; for the prosecution is not grounded upon the damage, but on the abuse of public justice; neither is it material whether the thing sworn, be true or false.

By stat. 5 Eliz. c. 9. persons guilty of perjury, or subornation of perjury, are to be punished with one year's imprisonment, and stand in the pillory where the offence was committed. This offence is also punished by transportation.

PERMIT, a licence or warrant for persons to pass with or sell goods, having paid the duties of customs and excise.

PER MY ET PER TOUT, a joint tenant is said to be seized of land he holds jointly *per my et per tout,* that is by every parcel and the whole.

PERNOR OF PROFITS, he who takes or receives the profits.

PERPETUATING the testimony of witnesses, is, where the witnesses are old and infirm, and one of the parties institutes a suit to perpetuate their testimony; for it may be, a man's antagonist only waits for the death of some of them to begin his suit.

PERPETUITY, is, where if all that have interest join in the conveyance, yet they cannot bar or pass the estate; for, if by concurrence of all having interest, the estate may be barred, it is no perpetuity. 1 *Chan. Ca.* 213.

PERQUISITE, any thing acquired by a man's own industry, or purchased with his own money.

PERQUISITES OF COURTS, are the profits which grow to a lord of a manor, by virtue of his court baron, over and above the certain yearly profits of his land; as fines of copyholds, heriots, amerciaments, waifs, strays, &c.

PERSONABLE, one enabled to maintain plea in court; as, the defendant was judged *personable* to maintain his action.

PERSONAL, any moveable thing belonging to a man, be it quick or dead, as chattels *personal,* &c.

PERSONAL ACTION. See *Action.*

PERSONAL

PERSONAL TITHES, tithes paid of such profits as come by the labour of a man's person, as by buying and selling, gains of merchandize, and handicrafts, &c.

PERSONALITY, an action is in the *personality*, where it is brought against the right person, or the person against whom in law it lies.

PERSONATE, is the representing a person by a fictitious or assumed character, so as to pass for the person *represented*. Personating bail, is by stat. 21 Jac. I. c, 26. a capital felony. By various other statutes, personating seamen entitled to wages, prize-money, &c. is also a capital felony. See *Fraud.*

PETITION, no petition to the king, or to either house of parliament, for any alteration in church or state, shall be signed by above twenty persons, unless the matter thereof be approved, by three justices of the peace, or the major part of the grand jury in the country; and in London by the lord mayor, aldermen, and common council: nor shall any petition be presented by more than ten persons at a time.

PETITION IN CHANCERY, a request in writing, directed to the lord chancellor or master of the rolls, shewing some matter or cause, whereupon the petitioner prays somewhat to be granted him.

PETITION OF RIGHT. See 3 Car. I. c. 1.

PETTY or PETIT LARCENY. See *Larceny.*

PETTY SESSION. See *Sessions of the Peace.*

PETTY or PETIT TREASON. See *Treason.*

PEWS, in a church, are somewhat of the nature of heir-looms, which may descend by custom immemorial, from the ancestor to the heir, without any ecclesiastical concurrence 2 *Black.* 429.

PHEASANTS AND PARTRIDGES. See *Game.*

PHYSICIANS, no person within London, nor within seven miles of the same, shall exercise as a physician or surgeon, except he be examined and approved by the bishop of London, or by the dean of St. Paul's, calling to them four doctors of physic, and for surgery, other expert persons in that faculty, of them that have been approved; upon the pain of forfeiture for every month 5l. one half to the king, and the other half to any that will sue. 3 H. VIII. c. 11.

One that has taken his degree of doctor of physic in either

of the universities, may not practice in London, and within seven miles of the same, without licence from the college of physicians.

And it hath been holden, that if a person, not duly authorized to be a physician or surgeon, undertake a cure, and the patient die under his hands, he is guilty of felony; but he is not excluded from the benefit of clergy.

PIE-POWDER COURT. See *Fairs.*

PIGEONS, every person who shall shoot at, kill, or destroy a pigeon, may be committed to the common goal for three months, by two justices of the peace, or pay 20s. to the poor, 1 Jac. I. c. 27.

PILLORY, a very ancient instrnment of punishment in this kingdom: and they that have been adjudged to the pillory, are infamous, and not to be received as jurors or witnesses. 3 *Inst.* 219.

PILOT, all pilots must be examined and approved by the Trinity House. 3 Geo. I. c. 13.

For government of the pilots of the Trinity House at Deptford, see 5 Geo. II. c. 30.

PIPE, a roll in the exchequer, otherwise called the *great roll.*

PIRATE, one who maintains himself by pillage and robbing at sea.

By stat. 28 H. VIII. c. 15. all treasons, felonies, robberies, murders, and confederacies committed upon the sea, or in any haven, creek, or place, where the admiral hath jurisdiction, shall be tried in such shires, or places, as the king shall appoint by his commission, in like forms, as if such offence had been committed upon land, and according to the course of the common law, and the offenders shall suffer death without benefit of clergy.

And by stat. 6 Geo. I. made perpetual, it is enacted, that if any of his majesty's natural born subjects or denizens of this kingdom, shall commit any piracy or robbery, or any act of hostility, against other his majesty's subjects upon the sea, under colour of any commission from any prince or state, or pretence of authority from any person whatsoever; such offender shall be deemed to be a pirate, felon, and robber: and being duly convicted thereof

thereof according to this act, or the aforesaid act of 23 H. VIII. shall have and suffer such pains of death, loss of lands, goods, and chattels, as pirates, felons, and robbers, upon the seas ought to have and suffer.

By 18 Geo. II. c. 30. persons committing hostilities, or aiding enemies at sea, may be tried as pirates. Piracies at sea, are excepted out of the general pardon, by 20 Geo II. c. 52.

PIRATE'S GOODS, go to the admiral by grant, but not piratical goods, which go to the king, if the owner be not known.

PISCARY, is a right of fishing in another man's waters.

PLACE, where a fact was committed, is to be alledged in appeals of death, indictments, &c. and *place* is considerable in pleadings in some cases.

PLACITA, pleas, or pleading, or debates and trials at law.

PLAGUE. See *Quarantine.*

PLAINT, is the exhibiting any action personal or real in writing, and the party making this plaint, is called the plaintiff.

PLANTATIONS, colonies in distant countries; and are either such where the lands are claimed by right of occupancy only, by finding them desart and uncultivated, and peopling them from the mother country; or where, when already cultivated, they have been either gained by conquest, or ceded by treaties.

PLAYS AND GAMES. See *Gaming.*

PLEA, that which either party alleges for himself in court. These are divided into pleas of the crown and common pleas. *Pleas* of the crown, are all suits in the king's name, against offences committed against his crown and dignity, or against his crown and peace. *Common-pleas,* are those that are held between common persons.

Common-pleas, are either dilatory or pleas to the action.

Pleas Dilatory, are such as tend merely to delay, or put off the suit, by questioning the propriety of the remedy, rather than by denying the injury.

Pleas to the action, are such as dispute the very cause of suit. 3 *Black.* 301. See *Tidd's K. B. Practice.*

PLEADINGS, pleadings in general, signify the allegations of parties to suits when they are put into a proper and legal form; and are distinguished in respect to the parties who plead them,

by

by the names of bars, replications, rejoinders, sur-rejoinders, rebutters, sur-rebutters, &c. and though the matter in the declaration or court does not properly come under the name of pleading, yet, being often comprehended in the extended sense of the word, it is generally considered under this head. 4 *Bac. Abr.* 1. See *Tidd's K. B. Practice.*

PLEDGERY, suretyship.

PLEGIIS ACQUIETANDIS, a writ that formerly lay for a surety against him for whom he is surety, if he did not pay the money at the day. F. N. B. 137.

PLENARTY, is used in the common law in matters of benefices, and where a church is full of an incumbent; in such cases *plenarty* and vacation are direct contraries.

PLENE ADMINISTRAVIT, a plea pleaded by an executor or administrator, where they have administered the deceased's estate faithfully and justly before the action brought against them.

PLOUGH-BOTE, a right of tenants to take wood to repair ploughs, carts, and harrows.

PLOUGH-SILVER, was money anciently paid by some tenants, in lieu of service to plough the lord's land.

PLURALITY. If any person having one benefice with cure of souls of 8l. a year in the king's books, shall accept another of whatsoever value, and be instituted and inducted into the same, the former benefice shall be void; unless he have a dispensation from the archbishop of Canterbury who hath power to grant dispensations to chaplains of noblemen and other under proper qualifications, to hold two livings, provided they be not more than thirty miles distant from each other, and provided, that he reside in each, for a reasonable time every year, and that he keep a sufficient curate in that wherein he doth not ordinarily reside.

POISONING, is the most detestable of all kinds of murder; because it is most horrible and fearful to the nature of man, and of all others can be least prevented, either by resistance or foresight. See *Murder* under the article *Homicide.*

POLICE, is applied to the internal regulations of large cities and towns, particularly of the metropolis.

POLICY OF INSURANCE. See *Insurance Marine.*

POLL MONEY, a tax ordained by act of parliament. 18 & 19 Car. II. c. 1. & 5.

POLYGAMY, is where a man marries two or wore wives together; or a woman who has two or more husbands at the same time.

PONE, if a replevin be sued by a writ out of chancery, then if the plaintiff or defendant will move the plaint out of the county into the common-pleas or king's-bench, he ought to sue a writ out of the chancery, which is called a *pone*.

PONENDIS IN ASSIS, a writ to shew what persons, sheriffs ought to empanel upon assizes and juries, and what not; as also what number.

PONENDUM SIGILLUM AD EXCEPTIONEM, a writ whereby the king requires the justices, to put the seals to the exceptions exhibited by the defendant against the plaintiff's declarations, or against the evidence, verdict, or other proceedings before the justices.

PONTIBUS REPARANDIS, a writ directed to the sheriff, &c. requiring him to charge one or more to repair a bridge to whom it belongeth.

POOR. Where the last legal settlement of the father of a legitimate child is not known, the child may be sent to the place of its birth, as well as an illegitimate one. *Blackerby*. 246.

A legitimate child, shall necessarily follow the settlement of its parents as a nurse child or as part of the family, only till it be *seven* years of age; and after that age, it shall not be removed as part of the father's family; but with an adjudication of the place of its own legal settlement, as being deemed capable at that age of having gained a settlement of his own.

By the 13 & 14 Car. II c. 12. on complaint by the church-wardens or overseers of the poor, within 40 days after any person shall come to settle in any parish, or any tenement under 10l. a year, two justices, (one of the quorum) may remove him to the place where he was last legally settled, either as a native, householder, sojourner, apprentice, or servant, for the space of 40 days at the least.

If a person be bound apprentice by indenture, wherever he continues 40 days in the service of his master or mistress, there such apprentice gains a settlement; and where any person serves the

the last forty days of his apprenticeship, that is the place of his last legal settlement.

The 8 & 9 W. c. 30. explains, that as some doubts had arisen touching the settlement of unmarried persons, not having child or children, lawfully hired into any parish or town for *one year*, it was enacted, that no such person so hired as aforesaid, should be deemed to have a good settlement in any such parish or township, unless such person should continue and abide in such service, during the space of one whole year.

A general hiring, without any particular time agreed upon, is construed to be an hiring for a year, and therefore sufficient.

It is not the terms of the hiring, but the intention that is the criterion; for though a servant be hired for so much per week, yet if it be understood at the time, that he is to continue for the year, if approved of, it is equal to an hiring for a year.

A woman marrying an husband who has a known settlement, shall follow her husband's settlement.

The act of 9 & 10 W. c. 11. doth not require a person renting a tenement of 10l. a year, to occupy it: it is enough if he rent it and reside 40 days in the parish.

Poor-rate. The 43 Eliz. c. 2. enacts, that the churchwardens and overseers of the poor of every parish, or the greater part of them, shall raise weekly or otherwise (by taxation of every inhabitant, parson, vicar, and other, and of every occupier of lands, houses, tithes, mines, or saleable underwoods in the said parish) a convenient stock of flax, hemp, wool, thread, iron, and other ware and stuff, to set the poor on work: and also competent sums for the necessary relief of the lame, impotent, old, blind, and such other among them being poor as are not able to work, and also for the putting out poor children apprentices.

The concurrence of the inhabitants in making a rate is not necessary; for the churchwardens and overseers, with the consent of two justices, may make one without them.

The occupier of an house, or of an estate, ought to be rated according to its full value, with all its improvements; and not according to the price which he may have paid for it, without taking into the account the value of the improvements. K v. *Mast. Hill.* 35 Geo. III.

The 9 Geo. I. c. 7. enacts, that the churchwardens and overseers,

seers, in any parish, township, or place, with the consent of the major part of the parishioners or inhabitants, in vestry, or other parish or public meeting for that purpose assembled, or of so many of them as shall be so assembled, upon usual notice thereof first given, may purchase or hire any house or houses, in the same parish, township, or place, and contract with any person or persons, for the lodging, keeping, maintaining, and employing, any or all such poor in their respective parishes, townships, or places, as shall desire to receive relief or collection, and there to keep, maintain, and employ them, and take the benefit of the work, labour, and service, of any such poor persons, who shall be maintained in any such house or houses, for the better maintenance and relief of such poor persons who shall be there maintained. And any poor person who shall refuse to be lodged, kept, or maintained, in such house or houses shall be put out of the parish book, and shall not be entitled to receive relief from the churchwardens and overseers.

By stat. 3 W. c. 11. there shall be provided and kept in every parish, a book wherein the names of all persons who receive collection, shall be registered, with the day and year when they were first admitted to have relief, and the occasion which brought them under that necessity, and yearly in Easter week, or as often as shall be thought convenient, the commissioners shall meet in the vestry or other usual place of meeting in the parish, before whom the book shall be produced, and all other persons receiving collections to be called over, and the reasons of their taking relief examined, and a new list made and entered, of such persons as they shall allow and think fit to receive collections.

The churchwardens and overseers, shall within four days after the end of their year, and other overseers nominated, make and yield up to two justices, a true and perfect account, of all sums by them received, and of such stock as shall be in their hands, or in the hands of any of the poor to work, and of all other things concerning their office; and such sums of money as shall be in their hands, shall pay and deliver over to their successors. 43 Eliz. c. 2.

If any action shall be brought against any justice or constable, or against any churchwarden or overseer, or other person, who in their aid or by their command shall do any thing concerning their offices,

offices, he may plead the general issue, and give the special matter in evidence; and if a verdict shall pass for him, or the plaintiff be nonsuit, or suffer discontinuance, he shall have double costs. And such action shall be laid in the county where the fact was committed and not elsewhere. 7 & 21 Jac. c. 5 & 7.

POPERY. See *Papists*.

POPULAR ACTION, an action given in general to any person who will sue for a penalty on the breach of some penal statute.

PORT, an harbour or place of shelter, where ships arrive with their freight, and customs for goods are taken.

PORTERAGE, by stat. 39 G. III. c. 58, no innkeeper, warehouse-keeper, or other person, to whom any box, basket, package, parcel, truss, game, or other thing whatsoever, not exceeding fifty-six pounds weight, or any porter or other person employed by such inn-keeper, warehouse-keeper, or other person, in porterage, or delivery of any such box, parcel, &c. within the cities of London, Westminster, or Borough of Southwark, and their respective suburbs, and other parts contiguous, not exceeding half a mile from the end of the carriage pavement, in the several streets and places within the abovementioned limits, shall ask or demand, or receive or take, in respect of such porterage or delivery any greater rate or price than as follows:

Not exceeding a	quarter of a mile	*three-pence.*
....	half a mile	*four-pence.*
....	one mile	*six-pence*
....	one mile and a half	*eight-pence*
....	two miles	*ten-pence.*

For every further distance, not exceeding half a mile, three-pence additional.

Persons asking or receiving more than the above rates, shall for every such offence, forfeit a sum not exceeding 20s. nor less than 5s.

PORTGREVE, a magistrate in certain sea-port towns, with authority something similar to that of a mayor. See *Mayor*.

PORTION, that part or share of a person's estate, which was given or left to a child. See *Legacy*.

PORTIONER, where a parsonage is served by two or sometimes three ministers alternately, the ministers are called portioners,

ers, because they have but their portion, or proportion of the tithes or profits of the living.

PORT-TOLL, a payment for the liberty of bringing goods into a port.

POSSE, signifies a possibility, as *esse* signifies a thing in being. See *Esse*.

POSSE COMITATUS, the power of the county.

POSSESSION is two-fold, actual, and in law; *actual* possession, is, when a man actually enters into lands and tenements to him descended. *Possession in law*, is, when the lands or tenements are descended to a man, and he hath not as yet actually entered into them. *Staundf.* 198.

POSSIBILITY IN LAW, is defined to be an uncertain thing, which may or may not happen.

POST DIEM, a fee by way of penalty upon a sheriff for his neglect in returning a writ after the day assigned for its return.

POST DISSEISIN, a writ for him that having recovered land or tenements by *præcipe quod reddat*, upon default of reddition is again disseized by the former disseisor.

POSTEA, is the return of the proceedings by nisi prius into the court of common pleas after a verdict, and there afterwards recorded. *Plowd.* 211.

POSTERIORITY, a man holding lands or tenements of two lords, holds of his *ancienter* lord by *priority*, and of his latter lord by *posteriority*.

POST FINE, a duty to the king, for a fine formerly acknowledged before him in his court, which is paid by the cognizee, after the same is fully passed, and all things performed touching the same.

POSTHUMOUS CHILDREN, children born after the decease of their father.

A posthumous child, either of the whole, or half blood, shall take under the statute of distribution. 1 *Vez.* 156. 10 & 11 W. c. 16.

POST NATI, children of persons attainted of treason, born after the king's pardon, may inherit lands; though not those born before. *Co. Lit.* 391.

POST-OFFICE, a general post-office erected 12 Car. II. c. 35, made perpetual and part of the general fund. 3 G. I. c. 7.

No action can be maintained against the postmaster-general for the loss of bills or articles sent in letters by the post, and lost.

Many attempts have been made by postmasters in country towns, to charge an half-penny or penny each letter, on delivery at the houses in the town above the parliamentary rates, under pretence that they were not obliged to carry letters out of the office gratis: but it has been repeatedly decided, that such demand is illegal, and that they are bound to deliver the letters to the inhabitants within the usual and established limits of the town, without any addition to the rate of postage. 5 *Bur.* 5709.

POUND, a common pound belongs to a lordship, or village, and there ought to be such a pound in every township, kept in repair by those who have used to do it time out of mind; the oversight whereof is to be by the constable or steward of the leet. See *Distress*.

POUND-BREACH. See *Distress*.

POURPARTY, to make *pourparty*, is to divide and sever the lands that fall to parceners.

POURPRESTURE, is where a man takes to himself or incroaches any thing that he ought not, whether it be in any jurisdiction, land, or franchise; and generally when any thing is done to the nuisance of the king's tenants. *Kitchin.* 10.

POURSUIVANT, signifies a king's messenger, and also an herald, called *poursuivant at arms*.

POWER, is an authority which one man gives to another to act for him; and it is sometimes a reservation which a person makes in a conveyance for himself to do some acts, as to make leases or the like. 2 *Lil. Abr.* 339.

POWER OF ATTORNEY, an instrument or deed, whereby a person is authorized to act for another, either generally, or in a specific transaction. See *Agent, Broker, Deed.*

POWER OF THE COUNTY, contains the aid and attendance of all knights, gentlemen, yeomen, labourers, servants, apprentices, and all others above the age of fifteen years within the county. This the sheriff at any time may raise to assist him in the execution of a precept of restitution. The power of the county is also called the *posse comitatus*.

PRACTICE, the law loves plain and fair practice, and will not countenance

countenance fraud in proceedings, nor suffer advantage to be taken thereby. 2 *Lil. Abr.* 342.

PRÆCIPE, a writ commanding the defendant to do the thing required, or to shew cause why he hath not done it. 274.

PRÆMUNIRE. This punishment is inflicted upon him who denies the king's supremacy the second time; upon him who affirms the authority of the pope, or refuses to take the oath of supremacy; upon such as are seditious talkers of the inheritance of the crown; and upon such as affirm that there is any obligation by any oath, covenant, or engagement whatsoever, to endeavour a change of government either in church or state; or that both or either house of parliament have or hath a legislative power without the king, &c.

The judgment in *præmunire* at the suit of the king, against the defendant being in prison, is, that he shall be out of the king's protection; that his lands and tenements, goods and chattels, shall be forfeited to the king; and that his body shall remain in prison at the king's pleasure; but if the defendant be condemned upon his default of not appearing, whether at the suit of the king or party, the same judgment shall be given as to the being out of the king's protection and the forfeiture; but instead of the clause that the body shall remain in prison, there shall be an award of a *capiatur*. *Co. Lit.* 129.

Upon an indictment of a *præmunire*, a peer of the realm shall not be tried by his peers. 12 *Co.* 92.

PRÆPOSITUS VILLÆ, is used sometimes for the constable of a town, or petit constable.

PRÆSENTARE AD ECCLESIAM, denotes the patron's placing an incumbent in the church.

PREAMBLE, the beginning of an act of parliament is called the *preamble*.

PREBEND, the portion which every prebendary of a cathedral church, receives in the right of his place for his maintenance.

PRECARIÆ, day's work, which the tenants of some manors were bound, by reason of their tenure, to do for their lord in harvest.

PRECEDENCE, the right to a station of honour, which all the nobility enjoy, each according to his rank.

PRECEDENTS, are examples or authorities to follow, in judg-

 ments

ments and determinations in the courts of justice, which have always been greatly regarded by the sages of the law.

PRECEPT, a command in writing, by a justice of the peace, or other officer, for bringing a person or records before him.

PRECONTRACT OF MARRIAGE, no suit shall be had in any ecclesiastical court, to compel the celebration of any marriage, by reason of any contract of marriage, either *per verba de praesenti*, or *per verba de futuro*: although formerly the spiritual judge would compel a contract of present marriage to be carried into execution. 2 G. I. c. 23.

PREDIAL TITHES, those which are paid of things arising and growing from the ground only, as corn, hay, fruit of trees and the like.

PREGNANCY, is a plea in stay of execution, when a woman is convicted of a capital crime, alledging that she is with child: in which case, the judge must direct a jury of twelve discreet women to enquire of the fact: and if they bring in their verdict *quick with child* (for *barely with child* is not sufficient) execution shall be stayed generally, till either she be delivered, or prove by the course of nature, not to have been with child. 4 *Black.* 395.

PREMISSES, is that part in the beginning of a deed, the office of which is to express the grantor and grantee, and the land or thing granted. 5 *Rep.* 55. See *Deed.*

PREMIUM. See *Insurance Marine.*

PRENDER DE BARON, is used as an exception to deprive a woman from pursuing an appeal of murder against the killer of her former husband. *Standf.* 59.

PREPENSED, or forethought. See *Homicide.*

PREROGATIVE, is a word of large extent, including all the rights and privileges which by law the king hath, as chief of the commonwealth, and as intrusted with the execution of the laws. 4 *Bac. Abr.* 149.

All jurisdiction exercised in these kingdoms that are in obedience to our king, is derived from the crown; and the laws, whether of a temporal, ecclesiastical, or military nature, are called his laws; and it is his prerogative to take care of the due execution of them. Hence all judges must derive their authority from the crown, by some commission warranted by law; and must ex-

ercise

ercise it in a lawful manner, and without any the least deviation from the known and stated forms.

The king, as the fountain of justice, hath an undoubted prerogative in erecting officers, and all officers are said to derive their authority mediately, or immediately from him: but though all such officers derive their authority from the crown, and from whence the king is termed the universal officer or disposer of justice, yet it hath been held, that he hath not the office in him to execute it himself, but is only to grant or nominate; nor can the king grant any new powers or privileges to any such officers, but they must execute their offices according to the rules established and prescribed them by law. *Co. Lit.* 114.

PREROGATIVE COURT, the court wherein all wills are proved, and all administrations taken which belong to the archbishop by his prerogative; that is in case where the deceased had goods of any considerable value out of the diocese wherein he died; and that value is ordinarily 5l. except it be otherwise by composition between the said archbishop and some other bishop, as in the diocese of London it is 10l. and if any contention grow between two or more, touching any such will or administration, the cause is properly debated and decided in this court. 4 *Inst.* 335.

PRESCRIPTION, is a title acquired by use and time, and allowed by the law.

PRESENTATION. See *Advowson.*

PRESENTMENT *of offences*, is that which the grand jury find of their own knowledge, and present to the court, without any bill of indictment laid before them at the suit of the king; as a presentment of a nuisance, a libel, and the like; upon which the officer of the court must afterwards frame an indictment, before the party presented can be put to answer it. There are also *presentments* by justices of the peace, constables, surveyors of the highways, churchwardens, &c.

PRESIDENT OF THE COUNCIL, an officer created by letters patent under the great seal *durante bene placito*, whose business is to attend upon the king, to propose business at the council table, and report to his majesty the transactions there.

PREST, a duty in money, to be paid by the sheriff upon his

 account,

account, in the exchequer; or for money left, or remaining in his hands.

PRESUMPTION, a supposition, opinion, or belief, previously formed.

PRESUMPTIVE HEIR, is one who if the ancestor should die immediately, would in the present circumstances of things be his heir, but whose right of inheritance may be defeated by the contingency of some nearer heir being born; as a brother, whose presumptive succession may be destroyed by the birth of a child; or a daughter whose present expectation may be cut off by the birth of a son. 2 *Black.* 208.

PRETENDER. See *Abjuration.*

PRETENSED RIGHT OR TITLE, is where a person is in possession of lands or tenements, and another who is out claims it, and sues for it; here the *pretensed right and title,* is said to be in him who claims and sues.

PRIMER FINE, a sum due to the king, on sueing out a *præcipe* or writ of covenant, in order to the levying a fine.

PRIMOGENITURE, the title of an elder brother in the right of his birth.

PRINCE, is sometimes taken at large for the king himself, but more properly for the king's eldest son, who is *prince of Wales.*

PRINCIPAL AND ACCESSARY, the principal is the person who actually commits any crime; and the accessary is he who is not the chief actor, but is somewhat concerned therein, either before or after the felony committed, assisting to him in the doing thereof. 2 *Lil. Abr.* 355.

PRIORITY, an antiquity of tenure, in comparison of another not so ancient, as *to hold by priority,* is to hold of a lord more anciently than that of another.

PRIORITY OF DEBTS AND SUIT, a prior suit depending, may be pleaded in abatement of a subsequent action or prosecution.

PRISONS, places of confinement for persons guilty of offences, or for debtors. Each county has a prison, where persons taken within its limits are committed. There are prisons also belonging to the courts of chancery, king's bench, common pleas, exchequer and marshalsea.

PRIVATEERS,

PRIVATEERS, private ships of war, sailing under commission from the admiralty.

PRIVATION, a taking away, applied to a bishop or rector of a church, when by death or other act, they are deprived of their bishopric, or benefice.

PRIVEMENT ENSIENT, is where a woman is with child by her husband, but not quick with child.

PRIVILEGE, a particular exemption from the operation of a law, or a certain exclusive right granted to an individual, either for a time permanent, or for a certain period. See *Arrest*.

PRIVY, one who is partaker, or hath an interest in any action or thing; as privies of blood.

PRIVY COUNCIL, is the principal council belonging to the king, and is generally called by way of eminence the *council*.

Privy counsellors are made by the king's nomination, without either patent or grant; and on taking the necessary oaths, they become immediately privy counsellors, during the life of the king that chooses them, but subject to removal at his discretion. No inconvenience now arises from the extension of the number of privy council, as those only attend, who are especially summoned for that particular occasion.

PRIVY SEAL, is a seal that the king uses to such grants, or other things, as pass the *great seal*.

PROBATE OF WILLS, is the exhibiting and proving wills and testaments before the ecclesiastical judges, delegated by the bishop, who is ordinary of the place where the party dies.

PROBATOR, an accuser, or approver, or one who undertakes to prove a crime charged upon another.

PROCEDENDO, a writ which lies where a cause is removed out of an inferior to a superior court.

PROCEDENDO AD JUDICIUM, lies when the judges of any court delay the party, plaintiff, or defendant, and will not give judgment in a cause, when they ought to do it. *Wood's Inst.* 570.

PROCEDENDO ON AID PRAYER. If a man pray in aid of the king, in a real action, and the aid be granted: it shall be awarded, that he sue to the king in chancery, and the justices in the common pleas shall stay until the writ of *procedendo de loquela* come unto them; and if it appear to the judges by pleading or shewing

shewing of the party, that the king hath interest in the land, or shall lose rent or service, &c. there the court ought to stay until they have from the king, a *procedendo in lequela*: and then they may proceed in the plea, until they come to judgment; when the justice ought not to proceed to judgment without a writ for that purpose.

PROCESS, is the manner of proceeding in every cause, being the writs and precepts that *proceed*, or go forth upon the original upon every action, being either original or judicial. *Britton*. 138.

Process is only meant to bring the defendant into court, in order to contest the suit, and abide the determination of the law. See *Impey's Practice*.

PROCHEIN AMY, is the next of kin to a child in his nonage, and is in that respect allowed by law to conduct and manage his affairs.

PROCLAMATION, a notice publicly given of any thing, whereof the king thinks fit to advertise his subjects.

PROCLAMATION OF A FINE, is a notice openly and solemnly given at all the assizes held in the county, within one year after the engrossing it.

PRO CONFESSO, where a bill is exhibited in chancery, to which the defendant appears, and is afterwards in contempt for not answering, or makes an insufficient answer, the matter contained in the bill shall be taken as if it were *confessed* by the defendant.

PROCTOR, he who undertakes to manage another man's cause, in any court of the civil law or ecclesiastical, for his fee.

PROCTORS OF THE CLERGY, are those who are chosen and appointed to appear for the cathedral or other collegiate churches, as also for the common clergy of every diocese at the parliament to be their representatives in *convocation*.

PROCURATIONS, certain sums of money paid yearly by the inferior clergy, to the bishop or archdeacon, for the charges of visitation.

PROFANENESS, a disrespect shewn to the name of God, and to things and persons consecrated to him. *Wood's Inst.* 396. See *Blasphemy*.

PROFER. The time appointed for the accounts of sheriffs, and other officers in the exchequer, which is twice in the year.

PROFERT

PROFERT IN CURIA, is where the plaintiff in an action declares upon a deed, or the defendant pleads a deed, he must do it with a *profert in curia,* (producing it in court) to the end that the other party may at his own charges have a copy of it; and until then he hath at his request and charges gotten a copy of the deed, he is not bound to answer it. 2 *Lil. Abr.* 382.

PROFITS, a devise of profits of lands, is a devise of the land itself. *Dyer.* 210.

PROHIBITION, is a writ properly issuing only out of the court of king's bench, being the king's prerogative writ; but, for the furtherance of justice, it may now also be had in some cause out of the court of chancery, common pleas, or exchequer, directed to the judge and parties of a suit in an inferior court, commanding them to cease from the prosecution thereof, upon a suggestion, that either the cause originally, or some collateral matter arising therein, doth not belong to that jurisdiction, but the cognizance of some other court. 3 *Black.* 112.

Upon the court being satisfied that the matter alledged by the suggestion is sufficient, the writ of prohibition immediately issues; commanding the judge not to hold, and the party not to prosecute the plea. And if either the judge or party shall proceed after such prohibition, an attachment may be had against them for the contempt, by the court that awarded it, and an action will lie against them to repair the party in damages. 3 *Black.* 113.

PROHIBITIO DE VASTO DIRECTA PARTI, a judicial writ directed to the tenant, prohibiting him from making waste upon the land in controversy during the suit.

PRO INDIVISO. The possession or occupation of lands or tenements, belonging to two or more persons, whereof none knows his several portion; as *coparceners* before partition.

PROMISE, is, where upon a valuable consideration, persons bind themselves by words to do or perform such a thing *agreed* on: it is in the nature of a verbal covenant, and wants only the solemnity of writing and sealing to make it absolutely the same. Yet for the breach of it, the remedy is different; for instead of an action of covenant, there lies only an action upon the case, the damages whereof are to be estimated and determined by the jury.

PROMISSORY NOTE. See *Bills of Exchange.*

PROMULGE

PROMULGE A LAW, is first to make a law, then to declare, publish, and proclaim the same to public view.

PROOF, the shewing or making plain the truth of any matter alledged: either in giving evidence to a jury on a trial, or else on interrogatories, or by copies of records, or exemplifications of them.

PROPERTY, is the highest right that a man hath, or can have, to any thing, and no ways depending upon another. And there are three sorts of rights of property; viz. property absolute, property qualified, and property possessory.

An absolute proprietor, hath an absolute power to dispose of his estate as he pleases, subject to the laws of the land.

Property in possession absolute, may be in all inanimate things, and in all such animals as are naturally tame.

A qualified property is had under certain circumstances, in wild animals being tamed.

PROPRIETARY, was formerly chiefly applied to him who had the fruits of a benefice to himself, his heirs, and successors, as abbots, and priors.

PRO RATA, in proportion.

PROROGUE, to put off to another day. See *Parliament*.

PROTECTION, is used for that benefit and safety, which every subject, denizen, or alien, especially secured, hath, by the king's laws.

PROTECTION OF PARLIAMENT. See *Arrest*, and *Privilege*.

PROTEST, where one openly affirms, that he doth either not at all, or but conditionally yield his consent to any act, or unto the proceeding of a judge in court, wherein his jurisdiction is doubtful, or to answer upon his oath farther than by law he is bound.

Protest, is also that act by which the holder of a foreign bill of exchange declares that such bill is dishonoured.

Protest, is also that act of a master, on his arrival with his ship from parts beyond the seas, to save him and his owners harmless and indemnified from any damage sustained in the goods of her lading, on account of storms. See *Bills of Exchange* and *Insurance*.

PROTESTATION, is a form of pleading, when one doth not directly

directly affirm or deny any thing that is alledged by another, or which he himself alledges.

PROTESTANT CHILDREN OF PAPISTS AND JEWS. The lord chancellor is empowered to make an order on popish and jewish parents, refusing to allow their protestant children a maintenance.

PROTHONOTARY, is a chief officer or clerk of the common pleas and king's bench; the former hath three, and the latter but one; whose office is to record all civil actions, as the clerk of the crown office, doth criminal causes in that court. Those of the common pleas, enter and enroll all manner of declarations, pleadings, assizes, judgments, &c.

PROVINCE. A province is the circuit of an archbishop's jurisdiction, which is subdivided into bishoprics. The ecclesiastical division of this kingdom, is into two provinces; viz. Canterbury and York.

PROVINCIAL CONSTITUTIONS, in this kingdom, were decrees made in the provincial synods, held under divers archbishops of Canterbury.

PROVISO, is a condition inserted into a deed, upon the observance whereof the validity of the deed depends.

PROVOST MARSHAL, an officer of the king's navy, who hath charge of the king's prisoners taken at sea.

PROXIES, are persons appointed instead of others to represent them. Every peer of the realm called to parliament, hath the privilege of constituting a proxy to vote for him in his absence, upon a lawful occasion; but such proxies are to be licenced by the king.

PUBERTY. See *Age*.

PUBLIC ACCOUNTS, commissioners are to enquire of the accounts of the sheriffs, customers, and other the king's officers, after passed in the exchequer, and if detected of any fraud they shall pay treble damages.

PUBLICATION, is used of depositions of witnesses in a cause in chancery, in order to the hearing, and rules may be given to pass *publication*; which is a power to shew the depositions openly, and to give out copies of them, &c.

PUBLIC WORSHIP. All contemners of public worship shall be *ipso facto* excommunicated; and if any person shall disturb a preacher

preacher in his sermon by word or deed, he shall be apprehended and carried before a justice, who shall commit him to goal for three months.

PUIS DARRIEN CONTINUANCE, a plea of new matter, pending an action.

PUISNE, younger, junior.

PUNISHMENT, the penalty of transgressing the laws.

PUR AUTER VIE, where lands &c. are held by another's life.

PURCHASE, signifies the buying or acquisition of lands or tenements with money, or by deed or agreement; and not obtaining it by descent, or hereditary right.

An estate taken by purchase, will not make the heir answerable for the acts of his ancestor, as an estate by descent will.

PURGATION. See *Ordeal*.

PURPARTY. To make purparty is to divide the lands which belong to parceners, which till partition they held jointly and undivided.

PUTTING IN FEAR. See *Robbery*.

Q.

QUÆ PLURA, a writ which lay where an inquisition had been taken by an escheator in any county, of such lands or tenements as any man died seized of, and all that was in his possession was imagined not to be found by the office.

QUÆRY, or QUERY, implies a doubt.

QUÆRENS NON INVENIT PLEGIUM, a return made by the sheriff upon a writ directed to him.

QUÆCIUS, is that which a man hath by purchase, as *hæreditas* is what he hath by descent.

QUAKERS. By stat. 7 & 8 W. III. c. 27, and 8 G. I. c. 6, quakers making and subscribing the declaration of fidelity, mentioned in 1 W. & M. shall not be liable to the penalty against others refusing to take such oaths; and not subscribing the declaration of fidelity, &c. they are disabled to vote at the election of members of parliament.

By 7 & 8 W. III. c. 34, made perpetual by 1 G. I. c. 6, quakers, where an oath is required, are permitted to make a solemn affirmation or declaration of the truth of any fact; but they are not capable of being witnesses in any criminal cause, serving on juries, or bearing any office or place of profit under government, unless they are sworn like other protestants; but this clause does not extend to the freedom of a corporation. 1 *Lord Raym.* 337.

By stat. 22 G. II. c. 46, an affirmation shall be allowed in all cases (except criminal) where by any act of parliament an oath is required, though no provision be therein made, for admitting a quaker to make his affirmation.

QUALE JUS, a writ judicial, which lay where a man of religion had judgment to recover land, before execution was made of the judgment, it went to the escheator, between judgment and execution, to enquire whether the religious person had any right to recover, or whether the judgment was obtained by collusion between the parties, to the intent, that the true lord might not be defrauded.

QUAMDIU SE BENE GESSERIT, as long as he shall behave himself well in his office, is a clause frequently inserted in letters patent.

QUANTUM MERUIT, is an action on the case, grounded upon the promise of another, to pay him for doing any thing, so much as he should deserve or *merit*.

QUANTUM VALEBAT, is where goods and wares sold, are delivered by a tradesman at no certain price, or to be paid for them as much as they are worth in general; then *quantum valebat* lies, and the plaintiff is to aver them to be worth so much.

QUARE IMPEDIT, a writ which lies for him that hath purchased a manor, with the advowson thereto belonging, against him that disturbs him in the right of his advowson, by presenting a clerk thereto when the church is void.

QUARE INCUMBRAVIT, is a writ that lies, where two are in plea for the advowson of a church, and the bishop admits the clerk of one of them within six months after vacation of a benefice; then the other shall have this writ against the bishop, that he appear and shew cause why he hath incumbered the church. And if it be found by verdict that the bishop hath incumbered the church after a *ne admittas* delivered to him, and within six months after the avoidance, damages are to be awarded to the plaintiff, and the bishop directed to disincumber the church.

QUARE NON ADMISIT, a writ that lies against a bishop refusing to admit his clerk, that hath recovered in a plea of advowson.

QUARE NON PERMITTIT, a writ that lies for one who has right to present for a turn against the proprietary.

QUARANTINE, is the space of forty days, wherein any person coming from foreign parts infected with the plague, is not permitted to land or come on shore, until so many days are expired. See 40 G. III. c. 80.

QUARTER-SESSIONS. The sessions of the peace is a court of record holden before two or more justices, whereof one is of the *quorum*, for the execution of the authority given them by the commission of the peace, and certain statutes and acts of parliament.

The justices shall keep their sessions in every quarter of the year at least, and for three days if need be; to wit, in the first week after the feast of St. Michael, in the first week after the Epiphany, in the first week after Easter, and in the first week after St. Thomas, and oftener if need be.

Any two justices, one whereof is of the *quorum*, by the words of the commission of the peace, may issue their precept to the sheriff to summon a session for the general execution of their authority; and such session, holden at any time within that quarter of a year, is a general quarter-session. 4 *Burn*. 181.

And such precept should bear teste, or be dated fifteen days before the return. *Nels. Intr.* 35.

The sheriff also shall cause a jury to appear at such days and places as the said justices, or such two or more of them as aforesaid shall appoint.

There are many offences, which, by particular statutes, belong properly to this jurisdiction, and ought to be prosecuted in this court: as the smaller misdemeanours against the public or commonwealth, not amounting to felony; and especially offences relating to the game, highways, alehouses, bastard children, the settlement and provision of the poor, vagrants, servants' wages, apprentices and popish recusants. Some of these are proceeded upon by indictment; and others in a summary way, by motion and order thereupon, which order may, for the most part, unless

 guarded

guarded against by any particular statute, be removed into the court of king's bench by *certiorari*, and be there either quashed or confirmed.

QUASH, to overthrow or annul.

QUEEN. The *queen consort* is an exempt person from the king by the common law, and is of ability and capacity to purchase and grant without the king; and is capable of taking lands or tenements of the gift of the king. *Co. Lit.* 133. See *Charlotte.*

QUEEN ANNE'S BOUNTY. See *First Fruits.*

QUEEN DOWAGER. No man may marry the queen dowager without a licence from the king, on pain to forfeit his lands and goods: but if she marry any of the nobility, or under that degree she loses not her dignity; but by the name of a queen may maintain an action.

QUEEN-GOLD. See *Aurum Reginæ.*

QUE ESTATE. In common law it is a plea, whereby a man intitling another to land, &c. saith that the same estate he had, he hath from him.

QUEM REDDITUM REDDAT. A judicial writ that lies for him to whom a rent charge is granted, by fine levied in the king's court against the tenant of the land, who refuses to attorn to him, thereby to cause to attorn.

QUERELA, an action in a court of justice.

QUEST, an inquest, inquisition, or enquiry upon the oath of an impanelled jury.

QUIA IMPROVIDE, *supersedeas* granted in the behalf of a clerk of chancery, sued against the privilege of that court in the common pleas, and pursued to the *exigent.*

QUICK WITH CHILD. See *Pregnancy.*

QUID JURIS CLAMAT, a judicial writ issuing out of the record of the fine, which remains with the custos brevium of the common pleas, before it is engrossed; and it lies for a grantee of the reversion or remainder, when the particular tenant will not attorn.

QUID PRO QUO, the giving one thing of value, for another thing of like value, being the mutual consideration and performance of both parties in a contract.

QUIETUS, a word used by the clerk of the pipe, and auditors

of the exchequer, in their acquittances or discharges given to accomptants.

QUIETUS REDDITUS, a quit rent, or small acknowledgment paid in money, so called, because such payment acquitted the tenant from all other services or duties to the lord.

QUINTO EXACTUS, the fifth and last call of a defendant, who is sued to the outlawry; where if he appear not, he is by the judgment of the coroners returned outlawed.

QUI-TAM. See *Popular Action*.

QUOD EI DEFORCEAT, a writ that lies for the tenant in tail, tenant in dower, or tenant for term of life, having lost their lands by default, against him that recovered, or against his heir.

QUOD PERMITTAT, a writ that lies for one who is disseised of his common of pasture, against the heir of the disseisor.

QUO JURE, a writ that lies for him who has land wherein another challenges *common of pasture* time out of mind: and is to compel him to shew *by what title* he challenges it.

QUO MINUS, a writ that lies for him that hath a grant of housebote, and haybote, in another man's woods, against the grantor, making such waste as the grantee cannot enjoy his grant.

QUORUM, a word which often occurs in our statutes, and is much used in commissions both of justices of the peace, and others, and so called from the words of the commission, *quorum unum esse volumus.*

QUO WORRANTO, is in nature of a writ of right for the king, against him who claims or usurps any office, franchise, or liberty, to inquire by what authority he supports his claim, in order to determine the right.

R.

RACK RENT, the full extended yearly value of the land, &c. let by lease, payable by tenant for life or years.

RANSOM, was the sum formerly given by captains or passengers

gers for the redemption of a vessel captured by pirates. This is now prohibited by statute.

RAPE, a division of a county, similar to that of an hundred, and generally consists of more hundreds than one.

RAPE OF WOMEN, is where a man hath carnal knowledge of a woman by force, and against her will; by 18 Eliz. c. 7, if any person shall unlawfully and carnally know and abuse any woman child under the age of ten years, whether with her consent or against it, he shall be punished as for a rape. And it is not a sufficient excuse in the ravisher, to prove that she is a common strumpet; for she is still under the protection of the law, and may not be forced. Nor is the offence of a rape mitigated, by shewing that the woman at last yielded to the violence, if such her consent were forced by fear of death or duress; nor is it any excuse, that she consented after the fact. 1 *Haw.* 108.

RAPINE, to take a thing openly, or by violence. 14 Car. II. c. 22.

RASURE of a deed, so as to alter it in a material part, without consent of the party bound by it, will make the same void.

RATIFICATION, is used for the confirmation of a clerk in a prebend, &c.

RATIONALIBUS DIVISIS; a writ that lies where two lords, in divers towns, have seigniories joining together.

RAVISHMENT. See *Rape*.

RAVISHMENT DE GARD, a writ which lay for the guardian by knight service, or in socage, against him who took from him the body of his ward.

REAL ACTION. See *Action*.

REASON. If maxims of law admit of any difference, those are to be preferred, which carry with them the more perfect and excellent reason.

REASONABLE AID, was a duty that the lord of the fee claimed of his tenants holding by knight's service, or in socage, to marry his daughters, or make his son a knight.

RE-ATTACHMENT, a second attachment of him that was formerly attached and dismissed the court without day, as by the not coming of the justices, or some such casualty.

REBELLION, taking up arms traitorously against the king, be it by natural subjects, or by others once subdued.

 REBUTTER,

REBUTTER, is the answer of the defendant to the plaintiff's *sur-rejoinder*.

RECAPTION, where one hath deprived another of his property, the owner may lawfully claim and retake it, wherever he happens to find it, so it be not in a riotous manner, or attended with any breach of the peace.

RECEIPTS, are acknowledgments in writing of having received a sum of money or other value. A receipt is either a voucher for an obligation discharged or one incurred. Receipts for money above 40s. must be on stamps; but on the back of a bill of exchange or promissory note which is already stamped, is good without a farther duty. Writing a receipt on a stamp of greater value than the law requires, incurs no penalty, and the receipt is good; but if on a stamp of a lower value, or on unstamped paper, then a receipt is no discharge, and incurs a penalty. See *Stamp*.

RECEIVER, receiving stolen goods, knowing them to be stolen, is an high misdemeanour at the common law; and by several statutes, is made felony and transportation; and in some particular instances, felony without benefit of clergy.

RECEIVER OF THE FINES, an officer who receives the money of all such as compound with the king upon original writs in chancery.

RECITAL, is the rehearsal or making mention in a deed or writing, of something which has been done before. See *Deed*.

RECOGNISANCE, is an obligation of record, which a man enters into before some court of record, or magistrate duly authorized, with condition to the same particular act; as to appear at the assizes or quarter sessions, to keep the peace, &c.

RECORD, an act committed to writing in any of the king's courts; during the term wherein it is written, is alterable, being no record; but that term once ended, and the act duly enrolled, it is a *record*, and of that credit, which admits of no alteration or proof to the contrary.

RECORDARE, or RECORDARI FACIAS, a writ directed to the sheriff, to remove a cause depending in an inferior court, or court of ancient demesne, hundred, or county, to the king's bench or common pleas.

RECOVERY. *Common recoveries* were invented by the ecclesiastics

siastics to elude the statutes of mortmain; and afterwards encouraged by the finesse of the courts at law, in order to put an end to all fettered inheritances, and bar not only all estates tail, but also all remainders and reversions expectant thereon.

A common recovery is so far like a fine, that it is a suit or action, either actual or fictitious; and in it, the lands are recovered against the tenant of the freehold; which recovery by a supposed adjudication of the right, binds all persons, and vests a free and absolute fee-simple in the recoverer. And a common recovery is now looked upon as the best assurance, except an act of parliament, that purchasers can have. 2 *Black.* c. 21.

There must be three persons at least to make a common recovery, a *recoveror*, a *recoveree*, and a *vouchee*. The *recoveror* is the plaintiff or demandant, that brings the writ of entry. The *recoveree* is the defendant or tenant of the land, against whom the writ is brought. The *vouchee*, is he whom the defendant or tenant *voucheth* or calls to warranty of the land in demand, either defend the right, or to yield him other lands in value, according to a supposed agreement. *Wood.* b. 2. c. 3.

And this being by consent and permission of the parties, it is therefore said that a recovery is suffered.

A common recovery may be had of such things, for the most part, as pass by a fine. An use may be raised upon a recovery, as well as upon a fine; and the same rules are generally to be observed and followed for the guiding and directing the uses of a recovery, as are observed for the guidance and direction of a fine. 1 *Co.* 15. See *Fine*.

RECOUPE, signifies the keeping back or stopping something, for what is due; thus an innkeeper may keep back or detain his guests, horses, &c. till he pay for his entertainment. 1 *Cro.* 196.

RECTO, a writ of right, which is of so high a nature, that where as other rights in real actions are only to recover the possession of the land or tenements in question, which have been lost by our ancestor or ourselves; this aims to recover both the seisin which some of our ancestors or we had, and also the property of the hiring whereof the ancestor died not seised as of fee; and whereby are pleaded and tried both their rights together, viz. as well of possession as of property; so that if a man ever lose his cause

cause upon this writ, either by judgment, or assize, he is without remedy. *Pract. Lib.* 5

RECTO DE ADVOCATIONE ECCLESIÆ, a writ of right, lying where a man hath a *right of advowson,* and the parson of the church dying, a stranger presents his clerk to the church, and he not having brought his action of *quare impedit,* nor *darrein presentment,* within six months, but suffered the stranger to usurp upon him.

RECTO DE CUSTODIA TERRÆ ET HÆREDIS, a writ that lay for him, whose tenant holding of him in chivalry, died in nonage, against a stranger that entered upon the land and took the body of the heir.

RECTO DE DOTE, *a writ of right of dower,* which lies for a woman who hath received part of her dower, and purposes to demand the remainder in the same town, against the heir, or his guardian if he be a ward.

RECTO DE DOTE UNDE NIHIL HABET, a writ of right which lies in a case, where the husband having divers lands or tenements, hath assured no dower to his wife, and she thereby is driven to sue for her thirds, against the heir or his guardian.

RETCO QUANDO DOMINUS REMISIT, a writ of right, which lies in case where lands or tenements in the seigniory of any lord, are in demand by a *writ of right.*

RECTO SUR DISCLAIMER, a writ that lies where a lord in the king's court of common-pleas *avows* upon his tenant, and the tenant *disclaims* to hold of him; upon which *disclaimer* he shall have this writ; and if the lord aver and prove, that the land is holden of him, he shall recover the land for ever.

RECTORY, is taken for an entire parish-church, with all its rights, glebes, titles, and other profits whatsoever.

RECUSANT, a person who refuses to go to church, and worship God, after the manner of the church of England as by law established: to which is annexed the penalty of 20l. a month for nonconformity. 23 Eliz. c. 1.

REDDENDUM, a clause in a lease whereby the rent is reserved to the lessor. See *Deed.*

REDEMPTION. See *Mortgage.*

REDISSEISIN, a disseisin made by him who once before was found

found adjudged to have disseised the same man of his lands or tenements; for which there lies a special writ, called *disseisin*.

RE-ENTRY, signifies the resuming or retaking a possession lately lost.

RE-EXTENT, a second extent on lands and tenements, on complaint made, that the former extent was partially made.

REFERENCE, is where a matter is referred by the court of chancery to a master, and by the courts at law to a prothonotary or secondary, to examine and report to the court. 2 *Lit. Abr.* 432.

Reference, also signifies where a matter in dispute is *referred* to the decision of an arbitrator. See *Arbitration*.

REFUSAL, is where a person hath by law a right and power of having or doing something of advantage to him, and he refuseth it.

REGALIA, the royal rights of a king, which according to *Civilians* are six; power of judicature; power of life and death; power of war and peace; masterless goods as waifs, strays, &c. assessments; and minting of money.

REGE INCONSULTO, is a writ issued from the king to the judges, not to proceed in a cause which may prejudice the king, until he is advised.

REGENT, one who governs a kingdom during the minority or absence of the king.

REGIO ASSENSU, a writ whereby the king gives his royal assent to the election of a bishop.

REGRATING. See *Forestalling*.

REHEARING, in chancery, is when either of the parties to the suit thinks himself aggrieved by the decree; in which case, he may petition the lord chancellor for the cause to be heard again: but a petition for rehearing must be signed by two of the counsel, certifying that they apprehend the cause is proper to be reheard. 3 *Black.* 453.

REJOINDER, is where the defendant answers to the plaintiff's replication: it is an exception or answer thereto, and it ought to be a sufficient answer to the replication, and follow and enforce the matter of the bar pleaded; otherwise it is a departure from the plea, which the law will not allow. 2 *Lil. Abr.* 433.

RELATION, a fiction of law, to make a nullity of the thing

from

from the beginning (for a certain intent) which in truth had essence.

RELEASE, releases are distinguished into express releases indeed, and those arising by operation of law; and are made of lands and tenements, goods and chattels; or of actions real, personal, and mixed. *Co. Lit.* 264.

By a release of all demands, all actions real, personal, and mixed, and all actions of appeal, are extinct. *Lit.* 509.

RELEGATION, is taken for a banishment for a time only. *Co. Lit.* 133.

RELIEF, a certain sum of money which the tenant holding by knight's service, grand serjeantry, or other tenure (for which homage, or legal service is due), and being at full age at the death of his ancestor, paid to his lord at his entrance.

RELIGION, seditious words in derogation of the established religion are indictable, as tending to a breach of the peace. 1 *Haw.* 7.

RELINQUISHMENT, any person may relinquish an ill demand in a declaration; and have judgment for that which is well demanded.

REMAINDER, is an estate limited in lands, tenements, or rents, to be enjoyed after the expiration of another particular estate.

An estate in remainder, is an estate limited to take effect and be enjoyed after another estate is determined. As if a man seised in fee-simple grant lands to one for twenty years, and after the determination of the said term, then to another and his heirs for ever; here the former is tenant for years, remainder to the latter in fee. In the first place, an estate for years is created or carved out of the fee, and given to the former, and the residue and remainder of it is given to the latter. Both their interests are in fact only one estate; the present term of years, and the remainder afterwards, when added together, being equal only to one estate in fee. 2 *Black.* c. 11.

The word *remainder* is no term of art, nor is it necessary to create a remainder. So that any words sufficient to shew the intent of the party, will create a remainder; because such estates take their denomination of remainder more from the nature and manner of their existence, after they are limited, than from any previous

vious quality inherent in the word remainder. See *Fearne on Remainders.*

REMANET IN CUSTODIA, entry of an action in the marshal's book, by *reman. custod.* where a man is actually in custody is a good commencement of an action in B. R. 3 *Salk.* 150.

REMEDY, is the action or means given by law for recovery of a right; and whenever the law giveth any thing, it gives a remedy for the same.

REMITTER, is where one that hath right to lands, but is out of possession, hath afterwards the freehold cast upon him by some subsequent defective title, and enters by virtue of that title: in this case, the law *remits* him to his ancient and more certain right, and by an equitable fiction supposes him to have gained possession in consequence and by virtue thereof; and this because he cannot possibly obtain judgment at law, to be restored to his prior right, since he is himself the tenant of the land. 3 *Black.* 190.

RENDER, is used in levying a fine, which is either single whereby nothing is granted or rendered back again by the cognizee to the cognizor; or double which contains a grant or *render* back again of some real common, or other thing, out of the land itself, to the cognizor.

RENT, is a certain profit issuing yearly, out of lands and tenement corporeal.

There are at common law, three kinds of rents; *rent service, rent charge,* and *rent seck,* or *rack rent.*

Rent service, is where the tenant holds his land of his lord by fealty and certain rent; or by homage, fealty, and certain rent; or by other service and certain rent: and it is called a rent *service,* because it hath some corporal service incident to it, which at least is fealty.

Rent charge, is so called because the land for payment thereof is *charged* wtth a distress.

Rent seck, or *rack rent,* is where the land is granted without any clause of distress for the same. 1 *Inst.* 141.

The time for payment of rent, and consequently for a demand, is such a convenient time before the sun setting of the last day, as will be sufficient to have the money counted; but if the tenant meet the lessor on the land at any time of the last day of payment, and tender the rent, that is sufficient tender, because the money

money is to be paid indefinitely on that day, and therefore a tender on that day is sufficient. See *Distress.*

RENTAL, a roll wherein the rents of a manor are written, and by which the lord's bailiff collects the same.

RENTS ABSOLUTE, are accounted among the fee farm rents, to be sold by the statute 22 Car. II. c. 6. and are such rents or tenths at were anciently paid to the crown, from the lands of abbeys and religious houses.

REPARATIONS, a tenant for life or years may cut down timber trees to make reparations, although he be not compelled thereto; as where a house is ruinous at the time of the lease made, and the lessee suffer it to fall, he is not bound to rebuild it, and yet if he fell timber for *reparations*, he may justify the same. *Co. Litt.* 54.

REPARATIONE FACIENDA, a writ which lies in divers cases, whereof one is, where three are tenants in common or joint tenants, as *pro indiviso*, of a mill or house which is fallen into decay, and the one being willing to repair it, the other two will not: in this case, the party willing, shall have this writ against the other two. F. N. B. 127.

REPLEADER, whenever a repleader is granted the pleadings must begin *de novo* at that stage of them, whether it be the plea, replication, rejoinder, or whatever else, wherein there appears to have been the first default, or deviation from the regular course, when a repleader is awarded, it must be without costs. 3 *Black.* 395.

REPLEVIN, is the writ called *replegiare facias* by him who has cattle or other goods distrained by another, for any cause, and putting in surety to the sheriff, that upon delivery of the thing distrained, he will prosecute the action against the distrainer. *Co. Lit.* 12.

In this writ or action, both the plaintiff, and defendant, are called actors; the one, that is the plaintiff suing for damages, and the avowant or defendant to have a return of the goods or cattle. 2 *Bond.* 84.

That the avowant is in the nature of a plaintiff, appears, 1st. from his being called an actor, which is a term in the civil law, and signifies plaintiff; 2dly. from his being entitled to have judgment *de retorno habendo*, and damages as plaintiffs; 3dly. from this,

this, that the plaintiff might plead in abatement of the avowry, and consequently such avowry, must be in nature of an action. *Carth.* 112.

Replevins, by writ issue properly out of chancery, returnable into the courts of K. B. and C. B. at Westminster.

In order to obtain a replevin, application must be made to the sheriff, or one of his deputies, and security given that the party replevying will pursue his action against the distrainor, for which purpose by the ancient law, he is required to put in pledges to prosecute; and that if the right be determined against him, he will return the distress again, for which purpose he is to find pledges to make return These pledges are discretionary, and at the peril of the sheriff. 3 *Black.* 147.

After the goods are delivered back to the party replevying, he is then bound to bring his action of replevin against the distrainor; which may be prosecuted in the county court, be the distress of what value it may: but either party may remove it to the superior courts of king's-bench or common-pleas, the plaintiff at pleasure, and the defendant upon reasonable cause. 3 *Black.* 149.

If the sheriff be shewn a stranger's goods, and he takes them, an action of trespass lies against him, for otherwise he could have no remedy; for being a stranger he cannot have the writ *de proprietate probanda*, and were he not intitled to this remedy it would be in the power of the sheriff to strip a man's house of all his goods. 2 *Rol. Abr.* 552.

If it be determined for the plaintiff, namely, that the distress was wrongfully taken, he hath already got his goods back into his own possession, and shall keep them, and moreover recover damages. But if the defendant prevail, by the default on nonsuit of the plaintiff, then he shall have a writ *de retorno habendo*, whereby the goods or chattels which were distrained and then replevied, are returned again into his custody, to be sold, or otherwise disposed of, as if no replevin had been made. If the distress were for damage feasant, the distrainor may keep the goods so returned, until tender shall be made of sufficient amends. *Rol. Abr.* 146.

On a *retorno habendo* awarded, the party desiring to have the cattle or goods restored, must shew them to the sheriff; for otherwise the sheriff may not know them.

REPLICATION, an exception or answer of the plaintiff in a suit to the defendant's plea: and is also that which the complainant replies to the defendant's answer in chancery, &c.

The replication is to contain certainty, and not to vary from the declaration, but must pursue and maintain the cause of the plaintiff's ation; otherwise it will be a departure in pleading, and going to another matter. 1 *Inst* 304.

REPORTS, of *cases*, are histories of the several cases and decisions of the courts, with a short summary of the proceedings, which are reserved at large in the record, the argument on both sides, and the reasons the court gave for its judgment, taken down in short notes by persons present at the determination. 1 *Black*. 71.

REPRESENTATION, there is an heir by *representation*, where the father dies, in the life of the grandfather, leaving a son, who shall inherit the grandfather's estate, before the father's brother, &c.

REPRIEVE, to suspend a prisoner from the execution and proceeding of the law at that time. Every judge who hath power to order any execution, hath power to reprieve.

REPRISALS. See *Letters of Marque*.

REPUGNANT, what is contrary to any thing said before. *Repugnancy* in deeds, grants, indictments, verdicts, &c. makes them void. 3 *Nels*. 135.

REPUTATION or FAME. The security of reputation, or good name, from the arts of detraction and slander, are rights to which every man is intitled, by reason and natural justice; since, without these, it is impossible to have the perfect enjoyment of any other advantage or right. 1 *Black*. 134.

Reputation is properly under the protection of the law, as all persons have an interest in their good name: and scandal and defamation are injurious to it; though defamatory words are not actionable, otherwise, than as they are *a damage to the estate* of the person injured. *Wood's Inst*. 37.

REQUEST, of things to be done: where one is to do a collateral thing, agreed on making a contract, there ought to be a request to do it. 2 *Lil. Abr*. 464.

REQUESTS,

REQUESTS. See *Court of Requests.*

RESCEIT, is an admission, or receiving a third person to plead his right in a cause formerly commenced between other two.

RESCEIT OF HOMAGE, is the lord's receiving homage of his tenant at his admission to the land. *Kitchin.* 148.

RESCUE, or RESCOUS, is the taking away and setting at liberty against law, any distress taken for rent, or services, or damage feasant; but the more general notion of rescous is, the forcible freeing another from an arrest or some legal commitment; which being an high offence, subjects the offender not only to an action at the suit of the party injured, but likewise to fine and imprisonment at the suit of the king. *Co. Lit.* 160.

If goods be distrained without cause, or contrary to law, the owner may make rescue; but if they be once impounded, or even though taken without any cause, the owner may not break the pound and take them out, for then they are in custody of the law. 1 *Black.* 12. See *Distress.*

RESEISIR, a taking again of lands into the hands of the king, whereof a general livery, or *ouster le maine,* was formerly misused, contrary to the form and order of law. *Staundf. Prærog.* 26.

RESIDENCE, signifies a man's abode or continuance in a place.

Residence, is particularly used, for the continuance of a parson or vicar, on his benefice.

By stat. 13 Eliz. c. 20. and divers other subsequent statutes, if any beneficed clergyman be absent from his cure, above fourscore days in one year, he shall not only forfeit one year's profit of his benefice, to be distributed among the poor of the parish, but all leases made by him of the profits of such benefice, and all covenants and agreements of like nature, shall cease and be void; except in the case of licensed pluralists, who are allowed to demise the living on which they are nonresident, to their curates only.

RESIDUARY LEGATEE, is he to whom the residue of a personal estate is given by will. And such legatee being made executor with others, shall retain against the rest.

RESIGNATION, the giving up a benefice into the hands of the ordinary.

Every parson who resigns a benefice, must make the resignation to his superior; as an incumbent to a bishop, a bishop to an archbishop, and an archbishop to the king, as supreme ordinary. 1 *Rep.* 137.

RESPITE OF HOMAGE, the forbearance of homage which ought to be performed by the tenants holding by homage.

RESPONDEAS OUSTER, is to answer over in an action to the merits of the cause. If a demurrer be joined upon a plea to the jurisdiction, person, or writ, &c. and it be adjudged against the defendant, it is a *respondeas ouster*. *Jenk. Cent.* 306.

RESPONSALIS, he that appears for another in a court at a day assigned.

RESTITUTION, is the yielding up again, or restoring of any thing unlawfully taken from another.

Restitution is also where one being attainted of treason or felony (whereby the blood is stained or corrupted), he or his heirs is restored to his lands or possessions. The king by his charter may restore lands or goods forfeited to him by any attainder; but if by attainder the blood be corrupted, this can only be by an act of parliament.

There is also restitution of the possession of lands, in cases of forcible entry; a restitution of lands to an heir, on his ancestors being attainted of treason or felony; and restitution of stolen goods. *Wood. b.* 4. *c.* 5.

RE RESTITUTION, is when there hath been a writ of restitution before granted; and restitution is generally matter of duty, but re-restitution, may be granted upon motion, if the court see cause to grant it, and on quashing an indictment of forcible entry, the court of B. R. may grant a writ of re-restitution. 2 *Lil. Abr.* 474.

RESTITUTIONE TEMPORALIUM, a writ that lies where a man being elected and confirmed bishop of any diocese, and hath the king's royal assent thereto, for the recovery of the temporalities or barony of the said bishopric; and it is directed from the king to the escheator of the county.

RESULTING USE, is when an use limited by a deed expires, or cannot vest, it returns back to him who raised it.

RESUMMONS, signifies a *second summons*, and calling a man to to answer an action, where the first summons is defeated upon any occasion, as the death of the party or such like.

RETAINER OF DEBTS, an executor, among debts of equal degree, may pay himself first, by retaining in his hands, the amount of his debt.

RETAINING FEE, the first fee given to any counsellor, thereby to prevent his being engaged by the opposite party.

RETRAXIT, is where the plaintiff or demandant comes in person into the court, and says *he will proceed no farther*; and this is a bar of all other actions of like or inferior nature.

A *restraxit* is always of the part of the plaintiff or demandant, and cannot be, unless the plaintiff or demandant be in court in proper person.

RETURN, is most commonly used for the return of writs, which is the certificate of the sheriff made to the court of what he hath done, touching the execution of any writ directed to him; and where a writ is executed, or the defendant cannot be found, or the like, this matter is indorsed on the writ by the officer, and delivered into the court whence the writ issued, at the day of the return thereof, in order to be filed. 2 *Lil. Abr.* 176.

RETURNO HABENDO, a writ which lies for him who has avowed a distress made of cattle, and proved his distress to be lawfully taken, for returning to him the cattle distrained, which before were replevied by the party distrained, upon surety given to prosecute the action.

RETURNS OF MEMBERS TO PARLIAMENT. See *Election.*

RETURNUM IRREPLAGIABILE, a judicial writ sent out of the common-pleas to the sheriff, for the final restitution or return of cattle to the owner, unjustly taken by another, as *damage feasant*, and so found by the jury before justices of assize in the county, or otherwise by default of prosecution.

REVENUE, ROYAL, is that which the British constitution hath vested in the royal person, in order to support his dignity and maintain his power; being a portion which each subject contributes of his property, in order to secure the remainder.

REVERSAL, of a judgment, is the making it void for error, and when on the return of a writ of error, it appears that the judgment is erroneous, then the court will give judgment, *quod. judicium revocetur, adnulletur, et penitus pro nullo habeatur.*

REVERSION, hath a double acceptation in law; the *one* is, but an interest in the land when the possession shall fall; the *other* when the possession and estate, which was parted with for a time, ceases, and is determined in the person of the alienees, assignees, grantees, or their heirs, or effectually returns to the donor, his heirs, or assigns, whence it was derived. The difference between a reversion and remainder, is, that a remainder is general and may be to any man, but to him that grants or conveys the land, &c. for term of life only or otherwise. A reversion is to himself, from whom the conveyance of the land, &c. proceeded, and is commonly perpetual as to his heirs also. *Lit. Lib.* 2. See *Remainder.*

REVIEW, bill of, in chancery, is, where a cause hath been heard, and the decree signed and enrolled; and some error in law appears upon the decree, or new matter discovered in time after the decree made.

REVIVOR, bill of, is where a bill hath been exhibited in chancery against one who answers, and before the cause is heard, or if heard, before the decree enrolled, either party dies: in this case a bill of *revivor* must be brought, that the former proceedings may stand revived, and the cause be finally determined.

REVOCATION, a destroying or making void a deed or will which existed before the act of revocation.

Some things may be revoked of course, though they are made irrevokable by express words; as a letter of attorney, a submission to an award, a testament or last will; for these of their nature are revocable.

By the statute of frauds, 29 Car. II. c. 3, no devise of lands shall be revocable, otherwise than by some other will or codicil in writing, or other writing declaring the same, signed in the presence of three witnesses.

REWARDS, there are rewards given in many cases by statute, for the apprehending of criminals and bringing them to justice.

RIDER, is a schedule, or small piece of parchment added to some part of a record; as when on the third reading of a bill in parliament, a new clause is added, that is tacked to the bill, on a separate piece of parchment, and is called a *rider*.

RIDING ARMED, with dangerous and unusual weapons, is an offence at common law. 4 *Inst.* 160.

RIDING CLERK, one of the six clerks in chancery, who in his turn for one year, keeps the enrollment books of all grants that pass the great seal that year.

RIDINGS, are names of the divisions of *Yorkshire,* which are three, viz. the east riding, the west riding, and the north riding.

REINS ARREAR, a kind of plea used to an action of debt upon arrearages of amount, whereby the defendant alledges there is nothing in arrear.

RIENS PASSE PAR LE FAIT, nothing passes by the deed, is the form of an exception taken in some cases to an action.

RIENS PER DESCENT, is the plea of an heir, where he is sued for his ancestor's debt, and hath no land from him by *descent* or assets in his hands.

RIGHT, in general signification includes not only a right, for which a writ of right lies, but also any claim or title, either by virtue of a condition, mortgage, or the like, for which no action is given by law, but only on entry.

RIOT, ROUT, and UNLAWFUL ASSEMBLY. When three persons or more shall assemble themselves together, with an intent mutually to assist one another, against any who shall oppose them in the execution of some enterprize of a private nature, with force or violence, against the peace, or to the manifest terror of the people, whether the act intended were of itself lawful or unlawful; if they only meet for such a purpose or intent, though they shall after depart of their own accord without doing any thing, this is an unlawful assembly. 1 *Haw.* 155.

If after their first meeting, they shall move forwards towards the execution of any such act, whether they put their intended purpose into execution or not; this according to the general opinion is a rout. *Id.*

By 34 Ed. III. c. 1, it is enacted, that if a justice find persons riotously assembled, he alone has not only power to arrest the offenders, and bind them to their good behaviour, or imprison them if they do not offer good bail; but he may also authorize others to arrest them, by a bare verbal command, without other warrant; and by force thereof, the persons so commanded, may pursue and arrest the offenders in his absence as well as presence. It is also

also said, that after any riot is over, any one justice may send his warrant to arrest any person who was concerned in it, and that he may send him to goal till he shall find sureties for his good behaviour. 1 *Haw.* 160.

The punishment of unlawful assemblies, if to the number of twelve, may be capital; according to the circumstances which attend them: but from the number of *three to eleven*, is by fine and imprisonment only.

The same is the case by riots and routs by the common law, to which the pillory in very enormous cases, has been sometimes superadded. 4 *Black.* c. 11.

ROBBERY, is a felonious taking away of another man's goods from his person or presence against his will, putting him in fear, and of purpose to steal the same. *West. Symbol.*

To make a robbery there must be a felonious intention; and so it ought to be laid in the indictment. 1 H. H. 532.

It is immaterial of what value the thing taken is: a penny, as well as a pound, thus forcibly extorted, makes a robbery. 1 *Haw.* 34

If a man force another to part with his property, for the sake of preserving his character from the imputation of having been guilty of an unnatural crime, it will amount to a robbery, even though the party was under no apprehension of personal danger. *Leach's Cro. Law.* 257.

If any thing be snatched suddenly from the head, hand, or person of any one, without any struggle on the part of the owner, or without any evidence of force, or violence being exerted by the thief, it does not amount to robbery. But if any thing be broken or torn in consequence of the sudden seizure, it would be evidence of such force as would constitute a robbery: as where a part of a lady's hair was torn away, by snatching a diamond pin from her head, and an ear was torn by pulling off an ear-ring; each of these cases was determined to be a robbery. *Leach's Cro. Law.* 264.

By 7 G. II. c. 21, if any person shall, with any offensive weapon, assault, or by menaces, or in any forcible or violent manner, demand any money or goods, with a felonious intent to rob another, he shall be guilty of felony, and be transported for seven years.

If any person being out of prison, shall commit any robbery,

 and

and afterwards discover two or more persons who shall commit any robbery, so as two or more be convicted; he shall have the king's pardon, for all robberies he shall have committed before such discovery. See *Burglary, Hundred,* and *Larceny.*

ROGUE. See *Vagrant.*

ROLLS, are parchment, on which all the pleadings, memorials, and acts of courts are entered and filed with the proper officer, and then they become records of the court. 2 *Lil. Abr.* 149.

ROLLS OFFICE OF THE CHANCERY. See *Master of the Rolls.*

ROLLS OF PARLIAMENT, the manuscript registers, or rolls of the proceedings of our old parliaments.

ROME, CHURCH OF. See *Papists.*

ROYAL ASSENT. See *Parliament.*

ROYALTIES, are the rights of the king. See *Prerogative.*

RULES OF COURT. Attornies are bound to observe the rules of the court, to avoid confusion; also the plaintiff and defendant in a cause, are at their peril to take notice of the rules made in the court touching the cause between them. See *Tidd's K. B. Practice.*

RUMOURS, spreading such as are false, is criminal and punishable by common law. 1 *Haw.* 234.

S.

SACRILEGE, is church robbery, or a taking of things out of an holy place, as where a person steals any vessels, ornaments, or goods of the church.

SAFE CONDUCT. A safe conduct is a security given by the king, under the great seal, to a stranger, for his safe coming into, and passing out of the realm. Passports however, under the king's sign manual, or licences from his ambassadors abroad, which are now more usual, are obtained with equal facility.

SALE OF GOODS. If a man agree for the purchase of goods, he shall pay for them, before he carries them away, unless some term of a credit is expressly agreed upon.

If one man say the price of this article is 100*l.* and the other says

says I will give you 100l. but does not pay immediately, it is at the option of the seller whether he shall have it or no, except a day were given for the payment.

If a man upon the sale of goods, warrant them to be good, the law annexes to this contract a tacit warranty, that if they be not so, he shall make compensation to the purchaser; such warranty, however, must be on the sale.

But if the vendor knew the goods to be unsound, and hath used any art to disguise them, or if in any respect, they differ from what he represents them to be to the purchaser, he will be answerable for their goodness, though no general warranty will extend to those defects that are obvious to the senses.

If two persons come to a warehouse, and one buys, and the other to procure him credit, promises the seller, *if he do not pay you, I will*; this is a collateral undertaking, and void without writing, by the statutes of frauds; but if he say, *let him have the goods, I will be your pay-master*, this is an absolute undertaking as for himself, and he shall be intended to be the real buyer, and the other to act only as his servant. 2 T. R. 73.

After earnest is given, the vendor cannot sell the goods to another without a default in the vendee; and therefore if the vendee do not come and pay, and take the goods, the vendor ought to give him notice for that purpose; and then if he do not come and pay, and take away the goods in convenient time, the agreement is dissolved, and he is at liberty to sell them to any other person. 1 *Salk*. 113.

An earnest only binds the bargain, and gives the party a right to demand; but demand without payment of money is void. See also *Auction*.

SALVAGE. See *Insurance Marine*.

SANCTUARY, was a place privileged for the safeguard of offenders' lives, being founded upon the law of mercy.

By 21 Jac. I. c. 28, all privilege and sanctuary, and abjuration consequent thereupon, is utterly taken away and abolished. 4 *Black*. 332.

SANE MEMORY, perfect and sound mind and memory, to do any lawful act. See *Ideots*.

SATISFACTION, is the giving of a recompence for an injury done, for the payment of money due on bond, judgment, &c.

SAVER

SAVER DEFAULT, to excuse a default.

SCANDALUM MAGNATUM, is the special name of a statute, and also of a wrong done to any high personage of the land, as prelates, dukes, marquisses, earls, barons, and other nobles; and also the chancellor, treasurer, clerk of the privy seal, steward of the house, justice of one bench or other, and other great officers of the realm, by false news or horrible or false messages, whereby debates and discord, betwixt them and the commons, or any scandal to their persons might arise. 2 R. II. c. 5.

This statute hath given name to a writ, granted to recover damages thereupon. *Cowel.*

It is now clearly agreed, that though there be no express words in the statute which give an action, yet the party injured may maintain one on this principle of law, that when a statute prohibits the doing of a thing, which if done might be prejudicial to another, in such case he may have an action on that very statute for his damages. 2 *Mod.* 152.

SILICET, that is to say, or to wit, and is frequently used in law proceedings.

SCIRE FACIAS, is a judicial writ, and properly lies after a year and a day after judgment given; whereby the sheriff is commanded to summon or *give notice* to the defendant, that he appear and shew cause why the plaintiff should not have execution. 1. *Inst.* 290.

A *scire facias*, is deemed a judicial writ, and founded on some matter of record, as judgments, recognizances, and letters patent, on which it lies to enforce the execution of them, or to vacate or set them aside; and though it be a judicial writ of execution, yet it is so far in nature of an original, that the defendant may plead to it, and is in that respect considered as an action; and therefore it is held, that a release of all actions, or a release of all executions is a good bar to a *scire facias*. See *Rol. Abr.*

SCOLD, a common scold, is a public nuisance to her neighbourhood; for which offence she may be indicted.

SCOT AND LOT, a customary contribution laid upon all subjects, according to their ability.

SCOTLAND, by 5 Anne, c. 8, the union of England and Scotland was effected, and the *twenty-five articles of union*, agreed to by the parliaments of both nations, were ratified and confirmed as follows; viz. the succession to the monarchy of Great Britan, shall be the same, as was before settled with regard to that of England. The united kingdoms shall be represented by one parliament. There shall be a communication of all rights and privileges between the subjects of both kingdoms, except where it is otherwise agreed. When England raises 2,000,000l. by land-tax, Scotland shall raise 48000l. The standards of the coin, of weights, and measures, shall be reduced to those of England, throughout the united kingdoms. The laws relating to the trade, customs, and the excise, shall be the same in Scotland as in England. But all the other laws of Scotland shall remain in force, though alterable by the parliament of Great Britain: and particularly laws relating to public policy, are alterable at the discretion of parliament: laws relating to private right are not to be altered, but for the evident utility of the people of Scotland. Sixteen peers are to be chosen to represent the peerage of Scotland in parliament, and forty-five members to sit in the house of commons.

The sixteen peers of Scotland shall have all privileges of parliament, and all peers of Scotland shall be peers of Great Britain, ranking next after those of the same degree at the time of the union, and shall have all privileges of peers, except sitting in the house of lords, and voting on the trial of a peer.

It was formerly resolved by the house of lords, that a peer of Scotland, claiming and having a right to sit in the British house of peers had no right to vote in the election of the sixteen Scotch peers: but it seems now settled, that a Scotch peer, made a peer of Great Britain, has a right to vote in the election of the sixteen Scotch peers: and that if any of the sixteen Scotch peers are created peers of Great Britain, they thereby cease to sit as representatives of the Scotch peerage, and new Scotch peers must be elected in their room.

SCRIPTURE, all profane scoffing at the holy scripture, or exposing any part thereof to contempt or ridicule, is punishable by fine and imprisonment. 1 *Haw.* 7.

SCRIVENERS. A scrivener is a kind of broker between those who want to borrow money on security, and those who have money to place out at interest.

SCUTAGE, tax or contribution, raised by those who held lands by knights' service, towards furnishing the king's army, at one, two, or three marks for every knight's fee.

SCUTAGE

SCUTAGIO HABENDO, a writ which lay for the king, or other lord, against the tenant that held by *knight's service*, to serve by himself, or else to send a sufficient man in his place, or pay, &c.

SCYRGEMOTE, a court held twice every year as the sheriff's torn is now, by the bishop of the diocese, and the ealderman (in shires that had ealdermen), and by the bishops and sheriffs, in such as were committed to the sheriffs that were immediate to the king, wherein both the ecclesiastical and temporal laws were given in charge to the country.

SEA. The sea shall be open to all merchants. The main sea beneath the low water mark, and round England, is part of England; for there the admiralty hath jurisdiction. 1 *Inst.* 260.

SEAL, is either in wax, impressed with a device and attached to deeds, &c. or the instrument with which the wax is impressed.

Sealing of a deed, is an essential part of it; for if a writing be not sealed, it cannot be a deed. See *Deed.*

SEALER, an officer in chancery appointed by the lord chancellor of England, to seal the writs and instruments there made in his presence

SEAMEN, by various statutes, sailors having served the king for a limited time, are free to use any trade or profession, in any town of the kingdom, except in *Oxford* or *Cambridge.*

By 2 G. II. c. 36, made perpetual by 2 G. III. c. 31, no master of any vessel shall carry to sea any seaman, his own apprentices excepted, without first entering into an agreement with such seaman for his wages, such agreement to be made in writing, and to declare what wages such seaman is to receive during the whole of the voyage, or for such time as shall be therein agreed upon; and such agreement shall also express the voyage for which such seaman was shipped to perform the same. The provisions of this act are enforced by a penalty of 10l. for each mariner carried to sea without such agreement, to be forfeited by the master to the use of Greenwich Hospital. This agreement is to be signed by each mariner within three days after entering on board such ship, and is, when executed, binding on all parties.

SECONDARY, an officer who is second, or next to the chief

 officer;

officer; as the secondaries to the prothonotaries in the courts of B. R. and C. B.

SECOND DELIVERANCE, a judicial writ that lies after non-suit of the plaintiff in a replevin, and a *retorno habendo* of the cattle replevied; adjudged to him that distrained them, for the replevying of the same cattle again upon security put in for the redelivery of them in case the distress be justified.

SECRETARY. A secretary of state, is a great officer under the king; but it doth not seem, that in that capacity he is any considerable degree the object of our laws, or hath any very important share of magistracy conferred upon him; except that he is allowed the power of commitment, in order to bring offenders to trial. 1 *Black* 338.

SECTA AD CURIAM, a writ that lies against him who refuses to perform his suit, either to the *county*, or *court baron*.

SECTA AD JUSTICIAM FACIENDAM, a service which a man is bound to perform by his fee.

SECTA CURIÆ, suit and service done by tenants at the court of their lord.

SECTA REGALIS, a suit so called, by which all persons were bound twice in a year to attend the sheriff's torn, that they might be informed of things relating to the peace of the public: it was called *regalis,* because the sheriff's torn was the king's leet; and it was a court held that the people might be bound by oath to bear true allegiance to the king: for all persons above twelve years old were obliged to take the oath of allegiance in this court.

SECTA UNICA TANTUM FACIENDA PRO PLURIBUS HÆREDITATIBUS, a writ that lies for that heir that is distrained by the lord to more suits than one, in respect of the land of divers heirs descended unto him.

SECTIS NON FACIENDIS, a writ that lies for a woman, who for her dower, ought not to perform suit or court.

SECURITATE PACIS, a writ that lies for one who is threatened with death or danger, against him that so threateneth, and is taken out of the chancery, and directed to the sheriff.

SE DEFENDENDO, a plea for him who is charged with the death of another, saying he was compelled to do that which he did, in his own defence. See *Homicide*.

SEIGNIOR

SEIGNIOR, denotes in the general signification as much as lord; but is particularly used for the lord of the fee, or of a manor.

SEISIN, is two-fold, seisin in law, and seisin in fact. *Seisin in fact*, is when an actual possession is taken; *seisin in law* when something is done, which the law accounts a seisin, as an enrollment.

SEISINA HABENDA, QUIA REX HABUIT ANNUM, DIEM, ET *VASTUM*, a writ which lies for delivery of seisin to the lord of his lands or tenements, after the king, in the right of his prerogative, hath had the year day and waste.

SEIZURE OF GOODS FOR OFFENCES, no goods of a felon or other offender can be seized to the use of the king, before forfeited; and there are two seizures, one verbal only, to make an inventory, and charge the town or place, when the owner is indicted of the offence; and the other actual, which is the taking of them away afterwards on conviction, &c. 3 *Inst.* 103.

SELF-PRESERVATION. See *Homicide*.

SENATORS, members of parliament. See *Parliament* and *Election*.

SEPARATION OF HUSBAND AND WIFE. See *Divorce*.

SEQUATOR SUB SUO PERICULO, a writ that lies where a summons *ad warrantisaudum* is awarded, and the sheriff returns that he hath nothing whereby he may be summoned; then issues an *alias*, and *pluries*, and if he come not at the *pluries*, this writ shall issue.

SEQUELA CAUSÆ, the process, and depending issue of a cause or trial.

SEQUELA CURIÆ, a suit of court.

SEQUELA VILLANORUM, all the retinue and appurtenances to the goods and chattels of servile tenants, which were at the arbitrary and absolute disposal of the lord.

SEQUESTER, is a term used in the civil law for renouncing, as when a widow comes into court, and disdains to have any thing to do, or to intermeddle with her husband's estate who is deceased, she is said to sequester.

SEQUESTRATION, is the separating or setting aside of a thing in controversy from the possession of both those who contend for it. And it is of two kinds, voluntary, or necessary; *voluntary* is is that which is done by consent of each party; *necessary*, is what the judge doth of his authority, whether the parties will or not. It is used also for the act of the ordinary disposing of the goods and chattels of one deceased, whose estate no man will meddle with.

A *sequestration* is also a kind of execution for debt, especially in the case of a beneficed clerk, of the profits of the benefice, to be paid over to him that had the judgment till the debt is satisfied.

SEQUESTRO HABENDO, a writ judicial, for dissolving a sequestration of the fruits of a benefice made by a bishop at the king's command, thereby to compel the parson to appear at the suit of another; for the parson upon his appearance may have this writ for the discharge of the sequestration.

SERJEANT, *at law*, is the highest degree taken in that profession, as that of a doctor is in the civil law. To these serjeants, as men of great learning and experience, one court is set apart for them to plead in by themselves, which is the court of common pleas, where the common law of England is most strictly observed; yet though they have this court to themselves, they are not restrained from pleading in any other courts, where the judges (who cannot be elevated to that dignity till they have taken the degree of serjeant at law) call them *brothers*, and hear them with great respect, next to the king's attorney and solicitor general. These are made by the king's mandate, or writ.

There are also serjeants at arms, whose office is to attend on the person of the king, to arrest persons of condition offending.

SERJEANTY, signifies in law a service that cannot be due from a tenant to any lord, but to the king only; and it is either grand serjeanty or petit serjeanty.

Grand serjeanty, is a tenure whereby a person holds his lands of the king by such services as he ought to do in person, as to carry the king's banner, or his lance, or to carry his sword before him at his coronation, or to do other like services; and is called grand serjeanty, because it is a more worthy service, than the service in the common tenure of escuage.

Petit serjeanty, is where a person holds his land of the king, to furnish him yearly with some small thing towards his wars, as a bow, lance, &c. And such service is but socage in effect, because such tenant by his tenure, ought not to go nor do any thing in his proper,

proper person, but to render and pay yearly, certain things to the king. *Lil.* 160.

SERVAGE, is when each tenant, besides the payment of a certain rent, finds one or more workmen for his lord's service.

SERVANTS. See *Master and Servant.*

SERVICE, that which the tenant by reason of his fee or estate, owes unto his lord.

SERVITIUM FEODALE, ET PRÆDIALE, was not a personal service, but only by reason of the lands which were held in fee.

SERVITIUM FORINSECUM, a service which did not belong to the chief lord, but to the king.

SERVITIUM INTRINSECUM, is that service which was due to the chief lord alone, from his vassals.

SERVITIUM LIBERUM, a service to be done by the feudatory tenants, who were called *liberi homines,* and distinct from vassals, so also was their service, for they were not bound to any of those base services, as to plough the lord's land, &c. but only to find a man and horse to go with the lord into the army, or to attend his court, &c.

SERVITIUM REGALE, royal service, or the rights and prerogatives that within such a manor belong to the lord of it, as were formerly annexed to some manors in their grant from the king.

SESSION OF PARLIAMENT. The session of parliament continues till it be prorogued or dissolved. 4 *Inst.* 27. See *Parliament.*

SESSIONS OF THE PEACE. See *Quarter Sessions.*

SESSIONS FOR WEIGHTS AND MEASURES. In London, *four justices* from among the mayor, recorder, and aldermen, (of which the mayor or recorder to be one) may hold a sessions to enquire into offences of selling by false weights and measures, contrary to the statutes; and to receive indictments, punish the offenders, &c.

SET-OFF, is when the defendant acknowledges the justice of the plaintiff's demand on the one hand, but on the other sets up a demand of his own, to counterbalance that of the plaintiff, either in the whole, or in part; as if the plaintiff sue for 10l. due on a note of hand, the defendant may *set-off* 9l. due to himself for merchandize sold to the plaintiff. 3 *Black.* 304.

The action in which a *set-off* is allowable upon the statutes 2 & 8 G. II. c. 22 & 24, are debt, covenant, and assumpsit, for the non payment of money; and the demand intended to be set-off, must be such as might have been made the subject of one or other of these actions. A *set-off*, therefore, is never allowed in actions upon the case, trespass, replevin, &c. nor of a penalty, in debt on bond conditioned for the performance of covenants, &c. nor of general damages in covenant or assumpsit; but where a bond is conditioned for the payment of an annuity, a *set-off* may be allowed. A debt barred by the statute of limitations, cannot be *set-off*; and if it be pleaded in bar to the action, the plaintiff may reply the statute of limitations; or if given in evidence, on a notice of *set-off*, it may be objected to at the trial. *Tidd's Pract.* K. B.

SEVERAL ACTION, is where two or more persons are severally charged in any action.

SEVERAL COVENANT, is a covenant by two or more severally; and in a deed where the covenants are several between divers persons, they are as several deeds, written in one piece of parchment. 5 *Rep.* 23.

SEVERAL INHERITANCE, an inheritance conveyed, so as to descend, or come to two persons severally by moieties, &c.

SEVERAL TAIL, that whereby land is given and intailed severally to two: for example, land is given to two men and their wives, and to the heirs of their bodies begotten, the donees have joint estates for their two lives, and yet they have several inheritances, because the issue of the one shall have his moiety, and the issue of the other, the other moiety.

SEVERAL TENANCY, is a plea or exception taken to a writ that is laid against two as joint, which are several.

SEVERANCE, the singling or severing of two, or more, that are joined in one writ. For example, if two join in a writ *de liberate probanda* and the one afterwards be nonsuit, here *severance* is permitted; so that notwithstanding the nonsuit of the one, the other may severally proceed. F. N. B. 78.

SHEADING, a riding, tithing, or division in the *Isle of Man.*

SHEEP. Any person who shall feloniously drive away, or feloniously steal any sheep or lamb; or wilfully kill any sheep or lamb, with a felonious intent to steal the carcase or any part thereof;

thereof; or assist or aid in committing any of the said offences, shall be guilty of felony without benefit of clergy. 14 Geo. II. c. 6.

Any person who shall apprehend and prosecute to conviction any such offender, shall have a reward of 10l. for which purpose, he shall have a certificate signed by the judge, before the end of the assizes, certifying such conviction, and where the offence was committed, and that the offender was apprehended and prosecuted by the person claiming the reward; and if more than one claim it, he shall therein appoint what share shall be paid to each claimant. And on tendering such certificate to the sheriff, he shall pay the same within a month, without deduction, or forfeit double, with treble costs. To be allowed in his accounts, or be repaid him out of the treasury.

And any person who shall in the night time, maliciously and wilfully maim, wound, or otherwise hurt any sheep, whereby the same is not killed, shall forfeit to the party grieved treble damages, by action of trespass, or on the case.

And by 28 Geo. III. c. 38. every person who shall export any live sheep or lambs, shall forfeit 3l. for every sheep or lamb, and shall also suffer solitary imprisonment for three months, without bail, and until the forfeiture be paid; but not to exceed twelve months for such non-payment: and for every subsequent offence 5l. a piece, and imprisonment for six months, and until the forfeiture be paid; but not to exceed two years for the non-payment thereof. And all ships and vessels employed therein shall be forfeited.

SHERIFF, as keeper of the king's peace, the sheriff is the first man in the county, and superior in rank to any nobleman therein, during his office. He may apprehend and commit to prison all persons who break the peace, or attempt to break it, and may bind any one in a recognizance to keep the king's peace. He may, and is bound *ex-officio* to pursue and take all traitors, murderers, felons, and other misdoers, and commit them to goal for safe custody. He is also to defend his country against any of the king's enemies, when they come into the land: and for this purpose, as well as for keeping the peace and pursuing felons, he may command all the people of his county to attend him; which is called the *posse comitatus*, or power of the county; which summons, every person above fifteen years of age, and under the degree of a peer, is bound to attend upon warning, on pain of fine and imprisonment. Yet he cannot exercise the office of a justice of the peace, for then this inconvenience would arise, that he should command himself to execute his own precepts. 1 *Black.* 343.

The sheriff hath a jurisdiction both in criminal and civil cases; and therefore he has two courts, his *torn* for criminal causes, which is the king's court; the other is his *county court,* for civil causes, and this is the court of the sheriff himself. 3 *Salk.* 322.

When the new sheriff is appointed and sworn, he ought at or before the next county court, to deliver a writ of discharge to the old sheriff; who is to set over all the prisoners in the goal, severally by their names, (together with all the writs), precisely, by view and indenture between the two sheriffs; wherein must be comprehended all the actions which the old sheriff has against every prisoner; though the executions are of record. And till the delivery of the prisoners to the new sheriff, they remain in the custody of the old sheriff; notwithstanding the letters patent of appointment, the writ of discharge, and the writ of delivery. Neither is the new sheriff obliged to receive the prisoners, but at the goal. But the office of the old sheriff ceases, when the writ of discharge is brought to him. *Wood.* b. 1. c. 7.

By 3 Geo. I. c. 15. it shall not be lawful for any person to buy, sell, let, or take to farm, the office of under-sheriff, or deputy-sheriff, or seal-keeper, county-clerk, shire-clerk, goaler, bailiff, or any other office pertaining to the office of high-sheriff, or to contract for any of the said offices, on forfeiture of 500l. one moiety to his majesty, the other to such as shall sue in any court at Westminster, within two years after the offence.

Provided that nothing in this act shall hinder any high-sheriff from constituting an under-sheriff, or deputy-sheriff, as by law he may; nor to hinder the under-sheriff in any case of the high-sheriff's death, when he acts as high-sheriff, from constituting a deputy; nor to hinder such sheriff, or under-sheriff, from receiving the lawful perquisites of his office, or for taking security for the due answering the same; nor to hinder such sheriff, or under-sheriff, deputy-sheriff, seal-keeper, &c. from accounting to the high-sheriff for all such lawful fees as shall be by them taken, nor

for

for giving security so to do, or to hinder the high-sheriff from allowing a salary to his under-sheriff, &c. or other officers.

And if any sheriff shall die before the expiration of his year, or before he be superseded, the under-sheriff shall nevertheless continue in his office, and execute the same in the name of the deceased, till another sheriff be appointed and sworn; and the under-sheriff shall be answerable for the execution of the office during such interval, as the high-sheriff would have been; and the security given by the under-sheriff and his pledges shall stand a security to the king, and all persons whatsoever, for the performing his office during such interval. *Id.*

SHERIFFALTY, is the sheriffship, or time of a man's being sheriff.

SHERIFFWICK, the extent of a sheriff's authority.

SHERIFFGELD, a rent formerly paid by the sheriff; and it is prayed that the sheriff in his account may be discharged thereof.

SHEWING, is especially used to be quit of an attachment in a court, in plaints *shewed* and not avowed.

SHIP MONEY, an imposition charged on the ports, towns, cities, boroughs, and counties of this realm, in the time of king Charles I. by writs commonly called ship-writs, under the great seal of England, in 1635 and 1636, for providing and furnishing certain ships for the king's service, &c. which was declared to be contrary to the laws and statutes of this realm, the petition of right, and liberty of the subject.

SHIPS, wilfully destroying a ship with intent to prejudice the insurers; plundering a ship in distress; stealing goods of the value of 40s. from on ship board; burning or destroying any of his majesty's shipping or stores; are by a variéty of statutes, made felony without benefit of clergy.

SHIRE, is a part or portion of this kingdom, called also a county.

SHIRE-CLERK, is he that keeps the county court; his office is so incident to the sheriff, that the king cannot grant it.

SHIRE-HALL, by 29 Geo. III. c. 20. the justices in sessions, on presentment of the grand jury at the assizes, of the ill state and condition of the shire-hall, or other building used for holding the assizes, and the necessity of repairing it, may order it to be repaired

paired as they shall think fit, and the money to be levied as for other county rates.

SHOOTING, maliciously at persons in any dwelling house, or other place, though death should not ensue, is felony without clergy, by the 9 Geo. I. c. 22. commonly called the *black act*.

SHOPLIFTERS, those who steal goods privately out of shops; which being to the value of 5l. though no person be in the shop, is felony without benefit of clergy. 10 & 11 W. III. c. 23.

SHROUD, stealing a shroud from a dead body, is felony; for the property thereof remains in the executor, or the person who was at the charge of the funeral. But stealing the corpse only, which has no owner, is not felony, unless some of the grave-cloaths be stolen with it. 2 *Black*. 419.

SHRUBS, wilfully to spoil or destroy any trees, roots, shrubs, or plants, is, for the two first offences, liable to pecuniary penalties; and for the third, the offender is guilty of felony, and transported for seven years. And stealing any of them by night, to the value of 5s. is felony for the first offence.

SICUT ALIAS, a second writ issued, where the first was not executed.

SIDEMEN or SYNODSMEN, those who are yearly chosen, according to the custom of every parish, to assist the churchwardens in the inquiry, and presenting such offenders to the ordinary, as punishable in the court christian.

SIGN MANUAL, the signature of the king on grants or letters patent, which first pass by bill, &c.

SIGNET, one of the king's seals, wherewith his private letters are sealed, which is always in custody of the king's secretaries; and there are four clerks of the *signet-office*, always attending. 2 *Inst*. 556.

SIGNIFICAVIT, a writ *de excommunicate capiendo*, issuing out of *chancery* upon a certificate given by the ordinary, of a man that stands obstinately excommunicated, by the space of forty days, for the laying him up in prison, without bail or mainprize, until he submit himself to the authority of the church. And it is so called, because the word *significavit*, is an emphatical word in the writ.

SIGNING, of deeds and wills, is necessary to make them binding.

SIMONY,

SIMONY, is the corrupt presentation of any one to an ecclesiastical benefice, for money, gift, reward, or benefit. It was not an offence punishable in a criminal way at the common law, it being thought sufficient to leave the clerk to ecclesiastical censures. But as these did not affect the simoniacal patron, none were efficacious enough to repel the notorious practice of the thing, divers acts of parliament have been made to restrain it by means of civil forfeitures; which the modern prevailing usage with regard to spiritual preferments, call aloud to put in execution. 2 *Black*. c. 18.

By one of the canons of 1603, every person, before his admission to any ecclesiastical promotion, shall, before the ordinary, take an oath, that he hath made no simoniacal contract, promise, or payment, directly, or indirectly, by himself or any other, for the obtaining of the said promotion; and that he will not afterwards perform or satisfy any such kind of payment, contract, or promise, by any other without his knowledge or consent.

To purchase a presentation, the living being actually vacant, is open and notorious simony; this being expressly in the face of the statute. *Moor*. 914.

The sale of an *advowson*, during a vacancy, is not within the statute of simony, as the sale of the next presentation is: but it is void by the common law. 2 *Black*. 22.

A bond of resignation, is a bond given by the person intended to be presented to a benefice, with condition to resign the same; and is special or general. The condition of a *special* one, is to resign the benefice in favour of some certain person, as a son, kinsman, or friend of the patron, when he shall be capable of taking the same. By a *general bond*, the incumbent is bound to resign on the request of the patron. 4 *Bac. Abr*. 470.

A bond with condition to resign within three months after being requested, to the intent that the patron might present his son when he should be capable, was held good; and the judgment was affirmed in the exchequer-chamber: for that a man may without any colour of simony bind himself for good reasons; as if he take a second benefice, or if he be non-resident, or that the patron present his son, to resign; but if the condition had been to let the patron have a lease of the glebe or tithes, or to pay a sum of money, it had been simoniacal.

SIMPL

SIMPLE CONTRACT, debts by simple contract, are such where the contract upon which the obligation arises, is neither ascertained by matter of record, nor yet by special deed or instrument, but by mere oral evidence, or by notes unsealed; whereas debts by specialty are such whereby the contract is ascertained by deed or instrument under seal. 2 *Black.* 462.

SIMPLER JUSTICIARIUS, this style was anciently used for any *puisne* judge, who was not chief in any court.

SIMUL CUM, together with, are words used in indictments, and declarations of trespass against several persons, where some of them are known, and others not.

SINE ASSENSU CAPITALI, a writ that lies where a dean, bishop, prebendary, abbot, prior, or master, of an hospital, alien the land holden in right of his house, *without the assent of the chapter, convent, and fraternity*; in which case his successor shall have this writ.

SINE CURE, is where a rector of a parish hath a vicar under him endowed and charged with the cure; so that the rector is not obliged either to do duty or residence.

SI NON OMNES, a writ of association, whereby, if all in commission cannot meet at the day assigned, it is allowed that two or more of them may finish the business.

SINKING FUND, a name given to the sum annually assigned for payment and diminishing the capital of the national debt. Its progress is that of compound interest, and very rapidly increases as it goes on. This fund was established by Mr. Pitt for counteracting national ruin, by the too great extent of the borrowing system.

SIX CLERKS IN CHANCERY. See *Chancery*.

SLAVERY, the law of England abhors, and will not endure the existence of slavery within this nation.

A *slave* or negro, the moment he lands in England, falls under the protection of the laws, and so far becomes a freeman. Yet with regard to any right which the master may have lawfully acquired to his perpetual service, that will remain exactly in the same state as before: for this is no more than the same state of subjection for life, which every apprentice submits to for the space of seven years, or sometimes for a longer term. 1 *Black.* 127.

SOCCAGE,

SOCAGE, a tenure of lands by or for certain inferior *services* of husbandry to be performed to the lord of the fee. This was a tenure of so large an extent, that all the lands in England, which were not held in knight's service, were held in *socage*.

SOCMANS, or SOKEMANS, such tenants as hold their lands and tenements by *socage tenure*.

SOLDIERS, the regulations respecting the soldiery, are principally contained in the annual acts against mutiny and desertion. See *Mutiny Act*.

SOLE TENANT, he or she who holds only in his or her own right, without any other joined: for example, if a man and wife, hold land for their lives, the remainder to their son, here the man dying, the lord shall not have heriot, because he dieth not sole tenant.

SOLICITOR, a person employed to take care of and follow suits depending in suits of equity: but he may be sworn and admitted an attorney in the court of king's-bench, or common-pleas. 23 Geo. II. c. 26.

SOMERSET-HOUSE, was assured to queen Charlotte for life, by 2 Geo. III. c. 1. but Buckingham-house has been since purchased and settled upon her in lieu thereof.

SON ASSAULT, a justification in an action of assault and battery; because the plaintiff made the first assault, and what the defendant did was in his own defence.

SOVEREIGN, in our constitution, the law ascribes to the king the attribute of sovereignty, but that it is to be understood in a qualified sense, *i. e.* a supreme magistrate, not as sole legislator; as the legislative power is vested in the king, lords, and commons, not in any of the three estates alone.

SOUTH-SEA COMPANY, a company of merchants established for the purpose of trading to the South-sea. This company was famous for the false speculations into which it led the public, in 1719-20.

SPATÆ PLACITUM, pleas of the word, or a court-martial for the speedy execution of justice on military delinquents.

SPEAKER. See *Election* and *Parliament*.

SPECIAL JURY. See *Jury*.

SPECIALTY, a bond, bill, or such like instrument; a writing or deed under the hand and seal of the parties. These are the next sort of debts after those of record; being confirmed by special evidence under seal. 2 *Black* c. 30.

SPINSTER, the addition usually given to all unmarried women, from the viscount's daughter downward.

SPIRITUALITIES OF A BISHOP, are those profits which he receives as a bishop, not as a baron of parliament.

SPOLIATION, a writ which lies for one incumbent against another, in any case where the right of the patronage comes not in the debate, as if a parson be made a bishop, and hath dispursation to keep his rectory, and afterwards the patron present another to the church, who is instituted and inducted. The bishop shall have against his incumbent a writ of spoliation in court christian. F. N. B. 36.

STABBING OF PERSONS, is made felony without benefit of clergy.

STAMPS. Actions, entry of, in inferior courts for 40s. and upwards, *one shilling and sixpence.* 12 Geo. c. 22.

Acts. See *Notarial Acts.*

Adjudication, apprisings, charter, resignation, clare-constat, cognition of heirs, heritable right, confirmation, novodamas, principal and original instrument of surrender, retour, sasine, and service in Scotland, *nine shillings and sixpence.* 37 Geo. III. c. 90.

Administration. See *Probate.*

Admiralty, or Cinque Ports. Any answer exhibited in these courts, *seven shillings.* 41 Geo. III. c. 86.

Any libel, allegation, deposition, or inventory, exhibited in the courts of admiralty or cinque-Ports; *five shillings.* 37 Geo. III. c. 90.

Any copy of any citation, monition, or answer, made in the courts of admiralty or cinque-ports; *five shillings.* 37 Geo. III. c. 90.

Any copy of any libel, allegation, deposition, or inventory, exhibited in the courts of admiralty or cinque-ports; *five shillings.* 37 Geo. III. c. 90.

Any personal decree, warrant, or monition, in any court of admiralty or the cinque-ports, or any copy thereof; *ten shillings.* 27 Geo. III. c. 90.

Any sentence given in the courts of admiralty or cinque-ports, or or any attachment made out by the same, or relaxation thereof; *one pound.* 37 Geo. III. c. 90.

Any sentence or final decree exhibited in the courts of admiralty or cinque-ports, or any copy thereof; *four shillings.* 37 Geo. III. c. 90.

Admission into corporations or companies; *eight shillings.* 37 Geo. III. c. 90.

Admission into any inn of chancery; *four pounds two shillings.* 37 Geo. III. c. 90.

Admission into any of the four inns of court; *sixteen pounds four shillings.* 37 Geo. III. c. 90.

Admittance of fellow of college of physicians, attorney, clerk, advocate, proctor, notary, or other officer of any court whatsoever in Great Britain, except under 10l. per annum; *sixteen pounds.* 37 Geo. III. c. 50.

Advertisement in newspaper; *three shillings.* 37 Geo. III. c. 50.

Advertisement in periodical pamphlets; *three shillings.* 29 Geo. III. c. 50.

Advocate. See *Admittance.*

Affidavit in any court of law or equity, at Westminster, or in any court of great sessions for the counties in Wales, or in the court of the county palatine of Chester, or copies thereof; *two shillings.* 35 Geo. III. c. 30.

Affidavits in inferior courts; *one shilling.* 35 Geo. III. c. 30.

Agreements (except where the matter of agreement shall not exceed twenty pounds, and also except those for lease at rack rent), of messuages under five pounds, those for hire of labourers, artificers, manufacturers or menial servants, and those relating to sale of goods, &c. *ten shillings.* 37 Geo. III. c. 90.

No memorandum or agreement written upon an unstamped paper shall be deemed void, in case it be stamped at the head office and the duty paid within twenty-one days after the same shall have been entered into.

Allegation. See *Citation.*

Almanack, book or sheet; *eight pence.* 37 Geo. III. c. 90.

Answer in court of equity. See *Bills, Copy.*

Answer, sentence, and final decree, in ecclesiastical courts, and copies thereof, and copies of citation or monition; *two shillings.* 23 Geo. III. c. 58.

Appeal, writ of. See *Certiorari.*

Appeal from the admiralty, arches, or prerogative courts of Canterbury or York; *twelve pounds.* 37 Geo. III. c. 90.

Appearance on common bail, in the courts at Westminster, great sessions, or counties palatine; *one shilling and sixpence.* 32 Geo. II. c. 35. in all other courts, *one shilling.*

Appearance on special bail; *two shillings.* 10 W. III. c. 25.

Apprentices, the stamps upon apprentices' indentures, amount to 25s. for each indenture; except parish-apprentices, or charity children, for whom a *sixpenny* stamp is sufficient. Also where the fee given with the apprentice does not amount to 10l. each indenture is subject to a stamp of *fifteen shillings* only. See *Deeds.*

And if a fee be given with an apprentice, clerk, or servant, bound or articled for a term of years, the following duty must be paid in respect of such fee.

From 1l. to 50l. *six-pence for every pound.*

All above 50l. and upwards, *one shilling for every pound*; to be paid by the master or mistress.

The full sum given, must be set down in the indentures, or forfeit double the amount, if the deception can be discovered.

And the indentures must be brought to the stamp-office; if executed within the bills of mortality, within one month; or if executed in the country, to their agents within two months after binding, and the duty paid, or the indentures become void and forfeit 50l. besides.

Apprisings. See *Adjudication.*

Articles of clerkship. See *Attorney's Clerks.*

Assignments. See *Deeds.*

Assignments of bail-bonds; *one shilling.* 10 W. III. c. 25.

Assurance of houses and policy. See *Insurance.*

Attachment in admiralty or cinque-ports; *one pound.* 37 Geo. III. c. 90.

Attested copies. See *Copy.*

Attorney, letter of. See *Deeds.*

Attorney, admittance of. See *Admittance.*

Every solicitor, attorney, notary, proctor, agent, or procurator, practising in any of the courts at Westminster, ecclesiastical, admiralty, or cinque-port courts, in his majesty's courts in Scotland, the great sessions in Wales, the courts in the counties palatine, or any other courts holding pleas to the amount of 40s. or more;

shall

shall take out certificates annually, upon which there shall be charged, if the solicitor, &c. reside in any of the inns of court, or in London, Westminster, Southwark, St. Pancras, St. Mary-le-bone, or within the bills of mortality, a stamp-duty of 5l. in any other part of Great Britain 3l. 25 Geo. III. c. 80.

And every solicitor, attorney, notary, proctor, agent, or procurator, in any court in England, holding plea of 40s. shall annually, between Nov. 1 and the end of Michaelmas term, deliver at the head office for stamps, a note containing his name and place of abode, and thereupon, and upon payment of the duties in respect of his abode, every such person shall be entitled to his certificate, to be issued by the commissioners of stamps, or their proper officer. 37 Geo. III. c. 90.

And every such certificate so obtained shall be entered with the proper officer of the court where the party shall practice, who shall be paid *one shilling* for the entry, and the books of such entry may be inspected by all persons gratis.

And every such certificate shall bear date the 2d day of November, and shall cease on the 1st day of November, next following.

Persons who shall from and after the first day of November, 1797, act without obtaining a certificate, or without entering the same as aforesaid, or shall deliver in to any person at the stamp-office, any account of a residence with intent to evade the higher duties, shall forfeit 50l. and be incapable of suing for any fees.

And every person, admitted, sworn, inrolled, or registered in any of the courts, who shall neglect to obtain his certificate in manner aforesaid for the space of one whole year, shall from thenceforth be incapable of practising in his own name, or in the name of any other; but the courts may re-admit him on payment of the duty accrued since the expiration of his last certificate, and such further sum as the court shall order by way of penalty.

And by 39 & 40 Geo. III. c. 72. from and after Nov. 1, 1800, every person who shall act as a public notary, or use or exercise the office of a notary in any manner, or do any notorial act whatsoever, without having been duly admitted in the court where notaries are usually admitted, and without having delivered in his name and usual place of residence, and taken out such certificate as is directed by the acts; shall forfeit 50l. and be incapable to do any act as a notary-public, or recover any fee.

Attornies clerks, by 34 Geo. III. c. 14. there shall be paid for every contract in writing, whereby any person shall become bound to serve as a clerk, in order to his admission as a solicitor or attorney, the additional duties following, viz. for every piece of vellum, parchment, or paper, upon which shall be written any such contract, whereby any person shall become bound to serve as a clerk as aforesaid, in order to his admission as a solicitor or attorney in any of the courts at Westminster, there shall be charged a stamp-duty of *one hundred pounds.*

And in order to his admission as a solicitor or attorney in any of the courts of great sessions in Wales, or in the counties palatine of Chester, Lancaster, or Durham, or in any court of record in England, holding pleas to the amount of 40s. and not in any of the said courts at Westminster, there shall be charged a stamp-duty of *fifty pounds.*

Award, *ten shillings.* 37 Geo. III. c. 90.

Bail-bonds and assignments thereof, *one shilling.* 10 W. III. c. 25.

Beneficial warrant under sign manual (except for navy, army, or ordnance), *one pound five shillings.* 37 Geo. III. c. 90.

Bill of exchange, promissory or other note, draft, or order, where the sum amounts to 40s and does not exceed 5l. 5s. *sixpence.* 41 Geo. III. c. 10.

Above 5l. 5s. and not exceeding 30l. *one shilling.* 41 Geo. III. c. 10.

Above 30l and not exceeding 50l. *one shilling and sixpence.* 41 Geo. III. c. 10.

Above 50l. and not exceeding 100l. *two shillings.* 41 Geo. III. c. 10.

Above 100l. and not exceeding 200l. *three shillings.* 41 Geo. III. c. 10.

Bills and notes not exceeding 200l. *value,* and for every bill of exchange, promisory or other notes, draft or order, payable on demand, or otherwise, where the sum shall exceed 200l. there shall be charged *four shillings.* 41 Geo. III. c. 10.

Foreign

Foreign bills of exchange, drawn in sets according to the custom of merchants, where the sum shall not exceed 100l. *one shilling and a penny*. 41 Geo. III. c. 10.

Above 100l. and not exceeding 200l. *one shilling and sixpence*. 41 Geo. III. c. 10.

And exceeding 200l. *two shillings*. 41 Geo. III. c. 10.

Bill of lading, *two shillings*. 37 Geo. III. c. 90.

Bill of Middlesex. See *Original Writ*.

Bills, answers, replications, rejoinders, demurrers, interrogatories, depositions taken by commissions, and other proceedings in courts of equity; *two shillings and sixpence*. 23 Geo. III. c. 58.

Bonds (except such as are given as security for money); *fifteen shillings*. 41 Geo. III. c. 86.

Coast bonds, and bonds on wills or administrations not exceeding 20l. and bonds given by the widow of any soldier or sailor, are exempt from the duty imposed by 37 Geo. III. c. 90.

Bonds given as security for payment of money if not above 100l. *fifteen shillings*. 41 Geo. III. c. 86.

Above 100l. and under 500l. *one pound*. 37 Geo. III. c. 90.

If of 500l. or upwards, *one pound ten shillings*. 37 Geo. III. c. 90.

When the amount shall be of the value of 100l. or upwards, *two pounds*. 37 Geo. III. c. 90.

When the amount shall be of the value of 200l. or upwards, *three pounds*. 37 Geo. III. c. 90.

When the amount shall be of the value of 5000l. or upwards, *five pounds*. 37 Geo. III. c. 90.

Briefs for collecting charitable benevolence, &c. *four pounds*, 23 Geo. III. c. 58.

Capias writ. See *Original Writ*.

Cards per pack, *two shillings and sixpence*. 41 Geo. III. c. 86.

Catalogue. See *Inventory*.

Certificate of barrister in any of the inns of court, *twenty-eight pounds*. 37 Geo. III. c. 90.

Certificate or debenture for drawback, *four shillings*. 37 Geo. III. c. 90.

Certificate of marriage except of seamen's widows, *five shillings*. 5 W. III. c. 21.

Certificate

Certificate See *Register, Registry, Sacrament.*

Certiorari, writ of error, or writ of appeal, except to delegates, *ten shillings.*

Certificate to kill game, *three pounds three shillings.* See *Game.*

Certificate of appointment of game-keeper, *ten shillings and sixpence.*

Certificate for wearing hair-powder, *one pound one shilling.* 41 Geo. III. c. 69.

Certificate for attornies. See *Attorney.*

Charter. See *Adjudication.*

Charter-party. See *Deeds.*

Charity-children's indenture. See *Apprentice.*

Citation or monition, libel, or allegation, deposition, or inventory, exhibited in any ecclesiastical court, and all copies thereof (except copies of citation or monition for which see *Answer* (*two shillings and sixpence.* 23 Geo. III. c. 58.

Clare-constat. See *Adjudication.*

Clerk. See *Admittance.*

Clerks to attornies. See *Attornies Clerks.*

Cognition of heirs. See *Adjudication.*

Collation, donation, or presentation to any ecclesiastical dignity, promotion, or benefice of the yearly value of 10l. and upwards in the king's books, *twelve pounds.* 37 Geo. III. c. 90.

And to any other benefice, dignity, or spiritual, or ecclesiastical promotion, *six pounds.* 37 Geo. III. c. 90.

Commission ecclesiastical, *five shillings.* 10 W. III. c. 25.

Common bail in the courts at Westminster, great sessions, or county palatine, *one shilling and sixpence.* 32 Geo. II. c. 35.

Confirmation. See *Adjudication.*

Contract. See *Deed.*

Conveyance, surrender, of grants of offices, release, or other deed inrolled in any court of record, or by any custos rotulorum, or clerk of the peace, *one pound.* 37. Geo. III. c. 90.

Copy of court-roll. See *Surrender.*

Copy of depositions in chancery, or other court of equity at Westminster, copy of any bill, answer, plea, demurrer, replication, rejoinder, interrogatories, or other proceedings whatsoever, in such courts of equity, *three-pence.* 19 Geo. III. c. 66.

Copies

Copies of wills, *sixpence.* 37 Geo. III. c. 90.

Any copy purporting to be a true copy, or attested to be a true copy, of any indenture, lease, or other deed, or any part thereof, for the security or use of any person, being a party to the same deed, and not having the custody of the original, or where such copy shall not be made in lieu of such original, *six shillings and eight-pence.* 40 Geo. III. c. 72.

And the number of stamps required to be used for such copies of deeds, are one for every ten common law sheets of 72 words; but if after a calculation in that number, there shall remain a number of words, less in quantity than 10 common law-sheets, no further stamp is required for the excess.

And by 39 & 40 Geo. III. c. 72. from Aug. 1, 1800, in lieu of the stamp-duty of *six shillings and eight-pence,* upon the copy of any deed, when it is for the use of any person, other than any of the parties to the same deed, and who shall not have the custody of the original, or where such copy shall not be made in lieu of such original, then shall be paid a stamp-duty of *six-pence,* on every piece of vellum or parchment, or sheet or piece of paper, on which any such copy shall be written.

And the number of stamps to be put upon every copy, is to be calculated according to the last act.

And by 39 & 40 Geo. III. c. 34. copies of indentures or other deeds, liable to the duties granted, by 37 Geo. III. c. 90. may be stamped within sixty days after date of the attestation, on payment of the duty only.

Copy of any surrender of, and admittance to, any custom-right estate, not being copyhold, which shall pass by surrender and admittance only, and which shall not pass by deed, within England, Wales, and town of Berwick-upon-Tweed, *twelve shillings.* 41 Geo. III. c. 86.

Copyhold estate. See *Surrender.*

Covenant writ of. See *Writ of Covenant.*

Debenture for drawbacks. See *Certificate.*

Declaration, plea, replication, rejoinder, demurrer, or other pleading whatsoever, in any court of law at Westminster, or in any of the courts of the principality of Wales, or in any of the counties palatine of Chester, Lancaster, or Durham, and copies thereof, *three-pence.* 32 Geo. II. c. 35.

Declaration, plea, replication, rejoinder, demurrer, or other pleading

pleading whatsoever, in any inferior court of law, and copies thereof, *two-pence.* 10 W. III. c. 15.

Decree personal. See *Warrant.*

Dedimus potestatem. See *Original Writ.*

Deeds, any indenture (except parish-indentures) lease or deed-poll; and any charter-party, release, contract, or other obligatory instrument; or any procuration of letters of attorney, for every 15 common law-sheets, of 72 words each, *fifteen shillings.* 41 Geo. III. c. 86.

And moreover by 37 Geo. III. there shall be paid upon every deed which shall be made after Aug. 1, 1797, an additional stamp-duty of 10s. over and above all duties now payable on the vellum or paper, whereon such deed shall be engrossed (but this is upon the first skin only) the provisions of this act being as follow:

It shall not extend to any bond or letter of attorney, bearing date before Aug. 1, 1797.

Also it shall not extend to any indenture of apprenticeship, where a sum not exceeding 10l. shall be given; nor to any lease for not exceeding twenty-one years, the full and improved value whereof, and rent reserved thereby, shall not be more than 10l. nor to any lease for lives, or years determinable on lives, where the fine shall not exceed 20l. nor the rent reserved 40.

But by 39 and 40 Geo. III. c. 42. the above duties shall extend to every deed, which by lease may form, or is intended to form, a part of any conveyance of lands or tenements, whereby a greater interest in the same shall be conveyed, than a term of twenty-one years, whatever may be the value thereof.

Nor shall any deed be subject to the payment of any greater duty than the sum before mentioned, or to be stamped on more than one skin, with the additional stamp; or to be stamped with more than one such stamp.

Nor shall the duty by this act imposed, be liable to the regulations respecting the stamping of parchment and paper, according to the number of common law-sheets engrossed thereon.

Upon payment within 60 days, after the date of the deed, of the duty hereby imposed, the stamp-officers may stamp any vellum, parchment, or paper, to which any deed shall have been engrossed, or on which any deed shall be intended to be engrossed, with the additional stamp.

And

And if the duty shall not be paid within sixty days, then it shall be lawful to send the deed to the head office, and on payment of the duty, and the further sum of 10l. by way of penalty, the same may be stamped.

But grants, conveyances, and assurances, under the seal of the duchy of Lancaster, according to 19 Geo. III. c. 45. where the consideration does not exceed 10l. are exempted by that act and 39 & 40 Geo. III. c. 72. from all duty.

The number of stamps required to be used on deeds, are one for every fifteen common law-sheets (of 72 words each) contained in the deed, or in any schedule or instrument annexed thereto, or any indorsement thereon.

Deeds to be inrolled. See *Conveyance.*

Degrees in universities. See *Register.*

Demurrer at law. See *Declaration.*

Demurrer in equity. See *Bills, Copy.*

Depositions in courts of equity. See *Bills.*

Depositions in ecclesiastical court. See *Citation.*

Dice per pair, and all other things used for any game of chance, *seventeen shillings and six-pence.* 41 Geo. III. c. 86.

Dispensation to hold two ecclesiastical dignities, or benefices, or other dispensation from the archbishop of Canterbury, *twenty pounds.* 37 Geo. III. c. 90.

Donation. See *Collation.*

Draft for money. See *Bill of Exchange.*

Drawbacks. See *Certificate.*

Ecclesiastical commission. See *Commission.*

Entry of writ. See *Writ of Covenants.*

Error writ of. See *Certiorari.*

Exemplifications under the seal of any court, *two pounds.* 37 Geo. III. c. 90.

Faculty from the archbishop of Canterbury, or master of the faculties, *twenty pounds.* 37 Geo. III. c. 90.

Fellow of the college of physicians. See *Admittance.*

Final decree. See *Answer.*

Grant or letters patent, any grant or letters patent, under the great seal, or the seal of the duchy of Lancaster, of any honour, dignity, promotion, franchise, liberty, or privilege, or the exemplification thereof, *sixteen pounds.* 37 Geo. III. c. 90.

Grant

Grant from his majesty of money exceeding one hundred pounds, which shall pass the great seal or privy seal, *twelve pounds.* 37 Geo. III. c. 90.

Grant of land in fee, lease for years, or other profits, not particularly charged under the great seal, seal of exchequer, duchy or county palatine of Lancaster, or privy seal, *ten pounds.* 37 G. III. c. 90.

Grant of office or employment above 50l. a year, *six pounds.* 12 Anne. c. 9.

If above 100l. (to be calculated on the salary, fees, and perquisites, *twelve pounds.* 37 Geo. III. c. 90.

Habeas corpus, *five shillings.* 5 W. III. c. 21.

Hats, duty on every hat of 4s. or under, *three-pence.* 36 Geo. III. c. 12.

Above 4s. and not exceeding 7s. *six-pence.* 36 Geo. III. c. 12.

Above 7s. and not exceeding 12s. *one shilling.* 36 Geo. III. c. 12.

Above 12s. and upwards, *two shillings.* 36 Geo. III. c. 12.

Heretable right. See *Adjudication.*

Horses. See *Race-horses.*

Indenture. See *Deeds.*

Indentures, parish or charity. See *Apprentices.*

Institution, or licence ecclesiastical in England, Wales, or Berwick-upon-Tweed (except licences of any ecclesiastical court or ordinary, appointing any stipendiary curate, in which the annual amount of the stipend shall be inserted, *one pound ten shillings.* 37 Geo. III. c. 90.

Instrument obligatory. See *Deed.*

Insurance of horses or goods from fire, *two shillings per cent.* 37 Geo. III c. 90.

Insurance upon any ship, goods, or merchandize, when the sum shall amount to one hundred pounds, *five shillings.* 41 Geo. III. c. 10. and so progressively for every sum of one hundred pounds insured.

And where the sum to be insured shall not amount to one hundred pounds, a like duty of *five shillings.* 41 Geo. III. c. 10.

And where the sum to be insured shall exceed one hundred pounds, or any progressive sums of one hundred pounds each, by

any

any fractional part of one hundred pounds, at like duty for each fractional part of one hundred pounds; *five shillings.* 41 G. III. c. 10.

And upon every insurance where the premium shall not exceed the rate of 20s. there shall be paid where the sum shall amount to 100l. a duty of *two shillings and six-pence*; and so progressively for every sum of one hundred pounds so insured. 41 G. III. c. 10.

And where the sum so to be insured, shall not amount to 100l. a like duty of *two shillings and six-pence.*

And where the sum so to be insured shall exceed 100l. or any progressive sums of 100l. each, by any fractional part of 100l, a like duty of *two shillings and six-pence.* 41 G. III. c. 10.

Which duties shall be payable by the assured.

This does not extend to any insurance of houses, furniture, goods, wares, merchandizes, or other property, from loss by fine, already subject to duty, nor any insurance on lives. 41 G. III. c. 10.

Interrogatories. See *Bills, Copy.*

Inventory or catalogue of furniture with reference to any agreement; *five shillings.* 37 G. III. c. 90.

Inventory in ecclesiastical court. See *Citation.*

Judgment. See *Record.*

Lading. See *Bill of Lading.*

Latitat. See *Original Writ.*

Lease of land, house, &c. See *Deed.*

Lease for years, or other profits, not particularly charged, under the great seal, seal of exchequer, duchy or county palatine of Lancaster, or privy seal; *ten pounds.* 37 G. III. c. 90.

Lease by copy of court roll. See *Surrender.*

Legacies, wives, children, and grandchildren, to pay for a legacy or share of a personal estate:

Of the value of 20l. or under, *two shillings and six-pence.* 20 G. III. c. 28.

Above 20l. and under 100l. *five shillings.* 20 G. III. c. 28.

For 100l. and upwards, *one pound.* 20 G. III. c. 28.

Any other lineal descendant, or the father, mother, and other lineal ascendant, or the husband of the deceased, to pay for a legacy or share of a personal estate:

Of the value of 20l. or under; *five shillings.* 23 G. III. c. 58.

Above 20l. and under 100l. *ten shillings.* 23 G. III. c. 58.

For 100l. *two pounds.* 23 G. III. c. 58.

For 200l. *three pounds.* 23 G. III. c. 58.

For 300l. *four pounds.* 23 G. III. c. 58.

And for every further sum of 100l. *two pounds.* 29 G. III. c. 51.

All collateral relations, and strangers, to pay for a legacy or share of a personal estate; under the value of 20l. *five shillings.* 23 G. III. c. 58.

Letter of attorney for transfer or disposal of stock, or any other purpose; *fifteen shillings.* 41 G. III. c. 86.

Letters of administration. See *Probate.*

Letters of Mart. See *Mart.*

Letters patent. See *Grant.*

Libel. See *Citation.*

Licence ecclesiastical. See *Institution.*

Licence to pawnbrokers within the bills of mortality; 10l. per annum.

Out of the bills, 5l. per ann. 25 G. III. c. 48.

Licence for marriage, *five shillings.* 5 W. III. c. 21.

Licence for selling quack medicines. See *Medicines.*

License for retailing beer and ale; *two pounds two shillings.*

Licences, for spirituous liquors, sweets, and wines, to be taken out annually at the excise office.

Licence for a mad house; *five shillings.*

Licence to keep lying-in hospitals; *five shillings.*

Licence to keep lottery office, in London, Edinburgh, or Dublin; *fifty pounds,* elsewhere, *ten pounds.*

Mandate. See *Original Writ.*

Marine Insurance. See *Insurance.*

Marriage licence. See *Licence.*

Mart, letters of, *one pound ten shillings.* 37 G. III. c. 90.

Matriculation in the universities; *eight shillings.* 37 G. III. c. 90.

Medicines. See *Quack Medicines.*

Middlesex, bill of. See *Original.*

Monition. See *Citation, Warrant.*

Newgate,

Newgate, and general circuit pardon, *four pounds*. 23 G. III. c. 58.

Newspapers, every newspaper, or paper containing public news, intelligence, or occurrences, contained in half a sheet or less; *three-pence half-penny*. 37 G. III. c. 90.

Being larger than half a sheet and not exceeding an whole sheet; *four-pence*. 37 G. III. c. 90.

Nisi prius. See *Record*.

Notary. See *Admittance and Attorney*.

Notarial acts; any protest, or notarial act whatever; *four shillings*. 37 G. III. c. 90.

Note promissory. See *Bills of Exchange*.

Novodamus. See *Adjudication*.

Obligatory instrument. See *Bond*.

Officer of any court. See *Admittance*.

Order for payment of money. See *Bills of Exchange*.

Order in any court of Westminster, and copy; *one shilling and sixpence*. 32 G. II. c. 35.

Original writ (unless prœ capias), subpœna, bill of Middlesex, latitat, writ of capias, quo minus, writ of dedimus potestatem, every other writ, process, or mandate, for forty shillings or upwards; *three shillings and sixpence*. 35 G. III. c. 30.

Pamphlets of half a sheet or less; *an halfpenny*.

.... of one sheet, *one penny*.

.... per sheet, for every sheet in one copy of every pamphlet not exceeding six sheets in octavo, or a less size, twelve sheets in quarto, and twenty in folio; *two shillings*.

Pardon of corporal punishment, crime, forfeiture, offence, or money above 100l. *twelve pounds*. 37 G. III. c. 90.

Pardon. See *Newgate Pardon*.

Parish, charity indentures. See *Apprentice*.

Passports; *two shillings*. 37 G. III. c. 90.

Patents. See *Grant*.

Personal decree. See *Warrant*.

Plate. All gold plate made or wrought in Great Britain, except watch cases, per oz. troy; *sixteen shillings*. 37 G. III. c. 90.

And for every ounce troy of all silver plate; *one shilling*. 37 G. III. c. 90.

Plea at law. See *Declaration*.

Plea in equity. See *Copy*.

Pleadings in superior courts. See *Bills, Copy, Declaration.*

Pleadings in inferior courts. See *Declaration.*

Policy of assurance; on house, goods, or life, on any sum not exceeding 1000l. *six shillings.* 25 G. III. c. 58.

If above 1000l. *eleven shillings.* 17 G. III. c. 50.

But by stat. 37 G. III. c. 90. the above duties on policies, so far as the same relate to policies for insuring houses, furniture, goods, wares, merchandize, or other property, *from loss by fire,* are repealed from and after July 5, 1797, and from that period there shall be paid in lieu thereof:

For every policy of assurance, where the sum insured shall not amount to 1000l. the sum of *three shillings.*

And where it shall amount to 1000l. or upwards, *six shillings.* These policies are exempted from the additional ten shillings duty on deeds.

Policy of assurance upon ships. See *Insurance.*

Postsea. See *Record.*

Presentation to any ecclesiastical dignity, promotion or benefice, of the yearly value of 10l. and upwards in the king's books; *twelve pounds.* 37 G. III. c. 90.

And to any other benefice, dignity, or spiritual or ecclesiastical promotion, *six pounds.* 37 G. III. c. 90.

Probate of wills, or letters of administration, of any estate above 24l. and under 100l. *ten shillings.*

If the estate be of the value of 100l. and under 300l. *two pounds ten shillings.*

If the estate be of the value of 300l. and under 600l. *eight pounds.* 37 G. III. c. 90.

If the estate be of the value of 600l. and under 1000l. *fifteen pounds.* 41 G. III. c. 86.

If the estate be of the value of 1000l. and under 2000l. *thirty pounds.* 41 G. III. c. 86.

If the estate be of the value of 2000l. and under 5000l. *fifty pounds.* 41 G. III. c. 86.

If the estate be of the value of 5000l. and under 10,000l. *seventy-five pounds.* 41 G. III. c. 86.

If the estate be of the value of 10,000l. and under 15,000l. *one hundred and ten pounds.* 41 G. III. c. 86.

If

If the estate be of the value of 15,000l. and under 20,000l. *one hundred and sixty pounds*. 41 G. III. c. 86.

If the estate be of the value of 20,000l and under 30,000l. *two hundred and ten pounds*. 41 G. III. c. 86.

If the estate be of the value of 30,000l. and under 40,000l. *three hundred and ten pounds*. 41 G. III. c. 86.

If the estate be of the value of 40,000l. and under 50,000l. *four hundred and ten pounds*. 41 G. III. c. 86.

If the estate be of the value of 50,000l. and under 60,000l. *five hundred and ten pounds*. 41 G. III. c. 86.

If the estate be of the value of 60,000l. and under 70,000l. *six hundred and ten pounds*. 41 G. III. c. 86.

If the estate be of the value of 70,000l. and under 80,000l. *seven hundred and ten pounds*. 41 G. III. c. 86.

If the estate be of the value of 80,000l. and under 90,000l. *eight hundred and ten pounds*. 41 G. III. c. 86.

If the estate be of the value of 90,000l. and under 100,000l. *nine hundred and ten pounds*. 41 G. III. c. 86.

If the estate be of the value of 100,000l. and upwards; *one thousand pounds*. 41 G. III. c. 86.

And if any person shall administer any personal estate, without proving the will, or taking out letters of administration, within six months after the death of the party, such person shall forfeit 50l. to be recovered by action or information. 37 G. III. c. 90.

Proctor. See *Admittance*.

Quack medicines, by 25 G. III. c. 79. For every packet, box, bottle, pot, phial, or other inclosure, containing drugs, herbs, pills, waters, essences, tinctures, powders, or other preparation or composition whatsoever, used or applied externally or internally, as medicines, or medicaments, for the prevention, cure, or relief, of any disorder or complaint incident to, or in any wise affecting the human body, which shall be uttered or vended in Great Britain, there shall be charged a stamp duty, after the rates following: viz.

Where the contents of any such packet, box, &c. shall not exceed the price of 1s. there shall be charged a stamp duty of *one penny halfpenny*.

Above 1s. and not exceeding 2s. 6d. *three-pence*.
.... 2s. 6d. .... 4s. *six-pence*.

Above 4s	and not exceeding	10s.	*one shilling.*
.... 10s.	....	20s.	*two shillings.*
.... 20s.	....	30s.	*three shillings.*
.... 30s.	....	50s.	*ten shillings.*

And above 50s. *twenty shillings.*

Quo minus. See *Original Writ.*

Race horses, for every horse entered to start or run for any plate, prize, sum of money, or any thing whatsoever, *two pounds two shillings.*

Receipts, by 31 G. III. c. 25, the following stamp duties shall be paid upon receipts.

For every piece of paper, &c. upon which shall be written, &c. any receipt, discharge, or acquittance for money, amounting to 40s. and not amounting to 10l. *two-pence.*

Amounting to 10l.	and not exceeding	20l.	*four-pence.*
.... 20l.	....	50l.	*eight-pence.*
.... 50l.	....	100l.	*one shilling.*
.... 100l.	....	200l.	*two shillings*
.... 200l.	....	500l.	*three shillings.*

If amounting to 500l or upwards, *five shillings.*

Receipt or discharge for legacies See *Legacies.*

Recognizances and entries thereof, statute staple, or statute merchant, *one pound.* 37 G. III. c. 90.

Record of nisi prius and postea; *five shillings.* 10 W. III. c. 25.

Register, entry, testimonial, or certificate of degree in any inn of court; *twenty-eight pounds.* 37 G. III. c. 90.

Rejoinder at law. See *Declaration.*

Rejoinder in equity. See *Bills, Copy.*

Release. See *Deed.*

Release, enrolled See *Conveyance.*

Replication at law. See *Declaration.*

Replication in equity. See *Bills, Copy.*

Reprieve, *twelve pounds,* 37 G III. c. 90.

Resignation. See *Adjudication.*

Retour. See *Adjudication.*

Rule or order in any of the courts at Westminster, and copies thereof, *one shilling and sixpence.* 32 G. II. c. 35.

Running horses. See *Race horses.*

Sacrament certificate, *one shilling.*

Sasine and service. See *Adjudication.*

Sentence. See *Answer.*

Sentence,

Sentence, in the admiralty. See *Admiralty.*

Significavit pro corporis deliberatione ; *ten shillings.* 10 W. III. c. 25.

Special bail, and appearance therein. See *Appearance.*

Statute merchant. See *Recognizance.*

Statute staple. See *Recognizance.*

Subpœna. See *Original Writ.*

Surrender of, or admittance to, any copyhold land or tenement in England, Wales, or Berwick upon Tweed ; or grant, or lease, by copy of court roll, or any other copy of court roll, of any honour or manor, within the same parts, except the original surrender to the use of a will, and the court book or roll itself; *ten shillings.* 37 G. III. c. 90.

And for every copyhold tenement of 20s. per annum mentioned in any surrender, for which a several fine shall be due, a distinct stamp duty shall be charged, if the tenements mentioned in the surrender, shall before June 22, 1797, have been surrendered by different surrenders, and from and after 28 June, 1798, shall be added to any other tenement, or mentioned therewith, to be surrendered by the same surrender, 38 G. III. c. 85 ; and if any officer of a copyhold or customary court, shall receive a fine for any surrender without demanding the duty for each distinct tenement, he shall forfeit 20l. and if he shall receive the duties, and neglect to purchase the proper stamps for three months, he shall forfeit 5l. and double duty. 37 G. III. c. 90.

Surrender, copy of. See *Copy.*

Surrender of grants or offices. See *Conveyance.*

Surrender, principal and original instrument of. See *Adjudication.*

Testimonial. See *Register* and *Registry.*

Transfer of stock in any company, society, or corporation, except the bank of England, or south-sea company ; *one pound.* 73 G. III c. 90.

Transfers at the bank of England ; *seven shillings and ninepence.* 23 G. III. c. 58.

Universities, degrees in. See *Register.*

Warrant beneficial. See *Beneficial Warrant.*

Warrant, mandate, or authority, given to an attorney or solicitor, to carry on or defend a suit, &c. in any of the courts at Westminster, ecclesiastical, admiralty, or cinque port courts, or in his majesty's majesty's courts in Scotland, the grand session in Wales, or courts in the counties palatine, wherein the debt shall amount to 40s. or more; *two shillings and sixpence*, to be paid by the attorney, and not charged to the client. 25 G. III. c. 80.

Warrant of attorney to enter up judgment. See *Letter of Attorney*.

Wills. See *Copy*.

Wills, probate of. See *Probate*.

Writ. See *Original Writ*.

Writ of covenant for levying fines, *one pound ten shillings*. 37 G. III. c. 90.

Writ of entry; *one pound ten shillings*.

Writ of error. See *Certiorari*.

Writ of habeas corpus, *five shillings*.

STANNARIES. See *Cornwall*.

STAPLE. The staple goods of England, are wool, woolsells, leather, lead, tin, cloth, butter, cheese, &c.

STAR-CHAMBER, was a very ancient court, but new modelled afterwards by divers statutes. It consisted of several of the lords spiritual and temporal, being privy counsellors, together with two judges of the courts of common law, without the intervention of any jury. The legal jurisdiction extended over riots, perjury, misbehaviour, of public officers, and other notorious misdemeanours. But afterwards, they stretched their power beyond the utmost bounds of legality, vindicating all the encroachments of the crown in granting monopolies, in issuing proclamations which should have the force of laws, in punishing small offences, or no offences at all, but of their own creating, by exorbitant fines, imprisonment, and corporal severities; until at last this court became so odious, that it was finally abolished by the 16 Car. I. c. 10. 4 *Black.* 264.

STATUTE, is a written law, made with the concurrence of the king and both houses of parliament. 2 *Bac. Abr.* 633.

Divers acts of parliament have attempted to bar, restrain, suspend, qualify, or make void, the acts of subsequent parliaments: but this could never be effected, for a latter parliament hath ever power, to abrogate, suspend, qualify, or make void, the acts of a former, in the whole, or any part thereof, notwithstanding any

words

words of restraint or prohibition in the acts of the former. 4 *Inst.* 43.

When a statute is repealed, all acts done under it, while it was in force, are good: but if it is declared null all these are void. *Jenk.* 233, *pl.* 6.

Where a statute before perpetual, is continued by an affirmative statute, for a time, this does not amount to a repeal of it at the end of that time. *Lord Raym.* 397.

Where two acts contradictory to each other, are passed in the same session, the latter only shall take effect. 6 *Mod.* 287.

STATUTE MERCHANT, is a bond of record, acknowledged before one of the clerks of the statute merchant, and lord mayor of the city of London, or two merchants of the said city, for that purpose assigned, or before the mayor or warden of the towns, or other discreet men for that purpose assigned. This recognizance is to be entered on a roll, which must be double, one part to remain with the mayor, and the other with a clerk, who shall write with his own hand a bill obligatory, to which a seal of the king for that purpose appointed, shall be affixed, together with the seal of the debtor. 2 *Bac. Abr.* 331.

The design of this security, was to promote and encourage trade, by providing a sure and speedy remedy for merchant strangers, as well as natives, to recover their debts at the day assigned for payment.

But though the statute merchant seems first to be introduced, and wholly calculated for the ease and benefit of merchants, as the name itself imports; yet they were not long engrossed by them, for other men finding from their own observation, that they have much of the same nature with judgments in Westminster-hall, but obtained, with less trouble and expence, out of regard to their own interest and quiet, easily fell into this way of contracting, and by degrees it came to be improved into a *common assurance*, as we find it at this day. *Winch.* 83. See *Insurance*.

STATUTE STAPLE, is a bond of record, acknowledged before the mayor of the staple, in the presence of all or one of the constables. But now *statute staple* as well as *statute merchant*, are in a great measure become obsolete.

STATUTES, or STATUTES SESSIONS, otherwise called petit sessions, are a meeting in every hundred, of all the shires in England,

gland, where by custom, they have been used, whereto the constables and others, both householders and servants repair for the debating of differences between masters and servants, the rating of servants' wages, and bestowing such people in service, as being fit to serve, either refuse to seek or get masters. Stat. 5 Eliz. c. 5.

STEALING, the fraudulent taking away of another man's goods, with an intent to steal them, against, or without the will of him, whose goods they are. See *Burglary, Larceny, Robbery.*

STERLING, was the epithet for gold or silver money current within this realm.

STEWARD, a man appointed in a place or stead, and always signifies a principal officer within his jurisdiction.

The greatest of these, is the lord high steward of England; but the power of this officer being very great, of late he has not usually been appointed for any length of time, but only for the dispatch of some special business, as the trial of some nobleman in cases of treason, &c. after which his commission expires.

STINT, is the proportionable part of a man's cattle, which he may keep upon the common. The general rule is, that the commoner shall not turn more cattle upon the common, than are sufficient to manure and stock the land, to which his right of common is annexed. 3 *Black.* 239.

STOCK-JOBBING AND STOCKS, contracts relating to stock made void, and the premium to be restored. Bills for discovery of such contracts, how to be answered; and the plaintiff's security to answer costs; and persons executing such contracts to forfeit 500l. stock sold for a certain day, and not paid for according to agreement, may be sold to any other person, and the seller recover damages; and the buyer may purchase the like quantity, where the seller refuses to transfer the stock sold, and shall recover damages; penalties on persons selling stock, which they are not possessed of, and on brokers negociating such contracts; or not entering contracts. 7 G. II. c. 8.

STOCKS, every vill within the precinct of a torn is indictable for not having a pair of stocks, and shall forfeit 5l. By the common law, a constable may confine offenders in the stocks, by way of security, but not by way of punishment.

STOLEN

STOLEN GOODS, to help people to stolen goods for reward without apprehending the felon, is felony. 4 G. I. c. 11.

Persons having or receiving, lead, iron, copper, brass, bell-metal, or solder, knowing the same to be stolen, shall be transported. 29 G. II. c. 30.

STORES. If any person who has the charge or custody, of any of the king's armour, ordnance, ammunition, shot, powder, or habiliments of war, or of any victuals for victualling the navy, shall to hinder his majesty's service, embezzle, purloin, or convey away the same to the value of 20s. or shall steal or embezzle any of his majesty's sails, cordage, or any other of his naval stores, to the value of 20s. he shall be adjudged guilty of felony without benefit of clergy. 22 Car. II. c. 5.

The treasurer, comptroller, surveyor, clerk of the acts, or any commissioner of the navy may act as justices in causing the offender to be apprehended, committed, and prosecuted for the same. 9 G. III. c. 30.

If any person shall wilfully and maliciously set on fire, burn, or destroy, any of his majesty's military, naval, or victualling stores, or other ammunition of war, or any place, where any such stores or ammunition shall be kept; he and his abettors, shall be guilty of felony without benefit of clergy 12 G. III. c. 24.

STRANDED, ships stranded. See *Insurance Marine.*

STRANGER, a person born out of the land. See *Alien.*

STYLE, to call, name, or entitle one.

SUBJECTS, the members of the commonwealth and the king their head.

SUBMARSHAL, an officer in the marshalsea, who is deputy to the chief marshal of the king's house, commonly called the knight marshal, and hath the custody of the prisoners there.

SUBORNATION, a secret or underhand preparing, instructing, or bringing in a false witness, or corrupting or alluring to do such a false act. See *Perjury.*

SUBPŒNA, is a writ whereby all persons under the degree of peerage, are called into chancery, in such case only where the common law fails, and hath made no provision; so as the party who in equity hath wrong, can have no other remedy by the rules and course of common law. But the peers of the realm in such cases, are called by the lord chancellor's, or lord keeper's letters, giving notice of the suit intended against them, and requiring them to appear. There is also a *subpœna ad testificandum* for the summoning of witnesses as well in chancery as other courts.

There is also a *subpœna* in the exchequer, as well in the court of equity there, as in the office of pleas.

SUBSIDY, an aid, tax, or tribute, granted by parliament to the king, for the urgent occasions of the kingdom, to be levied on every subject of ability, according to the value of his lands or goods.

SUBSTANCE, the substance of things is most to be regarded; and therefore our law prefers matter of substance, before matters of circumstance.

SUCCESSOR, he who follows or comes in another's place.

An aggregate corporation may have a fee-simple estate in succession, without the word *successors*; and take goods and chattels in action or possession, and they shall go to the successors. *Wood's Inst.* 111.

SUFFERANCE. Tenant at sufferance, is he who holdeth over his term at first lawfully granted. A person is tenant at sufferance who continues after his estate is ended, and wrongfully holds against another, &c. 1 *Co. Inst.* 57.

Tenants holding over, after determination of their term, and after demand made in writing to deliver possession, are rendered liable to pay double the yearly value. And tenants giving notice of their intention to quit, and not accordingly delivering up the possession at the time in such notice contained, are rendered liable to pay double rent. And it hath been held, that under this act, the notice need not be in writing, and that the landlord may levy his double rent by distress. *Bur.* 1603.

SUFFRAGAN, a titular bishop, appointed to aid and assist the bishop of the diocese.

SUGGESTION, a surmise or representation of a thing.

Though matters of record ought not to be stayed upon the bare suggestion of the party, there ought to be an affidavit made of the matter suggested, to induce the court to grant a rule for staying the proceedings upon the record. 2 *Lil. Abr.* 536.

SUICIDE, or SELF-MURDER. See *Felo de se.*

SUIT, is used in divers senses; *first* in a suit of law, and is divided into real and personal, and is the same with action *real*, and

personal

personal; *secondly, suit of court*, or suit service, is an attendance that tenants owe to the court of their lord. *Thirdly, suit covenant*, is where the ancestor hath covenanted with another, to sue to his court. *Fourthly, suit custom*, when a man and his ancestors have beein seized time out of mind, of his suit. *Fifthly, suit real*, or regal, when men come to the sheriff's torn or leet. *Sixthly, suit* signifies the following one in chase, as fresh suit. *Lastly*, it signifies as a petition made to the king or any great person. *Cowel.*

SUIT OF COURT, that is, suit to the lord's court, is that service which the feudatory tenant was bound to do at the lord's court.

SUIT OF THE KING'S PEACE, is the pursuing a man for the breach of the king's peace, by treasons, insurrections or trespasses.

SUMMONER, a petty officer who calls or cites a man to any court.

SUMMONS, in general, is a writ to the sheriff to warn one to appear at a day.

There is a summons in writs of formidon, &c. and on every summons upon the land in a real action, fourteen days before the return, proclamation is to be made thereof on a Sunday, at or near the door of the church or chapel of the place where the land lies, which must be returned with the names of the summoners, and if such proclamation shall not be had, then no *grand cape* shall issue, but an *alias* and *pluries* summons, until a summons and proclamation be duly made and returned. 2 *Lil, Abr*. 538.

SUMMONS AND SEVERANCE. The summons is only a process, which must in certain cases, issue before judgment of severance can be given.

Severance is a judgment, by which, where two or more are joined in an action, one or more of these are enabled to proceed in such action without the other or others. See *Joint Tenant* and *Severance.*

SUNDAY. No arrest can be made or process served upon a Sunday, except for treason, felony, or breach of the peace, nor can any proceedings be had, nor judgment given, nor supposed to be given on Sunday.

SUPER INSTITUTION, one institution upon another; as where *A*. is admitted and instituted to a benefice upon one title,

 and

and *B.* is admitted, instituted, &c. by the presentment of another.

SUPER JURARE, when a criminal endeavoured to excuse himself by his own oath, or by the oath of one or two witnesses, and the crime was so notorious, that he was convicted by the oaths of *many more* witnesses, this was called *super jurare.*

SUPER PRÆROGATIVA REGIS, a writ which anciently lay against the king's widow, for marrying without his licence.

SUPERSEDEAS, a writ that lies in a great many cases, and signifies in general, a command to stay proceedings, on good cause shewn, which ought otherwise to proceed.

By a *supersedeas,* the doing of a thing, which might otherwise have been lawfully done, is prevented; or a thing that has been done, is (notwithstanding it was done in a due course of law) thereby made void. 4 *Bac. Abr.* 667.

A *supersedeas* is either expressed or implied; an express supersedeas, is sometimes by writ, sometimes without a writ; where it is by writ, some person to whom the writ is directed, is thereby commanded to forbear the doing something therein mentioned, or if the thing has been already done, to revoke, as that can be done, the act. 4 *Bac. Abr.* 668.

SUPER STATUTO DE ARTICULIS CLERI, a writ lying against the sheriff or other officer, who distrains in the king's highway, or in the glebe land anciently given to rectories.

SUPERSTITIOUS USES. See *Mortmain.*

SUPPLICAVIT, a writ issuing out of the chancery, for taking the surety of the peace against a man: it is directed to the justices of the peace of the county, and the sheriffs.

SUPREMACY. See *King* and *Papists.*

SURCHARGE OF THE FOREST, is when a commoner puts on more beasts in the forest, than he has a right to do.

SURETY OF THE PEACE. A justice of the peace may, according to his discretion, bind all those to keep the peace, who in his presence shall make any affray, or shall threaten to kill or beat any person, or shall contend together in hot words, and all those who shall go about with unlawful weapons, or attendance to the terror of the people; and all such persons as shall be known by him to be common barrators; and all who shall be brought before him by a constable, for a breach of the peace in the presence of of such constable; and all such persons, who having been before bound to keep the peace, shall be convicted of having forfeited their recognizance. *Lamb.* 77.

When surety of the peace is granted by the court of king's bench, if a *supersedeas* come from the court of chancery to the justices of that court, their power is at an end; and the party as to them discharged.

If security of the peace be desired against a peer, the safest way is to apply to the court of chancery, or king's bench. 1 *Haw.* 127.

If the person against whom security of the peace be demanded, be present, the justice of the peace may commit him immediately, unless he offer sureties; and *a fortiori* he may be commanded to find sureties, and be committed for not doing it. *Id.*

SURETY OF THE GOOD BEHAVIOUR, includes the peace; and he that is bound to the *good behaviour,* is therein also bound to the *peace*: and yet a man may be compelled to find sureties both for the good behaviour and peace. *Dalt.* c. 122. See *Good Behaviour.*

SUR LUI JUR, upon his oath.

SURMISE, something offered to a court to move it, to grant a prohibition, *audita querela,* or other writ grantable thereon.

SURPLUSAGE, a superfluity or addition more than needful, which sometimes is the cause that a writ abates; but in pleading, many times it is absolutely void, and the residue of the plea shall stand good. *Plowd.* 63.

SURREBUTTER, a second *rebutter.*

SUR-REJOINDER, as a rejoinder is the defendant's answer to the replification of the plaintiff; so a sur-rejoinder is the plaintiff's answer to the defendant's rejoinder. *Wood's Inst.* 586.

SURRENDER, a deed or instrument, testifying that the particular tenant of lands or tenements for life, or years, doth sufficiently consent and agree, that he which has the next or immediate remainder or reversion thereof, shall also have the present estate of the same in possession; and that he yields and gives up the same unto him; for every *surrenderer* ought forthwith to give possession of the things surrendered. *West. Sym.*

SURROGATE, one who is substituted or appointed in the room of another; as the bishop or chancellor's surrogate.

SURVIVOR, signifies the longer liver of two joint tenants.

SUSPENSION, that suspension which relates solely to the clergy, is suspension from office and benefice jointly, or from office or benefice singly, and may be called a temporary degradation or deprivation, or both.

SUSPICION, a person may be taken up on suspicion, where a felony is done, &c. but those who are imprisoned for a light suspicion of larceny or robbery, are bailable by statute. 2 *Haw.* 101.

SWANS. See *Game.*

SWANIMMOTE, or SWAINMOTE. See *Forest.*

SWEARING AND CURSING, punishable by fine on oath of one witness before any justice of peace, or before any mayor, justice, bailiff, or other chief magistrate, of any city or town corporate.

SYNOD, a meeting or assembly of ecclesiastical persons concerning religion.

SYNODALES TESTES, synodsmen. See *Sidesmen.*

T.

TABLE RENTS, rents paid to bishops, &c. appropriated to their table or house keeping. See *Board Land Rents.*

TABLING OF FINES, is the making a table for every county where his majesty's writ runs, comprising the contents of every fine passed in any one term; as the name of the county, towns and places, wherein the lands or tenements lie; the name of the demandant and deforceant, and of every manor named in the fine.

TAIL. See *Estate.*

TAIL AFTER POSSIBILITY OF ISSUE EXTINCT. See *Estate.*

TALES, is used in law for a supply of men impanelled on a jury, and not appearing, or on their appearance challenged and disallowed, when the judge upon motion orders a supply to be made by the sheriff of one or more such persons present in court, to make up a full jury.

TALLEY, a stick cut in two parts; each of which is marked by notches

notches or otherwise, what was due between debtor and creditor; and this was the ancient way of keeping all accounts.

TAVERN. See *Alehouses* and *Inns*.

TAX, may now be defined to be a certain aid, subsidy, or supply, granted by the commons of Great Britain in parliament assembled, constituting the king's extraordinary revenue, and paid yearly towards the expences of government. 1 *Black.* c. 8.

TAX UPON LAND. See *Land tax*.

TELLER, an officer of the exchequer, of which there are four, whose office is to receive all monies due to the king, and to give the clerk of the pells, a bill to charge him therewith. They also pay to all persons any money payable by the king, by warrant from auditor of the receipt; and make weekly and yearly books, both of their receipts and payments, which they deliver to the lord treasurer.

TEMPLARS. See *Knights Templars*.

TEMPORALITIES OF BISHOPS, are such revenues, lands, and tenements, and lay fees, as have been added to bishop's fees, by kings and other great personages of this land, from time to time, as they are barons and lords of parliament.

This revenue of the king, which was anciently very considerable, is now, by a customary indulgence, almost reduced to nothing: for at present, as soon as the new bishop is consecrated and confirmed, he usually receives from the king, the restitution of his temporalities entire and untouched; and then and not sooner he has a *fee-simple* in his bishopric, and may maintain an action for the profits. 1 *Black.* 283.

TENANT, signifies one who holds or possesses, lands or tenements by any kind of right, either in fee, for life, years, or at will.

TEND, to offer, tender, or present.

TENDER, is an offer to pay a debt, or perform a duty. In every plea of tender, where money is the thing demanded by the action, and the debt or duty is not discharged by the tender and refusal, money may be brought in without leave of the court: but as other things as well as money, may where a tender is pleaded, be brought into court, this is with more propriety called bringing into court generally, than a bringing money into court. In all other cases, the leave of the court must be had, before money can be brought into court. The rule, under which this leave is granted, is, as in the case of an ejectment by a mortgagee, founded upon a particular act of parliament. In other cases, it is founded upon that discretionary power, which is, for the furtherance of justice, vested in the court. By the discretionary rule, it is sometimes ordered, that upon bringing money into court, all proceedings in an action shall be stayed. At other times it is ordered, that the money brought into court, shall be struck out of the plaintiff's declaration, and that the plaintiff shall not, at the trial of the issue, be permitted to give any evidence as to this money. This rule, by which the money brought into court, is ordered to be struck out of the declaration, is from its being more frequently granted, than that by which it is ordered that the proceeding shall be stayed, called the common rule. 5 *Bac. Abr.* 1.

If bank notes have been offered, and no objection made on that account, it has been considered by the court of king's bench as good tender. 3 *Durnf. & East.* 554.

TENEMENT, in its common acceptation, is applied only to houses and other buildings; but in its original, proper, and legal sense, it signifies every thing that may be *holden*, provided it be of a permanent nature, whether it be of a substantial, or of an unsubstantial and ideal kind. Thus *frank tenement*, or freehold, is applicable not only to lands and other solid objects, but also to offices, rents, commons, and the like; and as lands and houses are tenements, so is an advowson a tenement; and a franchise, or office, a right of common, a peerage, or other property of the like unsubstantial kind, are all of them, legally speaking, *tenements*. 2 *Black.* 17.

TENEMENTIS LEGATIS, a writ that lies to London, or any other corporation (where the custom is, that men may demise tenements as well as goods and chattels by their last will) for the hearing any controversy touching the same, and for rectifying the wrong.

TENENDUM, is a clause in a deed, wherein, the tenure of the land is created or limited. See *Deed.*

TENENTIBUS IN ASSISA NON ONERANDIS, a writ which lies for him to whom a disseisor hath alienated the land, whereof he disseised another; that he may be not molested for the

damages

damages awarded, if the disseisor have wherewith to satisfy them himself.

TENOR, of writs, records, &c. is the substance or purport of them, or a transcript or copy.

TENORE INDICTAMENTI MITTENDO, a writ whereby the record of an indictment, and the process thereupon, is called out of another court into the chancery.

TENORE PRESENTIUM. The tenor of these presents, is the matter contained therein, or rather the true intent and meaning thereof.

TENTHS, that yearly portion or tribute which all ecclesiastical livings, anciently paid to the king. See *First Fruits*.

TENURE, the manner whereby lands or tenements are holden, or the service that the tenant owes to his lord.

Under the word tenure, is included every holding of an inheritance; but the signification of this word, which is a very extensive one, is usually restrained by coupling other words with it; this is, sometimes done by words which denote the duration of the tenant's estate: as if a man hold to himself and his heirs, it is called tenure in fee-simple. At other times the tenure is coupled with words pointing out the instrument by which an inheritance is held: thus, if the holding be by copy of court roll, it is called tenure by copy of court roll. At other times, this word is coupled with others that shew the principal service by which an inheritance is held: as where a man held by knight's service, it is called tenure by knight's service. 5 *Bac. Abr.* 34.

TERMOR, he who holds lands or tenements for term of years or life. *Lil.* 100.

TERMS, are those spaces of time, wherein the courts of justice are open for all that complain of wrongs or injuries, and seek their rights by course of law or action, in order to their redress; and during which, the courts in Westminster-hall sit and give judgments, &c. but the high court of parliament, the chancery, and inferior courts, do not observe the terms; only the courts of king's bench, common pleas, and exchequer, the highest courts at common law. Of these terms there are four in every year; viz. *hilary* term, which begins the 23d of January, and ends the 12th of February; unless on Sundays, and then the day after; *Easter* term, which begins the Wednesday fortnight after *Easter* day, and

and ends the Monday next after ascension day; trinity term, which begins the Friday after trinity Sunday, and ends the Wednesday fortnight after; and *Michaelmas* term, begins the 6th and ends the 28th of November.

There are in each of these terms, stated days, called days in *bank*, that is days of appearance in the court of common pleas, called usually *bancum*, or *commune bancum*, to distinguish it from *bancum regis*, or the court of king's bench. They are generally at the distance of about a week from each other, and regulated by some festival of the church. On some of these days in bank, all original writs must be made returnable, and therefore they are generally called, the returns of that term. 3 *Black*. 227.

The first return in every term, is properly speaking, the first day in that term; and thereon the court sits to take *essoins*, or excuses, for such as do not appear according to the summons of the writ; wherefore this is usually called the *essoin* day of the term. But the person summoned hath three days grace, beyond the return of the writ, in which to make his appearance; and if he appear on the fourth day inclusive, *quarto die post*, it is sufficient. Therefore, at the beginning of each term, the court doth not sit for dispatch of business till the fourth day, and in trinity term, by stat. 32 H. VIII. c. 21 not till the sixth day. 3 *Black*. 227.

TERMS OF THE LAW, artificial or technical words and turns of art, particularly used in and adapted to the profession of the law.

TERRA EXTENDENDA, is a writ directed to the escheator, &c, requiring him to enquire and find out the true yearly value of any land, &c. by the oath of twelve men, and to certify the extent into the chancery.

TERRÆ TESTIMENTALES, lands that were held free from feudal services, *in allodio, in socogio*, descendible to all the sons, and therefore called gavel kind, were devisable by will, and therefore called *terræ testimentales*.

TERRAR, a book, or roll, wherein the several lands either of a single person, or of a town are described, containing the quantity of acres, boundaries, tenants' names, &c. 18 Eliz. c. 17.

TERRE TENANT, he who has the actual possession of the land, which we otherwise call the occupation.

TERRIS

TERRIS LIBERANDIS, a writ that lies for a man convicted by attaint, to bring the record and process before the king, and to take a fine for his imprisonment to deliver him his lands and tenements again, and to release him of the *strip* and *waste*.

TEST. By the act of king Car. II. commonly called the *test act*, all officers civil and military, are to take the oaths and *test*.

TESTAMENT, is a voluntary disposition of what one would have to be done, concerning his goods and chattels, real and personal, after his decease, with the appointment of an executor.

TESTATOR, he that makes a testament or will. See *Will*.

TESTATUM, a writ in personal actions, as if the defendant cannot be arrested upon a *capias* in the county where the action is laid, but is returned *non est inventus* by the sheriff: this writ shall be sent out into any other county where such person is thought to have wherewith to satisfy; and this is termed a *testatum*, because the sheriff hath formerly testified, that the defendant was not to be found in his bailiwick.

TESTE, that part of a writ wherein the date is contained, which begins with these words, *teste me ipso, &c.* if it be an original writ; or if judicial, *teste*, chief justice, &c.

THANE, the title of those who attended the English Saxon kings in their courts, and who held their land immediately of those kings.

THEFT, is an unlawful felonious taking away of another man's moveable and personal goods, against the owner's will, with an intent to steal them; and this is divided into *theft* simply so called, and *petit theft*, whereof the one is of goods above the value of 12d. and is felony; the other under that value, and is no felony, but is called petit larceny. See *Larceny and Felony*.

THEFT BOTE, is the receiving of a man's goods or other things, from a thief after stolen, not to prosecute the felon, that the thief may escape; which is an offence punishable with fine and imprisonment, &c. *Hale's Pl. Cor.* 130.

THELONIUM, or BREVE ESSENDI QUIETI DE THELONIO, a writ lying for the citizens of any city, or burgesses of any town, that have a charter or prescription to free them from toll, against the officers of any town or market, who would constrain them to pay toll of their merchandize contrary to the said grant or prescription.

THIRD-

THIRDBOROW, was the same officer in former times, as is at present called constable.

THREATENING LETTER, if any person shall *send* any letter threatening to accuse any other person of a crime punishable with death, transportation, pillory, or other infamous punishment, with a view to extort money from him, he shall be punished at the discretion of the court, with fine, imprisonment, pillory, whipping, or transportation. 30 G. II. c. 24.

But if the writer of a threatening letter, *deliver it himself*, and do not send it, he is guilty of felony under this act. *Leach's Cro. Law.* 351.

TIDING PENNY, a small tax or allowance to the sheriff from each tithing, towards the charge of keeping courts, &c.

TILTING, where one kills another by fighting at tilting by the king's command, the accident is excusable; but if it be by tilting without the command of the king, it will be felony of manslaughter.

TIMBER TREES, are properly oak, ash, and elm. In some particular countries, by local custom, other trees, being commonly there made use of for building, are considered as timber. 2 *Black.* 28. Of these, being part of the freehold, larceny cannot be committed; but, if they be severed at one time, and carried away at another, then the stealing of them is larceny. And by several late statutes the stealing of them in the first instance, is made felony, or incurs a pecuniary forfeiture. 4 *Black.* 233.

For the better preservation of roots, shrubs, and plants, it is by the 6 G. III. c. 48, enacted, that from and after the 24th day of June, 1766, every person convicted of damaging, destroying, or carrying away any timber tree, or trees, or trees likely to become timber, without consent of the owner, &c. shall forfeit for the first offence not exceeding 20l. with the charges attending; and on nonpayment, shall be committed for not more than twelve, nor less than six months; for the second offence, a sum not exceeding 30l. and on non payment shall be committed for not more than eighteen, and not less than twelve months; and for the third offence, is to be transported for seven years.

All oak, beech, chesnut, walnut, ash, elm, cedar, fir, asp, lime, sycamore, and birch trees, shall be deemed and taken

to

to be timber trees, within the true meaning and provision of this act.

Persons convicted of plucking up, spoiling, or taking away, any root, shrub, or plant, out of private cultivated ground, shall forfeit for the first offence, any sum not exceeding 40s. with the charges; for the second offence, a sum not exceeding 5l. with the charges; and for the third offence are to be transported for seven years. *Id.*

Power given to justices of the peace to put this act in execution.

TIPSTAFFS, officers appointed by the marshal of the king's bench, to attend the judges with a kind of staff, tipped with silver, who take into their custody all prisoners, either committed or turned over by the judges at their chambers, &c.

TITHES, are the tenth part of the increase yearly arising and renewing from the profits of lands, the stock upon lands, and the personal industry of the inhabitants. And hence they are usually divided into three kinds; prædial, mixed, and personal.

Prædial tithes, are such as arise merely and immediately from the ground, as grain of all sorts, hay, wood, fruits, herbs; for a piece of land or ground, being called in Latin prædium, whether it be arable, meadow, or pasture, the fruit or produce thereof is called prædial, and consequently the tithe payable for such annual produce, is called a prædial tithe.

Mixed tithes, are those which arise not immediately from the ground, but from things immediately nourished from the ground; as by means of goods depastured thereupon, or otherwise nourished with the fruits thereof; as colts, calves, lambs, chickens, milk, cheese, eggs.

Personal tithes, are such as arise from the honest labour and industry of man, employing himself in some personal work, artifice, or negotiation; being the tenth part of the clear gain, after charges deducted. *Watts*. c. 59.

Tithes with respect to value, are divided into great and small: *great tithes*, as corn, hay, wood: *small tithes*, as the prædial tithes of other kinds, together with those that are mixed, and personal.

Tithes of common right belong to that church, within the precincts of whose parish they arise. But one person may prescribe to to have tithes within the parish of another; and this is what is called a portion of tithes.

No tithe is due *de jure* of the produce of a mine, or of a quarry; because this is not a fruit of the earth, renewing annually; but is the substance of the earth, and has perhaps been so for a great number of years. 1 *Rol. Abr.* 637.

But in some places tithes are due by custom of the produce of mines. 2 *Vern.* 46.

No tithe is due of lime: the chalk of which this is made being part of the soil. 1 *Rol. Abr.* 637.

Tithe is not due of bricks, which are made from the earth itself. 2 *Mod.* 77.

Nor is tithe due of turf, or of gravel: because both these are part of the soil 1 *Mod.* 35.

It has been held, that no tithe is due of salt, because this does not renew annually. 1 *Rol. Abr.* 642.

But every one of these, and all things of the like kind, may by custom become tithable. 1 *Rol. Abr.* 642.

Barren land converted into tillage; no tithe shall be paid for the first seven years; but if it be not barren in its own nature, as if it be woodland grubbed and made fit for tillage; tithes shall be paid presently; for wood-land is fertile, not barren. 1 *Rol. Abr.*

Glebe lands, in the hands of the parson, shall not pay tithe to the vicar, nor being in the hands of the vicar, shall they pay tithe to the parson; because the church shall not pay tithes to the church. But if the parson let his rectory, reserving the glebe lands, he shall pay the tithes thereof to the lessee. *Gibs.* 661.

No tithes are due for houses; for tithes are only due of such things as renew from year to year. 11 *Rep.* 16.

But houses in London are, by decree, which was confirmed by an act of parliament, and made liable to the payment of tithes. 2 *Inst.* 659.

There is likewise in most ancient cities and boroughs, a custom to pay tithes for houses: without which there would be no maintenance in many parishes for the clergy. 11 *Rep.* 16.

As to mills, it is now settled by a decree of the house of lords, upon an appeal from a decree of the court of exchequer, that only personal tithes, are due from the occupier of a corn-mill. 2 *Pere. Will. Rep.* 463.

The occupier of a new-erected mill, is liable to tithes, although such mill is erected upon land discharged of tithes. *Cro. Jac.* 429.

Agistment, agisting in the strict sense of the word, means the depasturing of a beast the property of a stranger: but this word is constantly used, in the books, for depasturing the beast of an occupier of land, as well as that of a stranger. 5 *Bac. Abr.*

An occupier of land, is not liable to pay tithe for the pasture of horses, or other beasts, which are used in husbandry in the parish in which they are depastured; because the tithe of corn is by their labour increased. 1 *Roll. Abr.* 646.

But if horses or other beasts are used in husbandry out of the parish in which they are depastured, an agistment tithe is due for them. 7 *Mod,* 114.

No tithe is due for the pasture of milk-cattle which are milked in the parish in which they are depastured; because tithe is paid of the milk of such cattle. *Lord Raym.* 130.

No tithe is due for the pasture of a saddle-horse which an occupier of land keeps for himself or servants to ride upon. *Cro. Jac.* 430.

An occupier of land is liable to an agistment tithe for all such cattle as he keeps for sale. *Cro. Eliz.* 446.

Milk-cattle which are reserved for calving, shall pay no tithe for their pasture whilst they are dry; but if they be afterwards sold, or milked in another parish, an agistment tithe is due for the time they were dry. *Lord Raym.* 130.

No tithe is due from an occupier of land for the pasture of young cattle, reared to be used in husbandry or for the pail. *Cro. Eliz.* 476.

But if such young beasts be sold, before they come to such perfection as to be fit for husbandry, or before they give milk, an agistment tithe must be paid for them. *Het.* 86.

An occupier of land, is liable to an agistment tithe for all such cattle as he keeps for sale. *Cro. Eliz.* 446.

But if cattle, which have neither been used in husbandry, nor for the pail, are, after having been kept sometime, killed, to be spent in the family of the occupier of the land on which they are depastured, no tithe is due for their pasture. *Jenk.* 281.

No tithe is due for the cattle, either of a stranger or an occupier, which are depastured in grounds, that have in the same year paid tithe of hay. 2 *Rol Rep*. 191.

But it is generally true, that an agistment tithe is due, for depasturing any sort of cattle the property of a stranger. *Cro. Eliz.* 276.

No agistment-tithe is due for such beasts, either of a stranger or an occupier, as are depastured on the head-lands of ploughed-fields: provided that these are not wider, than is sufficient to turn the plough and horses upon. 1 *Rol. Rep*. 646.

No tithe is due for such cattle as are depastured upon land, that has the same year paid tithe of corn. 1 *Mod*. 216.

If land, which has paid tithe of corn one year, is left unsown the next year, no agistment is due for such land; because by this lying fresh, the tithe of the next crop of corn is increased. 1 *Rol. Rep*. 642.

But if land which has paid tithe of corn in one year, be left unsown the next year, no agistment is due for such land, but if suffered to lie fallow longer than by the course of husbandry is usual, an agistment-tithe is due for the beasts depastured upon such land. *Shep. Abr*. 1008.

Sheep after paying tithe of wool, had been fed upon turnips not severed, by which they were bettered to the value of five shillings each, and were then sold; it also appeared, that before the next shearing-time, as many had been brought in, as were sold, and that of these tithe of wool had been paid. It was insisted, that if an agistment were to be paid for the sheep sold, it would be a double tithing: but the court held that this was a new increase, and decreed the defendant to account for an agistment-tithe. *Gibs. Rep. in Equi*. 231.

But in a later case the court held, that no agistment-tithe should be paid, because sheep are *animalia fructuosa*. *Bunb*. 278.

Corn. It is held, that no tithe is due of the rakings of corn involuntarily scattered. *Cro. Eliz*. 278.

But if more of any sort of corn, be fraudulently scattered, than there would have been scattered if proper care had been taken, tithe is due of the rakings of such corn. *Cro. Eliz*. 475.

No tithes are due of the stubbles left in corn-fields, after mowing or reaping of corn. 2 *Inst*. 261.

Tithe

Tithe of *hay*, is to be paid, though beasts of the plough or pail, or sheep, are to be foddered with such hay. 12 *Mod.* 197.

But no tithe is due of hay upon the headlands of ploughed-grounds, provided that such headlands, are not wider than is sufficient to turn the plough and horses upon. 1 *Rol Abr.* 646.

It is laid down in an old case, that if a man cut down grass, and while it is in the swathes, carry it away, and give it to his plough-cattle, not having sufficient sustenance for them otherwise, no tithe is due thereof. 1 *Rol Abr.* 645.

And in a modern case, the court of exchequer was of opinion, that no tithe is due of vetches, or of clover, cut green and given to cattle in husbandry. *Rumb.* 279.

Wood. Tithe of wood is not due in common right, because wood does not renew annually: but it was in ancient times paid in many places by custom. 2 *Inst.* 645.

Exemptions from tithes are of two kinds; either to be wholly exempted from paying any tithes, or from paying tithes in kind. The former is called *de non decimando*: the latter *de modo decimandi.*

Prescription de non decimando, is to be free from the payment of tithes, without any recompense for the same. Concerning which, the general rule is, that no layman can prescribe *in non decimando*; that is, to be discarged absolutely of the payment of tithes, and to pay nothing in lieu thereof; unless he begin his prescription in a religious or ecclesiastical person. But all spiritual persons, as bishops, dean, prebendaries, parsons, and vicars, may prescribe generally *in non decimando.* 1 *Rol. Abr.* 653.

A modus decimandi, usually called by the name of *modus* only, is where there is by custom a particular manner of tithing, different from the general laws of taking tithes in kind. This is sometimes a pecuniary compensation, as so much an acre for the tithe of land: sometimes a compensation in work and labour; as that the parson shall have only the twelfth cock of hay, and not the tenth, in consideration of the owner's making it for him: sometimes in lieu of a large quantity, when arrived to great maturity; as a couple of fowls in lieu of tithe-eggs and the like. Any means in short, whereby the general law of tithing is altered, and a new method of taking them is introduced, is called *modus decimandi,* or special method of tithing. 2 *Black.* 29.

In order to make a *modus* or prescription good, several qualifications are requisite. It must be supposed to have had a reasonable commencement, as that at the time of the composition, the modus was the real value of money, it is now become much less. It must be something for the parson's benefit; therefore the finding straw for the body of the church, the finding a rope for a bell, the paying 5s. to the parish-clerk, have been adjudged not to be good. But it is a good modus to be discharged, that one hath time out of mind been used to employ the profits, for the repair of the chancel, for the parson hath a benefit by that.

A *modus* must be *certain*: so a prescription to pay a penny or *thereabouts*, for every acre of land, is void for the uncertainty. And it has been held, that if a precise day of payment be not alledged, the *modus* will be ill; but now it is holden, that where an amenial modus hath been paid, and no certain day for the payment thereof is limited, the same shall be due and payable, on the last day of the year.

A *modus* must be *ancient*; and therefore, if it be any thing near the value of the tithe, it will be supposed to be of late commencement, and for that reason will be set aside.

A *modus* must be *durable*, for the tithe in kind, being an inheritance certain, the recompense for it, should be as durable, therefore a certain sum, to be paid by the inhabitants of such an house, hath been set aside, because the house may go down and none inhabit it.

And it must be *constant* and uninterrupted; for if there have been frequent interruptions, no custom or prescription can be obtained. But after it hath been once duly obtained, a disturbance for ten or twenty years shall not destroy it.

When a common is divided and inclosed, a modus shall only extend to such tithes as the common yielded before inclosure, such as the tithes of wool, lambs, or agistment; but not to the tithes of hay and corn, which the common, whilst it was common, did never produce. *Bur.* 1735.

The parson cannot come himself and set out his tithes, without the consent of the owner; but he may attend and see it set out; yet the owner is not obliged to give him notice when he intends to set it out, unless it be by special custom. *Id.* 1891.

After it is set out, the care thereof as to wasting or spoiling,

rests

rests upon the parson, and not upon the owner of the land; but the parson may spread, dry, and prepare his corn, hay, or the like, in any convenient place upon the ground, till it be sufficiently weathered, and fit to be carried into the barn.

And he may carry his tithes from the ground, either by the common way, or such other way as the owner of the land uses to carry away his nine parts.

If the parson suffer his tithe to stay too long upon the land, the other may distrain the same as doing damage; or he may have an action on the case: but he cannot put in his cattle and destroy the corn or other tithe, for that would be to make himself judge what shall be deemed a convenient time for taking it away. *Lord Raym.* 189.

Payment of tithes, by 1 Geo. I. c. 6. all customary payments due to clergymen, the payment of tithes, &c. is enforced; and the prosecution in this case may be, for any tithes or church-rates, or any customary or other rights, dues, or payments, belonging to any church or chapel, which of right by law and custom, ought to be paid for the stipend or maintenance of any minister or curate, officiating in any church or chapel; provided that the same do not exceed 20l.

But the time is not limited, within which the same shall become due.

And if any quaker shall refuse, to pay or compound for the same, any parson, vicar, curate, farmer, or proprietor of such tithes, or any churchwarden, chapelwarden, or other person who ought to have, receive, or collect, any such tithes, rates, dues, or payments, may make complaint to any two justices, other than such as is patron of the church or chapel, or interested in the tithes.

The number of days is not limited between the time of refusal, and the complaint; nor is it hereby required, that such complaint shall be in writing. But it will be more conformable to the usual practice in like cases, if it be in writing.

Upon which complaint, the said justices are required to summon in writing under their hands and seals, by reasonable warning, such quaker, against whom such complaint shall be made.

And after appearance, or on default of appearance (the warning or summons being proved before them upon oath), they may proceed to examine on oath the truth of the complaint, and to ascertain and state what is due and payable.

And by order under their hands and seals, they may direct and appoint the payment thereof, so as the sum, ordered as aforesaid, do not exceed 10l. And also such costs and charges, as upon the merits of the cause shall appear, not exceeding 10s.

And on refusal to pay, any one of the two next justices, by warrant under his hand and seal, may levy the same by distress and sale, rendering the overplus, the necessary charges of distraining being first deducted and allowed by the said justice; unless it be in the case of appeal, and then no warrant of distress shall be granted, till the appeal shall be determined.

As no time is limited for detaining the distress, nor charges allowed for keeping it, it may be sold immediately.

Any person, who shall think himself aggrieved by the judgment of the two justices, may appeal to the next sessions; where if the judgment shall be affirmed, they shall decree the same by order of sessions, and give costs against the appellant, to be levied by distress and sale, as to them shall seem reasonable.

And no proceeding herein, shall be removed by *certiorari*, or otherwise, unless the title of such tithes shall be in question.

The withholding of tithes from the parson or vicar, whether the former be a clergyman or lay-appropriator, is among the pecuniary causes cognizable in the ecclesiastical court. But herein a distinction must be taken; for the ecclesiastical courts have no jurisdiction to try the right of tithes, unless between spiritual persons, between spiritual men and lay men, and are *only* to compel the payment of them, when the right is not disputed. 2 *Inst.* 364.

TITHING MEN, in the Saxon times, for the better conservation of peace, and the more easy administration of justice, every hundred was divided into ten districts or *tithings*, each tithing consisting of ten *friborgs*, each friborg of ten families; which *tithing-men*, or civil deans, were to examine and determine all smaller differences between villages and neighbours, but to refer all greater matters to the superior courts, which had a jurisdiction over the whole hundred. See *Decennary*.

TITLE, properly is, when a man hath lawful cause of entry into lands, whereof another is seized, for which he can have no action,

action, as *title* of mortmain, or *title* to enter for a breach of condition: but legally, this word title includes a right.

TITLE OF ENTRY, is when one seised of land in fee, makes a feoffment thereof, on condition, and the condition is broken; after which the feoffor hath title to enter into the land, and may do so at his pleasure, and by his *entry*, the freehold shall be said to be in him presently.

TOBACCO, not to be planted in England or Ireland, &c. under the penalty of 12l. for every pole, and the forfeiture thereof. See *Complete Abridgment of the Excise Laws.*

TOFT, a messuage, or rather a place where a messuage formerly stood, but is decayed or casually burnt, and not rebuilt.

TOLL, a payment in towns, markets, and fairs, for goods bought and sold.

TOLL, or PORT TOLL, a prescription to have port toll for all goods coming into a man's port, may be good; and this it is said, without any consideration. 2 *Lev.* 96.

TOLL, or THOROUGH TOLL, is properly where a toll is taken of men for passing through a vill in the high street. 2 *Roll. Abr.* 522.

TOLL TRAVERSE, is properly when a man pays certain toll for passing over the soil of another man in a way not an high street. *Mod.* 232.

TOLL TRADERS, is when a person claims toll for every beast driven over his ground; for which a man may prescribe, and distrain for it *in via regia*. *Cro. Eliz.* 710.

TOLL, or TURN-TOLL, a toll paid for beasts that are driven to a market to be sold, and return unsold. 6 *Rep.* 46.

TOLLAGE, any manner of custom or imposition.

TOLL-CORN, an indictment lies against a miller for taking too much toll. 5 *Mod.* 13. See *Mill.*

TOLT, is a writ whereby a cause depending in a court baron, is removed to the county court.

TONNAGE, is a custom or import paid to the king for merchandize, imported or exported, according to a certain rate upon every ton.

TOURN, the sheriff's tourn, is the king's court of record, holden before the sheriff, for redressing of common grievances within the county. 2 *Haw.* 55.

TRADE,

TRADE, in general signification, is traffic or merchandize: also a private art, and way of living.

TRANSCRIPT, the copy of an original deed, written again or exemplified, as the transcript of a fine.

TRANSGRESSIONE, a writ commonly called a writ or action of trespass; which is to be sued in the court of king's-bench or common-pleas.

TRANSITORY, transitory actions are such as may be laid in any county or place; as for debt, detinue, slander, or the like, which are injuries that might happen any where; whereas a *local* action is restricted to that particular county where the injury was actually done, as for waste, trespass, or the like.

TRANSLATION, is the removal of a bishop to another diocese.

TRANSPORTATION, is the banishing or sending away a criminal into another country.

If any offender ordered to be transported, shall return into Great Britain or Ireland, before the end of his term, he shall be liable to be punished as a person attainted of felony, without benefit of clergy, and execution shall be awarded against him accordingly. 24 Geo. III. c. 56.

TRAVERSE, signifies sometimes to deny, sometimes to overthrow or undo a thing, or to put one to prove some matter; much used in answers to bills in chancery; or it is that which the defendant pleads or saith in bar to avoid the plaintiff's bill, either by confessing and avoiding, or by denying and traversing the material parts thereof.

TRAVERSE AN INDICTMENT, is to take issue upon the chief matter, and to contradict or deny some point of it.

A traverse must be always made to the substantial part of the title. Where an act may indifferently be intended to be at one day or another, there the day is not traversable. In an action of trespass, generally the day is not material; though if a matter be done upon a particular day, there it is material and traversable. *2 Roll's Rep. 37.*

TRAVERSE AN OFFICE, is to prove that an inquisition made of lands or goods by escheator, is defective and untruly made.

TRAYLBASTON. See *Justices of Traylbaston.*

TRAYTOR;

TREYTOR. See *Treason*.

TREASON, is divided into high treason, and petty treason; *high treason* is defined to be an offence committed against the security of the king or kingdom, whether it be by imagination, word or deed; as to compass or imagine the death of the king, queen, or prince, or to deflower the king's wife, or his eldest daughter unmarried; or his eldest son's wife; or levy war against the king in his realm, adhere to his enemies, counterfeit his great seal, privy seal, or money, or wittingly to bring false money into this realm counterfeited like the money of England, and utter the same. To kill the king's chancellor, treasurer, justices of either bench, justices in eyre, of assize, or of *oyer* and *terminer*, being in their place doing this office. Forging the king's sign manual, or privy signet, privy seal, or foreign coin current here, or diminishing or impairing current money. In case of treason, a man shall be drawn, hanged, and quartered, and forfeit his lands and goods to the king. 25 Ed. III.

Petit treason, whenever a wife murders her husband, a servant his master or mistress, or an ecclesiastic a prelate, or to whom he owes obedience, every one of these offences is *petit treason*.

As every petit treason implies a murder, it follows, that the mere killing of an husband, master or prelate, is not always petit treason; for if there are not such circumstances, in the case of killing one of these persons, as would have made it murder in the case of killing any other person, it does not amount to this offence. 1 *Haw*. 88.

There can be no accessary in high treason. 2 *Haw*. 310.

And it seems to be always agreed, that, what would have made a man an accessary before the fact in any other felony, makes him a principal in high treason. 3 *Inst*. 21.

As the person of his majesty was imagined in iminent danger it was thought necessary to enact two law statutes, viz. 36 G. III. c. 7. and 36 G. III. c. 8. the former to enlarge the clauses in the stat. 25 Ed. III. *for the greater safety of his majesty's person*; the latter *for the preventing seditious meetings*. But on account of the too great length of the acts, we are obliged to refer the reader thereto.

TREASURER OF THE COUNTY. The justices of the peace in sessions, may appoint treasurers from time to time, of the

the county rates, and allow them salaries not exceeding 20l. a year; which treasurers shall keep books of entries of all receipts and disbursements by them made, and account for the same to the said justices in sessions.

There are two treasurers in each county, chosen by the major part of the justices of the peace, &c. at Easter sessions. They must have 10l. a year in land, or 50l. in personal estate; and shall not continue in their office above a year; and they are to account yearly at quarter-sessions, or within ten days after, to their successors under penalties.

TREASURE TROVE, is where any money or coin, gold, silver, plate, or bullion, is hidden in the earth, or other private place the owner thereof being unknown; in which case, the treasure belongs to the king, or some other who claims by the king's grant, or by prescription. *Blac. Lib.* 3.

But if he that hid it be known, or afterwards found out, the owner and not the king is entitled to it. 1 *Black.* 295.

If it be found in the sea, or *upon* the earth, it doth not belong to the king, but to the finder, if no owner appear. *Black.* 295.

TREES. See *Timber.*

TRESPASS, is any transgression of the law, under treason, felony, or misprision of either. *Staundf. Pl. Cor.* 38.

Trespass signifies going beyond what is lawful; hence it follows, that every injurious act is, in the large sense of this word, a trespass. But as many injurious acts are distinguished by particular names, as treason, murder, rape, and other names, the legal sense of the word *trespass*, is confined to such injurious acts, as have not acquired a particular name. Some trespasses are not accompanied with any force; a trespass of this sort is called a trespass upon the case: and the proper remedy for the party injured, is by an action upon the case. Other trespasses are accompanied with force, either actual or implied. If a trespass, which was accompanied with either actual or implied force, have been injurious to the public, the proper remedy in every such case, is by an indictment, or by information. And if a trespass that was accompanied with an actual force, have been injurious only to one or more private persons, the offender is in every such case liable to an indictment; or to an information; for although the injury has in such case been only done to one or more private persons, as every trespass accompanied with actual force is a breach of the peace, it is to be considered and punished as an offence against the public. 5 *Bac. Abr.* 150.

A man is answerable for not only his own trespass, but that of his cattle also. 3 *Black.* 211.

And the law gives the party injured, a double remedy in this case; by permitting him to distrain the cattle thus doing damage, till the owner shall make him satisfaction, or else by leaving him to the common remedy by action. And in either of these cases of trespass committed on another's land, either by a man himself or his cattle, the action that lies, is the action of trespass, *with force and arms*; for the law always couples the idea of force, with that of intrusion upon the property of another. 3 *Black.* 210.

In some cases, trespass is justifiable; or rather entry on another's land or house, shall not in these cases be accounted trespass; as if a man came there to demand or pay money there payable, or to execute in a legal manner the process of the law. 3 *Black.* 219.

To prevent trifling and vexatious actions of trespass, it is enacted by 43 Eliz. c. 6. 22 and 23 Car. II. c. 9. and 8 & 9 W. c. II. that where a jury who try an action of trespass, give less damages than 40s. the plaintiff shall be allowed no more costs than damages; unless the judge shall certify on the back of the record, that the freehold or title of the land came chiefly in question. But if it shall appear, that the trespass was wilful and malicious, the plaintiff shall have his full costs. And every trespass is *wilful*, where the defendant has been *forewarned*, and *malicious* where the intent of the defendant appears to be to harass or injure the plaintiff. 3 *Black.* 370.

TRIAL, the proceeding of a court of law, when the parties are at issue, such as the examination of witnesses, &c. to enable the court, deliberately weighing the evidence given on both sides, to draw a true conclusion, and administer justice accordingly. See *Tidd's Practice*, K. B.

TRITHING, the third part of a shire or county.

TRINITY-HOUSE, a college belonging to a company or corporation of seamen, who are empowered by charter to take cognizance of those who destroy sea-marks, to regulate the rates of ballastage, pilots, light-houses, &c. 5 Geo. II. c. 20.

TRONAGE,

TRONAGE, the mayor and commonalty of the city of London, are ordained keepers of the beams and weights for weighing merchants' commodities, with power to assign clerks, porters, &c. of the great beam and balance; which weighing of goods and wares, is called *tronage*.

TROVER, is the remedy prescribed by the law, where any person is in possession of the property of another, which he unlawfully detains. Previous to commencing this action, a demand of the property so detained, must be made in writing by some person properly authorized by the owner of the property; and upon refusal to restore it, the law presumes an unlawful conversion; and the party is entitled to this action, and will recover damages to the value of the property detained. As trover implies trespass, the smallest damages will carry costs. A similar action may be brought for the unlawful detention of any property, on which the specific articles so detained, may be recovered; but as articles detained, must be precisely stated in the declaration, and is attended with some difficulty, this action is very seldom brought.

TRUST, is a right to receive profits of land, and to dispose of the land in equity. And one holding the possession and disposing thereof at his will and pleasure, are signs of trust. *Chan. Rep.* 52.

A trust is but a new name given to an use, and invented to evade the statute of uses. 21 *Vin.* 493.

What is a declaration of trust, and when a trust shall be raised. By stat. 29 C. II. c. 3. all declaration or creation of trusts shall be manifested by some writing signed by the party, or by his last will in writing, or else shall be void. And by *sect.* 9. of the same act, assignments of trusts shall be in writing, signed by the party assigning the same, or by his last will, or else shall be of no effect.

What shall be deemed a trust by implication. By 29 Car. II. all declarations of trusts were to be made in writing: but in the said act there is a saving with regard to trusts resulting by implication of law, which are left on the footing whereon they stood before the act; now a bare declaration by parol before the act, would prevent any resulting trust. 2 *Vern.* 294.

If a man purchase lands in another's name, and pay the money,

4 it

it will be a trust for him that paid the money, though there be no deed made, declaring the trust thereof; for the statute of frauds and perjuries extends not to trusts raised by operations of law. 2 *Vent.* 361.

TRUSTEES OF PAPISTS, are disabled to make presentations to churches by stat. 12 Anne. c. 4.

TURBARY, a right to dig turfs on another man's ground.

TURNIPS, penalties on stealing. See *Cabbage.*

TURNO VICECOMITUM, a writ that lies for those who are called to the sheriff's *tourn,* out of their own hundred.

TURNPIKES, if any person shall pull down, or otherwise destroy any turnpike-gate, post, chain, bar, or other fence, or any house erected for the use of such gate, he shall be guilty of felony, and transported for seven years. 13 G. III. c. 84.

TWELVE MEN, a jury. See *Jury.*

TYTHES. See *Tithes.*

V.

VACATION, is all the time between the end of one term, and the beginning of another, it begins the last day of every term, as soon as the court rises.

VADIUM MORTUUM, a mortgage or dead pledge; which is, where a man borrows money of another, and grants him an estate fee, on condition, that if the money be not repaid, the estate so put in pledge shall continue to the lender as dead and gone from the mortgagor. 2 *Black.* 157. See *Mortgage.*

VAGABOND, one who wanders about and has no certain dwelling.

VAGRANTS, are all persons threatening to run away and leave their wives and children to the parish: All persons unlawfully returning to the parish or place whence they have been legally removed by order of two justices, without bringing a certificate from the parish or place whereunto they belong: All persons who have not wherewith to maintain themselves, live idle, and refuse to work for the usual wages given to other labourers in the like work, in the parishes or places where they are: All persons going from door to door, or placing themselves in the streets, highways, or passages, to beg or gather alms in the parishes or places where they dwell.

All these shall be deemed idle and disorderly persons. And one justice may commit such offenders (being thereof convicted before him, by his own view, confession, or oath of one witness) to the house of correction, to hard-labour not exceeding one month. And any person may apprehend, and carry before a justice, any such persons going from door to door, or placing themselves in the streets, highways, or passages, to beg alms in the parishes or places where they dwell; and if they shall resist, or escape from the person apprehending them, they shall be punished as rogues and vagabonds. And the said justice, by warrant under his hand and seal, may order any overseer where such offender shall be apprehended, to pay 5s. to any person in such parish or place so apprehending them, for every offender so apprehended; to be allowed in his accounts, on producing the justice's order, and the person's receipt to whom it was paid. 17 G. II. c. 5.

The same statute also enacts, that such justice, shall order the person so apprehended, to be publicly whipped by the constable, petit-constable, or some other person to be appointed by such constable or petit-constable, of the place where such offender was apprehended; or shall order him to be sent to the house of correction (and by 27 G. III. c. 11.) the common goal, till the next sessions, or for any less time, as such justice shall think proper.

To defray the expences of apprehending, conveying, and maintaining rogues, vagabonds, and incorrigible rogues, and all other expences necessary, the justices in sessions, may cause such sums as shall be necessary to be raised, in the same manner as the general county rate. 17 G. III. c. 5. See *Burn. Tit. Rogue.* and *Vagrant.*

VALUE, has two different meanings. It sometimes expresses the utility of an object, and sometimes the power of purchasing other goods with it. The first may be called value in use, the other value in exchange.

Value in *use* is a mere simple effect, arising from the nature of an object, and its being more or less conducive to the necessities, the comforts, or enjoyments of men. The other value is of a compound nature, composed of the value in use, and the labour necessary to procure the object in question. Values are measured by money, which has become a common standard of comparison for all different commodities.

A man cannot say another owes him so much, when the value of the thing owing is uncertain; for which reason actions in these cases are always brought in the *detinet*, and the declaration *ad valentiam*, &c. 1 *Lutw.* 484.

VARIANCE, signifies any alteration of a thing formerly laid in a plea, or where the declaration in a cause differs from the writ, or from the deed upon which it is grounded. 2 *Lil. Abr.* 629.

If there be a variance between the declaration and the writ, it is error; and the writ shall abate. And if there appear to be a material variance between the matter pleaded, and the manner of pleading it, this is not a good plea; for the manner and matter of pleading ought to agree in substance, or there will be no certainty in it. *Cro. Jac.* 479.

VASSAL, signifies him that holds land in fee of his lord; we call him more usually a *tenant in fee*, whereof some owe fidelity and service.

VASTO, a writ which lies for the heir against the tenant, for a term of life or of years, for making waste; or for him in the reversion or remainder. F. N. B. 55.

VEJOURS, are such persons as are appointed to view an offence, as a man murdered, &c.

VELLUM AND PARCHMENT. See *Excise*.

VENDITIONE EXPONAS, a writ judicial, directed to the under sheriff, commanding him to sell goods, which he hath formerly taken into his hands, for satisfying a judgment given in the king's court.

VENDITOR REGIS, the king's salesman; being the person who exposed to sale those goods and chattels which were seized and distrained, to answer any debt due to the king.

VENDOR AND VENDEE. *Vendor* is a person who sells any thing, and *vendee* the person to whom it is sold. Where a man sells any thing to another, it is implied that the vendor shall make assurance by bill of sale to the vendee, but not unless it be demanded.

VENIRE FACIAS, a writ judicial awarded to the sheriff to cause a jury of the neighbourhood to appear, when a cause is brought to issue, to try the same, and if the jury come not at the day of this writ, then there shall go an *habeas corpora*, and after a distress till they appear. 2 *Haw.* 298.

Venire facias, is also the common process upon any presentment, being in nature of a summons for the party to appear; and this is a proper process to be first awarded on an indictment for any crime, under the degree of treason, or felony, or *maihem*, except in such cases wherein other process is directed by statute. And if by the return to such *venire*, it appear that the party hath lands in the county, whereby he may be distrained, then a *distress infinite* shall be issued from time to time till he appear. But if the sheriff return that he hath no lands in his bailiwick, then upon his non-appearance, a writ of *capias* shall issue to take his body. 4 *Black.* 313.

VENTER, is used in the law for the children by a woman of one marriage; there is a first and second *venter*, &c. where a man hath children by several wives. See *Descent*.

VENTRE INSPICIENDO, a writ to search a woman that saith she is with child, and thereby withholds lands from the next heir. As if a man having lands in fee-simple, die, and his widow soon after marry again, and say she is with child by her former husband; in this case, this writ *de ventre inspiciendo* lies for the heir against her. By which writ the sheriff is commanded, that in presence of twelve men, and as many women, he cause examination to be made, whether the woman is with child or not; and if with child, then about what time it will be born; and that he certify the same to the justices of the assize, or at Westminster, under his seal, and under the seals of two of the men present. *Cro. Eliz.* 506.

This writ is now granted, not only to an heir at law, but to a devisee, whether for life, in tail, or in fee.

VENUE, the *neighbourhood*, from whence juries are to be summoned for trial of causes. In *local* actions, as of trespass and ejectment, the venue is to be from the neighbourhood of the place, where the lands in question lie; and in all real actions, the venue must be laid in the county where the thing is for which the action is brought. But in transitory actions, for injuries that may have happened any where, as debt, detinue, slander, or the like, the plaintiff may declare in what county he pleases; and then the trial must be in that county in which the declaration is laid. Though if the defendant will make affidavit, that the cause of action, if any, arose not in that, but in another county, the court will direct *a change of the venue,* and oblige the plaintiff to declare in the proper county. And the court will sometimes move the venue from the proper jurisdiction (especially of the narrow and limited kind) upon a suggestion duly supported, that a fair and impartial trial cannot be had therein. 3 *Black.* 294.

With respect to criminal cases, it is ordained by stat. 21 Jac. I. c. 4, that all informations on penal statutes shall be laid in the counties were the offences were committed.

VERDEROR, a judicial officer of the king's forest, chosen by the king's writ in the full county of the same shire, within the forest where he dwells; and is sworn to maintain and keep the assizes of the forest, and to view, receive, and enrol the attachments and presentments, of all manner of trespasses of vert and venison in the forest.

VERDICT, the answer of a jury, made upon any cause, civil, or criminal, committed by the court to their examination, and this is twofold, general, or special.

A general verdict is that which is given or brought into the court in like general terms to the general issue; as in an action of disseisin, the defendant pleadeth *no wrong, no disseisin*; then the issue is *general,* whether the fact be wrong or not, which being committed to the jury, they upon consideration of the evidence come in and say, either for the plaintiff, that is a wrong and disseisin; or for the defendant, that it is no wrong, no disseisin

A special verdict, is when they say at large, that such a thing and such a thing they find to be done by the defendant or tenant, so declaring the course of the fact, as in their opinion it is proved; and as to the law upon the fact, they pray the judgment of the court; and this *special verdict,* if it contain any ample declaration of the cause from the beginning to the end, is also called a verdict at large. *Co. Lit.* 128.

A special verdict is usually found where there is any difficulty or doubt respecting the laws when the jury state the facts as proved, and pray the advice of the court thereon. A less expensive, and more speedy mode however, is to find a verdict generally for the plaintiff, subject nevertheless to the opinion of the judge, or the court above, on a special case drawn up and settled by counsel on both sides.

VERGE, the compass of the king's court, which bounds the jurisdiction of the lord steward of the king's houshold, and of the coroner of the king's house, and that seems to have been twelve miles compass. See *Marshalsea Court.*

Verge, hath also another signification, and is used for a stick or rod, whereby one is admitted tenant, and holding it in his hand, swears fealty to the lord of the manor, who for that cause is called *tenant by the verge.*

VERGERS, such as carry white wands before the justices of either bench.

VERT, cover for deer and also that power which a man hath by the king's grant, to cut green wood in the forest.

VERY LORD AND VERY TENANT, they that are immediate lord and tenant one to another.

VESTRY, a place adjoining to a church, where the vestments of the minister are kept; also a meeting at such place where the minister, churchwardens, and principal men of most parishes, do at this day make a parish vestry. On the Sunday before a vestry is to meet, public notice ought to be given, either in the church, or after divine service is ended, or else at the church door as the parishioners come out; both of the calling of the said meeting, and also the time and place of the assembling of it: and it is reasonable then also to declare for what business the said meeting is to be held, that none may be surprized, but that all may have full time before, to consider of what is to be proposed at the said meeting. *Wats.* c. 39.

VETITUM NAMIUM, *forbidden distress,* as when the bailiff of a lord distrains beasts or goods, and the lord forbids him to deliver them, when the sheriff comes to replevy them, and to that end drives them to places unknown; or when they are so eloined, as they cannot be replevied.

VIA REGIA, the highway or common road, called the king's way, because authorized by him, and under his protection.

VICAR, one who supplies the place of another. The priest of every

every parish is called rector, unless the prædial tithes are appropriated, and then he is stiled vicar; and when rectories are appropriated, vicars are to supply the rector's place. For the maintenance of the vicar, there was then set apart a certain portion of the tithes, commonly about a third part of the whole, which are now what are called the vicarial tithes, the rest being reserved to the use of those houses, which for the like reason are determinated the rectorial tithes.

VICARAGE. For the most part vicarages were endowed upon appropriations; but sometimes vicarages have been endowed without any appropriation of the parsonage; and there are several churches where the tithes are wholly impropriated, and no vicarage endowed; and there, the impropriators, are bound to maintain curates to perform divine service, &c. The parsons, patron, and ordinary, may create a vicarage, and endow it; and in time of vacancy of the church, the patron and ordinary may do it; but the ordinary alone cannot create a vicarage, without the patron's assent.

VICAR GENERAL, an officer under the bishop, having cognizance of spiritual matters, as correction of manners, and the like; as the *official principal* hath jurisdiction of temporal matters, as of wills and administrations, and both of these are commonly united under the name of chancellor.

VICINAGE, *common of vicinage,* is, where the inhabitants of two townships, which lie contiguous, have usually intercommoned with one another, the beasts of the one straying mutually into the other's fields without any molestation from either. This indeed, is only a permissive right, intended to excuse, what in strictness is a trespass in both, and to prevent a multiplicity of suits; and therefore either township may inclose and bar out the other, though they have intercommoned time out of mind. Neither hath any person of one town a right to put his beasts originally, into the other's common; but if they escape and stray there of themselves, the law winks at the trespass. 2 *Black.* 34. See *Common.*

VICONTIEL JURISDICTION, that jurisdiction which belongs to the officers of a county, as sheriff's, coroner, escheator, &c.

VIDELICET. A videlicit in a deed may make a separation, as well as an *habendum*: and if there be a several *habend,* of an annuity

annuity of 20l. to one, and so to four others; it will be to the same effect, though it say *habendum* 100l. to them, to be equally divided; *viz.* 20l. to one and so to the rest. 5 *Rep.* 29.

VI ET ARMIS, *with force and arms*, are words used in indictments, &c. to express the charge of forcible and violent committing any crime or trespass: but on appeal of death, on a killing with a weapon, the words *vi et armis* are not necessary, because they are implied; so in an indictment of forcible entry alledged to have been made, *manu forti*, &c. 2 *Haw.* 179.

VIEW, is generally where a real action is brought in any of the courts of record at Westminster, and it shall appear to the court to be proper and necessary that the jurors should have a view, they may order special writs of *distringas*, or *habeas corpora* to issue, commanding the sheriff to have six of the first twelve of the jurors therein named, or of some greater number of them at the place in question, &c. But as the having a view was not a matter of course, though such a practice had prevailed, and had been abused to the purposes of delay, the court thought it their duty to take care that their ordering a view should not obstruct justice, and prevent the cause from being tried: and they resolved not to order one any more, without a full examination into the propriety and necessity of it. For they were all clearly of opinion, that the act of parliament meant that a view should not be granted, unless the court were satisfied that it was *proper and necessary*; and they thought it better that a cause should be tried upon a view had by any six, or by fewer than six, or even without any view, than be delayed for any greater length of time. *Burr.* 256.

VIEW OF FRANK PLEDGE, the office which the sheriff in his county court, or the bailiff in his hundred, performs in looking to the king's peace, and seeing that every man be in some pledge.

VI LAICA REMOVENDA, a writ which lies where two persons contend for a church, and one of them enters into it with a great number of laymen, and holds out the other *vi et armis*; then he that is holden out, shall have this writ directed to the sheriff, that he remove the force.

VILL, or VILLAGE, was anciently a precinct consisting of ten tenants, on which account they are sometimes called tithings.

By

By intendment of law, every parish is a vill unless it be shewn to the contrary. *Co. Lit.* 125.

Every vill must have a constable; otherwise it is but an hamlet. 12 *Mod.* 18.

VILLAIN or VILLEIN, a man of servile or base degree.

Of these bondmen or villeins, there were two sorts in England, one termed a *villain in gross*, who was immediately bound to the person of his lord and his heirs. The other *villein regardant* to a manor, being bound to his lord as a member belonging and annexed to a manor whereof the lord was owner.

Both villains regardant, and villains in gross were transferable by deed from one owner to another. They could not leave their lord without his permission; but if they ran away or were purloined from him, might be claimed and recovered by action like beasts or other chattels. They held indeed small portions of land to sustain themselves and families; but it was at the mere will of the lord, who might dispossess them whenever he pleased. A villain could acquire no property either in lands or goods; but if he purchased either, the lord might enter upon him, and seize them to his own use. 1 *Black.* 93.

VILLANOUS JUDGMENT, is that which casts the reproach of villany upon him against whom it is given; and it was an ancient judgment given by the common law in attaint, or in cases of conspiracy, whereby the offender lost his *liberam ligem*, and became infamous, disabled to be a juror, or witness, forfeited his goods and chattels, and his lands during life, and to have those lands wasted, his houses rased, his trees rooted up, and his body committed to prison. *Staundf. Pl. Cor.* 157.

The punishment at this day appointed for perjury, may partake of the name of *villanous judgment*; as it hath somewhat more in it than corporal, or pecuniary pain, viz. the discrediting the testimony of the offender for ever.

VIOLENCE. All violence is unlawful; if a man assault another with an intention of beating him only, and he die, it is felony.

VISITATION, that office which is performed by the bishop of every diocese once every three years, or by the archdeacon once a year, by visiting the churches and their rectors, throughout the whole diocese.

VISITOR,

VISITOR, an inspector of the government of a corporation, &c. the ordinary is visitor of spiritual corporations; but corporations instituted for private charity, if they are lay, are visitable by the founder, or by whom he shall appoint, and from the sentence of such visitor there lies no appeal. 3 *Salk.* 381.

VIVA VOCE, is where a witness is examined personally in open court. See *Evidence.*

UMPIRAGE, is where two persons being appointed arbitrators in consequence of not agreeing in opinion, appoint some person to decide the difference; the party so appointed, is in such case, termed the umpire, and his determination the umpirage. See *Award* and *Arbitration.*

UNA CUM OMNIBUS ALIIS, in the grant of a deed, is a new edition of other things, than were granted before; and hath its own conclusion attending it. *Hob.* 175.

UNCORE PRIST, or ENCORE PRIST, is a plea for the defendant, being sued for a debt, due at a day past, to save the forfeiture of his bond, saying that he tendered the debt at the time and place, and that there was none to receive, and that he is still ready to pay the same.

UNDERSHERIFF. See *Sheriff.*

UNIFORMITY, one form of public prayers, and administration of sacraments, and other rites and ceremonies of the church of England, to which all must submit, prescribed by statutes. 1 c. 2: and 14 Car. II. c. 4.

UNION OF ENGLAND AND IRELAND. See *Ireland.*

UNION OF ENGLAND AND SCOTLAND. See *Scotland.*

UNITY OF POSSESSION, signifies *joint possession* of two rights, by several titles. As for example, if a man take a lease of land from another person at a certain rent, and afterwards buy the fee-simple, this is an *unity of possession,* by which the lease is extinguished, by reason that he, who before had the occupation only for his rent, is become lord of the same, and is to pay rent to none but himself.

UNIVERSITY. By universities in general, we understand those seminaries of learning, where youth are sent to finish their education, and to be instructed in the liberal sciences. With us, by universities, are more particularly denoted those two learned

bodies

bodies of *Oxford* and *Cambridge*, which are invested with several peculiar privileges. 5 *Bac. Abr.* 330.

UNLAWFUL ASSEMBLY. See *Riots*.

UNQUES PRIST, *always ready*, a plea whereby a man professes himself always ready to do or perform that which the demandant requires. For example, a woman sues the tenant for her dower, and he coming in at the day, offers to aver, that he was always ready, and still is, to perform it. In this case, except the demandant will aver the contrary, he shall recover no damages. *Kitch.* 243.

VOCIFERATIO. See *Hue and Cry*.

VOIDANCE, a want of an incumbent upon a benefice, and this is double, either *in law* as when a man hath more benefices incompatible, or *in deed*, as when the incumbent is dead, or actually deprived. *Bro.* 51.

VOID AND VOIDABLE, in the law, some things are absolutely void, and others only voidable. A thing is void which is done against law at the very time of doing it, and no person shall be bound by such an act; but a thing is only voidable which is done by a person who ought not to have done it, but who nevertheless cannot avoid it himself after it is done; though it may be by some act in law made void by his heir, &c. 2 *Lil. Abr.* 807.

VOIR DIRE, is where the party is examined upon oath, to speak the truth, or make true answer to such questions as the court shall demand of him: so where it is prayed upon a trial at law, that a witness may be sworn, whether he shall get or lose by the matter in controversy, this is called a *voir dire*; and if it appear that the witness be disinterested, his testimony is allowed, otherwise not. 3 *Black.* 332.

VOLUMUS, the first word of a clause in the king's writs of protection, and letters patent.

VOLUNTARY, when applied to a deed, is where any conveyance is made, without a consideration of either money, marriage, &c. Thus remainders limited in settlements, to a man's right heirs, &c. are deemed voluntary in equity, and the persons claiming under them are called *volunteers*.

VOLUNTAS, is when the tenant holds at the will of the lessor, or lord, which may be done in two different ways; one is, when a person a person makes a lease to a man of lands to hold at *his will*, then he may put him out at his pleasure, but if the tenant sow the ground, and he put him out, then the tenant shall have his corn with egress and regress, till it be ripe to cut, and carry out of the ground. And such tenant at will, is not bound to sustain and repair the house, as tenant for years is. But if he make wilful waste, the lessor shall have against him an action of trespass.

The other *tenant at will of the lord*, is, by copy of court roll, according to the custom of the manor; and such a tenant may surrender the land into the hands of the lord, according to the custom, to the use of another for life, in fee, or in tail; and then he shall take the land of the lord, or his steward, by copy, and shall make fine to the lord.

VOUCHER, a term of art, when the tenant in a writ of right, calls another into the court who is bound to him to warranty. And that is either to defend the right against the demandant, or to yield him other lands, &c. in value; and extends to lands or tenements of freehold or inheritance: he that voucheth, is called *voucher*, and he that is vouched, is called the *vouchee*. See *Recovery*.

USAGE, differs from custom and prescription: no man may claim a rent, common, or other inheritance, by usage though he may by prescription. *B. Co.* 65.

USANCE. See *Bills of Exchange*.

USE, is a trust and confidence reposed in another who is tenant of the land, that he shall dispose of the land according to the intention of *cestuy que use*, or him to whose use it was granted, and suffer him to take the profits. 2 *Black.* 328.

By stat 27 H. VIII. c. 10, commonly called *the statute of uses or the statute for transferring uses into possession* the *cestuy que use* is considered as the real owner of the estate; whereby it is enacted that, when any person is seized of lands to the use of another, the person intitled to the use in fee-simple, fee-tail, for life or years, or otherwise, shall stand and be seized or possessed of the land, in the like estate, as he hath of the use, trust or confidence. And thereby the act makes *cestuy que use* complete owner both at law and in equity. 2 *Black.* 302.

USES, SUPERSTITIOUS. See *Mortmain*.

USUCAPTION,

USUCAPTION, the enjoying a thing by continuance of time, or receiving the profits, long possession, or prescription.

USURIOUS CONTRACT, any bargain or contract, whereby any man is obliged to pay more than legal interest. See *Usury*.

USURPATION, the using that which is another's; an interruption, or disturbing a man in his right and possession, &c.

USURPATION OF FRANCHISES, is when a subject unjustly uses any royal franchises, &c. And it is said to be an usurpation upon the king; who shall have the writ of *quo warranto* against the usurpers.

USURY, in a strict sense, is a contract upon the loan of money, to give the lender a certain profit for the use of it, upon all events whether the borrower made any advantage of it, or the lender suffered any prejudice for want of it, or whether it be repaid on the appointed time or not; and in a large sense, it seems, that all undue advantages, taken by a lender against a borrower, came under the notion of usury. *Haw.* 245.

The stat. 12 Anne c. 16, enacts that no person upon any contract which shall be made, shall take for loan of any money, wares, &c. above the value of 5l. for the forbearance of 100l. for a year; and all bonds and assurances for the payment of any money to be lent upon usury, whereupon or whereby, there shall be reserved or taken, above five pounds in the hundred, shall be void; and every person who shall receive, by means of any corrupt bargain, loan, exchange, shift, or interest, of any wares or other things, or by any deceitful way, for forbearing, or giving day of payment for one year, for their money or other things, above 5l. for 100l. for a year, &c. shall forfeit treble the value of the monies or other things lent.

But if a contract, which carries interest, be made in a foreign country, our courts will direct the payment of interest, according to the law of that country in which the contract was made. Thus, *Irish, American, Turkish,* and *Indian* interest have been allowed in our courts, to the amount of each 12l. per cent. For the moderation or exorbitance of interest depends upon local circumstances; and the refusal to enforce such contracts, would put a stop to all foreign trade. 2 *Black.* 463.

UTLAGATO CAPIENDO QUANDO UTLAGATUR IN UNO COMITATU, ET POSTEA FUGIT IN ALIUM. A writ for the taking of an outlawed person in one county, who afterwards flies into another.

W.

WAGE, signifies the giving security for the performance of a thing.

WAGER OF LAW, is a particular mode of proceeding, whereby in an action of debt brought upon a simple contract between the parties, without any deed or record, the defendant may discharge himself by swearing in court in the presence of compurgators, that he owes the plaintiff nothing, in manner and form as he has declared, and his compurgators swear, that they believe what he says is true. And this waging his law, is sometimes called making his law. *5 Bac. Abr.* 428.

It being at length considered, that this waging of law, offered too great a temptation to perjury, by degrees new remedies were devised, and new forms of action introduced, wherein no defendant is at liberty to wage his law.

Instead of an action of debt upon a simple contract, an action is now brought for the breach of a promise, or assumpsit, wherein though the specific debt cannot be recovered, yet damages may, equivalent to the specific debt: and this being an action of trespass, no law can be waged therein. So instead of an action of detinue to recover the very thing detained, an action of trespass upon the case, in trover, and conversion is usually brought, wherein though the specific thing cannot be had, yet the defendant shall pay damages for the conversion equal to the value thereof; and for this trespass, also no wager of law is allowed. In the place of actions of account, a bill in equity is usually filed, wherein, though the defendant answers upon his oath, yet such oath is not conclusive to the plaintiff, but he may prove every article, by other evidence, in contradiction to what the defendant hath sworn. So that wager of law is now quite out of *use*, being avoided by the mode of bringing the action, but still is not out of *force*. And therefore when a new statute inflicts a penalty, and gives an action of of debt to recover it, it is usual to add, *in which no wager of law shall be allowed.* 3 *Black.* 347.

WAGERS. In general a wager may be considered as legal, if it be not an incitement to a breach of the peace, or to immorality; or if it do not affect the feelings or interest of a third person, or expose him to ridicule: or if it be not against sound policy. 2 *Durnf. & East.* 610. See *Insurance, Wager, Policy.*

WAGES, what is agreed upon by a master to be paid to a servant, or any other person that he hires to do his business for him. 2 *Lil. Abr.* 677. See *Master and Servant.*

WAIFS, are goods which are stolen and waved by a felon in his flight from those who pursue him, which are forfeited: and though waif is generally spoken of goods stolen; yet if a man be pursued with hue and cry as a felon, and he flee and leave his own goods, these will be forfeited as goods stolen; but they are properly fugitive's goods, and not forfeited till it be found before the coroner, or otherwise of record, that he fled for the felony. 2 *Haw.* 450. See *Estrays.*

WAINAGE. The reasonableness of fines or amercements having been regulated by *magna charta,* that no person shall have a larger amercement imposed upon him than his circumstances or personal estate will bear, it is added, saving to the freeholder his contenement or land; to the trader his merchandize; and to the countryman his *wainage,* or team and instruments of husbandry. 4 *Black.* 379.

WAIVE in the general signification, is to forsake, but is specially applied to a woman, who for any crime for which a man may be outlawed, is termed waived.

WAIVER, signifies the passing by of a thing, or a refusal to accept it; sometimes it is applied to an estate, or something conveyed to a man, and sometimes to plea, &c. And a waiver or disagreement as to goods and chattels, in case of a gift, will be effectual. *Lil.* 710.

WALES, by stat. 27 H. VIII. c. 26, and other subsequent statutes, the dominion of Wales shall be incorporated with, and part of the realm of England; and all persons born in Wales, shall enjoy all liberties and privileges as the subjects in England do. And the lands in Wales shall be inheritable after the English tenure, and not after any Welch laws or customs. And the proceedings

proceedings in all the law courts, shall be in the English tongue. A session is also to be held twice a year in every county, by judges appointed by the king, to be called the great sessions of the several counties in Wales, in which all pleas of real and personal actions shall be held, with the same form of process, and in as ample manner, as in the court of common pleas at Westminster; and writs of error shall lie from judgments therein to the court of king's bench at Westminster. But the ordinary original writs, or process of the king's courts at Westminster, do not run into the principality of Wales; though process of execution does, as also all prerogative writs; as writs of *certiorari, quo minus, mandamus,* and the like. 3 *Black.* 77.

Murders and felonies in any part of Wales, may be tried in the next adjoining English county; the judges of assize, having a concurrent jurisdiction throughout all Wales, with the justices of the grand sessions. *Str.* 553.

All local matters arising in Wales, triable in the king's bench, are by the common law to be tried by a jury, returned from the next adjoining county in England. *Burr.* 859.

No sheriff or officer in Wales, shall upon any process out of the courts at Westminster, hold any person to special bail, unless the cause of action be *twenty pounds or upwards.* 11 & 12 W. c. 9.

WALTHAM BLACKS, in the reign of king George the First, there sprang up a set of desperate villains, called *Waltham blacks,* who blacking their faces, and using other disguises, robbed forests, parks, and warrens, destroyed cattle, levied money on their neighbours, by threats and menaces to fire their houses, and committed divers other violences, but they were suppressed and declared felons by 9 G. I. c. 22, commonly called the *black act.*

WAPENTAKE, is the same with what we call an hundred, specially so used in some of the northern counties.

WARD, is variously used, in one sense signifying a guardian, in a second a prison, in a third the ward of a forest, and in a fourth a district or division of the city of London.

WARDEN, is he who hath the keeping or charge of any persons or things by office.

WARDMOTE, a court kept in every ward in London; usually called the wardmote court: and the wardmote inquest hath power every year to enquire into, and present all defaults concerning the

the watch, and constables not doing their duty; that engines, &c. be provided against fire; persons selling ale and beer be honest and suffer no disorders, nor permit gaming, &c. that they sell in lawful measures; and searches be made for vagrants, beggars, and idle persons, &c. who shall be punished.

WARDS, was a court first erected in the reign of H. VIII. and afterwards augmented by him with the issue of liveries; whence it was stiled the court of wards and liveries, but dissolved by 12 Car. II.

WARDSHIP, when the tenant died, and his heir was under the age of twenty-one, being a male, or fourteen, being a female, the lord was entitled to the wardship of the heir, and was called the guardian in chivalry. This wardship consisted in having the custody of the body and lands of such heir, without any account of the profits, till the age of twenty-one in males, and fourteen (which was afterwards advanced to sixteen) in females. For the law supposed the heir male unable to perform knight's service till twenty-one; but as for the female, she was supposed capable at fourteen to marry, and then her husband might perform the office. 2 *Black*. 67.

WARRANT, a præcipe under hand and seal to some officer to bring any offender before the person granting it; and warrants of commitment are issued by the privy council, a secretary of state, or justice of peace, &c. where there hath been a private information, or a witness had deposed against an offender. *Wood's Inst.* 614.

Any one under the degree of nobility may be arrested for a misdemeanour, or any thing done against the peace of the kingdom, by warrant from a justice of the peace; though if the person be a peer of the realm, he must be apprehended for a breach of the peace by warrant out of B. R. *Dalt. Just.* 263.

A constable ought not to execute a justice's warrant, where the warrant is unlawful, or the justice hath no jurisdiction; if he do he may be punished. *Plowd*. 394.

But if any person abuse it, by throwing it in the dirt, &c. or refuse to execute a lawful warrant, it is a contempt of the king's process, for which the offender may be indicted and fined. *Crompt.* 149.

A *general* warrant to apprehend all persons suspected, without

 naming

naming or particularly describing any person in special, is illegal and void for its uncertainty: for it is the duty of the magistrate, and ought not to be left to the officer, to judge of the ground of the suspicion. Also a warrant to apprehend all persons *guilty of such a crime*, is no legal warrant; for the point upon which its authority rests, is a fact to be decided on a subsequent trial; namely, whether the person apprehended thereupon be guilty or not guilty. 4 *Black.* 291.

A warrant may be lawfully granted by any justice, for treason, felony, or præmunire, or any other offence against the peace, and it seems clear, that where a statute gives any one justice a jurisdiction over any offence, or a power to require any person to do a certain thing ordained by such a statute, it impliedly gives a power to every such justice to make out a warrant to bring before him any one accused of such offence, or compelled to do any thing ordained by such statute; for it cannot but be intended, that a statute which gives a person jurisdiction over an offence, means also to give him the power incident to all courts of compelling the party to come before him. 2 *Haw.* 84.

But in cases where the king is not a party, or where no corporal punishment is appointed, as in cases for servants' wages and the like, it seems that a summons is the more proper process; and for default of appearance, the justice may proceed; and so indeed it is often directed by special statutes.

A warrant from any of the justices of the court of king's bench extends over all the kingdom, and is tested or dated *England*: but a warrant of a justice of peace in one county, must be backed, that is, signed, by a justice of another county, before it can be executed there. And a warrant for apprehending an English or a Scotch offender, may be indorsed in the opposite kingdom, and the offender carried back to that part of the united kingdom in which the offence was committed. 4 *Black.* 291.

WARRANT OF ATTORNEY is an authority and power given by a client to his attorney, to appear and plead for him; or to suffer judgment to pass against him by confessing the action, by *nil dicit, non sum informatus, &c.* And although a warrant of attorney given by a man in custody to confess a judgment, no attorney being present, is void as to the entry of judgment; yet it may

may be a good warrant to appear and file common bail. 2 *Lil. Abr.* 682.

WARRANTIA CHARTÆ, a writ that lies where a man is enfeoffed of lands with warranty, and then he is sued or impleaded. And if the feoffee be impleaded in assize, or other action, in which he cannot vouch or call to warranty, he shall have this writ against the feoffer, or his heirs, to compel them to warrant the land to him; and if the land be recovered from him, he shall recover as much lands in value against the warrantor, &c. But the *warrantia chartæ* ought to be brought by the feoffee, depending the first writ against him, or he hath lost his advantage. F. N. B. 134.

WARRANTIA CUSTODIÆ, a writ judicial, and lay for him who was challenged to be a ward to another, in respect of land said to be holden in knight's service, which, when it was brought by the ancestors of the ward, was *warranted* to be free from such thraldom, and it lay against the warrantor and his heirs.

WARRANTIA DIEI, a writ lying in case, where a man having a day assigned, personally to appear in court to any action wherein he is sued, is in the mean time employed in the king's service, so that he cannot come at the day assigned. This writ is directed to the justices to this end, that they neither take nor record him in default for that day.

WARRANTY, a promise or covenant by deed, made by the bargainor, for himself and his heirs, to warrant or secure the bargainee and his heirs against all men, for the enjoying any thing agreed on between them.

Warranty is either real or personal; *real*, when it is annexed to lands or tenements granted for life, &c. And this is either *in deed*, as by the word *warrantizo* expressly; or *in law*, as by the word *dedi*, or some other amplification.

Personal, which either respects the property of the thing sold, or the quality of it. *Cowel.*

Warranties in their more general divisions are of two kinds: first, a warranty *in deed*, or an express warranty, which is when a fine, or feoffment in fee, or a lease for life is made by deed, which has an express clause of warranty contained in it, as when a conusor, feoffor, or lessor, covenants to warrant the land to the conusee, feoffee, or lessee; secondly, a warrant *in law*, or an implied

plied warranty, which is, when it is not expressed by the party, but tacitly made and implied by the law. 1 *Inst.* 365.

A warranty in deed is either lineal or collateral. A *lineal* warranty is a covenant real, annexed to the land by him, who either was owner of or might have inherited the land, and from whom his heir lineal or collateral, might possibly have claimed the land as heir from him that made the warranty, A *collateral* warranty is made by him that had no right, or possibility of right, to the land, and is collateral to the title of the land. 1 *Inst.* 370.

WARREN, is a franchise or place privileged, by prescription or grant from the king, for the keeping of beasts and fowls of the warren; which are conies, partridges, pheasants, and some add quails, woodcocks, and water-fowl. 1 *Inst.* 233.

These were looked upon as royal game, and the franchise of free warren, was invented to protect them, by giving the grantee a sole and exclusive power of killing such game, so far as his warren extended, on condition of his preventing other persons; for, by the common law, no man, not even a lord of a manor, could justify killing game on another man's soil, unless he had the liberty of free warren. 2 *Black.* 39.

WASTE, is the committing any spoil or destruction in houses, lands, &c. by tenants, to the damage of the heir, or of him in reversion or remainder: whereupon the writ or action of waste, is brought for the recovery of the thing wasted, and damages for the waste done. 5 *Bac. Abr.* 459.

There are two kinds of waste, *voluntary* or actual, and *negligent* or permissive. *Voluntary waste* may be done by pulling down or prostrating houses, or cutting down timber trees: *negligent waste* may be, by suffering an house to be uncovered, whereby the spars or rafters, planches or other timber of the house are rotten. 1 *Inst.* 53.

A writ of waste, to punish the offence after it has been committed, is an action partly founded upon the common law, and partly upon the statute of *Gloucester,* and may be brought by him that has the immediate state of inheritance in reversion or remainder, against the tenant for life, tenant in dower, tenant by the courtesy, or tenant for years. 3 *Black.* 227.

This action of waste is a mixed action; partly real, so far as it recovers land, and partly personal, so far as it recovers damages,

for

for it is brought for both those purposes; and if the waste be proved, the plaintiff shall recover the thing or place wasted, and also treble damages by the said statute. 6 Ed. I. c. 5.

The writ of waste, calls upon the tenant to appear and shew cause why he hath committed waste and destruction in the place named, to the dishersion of the plaintiff. And if the defendant make default, or do not appear at the day assigned him, then the sheriff is to take with him a jury of twelve men, and go in person to the place allcdged to be wasted, and there enquire of the waste done, and the damages; and make a return or report of the same to the court, upon which report the judgment is founded. 3 *Black.* 223.

WATCH AND WARD. Watching is properly intended in the night, and warding for the day time. *Dalt.* 104.

Persons aggrieved by assessments, for watch and ward, may appeal to the mayor. 11 G. I. c. 18.

WATCHES, made by artificers are to have the makers' names, &c. under the penalty of 20l. 9 & 10 W. III. c. 28.

WATER BAILIFF, an officer in port towns, for the searching of ships.

WATER COURSE. A water course does not begin by prescription, nor assent, but begins, *ex jure naturæ*, having this course naturally, and cannot be divested. 3 *Bulst.* 340.

WATERMEN. In London the lord mayor and court of aldermen have much power in governing the company of watermen, and appointing the fares for plying on the river Thames; and justices for Middlesex, and other adjoining counties, have also power to hear and determine offences, &c. See 10 G. II. c. 31.

WATER ORDEAL. See *Ordeal.*

WAY. A way may be by prescription, as if the owners and occupiers of such a farm have immemorially used to cross another's ground; for this immemorial usage supplies an original grant. A right of way may also arise by act and operation of law; for if a man grant to another, a piece of ground in the middle of his field, he at the same time tacitly gives him a way to come at it, for where the law gives any thing to any person, it gives implied

implied whatever is necessary for enjoying the same. 2 *Black.* 35.

WEAVERS. The wages of journeymen weavers in London, are to be settled by the lord mayor, recorder, and aldermen. Masters giving more wages than is appointed, to forfeit 50l. and journeymen demanding, or combining to demand more, to forfeit 40s. or be imprisoned three months.

WEIGHTS AND MEASURES, the standard of measures, was originally kept at *Winchester*, which measure was by the law of king Edgar, ordained to be observed through the kingdom.

By stat. 35 G. III. c. 102. the justices in quarter-sessions in every county, are required to appoint persons to examine the weights and balances within their respective jurisdictions. These inspectors may seize and examine weights in shops, &c. and seize false weights and balances, and the offender, being convicted before one justice, shall be fined from 5s. to 20s. Persons obstructing the inspectors, to forfeit from 5s. to 40s. Inspectors to be recompensed out of the county-rate. Standard weights to be purchased by the sessions out of the county-rate, and produced to all persons paying for the production thereof: Informations to be within one month.

WESTMINSTER, was the ancient seat of our kings, and is now the well-known place, where the high court of parliament, and courts of judicature sit.

WHARFAGE, money paid for landing wares at a *wharf*, or for shipping or taking goods into a boat or barge from thence. See 22 Car. II. c. 11.

WHITE RENT, a duty or rent of eight-pence, payable by every tinner in the county of Devon, to the duke of Cornwall.

WIDOW, a woman who has lost her husband by death: in London and throughout the province of York, the widow of a freeman, is by custom, entitled to her apparel, and the furniture of the bed-chamber, called the widow's chamber.

WIFE, after marriage, all the will of the wife, in judgment of law, is subject to the will of the husband; and it is commonly said, a feme covert hath no will. See *Husband and Wife.*

WILL AND TESTAMENT, is that disposition of property which is made by a person to take place after his decease. Every person

person capable of binding himself by contract, is capable of making a will.

Also a male infant of the age of 14 years and upwards, and female of twelve years or upwards, are capable of making a will respecting personal estates only.

But a married woman cannot make a will, unless a power be reserved in a marriage settlement; but wherever personal property, however, is given to a married woman for her sole and seperate use, she may dispose of it by will.

If a feme sole make her will, and afterwards marry, such marriage is a legal revocation of the will.

Wills are of two kinds, written and verbal; the former is most usual and secure.

It is not absolutely necessary that a will should be witnessed; and a testament of chattels, written in the testator's own hand, though it have neither the testator's name nor seal to it, nor witnesses present at his publication, will be good, provided sufficient proof can be had that it is his hand-writing. *Gilb.* 260.

By stat. 29 Car. II. c. 3. all devises of lands, and tenements, shall not only be in writing, but shall also be signed by the party so devising the same, or by some other person in his presence, and by his express direction, and shall be witnessed and subscribed in the presence of the person devising, by three or four credible witnesses, or else the devise, will be intirely void, and the land will descend to the heir at law.

A will, even if made beyond sea, bequeathing land in England, must be attested by three witnesses. 2 *Perc. Wms.* 293.

A will, however, devising copyhold land, does not require to be witnessed; it is sufficient to declare the uses of a surrender of such copyhold land made to the use of the will. The party to whom the land is given, becomes entitled to it by means of the surrender, and not by the will. 2 *Atk.* 37.

A codicil is a supplement to a will, or an addition made by the person making the same, annexed to, and to be taken as part of the will itself, being for it's explanation or alteration, to add something to, or take something from the former disposition, and which may also be either written or verbal, under the same restrictions as regard wills.

If two wills are found, and it does not appear which was the former

former or latter, both will be void ; but if two codicils are found, and it cannot be ascertained which was the first, but the same thing is devised to two persons, both ought to divide ; but where either wills or codicils have dates, the latter is considered as valid, and revokes the former. See *Administrator, Executor, Legacy.*

WITCHCRAFT, by 9 G. II. c. 5. no prosecution shall be commenced or carried on against any person for witchcraft, sorcery, inchantment, or conjuration, or for charging another with any such offence.

But if any person shall pretend to exercise or use, any kind of witchcraft, sorcery, inchantment, or conjuration; or undertake to tell fortunes, or pretend from his skill or knowledge in any occult or crafty science, to discover where, and in what manner, any goods supposed to have been stolen or lost, may be found ; he shall be imprisoned for a year, and once in every quarter of that year, stand openly on the pillory for an hour, further shall be bound to the good behaviour as the court shall award.

WITHERNAM, is a forbidden taking, as the taking or driving a distress to hold, or out of the county, so that the sheriff cannot upon the replevin, make deliverance thereof to the party distrained.

WITNESS, one who is sworn to give evidence in a cause.

If a man be subpœnaed as a witness upon a trial, he must appear in court on pain of 100l. to be forfeited to the king, and 10l. together with damages equivalent to the loss sustained by the want of his evidence to the party aggrieved. 3 *Black. Com.* 369.

But witnesses ought to have a reasonable time, that their attendance upon the court, may be of as little prejudice to themselves as possible ; and the court of king's-bench held, that notice at two in the afternoon to attend the sitting, that evening at Westminster, was too short a time. *Str.* 510.

Where a witness cannot be present at a trial, he may by consent of the plaintiff and defendant, or by rule of court, be examined upon interrogatories at the judge's chambers.

No witness is bound to appear to give evidence in a cause, unless his reasonable expence be tendered him, and if he appear, till such charge is actually paid him, except he both resides, and

is

is summoned to give evidence within the bills of mortality. See *Arrest, Evidence, Privilege.*

WOMEN, by the 26 G. II. c. 33. no suit shall be had in any ecclesiastical court, to compel a celebration of marriage in *facie ecclesiæ*, by reason of any contract of matrimony whatsoever, whether *per verba de presenti*, or *per verba de futuro*: and the marriage of any person under the age of twenty-one, without the consent of parents or guardians, shall be null and void.

By 20 H. VI. c. 9. peeresses shall be tried as peers for treason or felony.

And by stat. 3 W. c. 9. a woman being convicted of an offence, for which a man may have his clergy, shall suffer the same punishment that a man should suffer, who has the benefit of his clergy allowed; that is, shall be burnt in the hand, and further kept in prison as the court shall think fit, not exceeding one year.

But she shall be only once intitled to the benefit of the said statute. See *Heiress, Maid,* and *Quick with Child.*

WOOD. See *Trees* and *Timber.*

WOOL, either in a raw or manufactured state, has always been the principal of the staple articles of this country. The price of wool was in very early times, much higher in proportion to the wages of labour, the rent of land, and the price of butcher's meat than at present. It was before the time of Edward III. always exported raw, the art of working it into cloth and dying being so imperfectly known, that no persons above the degree of working-people could go dressed in cloth of English manufacture.

The first steps taken to encourage the manufacture of woollen cloths was by Edward the Third, who procured some good workmen from the Netherlands by means of protection and encouragement. The value of wool was considered as so essentially solid, that taxes were voted in that commodity, reckoning by the number of sacks; and in proportion to the price of the necessaries of life and value of silver, wool was at least three times dearer then, than it is now. The manufacturing of cloth being once introduced into the country, the policy of preventing the exportation of the raw material was soon evident; and the first act, was that of H. IV. c. 2. by which the exportation of sheep, lambs, or rams, is forbidden under very heavy penalties.

By stat. 28 G. III. all former statutes respecting the exportation of wool and sheep are repealed, and numerous restrictions are consolidated in that statute.

By this act if any person shall send or receive any sheep on board any vessel to be carried out of the kingdom, such vessel shall be forfeited, and the person so offending, shall forfeit 3l. for every sheep, and suffer solitary imprisonment for three months. But wether sheep, by a licence from the collector of the customs may be taken on board for the use of the ship's company; and every person who shall export any wool, or woollen articles slightly made up, so as easily to be reduced again to wool, or any fuller's-earth or tobacco-pipe clay, and every carrier, ship-owner, commander, mariner, or other person, who shall knowingly assist in exporting or attempting to export these articles, shall forfeit *three shillings* for every pound weight, or the sum of 50l. in the whole, at the election of the prosecutor, and shall also suffer solitary imprisonment for three months. But wool may be carried coastwise upon being duly entered, and security being given according to the directions of the statute, to the officer of the port from whence the same shall be conveyed; and the owners of sheep within five miles of the sea, and ten miles in Kent and Sussex, cannot remove the wool, without giving notice to the officer of the nearest port, as directed by the statute.

WOOLLEN CLOTH, interment in, the 30 G. II. c. 3. (an act which is required to be given in charge at the assizes and sessions, and to be read four times publicly each year in the church by every parson) no corpse of any person (except of those who die of the plague) shall be buried in any shirt, shift, sheet, or shroud, or any thing made or mingled with flax, hemp, silk, hair, gold, or silver, or in any stuff or thing not made of sheep's wool only; or be put into any coffin lined or faced with any sort of clothier stuff, or any other thing, made of any other material, than sheep's wool only, under penalty of 5l. to be recovered by distress and sale of the goods and chattels of the party deceased.

WOOL-COMBERS, by 35 G. III. c. 124. all those who have served an apprenticeship to the trade of a wool-comber, or who are by law entitled to exercise the same, and also their wives and children, may set up and exercise such trade, or any other trade or business they are apt and able for, in any town or place within this kingdom, without any molestation; nor shall such wool-combers,

combers, their wives or children, while they exercise such trades be removable from such place to their last legal settlement, till they shall actually become chargeable to such parish.

WORDS, which may be taken or interpreted by law in a general or common sense, ought not to receive a strained or unusual contruction: and ambiguous words are to be construed so as to make them stand with law and equity; and not be wrested to do wrong. 2 *Lill.* 711. See 16 *Vin. Abr.*

WORDS DEFAMATORY, are in some cases indictable, as calling a justice of the peace a rogue; and in others actionable, as to say such an attorney is a rogue.

WORKING IN HARVEST, a person may go abroad to work in harvest, carrying with him a certificate from the minister, and one churchwarden or overseer, that he hath a dwelling-house or place, in which he inhabits, and hath left wife and children, or some of them there (or otherwise as his condition shall require) and declaring him an inhabitant there.

A person carrying such certificate with him, shall not be apprehended under the stat. 17 G. II. c. 5. commonly called *the vagrant act.*

WRECK, such goods as after a shipwreck are cast upon the land by the sea, and left there within some county, for they are not wrecks so long as they remain at sea, being within the jurisdiction of the admiralty.

Various statutes have been made relative to wreck, which was formerly a perquisite belonging to the king, or by special grant to the lord of the manor; it is now however held, that if proof can be made of the property of any of the goods or lading which come to shore they shall not be forfeited as wreck.

By the 3 Ed. c. 4. the sheriff of the county shall be bound to keep the goods a year and a day, that if any man can prove a property in them, either in his own right, or by right of representation, they shall be restored to him without delay.

By stat. 26 G. II. c. 19. plundering any vessel either in distress or wrecked, and whether any living creature be on board or not, or preventing the escape of any person that endeavours to save his life, or putting out false lights to bring any vessel into danger, are all declared to be capital felonies; and by this statute, pilfering any goods cast ashore, is declared to be petty larceny. See *Insurance. Salvage.*

WRIT, is the king's precept, whereby any thing is commanded touching a suit or action; as the defendant or tenant to be summoned, a distress to be taken, a disseisin to be redressed, &c. And these writs are diversly divided; some in respect of their order, or manner of granting, are termed original, and some judicial.

Original writs, are those that are sent out for the summoning of the defendant in a personal, or the tenant in a real action, before the suit begins or rather to begin the suit.

The *judicial* writs are those which are sent out by order of the court where the cause depends, upon occasion after the suit begun.

Original writs are issued out in the court of chancery, for the summoning a defendant to appear, and are granted before the suit is begun, to begin the same: and judicial writs issue out of the court where the original is returned, after the suit is begun. The originals bear date in the name of the king; but the judicial writs bear *teste* in the name of the chief justice.

WRIT OF ASSISTANCE, issues out of the exchequer, to authorize any person to take a constable, or other public officer, to seize goods, or merchandize prohibited and uncustomed.

Also a writ issuing out of the chancery to give a possession.

WRIT OF ENTRY. See *Entry*.

WRIT OF INQUIRY OF DAMAGES, a judicial writ that issues out to the sheriff, upon a judgment by default, in action of the case, covenant, trespass, trover, &c. commanding him to summon a jury to inquire what damages the plaintiff hath sustained *occasione præmissorum*; and when this is returned with the inquisition, the rule for judgment is given upon it; and if nothing be said to the contrary; judgment is thereupon entered. 2 *Lill. Abr.* 721.

A writ of inquiry of damages, is a mere inquest of office, to inform the conscience of the court; who, if they please, may themselves assess the damages. And it is accordingly the practice, in actions upon promissory notes and bills of exchange, instead of executing a writ of inquiry, to apply to the court for a rule to shew cause, why it should not be referred to the master to see what

what is due for principal and interest, and why final judgment should not be signed for that sum, without executing a writ of inquiry; which rule is made absolute on an affidavit of service, unless good cause be shewn to the contrary. *Tidd's Pract.* K. B.

WRITING, a simple writing or declaration, *not* in the manner of a deed, made to a certain person, &c. shall be good in law. *Hob.* 312.

WRONG, any damage or injury; being the contrary to that which is right and strait.

WRONG STAMP. By 37 G. III. c. 136. any instrument (except bills of exchange, promissory notes, or other notes, drafts, or orders) liable to stamp-duty, whereon shall be impressed any stamp of a *different denomination*, but of an *equal* or *greater value* than the stamp required, may be stamped with the proper stamp after the execution, on payment of duty and five pounds penalty, but without any allowance for the wrong stamp.

Likewise any such instrument (except as aforesaid) being ingrossed without having been first stamped, or having a stamp thereon of *less value* than required, the same may be stamped after the execution, on payment of the duty and ten pounds penalty only, for each skin thereof: but in case it shall be satisfactorily proved to the commissioners of stamps, that the same hath been so ingrossed either by accident or inadvertency, or from urgent necessity or unavoidable circumstances, and without any intention of fraud, the commissioners are authorized to stamp the same within sixty days after the execution, to remit the penalty in part, or in all, and to indemnify persons so ingrossing the same.

Y.

YARDLAND, a quantity of land, different according to the place, or county, as in Surry, it is but fifteen acres, in some counties twenty, and twenty-four, and in others thirty. *Bract. Lib.* 2. c. 10.

YARN, no person shall buy yarn or wool, but he that makes cloth

cloth of it. And none may transport yarn beyond the sea, by stat. 8 H. VI. c. 5. and 33 H. VIII. c. 16. See *Wool.*

YEAR, by 24 G. II. c. 23. the year shall begin on the first day of January, and not as heretofore on the twenty-fifth of March. And in legal proceedings, the year shall be computed according to the calendar, and not according to twenty-eight days in the month. 2 *Inst.* 320.

YEAR AND DAY, is a time that determines a right in many cases; and in some, works an usurpation, and in others, a prescription; as in case of an *estray,* if the owner, proclamation being made, challenge it not within the time, it is forfeited.

So is the *year and day,* given in case of appeal; in case of descent after entry or claim; if no claim upon a fine or writ of right at the common law; so if a villain remaining in ancient demesne; of a man sore bruised or wounded; of protections; essoins in respect of the king's service; of a wreck; and divers other cases. *Co.* 6. *Rep. Fol.* 107.

YEAR BOOKS, reports in a regular series, from Ed. II. inclusive, to the time of Hen. VIII. which were taken by the prothonotaries of the court, at the expence of the crown, and published annually.

YEAR DAY AND WASTE, is a part of the king's prerogative whereby he challengeth the profits of their lands and tenements *for a year and a day,* that are attainted of petty-treason or felony; whoever is lord of the manor where the lands or tenements belong; and not only so, but in the end may *waste* the tenements, destroy the houses, root up the woods, garden, and pasture; and plough up the meadows, except the lord of the fee agree with him for redemption of such *waste,* afterwards restoring it to the lord of the fee. *Staundf. Prærog.* c. 16.

YEARS (estate for): Tenant for term of years, is where a man letteth lands or tenements to another, for a certain term of years agreed upon between the lessor and lessee; and when the lessee entereth by force of the lease, then he is tenant for term of years. *Litt. Sect.* 58.

If tenements be let to a man for term of half a year, or for a quarter of a year, or any less time; this lessee is respected as tenant for years, and is styled so in some legal proceedings: a year being the shortest term, which the law in this case takes notice of. *Litt. Sect.* 67.

Generally

Generally, every estate which must expire at a period certain and prefixed, by whatever words created, is an estate for years; and therefore this estate is frequently called a *term*; because its duration or continuance, is bounded, limited, and determined. 2 *Black*. 143.

For every such estate must have a certain beginning, and certain end. If no day of commencement be named in the creation of this estate, it begins from the making, or delivery of the lease. A lease for so many years as such an one shall live, is void from the beginning; for it is neither certain, nor can it ever be reduced to a certainty, during the continuance of the lease. *Id.*

And the same doctrine holds, if a person make a lease of his glebe for so many years as he shall continue parson of such a church, for this is still more uncertain. But a lease for twenty or more years, if the parson shall so long live, or if he shall so long continue parson, is good; for there is a certain period fixed, beyond which it cannot last, though it may determine sooner, on the parson's death, or his ceasing to be parson there. 2 *Black.* 143.

An estate for years, though never so many, is inferior to an estate for life. For as estate for life, though it be only for the life of another person, is a freehold; but an estate, though it be for a thousand years, is only a chattel, and reckoned part of the personal estate. *Id.*

Hence it follows, that a lease for years may be made to commence *in futuro*, though a lease for life cannot. As if I grant lands to one from Michaelmas next for twenty years, this is good; but to hold from Michaelmas next for the term of his natural life, is void. *Id.*

For no estate of freehold can commence *in futuro*, because it cannot be created at common law without livery of seisin, or corporal possession of the land; and corporal possession cannot be given of an estate now, which is not to commence now, but hereafter. And because no livery of seisin is necessary for a lease for years, such a lessee is not said to be seized, or to have true legal seisin of the lands. Nor indeed doth the bare lease, vest any estate in the lessee, but only gives him a right of entry on the tenement, which right is called his *interest in the term*: but when he has actually so entered, and thereby accepted the grant, the estate is then and not before, vested in him; and he is *possessed*, not properly of the land, but of the term of years, the possesion or seisin of the land, remaining still in him who has the freehold. *2 Black.* 144.

YEOMAN, is defined to be one, that hath fee land of 40s. a year; who was thereby heretofore, qualified to serve on juries, and can yet vote for knights of the shire, and do any other act where the law requires one, that is *probus et legalis homo.* Below yeomen, are ranked tradesmen, artificers, and labourers. *2 Inst.* 668.

YIELDING AND PAYING. See *Reddendum under the Title, Deed.*

YORK, in the county of York, only one panel of 48 jurors shall be returned to serve on the grand jury at the assizes; and at the quarter-sessions not above 40, either upon the grand jury or other service there. 7 & 8 W. III. c. 32.

And no person, having 150l. a year, shall be summoned to the sessions, but only persons less liable to bear the expence of attending at the assizes. 1 Anne. c. 13.

By stat. 4 W. III. c. 2. the inhabitants of the province of York, have power to dispose of their whole personal estate by will; which before they had not, further than the testator's own proportionable part, called the *dead man's* or *death's part.* For if the testator had a wife, and a child, or children, the wife should have one third, the child or children another third, and the remaining third, was all that the testator had to dispose of. If he had a wife and no child, then she should have one moiety, and the other moiety remained to him, to dispose of by his testament: so if he left a child or children, and no wife. But if he had neither wife or child, he might dispose of the whole. In case of intestacy, the same proportions continue to the wife and children to this day; but the dead man's part shall be distributed according to the stat. 22. & 23 Car. II. c. 10. commonly called the *statute of distributions.*

THE END.

J. CUNDEE, PRINTER,
Ivy-Lane.

www.ingramcontent.com/pod-product-compliance
Lightning Source LLC
LaVergne TN
LVHW102012210926
848483LV00011B/275
* 9 7 8 1 5 8 4 7 7 4 3 3 4 *